LA VIDA

*A Puerto Rican Family
in the Culture of Poverty—
San Juan and New York*

VINTAGE BOOKS

A Division Of Random House

New York

LA VIDA

A Puerto Rican Family
in the Culture of Poverty—
San Juan and New York

by

OSCAR LEWIS

Manufactured in the United States of America

Vintage Books are published by
Alfred A. Knopf, Inc. and Random House, Inc.

IN ORDER to maintain the anonymity of the subjects of this study, the names of all the family members, their friends and neighbors have been changed. I have also changed the name of the slum and the names of some of the streets, Stop numbers, bars, hotels and other public places. The names of historical figures and public officials have not been changed.

Acknowledgments

IN WRITING THIS BOOK I have incurred many obligations. For research grants and fellowships which facilitated this study I am grateful to the John Simon Guggenheim Memorial Foundation, the Research Institute for the Study of Man, the Wenner-Gren Foundation for Anthropological Research, the Social Security Administration and Welfare Administration Research Grants Program, and the University of Illinois Research Board. I also want to thank the Department of Anthropology of the University of Illinois for a two-year leave of absence which made the research possible.

I am grateful to my students Douglas S. Butterworth and Rosita González for their assistance in all phases of the research project but especially for their help with the field work in the slums of San Juan and in New York City. I am also grateful to Elizabeth Hegeman, Frank Franco, Anadel Snyder and Aida Torres de Estepan for their assistance with some aspects of the field work.

To Muna Muñoz Lee I am deeply grateful for her excellent translation of the field data upon which this volume is based. I also want to thank Asa Zatz, the principal translator of the research materials for my earlier volumes *The Children of Sánchez* and *Pedro Martínez*, for his translation assistance on this volume. I am grateful as well to Agnes Colón, Helen Tooker and my wife, Ruth M. Lewis, for their assistance with translations. In preparing this volume a total of over six thousand pages of my interview data was translated from Spanish into English.

I am indebted to Dr. Rosa Celeste Marín of the Puerto Rico School of Social Work for sharing with me her knowledge of lower-class family life and for inviting me to collaborate in a study of some of the families of her own research project. In addition I want to thank the members of Dr. Marín's staff for their assistance. I am grateful to Hugh Barton for providing me with statistical data on the economic development of Puerto Rico and to Edna Torres de Ranck for helpful data on urban renewal.

For editorial assistance I am grateful to Helen Kuypers, Margaret Larkin, Starry Krueger, Barbara Willson and Ruth M. Lewis. For secretarial assistance in the transcription of the tape recordings I want to thank Selenia Cabrera, Aida Muñoz, Rosa Morales and Etanislá Rivera. And I thank Terry Butterworth, Gwendolin Pierce and Susan Holper for secretarial assistance.

To Dr. Alberto Tristani and Caroline Luján I am grateful for their administration of psychological tests to members of the Ríos family and to other sample families of the larger research project. I am particularly grateful to Mrs. Luján for her profound analysis of the Rorschach and Thematic Apperception Test protocols and of the life histories. I hope to publish this analysis separately at a later date.

I am indebted to a number of friends and colleagues for reading portions of the manuscript and providing me with helpful comments and suggestions. In this connection I want to thank Douglas S. Butterworth, Joseph B. Casagrande, Jason Epstein, Father Joseph P. Fitzpatrick, Herbert Gans, Allean Hale, Elizabeth Herzog, Reuben Hill, Berenice Hoffman, Gordon K. Lewis, Caroline Luján, Albert Maltz, Muna Muñoz Lee, Harriet Magil, Lloyd E. Ohlin, Helen Harris Perlman, Lloyd H. Rogler, Vera Rubin, Julian H. Steward, Paul Webbink and, finally, my son Gene L. Lewis.

I am grateful to many friends in Puerto Rico for their hospitality and kindness to me and my family during the field work on the island. I am especially grateful to the Honorable Luis Muñoz Marín and to his wife doña Inés for their sympathetic interest in my research. I should also like to thank José Alonso, Manuel Maldonado Denis, René Marqués, Thomas G. Mathews, José Nieto and his wife María Teresa Babín, Dr. Angel G. Quintero Alfaro, Beata Salz, Pedro Juan Soto, Howard Stanton and his wife Hazel, Nilita Vientos, Kal Wagenheim, Fred Wales and Charles Zimmerman.

I am profoundly grateful to my wife for her patience and for her generous and untiring collaboration in all phases of the preparation of this book.

To the Ríos family I am grateful for their co-operation and friendship and for their permission to publish the research data on their lives.

Contents

CONTENTS

Contents

Introduction

IN THE COURSE of my anthropological studies of poverty and family life in Mexico, a number of my Mexican and other Latin American friends have sometimes delicately suggested that I turn to a study of poverty in my own country, the United States. My study of Puerto Ricans is a first step in that direction. Puerto Rico has been under the control and influence of the United States since 1898, an "unincorporated territory" since 1901, and a commonwealth since 1952. Puerto Ricans have been American citizens since 1917. Of three and a half million Puerto Ricans, one million live in the United States and over 600,000 in New York City, where most of them live in poverty. They have a very low educational level (the lowest of any ethnic group in the city), a high incidence of mental disability, and a relatively high rate of tuberculosis —conditions which reflect the poverty of their native land.

Because of the great publicity given to the dramatic and inspiring progress of Puerto Rico since 1940, we tend to forget that it is still a very poor country, twice as poor as the poorest state in the United States, and that many of the problems of Puerto Ricans in New York have their origin in the slums of Puerto Rico. In 1960, 42.7 percent of all families in Puerto Rico reporting monetary income earned less than $1,000 a year; 80 percent had less than $3,000. Fourteen percent of the population were still unemployed, 15 percent of all families were on relief, and 20 percent received food allotments.* In

* In 1962 approximately 300,000 people on the island were receiving public assistance, and over 650,000 were receiving surplus food from the Federal Commodities program.

1960 almost 160,000 young Puerto Ricans between the ages of fourteen and nineteen were not in school. Of these, over 100,000 (58.5 percent of the males and 85.1 percent of the females) were also not in the labor force. These are much higher figures than for 1950 and probably reflect the increased urbanization and the reduction in the number of agricultural jobs.

The persistence of a Puerto Rican way of life, especially among the low-income group, even after many years of residence in the United States, is the result of several factors, one of which is the maintenance of close ties with Puerto Rico. One of the most distinctive characteristics of the Puerto Rican migration to the States is that it is a two-way rather than a one-way movement. In 1960 there was a total net migration to the United States of 20,000, but Puerto Ricans made almost a million trips back and forth, taking advantage of the inexpensive plane fare between New York and San Juan.

Although Puerto Ricans have been among the most surveyed and studied groups, most of the studies on the island have been of the rural population.[1] * The urban scene and especially the urban slums have received very little attention.[2] Much more has been written on Puerto Ricans in New York City than on Puerto Ricans in San Juan.[3] The recent study of Hollingshead and Rogler[4] is a welcome addition to a neglected and almost virgin field. However, we have not had a single full-length portrait of a Puerto Rican urban slum family. The nearest approach to a family study is Professor Sidney Mintz's interesting biography of a rural sugar-cane worker.[5]

In this tape-recorded story of a low-income Puerto Rican slum family in San Juan and New York, I have tried to give a voice to people who are rarely heard, and to provide the reader with an inside view of a style of life which is common in many of the deprived and marginal groups in our society but which is largely unknown, ignored or inaccessible to most middle-class readers. Indeed, one of the major objectives of this volume is to bridge the gap in communication between the very poor and the middle-class personnel—teachers, social workers, doctors, priests, and others—who bear the major responsibility for carrying out the anti-poverty progams. It is my hope that a better understanding of the nature of the culture of poverty will eventually lead to a more sympathetic view of the poor and their problems and will provide a more rational basis for constructive social action.

I am aware that an intensive study of poverty and its multiple facets and problems, particularly one which reveals its effects upon character, runs the risk of offending some Puerto Ricans who have dedicated themselves to the elimination of poverty and who are trying to build a positive public image of an often maligned minority group. I am also aware of the danger that my findings may be misinterpreted or used to justify prejudices and negative stereotypes about Puerto Ricans which, unfortunately, are still held by some Amer-

* This and subsequent numerals refer to Notes at the end of the Introduction.

icans. I should like to emphasize that this study deals with only one segment of the Puerto Rican population and that the data should not be generalized to Puerto Rican society as a whole. Much of the behavior described in these pages goes counter to some of the most cherished ideals of the larger society. There may be some people who, for various reasons, would prefer to conceal the conditions described in this book. However, if anything is to be done to improve these conditions, the first step is to know about them. There is a popular Puerto Rican saying that is appropriate here: *No se puede tapar el cielo con la mano,* or "You can't cover up the sky with your hand." Indeed, you can't cover up slums, poverty and ugliness.

On the other hand, this book is not intended to detract from the real progress made by Puerto Rico since 1940 under the able leadership of Muñoz Marín. The economy has been growing twice as fast as that of the United States and has been transformed from a predominantly one-crop agricultural economy to one which is increasingly dependent upon industries and manufacturing. Before World War II agriculture accounted for almost a third of the total net income and manufacturing accounted for less than 12 percent. By 1964 there were over 1,000 industrial plants which had been promoted or aided by the Economic Development Administration and which gave employment to over 100,000 workers. By 1964 the national income from manufacturing was greater than that from agriculture and accounted for almost one-fourth of the total net income. Puerto Rican leaders proudly announce that in over half of their industrial plants there are Puerto Rican managers, engineers, technicians and foremen. Puerto Ricans are also proud that in the past fifty years they have been hosts to thousands of observers and technicians who have come from many countries to study development techniques in Puerto Rico.

All indices—demographic, economic and social—point to the rapid strides that have been made. Between 1940 and 1960 life expectancy increased from about 46 years to about 70 years and the number of doctors in proportion to the population tripled. The rate of tuberculosis has been reduced to almost the same level as that of the United States and malaria has practically been wiped out.* As one observer has pointed out, Puerto Rico has become so modern that by 1960 heart disease and cancer had replaced tuberculosis and pneumonia as the principal killer diseases. Also, the people have become less resistant to the use of hospitals, health centers and clinics. Eighty-two percent of all births now occur in hospitals, and ambulance service reaches into most of the slum areas.

In 1940 Puerto Rico had an annual per capita income of $120; by 1963 it was $740, about twice the average for Latin American countries. Today the

---

* Deaths from diarrhea and enteritis decreased from 409.5 per 100,000 for the period 1930-39 to 39.5 in 1960; infant mortality from 88.3 to 43.7; and general mortality from 19.7 during 1930-39 to 6.7 in 1960.

Puerto Rican consumer spends more than $400 yearly per capita for imported products; this is several times his total per capita income of twenty years ago.

The progress in the educational system has also been notable. In 1940, 285,000 children of school age (40 percent) were still not in school. By 1964 well over 90 percent were attending school. Illiteracy dropped from 32 percent in 1940 to less than 17 percent in 1960, and to 11 percent in 1965.

However, the social and economic progress of Puerto Rico has not equally benefited all segments of society, and the figures cited above tend to conceal conditions of human misery which are still the lot of many Puerto Ricans, especially those who live in the urban slums. Over 90,000 still live in the slums of Greater San Juan alone.* Although Puerto Rico can point to an admirable record of building public housing projects, the rate of increase in the urban slums has just about kept up with the rate of new building. If the present ratio persists, it will take over fifty years to make any real progress toward the elimination of the slums.†

The story of the Ríos family presented in this volume shows in painful and dramatic form the terrible conditions of poverty and social pathology which existed on a mass scale in Puerto Rico prior to the 1940's and which still persist today in the slums. The life histories of the individuals who were born between 1900 and 1930 reveal a picture of family disruption, violence, brutality, cheapness of life, lack of love, lack of education, lack of medical facilities —in short, a picture of incredible deprivation the effects of which cannot be wiped out in a single generation.

Most of the characters in this book feel that progress has passed them by, that they were better off before, "when food cost less." They are generally hostile to government and find the idea of the Commonwealth difficult to understand.‡ There is no doubt in my mind, however, that the children are better

* Greater San Juan includes Old San Juan, Santurce and Río Piedras. Together they comprise the urban core of the San Juan metropolitan area, which had a population of over 600,000 inhabitants in 1962 and which includes the five municipalities of Cataño, Bayamón, Guaynabo, Trujillo Alto and Carolina.

† This is a conservative estimate. A recent study by United States sociologists is much more pessimistic. "It will come as a shock to many Puerto Ricans who have watched their government's gigantic efforts at slum clearance in recent years to realize that, although the growth of the Slum Belt has been checked, only trifling progress has been made towards its removal. The decline of the slum population has recently averaged less than one-half of one percent per year—a rate that, if continued, would give the Slum Belt two centuries more of existence." Caplow, Stryker and Wallace, p. 228.[4]

‡ Our findings on the Ríos family and on other families are in sharp contrast with the rather broad and overly optimistic generalization of Tumin and Feldman[1] (pp. 164-65), who wrote: "There is very high morale in all segments of the Puerto Rican community. The present inequalities are not perceived as insuperable obstacles. The social order is viewed at all levels of the class structure as a fair and

off than their parents and that the parents are better off than the grandparents. One has only to compare the lives of Fernanda and her mother Luisa with those of Fernanda's children and grandchildren to realize what a great rise in aspiration level has occurred in Puerto Rican society as a whole. But the findings in this book leave no room for smugness or complacency about past accomplishments. So long as there are families like the Ríos family in Puerto Rico and in New York, a great deal remains to be done.

The intensive study of the life of even a single extended family by the methods used in this volume tells us something about individuals, about family life, about lower-class life as a whole, and about the history and culture of the larger society in which these people live. It may also reflect something of national character, although this would be difficult to prove. Most studies of national character have focused upon the middle class, on the assumption that this class reflects the dominant values of the society. However, I am suggesting the possibility that studies of the lower class may also reveal something that is distinctive of a people as a whole.

At one time I would have been quite skeptical about such a proposition. Indeed, it was my dissatisfaction with the high level of abstraction inherent in the concept of culture patterns which led me to turn away from anthropological community studies to the intensive study of families. It seemed to me that descriptions of a way of life on the abstract level of culture patterns left out the very heart and soul of the phenomena we were concerned with, namely, the individual human being. In describing total culture patterns there is an almost inevitable neglect of the range of variation in custom and in behavior which may lead all too readily to overdrawn configurations that play up differences between cultures and tend to ignore the fundamental human similarities. However, after having worked for a number of years on the level of family analysis, I find it helpful to return again to the higher conceptual level of history and culture. When I compare my findings on the Ríos family and the other families that I have studied in Puerto Rico with my findings on my Mexican families, a number of differences emerge, differences which are undoubtedly related to the different histories of Mexico and Puerto Rico.

Although Puerto Rico and Mexico are both Latin American countries and share a Hispanic tradition, there are great contrasts between them in size, in geography, in natural resources, in the racial composition of their population, in their political system and in the general character of their people. It would be difficult to find two Latin American countries with greater contrast. Some of the differences in culture date back to the pre-Hispanic period. In

---

reasonable arrangement. Members of all classes feel well integrated and feel it is worth giving their loyalty to the society and their effort toward its development. In these terms, though they are decidedly unequally equipped with the required skills, people at all levels are relatively equally equipped for the future with the spirit required."

Puerto Rico the native culture was relatively simple and never reached the high degree of civilization achieved by Mexico in pre-Hispanic times. The Spanish conquest was much more devastating for Puerto Rico than for Mexico because the Spaniards wiped out most of the Indian population. Within fifty years after the conquest there was little Indian culture left to speak of in Puerto Rico, whereas in Mexico the Indian population and culture persisted and its influence was to be one of the major factors in the history of the nation. This has its irony because the native Puerto Rican Indian society was probably much more democratic and egalitarian than the Mexican, which was highly stratified and exploitative.

Because of the large Indian population in Mexico, the Spanish conquerors and immigrants throughout the three hundred years of the colonial period were absorbed by the native population. The Mexican population is a fusion of the Indian and Spaniard, with only a minimal admixture of Negroes. In Puerto Rico, where Negroes were brought in as slaves by the Spaniards soon after the conquest, the population is a fusion of the Spaniard and the Negro with very little of the Indian.

Both the Indian in Mexico and the Negro slaves in Puerto Rico were a depressed and exploited group during the colonial period, but the Mexican Indians had a relatively higher status and lived under more favorable conditions. In Puerto Rico both colonialism and slavery lasted much longer than in Mexico. Whereas Mexico takes pride in its Indian tradition, Puerto Rico cannot point to a great Indian or Negro past. Nor are Puerto Rican Negroes especially conscious of their own distinctive African origins. In part this is due to the long process of racial integration of which Puerto Ricans are so proud. It is interesting to note in this connection that in Puerto Rico, unlike Cuba, there has never developed a comparable interest and specialization in the field of Negro studies or in the African cultural background of some of its people.[6]

Puerto Rico's small size, its small population and its paucity of natural resources, especially minerals, were a great disadvantage from the very beginning of the colonial period. Because the island was not a source of great wealth, it was treated by the mother country as a fourth-rate colony and was neglected in many ways. But perhaps the crucial difference in the history of the two countries was the development of a great revolutionary tradition in Mexico and its absence in Puerto Rico.* Puerto Ricans sought greater autonomy from Spain during the nineteenth century, but they were never able to organize

---

* Muñoz Marín has suggested that the failure to develop a successful revolutionary movement against Spain in the nineteenth century was due, in part, to the tiny size of the island, because in Puerto Rico, unlike Cuba, there was no place for guerrilla warriors to hide. René Marqués, a leading Puerto Rican writer, apparently rejects this type of geographical determinism and suggests instead a basic docility in Puerto Rican character. See his "El puertorriqueño dócil," *Cuadernos Americanos* CXX (1962), pp. 144-95.

a revolutionary struggle for their freedom, and the single attempt along this line, at Lares, was short-lived and never received mass support.* By contrast the Mexicans fought for their independence from Spain between 1810 and 1821, drove out the French in 1866 and later produced the great revolution of 1910-20 with its glorious ideals of social justice. In the course of these struggles great heroes emerged, men who have become symbols of the Mexican spirit of revolution and independence.

In Mexico even the poorest slum dwellers have a much richer sense of the past and a deeper identification with the Mexican tradition than do Puerto Ricans with their tradition. In both countries I presented urban slum dwellers with the names of national figures. In Mexico City quite a high percentage of the respondents, including those with little or no formal schooling, knew about Cuauhtémoc, Hidalgo, Morelos, Juárez, Díaz, Zapata, Villa, Carranza and Cárdenas. In San Juan the respondents showed an abysmal ignorance of Puerto Rican historical figures. Some knew more about George Washington and Abraham Lincoln than about their own heroes. The names of Ramón Power, José de Diego, Baldiorioty de Castro, Ramón Betances, Nemesio Canales, Lloréns Torres, rang no bell. Many knew about Albizu Campos, the Nationalist leader. However, for most lower-income Puerto Rican slum dwellers history begins and ends with Muñoz Rivera, his son Muñoz Marín, and *doña* Felisa Rincón de Gautier, mayoress of San Juan!

One of the most striking differences in the language of the Mexican and Puerto Rican slum dwellers is the latter's mixture of English and Spanish and the Hispanization of many English words. This mixture of the two languages has been decried by many Puerto Rican leaders and intellectuals as a symptom of cultural breakdown and as a threat to the Spanish language, which is the single most important basis of Puerto Rican cultural identity. Most of the

* Anderson describes the Puerto Rican political scene in the nineteenth century as follows: "As the Spanish pendulum swung back and forth between monarchical absolutism and constitutional liberalism, Puerto Rican politicians showed remarkable patience and flexibility in adjusting their claims and expectations to the vagaries of peninsular politics. It is noteworthy that throughout this period there was no significant open movement of national rebellion in Puerto Rico, as there was in Cuba. The long and bloody civil war in Cuba, which broke out in 1868 and again in 1895, dramatized the dilemmas and failures of Spain in her leftover colonies. Except for a brief and rather pathetic flurry of revolt in the mountain town of Lares in 1868, to which the Puerto Rican people and their principal leaders responded with an eloquent apathy, national independence was hardly mentioned as a possible solution to Puerto Rico's problems. The island's political leaders tended to advocate either a more complete assimilation into the Spanish system or a higher degree of autonomy for the island, but within the context of a legal and moral tie to Spain." Robert W. Anderson, *Party Politics in Puerto Rico* (Stanford, Stanford University Press, 1965).

"loan" words used by Puerto Ricans are derived from their experiences in New York and fall into a number of categories: housing and furniture, factories and work, government and military, school, food and clothing, city and transport. A few examples of loan words most frequently used in each category follow:

Housing and furniture: *el caucho* (derived from the English "couch," this means a cot or folding bed), *el closet, el hall, el ground floor, el building, el landlord, el basement, el mattress, la furnitura* and *el super* (for "superintendent"). Factory: *la overtime, el boss* or *el bosso, la bossa, busy, steady, slow, el watchman* (often pronounced *wáchiman*), *el foreman* and *la floorlady*. Government and military: *social security* (often pronounced *sekiúriti*), *Army, Navy, Merchant Marine, el welfare,* etc. School: *la high, teacher, la Miss, la Mrs., la sister* and *la norsa* (for nurse). Food and clothing: *el hamburger, el sandwich, lonchear* (to eat lunch) and *el supermarket; el coat, los panties, el sweter, la T-shirt, el jacket, el lipstick.* City and transport: *el east side, el west side, downtown, uptown, el subway* and *el trolley.*

Other common loan words which are usually inserted in a Spanish sentence are *la Gem, el party, el trouble, el laundry, dry cleaning, nice, easy, anyway, el appointment, las Christmas, brown* and *blue.* A typical sentence in Spanish would be *"Qué bonitos ojos brown tienes"* ("What pretty brown eyes you have"). Or *"Toma la vida easy, muchacha"* ("Take life easy, girl").

Methods

THIS BOOK is the first of a series of volumes based upon a study of one hundred Puerto Rican families from four slums of Greater San Juan and of their relatives in New York City. The major objectives of the study were to contribute to our understanding of urban slum life in San Juan; to examine the problems of adjustment and the changes in the family life of migrants to New York; to develop a comparative literature on intensive family case studies; to devise new field methods and new ways of organizing and presenting family data; and finally, to test and refine the concept of a culture of poverty by a comparison of my Mexican and Puerto Rican data.

The one hundred families in Greater San Juan were selected from slums which represented significant ecological, racial, socio-economic and religious variables. We wanted old and new slum settlements, slums on dry land as well as those on the ocean front or on bay inlets, slums with both Negroes and whites, with Protestants, especially Pentecostal and Evangelical sects, as well as Catholics.

The principal criteria in the selection of families were low income, relatives in New York, and a willingness to co-operate in the study. We located the poorest families with the help of social workers who introduced us to their local *barrio comisarios*.* In our initial reconnaissance survey we found a remarkably wide range of income within the slums. A substantial number of families had comparatively high incomes and owned such luxury items as refrigerators, television sets, washing machines and even cars. Although our primary interest was in low-income families, we decided to include some families in each of the income groups reported in the U. S. Census so that at some later time we would be able to compare high-income families with low-income families to determine the factors involved in upward mobility.

The task of locating and working with the New York relatives of the Puerto Rican sample families proved to be a time-consuming and frustrating process. In Puerto Rico we had the great advantage of working with families within four or five small slum communities. In New York our families were scattered from Coney Island to the Bronx. Moreover, the people in New York seemed to have less free time and were more suspicious and not as readily available for interviews. Because of these field-work difficulties and our limited staff, we decided to concentrate on fewer families in New York and to study related family clusters in greater depth.

The methods used in this study are a combination of the traditional techniques used in sociology, anthropology and psychology, and include questionnaires, interviews, participant-observation, biographies, a limited number of intensive whole-family case studies, and the application of selected psychological tests, such as the Thematic Apperception, Rorschach and the Sentence Completion. A novel aspect of the project was the use as research assistants of two lower-class Mexicans whose families I had studied in previous research. These assistants gave me a Mexican view of Puerto Rican slum culture and helped point up the similarities and differences between Mexican and Puerto Rican subcultures.

Four basic schedules were applied to each sample family. The schedules dealt with household composition, an inventory of major household items, a summary of the residence and employment history of each adult, and information concerning migration to New York.

In addition to the four basic questionnaires administered to each family, fifteen other schedules containing over five hundred questions were also used. These questionnaires dealt with the following subjects: complete household

---

* A *barrio* "commissar" or "inspector," who is usually an active worker in the Popular Party as well as a municipal employee. The *comisario* serves as a liaison officer between the city administration, the local political leaders and the people of the *barrio*.

inventory, including clothing, animals, religious objects, books, etc.; friendship patterns within the neighborhood; patterns of *compadrazgo;** family relations; income and expenditures; division of labor; recreational patterns; cosmopolitanism; health and treatment of disease; politics; religion; and world view. The administration of the nineteen schedules took about twelve hours per informant.

The intensive studies of families involved the establishment of deep personal ties without which we could never have obtained the intimate data presented in this volume. My assistants and I spent many hours attending family parties, wakes and baptisms, and responding to emergency calls. We took people to the hospital, secured their release from jail, filled out applications for them, arranged doctors' appointments, helped get apartments and jobs, and helped get families on relief.

The tape recordings of the life histories were begun only after we knew the family well. In some cases we visited the family regularly for a few months and learned a great deal about their lives in casual conversations. Later, in the recordings, we would ask the informants to repeat stories which we already knew so that we could have them in their own words.

My approach to family studies requires exhaustive research which by its nature precludes large samples. The study of the one hundred families was conducted by the questionnaire method in order to gain background material for the much more detailed study of a smaller group of families. The intensive study of the family has many methodological advantages. Because the family is a small social system, it lends itself to the holistic approach of anthropology. The family is a natural unit of study, particularly in a large metropolis like San Juan or New York. In studying a culture through the intensive analysis of specific families we learn what institutions mean to individuals. It helps us get beyond form and structure to the realities of human life. Whole-family studies bridge the gap between the conceptual extremes of culture at one pole and the individual at the other; we see both culture and personality as they are interrelated in real life.

Family studies also serve to delineate the social networks within which families transact their lives, and to this extent the family-study approach and the social-network-study approach are overlapping and mutually reinforcing. Relatives, neighbors, friends, *compadres,* fellow workers, employers, teachers, priests, spiritualists, policemen, social workers, shopkeepers all come and go in these autobiographies. On the whole, however, most interpersonal relations occur within a fairly narrow circle of close relatives, which serves as a defense in economic and emotional crises.

In an earlier book[7] I suggested four separate but related approaches

* *Compadrazgo* is a system of relationships and obligations between godparents (*padrinos*) and godchildren (*ahijados*), and between godparents and parents, who are *compadres.*

which, when combined, may provide a rounded and integrated view of family life. The first or topical approach applies most of the conceptual categories used in the study of an entire community to a single family. A second approach records long, intensive autobiographies of each member of the family. This technique permits us to see the family through the eyes of each of its members and gives us insight into individual psychology and family dynamics. The independent versions of similar incidents in family life serve to check the validity and reliability of the data.

The third approach is to study intensively a particular problem or a special event or crisis within the family. The way a family meets new situations reveals many latent aspects of individual and family psychodynamics.

A fourth approach to the study of a whole family is the detailed observation and recording of a typical day in the life of the family. The selection of the day is arbitrary, practically a random choice; it may be an ordinary day or one marked by an unusual event such as a birth, a baptism, a fiesta, a funeral or a move to a new house.

The use of the day as the unit of study has been a common device of the novelist. As I have pointed out elsewhere, it has as many advantages for science as for literature, and provides an excellent medium for combining the scientific and humanistic aspects of anthropology. The day universally orders family life; it is a small-enough time unit to permit intensive and uninterrupted study by the method of direct observation, and it is ideally suited for controlled comparisons. It makes possible a quantitative analysis of almost any aspect of family life. For example, one can study the amount of time devoted to the preparation of food in different families, the amount of conversation between husband and wife or between parents and children, the amount of laughter, the extent and kind of table talk, and so on. One can also study the more subtle and qualitative aspects of interpersonal family relations, the tensions and shifting moods, as well as the variety of activities and the number of outside contacts.

As a background for the observation and recording of days in these Puerto Rican families I have added a further elaboration of method, namely, the reconstruction of days through intensive interviewing of the heads of households. Each morning for a week or more, the field worker studying a particular family questioned the informant about the details of events of the previous day. These reconstructed days were useful in several ways. First, they enabled us to see the actually observed and recorded days in better perspective as to typicality, and it helped us to estimate the effect of the investigator's presence on the normal routines of family life. Second, the reconstructed days gave us new insights and leads which at times opened up an entirely new line of investigation. Third, the repeated questioning served to sensitize the informant to the type of detailed information we wanted and to improve the content and orderliness of his or her subsequent narrations.

Before attempting to record an actual day with a family, rapport must be sufficiently good so that the normal behavior and routines of family life are only minimally disturbed. Although the controlled laboratory procedures of small-group studies with built-in microphones and one-way screens were not used and are not possible, well-trained observers can succeed in giving camera-like views of the movements, conversations and interactions that occur in a family. In the study of the Ríos family I was fortunate in having the assistance of a talented Puerto Rican graduate student with an excellent memory for dialogue and detail. Note-taking during the day was minimal and had little effect upon her rapport with the family. In my study of other families, in addition to an observer I used a skilled stenographer to record all conversation.

In the autobiographies I have placed great reliance upon tape-recorded interviews. The value of this approach was discussed in the Introduction to *The Children of Sánchez*.[8] Briefly, I believe it captures the full flavor of the speech of the people, the slang, the nuances, the hesitations, the laughter, the tears. Autobiographies based on tape transcriptions present living documents of a type that are difficult to match by any other method.

In studying the extended family, it is highly desirable to have a complete family genealogy, including the names and relationship of all relatives, living or dead, known to the informant; their age, place of birth, civil status, occupation, place of residence, and years of schooling; frequency of visits; what assistance they are to the informant; whether they are house and/or landowners; and whether they have been to the United States. Since a single informant may have knowledge of over one hundred relatives (some know more than three hundred!), the preparation of genealogies is a time-consuming, painstaking, technical labor. A special research assistant worked for many months preparing genealogies on my most important families.

As part of the study of a hundred families in Greater San Juan I made a detailed analysis of their material possessions and also those of their relatives in New York. I was especially interested in the changes in New York as an index of acculturation. Studies of the material possessions of urban dwellers on a household basis have generally been neglected by anthropologists and other students of society. Actually, the study of the material possessions of the poor may give us another important dimension for the definition of poverty. It can tell us about their buying and spending habits, their definition of luxury items, the relationship between income and material wealth, the proportion of goods bought in stores, markets, street stands, or from hawkers; the extent of trade or exchange of goods within slum settlements or neighborhoods, and the social consequences and concomitants thereof; the distances which they go to make purchases; the periods of economic crisis within the family as revealed by the history of pawned objects, the range and variation in the distribution of "wealth" among families who seem desperately poor; and finally, the values of the people as reflected in the relative amount of their income spent on various types of objects—for example, religious items versus modern appliances.

In this connection I designed an inventory form which calls for the following information on each item found in a household: number or quantity of each article; description and condition; length of time in possession; cost; method of purchase (installment plan or cash); item new or used at time of purchase, where purchased, who purchased the item; if a gift, when given, by whom, for what occasion, new or used, and approximate value; if homemade, who made the item, when made and value; cost of replacing the item and approximate present value; whether the item had been pawned and/or redeemed; other comments.

The approach outlined above is analagous to that of the archaeologist trying to reconstruct the culture of past civilizations through the analysis of material remains. The study of potsherds, for example, may enable him to draw inferences about trade patterns, sources and directions of cultural influences, economic levels, residence patterns, artistic achievements and degrees of social stratification. Similarly, an analysis of the material possessions of a living people can tell us a great deal which may pass unnoticed or is unverifiable in a standard ethnographic account.

Of course, the "archaeology" of living peoples has an important advantage over traditional archaeology, that is, the ability to question the people directly about their possessions. Thus a question about a clay bowl might lead to an understanding of gift-giving between godparents, whereas the sherds unearthed by an archaeologist will more than likely yield little or no specific information along social lines. However, quantitative analysis in both instances enables us to make important generalizations about the society.

The study of the material possessions of contemporary peoples further enables us to make distinctions between what has been called the "real" and the "ideal" culture. For example, informants might tell the investigator that godparents always give gifts to their godchildren on the Day of the Three Kings. But if the inventories show that only a few children have in fact received gifts from their godparents, we are able to make a definitive statement on this point. In addition, we would be able to see which godparents did present gifts to their godchildren over a certain period of time, and perhaps draw some salient facts about social organization from several such bodies of data.

In summary, the major steps involved in producing a well-rounded family study are as follows: (1) census-type data are gathered on a large number of families selected on the basis of the major variables of interest to the study; (2) from this sample, a smaller group of families are selected for more intensive study; (3) interviews are conducted with each family member to record their life stories and to question them on a wide range of topics; (4) a week or more of consecutive days are reconstructed on the basis of intensive interrogation; (5) complete days in the life of the family are observed and recorded; (6) recorded interviews are transcribed from the tapes; (7) typed data are translated, edited and organized; (8) reinterviewing is done to fill in gaps in the data; significant new data are translated and inserted; (9) the final versions of the autobiographies and days are edited for publication.

The Ríos Family

THE RÍOS FAMILY presented in this volume consists of five households, a mother and two married daughters in Puerto Rico and a married son and daughter in New York City. The mother, Fernanda Fuentes, a Negro woman of forty, is now living with her sixth husband in La Esmeralda, a San Juan slum. Her children—Soledad, twenty-five; Felícita, twenty-three; Simplicio, twenty-one; and Cruz, nineteen—were born to Fernanda while she was living in free union with her first husband, Cristóbal Ríos, a light-skinned Puerto Rican.

In addition to the five major characters, I have included the views of the spouses, of two young grandchildren, ages seven and nine, of a maternal aunt, and of a close friend of the family. In all, sixteen Puerto Ricans, ranging in ages from seven to sixty-four and representing four generations, tell their life stories and those of their parents and grandparents.* This gives the reader a historical depth of well over one hundred years, reveals the patterns of change and stability over many generations, and provides some contrasts between rural and urban family patterns.

Although I call this book a family study, the number of people involved is greater than the population of some village communities described in anthropological monographs. Nineteen related households, eleven in San Juan and eight in New York City, with a total population of fifty-five individuals, were studied in preparing this volume. The book also includes data on twelve other households. In all, over three hundred individuals appear in these pages.

The organization of the book reflects the actual movement of Puerto Ricans back and forth between San Juan and New York. Part I begins with the mother, Fernanda, in San Juan; Part II moves to New York for a view of

* I have also studied the life history of Fernanda's great-aunt Funeraria (age eighty), a country woman, and the only surviving family member of her generation. Because of space limitation, however, I have not included her story. Funeraria's story takes us back two generations, to her grandfather, and thereby gives us the perspective of seven generations.

Soledad, the eldest daughter; Part III shifts back to San Juan with Felícita; Part IV returns to New York for a view of the son, Simplicio; and Part V is again set in San Juan with the youngest daughter, Cruz. The book ends with an epilogue by Cruz, who describes her move from the slum La Esmeralda to a beautiful public housing project, and tells of her experiences and problems of adjustment in her new environment.

Perhaps the most important methodological innovation in this volume as compared to my earlier studies, *Five Families, The Children of Sánchez* and *Pedro Martínez*,[9] is the much broader canvas of the family portrait, the intensification of the technique whereby individuals and incidents are seen from multiple points of view, and the combination of multiple biographies with observed typical days. The biographies provide a subjective view of each of the characters, whereas the days give us a more objective account of their actual behavior. The two types of data supplement each other and set up a counterpoint which makes for a more balanced picture. On the whole, the observed days give a greater sense of vividness and warmer glimpses of these people than do their own autobiographies. And because the days include a description not only of the people but also of the setting, of the domestic routines and material possessions, the reader gets a more integrated view of their lives.

In the selection of the Ríos family there was an inadvertent but fortunate convergence of two independent sampling procedures. Three households of the Ríos family were part of a sample of thirty-two families which we selected for study in La Esmeralda slum. Shortly after we began to work with the Ríos family, Dr. Rosa C. Marín of the School of Social Work, University of Puerto Rico, invited me to do an independent study of some of her 225 low-income, multiple-problem families which had been carefully selected from the rolls of social agencies for her Family-Centered Treatment, Research and Demonstration Project. I agreed to study ten of her sample families in La Esmeralda, and was introduced to each of them by a social worker. Cruz Ríos and her children, whom we had already been studying for about a week, was one of the ten families.

The Ríos family, their friends and neighbors, reflect many of the characteristics of the subculture of poverty, characteristics which are widespread in Puerto Rico but which are by no means exclusively Puerto Rican. They are also found among urban slum dwellers in many parts of the world. Indeed, the Ríos family is not presented here as a typical Puerto Rican family but rather as representative of one style of life in a Puerto Rican slum. The frequency distribution of this style of life cannot be determined until we have many comparable studies from other slums in Puerto Rico and elsewhere.

The language used by the Ríos family in this volume, as well as that used by the other families of our study, is simple, direct and earthy. There is relatively little use of metaphor or analogy except that contained in some of the popular proverbs. And while the language is strong and vivid, it never reaches the poetic levels of the language of the Mexicans I have studied. Most of the linguistic creativity in the San Juan slums seems inspired by bodily functions, primarily anal and genital. The description of the most intimate sexual scenes is so matter-of-fact that it soon loses the quality of obscenity and one comes to accept it as an intrinsic part of their everyday life.

The people in this book, like most of the other Puerto Rican slum dwellers I have studied, show a great zest for life, especially for sex, and a need for excitement, new experiences and adventures. Theirs is an expressive style of life. They value acting out more than thinking out, self-expression more than self-constraint, pleasure more than productivity, spending more than saving, personal loyalty more than impersonal justice. They are fun-loving and enjoy parties, dancing and music. They cannot be alone; they have an almost insatiable need for sociability and interaction. They are not apathetic, isolated, withdrawn or melancholy. Compared with the low-income Mexicans I have studied, they seem less reserved, less depressive, less controlled and less stable.

The Ríos family is closer to the expression of an unbridled id than any other people I have studied. They have an almost complete absence of internal conflict and of a sense of guilt. They tend to accept themselves as they are, and do not indulge in soul-searching or introspection. The leading characters in *The Children of Sánchez* seem mild, repressed and almost middle-class by comparison.

In the Ríos family, uncontrolled rage, aggression, violence and even bloodshed are not uncommon; their extreme impulsivity affects the whole tenor of their lives. There is an overwhelming preoccupation with sex, the most frequent cause of quarrels. Sex is used to satisfy a great variety of needs —for children, for pleasure, for money, for revenge, for love, to express *machismo* (manliness), and to compensate for all the emptiness in their lives. Even family unity, one of the most sacred values in this family-oriented culture, is sometimes threatened by the danger of seduction by stepfathers, the sexual rivalry between sisters, between mother and daughters, and occasionally even between grandmothers and granddaughters. There is a remarkable frankness and openness about sex, and little effort is made to hide the facts of life from children. Although the children in the Ríos family have many problems, they do not suffer from parental secrecy and dishonesty about sex. The male children are erotically stimulated by their mothers and by other members of the family, who take pride in the child's every erection as an indication of his virility and *machismo*. Masturbation is generally not punished. In the Ríos family early sexual experience for boys and girls is accepted as almost inevitable, even though ideally mothers are supposed to keep their young daughters under control.

The women in this book show more aggressiveness and a greater violence of language and behavior than the men. The women are more demanding and less giving and have much less of a martyr complex than the Mexican women I have studied. In the Ríos family it is the women who take the initiative in breaking up the marriages. They call the police during family quarrels and take their husbands into court for nonsupport of the children. Indeed, a great deal of the aggressiveness of the women is directed against men. The women continually deprecate them and characterize them as inconsiderate, irresponsible, untrustworthy and exploitative. The women teach children to depend upon the mother and to distrust men.

The failure of the women in the Ríos family to accept the traditionally submissive role of women in Puerto Rican society creates tensions and problems in their marital relations, especially in the case of Fernanda and her daughters because of the bizarre ways in which they express their independence. Their behavior is caused by a deep ambivalence about their role as women, by their occupational history and by their experience as heads of matrifocal households, a common occurrence in the culture of poverty. It also reflects the general trend toward the greater freedom and independence of women which has accompanied the increasing urbanization, industrialization and Americanization of Puerto Rico.

On the whole, the men seem to be more passive, dependent and depressed than the women. It is the men who often express greater interest in having a stable family life and who resist their wives' attempts to separate. This role reversal cannot entirely be explained by the fact that some of these men have married women who have been "in the life"—that is, prostitutes. Many of the men who did not marry this type of woman also showed the same pattern of dependency.

Compared to the lower-class Mexican men, the Puerto Rican men in this volume were less stable, less responsible, and except when goaded, less concerned with *machismo*. In Mexico, although the men were more controlled, their quarrels more often led to killings, usually by shooting or stabbing. The intention was to destroy. In Puerto Rico the men were more explosive but they generally limited themselves to cutting the face of their opponent with a Gem razor. The intention was to disfigure and to demean.

The remarkable stability in some of the behavior patterns of the Ríos family over four generations, which span a period of rapid change in Puerto Rican society, suggests that we are dealing with a tenacious cultural pattern. This can be seen clearly in the high incidence of early marriages, of free unions, of multiple spouses and of illegitimate children. For example, Fernanda's maternal great-grandfather had children with six women—one a legal wife, three wives in free union and two concubines. Fernanda's maternal aunt Amparo has had six husbands, all in free union, and thirteen children by four of them. Fernanda herself has had six husbands, with children by two of them. Her daughter Soledad has had six husbands in free union and four children.

Another daughter, Felícita, has had five children by three men; and the youngest daughter, Cruz, had had three husbands by the time she was seventeen. This marriage pattern is not peculiar to the Ríos family. It is also true of many of the other characters in this book. For example, Soledad's present husband Benedicto has had six wives, five of them in free union, with children by three of them; Flora, Simplicio's wife, has had four husbands, all in free union. In summary, the five major characters, Fernanda and her children, have had a total of twenty marriages, seventeen of which were consensual and three legal. This is a large number when one considers that Fernanda's children were twenty-five years or younger. The nine secondary adult characters who tell their life stories have had a total of twenty-seven marriages, twenty-four in free union and three legal marriages. If we include twelve additional characters mentioned in the life stories, we find that twenty-six adults have had a total of eighty-nine unions, seventy-six of which were consensual and thirteen legal.

The history of the Ríos family, as well as other data, suggests that the pattern of free unions and multiple spouses was not limited to the poor. It has been a widespread pattern among wealthy rural families; Fernanda's great-grandfather, a well-to-do landowner, is a case in point. This illustrates a general proposition which has impressed me in Puerto Rico and elsewhere, namely, the remarkable similarities between some aspects of the lives of the very poor and of the very rich.

In writing about multiproblem families like the Ríos family, social scientists often stress the instability, the lack of organization, lack of direction and lack of order. Certainly there are many contradictory attitudes and inconsistencies expressed in these autobiographies. Nevertheless, it seems to me that their behavior is clearly patterned and reasonably predictable. Indeed, one is often struck by the inexorable repetitiousness and the iron entrenchment of their behavior patterns.

It has been my experience over many years that the psychiatrists, clinical psychologists and social workers who have read the autobiographies and psychological tests of the people I have studied, have often found more negative elements and pathology than I am willing to grant. This has also been the case with the present volume. Their findings may reflect some bias inherent in the tests themselves, but perhaps more important, it seems to me, is the failure to see these people within the context of the culture of poverty.

It is true that the Ríos family, like so many slum families, has a history of psychopathology which goes back a few generations. Fernanda's maternal grandmother, Clotilde, was described by her relatives as having been strange and difficult. After the death of one of her children her behavior became bizarre and she reportedly was "crazy" for some time. Fernanda's uncle had an episode of mental illness which was attributed to sorcery, and her cousin Adela "went crazy" for a period of two years. Fernanda's daughter, Soledad, has had a number of epileptic-type hysterical seizures, commonly known as the "Puerto Rican syndrome," and has been hospitalized several times for this. Another daughter, Felícita, has also had one or two seizures of a milder nature. There was a very high incidence of asthma in the Ríos family, especially among Fernanda's children and grandchildren. There was also a high incidence of asthma in our larger sample of a hundred families. In all my years of travel and research I have never seen as much asthma as in Puerto Rico. In Mexico I rarely found it.*

The Ríos family would probably be classified as a multiproblem family by most social workers, but it is by no means an extreme example nor is it the worst I have encountered in the Puerto Rican slums. None of the major characters are drug addicts, alcoholics, professional thieves or criminal types. Most of them work for a living and are self-supporting. Only two of the nine households, represented by the sixteen individuals who tell their life stories, were on relief. On the whole, there is remarkably little delinquency and relatively little involvement with gangs or gangsters. Despite the many violent incidents that occur, there have been no murders or suicides.

In spite of the presence of considerable pathology, I am impressed by the strengths in this family. I am impressed by their fortitude, vitality, resilience and ability to cope with problems which would paralyze many middle-class individuals. It takes a great deal of staying power to live in their harsh and brutalizing environment. They are a tough people, but they have their own sense of dignity and morality and they are capable of kindness, generosity and

---

* Another striking difference between Puerto Rico and Mexico is the attitude toward the giving away and the adoption of children. In Mexico City slums I found a great reluctance on the part of mothers to give away a child or to adopt a child from a neighbor. Even the sacred obligations of the *compadrazgo* system, which include the adoption of orphan children, are rarely honored. In most cases an orphan in a Mexican slum goes to live with a relative. In Puerto Rico, however, there is a much greater readiness to give children away and there are always women available who want to accept them. A sharp distinction is made between formal adoption and informal, nonlegal adoption. The latter is more common. Children who are adopted informally are called *hijos de crianza* (foster children). Adult Puerto Ricans never think of this custom of giving away a child as abandonment, but studies suggest that some children feel it as such.

Hijos de crianza were present in a large percentage of our sample families. It is not only childless women who adopt *hijos de crianza*. Often women with five or six children of their own will take in another child. The custom is widespread in Puerto Rico on all class levels, but I found it especially common in the slums. This system gives the woman a certain amount of freedom and mobility. Many young mothers have been able to go to New York by giving their children away to a neighbor or relative as *hijos de crianza*. Often a *compadrazgo* relationship is established between the donor mother and the receiving mother, who become *comadres*.

compassion. They share food and clothing, help each other in misfortune, take in the homeless and cure the ill. Money and material possessions, although important, do not motivate their major decisions. Their deepest need is for love, and their life is a relentless search for it.

Unfortunately, because of their own negative self-image, the Ríos family do not always present themselves in the best light. Even in the recorded days, their particular style of communication and the crudeness of their language make them appear less attractive than they really are. When Cruz screams at her three-year-old daughter, "I'll pull out your lungs through your mouth!" and the child continues to disobey without apparent fear, it suggests that perhaps the child is quite secure in her mother's love. When Felícita sings a "dirty" song to her children instead of a traditional lullaby, the reader may be so disconcerted by the sexual imagery that he forgets the healthier aspects of the scene, children dancing and clapping happily to their mother's music. And if the children's hurts go unattended, it is equally true that in the long run their mother's lack of concern is not entirely inappropriate in an environment where toughness is necessary for survival. Soledad may seem like a harsh, cruel, inconsistent mother by middle-class standards, but one should also note how much time, energy and attention she gives to her children and how hard she tries to live up to her own ideal of a good mother. With much effort she has managed to provide them with a home, food and clothing, even with toys. She has not abandoned them, nor permitted anyone to abuse them, and she is devoted to them when they are ill.

When I began the study of the Ríos family I was not aware of its history of prostitution. Indeed, the social worker who had worked with Cruz Ríos for over a year did not know that Cruz's mother and sisters had once been prostitutes. The mother, Fernanda, and her daughter Soledad were not working as prostitutes during the two-year period of our study. Fernanda was a cook's assistant in a restaurant in San Juan for a short time and Soledad worked in a factory in New York. Fernanda's son, Simplicio, and his wife, Flora, both worked in a factory in New York. Felícita had a night job at a bar in San Juan. Only later did I learn that she was also working as a prostitute.

In considering the extent to which the presence of prostitution in the Ríos family has affected or distorted the general lower-class pattern of their family life—the relationships between husbands and wives, parents and children, siblings, grandparents and grandchildren and in-laws—we must view prostitution in the context of a slum community and the culture of poverty rather than in terms of middle-class values and stereotypes. Prostitution has a different meaning in a slum community like La Esmeralda, where about a third of the households have had a history of prostitution, than it does in a slum or other local community where it is rare. For unskilled, often illiterate women, whose lives are a struggle for survival, prostitution is a tempting economic alternative which does not necessarily ostracize them from their neighbors or social group, and which does not represent as sharp a break from ordinary life as it does for middle-class women. In the culture of poverty, with its free unions, unstable marriages and high rate of illegitimacy, the line between the routine life and the "gay life" is sometimes a very thin one.

It seems to me that the history of prostitution in the Ríos family has not caused any major changes in the basic patterns of their family life. This conclusion is based on a comparison of their lives before and after they became prostitutes. Fernanda was married for seven years to her first husband and had four children with him before she went into the life. Soledad was married almost eight years and had three children before she turned to prostitution to help support them. Felícita had five children before she became a prostitute. Clearly, then, most of the children were raised during the crucial early years of their lives by mothers who were not prostitutes at the time. Moreover, all of these women had had difficulties with their husbands well before they became prostitutes. The domestic discord marking their later marriages represents a continuation of an earlier pattern and was not necessarily due to their having been in the life.

However, prostitution has certainly made a difference in the Ríos family. Their income has been higher but more variable; the women have spent more on clothing than do most women in the slums; the children have had a somewhat greater exposure to sex and to rough and obscene language, and have suffered from neglect because they were left alone at night when their mothers went out to work. Prostitution has tended to reinforce the negative self-image of the women and their children. Also, there has been a selective factor in the type of men who married into the family, especially when the man knew he was marrying a woman who had been a prostitute. However, one of the most common rationalizations of the men was the belief that ex-prostitutes sometimes become the most loyal wives.

Prostitution is regarded as a degraded occupation by most people in the slums as well as by the Ríos family themselves. Yet the prostitute is by no means at the lowest rung of the status ladder in La Esmeralda. Drug addicts, thieves, chronic alcoholics and homosexuals have lower status. On the whole the residents of La Esmeralda have accepted the Ríos family as neighbors and friends and have not discriminated against them because of their occupation. The fact that the Ríos women generally worked outside of La Esmeralda and were rather discreet about their profession helped their social position in the community. On the other hand, if we use the number of godchildren a person has as an index of social status, then the Ríos family had low status, because they had few godchildren. Most families would hesitate to ask a prostitute to be a godmother.

The data in this book suggests that we have to modify some of our stereotypes about prostitutes. One normally thinks of the role of a mother and the role of a prostitute as being contradictory, if not mutually exclusive. In these life histories the two roles coexist without too much conflict. Indeed, the relative ease with which the Ríos women move back and forth between the role of wife and mother and that of prostitute is remarkable.

The Setting

THE SETTING for the story of the Ríos family is La Esmeralda, an old and colorful slum in San Juan, built on a steep embankment between the city's ancient fort walls and the sea. Squeezed into an area not more than five city blocks long and a few hundred yards wide are nine hundred houses inhabited by 3,600 people. The area forms a kind of narrow rectangle, with seven rows of one- and two-story houses running from east to west. The rows of houses on the higher ground nearest the wall are straight and give some semblance of order and pattern like the houses on any city block. Farther down toward the sea, however, where the embankment is steeper, the houses stand helter-skelter along cement alleyways that turn and twist up and down and across the slope or come to a dead end.

Seen from the wall above, the slum looks almost prosperous. This is because all the houses have roofs of new green tar paper, a contribution from the mayoress, *doña* Felisa Rincón. And from this distance the cement walks or alleyways look clean, and one can see the ocean far below, with its white breakers foaming against the rocks.

Most of the houses are fairly large wooden structures with overhanging porches and balconies. The houses near the top of the embankment are set on cement bases; those nearer the sea are raised on stilts to protect them from high tides. Many of them have been painted in various shades of blue or green, with here and there a yellow or a saffron-colored building. Tall wooden poles, loaded with electric wires, run from east to west, and on many of the houses there are TV aerials.

Within the larger settlement are three subdivisions, known as San Nicolás, the New Esmeralda and the Old Esmeralda. These subdivisions are connected with San Juan by four entrances. The first two are steep, rough cement steps that lead down from the wall to San Nicolás on the east. There are over fifty of these steps, interrupted at intervals by small landings; it is a long, difficult climb or descent for the older inhabitants of La Esmeralda. At the foot of each stairway is an open space with a little grass, about one hundred by two hundred feet. Here, especially on Sundays, groups of men from La Esmeralda hold cockfights, gamble or play baseball. The third entrance is a paved road which passes under an arch and leads to the New Esmeralda. It is the only paved street running the length of the settlement. Old Esmeralda, on the west, is reached by a cement stairway similar to the ones which lead to San Nicolás.

Even though La Esmeralda is only ten minutes away from the Governor's Palace and the heart of San Juan, it is physically and socially marginal to the city. The wall above it stands as a kind of symbol separating it from the city. La Esmeralda forms a little community of its own, with a cemetery, a church, a small dispensary and maternity clinic, and one elementary school. There are many small stores, bars and taverns. The houses are decrepit and the alleyways littered with refuse.

From the wall down to the sea, the physical condition of the houses becomes poorer and poorer, and the social status of the people grows correspondingly lower, until on the beach itself the poorest people live in the most dilapidated houses. To live on the beach is dangerous, for there is the constant threat of a high tide which may wipe out the houses. Only recently fifty homes were destroyed by high waves during one night, and the residents had to be removed to public housing projects. The beach is also the dirtiest part of La Esmeralda. Several large conduits, broken in places, carry sewage down to the sea, and the beach swarms with flies and is littered with trash—garbage, human feces, beer bottles, condoms, broken beds and rotted pieces of wood. It is a refuge for dope addicts (the so-called *tecatos*) who gather under the houses to inject themselves. Nevertheless, the people of La Esmeralda use the beach for bathing, for love-making, for fishing and, when hungry, for collection of snails and crabs. And they raise pigs on the beach because of the abundant supply of garbage.

To the people of Greater San Juan, La Esmeralda has a bad reputation. It is known as the home of murderers, drug addicts, thieves and prostitutes. Most middle-class people are afraid of La Esmeralda and have never visited it. Yet conditions are said to have been much worse twenty years ago; at that time it was not uncommon to kill people and bury them under the houses. Today the residents of La Esmeralda think of it as a relatively elegant and healthful place, with its beautiful view of the sea, its paved streets, its new roofs, the absence of mosquitos, the low rentals and its nearness to their places of work.

In spite of the deprivation, poverty, violence and occasional murders, the general mood of the people of La Esmeralda is one of gaiety and exuberance. They seem outgoing, friendly and expressive, with relatively little distrust of outsiders. They live amid constant noise from radios, juke boxes and television sets, and spend a great deal of time in the stores and bars, where they drink and play dominoes.

The residents of La Esmeralda, like most slum dwellers, suffer from inadequate housing, poor education, illiteracy and low income.* According to U.S. Census data of 1960, 22 percent of the families had annual incomes of less than $500; 15 percent had incomes of from $500 to $999; 32 percent from $1,000 to $1,999; 27 percent from $2,000 to $3,999; only 4 percent had incomes of over $4,000. The income distribution in La Esmeralda as a whole closely paralleled that of our thirty-two sample families there, as well as our hundred-family sample from four San Juan slums. However, our thirty-two sample families from La Esmeralda were weighted somewhat toward the lower-income groups. About 47 percent of our sample families had annual incomes of less than $1,000, as compared to 37 percent for La Esmeralda as a whole. The thirty-two families in our sample had a median annual income of $1,100.

The people in La Esmeralda earned their living from a large number of occupations, but by far the greater proportion of the men were laborers and longshoremen working on the nearby city docks. Over 50 percent of all employed men and women worked in restaurants, hotels or other service occupations. This is well above the average for other slums in San Juan. As in other slums, though, very few men or women worked in factories. Some women were maids in private homes; some were sales workers or clerks. Many of the women worked within La Esmeralda, taking in washing and ironing. An un-

* La Esmeralda was one of our four sample slums in Greater San Juan. In 1964 the mean annual income of the one hundred sample families from the four slums was $1,400, with an average per capita income of $20 per month. Seventy-two percent of the families earned less than $1,999 per year. The ten poorest families had incomes ranging from $48 to $192; the ten richest families from $4,224 to $7,128.

The value of the material goods of the sample families showed the same wide range as the income distribution. The amount of money spent for household goods ranged from zero to $2,871. The ten families with the lowest expenditures on household goods had spent an average of $48. Most of the items in their homes were gifts from friends, neighbors and relatives. The ten families with the highest expenditures ranged from $1,705 to $2,871, with an average of $2,247.

The educational level of the families was low, ranging from zero to twelve years of schooling. The average number of grades completed was 3.6 years. One of four adults over eighteen had not finished the first grade; eight of ten had not gone beyond the sixth grade; only four of the 176 adults had gone beyond the ninth grade. About half of the adults had three years or less of formal schooling, and a quarter had no schooling at all.

Adult rural migrants averaged 3.4 years of schooling, compared with 5.6 years for city-born adults. Among the rural-born, 28 percent had less than one year of schooling or none at all. Only 7 percent of city-born adults were in this category. Our data show that in general, as education goes up, income goes up. Of the fifty families with less than $20 per capita monthly income, the average number of years of schooling was 2.8; of the fifty families with more than $20 per capita income, the average schooling was 4.4 years.

usually large number of women in La Esmeralda, compared to other San Juan slums, worked as prostitutes in San Juan, catering to the longshoremen and to visiting sailors and soldiers. Thirty-three percent of our sample families in La Esmeralda turned out to have a history of prostitution.

About seven out of every ten houses in La Esmeralda were classified in 1960 as dilapidated, deteriorated, of inadequate construction, and lacking some or all sanitary facilities. Because it was an older slum and did not have space for expansion, housing conditions were somewhat worse there than in other slums of the metropolitan area. Overcrowding was more acute, with about 50 percent of the houses having no separate bedroom and 40 percent having only one bedroom. The average size of the households, however, was 3.7 persons per unit, compared to the mean of 6 per unit in our hundred-family sample. This smaller average size of household was due to the unusually large number of people (28 percent) who lived alone in La Esmeralda. There were almost three times as many one-person households as in the other slums studied.

The average household in La Esmeralda contained about $500 worth of furnishings. The range of expenditures, like that of other slums studied, varied from zero to a high of over $2,000. Of our sample, the eight families with the lowest expenditures on household goods spent between zero and $149; the next group of eight families spent between $157 and $455; the third group of eight, between $457 and $825; and the last group, with the highest expenditures, between $1,001 and $2,416.

Unlike the other slums studied, in which four out of five families were illegal squatters who had built or purchased their homes on government land, in La Esmeralda only about 15 percent of the residents owned their house. According to the U.S. Census, the average value of these homes was about $700. Seven out of every ten dwellings were renter-occupied. Seventy-five percent of the rentees paid less than $20 rent per month; the average rental was approximately $15 a month.

La Esmeralda differed from the other slums studied in that over half of its adult residents were born in the metropolitan area. In the other slums, four out of five adults came from rural areas of Puerto Rico and had migrated to San Juan in their early twenties. In La Esmeralda, on the other hand, two-thirds of the adults born in the city were under thirty-five years of age, while most of those born in rural areas belonged to the older generation.

On the whole, residence in the four slums was remarkably stable. Although movement about the city was common at first, slum dwelling soon became a persistent way of life. Rural-born adults had lived an average of fourteen years in their slum. Some heads of families in La Esmeralda had lived there for more than forty years, the majority from eight to fifteen years. In our sample of thirty-two families, the household heads had lived in La Esmeralda for an average of twenty-seven years.

Over 50 percent of the marriages in La Esmeralda were of the consensual or free union type, a proportion much higher than that of the other slums studied. Almost seven out of ten family heads in La Esmeralda had had more than one union, legal or consensual. One of every five households in the slum was headed by a female, usually widowed or separated from her husband. This high incidence of mother-centered households was also found throughout the other slums.

In La Esmeralda, as in the other slums, one out of five families was receiving relief in the form of money payments and surplus food allotments.

According to the 1960 census for La Esmeralda as a whole, 82 percent of the children between seven and thirteen years of age were attending school. However, 66 percent of the boys and girls between ages fourteen and nineteen were school dropouts. About 20 percent of all those fourteen years of age or over were illiterate. Only 16.7 percent of the adults over twenty-five had gone beyond elementary school.

The educational achievement of our sample group of thirty-two families was lower than that of La Esmeralda as a whole. The average number of grades completed by adults over twenty-five was 3.5 years. Seventeen of the fifty-two adults (33 percent) had completed elementary school. The men had approximately twice as much schooling as the women. Almost half of the women over twenty-five had no formal education whatever.

How do the Ríos households in La Esmeralda and in New York compare with other Puerto Rican households we studied? In many ways the three households of Fernanda, Felícita and Cruz in La Esmeralda were quite typical of all the families studied. Forty-seven percent of the families in La Esmeralda had incomes which fell well within the middle range of the annual-income distribution curve, that is, between $500 and $1,999. Fernanda earned $15 a month when she worked as a maid, and her husband Junior earned $140 a month as a messenger. Their combined annual income was $1,980. We estimated that Felícita earned between $1,400 and $1,700 a year working as barmaid and prostitute. Cruz's annual income in 1964 was between $500 and $600; this placed her at the lower end of the middle-income group. All three of the Ríos households were below the $1,999 income level, along with 72 percent of the hundred-family sample and 69 percent of La Esmeralda families. Despite Cruz's low income, she was by no means among the lowest in La Esmeralda; 22 percent of the people had incomes of less than $500. Cruz was the only one in the Ríos family to receive public assistance; she was allotted $11 a month, a sum that barely paid her rent. Twenty percent of our hundred-sample families were on relief. The proportion for the country as a whole in 1960 was 15 percent.

In terms of the total value of possessions other than clothing, the three Ríos households fell in the lower half of the La Esmeralda sample of thirty-two families. Fernanda spent $436 on household goods, Felícita $149, and Cruz $120, compared to a range of from zero to $2,416 for the sample group. Cruz's possessions were at the poorer extreme, and most of what she owned were gifts. Neither she nor Felícita owned a refrigerator or, for that matter, any of the luxury items which were found among some slum families.

One of the more striking data to come out of our study is the disproportionately large amounts spent on clothing by low-income Puerto Rican families. Felícita, for example, spent over three times more ($496.36) on clothing than on household goods, and Cruz spent $70.23—over half of what she spent on other possessions. Fernanda spent only $53 on her own clothing, perhaps because she and Junior had to buy many household items to set up their new home. It should be remembered that Felícita and Cruz had children's clothing to buy as well as their own. Cruz spent only $13 on herself out of the $70.23 for clothing. Felícita, on the other hand, spent over 80 percent of her total clothing expenditures on herself. At the time of our inventory Felícita had twenty-five dresses, seven skirts and seven blouses, twelve pairs of shoes, seven brassières, twenty-two panties and three gold rings, in addition to other items. Nine months later she had bought twenty new dresses at a cost of $188!

The emphasis upon clothing and appearance was too widespread a pattern to be explained by the occupational requirements of a prostitute. In part it may also have been caused by inferiority feelings and reparative needs and by imitation of the Puerto Rican middle class, which stresses the importance of clothing.

The three Ríos households were typical of La Esmeralda in many other ways—in their crowded quarters, low rental, inadequate sanitary facilities, size and composition of household, matrifocality, and the pattern of free unions and multiple spouses.

The educational level of the Ríos family was slightly higher than the average for our sample group, which was 3.6 years of schooling. The average for the Ríos was 4.2 years. Fernanda reached Grade 3, Soledad Grade 2, Felícita and Cruz Grade 6 and Simplicio Grade 4. Their spouses averaged a year more in school but with a wider range between individuals, from Erasmo's and Edmundo's complete lack of schooling to Junior's second-year high school education. Flora, Amparo and Marcelo had only one year, while Hortensia had nine.

The religious beliefs and practices of the Ríos family as nominal Catholics, with an emphasis upon devotion to the saints in combination with a belief in spiritualism and sorcery, are typical of the families studied and of most low-income Puerto Ricans.

On the New York side, we located and studied fifty families of migrants who were related to families in our Puerto Rican sample. Although economic factors, such as low income and unemployment, created an atmosphere conducive to migration, we found that noneconomic factors were actually the more important. One of the more interesting findings of our study was the realization that the precipitating factor for leaving Puerto Rico was most often a personal social-psychological crisis. The three members of the Ríos family in New York—Soledad, Simplicio and Aunt Amparo—exemplified the kinds of factors involved in the decision to migrate. Soledad was trying to forget her deceased husband; Simplicio wanted to get away from friends who were having a bad influence upon him; and Amparo was having marital difficulties. Flora left Puerto Rico to join her husband, Simplicio; and Benedicto, Soledad's husband, had recently separated from his first wife.

Each of these individuals had spent a good part of their lives in Puerto Rico and did not differ significantly in personal and cultural traits from their relatives in Puerto Rico. Soledad was about twenty years old when she first went to the United States, Simplicio was sixteen and already married, Flora was twenty-four, Amparo was thirty-six, and Benedicto was nineteen. Almost half of the individuals in our New York sample had left Puerto Rico between the ages of fifteen and twenty-four.

The majority of migrants in the New York sample had made a three-step migration—from a rural birthplace in Puerto Rico to a San Juan slum to New York. Amparo, Flora, Erasmo and Edmundo were the only ones in the Ríos family to conform to this pattern, since all the others were born in the San Juan metropolitan area and went directly from there to New York.

The average household size in New York, four per dwelling unit, was smaller than in Puerto Rico. Simplicio's and Amparo's households had three members, and Soledad's had five. Family composition tended to be similar to Soledad's and Simplicio's, that is, variations on the simple nuclear family of a man, his wife and their children. Households like Amparo's, where a woman lived alone with her children, comprised 14 percent of the New York households.

Every family in the sample, including the Ríos', rented apartments in New York, all but four unfurnished. The families had moved an average of four times, usually within the same borough and often in the same neighborhood. The Ríos family stuck closely to this pattern, except that unlike most of the migrants in our sample, Soledad and Simplicio had lived outside of New York City. Simplicio had lived in New Jersey and Pennsylvania, and Soledad had lived in New Jersey and Florida.

Almost a third of the New York families paid rent within the $40- to $59-a-month range. Simplicio paid $47 a month and Soledad $56. Amparo's rent of $90 was paid by the city welfare agency. The average rent paid by the three Ríos households in New York was $64, almost exactly the same as the average for the whole sample ($62.50).

The percentage of couples living in free union increased in New York, compared to the Puerto Rican slums, as did the number of women who were divorced, separated or abandoned. Half the marriages in our New York sample were of the consensual variety, and 26 percent of the households were headed by a woman who had separated from her husband. Both Soledad and her brother, Simplicio, lived in free union with their spouses, and Amparo was separated from her husband.

The Puerto Ricans in our New York sample found that the range of employment opportunities open to them was limited although greater than in Puerto Rico. All but seven of the adults' occupations were jobs which required few formal skills or education. Two-thirds of the employed adults were in occupations technically known as operatives. Almost all of these were factory workers. In marked contrast to Puerto Rico, 40 percent of the wives in New York worked, mostly in factories. Flora and Soledad worked in a factory, and Amparo had worked before going on relief. Simplicio worked as a delivery boy, and Benedicto was in the merchant marine. All but Simplicio belonged to unions. Our general survey showed that 80 percent of all working adults were unionized. Few, however, were more than dues-paying members: many felt exploited by the union leaders.

With the exception of one woman who worked as a maid, all working adults paid unemployment insurance, and over 70 percent of them had received Social Security insurance at least once. Many had received it three or more times. Almost none knew how much was deducted from his wages either for the insurance or for union dues or income taxes.

The striking contrast in income between the families we studied in Puerto Rico and their relatives in New York can be seen in the following table:

ANNUAL FAMILY INCOME OF SAMPLE GROUPS
STUDIED IN NEW YORK AND SAN JUAN

Annual Family Income	32 Sample Families La Esmeralda 1964	All Families La Esmeralda 1960	100 Sample Families 4 Puerto Rican slums* 1964	50 Families of Relatives in New York 1964
	Percent	Percent	Percent	Percent
Less than $500	15.7	22	20	0
$500-$999	31.2	15	20	2
$1,000-$1,999	31.2	32	32	4
$2,000-$3,999	18.8	27	18	50
Over $4,000	3.1	4	10	44

* 25 families from La Esmeralda are included in the 100-family sample.

The incomes of the New York families were three to four times larger than those of the families in San Juan. Only 2 percent of the New York sample had incomes below $1,000, as compared to an average of 41.3 percent of our groups in San Juan. Most impressive is the high percentage (44 percent) of those with incomes of $4,000 or over, compared with 4 percent of all families in La Esmeralda slum. The mean annual income for all the New York families was $3,678, with a monthly per capita income of a little over $100.

Both Simplicio's and Soledad's households earned significantly above these levels, the result of both partners in the marriage holding steady jobs. Simplicio and his wife made about $5,000 a year, and Benedicto and Soledad brought in over $8,000 between them. One of Amparo's sons worked part time to supplement her relief payments. The annual family income in her case was a little over $3,000, the per capita income was about $85 a month, both below the average. Amparo had been on relief for a number of years. In our New York sample as a whole, one in five households were on relief.

Despite their comparatively high income, the households of Soledad and Simplicio had invested less in material goods than the average New York families of our sample. The amount they did spend (Soledad $1,185 and Simplicio $916), however, was three times greater than the combined expenditures of their mother and two sisters in Puerto Rico. The New York household expenditures did not include a refrigerator or stove, as these were provided by the landlord. Amparo had spent practically nothing on household goods, relying almost exclusively upon gifts from her friends.

Soledad and Simplicio also spent far more on clothing than did their relatives in Puerto Rico. Simplicio and Flora bought $1,051 worth of clothing; Soledad and Benedicto bought clothing and jewelry which cost $3,035 for themselves alone. A breakdown of some of these possessions is instructive.

SOLEDAD		BENEDICTO	
Item	*Cost*	*Item*	*Cost*
27 dresses	$304	5 suits	$530
3 suits	44	10 pr. pants	165
11 skirts	43	23 shirts	124
11 blouses	26	25 undershorts	?
11 half-slips	17	25 undershirts	?
16 panties	8	4 prs. shoes	77
7 prs. shoes	45	40 prs. socks	?
2 wrist watches	115	2 wrist watches	280
		1 gold chain	225
		3 gold rings	495

We found the educational level of the New York sample to be above the Puerto Rican average—6.5 years of schooling compared to 3.6 in Puerto Rico. The Ríos families in New York averaged 3.4 years of formal education, ranging from Amparo's one year to Benedicto's eight years of schooling. School dropouts among the migrants were high and only 4 percent of our New York families had children in school beyond the tenth grade.

Our survey indicated that there was little important change in customs and language among lower-income Puerto Ricans in New York. They formed small islands in the city and perpetuated their culture. Contacts with North Americans were few and often limited to landlords, government officials and other functionaries. The process of adjustment and assimilation to North American culture was slow and often difficult. Amparo typifies this in the extreme. After living for twenty-eight years in New York City, she spoke no English, had no American friends and few acquaintances, rarely left her home, and in general remained a Puerto Rican who had no roots in foreign soil. Soledad and Flora, too, were conservative, although to a lesser extent. Neither had learned more than very rudimentary English in spite of outside employment. They expressed negative feelings toward North Americans and their contacts with them on other than an official plane were few. These attitudes, particularly in regard to language, were true of most of the women in our New York survey. Two out of three women knew little or no English.

The men, on the other hand, were much less conservative. Simplicio and Benedicto spoke some English and understood it quite well. Both had one or two American friends and generally had positive attitudes toward North Americans, although they were critical of racial and ethnic prejudice. In our survey group over half of the men had some degree of fluency in English. Some negativism toward Americans and the American way of life was expressed by both men and women, although there were many who had very positive feelings toward the United States. Almost all of the migrants expressed satisfaction with the higher standard of living in New York despite the fact that they were almost at the bottom of the income level in the city.

The Puerto Ricans in New York showed a trend toward increased participation in voluntary organizations, particularly Parent-Teacher Associations and church groups. Twelve percent belonged to a church group and 12 percent to a school group. Only 4 percent reported having belonged to either of these organizations in Puerto Rico. In New York 4 percent joined a sports club; in Puerto Rico none of the migrants had been a member of such a club.

Three of every four household heads in the New York sample hoped to return to Puerto Rico some day to live. Benedicto and Soledad planned to stay in New York, but Simplicio, Flora and Amparo expressed a strong desire to go back to Puerto Rico. In fact, most of the families in our sample had already made return trips to Puerto Rico to visit friends and relatives. Simplicio had gone back once, Amparo twice, and Soledad five times. Benedicto went frequently because of his work, but Flora had never been able to afford a trip to the island.

In New York the Puerto Ricans visited each other with some frequency, but visiting patterns were directly connected with distance and travel time and were usually restricted to relatives. There was a general feeling that family bonds had weakened in New York. The Ríos family visited each other on weekends, although Amparo disliked to leave her house and visited much less often. Both Benedicto and Simplicio had fairly close friends outside the family in addition to women friends. Friction between the Ríos households was common, but it was no worse than in La Esmeralda.

We found marital conflict to be at a high level among the Puerto Rican families in New York. While this is by no means unusual among slum families, it seemed to have increased in New York as the result of wives working. Employment outside the home made the women more demanding of their husbands and gave them a new sense of independence. Soledad's and Simplicio's households typify the strains incurred under the new conditions.

The position of the male was further weakened in New York by the stricter enforcement of laws against wife- and child-beating and by a more adequate family relief and child-aid program. This, in large part, explains the increase in the number of abandonments, separations, consensual unions and matrifocal families.

The Culture of Poverty

BECAUSE the research design of this study was concerned with testing the concept of a culture of poverty in different national contexts and because this concept is helpful in understanding the Ríos family, I shall briefly summarize some of its dimensions here.

Although a great deal has been written about poverty and the poor, the concept of a culture of poverty is relatively new. I first suggested it in 1959 in my book *Five Families: Mexican Case Studies in the Culture of Poverty*. The phrase is a catchy one and has become widely used and misused.* Michael Harrington used it extensively in his book *The Other America* (1961), which played an important role in sparking the national anti-poverty program in the United States. However, he used it in a somewhat broader and less technical sense than I had intended. I shall try to define it more precisely as a conceptual model, with special emphasis upon the distinction between poverty and the culture of poverty. The absence of intensive anthropological studies of poor families from a wide variety of national and cultural contexts and especially from the socialist countries, is a serious handicap in formulating valid cross-

* There has been relatively little discussion of the culture of poverty concept in the professional journals, however. Two articles deal with the problem in some detail: Elizabeth Herzog, "Some Assumptions About the Poor," in *The Social Service Review*, December 1963, pp. 389-402; Lloyd Ohlin, "Inherited Poverty," Organization for Economic Cooperation and Development (no date), Paris.

cultural regularities. The model presented here is therefore provisional and subject to modification as new studies become available.

Throughout recorded history, in literature, in proverbs and in popular sayings, we find two opposite evaluations of the nature of the poor. Some characterize the poor as blessed, virtuous, upright, serene, independent, honest, kind and happy. Others characterize them as evil, mean, violent, sordid and criminal. These contradictory and confusing evaluations are also reflected in the in-fighting that is going on in the current war against poverty. Some stress the great potential of the poor for self-help, leadership and community organization, while others point to the sometimes irreversible, destructive effect of poverty upon individual character, and therefore emphasize the need for guidance and control to remain in the hands of the middle class, which presumably has better mental health.

These opposing views reflect a political power struggle between competing groups. However, some of the confusion results from the failure to distinguish between poverty *per se* and the culture of poverty and the tendency to focus upon the individual personality rather than upon the group—that is, the family and the slum community.

As an anthropologist I have tried to understand poverty and its associated traits as a culture or, more accurately, as a subculture* with its own structure and rationale, as a way of life which is passed down from generation to generation along family lines. This view directs attention to the fact that the culture of poverty in modern nations is not only a matter of economic deprivation, of disorganization or of the absence of something. It is also something positive and provides some rewards without which the poor could hardly carry on.

Elsewhere I have suggested that the culture of poverty transcends regional, rural-urban and national differences and shows remarkable similarities in family structure, interpersonal relations, time orientation, value systems and spending patterns. These cross-national similarities are examples of independent invention and convergence. They are common adaptations to common problems.

The culture of poverty can come into being in a variety of historical contexts. However, it tends to grow and flourish in societies with the following set of conditions: (1) a cash economy, wage labor and production for profit; (2) a persistently high rate of unemployment and underemployment for unskilled labor; (3) low wages; (4) the failure to provide social, political and economic organization, either on a voluntary basis or by government imposition, for the low-income population; (5) the existence of a bilateral kinship system rather than a unilateral one;† and finally, (6) the existence of a set of

* While the term "subculture of poverty" is technically more accurate, I have used "culture of poverty" as a shorter form.

† In a unilineal kinship system, descent is reckoned either through males or

values in the dominant class which stresses the accumulation of wealth and property, the possibility of upward mobility and thrift, and explains low economic status as the result of personal inadequacy or inferiority.

The way of life which develops among some of the poor under these conditions is the culture of poverty. It can best be studied in urban or rural slums and can be described in terms of some seventy interrelated social, economic and psychological traits.[10] However, the number of traits and the relationships between them may vary from society to society and from family to family. For example, in a highly literate society, illiteracy may be more diagnostic of the culture of poverty than in a society where illiteracy is widespread and where even the well-to-do may be illiterate, as in some Mexican peasant villages before the revolution.

The culture of poverty is both an adaptation and a reaction of the poor to their marginal position in a class-stratified, highly individuated, capitalistic society. It represents an effort to cope with feelings of hopelessness and despair which develop from the realization of the improbability of achieving success in terms of the values and goals of the larger society. Indeed, many of the traits of the culture of poverty can be viewed as attempts at local solutions for problems not met by existing institutions and agencies because the people are not eligible for them, cannot afford them, or are ignorant or suspicious of them. For example, unable to obtain credit from banks, they are thrown upon their own resources and organize informal credit devices without interest.

---

through females. When traced exclusively through males it is called patrilineal or agnatic descent; when reckoned exclusively through females it is called matrilineal or uterine descent. In a bilateral or cognatic system, descent is traced through males and females without emphasis on either line.

In a unilineal system, the lineage consists of all the descendants of one ancestor. In a patrilineal system, the lineage is composed of all the descendants through males of one male ancestor. A matrilineage consists of all the descendants through females of one female ancestor. The lineage may thus contain a very large number of generations. If bilateral descent is reckoned, however, the number of generations that can be included in a social unit is limited, since the number of ancestors doubles every generation.

Unilineal descent groups ("lineages" or "clans") are corporate groups in the sense that the lineage or clan may act as a collectivity: it can take blood vengeance against another descent group, it can hold property, etc. However, the bilateral kin group (the "kindred") can rarely act as a collectivity because it is not a "group" except from the point of view of a particular individual, and, furthermore, has no continuity over time.

In a unilineal system, an individual is assigned to a group by virtue of his birth. In contrast, a person born into a bilateral system usually has a choice of relatives whom he chooses to recognize as "kin" and with whom he wants to associate. This generally leads to a greater diffuseness and fragmentation of ties with relatives over time.

The culture of poverty, however, is not only an adaptation to a set of objective conditions of the larger society. Once it comes into existence it tends to perpetuate itself from generation to generation because of its effect on the children. By the time slum children are age six or seven they have usually absorbed the basic values and attitudes of their subculture and are not psychologically geared to take full advantage of changing conditions or increased opportunities which may occur in their lifetime.

Most frequently the culture of poverty develops when a stratified social and economic system is breaking down or is being replaced by another, as in the case of the transition from feudalism to capitalism or during periods of rapid technological change. Often it results from imperial conquest in which the native social and economic structure is smashed and the natives are maintained in a servile colonial status, sometimes for many generations. It can also occur in the process of detribalization, such as that now going on in Africa.

The most likely candidates for the culture of poverty are the people who come from the lower strata of a rapidly changing society and are already partially alienated from it. Thus landless rural workers who migrate to the cities can be expected to develop a culture of poverty much more readily than migrants from stable peasant villages with a well-organized traditional culture. In this connection there is a striking contrast between Latin America, where the rural population long ago made the transition from a tribal to a peasant society, and Africa, which is still close to its tribal heritage. The more corporate nature of many of the African tribal societies, in contrast to Latin American rural communities, and the persistence of village ties tend to inhibit or delay the formation of a full-blown culture of poverty in many of the African towns and cities. The special conditions of apartheid in South Africa, where the migrants are segregated into separate "locations" and do not enjoy freedom of movement, create special problems. Here the institutionalization of repression and discrimination tend to develop a greater sense of identity and group consciousness.

The culture of poverty can be studied from various points of view: the relationship between the subculture and the larger society; the nature of the slum community; the nature of the family; and the attitudes, values and character structure of the individual.

1. The lack of effective participation and integration of the poor in the major institutions of the larger society is one of the crucial characteristics of the culture of poverty. This is a complex matter and results from a variety of factors which may include lack of economic resources, segregation and discrimination, fear, suspicion or apathy, and the development of local solutions for problems. However, "participation" in some of the institutions of the larger society—for example, in the jails, the army and the public relief system—does not *per se* eliminate the traits of the culture of poverty. In the case of a relief

system which barely keeps people alive, both the basic poverty and the sense of hopelessness are perpetuated rather than eliminated.

Low wages, chronic unemployment and underemployment lead to low income, lack of property ownership, absence of savings, absence of food reserves in the home, and a chronic shortage of cash. These conditions reduce the possibility of effective participation in the larger economic system. And as a response to these conditions we find in the culture of poverty a high incidence of pawning of personal goods, borrowing from local moneylenders at usurious rates of interest, spontaneous informal credit devices organized by neighbors, the use of second-hand clothing and furniture, and the pattern of frequent buying of small quantities of food many times a day as the need arises.

People with a culture of poverty produce very little wealth and receive very little in return. They have a low level of literacy and education, usually do not belong to labor unions, are not members of political parties, generally do not participate in the national welfare agencies, and make very little use of banks, hospitals, department stores, museums or art galleries. They have a critical attitude toward some of the basic institutions of the dominant classes, hatred of the police, mistrust of government and those in high position, and a cynicism which extends even to the church. This gives the culture of poverty a high potential for protest and for being used in political movements aimed against the existing social order.

People with a culture of poverty are aware of middle-class values, talk about them and even claim some of them as their own, but on the whole they do not live by them. Thus it is important to distinguish between what they say and what they do. For example, many will tell you that marriage by law, by the church, or by both, is the ideal form of marriage, but few will marry. To men who have no steady jobs or other sources of income, who do not own property and have no wealth to pass on to their children, who are present-time oriented and who want to avoid the expense and legal difficulties involved in formal marriage and divorce, free unions or consensual marriage makes a lot of sense. Women will often turn down offers of marriage because they feel it ties them down to men who are immature, punishing and generally unreliable. Women feel that consensual union gives them a better break; it gives them some of the freedom and flexibility that men have. By not giving the fathers of their children legal status as husbands, the women have a stronger claim on their children if they decide to leave their men. It also gives women exclusive rights to a house or any other property they may own.

2. When we look at the culture of poverty on the local community level, we find poor housing conditions, crowding, gregariousness, but above all a minimum of organization beyond the level of the nuclear and extended family. Occasionally there are informal, temporary groupings or voluntary associations within slums. The existence of neighborhood gangs which cut across

slum settlements represents a considerable advance beyond the zero point of the continuum that I have in mind. Indeed, it is the low level of organization which gives the culture of poverty its marginal and anachronistic quality in our highly complex, specialized, organized society. Most primitive peoples have achieved a higher level of socio-cultural organization than our modern urban slum dwellers.

In spite of the generally low level of organization, there may be a sense of community and *esprit de corps* in urban slums and in slum neighborhoods. This can vary within a single city, or from region to region or country to country. The major factors influencing this variation are the size of the slum, its location and physical characteristics, length of residence, incidence of home and landownership (versus squatter rights), rentals, ethnicity, kinship ties, and freedom or lack of freedom of movement. When slums are separated from the surrounding area by enclosing walls or other physical barriers, when rents are low and fixed and stability of residence is great (twenty or thirty years), when the population constitutes a distinct ethnic, racial or language group, is bound by ties of kinship or *compadrazgo,* and when there are some internal voluntary associations, then the sense of local community approaches that of a village community. In many cases this combination of favorable conditions does not exist. However, even where internal organization and *esprit de corps* is at a bare minimum and people move around a great deal, a sense of territoriality develops which sets off the slum neighborhoods from the rest of the city. In Mexico City and San Juan this sense of territoriality results from the unavailability of low-income housing outside the slum areas. In South Africa the sense of territoriality grows out of the segregation enforced by the government, which confines the rural migrants to specific locations.

3. On the family level the major traits of the culture of poverty are the absence of childhood as a specially prolonged and protected stage in the life cycle, early initiation into sex, free unions or consensual marriages, a relatively high incidence of the abandonment of wives and children, a trend toward female- or mother-centered families and consequently a much greater knowledge of maternal relatives, a strong predisposition to authoritarianism, lack of privacy, verbal emphasis upon family solidarity which is only rarely achieved because of sibling rivalry, and competition for limited goods and maternal affection.

4. On the level of the individual the major characteristics are a strong feeling of marginality, of helplessness, of dependence and of inferiority. I found this to be true of slum dwellers in Mexico City and San Juan among families who do not constitute a distinct ethnic or racial group and who do not suffer from racial discrimination. In the United States, of course, the culture of poverty of the Negroes has the additional disadvantage of racial discrimination, but as I have already suggested, this additional disadvantage contains a great potential for revolutionary protest and organization which seems to be

absent in the slums of Mexico City or among the poor whites in the South.

Other traits include a high incidence of maternal deprivation, of orality, of weak ego structure, confusion of sexual identification, a lack of impulse control, a strong present-time orientation with relatively little ability to defer gratification and to plan for the future, a sense of resignation and fatalism, a widespread belief in male superiority, and a high tolerance for psychological pathology of all sorts.

People with a culture of poverty are provincial and locally oriented and have very little sense of history. They know only their own troubles, their own local conditions, their own neighborhood, their own way on life. Usually they do not have the knowledge, the vision or the ideology to see the similarities between their problems and those of their counterparts elsewhere in the world. They are not class-conscious, although they are very sensitive indeed to status distinctions.

When the poor become class-conscious or active members of trade-union organizations, or when they adopt an internationalist outlook on the world, they are no longer part of the culture of poverty, although they may still be desperately poor. Any movement, be it religious, pacifist or revolutionary, which organizes and gives hope to the poor and effectively promotes solidarity and a sense of identification with larger groups, destroys the psychological and social core of the culture of poverty. In this connection, I suspect that the civil rights movement among the Negroes in the United States has done more to improve their self-image and self-respect than have their economic advances, although, without doubt, the two are mutually reinforcing.

The distinction between poverty and the culture of poverty is basic to the model described here. There are degrees of poverty and many kinds of poor people. The culture of poverty refers to one way of life shared by poor people in given historical and social contexts. The economic traits which I have listed for the culture of poverty are necessary but not sufficient to define the phenomena I have in mind. There are a number of historical examples of very poor segments of the population which do not have a way of life that I would describe as a subculture of poverty. Here I should like to give four examples:

1. Many of the primitive or preliterate peoples studied by anthropologists suffer from dire poverty which is the result of poor technology and/or poor natural resources, or of both, but they do not have the traits of the subculture of poverty. Indeed, they do not constitute a subculture because their societies are not highly stratified. In spite of their poverty they have a relatively integrated, satisfying and self-sufficient culture. Even the simplest food-gathering and hunting tribes have a considerable amount of organization, bands and band chiefs, tribal councils and local self-government—traits which are not found in the culture of poverty.

2. In India the lower castes (the Chamars, the leather workers, and the Bhangis, the sweepers) may be desperately poor, both in the villages and in the cities, but most of them are integrated into the larger society and have their own *panchayat* * organizations which cut across village lines and give them a considerable amount of power.† In addition to the caste system, which gives individuals a sense of identity and belonging, there is still another factor, the clan system. Wherever there are unilateral kinship systems or clans one would not expect to find the culture of poverty, because a clan system gives people a sense of belonging to a corporate body with a history and a life of its own, thereby providing a sense of continuity, a sense of a past and of a future.

3. The Jews of eastern Europe were very poor, but they did not have many of the traits of the culture of poverty because of their tradition of literacy, the great value placed upon learning, the organization of the community around the rabbi, the proliferation of local voluntary associations, and their religion which taught that they were the chosen people.

4. My fourth example is speculative and relates to socialism. On the basis of my limited experience in one socialist country—Cuba—and on the basis of my reading, I am inclined to believe that the culture of poverty does not exist in the socialist countries. I first went to Cuba in 1947 as a visiting professor for the State Department. At that time I began a study of a sugar plantation in Melena del Sur and of a slum in Havana. After the Castro Revolution I made my second trip to Cuba as a correspondent for a major magazine, and I revisited the same slum and some of the same families. The physical aspect of the slum had changed very little, except for a beautiful new nursery school. It was clear that the people were still desperately poor, but I found much less of the despair, apathy and hopelessness which are so diagnostic of urban slums in the culture of poverty. They expressed great confidence in their leaders and hope for a better life in the future. The slum itself was now highly organized, with block committees, educational committees, party committees. The people had a new sense of power and importance. They were armed and were given a doctrine which glorified the lower class as the hope of humanity. (I was told by one Cuban official that they had practically eliminated delinquency by giving arms to the delinquents!)

* A formal organization designed to provide caste leadership.
† It may be that in the slums of Calcutta and Bombay an incipient culture of poverty is developing. It would be highly desirable to do family studies there as a crucial test of the culture-of-poverty hypothesis.

It is my impression that the Castro regime—unlike Marx and Engels—did not write off the so-called lumpen proletariat as an inherently reactionary and anti-revolutionary force, but rather saw its revolutionary potential and tried to utilize it. In this connection, Frantz Fanon makes a similar evaluation of the role of the lumpen proletariat based upon his experience in the Algerian struggle for independence. In his recently published book [11] he wrote:

> It is within this mass of humanity, this people of the shanty towns, at the core of the lumpen proletariat, that the rebellion will find its urban spearhead. For the lumpen proletariat, that horde of starving men, uprooted from their tribe and from their clan, constitutes one of the most spontaneous and most radically revolutionary forces of a colonized people.

My own studies of the urban poor in the slums of San Juan do not support the generalizations of Fanon. I have found very little revolutionary spirit or radical ideology among low-income Puerto Ricans. On the contrary, most of the families I studied were quite conservative politically and about half of them were in favor of the Republican Statehood Party. It seems to me that the revolutionary potential of people with a culture of poverty will vary considerably according to the national context and the particular historical circumstances. In a country like Algeria which was fighting for its independence, the lumpen proletariat was drawn into the struggle and became a vital force. However, in countries like Puerto Rico, in which the movement for independence has very little mass support, and in countries like Mexico which achieved their independence a long time ago and are now in their postrevolutionary period, the lumpen proletariat is not a leading source of rebellion or of revolutionary spirit.

In effect, we find that in primitive societies and in caste societies, the culture of poverty does not develop. In socialist, fascist and in highly developed capitalist societies with a welfare state, the culture of poverty tends to decline. I suspect that the culture of poverty flourishes in, and is generic to, the early free-enterprise stage of capitalism and that it is also endemic in colonialism.

It is important to distinguish between different profiles in the subculture of poverty depending upon the national context in which these subcultures are found. If we think of the culture of poverty primarily in terms of the factor of integration in the larger society and a sense of identification with the great tradition of that society, or with a new emerging revolutionary tradition, then we will not be surprised that some slum dwellers with a lower per capita income may have moved farther away from the core characteristics of the culture of poverty than others with a higher per capita income. For example,

Puerto Rico has a much higher per capita income than Mexico, yet Mexicans have a deeper sense of identity.

I have listed fatalism and a low level of aspiration as one of the key traits for the subculture of poverty. Here too, however, the national context makes a big difference. Certainly the level of aspiration of even the poorest sector of the population in a country like the United States with its traditional ideology of upward mobility and democracy is much higher than in more backward countries like Ecuador and Peru, where both the ideology and the actual possibilities of upward mobility are extremely limited and where authoritarian values still persist in both the urban and rural milieus.

Because of the advanced technology, high level of literacy, the development of mass media and the relatively high aspiration level of all sectors of the population, especially when compared with underdeveloped nations, I believe that although there is still a great deal of poverty in the United States (estimates range from thirty to fifty million people), there is relatively little of what I would call the culture of poverty. My rough guess would be that only about 20 percent of the population below the poverty line (between six and ten million people) in the United States have characteristics which would justify classifying their way of life as that of a culture of poverty. Probably the largest sector within this group would consist of very low-income Negroes, Mexicans, Puerto Ricans, American Indians and Southern poor whites. The relatively small number of people in the United States with a culture of poverty is a positive factor because it is much more difficult to eliminate the culture of poverty than to eliminate poverty *per se*.

Middle-class people, and this would certainly include most social scientists, tend to concentrate on the negative aspects of the culture of poverty. They tend to associate negative valences to such traits as present-time orientation and concrete versus abstract orientation. I do not intend to idealize or romanticize the culture of poverty. As someone has said, "It is easier to praise poverty than to live in it"; yet some of the positive aspects which may flow from these traits must not be overlooked. Living in the present may develop a capacity for spontaneity and adventure, for the enjoyment of the sensual, the indulgence of impulse, which is often blunted in the middle-class, future-oriented man. Perhaps it is this reality of the moment which the existentialist writers are so desperately trying to recapture but which the culture of poverty experiences as natural, everyday phenomena. The frequent use of violence certainly provides a ready outlet for hostility so that people in the culture of poverty suffer less from repression than does the middle class.

In the traditional view, anthropologists have said that culture provides human beings with a design for living, with a ready-made set of solutions for human problems so that individuals don't have to begin all over again each generation. That is, the core of culture is its positive adaptive function. I, too, have called attention to some of the adaptive mechanisms in the culture of poverty—for example, the low aspiration level helps to reduce frustration, the legitimization of short-range hedonism makes possible spontaneity and enjoyment. However, on the whole it seems to me that it is a relatively thin culture. There is a great deal of pathos, suffering and emptiness among those who live in the culture of poverty. It does not provide much support or long-range satisfaction and its encouragement of mistrust tends to magnify helplessness and isolation. Indeed, the poverty of culture is one of the crucial aspects of the culture of poverty.

The concept of the culture of poverty provides a high level of generalization which, hopefully, will unify and explain a number of phenomena viewed as distinctive characteristics of racial, national or regional groups. For example, matrifocality, a high incidence of consensual unions and a high percentage of households headed by women, which have been thought to be distinctive of Caribbean family organization or of Negro family life in the U.S.A., turn out to be traits of the culture of poverty and are found among diverse peoples in many parts of the world and among peoples who have had no history of slavery.

The concept of a cross-societal subculture of poverty enables us to see that many of the problems we think of as distinctively our own or distinctively Negro problems (or that of any other special racial or ethnic group), also exist in countries where there are no distinct ethnic minority groups. This suggests that the elimination of physical poverty *per se* may not be enough to eliminate the culture of poverty which is a whole way of life.

What is the future of the culture of poverty? In considering this question, one must distinguish between those countries in which it represents a relatively small segment of the population and those in which it constitutes a very large one. Obviously the solutions will differ in these two situations. In the United States, the major solution proposed by planners and social workers in dealing with multiple-problem families and the so-called hard core of poverty has been to attempt slowly to raise their level of living and to incorporate them into the middle class. Wherever possible, there has been some reliance upon psychiatric treatment.

In the underdeveloped countries, however, where great masses of people live in the culture of poverty, a social-work solution does not seem feasible. Because of the magnitude of the problem, psychiatrists can hardly begin to cope with it. They have all they can do to care for their own growing middle class. In these countries the people with a culture of poverty may seek a more revolutionary solution. By creating basic structural changes in society, by redistributing wealth, by organizing the poor and giving them a sense of belonging, of power and of leadership, revolutions frequently succeed in abolishing some of the basic characteristics of the culture of poverty even when they do not succeed in abolishing poverty itself.

Notes

[1] There is a vast bibliography on Puerto Rico. Among the better anthropological and sociological studies are:

Theodore Brameld, *The Remaking of a Culture: Life and Education in Puerto Rico*. New York, Harper & Bros., 1959. 478 pp.

Reuben Hill, J. Mayone Stycos and Kurt W. Back, *The Family and Population Control: A Puerto Rican Experiment in Social Change*. Chapel Hill, University of North Carolina Press, 1959. 481 pp.

David Landy, *Tropical Childhood, Cultural Transmission and Learning in a Rural Puerto Rican Village*. Chapel Hill, University of North Carolina Press, 1959.

Gordon K. Lewis, *Puerto Rico: Freedom and Power in the Caribbean*. New York, Monthly Review Press, 1963. 626 pp.

Lydia J. Roberts and Rosa Luisa Stefani, *Patterns of Living in Puerto Rican Families*. Río Piedras, P. R., University of Puerto Rico, 1949. 410 pp.

C. C. Rogler, *Comerio, A Study of a Puerto Rican Town*. Lawrence, University of Kansas Press, 1940.

E. Seda Bonilla, *Interacción social y personalidad en una comunidad de Puerto Rico*. San Juan, P. R., Ediciones Juan Ponce de Leon, 1964.

Julian H. Steward, ed., *The People of Puerto Rico*. Urbana, University of Illinois Press, 1956. 540 pp.

J. M. Stycos, *Family and Fertility in Puerto Rico: A Study of the Lower Income Group*. New York, Columbia University Press, 1955.

Melvin M. Tumin and Arnold Feldman, *Social Class and Social Change in Puerto Rico*. Princeton, Princeton University Press, 1961. 548 pp.

[2] Puerto Rican writers have given us some of the best descriptions of urban slum life. See for example René Marqués, *La carreta* (*Asomante*, San Juan, 1953) and his short stories "Dos vueltas de llave y un arcángel" in *En una ciudad llamada San Juan* (Imprenta Universitaria, Universidad Nacional de México, 1960), which also appeared in English translation as "Two Turns of a Key and an Archangel"

(*San Juan Review*, September 1964); "El delator," "El cuchillo y la piedra" and "En una ciudad llamada San Juan" appear in *En una ciudad llamada San Juan* and "La chiringa azul" (*Américas*, Washington, D. C., May 1965). See also Emilio Belaval, *Cuentos de la Plaza Fuerte* (*San Juan Review*, November 1965 and March 1966; Florángel Cárdenas, "El Fanguito" (*San Juan Review*, April 1964); José Luis González, "A Lead Coffin That Couldn't Be Opened" (*San Juan Review*, January 1965) and "There's a Little Colored Boy in the Bottom of the Water" (*San Juan Review*, April 1964); Salvador de Jesús, "Swamp Tears" (*San Juan Review*, August 1964); Luis Rafael Sánchez, "It Tastes of Paradise" (*San Juan Review*, July 1965) and Pedro Juan Soto and Kal Wagenheim, eds., "The Addict" (*San Juan Review*, November 1964).

[2] There are a few hundred articles, essays, monographs and reports on Puerto Ricans in the United States. Among the best are:

Beatrice B. Berle, *80 Puerto Rican Families in New York City*. New York, Columbia University Press, 1958. 331 pp.

David Caplovitz, *et al.*, *The Poor Pay More*. New York, Free Press of Glencoe, 1963. 220 pp.

Nathan Glazer and Daniel Patrick Moynihan, *Beyond the Melting Pot*. Cambridge, Harvard University Press, 1963.

Oscar Handlin, *The Newcomers: Negroes and Puerto Ricans in a Changing Metropolis*. Cambridge, Harvard University Press, 1959. 171 pp.

C. Wright Mills, Clarence Senior, and Rose Golden, *The Puerto Rican Journey: New York's Newest Migrant*. New York, Harper & Bros., 1950. 238 pp.

Elena Padilla, *Up from Puerto Rico*. New York, Columbia University Press, 1958. 317 pp.

Cristopher Rand, *The Puerto Ricans*. New York, Oxford University Press, 1958. 178 pp.

Clarence Senior, *The Puerto Ricans: Strangers—Then Neighbors*. Quadrangle Books, 1965. 128 pp.

Patricia Sexton, *Spanish Harlem: Anatomy of Poverty*. Harper & Row, 1965. 208 pp.

Dan Wakefield, *Island in the City: Puerto Ricans in New York*. Boston, Houghton Mifflin Co., 1959. 278 pp.

[4] A. B. Hollingshead and L. H. Rogler, *Trapped: Families and Schizophrenia*. New York, John Wiley and Sons, 1965. 436 pp. *See also:*

Theodore Caplow, Sheldon Stryker and Samuel Wallace, *The Urban Ambience: A Study of San Juan, Puerto Rico*. Totowa, The Bedminster Press, 1964.

Kurt W. Back, *Slums, Projects and People: Social Psychological Problems of Relocation in Puerto Rico*. Durham, Duke University Press, 1962.

[5] Sidney W. Mintz, *Worker in the Cane: A Puerto Rican Life History*. New Haven, Yale University Press, 1960. 288 pp.

[6] Some attention to the African heritage is found in the poetry of Luis Palés-Matos and in the work of later Negro poets like Victorio Llanes Allende (see *El Mundo, Suplemento Sabatino*, December 1, 1962). See also the study of the Puerto Rican Negro in his Hispanicized milieu, in Cesáreo Rosa-Nieves, *Diapasón Negro* (San Juan, Editorial Campos, 1960). There is also the work of Ricardo Alegría on the

African background of the Loíza Aldea festival tradition. See his *La Fiesta de Santiago Apóstol en Loíza Aldea* (Colección de Estudios Puertorriqueños, 1954).

[7] Oscar Lewis, *Five Families: Mexican Case Studies in the Culture of Poverty.* New York, Basic Books, 1959.

[8] Oscar Lewis, *The Children of Sánchez.* New York, Random House, 1961, and Vintage ed.

[9] Oscar Lewis, *Pedro Martínez.* New York, Random House, 1964.

[10] "The Culture of Poverty," in John J. TePaske and S.N. Fischer, eds., *Explosive Forces in Latin America.* Columbus, Ohio State University Press, 1964, pp. 149-173.

[11] Frantz Fanon, *The Wretched of the Earth.* New York, Grove Press, 1965, p. 103.

PART I

FERNANDA

A Day with Fernanda in San Juan

ON A SATURDAY morning in May 1964, Rosa González* went into La Esmeralda to spend a day with Fernanda Fuentes. It was about half past seven. She approached the slum by way of the paved road, then walked down through the short tunnel that had been cut out of the old fort wall. The tunnel led directly to an open space that served as a plaza, a bare paved area without flowers, bushes or trees. A long cement bench standing against the fort wall was used by people of the slum to rest, to visit with their neighbors, to wait for a taxi or an ambulance or to watch television on a large public TV set which had been placed there by the municipal government. Television watching went on day and night. Near by were a few small bars and the office of the Popular Party of Muñoz Marín, where flags and posters were displayed.

Two roads led off from the plaza. Rosa took the smaller road that turned east and down to the beach. Here the slum became poorer and shabbier. The pavement was broken, and dirty drainage water ran down the slope. Flimsy shacks with uneven roofs and sagging second-floor balconies supported by high

* This is a pseudonym for my research assistant who helped me in the observation and recording of the field data used in the "days" presented in this volume.

poles lined the road. Rosa passed several barefoot children and hungry-looking dogs. The road led to Bonilla's grocery store, which served as the local post office and as a social center, where people came for their mail, met friends and listened to a juke box that blared from early morning until late at night.

Across the road from Bonilla's, Rosa went down a flight of uneven steps and turned left onto a short, crudely paved street ending in a smaller plaza that slanted gently toward the sea. This plaza was paved with old Spanish cobblestones, bluish in color and slippery from long use. Two of Fernanda's daughters lived near by. High on a ledge to the south was Cruz's apartment; to the west, at the corner of *doña* Yolanda's bar, a narrow crooked alley led to Felícita's house. Next door was the house where Fernanda and her husband Junior had been living. Today they were moving to an apartment almost on the beach, and that was where Rosa was going.

Making her way carefully over the cobblestones, Rosa came to an open cement drain which carried sewage to the beach and the sea. A half-inch pipe, pierced with holes for flushing the sewage, lay in the center of the drain, but this primitive system of sanitation was no longer functioning. Garbage, empty cans, old newspapers, a ragged pair of child's panties littered the dry drain.

Rosa stepped over the drain and continued along a rough cement walk until she came to a paved open space, about twenty-five square feet, enclosed by surrounding houses. From this spot the houses on the steep slope seemed almost to sit on top of one another. In less than a hundred yards one could count ten levels of rooftops, in a crazy juxtaposition of angles and lines, roofs and walls and balconies jutting over one another in haphazard fashion. Most of the houses were wooden, many unpainted, with gabled roofs and shuttered doors and windows, some open or half open, some shut. Crisscrossed in front of the hill of houses, with no semblance of design or order, electric wires were strung in a dense mesh. As this was an election year, Republican Statehood Party and Popular Party flags, blown ragged by the wind, waved from tall bamboo poles on the roofs of many houses.

Fernanda's apartment was one of four in a long cement-block building. The door of each apartment had been painted a different color (Fernanda's was a bright green), and each door opened outward from the middle like a Dutch door, with one panel divided again, so that the top half could serve as a window. The inner side of Fernanda's door, which stood open, was painted a bright pink.

In front of her apartment, blocking the view of the sea, was the small, unpainted shack of her neighbor, *doña* Juli. A paved alleyway, about four feet wide, separated the two houses. To the left of Fernanda's building, at the dead end of the alleyway, stood the wooden house of Junior's parents.

As Rosa approached Fernanda's house, Fernanda came to the door with a mop in her hand. She was a good-looking, dark Negro woman of about forty with a stocky, youthful figure. Her neck was short and muscular. Her kinky hair was pinned into little knots on her round head. She had dull black eyes, heavy eyebrows and full lips. She was wearing an old checked dress, and she was barefoot.

Fernanda greeted Rosa cordially. "I don't move into a house until I give it a good scrubbing," she said. "I want to burn some herbs, too, in case the people who lived here before were unlucky. I don't want to catch anybody else's bad luck. Or who knows? Maybe somebody with tuberculosis lived here, or one of those dirty people who shit anywhere."

The new apartment consisted of two small, windowless rooms connected by an open doorway. The only source of ventilation and light was the outside door, which Fernanda had opened wide.

"I'll help you clean." Rosa said. She picked up a broom and started sweeping the cement floor in the dark bedrom. "Where's Junior?" she asked.

"Oh, he isn't up yet. He went to bed so late last night. And after all, today is his birthday. Damn this place. It's so small. Fuck it! How will Junior manage to get all our things in here? And the worst of it is that we have no water inside. Junior says he can fix up a shower right in front, though, because the outside faucet is so near. But we have no toilet either. We'll have to go screwing around to Junior's mother's house. That's the main reason I didn't want to move here, so as not be bothering them all the time. And I don't like their bunch of puny brats hanging around. I like to keep my house nice and pretty with my ornaments and knickknacks, and you know how kids are." She stopped mopping the floor to wipe perspiration from her forehead with the back of her hand.

"And another thing. Junior and I like to neck all the time and that looks bad in front of children. Well, I'll just hang a curtain over the door and I won't let the kids in. I'll have to hang a curtain over the bedroom doorway, too, but it won't do much good. The neighbors can hear the whole thing through the wall."

Junior walked in, his youthful face puffy with sleep and his hair uncombed. He was wearing dirty blue jeans, a sweatshirt and rubber sandals. The tight jeans made him look taller than his five-foot-nine.

"Good morning, *mi vida,*" Fernanda said, hugging him vigorously. "*Ay,* how much I love my man!" She kissed him on the lips. He put his arms around her, and ignoring Rosa's presence, they kissed for several long moments. Then they sat down on the front stoop.

"Happy birthday, my darling," Fernanda said. "I hope you'll last many, many more years, as long as you spend them with me and not with some other woman. Forgive me for not getting you a little gift. But never mind, I'll give you something tonight when there's nobody around to see." They both laughed.

Soon Junior said, "Well, I'd better be going back. Our things have to be carried over here. Aren't you going to help me, Fernanda?"

"I should say not. Wouldn't that be something? That's all right for a woman without a man of her own. But I have my man, and he's a good one."

"But look, I haven't had any coffee yet," Junior said.

"Well, son, that's the trouble when one's moving. I can't warm any coffee for you, unless I heat it down here between my legs. Would you like that?"

Junior took her face between his hands. "Don't get fresh, now."

"Well, I do have my little straw hut down there. So we don't have to move unless we want to. The only trouble is, being made of straw, it leaks."

"Stop, stop, or we'll never finish today!" Junior said. "And I'm dying to finish because I'm so tired."

"But, *cristiano*, who's keeping you? Hurry up and see if one of those drunks who's always hanging around will help you. And take the children too. They can help carry the light things. Only tell them not to break my dishes or ornaments, see?"

"*Muchacha*, you give more orders than a general," Junior said as he got up to go. "If you were my boss, I'd have smashed your face in already."

A few minutes after Junior had left, Fernanda's daughter Cruz arrived, her baby son, Chuito, on one arm, and her three-year-old daughter Anita tagging along behind. Cruz was eighteen, dark-skinned and only about four feet nine inches tall. One of her legs was shorter than the other, causing her to limp badly. Her crooked spine made her buttocks protrude and her shoulders arch back in an ungainly way. She held out a string that had several live crabs tied to it. "Look, I brought these because I know how much you like them," she said to Fernanda.

Fernanda's face lit up as she took the crabs and hung them on a nail in the front room. "Thank you, child."

"A man was going around selling them and he let me have them cheap," Cruz said. "I guess he liked me, and anyway, these were the last he had."

"Anita, come here," Fernanda said. "What's the matter with you, young lady? Don't you know how to greet your grandmother?"

"Anita, you damned brat, ask your grandmother for her blessing," Cruz said. "Who do you think you are, anyway?"

"Bless me," Anita said timidly, hanging her head.

"May the Lord favor you. *Ave María*, what a kinky mess that child's hair is today! By the Blessed God, her hair is the kinkiest in the family. Pin it up in two buns so it won't show so much."

Cruz laughed. Sitting down on the stoop, she pulled her daughter to her. "Oh, Nanda, you know that a cat's kit hunts mice," she said to her mother. "And remember that the *cabrón* that made her is black as they come! But they don't come any tastier either. See this little fellow on my arm? Little as he is, he already falls in love. I tell you, the damn kid really does. You should see the way he stares at the girls."

"He's a real *macho*, a real he-man," Fernanda said. "He doesn't come from a family of sissies."

"Well, I have to go sell *bolita* numbers," Cruz said. "Nanda, are you going to play the numbers today or aren't you?"

"Of course I will," her mother answered. "I'll play even if I go broke. Look, today I have a dollar-fifty and I'm going to play it all. The three or four dollars I keep for the *bolita* are sacred, *coño*. I never touch them for anything else. Yet I've never hit it. If I only could, one of these days! I'd build a little house of my own and then nobody would come screwing around. We only need about three hundred dollars. It's election time now, so anybody who wants help to build a house can have it. They don't dare say no to anybody for fear he'll change over to another party. With what Junior knows about carpentry, all we'd have to pay for is the wood. But no. I never hit it. If you play out of need, you never win. But one shouldn't lose faith. Let's see if that *cabrón* Saint Expedito will favor me this time."

Junior returned, carrying on his back a small red plastic sofa with wooden arms. This sofa and nearly all of Fernanda's furniture had been given her by *doña* Ofelia, in whose restaurant she had worked as cook and maid. Fernanda ran to help her husband, and together they placed the sofa in the front room against the left wall. Junior sat down to rest.

"*Señora,* don't you have any shoes?" he asked Fernanda disapprovingly. "You know I don't like you to go barefoot. And you haven't been feeling well lately."

"Yes, my darling, I'll put them on as soon as the floor dries," Fernanda answered.

Junior's younger brothers and sisters began to arrive with cartons full of household objects. Fernanda yelled, "You devils! Don't bang those boxes down so hard! If you break any of my ornaments I'll pull them out of your lungs. I'll break every tooth in your heads. No, no, I'm just joking. But if you do it well and don't break anything, I'll give you each a quarter." The children hurried out and Junior followed, saying, "I'll go back for some more." In a few minutes they all returned, Junior with an armchair that matched the sofa and the children with various small objects.

"Say, why don't you get to work and start taking out the stuff?" Junior asked Fernanda. "What are you waiting for? It's nearly nine o'clock."

"Let me do things my own way, *mi vida,*" Fernanda said placidly. "Men don't know a thing about housekeeping, and what's more, you shouldn't go sticking your nose into these things. In the first place, how am I to take the things out while the floor's still wet? And in the second place, I want to have everything here before I begin."

"I still haven't done the nicest little job of all, bringing the refrigerator," Junior said. "How am I ever going to carry that heavy thing all the way here?"

"Chuito, you go fetch Nanda's refrigerator," Cruz said to her baby.

"Look, Junior, see what Crucita brought us," Fernanda said, pointing to the string of crabs.

Junior looked pleased. "Well, so you finally gave somebody something! Tell me, what fly bit you? Are you sick? You must be burning up with fever. Nanda, run, get me a black bottle. I have to make a mark to remember this great day."

"Oh, go to hell," Cruz replied good-humoredly. "I'm going now before it gets too late to sell my *bolita* tickets. I have to get to the men when they're a bit high, but before they're drunk and broke. But first I have to make myself pretty. That's how you sell something to a man. They buy just because it gives them a chance to look at you."

"All right, beat it, nobody's holding you," Junior said. "But be sure to come back later with our *bolita* book and taste the crabs. But only to taste them, because I'm not going to give you much."

"Be careful, or you'll be the one who doesn't get a taste," Cruz said, starting to walk out with Chuito. She called to her daughter, "Come on, Little Tail, don't lag too far behind."

Fernanda walked with them until they reached the drain. When she returned, she said to Junior, *"Hombre,* why don't you go get Darío to help you with the moving? I hope he isn't drunk already, although he's a problem, drunk or sober. You know, Rosa, that cousin of mine steals like anything, but only from his own relatives. He stole twenty dollars from Fela on Mother's Day. But go get him anyway, Junior."

"I'll think about it," the young man said and left.

Fernanda settled down on the stoop with a cigarette. *"Ave María,* I hope I don't have to move soon again," she said. "First we were in Cataño, then we moved to Felícita's house, then to the place up there, and now here. But I won't stay here either if Junior's *mamá* and *papá* come screwing around all the time. But it's nice here, you know. The sea is calm today, but it can be wild and treacherous! See that gray house there on the right? There's a whirlpool there at high tide that can swallow up everything. That's the third house that's been built there. The sea took the other two. Before the hurricane this place down here was a town in itself. Wherever you see those posts sticking up in the sand, there used to be a house. People lived like sardines in a can but we were really happy then, gayer. You saw a crap game going on wherever you looked. We used to go at low tide to get those big clams. That's the best thing you ever tasted in a salad. Oh, we had fun! You know, on the beach there's a kind of shellfish that looks like a cunt and another animal that looks like a cock. And do you know what? When you put one next to the other, why *muchacha,* the 'cock' goes right to the 'cunt' and the 'cunt' sucks it in. It used to be our big joke."

Fernanda was still smoking and talking to Rosa when Junior came back with Darío and two other men. They were carrying the bed and mattress, several little tables, a stack of boards and miscellaneous objects. They set down the things and left. Cruz walked in. "I've come to help," she said. "Angelito's taking care of the children. So what shall I do?"

"Nothing, there isn't a thing to be done yet, *muchacha*," Fernanda answered. "I want to wait till Junior puts up the shelves. Say, Rosa, did you see the dress Fela gave me for Mother's Day? It's so pretty. Only, I don't know when I'll ever get to wear it. It's too nice to wear around here. *Bendito*, all my daughters gave me something except Soledad. She just wrote a scolding sort of letter from New York. She wouldn't dare do that if she were here. She knows I'd smash her face in if she did. Whoever heard of a daughter scolding her mother? It isn't like a son's doing it, because he's a man. Even so it wouldn't be right. And all over nothing! Just that she's upset because I'm living with Junior. What's wrong with that, if I'm happy with him? He works, he doesn't beat me, he treats me like a queen. The best thing about him is that he doesn't have any vices. That's the truth. He even smokes less than I do. And another good thing about him is that I caught him young and ignorant. I taught him everything and formed him to my taste."

"Say, Nanda, how about that comb you were going to give me," Cruz said.

"Oh Lord, I forgot," Fernanda answered. "But even if I'd remembered I couldn't have bought it this week. I almost drew a blank because there wasn't much ironing to do. Only washing. And you know washing pays less and I'm slower at it anyway. I didn't even earn sixteen dollars this week. Damn that job! I kill myself working for nothing. What can I do with sixteen dollars? I have to give at least six to Junior's mother for food. And we have so many debts. Damn money, anyway! It still hurts me to think I couldn't get Junior a present for his birthday. He's nineteen today. May he have many more birthdays by my side!"

"So much damn foolishness over a birthday!" Cruz said angrily. "Since when have you cared? Our birthdays have always passed under the table—they come and go and you never give them a thought. You never have. And we're your own children. Right now I bet you don't know what day you bore any of us. Yet you make such a fuss over Junior's birthday. You only care about his family. The Ríos' don't mean a thing to you any more."

Rosa was surprised at this outburst. Whatever their real feelings were, Fernanda's children usually spoke to their mother with great respect. Fernanda's answer was mild. "Of course I remember your birthdays. But if I don't have any money, what can I do? And anyway, you can't compare a husband with children. When you were with Emilio, who came first? Of course you have to show more affection to your husband than to your children."

"Oh, let's leave it there," Cruz said. "I don't want to argue with you, and anyway, I've got to go now or it really will be too late to sell any numbers. Besides, I have to see about my children."

Cruz left, almost at a run.

It was about ten-thirty when Junior and the other men returned with a large, old-fashioned refrigerator.

"Put it here," Fernanda said, pointing to a corner of the front wall near the sofa. "We have to use this room for the kitchen as well as for our dining room and parlor. Well, I'd better begin, everything's here now."

Junior lay down to rest on the floor near the front door. With Rosa's help, Fernanda began to arrange the furniture. They set the red armchair opposite the sofa and completed the "living room" unit with an end table and a coffee table. Fernanda hunted through the cartons until she found a vase and a bunch of plastic flowers to place on the coffee table. A mahogany-painted step table was shoved into the right-hand corner at the rear. "This is where I'll have my little garden, all my little ornaments," Fernanda said happily. A table with the two-burner kerosene stove on top of it was put in the corner opposite the refrigerator. Fernanda and Rosa pushed a large trunk against the right-hand wall. The only furniture for the inner room was the bed which Junior's helpers had set up. Fernanda planned to hang clothes from broomsticks fastened across the corners of the room, and shoes, purses and other small objects from nails on the walls. When all of the furniture was arranged, Fernanda began to unpack the cartons, humming as she worked.

"Junior, you aren't through yet," she said. "Get up and drive some nails here in the corner for my pots and pans. The trouble is, Rosa, I have no pots and pans. When I took off with my skinny darling here, they were selling six of these pans for two-fifty, but they turned out to be pure junk. They're full of holes already. I would throw them out but they remind me of that day. *Ay,* we were so happy! We were dying to be alone together so we could get our fill of the thing we wanted! We felt like flying. When we finally got home, we dived for the bed. And then, well, to get that man's prick down I would have had to cut it off with a machete."

"Fernanda, don't be so fresh," Junior protested. "Stop talking like that."

"I'm not fresh and it happens to every married couple," Fernanda said, laughing.

She picked up a small cooking pot and took it to the public faucet which was almost at her doorstep. She wanted water to clean the stove, and while she worked she talked to Junior, who had begun to put up the shelves she had asked for.

"You know," she said, "that other woman who irons in *el laundry* is just a beast. Why, even the owner said so. But he has a lot of respect for her because she practically grew up there, working for him. And she's fast as anything. Her temper is even worse than mine, so you can imagine! When she doesn't like one of the other women she makes her quit. But believe it or not, she gets along fine with me. She even gives me some of the pieces she's supposed to iron so I can earn more."

"Well, don't cross her or get too friendly with her either," Junior said. "And don't let her come screwing around. I don't let anybody screw me on my job, not even the boss. Slavery was abolished a long time ago. I work but not to kill myself. Why should I? To make someone else rich? Not on your life, *hombre!*"

"Oh, but those people at *el laundry* are nice," Fernanda said. "This isn't my first job, anyway. So who do you think you're teaching, *hombre?*"

"If I could get a job where I earned a little more, I wouldn't let you work at all. I don't like it a bit. Better that you stay home and give me a baby."

"Oh no, not me," Fernanda said. "As soon as I'd have a baby you'd take off with another woman."

"Quit your kidding, Nanda. You're always fooling around. Want to bet I'll make that baby right now?"

Fernanda smiled. "That's not the way it's done, son. You need time to do it right."

She began to unpack another carton. "Junior, do you know what we have to do? We have to buy a cot in case Simplicio or Soledad comes from New York to visit us."

"Well, we'll do that when we can afford it," Junior said firmly. "And if we never can, all the better. If there's no bed, nobody can stay with us. We're happier by ourselves."

"Hold your tongue, Junior. I'm speaking about my children, no less. If they come and there's no extra bed, then we'll have to give them ours. You know, Rosa, the last time Soledad came she couldn't stay with us, but next time it's going to be different.

"Now, if Felícita moves to the room on the left here, there will be only a wall between us. I figure I'll have to let her use our electric current. That's no problem, really, but I'd rather she didn't move here because there's no wedge worse than one from the same tree. And Felícita is so dirty and sloppy now. When I was staying with her, I couldn't stand the way the whole house stank of the children's shit. Felícita used to pile up their clothes without even scraping the shit off. I suppose she thought I'd wash them for her. But not me. I've already brought up one family and I'm not planning to bring up hers. Felícita enjoyed fucking to make those kids. Let her enjoy working to bring them up."

Junior was searching through a carton full of comic books. "Hey, give me that box," Fernanda said. "I'm not going to exchange those; they're for Simplicio. He loves them and maybe they'll keep him from drinking so much. I know he's drinking. Flora never writes me about that because she knows how I worry. But with so many people traveling back and forth, there's nothing I don't find out."

"And why shouldn't he drink?" Junior asked her. "Simplicio isn't a queer to be sitting around the house all the time. Real men drink and that's what he is, a *macho*. What's wrong is for a woman to drink. That really looks bad."

"If that shower's meant for me, you'd better dry up," Fernanda said. "I don't drink any more and I don't think I ever will again. *Ay,* what I wouldn't give to have Simplicio here now. That son of mine really loves me! Rosa, did you know that my grandson Gabi has gone to the States to live with him and Flora? It'll be heaven for Gabi, Flora is so good. But Felícita doesn't deserve to have people doing her favors and taking care of her son. I don't know how that girl got to be so cold. Going to the airport to see someone off, one feels sad and even cries because it isn't safe to travel in those machines. And that poor little boy was going all alone. Well, I cried, and do you know what that skinny bitch said? She said they were crocodile tears."

Doña Juli, Fernanda's neighbor, knocked on the door.

Fernanda called out, "Since when do you stand outside like a stick? Come on in."

The old woman walked in and sat down on the sofa. She was tall, thin and dark-skinned. She wore her hair pulled back into a tight bun that accentuated the look of weariness on her wrinkled face.

"*Ay,* Nanda!" she said. "Those children are driving me crazy! Well, I'm very glad you're my new neighbors. And you know that my house is yours."

"The same to you, *doña* Juli. Now we can stay up late and play bingo and thirty-one."

Doña Juli nodded. "I really believe those children want to kill me off with a wooden knife," she said. "Imagine, Maguie didn't want to go to school today because she doesn't have a new dress or any shoes. It's the last day of school, you know. Let her go barefoot, then. I do all I can but I can't buy her shoes. All I have is that miserable amount from Social Security and what I can make selling oranges sometimes. And I have Toña's girl and my granddaughter Julia's Ramoncito and her little baby, too."

"Excuse me, *doña* Juli, but I'm going to tell you something," Fernanda said. "It's your own fault that you're so screwed up. Why should you have to bring up the child of that great lump of a Julia? Or any of your great-grandchildren?"

"Why? For no reason. Just so Julia can spend her time chasing after her husband's ass. But, *cristiana,* how could I leave that baby as she was? When Francisco asked me to take her, she looked like a little corpse. She had watery diarrhea. I had to spend a whole day in the hospital while they gave her serum. They stuck needles into her bigger than she was. And I watched over that baby until she was strong and healthy. But when she's two years old, I'm going to give her back to Julia. They wanted me to adopt her, with ink and paper, but I said no. That's what mothers are for, to bring up their own children. And now Toña's pregnant again. That's all those granddaughters of mine are good for. They're like bitches in heat. I told Toña that I won't touch this new child with a ten-foot pole. I'm an old woman, and bringing up children is a lot of trouble."

"*Ay, doña* Juli, let her mother worry about her. I won't bring up anybody else's kids. Felícita wanted to wheedle me into taking Angelito but I can't do that. I have my husband to consider and Angelito is **terribly** spoiled. Junior doesn't get along with him."

Junior came in from the back room with a wooden crate that had been fitted with shelves. "Say, *doña* Juli, you might have some use for these shelves. Want them?"

"Oh yes, thank you. Everything has some use. I save everything, because people are bound to come asking, 'Do you have this? Do you have that?' And there it is . . . *doña* Juli has it for them. Well, I'm going now. That little flea of a Ramoncito wants to spend the whole day on the beach. He's bound to drown some day."

As *doña* Juli left, Junior's mother came to the door. "Give me your blessing, *mami*," Junior said to her.

"May the Lord bless you and protect you," the woman responded.

"Celestina, come on up and sit down," Fernanda said cordially.

Junior's mother was about Fernanda's age. She was pale and tired, and her hair looked as if it had not been combed for several days. She was about eight months pregnant. She sat down on the edge of the sofa.

"Well, you overgrown scamp, are you mad at coffee, or what?" she asked her son. "Why haven't you come over for breakfast?"

"Oh, *mami,* it's just that I haven't had time," Junior answered. "Tell Monse to bring me some."

"Blessed be Our Lady!" his mother exclaimed. "These youngsters sure like to be waited on. Any day now you'll ask me to hold the cup for you so you can drink."

"And what if I did. You'd do it gladly because I'm the first chick you ever hatched." He gave her a hug.

"Go on," his mother said, smiling. "And it's just as well you don't want coffee now because lunch is nearly ready. Listen, can you lend me a little vinegar for the fish?"

Junior searched through a box of groceries. "No, we don't have any, but take this and send for some." He handed her a dollar.

"Thank you, *mi vida.* I'm going now because Adán is home already." Celestina said good-bye and left.

Fernanda, who was still unpacking boxes, unwrapped six shot glasses. "Look, Rosa, Simplicio gave me these and a set of dishes for Mother's Day. I didn't take the dishes when I left Héctor to go off with Junior. They must be broken to bits by now, because his Leonor throws dishes whenever she gets mad. But these little glasses I wouldn't give to anybody, and nobody's going to drink from them. They're a keepsake."

She opened another carton and pulled out a transparent red nightgown.

"Look, Rosa, Soledad sent me this from New York for my birthday but I still haven't worn it. I need a robe to go with it."

"Ah yes, the egg needs salt," Junior said. "Why don't you say what you mean?"

"No, my darling, I know you'd buy me one if you could. So forget it, I was only talking to myself. Later on, maybe. There's plenty of time."

Junior's father, Adán, appeared at the door. He had white hair and a white beard, and a calm, fine-featured face. He was wearing a white nylon shirt, khaki trousers and beach sandals.

"Your blessing, *papi*," Junior said.

"God bless you and protect you," his father answered. "See how nice it is for you two to be near us? Now if anything happens, all you have to do is yell. Say, boy, can't you see that those nails are too long for your boards? I have some three-inch nails at home. Why don't you go over and get them? That nail you have there is going to bend."

"Thanks, *papi,* I'll get them later." Junior laid down his hammer.

"Say, Junior, give me the half dollar I had to pay the men for carrying the refrigerator," Adán said. "I had to treat each of them to a shot of rum and a pack of cigarettes besides."

"Sure, *hombre,* that's all right." Junior handed him the money.

"Who would think it, but such are the times we live in," Adán said. "In the old days nobody minded doing a little favor like that for somebody. But now it's different. Now people here won't help you unless you pay."

He noticed the string of crabs on the wall. *"Ave María,* how the price of crabs has gone up! Imagine, you have to pay a dollar-fifty for half a dozen. Well, I'm going home for my dinner. Come for the nails when you want them, Junior."

Junior went to sit beside Fernanda on the sofa, leaning his head against her shoulder. *"Ay,* I'm tired after all that carrying," he said. Gradually he slipped down until he was lying full length on the sofa with his head on Fernanda's lap. She began to play with his hair. "It looks like this child has lice," she said playfully. "I'll have to delouse him." She went on parting his hair, pretending to look for lice.

"Listen, yesterday my boss asked me why I didn't finish school," Junior said lazily. "He said I ought to finish the last year of high school and then he'd help me get a better job."

"But, my darling, that's just exactly what I want," Fernanda said. "You'll get out of work at five, come home to dinner, go to school and be back home by nine. That way you can finish in two years."

"Yes, and then they'll help me. My boss was saying that they haven't got any other messenger with as much schooling as I have. And they like educated people around those government offices. If I knew how to drive they'd have me driving. Know what I did the other day? I asked my boss to lend me his car and he handed me his keys right away."

"*Muchacho,* and what did you do then?"

"Oh, I laughed and said, 'Thank you, but I don't know how to drive yet. I'm just trying to see if I could learn.' "

"And then what did he say?"

"Nothing . . . to go ahead and learn and get a driver's license and then I could have the use of one of their cars whenever I wanted it. I'll learn in no time at all. You'll see."

"You know who you're like?" Fernanda said, smoothing Junior's hair. "You're like my son, Simplicio. Whenever he says he's going to do something, he goes ahead and does it."

"I already know most of the little book by heart," Junior went on. "When I know it real well I'll take the examination. What screws me up is that I'll have to have my picture taken and I don't like that."

"*Muchacho,* you're smart. You and Monse are the smartest ones in your family. That little girl is as clever as can be. You can tell how much brains a person is going to have from the time they're small."

Just then a tall, slender girl of about fourteen walked in. She was wearing a white blouse and a wine-colored skirt; her feet were bare.

"Rosa, this is Celeste, Junior's sister," Fernanda said. "She's a crazy kid. Imagine, she dropped out of school and doesn't want to go back. Adán spoke to her and advised her—I heard him myself. He told her, 'If you want to go back to school I'll send you, so that you can be somebody. But if you don't want to go, just stay home and be a donkey. Help your *mamá,* she's busy enough, goodness knows. And learn to cook. Because the only future for girls like you is to take off with some good-for-nothing!' "

"But, Nanda, we have so many children at home and so many problems," Celeste said.

"*Muchacha,* you can't imagine what a sad thing it is not to have an education," Fernanda said. "Like a woman here in La Esmeralda whose husband went to the States. It seems she was unfaithful to him, and he found out and sent her the dirtiest letters you can imagine. And what happened? The poor woman was illiterate and she handed those letters over to the first person who would read them to her. So everybody found out that she'd given her ass to her husband and that she'd put the horns on him. Well, that should show you."

"I can write letters, but not very well," Celeste said.

"Why don't you at least go to night school?" Fernanda suggested.

"How can I? *Papi* wants us in bed by seven. And that's when he's sober. When he's drunk he makes us go to sleep even earlier. What he wants is to have us in the house where he can pester us to death."

"Well, Celeste, just shut your eyes and take the plunge. Enroll next year.

You're already in the seventh grade, and in just two years you can finish the ninth and graduate from junior high school."

"And what good will that do?"

"Why, my child, it can help you get a job as a salesgirl or in a factory. Because if you keep on the way you're going, the only thing you can hope to get is a job as a housemaid. And you can't imagine how hard that is, with everybody ordering you around and you having to bend your neck under the yoke like an ox at the plow. Working like a Negro slave and earning almost nothing."

"Oh, I don't know, we'll see," Celeste said. "I'd better leave before *mami* shouts herself hoarse calling me." She ran out.

"You'll see, she won't ever go back to school," Fernanda said to Rosa. "She's already in love and she'll soon lose whatever she has to lose. But let me tell you, it's her mother's fault for being too soft with her. That girl doesn't do a lick of work at home except wash the dishes and scrub the floor. Her mother doesn't force her to do anything. And yet Junior, who is a man, had to wash his mother's bloody cloths after she had a baby. He had to do all kinds of work around the house, just like a girl. I don't know why he didn't turn out to be a queer."

Junior sat up, and Fernanda gave him several long kisses. Then she went over to the table at the back of the room and began to unwrap and arrange a number of ceramic figurines.

Junior took a clasp knife with a curved blade out of his pocket. "This used to belong to *papi* but he can forget it. It's mine now. I'm going to take out that bit of glass that got stuck in my foot this morning."

"Oh, dear God, such a long time I've had this little rabbit and now it had to go and break," Fernanda said. "I brought it from Cataño to La Esmeralda and nothing happened to it. And now it breaks on that short trip from the old house to this one."

"Girl, if I'd hurt myself you wouldn't feel it half as much," Junior said. "Why do you like those little things so much?"

"Well, son, things that people give you should be loved and appreciated. Do you want me to be ungrateful?"

Cruz dashed into the house again. It was now noon. She had changed into a very low-cut pink dress and wore sandals of interwoven beige and green straps. In spite of her deformed body she looked pretty.

"I got rid of all my numbers, Nanda," she said, out of breath. "They sold like hot cakes, and all for cash too. 'Here's your money, give me my number,' just like that. It's the best time to sell, but it's hot as hell outside. Here's your book. Pay me now, because I'm going to Lolo the 'Banker' right away. Say, Junior, don't you have a wallet to spare? Give it to me. Look, I've put all the money into the bosom of my dress and that way it's going to get lost. Oh Lord, if they catch me with all this cash they'll arrest me for sure!"

"I'll give you a couple of slaps in the face for being so fresh. That's all you'll get from me. Just look at that low neckline!" Junior said.

"You aren't my father," Cruz retorted. "Tell your wife to give you a child. Then you can hit him all you like. But, *Ave María,* the poor little brat would be uglier than the bogeyman because you're as ugly as they come. You look like a long-handled brush. All right, are you going to find a wallet for me or not?"

"*O.K.,* I'll lend it to you. Don't forget to return it." He handed her a leather wallet.

"Oh, I don't want that old thing," Cruz said. "The money would drop right out of it. I'd better keep it in my bosom."

"By the way, Crucita, can you lend me an extension cord?" Fernanda asked. "I need it to bring light from the bedroom into the parlor."

"I'll send one to you right away. Junior, pay me the three dollars for the numbers. I'm going."

"What's your hurry, girl? Is your sweetheart waiting for you?"

"Oh yes, and is he handsome!" Cruz said.

Angelito, one of Felícita's seven-year-old twins, appeared at the doorway. "Hey you, *puñeta,* masturbator, you left my kids alone," Cruz screamed at him. "If anything happens to them, I'll have your blood for it. What did I leave you in the house for, you idiot? I'm going to wring the bile out of you. And the way this boy eats!" she said to Rosa. "Like a dock hand, and he won't do a thing to earn his food. All he does is play. And I'm all screwed up, shoveling food into him to fill his belly. But that's going to end pretty soon because Felícita doesn't pay me a cent for that boy. She won't even buy clothes for him. It's not that she can't afford it. She can afford to go whoring all over the place. If she were grateful, at least, but she's not, no matter what you do for her. But I've learned my lesson. Remember what Soledad did to me? After I took such good care of her daughter and even enrolled her in school, she began to spread gossip about me. Just wait until she comes back to Puerto Rico. She'll hear from me then."

"All right, you two are sisters. You should forget and forgive," Fernanda said.

Cruz left, still scolding Angelito.

A large rat emerged from the back room and scuttled through the parlor. "Most Holy Mary!" Fernanda yelled, jumping up on the sofa. "What can I do in this fucking La Esmeralda? I left the other room because of the rats, and what's the first thing I see when I move? Junior, find that rat and kill it or I'm going to sleep somewhere else tonight."

Junior beat at the rat with the mop stick but it hid behind the refrigerator. "Rats don't harm anybody, child," he said, taking both Fernanda's hands in his and giving her a kiss.

Celeste returned, carrying two plates, and left. "She brought our lunch,"

Fernanda said to Rosa, calming down. "How nice! I'm starving, and Junior must be hungrier still because he didn't have any breakfast. That's fish, isn't it? Good!" Fernanda uncovered the plates. One was filled with fried fish and the other with pieces of boiled green bananas. She divided the food among the three of them but there was barely enough to go around.

"I'm going to cook those crabs right away," Fernanda said when they had eaten. "Junior, send one of your sisters to buy ten cents' worth of boiled bananas to eat with them." Junior went out and Fernanda filled a large pot at the outside faucet. When the water was boiling she dropped in the crabs. Soon Junior's sister Monse came in with the bananas. Fernanda took the crabs out of the pot, and she and Rosa began breaking the joints and picking the meat out of the shells.

"Take this to your *mamá*, Monse," Fernanda said, putting some crab meat on a plate. "You children can come and get your share here."

Monse soon returned with several smaller children, and Fernanda served a morsel or two of crab meat to each of them. Then she and Junior sat down on the sofa and fed each other from the same plate.

"Junior, I wish you'd go over to Loíza Aldea," Fernanda said when they had finished. "There are lots of crabs there free for the taking."

"All right, I'll go some day, but now I want to sleep for a while," Junior said.

"Yes, my darling, you do that. Rosa and I are going to see if I got a letter from New York."

Junior took a comic book and went to lie down on the bed. The two women went out.

"Isn't Junior's mother nice to me now?" Fernanda asked. "When I took off with Junior, Celestina wouldn't have anything to do with me. Junior's such a good son and he'd been so generous to his parents. They didn't want to have to stop sucking from such a full tit. At least that's what I think. Junior stood up to them and now they're as nice as can be. You saw how Celestina cooked for us today. It's only natural, since I don't forbid Junior to help them. On the contrary, I help them all I can. The other day a junkie passed by my house and dropped a five-dollar bill. *Muchacha,* I rushed out and grabbed it and went to Bonilla's to change it. I sent a dollar to Celestina right away. And let me tell you, she got all the rest, too, quarter by quarter."

As they walked along the narrow edge of the cement drain, the women passed some hogs rooting under a house. "Hell, what a small prick that hog has," Fernanda said. "They all do, I've heard. Well, look at ducks. They have tiny ones too, but they manage to get their females stirred up all right. Let's stop in here at old man Cayetano's house and see how he is."

They went up some steps and looked in at the open door. Cayetano, looking very feeble and ill, was talking to a thin blond young man. Fernanda

greeted him and then said to the young man, "You can see how much Cayetano needs you. The house looked like a pigpen all the time you were gone.
Stay with him. The Veterans Administration is now looking for somebody to
take good care of him, and who could do it better than you?"

"Yes, I already told him I'll stay if he wants me," the young man answered in a high, effeminate voice.

"Well, good-bye now, we're going to Bonilla's for the mail," Fernanda
said. As soon as they got out of earshot, she told Rosa, "That faggot kept
Cayetano's house real pretty until he had a fight somewhere and got arrested
for disturbing the peace. He's lived in Cayetano's house for a long time, but
you needn't think he gave it to the old man. No, he went out hustling and I'm
telling you, that fellow made more money than any whore. He had lovely long
hair, and when he dressed up like a woman he looked like a madonna. No one
could have imagined that he was a man. But now he's had a setback because
the first thing they did in jail was to give him a haircut and dress him like a
man. That's why he looks so sad. You know, there's no shame any more.
Those queers aren't a bit ashamed to kiss each other on every street corner.
Listen, I used to tell Simplicio, 'You go fall in love whenever you want to and
I'll be your go-between and even support your wife if need be. But don't come
to me with that shamelessness.' I'd a thousand times rather see my son dead,
with his legs stretched out stiff and candles lit around him, than have him
become a queer. As to my girls, I've always told them, 'Better be a whore than
a lesbian.' "

They walked on in silence for a few minutes. Then Fernanda, dropping
her voice, said, "Once, a long time ago, I had a strange dream about a lesbian.
I dreamed I had gone into a big warehouse to see what they kept there. They
closed the door and shut me in. I kept going farther in, crying, when suddenly
a man appeared and invited me to—you know. I refused and kept going. Then
a lesbian appeared and gave me the same invitation. I didn't want to, but then
she turned into a vampire. She showed her fangs and something like horns. She
said, "If you won't let me do it, I'll suck your blood.' Then she came nearer
and nearer and did everything she wanted to do with me. Next day I still felt
the sensation of that woman's body lying on me."

Rosa and Fernanda discussed the dream until they arrived at the grocery
store. "Bonilla, has the postman come?" Fernanda asked.

Bonilla, a dark, stout, round-faced man, was leaning on the counter.
"No, my child, not yet. Everybody is waiting for him."

Santa, a Negro woman of about seventy, spoke up. "That's because he
has a sweetheart up there. He'll come when he gets through with his petting.
At least that's what people say. I don't know."

"I'll tell you one thing, Santa, he's sure good-looking," Fernanda said.

"But, damn it, he should bring the letters first and then go do as he pleases, instead of keeping us here hours on end," Santa complained. "I'm waiting for a little check that's due today, and just look, it's two o'clock already. Now I'm going to miss today's serial on TV."

"And it's real good right now," said another woman who was also waiting.

"Yes, it's good, because now both of them are jealous. Now she's jealous of her cousin," Santa replied.

"Well, go ahead and watch it. I'll wait for the postman for you," Fernanda offered. "I don't like those dramas because of all the damn whining in them. The only program I ever liked was *Forgiveness for Woman*. None of the rest interests me."

Santa and the other woman left. Fernanda and Rosa crossed the street and sat on the cement steps leading to the road below. "We sure do need a post office here. There used to be one but they took it away. For a long time Bonilla would take the mail for us but then some letters got lost, so now he won't do it any more and we have to hang around all day. If you aren't here when the postman comes, he takes your letters back again."

Suddenly they heard Felícita's voice: "Nanda, I'm off to Hyde Park. I'm with the American. I'll be back Tuesday." Fernanda looked up and saw her daughter Felícita leaning out of a taxi which had pulled up in front of Bonilla's store. Beside her sat a fair-haired man of about fifty. Felícita was smartly dressed in a close-fitting red-checked dress, with white shoes and a bag to match. Her face was heavily made up and she wore her hair pulled back tightly. Three of her children were in the back seat, dressed in new clothes. Evita, the baby, was sucking her thumb and tears were rolling down her cheeks.

Felícita introduced her mother and then Rosa to Georgie, her companion. "Aren't you taking Angelito?" Fernando asked. Angelito had seen the taxi from Cruz's house and had come quickly to find out what was going on. The boy was standing beside the car, stroking the fender and gazing pleadingly at his mother.

"No."

"Oh, I see. He's not your son?"

"He's a big boy already," Felícita answered impatiently. "He's seven years old, practically a man. Cruz will give him his meals. Good-bye, we're leaving now."

As the car moved away, Angelito tore off his shirt and flung it to the ground. He watched the car angrily until it disappeared, then picked up the shirt, threw it over his shoulder and walked off with an air of unconcern. Fernanda seemed to feel Felícita's rejection of him as much as he did. She stood in silence for a few moments, with her head lowered and a frown contracting her heavy brows. Finally she said, "Fela's a bad mother. That's why God punishes her. And she's a bad daughter too. I'll never forget the time she told me right to my face that she didn't think of me as her mother and that she wanted to stay with her stepmother, Hortensia. I've never forgotten those words."

Santa came back up the steps and Fernanda greeted her. "You could see eighty programs and still that fucking postman wouldn't get here. I can't wait any longer. Junior will be awake by now."

"Don't worry. If there's anything for you, I'll take it," Santa answered. "I have to stay and wait no matter how late he comes. He's going to bring me my unemployment check and I can't risk having it sent back. I forgot to go for it when I was supposed to. When I went yesterday, they told me they already had mailed it."

As they walked across the plaza, Rosa and Fernanda came upon Adán sitting on a stone bench. He got up to join them. "I'll just tell you how unlucky I am," he said. "Today I played number thirty-eight in the daily double and what number do you think won? Eighty-three! And I've wasted the whole day looking for a man who had offered me a job. Believe it or not, I couldn't find him. That's how unlucky I am. I'm a man who's supported twenty-one children, because there was always work for a good plumber. Yes, with the labor of these hands that the earth will soon take, I've earned the bread that they eat. Yet Junior is the only one who has ever helped me out, may God bless and favor him! The others might as well not be my children. Take Juan now. That boy has a business selling cars and he's almost rich. He has telephones all over his house. But he doesn't do a thing for me except now and then, when he happens to come here and throws me a few pennies if he feels like it. When I'm down and out he doesn't come at all.

"One doesn't even have friends any more. You know, I was talking with one of them the other day in a perfectly friendly manner when he suddenly hauled off and hit me! It was so unexpected I couldn't defend myself. But no matter, I'll get even, if I have to wait twenty years. But don't you go telling my children about it, because if they ever find out there would be real trouble."

"*Bendito,* somebody always tells," Fernanda said. "I had already heard about it before Junior got home. That night I had to keep him from coming up here and getting into trouble."

When they got to Fernanda's place, Adán continued walking toward his own house. The women found Junior hammering at a set of shelves. He threw down his hammer.

"Come on, let's go play thirty-one," he said. "I'm tired of working."

"Yes, let's play outdoors. It's hot in here."

Junior carried the thirty-one board to a patch of cement in front of the house. "Who wants to play?" he called. Two players appeared, a tall slender man with a very pale face and jet-black hair, and a short, dark boy of about seventeen.

"Well, I haven't been able to get a job. But I've got thirty cents to play with. Let's see if I can win a dollar with it," the tall man said.

"I have a quarter," the boy said. "I've got to win seventy-five cents to have my new pants shortened."

"Well, let's see. Maybe I can clean you all out," Junior said, smiling. "I need money too."

"It's hard as hell to get a job these days," the tall man observed as Junior shuffled the deck of Spanish cards. "The docks are all screwed up. And my wife is going to have a baby any day now."

They began to play at a penny a point. Junior won the first three hands. He laughed aloud.

"Go ahead and laugh," Fernanda said. "You'll cry later."

"When you gamble, you should have no more feeling than a stick," Junior said seriously.

"Aren't you a beauty!" Fernanda mocked. "It's a wonder they don't put you in the comics. But don't worry, I'll win this hand. I have to win—shit on my mother if I don't—because if not, I'll be broke and have to drop out."

"Well, go ahead and shit on your mother," the tall man said. "I've just won. Look, I have the King of Cups. You can pick the cards over with a toothpick if you like. I'm not cheating."

"Well, lend me a penny. I'm broke," Fernanda said.

"All right, because you're the only woman playing. That is, if the *compai* will allow me."

"Sure, why not?" Junior said. "She can borrow from me for the next round."

"I shit on the horns of a cow!" Fernanda exclaimed. "What do you mean? I'm the one who's going to win the next round."

"We'll see. Whoever can, will win," the boy said. The tall man won again.

A short, squat, dark-skinned girl came running across the sand, calling Fernanda's name. She was a grossly deformed hunchback. Her large head rested on her chest and her breasts seemed to emerge directly from her abdomen. She wore a torn striped skirt and her hair was wild. "Nanda, Nanda, excuse me, can you come here?" she called excitedly. Her voice came in gasps, as if she were out of breath. "I have to tell you something."

Fernanda got up immediately, and she and Rosa accompanied Norma into the house. "Listen, Nanda," the girl said hysterically. "My stepmother gave me a terrible beating last night. Nicolás did his damage to me, you know, and she found out. Now I won't be able to go back to school. But even worse, I went straight to Nicolás last night and he beat me, too, because I told him I thought I was pregnant. What can I do now? I don't dare go home."

"Don't worry, child," Fernanda said. "Take off that torn skirt and blouse. I'll lend you some clothes. I can't offer you a home because I don't have an extra bed, as you can see. But come here to eat every day. You won't starve. And if you're going to have a baby, don't worry. Go ahead and have it. You won't be the first."

At this moment Junior burst in. He was obviously annoyed. He said, "That's enough, Fernanda. With all that chatter, you aren't playing."

"You said it, I'm not playing," Fernanda shouted at him. "And now you've been so rude I won't go back at all."

"I'll leave now to see what I can do," Norma said. "Look at me, I didn't even put my shoes on." She went out. Fernanda remained seated on the sofa. Her mood had changed and she glared angrily in the direction of her husband, who had gone outside. "That damn fool makes me so mad! God damn him. He's so rude! But I'll teach him a lesson. Wait and see."

A few minutes later Junior came back in. "Well, aren't you coming out to play?" he asked.

"Go to hell, you damn bastard," Fernanda cried. "Don't you speak to me, you insolent brat, you queer! What good did all that education do you? You sure didn't learn any manners in that school. What the devil do you want now? Go to hell. Beat it."

Junior, startled, moved back toward the door. He went out and sat on the steps. Fernanda went to the bedroom and began to make up the bed with furious energy. When she had finished, she came back to the sofa and smoked one cigarette after another. Finally Junior came in. Standing just inside the door, he said remorsefully, "Please, Nanda, please forgive me. I'll never do that again. *Coño,* this is the first time I've ever done it, and just look."

"Go on, beat it. The hell with you! Tonight you're going to sleep at your mother's house. That'll teach you. You must have stuck those high school lessons up your ass. I don't have much schooling but my manners are better than yours. So now you know. Tonight you sleep at your parents' house."

"*Ay,* Nanda, don't be like that." Junior was almost in tears. "Forgive me."

But Fernanda turned her back on him and he rushed out the door.

"It's the woman who teaches the man," Fernanda said to Rosa. She was much calmer now and apparently satisfied with her punishment of her husband. "Don't think Junior hasn't tried to hit me two or three times when we've quarreled. But I don't allow anyone to beat me, and I stopped him short every time. I hit him first and he'd better thank the saints that I wasn't drinking. If I had been, I'd have cut him up for sure. I'll fix him. I can upset him most by not kissing him good-bye when he goes to work. Then when he comes home, I won't speak to him. And I'll sleep ass to ass with him. Whenever I do that, *muchacha,* he begins to go round in circles because he thinks

I'm going to leave him. Finally I feel sorry for him and let him come back."

After a while Celestina entered, looking very upset. "Listen, Nanda, Junior is drunk over at Papo's bar. I sent Monse to get him, but Junior gave her a quarter and told her to go away and not bother him any more. What on earth can have happened to that boy? Maybe his birthday went to his head. Dear Lord, what a cross! I'm going to send him some black coffee. He isn't used to drinking, goodness knows. He must have got drunk on a couple of beers."

"Leave him alone so he'll learn his lesson," Fernanda said.

Monse had come in behind her mother. Seeming to relent, Fernanda said to her, "Monse, you go back to Junior and tell him, 'Nanda says you're to come to her at once.' Go quickly. I'll pay you something."

Monse went out with Celestina but soon returned. "He won't come. He's crying oceans and saying you don't love him, and he's paying for everybody's beer."

"I shit on God!" Fernanda exclaimed. "That queer who's taken over Papo's bar must be giving him credit. I'm going there right now." She rushed out of the house and Rosa followed. Inside the small bar, Fernanda went straight to the thin, straw-hatted man who stood behind the counter. "Say, you, what do you mean selling beer on credit to my husband? I want you to know right now that we aren't going to pay for it."

"I didn't sell the beer to you, lady," the bartender replied. "This is between him and me. Men's business is settled between men."

Fernanda went over to Junior, who was sitting at a corner table looking miserable. "Come on, Junior. Let's go home."

Junior looked up with his eyes full of tears. "No, I don't want to because you don't love me," he said timidly. "Oh, Fernanda. Forgive me! Please, please!"

"Yes, *hombre,* of course I will. Don't be so silly. Stop making a fool of yourself. Come on home."

She put her arm around him and led him out of the bar. At home, Junior sat down in the armchair and began to cry again. *"Muchacho,* come on, lie down on the bed," Fernanda said.

"Get me the chamber pot. I'm going to throw up."

"I shouldn't bring it to you at all," Fernanda said, going for it. "Nobody made you go and get drunk."

Junior vomited. Fernanda took the chamber pot outside, emptied it and washed it at the water tap.

"It's nine o'clock already and you have to get up early," she said in a matter-of-fact voice. "Junior, come to bed." Obediently the young man went into the inner room.

Fernanda said to Rosa, "You'll see, when he gets up in the morning he won't even turn on the light, so as not to wake me. I'll just lay out his clean shorts and socks and uniform for him. You see how I keep his things? As clean as a saint's." She turned toward the bedroom. "Like a saint. *Adiós,* Rosa. Good night."

Fernanda

———

You Can't Cover Up the Sky with Your Hand

———

I AM AS FRANK as I am ugly and I don't try to hide what I am because you can't cover up the sky with your hand. There is nothing good about me. I have a bad temper, why should I deny it? At times I become so angry no one dares come near me, so angry I cry, and in my rage I want to kill.

When I get into these rages, it makes no difference to me whether I kill or get killed. I never feel sorry or anything. I'm the kind of a woman that nobody can say anything to when she's drunk, because any little thing and I'm ready for a fight. If I have a husband and I'm drinking and he starts pestering me or being jealous without cause, or quarreling about any little thing my children do, I'd just as soon cut him with a razor, slash him with a bottle—anything. It makes no difference to me, see?

I often carry a razor because if someone tries to hit you, you have to defend yourself. When I was in the life, I kept a *Gem* blade in my mouth all the time. I could eat with it there, drink, talk and fight without anybody noticing it. I'd break off one corner of the blade to form a little handle and then I'd slip it between my lower gum and my cheek, with the cutting edge up. That way the edge doesn't touch your mouth, it's in the air, see? You can also hide a blade in your hair or you can slip it into the top of your stocking. The one place you should never carry a *Gem* is in your purse, because if you're arrested the cops will find it. When I know I'm going to get into a fight I have the *Gem* ready in my hand, hidden between my fingers. Then, when I get the chance, I quickly cut the cheek or lip.

I'm not afraid of anyone but God, and I'll never accept mistreatment from a man. I wasn't born for that. When I live with a man I'm faithful to the last, but if I find out he's cheating on me, I swear I'll do the same to him. You can count on it, I'll put the horns on him. Revenge! Because my *mamá* told me never to let men dominate me. "If they do it to you, do it to them. Never give in. Don't bow down." And I have the heart to do it.

I would rather be a man than a woman. If God had made me a man I would have been the worst son of a great whore ever born. Not a woman would have escaped me. *Ave María!* I'd have a woman everywhere, and if they didn't give me what I wanted I'd kick my way in. That's why God made me a woman, a real bitch of a one. I'm forty now and I've had six husbands, and if I want I can have six more. I wipe my ass with men.

I may be Negro and I may be getting old and, if we face facts, I was a whore. All this I cannot deny, but no one can come to me and say, "Fernanda, you took my man away from me." I can sing out with the greatest pride that I have never, never taken away another woman's husband. I have always preferred men who are free. I may kid around with married men but it's all in the open. I'm no home breaker because I'd never do to another woman what I wouldn't want her to do to me. That's why I feel that I am worth more than most women here in La Esmeralda.

The truth is, I am really soft-hearted. I have lots of friends. The fights I have are only with my husbands. If someone lives with me, he won't die of hunger or need or anything. If I have money I will give it to anyone near me who needs it, because I can't see them suffer. That's the kind of a heart I have. I feel compassion.

I've done favors for lots of people. Why, I've taken to the streets to get a few pesos for someone in need. I've made lots of money and I've spent it all. What would I want to keep it for? We're not made of stone and we all must die, right? Suppose I save money in the bank and then I die. Who is going to enjoy that money? The government! No, I'd rather eat up my money myself before they come and take care of it for me.

I was born in Río Grande, a little country town about fifty miles from San Juan. When I was only a few months old my parents separated, and my *mamá* went off to work as a maid in San Juan and left me behind with my father's mother. People tell me that my grandmother treated me badly and beat me, but I don't remember that. By the time I was three I was sickly and as skinny as a noodle. I had that illness that makes the belly stick out and the

ass cave in; rickets, they call it. Then one day someone went to see my *mamá*
at work and said to her, "If you don't get that child out of her grandmother's
house, she'll die." So my *mamá* went there and took me with her to San
Juan.

After that I never lacked food as a child because *mamá* always worked
and took care of me. The doctor she worked for prescribed extract of hemo-
globin and told her to give me good, nourishing food, like pigeon broth. I got
fat on that. I was so fat I could hardly get clothes to fit me! When I was a
little older I had asthma but my *mamá* cured it with a brew of manatee fish
bones, ground to a powder and boiled in water. Then, while I was still a little
girl, I had pains in my ovaries, and my *mamá* took me to the doctor often
because of that.

My mother kept on supporting me even after she got herself a new
husband. I was seven when she got together with Jorge. He was a charcoal
vendor, but at that time he and my *mamá* were servants for the Cordero
family. Jorge brought me up. He was very good to me. The first house we
lived in was in an alley at Stop 26.* Afterward we lived in a slum in Santurce in a house that was very poor. It had a charcoal stove and two beds.
There were no luxuries, no electricity, no radio, no television, no refrigerator.
Nobody had anything like that in those days. Later, when I became a
señorita, my *mamá* said that now that I was growing up it was time for me
to get used to having luxuries and to learn what they were for and how to
take care of them. So she bought a three-piece set of wicker furniture. After
that, I began to take an interest in fixing up the house and making it look
pretty.

My mother was a wonderful woman but she certainly had a temper!
You can't imagine how those old people of the past were. When she was
angry no one dared speak to her. I'd just disappear because she would hit me
as hard as if I were a boy. She whipped me with a piece of rope, really deadly
beatings. Afterward I didn't dare look her in the face for a week. Once she
threw a lighted gas lamp at me. Another time she asked me to prepare some
starch for her. I didn't know how and I put coffee in it. That made her so
angry she threw the pot of boiling starch at me. It didn't hit me because I ran
away and escaped. So long as I could get away I never had any problems in
my childhood.

My mother had a sad life because she was often sick and in pain. She
told me she had had a miscarriage and that the gut had come out before the
baby. So the doctor said she needed an operation. They opened her and took
out all her insides and she couldn't ever have her period again. After that,
because she was all hollow inside, she'd get into a rage every month. She'd

* The use of the word *Parada* for Stop is peculiar to San Juan. At the beginning of the century a trolley line went from Old San Juan to Río Piedras, and soon
the Stop numbers came to designate not only the Stop itself but the area around it.

stop speaking to me for a week or two, but later she would make up with me or I would make up with her. When I started to caress her she always said, "Go away, I won't have anything to do with you." But I answered, "Don't be like that, you know I'm your darling," until she stopped being angry.

My mother never taught me to do any kind of work, not even to cook a pot of rice. So I spent my childhood, until I was about eleven, playing all the time and never doing any work. I played with boys and fought with them. I knew how to use my fists. My mother never had any peace because someone was always going to her to complain, "*Doña* Luisa, your daughter's out here fighting with the boys. She's like a fighting cock and nobody can stop her." Then my mother had to drop whatever she was doing and rush off to catch me and beat me. I was really mischievous. I flew kites, spun tops, played marbles and I played with other girls' dolls because I never had one of my own. I got gifts on the Day of the Three Kings,* but everybody gave me clothing because my mother asked them not to give me dolls or toys. She always said that toys are broken in a day or two but clothes last a long time.

When I went to school for the first time, my mother took me. I started out at one of those private schools which charged twenty-five cents a week. They don't have that kind any more. I started when I was very small and kept going until I was seven. I was about eight when my mother enrolled me in a public school. In those days teachers really took an interest in the children. If a child did anything wrong, the teacher would give him a little slap on his bottom so that he would behave well and learn his lessons.

The teacher hit me only once. I didn't know how to write an *A* nicely, and she hit my hand hard with a ruler. When *mamá* saw my swollen hand and asked about it, I said I had hurt it playing during recess. I didn't tell her because I didn't want her to go to school and quarrel with my teacher. I never told my *mamá* when I was scolded or anything else that happened there. In school there are always fights among children and I fought often. They kept me back in the first grade because of my fighting.

My *mamá* sent me to her mother in Río Grande to see if I would change my ways there and be promoted to the second grade. So after that I lived with my grandmother Clotilde and my half sister Migdalia. Migdalia is three years younger than I am. She is my only sister but she's not my father's daughter. I found out how it all happened when I was grown up. After leaving my father, my mother became pregnant by Migdalia's father, but I never knew the man. Migdalia was born in the Municipal Hospital in Santurce, and from the time she was forty days old my grandmother Clotilde took care of her and brought her up.

Clotilde was black with very white hair. She was so crazy that if a visitor stayed a long time she'd come right out and say, "Get out of here!" Then,

* Epiphany, January 6.

if they stayed away two or three days, she sent for them and said, "You bastard, what's the matter with you? Why don't you ever come to my house any more?" When they said, "Why, *doña* Clotilde, you always kick out the people who go to visit you," she'd answer, "That's a lie and you know it." She had visitors every day; she'd quarrel with them, throw them out, send for them, and they always came back.

Her house was a wooden shack facing the street. It had three rooms and a smaller shack in the back. My grandmother kept all those rooms in case any of her relatives wanted to stay with her. She would often cry when she thought of my mother far away from her in Santurce. She cried because the days went by and my mother didn't come to see her and because she was always afraid that something might happen to her daughter. That's the way she was.

My grandmother wouldn't let my sister and me play with other children and she made us go to bed at five in the evening. If we didn't obey her, she would beat us with a rope or a blackjack. She said we would learn bad habits from other children. My sister and I played by ourselves in the back yard. On Saturdays she would buy food for us to prepare. We had our own kettles and charcoal stoves with three stones to hold the kettle over the fire. She gave us everything we needed so we wouldn't go looking elsewhere.

When she was drunk she would be very mean to us. She said we were shameless bitches, that we made her suffer and didn't love her. Then she'd beat us with sticks and chase us out into the street. Later she'd go get us and bring us back. Sometimes she tied us to a pole, feet up and head down, and beat us like that. Or else she sent us to the cemetery to get tamarind twigs and she whipped us with those. She sometimes scorched the soles of our feet with burning paper so that we wouldn't be able to run outside. She would also punish us by making us kneel with outstretched arms, holding a large stone in each hand.

While I was living with Clotilde, I visited my mother every fifteen days at the home of the Cordero family. A *público** would take me there and my mother paid him when we arrived. One day I returned to Río Grande from my *mamá*'s house, and as soon as I got back Clotilde began to curse me. I don't know whether she was drunk or what. She locked me out that night and left me to sleep in the street. Dead she is, but she knows I speak the truth. I told my *mamá* about it later and she said to me, "Just try to bear it until the school year is over and you get promoted, then you can come live with me."

The trouble with my grandmother was that she had been crazy once and afterward she was always nervous. I don't know much about her madness because I was living with my *mamá* when it happened, but I've heard that she went crazy when she gave birth to twins, and one of them died. It seems

* Public taxis which provide fast and inexpensive transportation around the island.

she did something that made her ill, and as we say, "the purge went to her head." That means that her menstrual blood rose instead of coming down as it should. Because of her madness, she lost some farms she had inherited. Her relatives took advantage of her condition and grabbed the land for themselves. All she had left was her house in Río Grande.

My grandmother never told us much about her life. She had two men that I know of, my grandfather, whom I never knew, and her second husband, Jaime, who still lives in Río Grande. He was a breeder of fighting cocks and spent a lot of time at cockfights. He also worked in the cane fields.

Jaime sold rum but didn't want to give any to Clotilde. He'd hide it from her, but she'd find it and drink it. Or she would go buy it somewhere else. I think she's the one that taught us to drink, because whenever we got a little cold she dosed us with *cañita** and burned sugar. When Clotilde got a bit high she chewed basil or mint, or paper and onions, to take away the smell of rum. It worked too; when she ate that stuff nobody could tell she had been drinking.

As long as she lived, Grandmother hardly loved me at all. She treated my sister better than me. Migdalia was her darling. My sister would ask for this or that, and every time she said, "Clotilde, give me——" my grandmother would drop whatever she was doing and go get what Migdalia wanted. But when I asked for something she'd say, "Go get it yourself." When my sister played some trick on me and we started to fight, my grandmother would beat me and say that I'd end up as a whore.

My mother's brother, Uncle Aurelio, lived near by. He had a good social standing in Río Grande. He had money and two stores, one of them a grocery. They were the best stores, always filled with customers, but he was a wicked man. One day there was nothing to eat at my grandmother's house, so at recess I went over to his store and asked him for a banana—you know how children are. He told me to get it at *mamá*'s house because she was hustling in Santurce and he didn't have to give me anything. I went back to school empty-handed, weeping and ashamed.

About fifteen days later I went to visit my *mamá* and I told her about it. She said, "Don't worry, sooner or later God will bring down a terrible punishment on him for telling such a terrible lie about me." And not much later, Uncle did show up at our house, crying. He'd had an attack of madness and everything he owned had to be sold; he went bankrupt. When my *mamá* saw him, she didn't say a word about what had happened. She gave him food and took him to see a number of spiritists. Because, you see, his trouble was due to a spell a woman had cast on him to make him go mad. Why, he even shaved his head. Crazy! And she made his testicles useless so that he couldn't take another woman. And he had been a ladies' man!

My *mamá* did everything she could until she finally cured him of the

* Raw bootleg rum.

curse. Then he knelt before her, weeping, and said, "Forgive me all the harm I have done you and your daughter."

"You know it is all forgiven," *mamá* answered. My *mamá* never bore a grudge.

One day when I was visiting my *mamá* in Santurce, she said, "I'll go back to Río Grande with you this time so you can meet your father. Maybe he'll help you, now that you are living there."

My father never took another woman after he and my *mamá* broke up. He lived with his mother all the rest of his life. The two of them were inseparable. My grandmother had several sons and daughters, but my father was her favorite. She was a strange woman. She'd be happy and then she'd get upset all of a sudden and everything bothered her. She was just like a little child. It was her fault that my parents broke up, because she didn't get on with my *mamá*.

My grandmother was named Fernanda like me. It was my *papá* who wanted to name me Fernanda but my *mamá* was against it. They had a big quarrel over that. When my *mamá* went to inscribe my name in the Registry, she found that my *papá* had already registered me. He had the right to do it because they were married, see?

About my *papá* I can truthfully say that I never knew a father's love. I don't know what it is to wear even a pair of *panties* bought by him. He refused to support me and it was all his mother's fault. That old woman was bad. She and my *papá* had comforts and they never shared any of them with me. Every time my *mamá* and I went there to ask my *papá* for money for my support, my grandmother would say, "Your father can't give you anything, he's not working now."

To get even, I played tricks on her. I would steal the eggs her chickens laid and I'd sell them. When I couldn't do that, I smashed them all. My grandmother never found out who did it.

My *papá* never gave me a thing but he was affectionate to me, in a way. He would take me on his lap and talk to me and caress me. Then he would kiss me and go off to drink rum.

Once he told me, "Nanda, wait for me at such and such a place. I'm going to take you to buy some shoes and *panties*." I waited a long time until I saw a man go by and asked him, "Have you seen my father around here?"

The man asked, "Who's your father?"

"Rogelio."

"Oh, you're Rogelio's daughter. Yes, go to such and such a bar. He's there drinking."

And there he was, flat broke, and drunk. I went in and snatched the glass of rum from his hand and broke the bottle he was holding. It made me angry to see him like that. I told him, "Aren't you ashamed to drink like that, an old man like you? And you deceive me as if I were a baby, promising to buy me something and getting drunk instead."

Then I said to the lady at the bar, "Don't sell him any more rum because he never spends a cent on me. He just takes his money and buys rum." Well, all my father did that time was pick me up and carry me home. He loved me a lot, but what's the use of loving if he didn't give anything?

When he was drunk he always went to his house and lay down to sleep. He didn't get up again until he was sober. Drunk or sober, he never swore or hurt anybody's feelings. He didn't like swearing and one couldn't even say a little word like *coño* in his hearing. My father was always solemn, but everyone was very fond of him anyway. He was a man who never knew what it was to go to court. He never fought and always behaved with propriety. That's the way he treated me too; he never once beat or slapped me. But, God forgive me, my father was never a father to me and I loved my mother more than anyone else in the world. Dear God, forgive me!

When I was promoted from the first grade, I said good-bye to my friends at school and went back to Santurce with my mother. My mother got me everything I needed for my graduation and even sent a bunch of white flowers for me to carry. Everything I wore that day was white, the head ornament, gloves, shoes, stockings, everything. I was very happy when they dressed me up. I even thought I was going to get married. *Ave María!* I was up in the clouds!

After the ceremonies I took my suitcase and went off to Santurce. I left without even changing my clothes. I didn't say good-bye to my father or my grandmother Fernanda, only to my aunt Sofía and my little friends. I was crazy to get back to my mother and I never wanted to return to Río Grande to live with my grandmother Clotilde.

When I got to Santurce the Corderos had a gift for me, a Mickey Mouse set with pen, pencils, ruler, a lot of things. My confirmation godmother, Emma Valdez, who was a daughter-in-law of the Corderos, had a gift for me too. My mother gave me clothes and I had a lot of other gifts—*panties,* soap, towels, and things like that.

My godmother had asked me to call on her, but even now I don't dare go because they're rich and white and all that, and they might think I went hoping for a handout. They have money and a farm and all kinds of wealth, and I don't like to lower myself before any rich person even if she happens to be my godmother. I never did call her "Godmother," I would have been ashamed to. I always called her *doña* Emma. My *mamá* didn't ask *doña* Emma to be my godmother, it was she herself who suggested it. After my confirmation she gave me two dollars every week. I always gave one to my mother and kept the other to buy candy. That's all I used the money for, because I've never cared for the movies or any other kind of amusement except playing with boys.

When I was in the third grade in school I had a fight with a boy. I still know the boy, he's a drug addict now. We were always getting into arguments with each other. One afternoon I told him, "Some day I'll beat you to a pulp, even though you're a boy and I'm a girl." I was doodling, and when I said that he grabbed my pencil and broke it. When school was out I went up to him and said, "Come here, you son of a bitch! Do now what you did to me in school." He called me "dirty black" and we started to fight. The teacher saw us and decided to take me home. I told her, "If you go home with me I will never again go to school." I always said that the day the teacher took me home would be my last day at school. She took me anyway, and I kept my word. I never went back to school. That's why I never studied beyond the third grade.

After leaving school, I stayed on at the Corderos', where *mamá* worked. I was living in a room at their house when I became a *señorita,* when I began to menstruate. For me, it was as if nothing at all had happened. Because when I became a *señorita* I went on playing with the boys as always, with kites, marbles, tops, and all that. I didn't feel I had become a young lady at all.

I did start having conversations with other girls about what I would do when I married. I said I'd always fix up a good breakfast for my husband and serve it to him in bed. I would treat him well, but I would never leave my mother. She and I would always be together, because the man who lived with me must allow my mother to be with us. If not, I said, I wouldn't stay with him even if we had fifty children, because I had to be at my mother's side forever. Those were my dreams because I loved my mother dearly and I loved only her.

Fernanda

———

Love and Marriage

———

THE ONLY man I was ever in love with was the first sweetheart I had. First love is never forgotten, you know. I even remember his name. Adalberto Flores. It was my dream to marry him, but my mother never liked him and I couldn't go against her. I had to be for her, you see. But he was the sweetheart I loved most.

He was the only sweetheart I sent letters to. I didn't write them myself. *Mamá* knew how to write well and in the beginning she wrote to Adalberto to help me out. But then something happened to make her think I wouldn't be happy with him, so she wrote a letter in my name, insulting him and breaking it off.

I don't know why my *mamá* objected to Adalberto. She said he was a gambler, a libertine and a drunkard, and I was a child compared to him. I believe I would have been happy with Adalberto. With him I would be living a better life, instead of suffocating as I am now. The only hopes and dreams I've ever had were all about Adalberto.

When I met my first husband, Cristóbal, he was working as a messenger. He came from Isabela but lived in Santurce with his brother. We met at a dance at my house and he began courting me right away. My *mamá* had vowed to the Three Holy Kings to go begging in the street, carrying their image. The money she collected she gave away to other people and to the church. When she had carried out her vow, we celebrated with a dance.

Cristóbal was there, and the minute he saw me he asked me to dance. That very day he gave me a jar of hair pomade and a comb, without our really knowing each other.

I don't know how I made my misstep with Cristóbal, because I never in my life loved him. He came to call on me every night. I didn't pay any attention to him but my *mamá* did. She was very fond of him, crazy about him, in fact. She would tell me, "Here, child, come and talk with him." I would answer, "I don't love him, tell him to go away." He would serenade me and my mother would open the door for him. I'd go right on sleeping. And still he had the nerve to keep calling on me.

That's the way things were between us. We were sweethearts but we never talked about anything that mattered. We would sit on opposite sides of the room and hardly open our mouths. If we talked at all it was of stupid things, his work and so forth, because that's all he ever talked about. We never even kissed. How could we, with *mamá* present? The most we could do was hold hands. We never went to a movie or anything. Then one day I took off with him. It was all my stepfather's fault.

You see, when I was about twelve years old, my stepfather Jorge fell in love with me. He never said anything but he tried to touch me. And he would give me such looks! He became very jealous when Cristóbal started visiting me. He didn't want Cristóbal in the house and he picked quarrels, dropped hints and said disagreeable things so that Cristóbal would go away and not come to see me any more.

Then one morning my *mamá* told me that she had surprised her husband standing beside my bed and looking at me as I slept. She said he was very startled when he saw her there. That was when my *mamá* realized that my stepfather wanted me.

The day Cristóbal and I took off, my *mamá* had gone to a wake and my stepfather had stayed home. He and Cristóbal had a big quarrel, I forget about what. So I just up and left. Cristóbal took me to the house of his brother Sergio, who is dead now. Cristóbal had his own private room in Sergio's house, so I was very well received. Cristóbal was twenty-two and I was fourteen.

I cried that first night I spent with him. He said, "Why are you crying? After all, you wanted to come with me and get away from that stepfather of yours. Do you want to go back and have to bear all his shameless ways?" I did want to, you see, because I still didn't feel any love for Cristóbal.

He taught me to be a woman. That first time I bled and it hurt a lot. He treated me kindly during the act and all, but I just didn't love Cristóbal. We had lived in that room about a week when my mother came weeping to ask me why I had done such a thing. She said that at home they gave me everything I needed, and so forth and so on.

I told her, "Look, I left home because my stepfather, your husband, was in love with me. And I'd rather belong to any other man than to him." But we went to live with my mother, anyway. There Cristóbal and I hardly ever spoke to each other because my mother slept beside us. My mother charged him with seducing a minor so he'd have to marry me. We never got married, though, because I refused to. I did go on living with him for seven years.

Cristóbal was hardly ever at home. He was always chasing after women, but he did set me up in a room of my own although it was my mother who paid the rent—two dollars a month. The room was in a big wooden house with seven rooms, all of them rented. We lived in a back room. The front rooms cost four dollars a month. My mother had the room beside mine. She was the one who bought clothes for me and the children.

I don't know why, but my mother quit working for the Cordero family and got herself a job ironing. I still couldn't wash or iron because my mother had never taught me how. The first time I ironed for Cristóbal, I burned a pair of his trousers. I finally learned by watching my next-door neighbors. That's the way I learned to do housework, watching other people. Because I'm stupid, see? It's no use trying to explain to me how to do a job. If I don't see someone else doing it, I don't learn.

At that time I never spoke to other men. I spent my time with my *mamá* or with young girls like myself. Cristóbal wasn't jealous of me. He had no reason to be because I didn't know anything of the world yet. I was the jealous one because he had women everywhere. We quarreled about that all the time. He cursed my mother and I cursed his. He told me to go to hell and I told him to go to hell. Whatever he said to me I'd give back as good as I got. I hit him, too, if I could catch him by surprise. When he wasn't looking I'd sneak up and bring a stick down hard on his head and I'd split his scalp. It was the only way I could hit him because he was so big.

I never loved him, not even when my first daughter, Soledad, was born. I always say that I had those four children with him just *because* I didn't love him. The minute he laid me I got pregnant, because Soledad was born in 1939, Felícita in '41, Simplicio in '42 and Cruz in '45.

While I was pregnant with Soledad he would take me to the movies. Cristóbal was the one who taught me to like movies. I'd never cared for them before. He also taught me to play dominoes, to shoot craps and to play bingo. We'd go out together to play bingo and sometimes it got to be three in the morning and we weren't home yet. My *mamá* would have to go get us, because if not, we'd stay up all night playing.

Cristóbal was a gambler but he worked hard too. Then he'd go spend the night somewhere with his women, even when I was pregnant. And when he came home in the morning he lied and told me he'd been in jail. It was easy for him to deceive me because I was so young and didn't know anything about life.

Soledad was born on my fifteenth birthday, January 22. I was a child, a snotty-nosed kid, and I didn't think giving birth was anything to make a fuss about. When my labor pains started at midnight, my *mamá* took me to the hospital. I was in labor all that night. I got scared and that delayed the birth. It was only by giving me a lot of injections that they finally managed to make the baby come at eleven o'clock the next morning.

My mother had a fritter stand by then, and she had to tend it. She had to grind the tubers and cook and sell the fritters and everything. So that morning while she was in the hospital with me, Cristóbal took over the stand. In the afternoon, when *mamá* got home, he came to see me. As long as I stayed in the hospital he flew to see how I was the minute he could get away. He always came, no matter what time it was. He couldn't stand to let a whole day go by without seeing me.

My mother always bought the babies' layettes. Cristóbal never bought a thing for his children. He was a very stingy man. Everything was given to me by my mother, everything. Cristóbal only gave me food, and that not too willingly. When Soledad was born, Cristóbal was working in a grocery store, delivering sacks of groceries to people's homes. That way he earned three dollars a week. If it hadn't been for my mother's help we'd never have made out. My mother earned eight dollars a month.

Soledad was a roly-poly baby, a regular little barrel. But Cristóbal wanted a boy and at first he didn't love her. Later on he became very fond of her. When Soledad was about a year old, she had a bad case of the drooling sickness. You know, when babies are teething their gums swell and they drool a lot. You shouldn't wipe off the saliva but I didn't know that, so I was always wiping her face. Then the spit stopped coming out and flowed back into her insides. That's what made her sick. *Mamá,* Cristóbal and I stayed up with her two nights. My *mamá* took her to a lady to make the sign of the cross over her. The lady prescribed calcium hypophosphite, castor oil and something else from the drugstore, I can't remember what, and Soledad got well.

After that she was fat and healthy and walked when she was about eight months old. She was always my mother's darling, the only one of my children *mamá* really cared for. I gave Soledad the breast for two years. When Felícita was born, Soledad weaned herself without any fuss. None of my children ever felt jealous when I suckled a new baby. They gave up the breast of their own free will. Simplicio gave up the tit for a rubber nipple. He never had a pacifier because those didn't exist then. What we had was the kind of rubber nipple you use on baby bottles. I nursed Simplicio for eight or nine months.

Cruz was the one who was weaned earliest. I nursed her only for two months, then started her on the bottle. But even while I suckled my babies I would give them a bottle oftener than the breast. And then, I never held them or carried them much, I just let them stay in their crib. That's why they were so easy to wean.

Soledad was an active and playful little girl, and mischievous. She'd hit the other children and run away before they could hit back. When she saw my *mamá* scrubbing the floor, Soledad would spill sand on it and litter it with old tin cans and stuff she brought in from the outside. And my mother would act as if what the child had done was cute. Well, she was *mamá*'s first grandchild and her darling. I hardly ever had that child with me. She was always in my *mamá*'s room. When *mamá* went out, she took Soledad with her and always bought her something.

Soledad was about two years old when I had her baptized. Her godfather is Humberto Reyes, and her godmother Judith. We had a party to celebrate the baptism and danced from six in the evening until midnight. A neighbor lent his house for the party, Humberto rented a juke box, and he and Judith bought ice cream. That was the only big celebration we had for a baptism. Later, Humberto and Judith went to New York and I haven't seen them since.

When I was pregnant with Felícita, Cristóbal had a mistress who was a maid. We lived on Loíza Street then and this woman lived right across the way. One night I got a craving, as pregnant women will. I wanted to eat some breadfruit, so my mother put some on to boil. Then I went out to call Cristóbal to come and eat. He just fell on me and beat me, pregnant as I was, right in front of his mistress. I went home crying and I told my mother that Cristóbal had beaten me in the street in front of everybody. Then Cristóbal came and tried to hit me again in the presence of my own mother. When she saw what he was up to, she threw the boiling water at him. He was so badly burned he had to stay in the hospital for three or four months. He still has the marks of those burns all over his chest, and his sight too was affected.

Cristóbal's brothers made an accusation against my mother. He has several brothers and I know only a few of them. There's Pablo, who is in Oregon now; Sergio, the one who died; and Simón, who now lives in New Jersey. Well, those three brought charges against my mother, but she never had to go to jail. She managed to arrange the whole thing in a roundabout way through a lawyer. She cooked and delivered meals, remember, and that's how she had met this lawyer.

The day of the trial Cristóbal himself testified in her favor. The judge asked him how he could stand there without dying of shame and defend the woman who had burned him. Cristóbal answered, "Well, after all, she's my mother-in-law."

My *mamá* only had to pay a fifteen-dollar fine. Cristóbal loved my mother dearly. They were both really fond of each other.

I had a very easy time during my second pregnancy, with Felícita. I went to the hospital and the delivery was easy too. We called Felícita "the lonely soul" because from the time she was very small she always liked to be alone. She never wanted to play with anybody, not even her sister. Her other nickname was "Breadfruit" because she was so fat that when she fell down, someone had to pick her up.

During my third pregnancy, with Simplicio, I was sick. I vomited all the time. Even smelling the food I was cooking made me vomit. From the fifth month on I felt perfectly well, and the labor and delivery were easy too but I had bad afterpains.

Later, Simplicio got sick. When he sat up he went limp, and his head would drop onto his feet. I took him to an aunt of his, Cristóbal's sister in Manatí. There we took him to a spiritist, and I also made a promise to the Virgin of Everlasting Mercy to wear her habit for three months if my baby got well. The spiritist examined the boy and told me, "Go now, señora, and remember you have a vow to keep. Your boy is well now." Simplicio was holding up his head and he sat up straight. Then we started to give him country remedies, such as herb teas, fruit juices, and things like that, to settle his little stomach. He got well and I brought him back to Santurce.

Later he got sick again. Cristóbal said it was because of malnutrition but it was the same illness all over again. We watched him day and night. Then one night he died. We placed him on a table to prepare him and to wrap him in his winding sheet. We were weeping and screaming when, about half an hour later, he came to life again. He opened his little eyes and started looking around. Then we put compresses of hot wine on his belly and on his head to revive him. We kept giving him this treatment and he became strong and healthy again.

That boy still isn't quite right in the head, though, because of this illness. He doesn't seem to understand things and he's stupid. When he says something is so, you have to say he's right even if he says black is white.

Once, before Cruz was born, we had no money in the house for food. Cristóbal told me, "Nanda, I'm going to call on a friend at Stop Fifteen to see if he'll lend me ten dollars." After he left I was sitting on the front stoop when a friend of mine came and said, "Nanda, let's go see if we find my husband. I think he has a woman over in Loíza Street." The children were asleep, so I went with her. We walked all over the place without seeing hide nor hair of her husband. Then she said, "Let's go to the market place." We went, and there was Cristóbal with a woman!

Then and there I went for her, although I didn't know how to fight at that time. If that woman had cut me I couldn't have done a thing to her because I didn't know how to use a razor yet. But I really hit her hard. She was big and fat and I was a skinny little kid. Cristóbal just crossed his arms and watched. Well, the woman went away, but before going she told my husband, "Good-bye, Toñito, I didn't know you had a wife and children." Then I told her, "His name isn't Toñito, it's Cristóbal."

Cristóbal never told any of his mistresses his real name. They kept sending kids all the time to ask for him by a lot of different names. I'd tell whoever brought the message, "Tell that woman to come here herself and ask for Cristóbal, because that's his real name." Then I'd follow the kid to try and catch the woman who'd sent him. But usually she saw me coming and hid. The one I found him with in the market was the only one I ever caught.

After that quarrel Cristóbal and I didn't speak to each other for three whole days. He didn't sleep at home during that time, but he'd come and speak to me as if nothing had happened. I never answered a word. We finally made up because of a bingo game. The game was held near my house and the children were sleeping. So I told my *comai,* "If the children wake up, send for me."

Cristóbal appeared at the game and said, "Oh, so you have money to gamble?" I told him, "I'm broke." I had been losing steadily. He gave me some of his money and we went on playing. He'd give me money when I needed it, and I'd give him some when I was winning. By the time the game was over we were friends again.

Soon after Cruz was born, Cristóbal was drafted into the Army. He's been in the Army nineteen years. The week they called him up I felt very bad because they said he would be sent overseas. That was during the war and I was afraid he'd have to fight. The day he said good-bye to us I was quite sad, but calm because after all I had my children. He kissed the children and cried when he had to go. I didn't shed a single tear.

After that I didn't have anything to do around the house; the children were no trouble because I didn't bring them up to be in the middle of everything. I never did get along very well with kids and I didn't let my children be close to me. They never dared cling to me because if they did I'd yank the hair off their scalps. So I had a lot of time on my hands and I'd go over to watch my *mamá* work.

My mother died forty-five days after Cruz was born. She was an old woman by then and she had heart disease. One day she came home from work, complaining that she felt a pain. Then she just flopped down on the bed. That was Thursday. On Friday she had aches and pains all over her body. I took her to the hospital twice in one day, once in the morning and once in the afternoon.

I went to my grandmother's house to tell her that *mamá* was sick, but Clotilde would not visit her in the hospital. "There's nothing wrong with that woman except that she's nasty and has a bad case of hot pants," she said. I told this to my *mamá* and she said that if she died I should not tell Clotilde. She didn't want anybody to know, not anybody at all.

That night the doctors told me that my *mamá* wouldn't live. And she was only forty! We never knew what was wrong with her, because after she died I wouldn't let them perform an autopsy. It all happened so quickly, just like that, and the earth and the sky came together for me.

Cristóbal was home on leave and he was the one who gave the news of *mamá*'s death to Uncle Pablito, and Uncle Pablito told Clotilde. Then we began the wake in my house in Santurce. Clotilde came and my aunt Amparo and all my mother's relatives. Had I known what a fuss they were going to kick up, I wouldn't have asked any of those people to the wake. I would have let them stay away instead of coming to disturb the peace as they did.

While *mamá*'s corpse was still in my house, my grandmother made a terrible scene because she thought my *mamá* had left some money. Clotilde said that I wanted to keep all the money myself and not give my sister her share, that I was a brazen bitch—all sorts of lies and insults. My uncle Aurelio and my aunt Sofía tried to reason with her. They told her that she shouldn't act like that, that she should show more respect for the dead. They pointed out that *mamá* could not possibly have left any money, because every cent she had went to buy food and little things for herself and Soledad. But Clotilde wasn't convinced. "Yes, yes, she did have money. Only this tramp won't share it, she wants it all for herself." I didn't say anything. I didn't dare, for fear she would beat me.

She made such a terrible fuss that I even cried. There were some clothes and household things my *mamá* had left and Clotilde wanted all of it. I said to her, "If you want them, take them. Don't bother to leave anything for me." And she took it all away.

I didn't even have enough money to buy the coffin. It was Uncle Aurelio and Tomás the Towhead, a numbers seller who was killed later on, who bought the coffin and helped with the funeral expenses. My mother was buried in Río Grande because my grandmother insisted on it.

After the funeral we continued the wake at my house at Stop 26 in Santurce. We didn't have any electricity, but a man let us tap his current so that we were able to stay up all night, praying and watching so nobody would come and break anything. We kept it up for the nine nights, and every night the house was full of people. I was out of my head, so I can't recall everybody who was there. My father didn't come, because he didn't know about it. His mother knew but she didn't tell him until five days later. The only people I never lost sight of were Uncle Aurelio and Aunt Sofía. Aunt Sofía took it very hard; of all the sisters, she and my *mamá* were the two who were fondest of each other.

Amparo

A Relative
Is a Relative

I AM FERNANDA'S aunt Amparo. Fernanda's mother, Luisa, was my eldest sister. I am sixty-four years old and I've lived in the Bronx for the past fifteen years. I stay in New York because my children are here and because I am getting help from *el Relief,* but there is no comparison between this country and Puerto Rico. The only advantage here is that you can earn good money. But so what? In my country you may earn less but you have more to show for it. There is no place in the world like Puerto Rico!

We were ten brothers and sisters altogether, children of Manuel Hernández and Clotilde Pozas. We lived in Río Grande with my mother's father, Nanda's great-grandfather Juan Pozas, until he died. He was a Negro but he was rich and had a farm and a store, animals, tenants and his own big house. He was an administrator of a hacienda. It was beautiful. He was good and everybody loved him. I was seven when he died and I loved him more than anybody. I've always said that if my grandfather hadn't died we would be living differently now.

That grandfather of mine! He had a heart like a saint. He treated everybody well. He would throw such good parties for his workers! I don't think there are any men like him left. He never spanked me, he never beat his wife, he never drank. He was a man amongst men. He couldn't read or write but he was a poet, that man. He took care of everything so well. The store was always busy and nobody could beat him at figures. He died of old age, struggling with life.

My grandfather used to say, "The day I die I want you to bring two guitars and a *guicharo* so you can play me a farewell." And we granted him his wish because he loved *fiestas* and he loved to dance a lot. The music played until dawn. His funeral was beautiful. Everybody cried for that old man. There were coaches and carts, drawn by horses with a black awning over them. On the sides were feathers and all the horses were dressed in black. A lot of people came, the sharecroppers, the godchildren and the children of the sharecroppers. It was tremendous.

They buried him in Trujillo Alto because Río Grande was just beginning to grow. It was still all woods, full of trees that had to be cut. Where we first lived, it was a tangle of wild growth springing from the mud. We had to clear a space to build our house. We helped build Río Grande.

My family was rich until my grandfather died. Then a brother of his, Ramiro, came and played my mother, Clotilde, a dirty trick. He took all the papers from her and had them put in his name. He kept everything and left her only the little house. When my mother tried to do something about it they said to her, "No, Ramiro Williams' name appears here," and she said, "Well, I hope he enjoys it." You can see how he enjoyed it—he is under the earth and another relative of his is enjoying it now. So it wasn't worth it.

My mother had a very strong character. Even when she was a child, she would do whatever she pleased. She would climb trees, urinate up there and sleep there. She was impossible, but she was good. As far as being respectful, ah, that was sacred, because she would get punished every time she misbehaved.

According to my mother, discipline was terrible in her day. People would be whipped with horses' reins. The slaves, the dark people, would be tied to a horse's tail and dragged. They would take pregnant women and put them in a hole in the ground, with their bellies down, and whip them. I'd ask my mother, "Why did they do this to them?" And she'd say, "Because of the color of their skin."

We were brought up so that we couldn't even give anybody a dirty look. If a person came to ask for water, we had to lower our heads and sometimes even kiss their hands. If they asked for a light, we took it to them, crossed our hands and withdrew quickly. If we disobeyed they would make us kneel on perforated cans, holding stones in our hands, or lock us up in a dark room. I don't even like to think of it, it was so sad. But children respected their parents then. There wasn't any of this disorder we have now.

My mother told us that she was about fourteen or fifteen when she fell in love with my father and ran away with him. There has never been anyone like my father. A saint, that's what he was and I'll never forget him. He was a very peaceful man. He did everything for the love of God, you understand? He came from a good family, and his parents were white and had "good" hair.

He had a beautiful mustache, which he would turn up. I don't say it because he was my father, but he was a good-looking man. He was so little I could pick him up. After he took my mother to live with him, he never had any other woman. He used to say that his wife was enough and that he didn't want any children besides the ones he had at home. And it was always like that.

Papá worked in a sugar mill, carrying the sacks of sugar up from the boilers. Before that he worked in the cane fields. He often told us of his youth at the time of the Spanish-American War, when he would go from one place to another looking for work and not finding any. There was no money to be had in those days. After the war it improved but when the Americans took over, things got better still. I should say they did! After that there was work, food, money—nobody went hungry any more. Working as I did as a servant from the time I was eight, I always provided my *papá* with the tidbits and food that he liked. I'd make a small bundle, tuck it into my bodice, and take it to him. He was always good to me so I looked out for him, too.

My mother never bothered about me. When I worked I would give her all the money I earned, about one dollar and fifty cents a week, and she'd buy me a dress of cloth so thin you could see the sun and the moon through it. But I wore it. What else could I do? My mother treated the other children well. I don't know why she didn't care for me.

My mother had fits of anger because she had lost her senses and was half crazy. After she gave birth to the twins, she quarreled with my father and ran outside in the rain and that's where her craziness came from. Whenever she fought with my father she would immediately dash out of the house and climb up the avocado tree. A few days later she tried to kill Victor, one of the twins, and my father said, "This woman is crazy." We took her to a curer who prepared some medicine that was supposed to quiet her, but it went to her head and that's when she really went mad. It lasted for about two months. The other twin died and we brought up Victorcito among us.

My mother didn't know how to treat my father. She exploited him and did as she pleased. She made him suffer too much. Poor *papá*, he took it in silence, without complaint. When he brought the groceries home she would throw them in the yard. She'd pick up a big tub and pour half a sack of rice in the water and it would be ruined. She did the same thing with the beans and everything else. She was unbearable, poor thing.

I know my *mamá* didn't love my *papá* because later, when he had his last illness, she didn't fight for his life. That illness was not sent by God, it was due to a spell that my sister Sofía's sweetheart worked on my father. My *papá* was against them marrying and they fixed a drink for him but the spell in it was too strong and killed him. The spiritist told me it was my *mamá* who handed him the drink, because of Sofía. I have never been sure whether to believe it or not, but the truth is that my *mamá* was on that man's side and against *papá*. She wasn't a good wife and didn't care that my *papá* was dying. When I took him to the hospital or to a spiritist she'd hang out black flags on the porch, as if to announce his death. She didn't care at all, may God keep her in His kingdom in Heaven.

But I admired my mother because she was kind to other people, even though she didn't have a thing to her name. If someone got sick she would always go to him, ready to give her life. If he died she would bathe and prepare him. Her temperament was a problem but in her heart she was good. I never saw my *mamá* do anything bad. She was always washing, ironing, cooking, and teaching us to do these things. She never had to go out to work. My *papá* supported all of us and my brothers worked and helped.

My sister Luisa was the goddess in our house and we always had to respect her because she was the eldest. She never did any work, but I had to work from the time I was eight. They sent me down to the river to wash the clothes, while Luisa stayed at home. We couldn't say a thing to her, but whatever she said had to be done. When my father wanted to buy me something my mother would object. She never cared about having me well dressed but Luisa was sacred to her.

Luisa and I were always fighting because she was so strong-willed, the kind of sister who tries to make you feel inferior. She didn't like us to go out with her and she didn't treat us as equals. In our house we were all different colors, and just because she was lighter-skinned and her hair was finer than ours, she thought she was better than us. Her hair was like silk, like my father's. Pitch-black. When she died, her hair was still completely black.

Luisa could be unbearable. She was always very fussy about eating, and when we went out she would spend most of the time kicking me under the table so that I would watch my manners. She was always the last one to finish eating.

Almost no one got along with Luisa. My heart felt no love for her because she had none for me. Sometimes I would ask her, "May I wear one of your dresses?" And she would answer, "No, leave my things alone." We loved her, yes, and we tried not to fight with her, but she was so difficult, so haughty, so arrogant. She tried to impress people but she couldn't. After all, she was poor, and you can only stretch your foot as far as it will reach. So everybody rejected her.

Luisa married Rogelio Fuentes, from Río Grande. He was a sugar-cane worker. I knew Rogelio's parents and also his grandparents. They all lived near our house. His mother, Fernanda, was an old lady, a good woman; her husband was a good man too. Nice people.

Luisa ran away with Rogelio, and two or three days later my father found them and made them get married by a justice of the peace.

Their life was a constant fight. His mother didn't approve of the marriage, I don't know why. There was something wrong there all the time. You know sometimes mothers object to having their sons or daughters fall in love. Rogelio's mother got along with me fine, she got along with my father, but she didn't approve of the marriage. She would say Luisa was too proud and wanted to be above others.

In the midst of that struggling they had Nanda. But Luisa got a job and abandoned the little girl and wouldn't even feed her. She brought her to my mother and just dumped her. My mother told her that she couldn't take her, so Luisa brought Nanda to her other grandmother. Rogelio's mother took the baby into her house but she didn't really want her either.

One day I went there and I saw Nanda covered with filth from head to toe, playing in a dirty box. I went to my mother and told her, "Look, if you only knew what condition that angel of God is in, with filth all caked down her back." And she said to me, "I'll go talk to Luisa to see what she can do. She should take that child to the house where she is working." We went and talked to her until we convinced her. She said, "Bring me the girl," and we did just that. She kept Nanda with her after that and took care of her like a good mother. This was her first child, and a mother can't throw away her children just like that. It's not their fault that they are brought into the world. They're innocent, and that's why you must take care of them until the end. My first three children died, it is true, but it wasn't because I had abandoned them, it was because of hunger.

So Luisa took care of her daughter until Nanda ran away with a man. I used to go to Santurce often to visit them, but they hardly ever came to Río Grande. They lived where Luisa was working, at the house of the Martínez family, a well-to-do Negro family. It was a big house. The Martínez family is that family of doctors who live at Stop 26. Luisa had a child by Dr. Martínez. She had Migdalia right at the house. We didn't know anything about it until one day we came to visit her and the lady of the house said, "She's in there. She just gave birth to a girl." We didn't know who the father was. We found out later. But Dr. Martínez denied his daughter and nothing could be done.

My mother wanted to know what she planned to do with the baby, and Luisa said, "Well, you have to take her with you because otherwise I'm going to give her away." My mother took her and Luisa forgot the little girl. She never sent the child anything. My mother bore all the expenses and had a hard time making ends meet.

Luisa had already been separated from Rogelio for years now, and they hardly ever saw each other. You could almost say that Nanda had no father. She was brought up by her mother. They lived in a little room, and Luisa worked at home, ironing for people with one of these small irons that you had to put on top of a coal stove. She did a lot of work.

Then Luisa took up with Jorge. They fell in love. He was a dark man, quite old. Jorge turned out to be a good husband and a good stepfather. He was crazy about Nanda. He treated Luisa well and took care of her, and they never had any arguments. My sister died in his arms.

Nanda was not a bad child. She was always respectful to me. She went to school and was sociable and cute, a very pretty girl. When I went to visit them in Santurce, Nanda was always nice, but her mother treated her badly although she wasn't as cruel to Nanda as before. No, she had gotten over that.

Nanda always had a strong character; she was like a man. She was outgoing, gay and bold. When she was thirteen she ran away with Cristóbal. I don't know if they got married but I do know that she was unfaithful to him. She betrayed him and he was so good! She acted as if she were more of a man than Cristóbal, and you can't live like that because what is the man going to do? Is she going to wear the pants and give him the skirt?

After she had Soledad, Nanda had another baby with a boxer she was seeing, and she gave it away before Cristóbal returned from Korea. She has given away two children from two different men. And while Cristóbal was fighting she was throwing away all his money.

Nanda behaved in a crazy way. Her children were always dirty and naked, roaming the streets at God's mercy. Simplicio, the smallest one, would be walking around with his balls showing while she visited the whole neighborhood, went to the movies and ran here and there.

Nanda's last child was a girl that she gave to the white woman at whose house she was working. They wrote to Cristóbal about it and that's why, when he returned from Panama, he almost killed her. He asked her for the money he had been sending to her for the house, and she told him, "There isn't any money, it has all been spent."

"But on what? You don't have a house and, even worse, there aren't any spoons or plates, and there's nothing to eat. Look at those children. They don't have clothes, they don't have anything." They fought and fought, until he said, "I'm leaving." Then people started telling him things about her.

When she separated from Cristóbal, Nanda went to Río Grande to my mother's house. No matter how bad she was, my family always welcomed her. A relative is a relative even if she is rolling in the mud.

Many years later, when my *mamá* was dying, I went back to Puerto Rico and I saw Nanda again. She was living with Erasmo. After *mamá's* funeral I went to see Nanda to settle the business of *mamá's* house. I had to get my niece's signature, because as the eldest daughter of my sister Luisa she had a share in the property. She signed right away.

That day, too, I met Soledad, Nanda's daughter, for the first time. She was a very shy girl, very shy, not brazen and shameless like she is now. There was no need for Soledad to grow up as she did. Nanda has been very mean to her and that's why she has turned out wild. That child has always worked to help her mother but Nanda never took care of her. Nanda would hit her and throw her out of the house. When I would ask for Soledad, Nanda would say, "No, she doesn't live here. That good-for-nothing has turned out to be a real tramp."

I'd say, "Nanda, I think you are to blame. Children have to be treated with love, not with blows and bad words."

I saw Soledad again here in New York, with her brother Simplicio. She has changed very much and I haven't had much to do with her. She is not sincere and she talks too much. She likes to make *trouble,* setting one relative against the other.

Once I had to tell Soledad I didn't want her here any more because she always came with a different man. So she said, "Well, Amparo, if you don't like it, don't eat it. I'll never set foot inside your house again." What do you think of that? I can't stand the woman's nasty temper. If she comes here I'll receive her politely, but not with the same open heart I receive Simplicio.

I met Simplicio only recently but I know I'll get along well with him all my life. He is very friendly and you can see he is sincere. He tries to please other people and finds ways of getting around them. He is just the opposite of Soledad.

I don't object to Soledad or Nanda because they were in the life. I have never avoided whores. On the contrary, I love to talk with them. I enjoy their gaiety, their dances, their nice clothes. I didn't come out of my mother's womb to become a whore, but it seems that other women did because it was their destiny. Everyone is born to a different fate. Some babies are born head first, some feet first. Take any five people and you'll always find two wrong-headed ones. That's the way it goes, three good to two bad. Looked at that way, a woman in the life is a woman like the rest of us. And why say "in the life"? Aren't we all alive and human? Aren't we all part of life, in life, too?

Fernanda

In the Life

Now MY MOTHER was dead and I hardly ever saw my husband. When Cristóbal came back from Panama, he was worse than ever. He almost never came home any more. Then I learned that he had set up housekeeping with another woman. As I've already said, I have a very jealous nature and in these matters I go the whole way. When I heard that he was living under one roof with another woman, I left him. I left him because I didn't love him. We broke up lightly, without any quarrel. I just told him I didn't want to have anything more to do with him, that I wanted to be free. I was about twenty-one years old.

I said I'd take the eldest, Soledad, who was about seven or eight, and leave the other three children with him, because you can fit in anywhere with one child but not with four. Cruz was only eight months old at the time. Felícita and Simplicio were crazy about their father, so they didn't cry because I left them. Soledad was the only one who didn't want to stay with him. Well, Cristóbal was in the Army so he turned the three youngest children over to their godmother Elsa, his brother Pablo's wife.

I would go to see Felícita, Simplicio and Cruz twice a month at their godmother's house. I guess they stayed with her until Cristóbal married Hortensia, about a year after we had separated. Then Hortensia took the children. They all lived at Stop 27; Cristóbal had his own house by then.

Hortensia and I knew each other well because we had been neighbors.

We used to visit each other and all. She's white and slender. When Cristóbal went to Panama he had a lot of mistresses but Hortensia wasn't one of those. He took up with her later. Hortensia and I get along well together. I don't bear her a grudge at all. I go to her house and she comes to mine.

When I left Cristóbal I went to Río Grande to my grandmother Clotilde, who was still alive at that time. I sent Soledad to school there. She was a good student. Soledad has always been the brightest among my children.

I had to leave my grandmother's house after a month because she kicked me out. It all came about because I had an abcess on my left breast and had to stay home one night when she went out. She went to a wake and I lay down with all my clothes on and Soledad beside me. Jamie, my grand-mother's husband, who always treated me with respect, was also in the house.

When my grandmother returned she began yelling in front of a lot of people. She said I had been waiting for her to leave so I could screw with Jaime the minute her back was turned. Maybe she was drunk when she said that, because she drank like a fish. That very night—it must have been eleven or twelve o'clock—she told me to get out. I didn't talk back to her or argue or anything. I'm always respectful to my older relatives. That's why they're all so fond of me on both sides of the family.

When she told me to leave, I burst out crying and went to my aunt Sofía's house and told her what had happened. She said, "*Ay*, you know *mamá* is crazy. Come stay with me and don't go back there." My aunt was all alone at the time because her husband, Esteban, was in jail for killing two men in Trujillo Alto. He served a fifteen-year sentence for that.

Well, I lived a long time at my aunt's house and she treated me very well. She gave me a bed that night, and Soledad and I went to sleep. She supported me as long as I stayed with her. I helped her and Adela, my cousin, with the housework but she never let me look for a job. She worked as a school janitor and she sold lottery tickets.

She used to beat my cousin Adela and me even though we were both grown women with children. One day Adela and I went to the movies, leaving Soledad and Adela's baby at home. Well, Aunt Sofía took the children to the movies and she beat us right then and there. We got out of the movie and she ran after us to whip us with tamarind twigs, which are the worst kind. When she beat me I never said anything. I had great respect for her. When she came home from work angry, or when she got mad at the children, God Himself wouldn't have dared look her in the face.

I finally got bored living there. I've never liked Río Grande much any-way. It's a dead town. It's not like San Juan, where you hear noise and there's always something going on. So one day when I met a friend of mine called Leonor, who told me about a dance she was going to in Santurce, I said, "Oh, wait for me, I'll go with you." My aunt said that if I went to dance and to whore around, I'd better not come back to her house. So I told her I was going to Santurce to stay. I didn't dare go back after that except to visit.

Soledad and I went to stay with my *comadre* Gilda, who took in washing and did housework for a well-to-do family. We got along very well with each other. While she washed the clothes I did the housework. Other times I'd wash and she'd do something else. She would always give me some of the money she earned so I could go to the movies or play bingo.

When Soledad was about eight, I asked her, "Would you like to go stay with your father now?" She didn't want to but then I said, "You'll be better off there because I have to get a job now and I won't be able to look after you." She agreed to go, on condition that I visit her every Sunday.

I went on living with *comai* Gilda. Then I got myself an old man who gave me everything I needed. His name was Valentín. He's dead now. I met him at Stop 26 because he used to walk by there. He'd give me gifts and I would joke with him. We never went out together, but he helped me because he had hopes of getting me to go live with him. He gave me money, and I divided it half and half with *comai* Gilda. This went on for about a month, but then I investigated and I learned he was married. I told him I was interested only in men who were free.

After I stopped seeing the old man I just had to get a job as a servant so I could help out with the expenses. I had been with Gilda for about a year. One day I was sitting reading the paper when I said, *"Ay, comadre,* I really feel like getting myself a job." And she answered, "I'm not asking you to leave. You don't have to work as long as I can take in washing. We can help each other." But I told her, "If I get a job we can really help each other."

Finally I went to work with a family living at Stop 19. This job didn't turn out well because the lady of the house was as angry as they make them. She wanted me to work seven days a week for fifteen dollars a month. I stayed only a week. After that I worked in a lot of houses.

I worked and worked but I saw that I never got ahead. I needed a lot of things that I couldn't afford to get. So I thought about what I could do to improve my situation and I decided to become a whore. Before that, it had never occurred to me. I had known several whores, but none of them had ever advised me to take up the profession. Gilda, my own *comadre,* had been a whore once, but she never suggested that I should be one. Gilda is very discreet about her affairs. She's a woman whom everybody thinks well of, and if she peddled her wares late at night, who was to know it? By the time I moved in with her, her whoring was a thing of the past. She gave it up because she had a little girl who was being brought up in the country and she didn't want to set her daughter a bad example.

I have a cousin called Virginia who was a whore too. She was my aunt Amparo's daughter. She used to come to Río Grande, but my grandmother Clotilde never wanted us to be friendly with her. "Don't talk to her," Clotilde would say. "She's a whore and she might advise you to do wrong and even take you with her." But Virginia never gave us any bad advice; on the contrary, her advice was always good. She had been a whore for a long time and she works at it even now. She has had a million men. She's way ahead of me and she's still in the profession.

I believe that I am now being punished because my grandmother forbade us to talk to Virginia or to any other whore. She didn't mind speaking with whores herself, but if one of those women bought candy for us she wouldn't let us take it. I don't know if my grandmother ever found out I was in the profession. After I left Río Grande, I didn't go back for a long time. What did I care about Río Grande? And knowing my grandmother, I thought, "She would probably treat me the way she treated Virginia." So I didn't go.

Before taking up the profession, whenever I saw whores I'd think, "I wonder what the hell those women are doing?" Once I was talking to somebody, I don't remember who, and I asked, "What are those women doing?" She told me, "They're peddling their wares." I said then, "Oh, so that's what whoring is like." And I thought, "I wonder why they do it? What is it like? What do they think about? How do they spend the money they get?" I asked all those questions, you see, but I had never thought of becoming a whore myself.

Well, what happened was that I started to work as kitchen help in a bar called El Molino in front of the Capitol. They've put up some buildings there now, but at that time there were a lot of wooden shacks and this bar was in one of them. They paid me twenty-five dollars a month. There were some whores in the bar but I didn't know much about it. I thought they led a gay life because they always seemed to be so happy. Then they gave me a job as waitress in that same bar. I did pretty well the first day, even though I didn't know much English. I got plenty of tips.

Well, I was a grown woman already and a free one to boot, so when a sailor I met there fell in love with me, I went out with him. That's how I got my start in the whoring profession. I was twenty-four years old. I was working in the bar that night and this American sailor told the owner that he liked me. He asked if I was willing to go out with any man or if I was a virgin. The bar owner told him no, I was not a virgin.

This sailor came and asked me if I wanted a drink. We started to drink together and he asked me if I went out with men. I thought this over a while and I looked at a man near me and at the bar owner before I answered, "Yes. Yes, I do."

He asked me in English how much I charged. The bar owner wanted **us** to be able to speak to the customers in English, so he told me how to answer the question. The customers would ask, *"You focking?"* and then *"How much?"* and the whore would answer, *"Two dollars to the room and five for me, at short time."*

I went upstairs with that sailor because it was the Christmas season, see, and I needed money for presents for my children for the Day of the Three Kings. I slept with him, but I didn't take off my clothes because I was ashamed. I just lowered my *panties* and I didn't look him in the face. He wanted to kiss me and I wouldn't let him. He gave me ten dollars, but he told the bar owner what had happened. Then the owner said to me, "Look, if you want to be a whore, you can't be that modest. And you need the money, Nanda. What you earn at the bar is a mere trifle. You're a new girl, so you have a better chance to get clients than the rest of the girls here. Try to be freer and more lively." He said, "Take a few drinks and that will give you courage."

He sent one of the other girls to give me advice. Her name was Josefina; she's in the States now. She told me, "When you're in a room with a *gringo,* kiss him, caress him and all that. And be sure to ask him to pay in advance or you mightn't get your money." I listened to her and said, "All right, I'll do it that way."

After that when I liked the looks of a customer I'd go and drink with him. All this was new to me, so I drank a lot and when we went upstairs he'd have to carry me. You understand that a whore is ashamed to be with a man she doesn't know. She has to be at least a bit high before she can go to bed with him. Well, I drank to get over the embarrassment and I kept it up after I stopped being a whore.

By the third day I no longer felt any shame. I'd take off my clothes right away, and I felt fine. I was gay. It didn't bother me a bit. Some women feel sad and ashamed, but not me.

Being in the profession is easier than being married. As long as you're a whore, nobody can interfere with you. You live alone, so there's nobody to tell you what to do or not to do. A whore can go anywhere, go to the movies as often as she likes, dance whenever she wants to and stay out as late as she pleases. If you want to take a holiday for a week or two, there's nobody to prevent it, unless you take up with a pimp.

If it weren't for the pimps, whoring would be a ball. The minute a whore gets herself a pimp, she isn't free to do what she likes any more. She must work only where he allows her to. If she stays too long with a customer, her pimp falls on her and beats her up. And then he takes all the money she earns. He doesn't work but stays in bed and sleeps as long as he likes while his whore is out on the job. A whore who has a pimp leads a dog's life. We have a rhyme about pimps that goes:

This pimp has come to think	Ese chulo se ha creído
The sun doesn't shine for me.	Que a mí no me alumbre el sol.
Four candles and a street lamp,	A mí me están alumbrando
That's all the light I see.	Cuatro velas y un farol.

I don't know why some women take up with pimps. To have a man of their own maybe, a man who can back them up and defend them if anybody tries to take advantage of them. That's the only thing a pimp can do well. But I say it isn't her pimp a whore loves, it's money. We had a couplet that said:

When the sailors come	Cuando vienen los marinos
The pimp sleeps in the street.	El chulo duerme al sereno.

And, you know, that's the truth. The sailors pay, so the pimp has to sleep outside.

A whore really doesn't feel pleasure, except when she feels the money in her hands. It's like not having a sex life at all. All that matters is the pay.

I didn't hang around much with other women. When they were together they'd always talk about their pimps. A woman who has a pimp must do whatever he asks. A pimp will force her to suck him or let him get into her ass whether she enjoys it or not. Almost every whore does it because many men like it that way. And people who don't want to have children do it. As the old saying has it, "That's not the way to get a woman pregnant."

But sometimes it harms a woman to do it that way. Like a girl I know whom we call Pupa. One day a lot of *gringos* arrived in San Juan. I told her, "A lot of ships came in today, Pupa. Wait for me tonight so that we can go out together."

Well, this Pupa was so selfish she went on ahead instead of waiting for me. She wanted to get the pick of the customers. As it happened, I got there late and all I could make that night was four *gringos* at five dollars apiece. I asked, "Well, where's Pupa?" And they told me, *"Muchacha,* they had to take Pupa to the hospital. She was with a man who had a lamppost for a penis and he tore her insides." She liked to do it up her ass and that night they had to carry her out of the hotel with her intestines hanging out. She had to have an operation and now that girl has a strange way of walking.

Whores are kind-hearted in a way. If you live near a prostitute you'll never lack for anything. A whore will help her neighbor even if she happens to be an honest married woman. A whore won't allow anyone who is near her to suffer. When I worked in the hotel, after I left the profession, the girls I knew would bring food and coffee up to me. I'd wash their sheets and all that. I knew a lot of girls whom I had helped, because when I was a whore I had more money than I knew what to do with. So when I gave up whoring, they helped me.

As long as I was in that life I never got pregnant. I never even had a miscarriage or an abortion. I can't explain it, because I never used any kind of contraceptive. I got sick once but I don't know who infected me. I went to the women's clinic in a sort of hospital or medical dispensary. The women's clinic was called *el detention*. The doctors treat you well there, not like whores but like respectable ladies. If a woman has a yellow discharge or something like that, they'll give her an injection of 800 cc. of penicillin every day. They tell me that now all whores get these injections whether they're sick or not.

One suffers a lot when one is in the life. I had to pay three dollars a night for a bed to sleep in, otherwise I had to sleep out in the street. Sometimes the owner of the bar would let me go up to sleep even if I had no money. But other times I would have to sit up at the bar until they closed at five or six in the morning.

The next day I'd go looking for customers right away. I worked in the daytime if I hadn't had any customers the night before. I'd go anywhere I saw a lot of people together, and I worked until I earned at least five or ten dollars so I could pay for my lunch and laundry. I had to change clothes every day and it cost me a dollar each time I had a dress washed or cleaned. The lady who did my clothes wouldn't give me credit, even if I didn't have a thing to wear that day.

There were times when I earned as much as fifty or sixty dollars in one night, but what was the good of that? I had to spend it all on clothes and on lodging. When I had enough money, I would pay ahead for a room so I would have a place to sleep in case I went broke. And I'd buy clothes or a new pair of shoes almost every day. All kinds of good-quality clothes, see? A whore doesn't really have to work. She just dresses up and peddles her goods. She lives sort of like a woman of means who doesn't have to do any housework.

I went hungry at times, but when I had no money I could usually get food from schooner crews. I'd go to a schooner that had come from Santo Domingo or St. Thomas and ask the captain or anybody on board for a meal and they'd give it to me. The men who work on schooners are very nice, especially the captains. If a lady of the streets goes to them and asks for something, the captain won't let the men curse her or use bad language. I had a lot of friends among the crews of schooners and they always had respect for me.

I was with an American one night at El Molino when I got into trouble and they put me in jail. One of the other girls just walked over to me and said that she liked my American and was going to lay him. I said she should ask him which of the two he liked better, her or me. She asked him and he said he liked me best. At that she hauled out and hit me and we began to fight. I had never used a razor before, but that time I grabbed one and cut her. It was the merest scratch, just a bit of a cut on the arm, but someone sent for the cops and they arrested me.

Well, my mother was dead and I had no one to bail me out, so I had to stay in jail until my case came up in court. I talked with the judge and with a man called Abel who was the marshal of the court. So when the case was heard, the judge only sentenced me to fifteen days in jail.

I cried all the time. Imagine, I'd never been in jail before, and I had to spend Christmas there. The very night I was jailed I thought of escaping through some steel drums I saw. But then I thought, "If I run away I will be killed or have to live as a fugitive. I'd better stay here." So I stayed. And the next day I felt better about it because the other girls there began to talk to me. They told me to be calm, not to mind too much spending Christmas there, because I had only a short sentence to serve. They begged me not to cry and I resigned myself to staying. During those fifteen days nobody visited me. But then, I didn't expect anyone to come.

In those days there were no beds in jail, only pallets made up on old doors which were laid on the floor. You can't say it wasn't clean though. We cleaned up the place every day. We would divide the work among us, scrubbing floors, cleaning out the toilets, washing the sink, cleaning the courtyard, planting, and so on. If a prisoner refused to follow orders she was put in solitary confinement. She would be locked up in a cell all by herself. Luckily I wasn't sent there. The guards treated us well. On weekdays we were given rice, beans and meat for dinner. On Sundays we would have chicken.

I've had only one fight with the police and that was much later, on account of my cousin Darío. He's my aunt Amparo's son. He's in jail now. When the cops came to arrest him, one of them tried to hit him and I got between them. The cop knocked me down and my daughter Soledad hit him. Then some more cops arrived and pushed me into the police wagon, but I escaped. They brought charges against me for having hit a policeman. And it was a big lie. It was my daughter who had hit him. She had bitten him too.

Well, they came to my house to arrest me. I stayed in jail a short time, about two weeks, and then I was bailed out. The day of the trial I was found not guilty because there was no evidence against me. The cop himself said he had nothing against me. I've never got into an argument with the police, see? All I had to do was to keep running when they were out arresting whores so they wouldn't put me in jail.

A whore's life is insecure. You're afraid all the time and you can't manage too well. Any time you are peddling your goods, you may suddenly find a cop beside you, to arrest you. You live scared. It's a dog's life. You have to be paying fines and serving jail sentences all the time. It's really terribly inconvenient. Sometimes I was fast asleep in a hotel and the owner of the place would wake me and tell me to beat it because the cops were on the way. And that night I'd have to stay out in the streets, hiding from the cops.

The truth is cops don't get along well with whores. They just won't let us alone. They'll arrest us without cause. They won't even let us earn a nickel in peace. They'll push the whores into the police wagon like dogs and treat them rough. If a whore curses a policeman, he'll charge her with assault and battery without her having lifted a finger.

Policemen are bullies. They like to hit people who aren't bothering them. A policeman will go into a bar on the sly and get drunk and then come out and bully you. There's no justice in the world. The really bad people are never caught, because they have money and can bribe the law and the police. So nobody does anything to them. But the poor souls who don't own anything, who don't do anything except get drunk—they get thrown into the cooler.

The lawyers are just as bad as the police. Thieves, every one of them. They fix up everything as between *compadre* and *compadre* and they get the rich off scot-free. But a poor client—why, after they eat up fifty or sixty dollars of his, they make him plead guilty. The lawyer tips the judge a wink and that's that! We used to be tried right out in the street. They'd say, "Did you disturb the peace? Well then, give me a quarter and you're free." Sometimes they said half a dollar or you had to leave something as a guarantee. They're all the same.

But we whores would get even with them. We had rhymes about them, which we'd sing. There was one that went like this:

When this judge reads my sentence	*Cuando este juez me sentencie*
I will confess my guilt	*Yo me declaro culpable*
And walking down the stairs	*Y bajando la escalera*
On his mother I will shit	*Yo me le cago en la madre*
When this judge reads my sentence	*Cuando este juez me sentencie,*
One question I'll ask him:	*Una pregunta le haré:*
"Didn't you like the whores	*Que si cuando el era chulo,*
When you were a pimp?"	*¿No le gustaban las putas?*

An honest whore is a rare thing. Most of them steal from the Americans. After making a big play for a *gringo* and all, they lift his billfold. They'll work out a plan with their pimp to take the American to their house and rob him there. I never did anything like that. And I never used heroin or marijuana or any kind of drug. My only vice is smoking cigarettes.

When I got out of jail that first time, I started drinking a lot. I went to La Marina, the dockyard section, to work in the Silver Cup Club. Whenever a ship came in, I didn't walk the streets but stayed in the Club, waiting for customers. I lived in a room right there at the Silver Cup and I didn't have to pay rent. They charged only two dollars for the bed. And every time I was with a man he paid me five dollars.

I earned twenty-five to thirty dollars a night. One night when I was at the Club an American wanted to screw me twice for five dollars. I refused and then he took my petticoat and my *panties* and hid them. He wouldn't give them to me, so the porters and a waiter came and bounced him out of the Club. That was the only time I had trouble with an American.

I liked Americans better than Puerto Ricans because Americans pay more. Puerto Ricans want to have a woman for only two dollars. But Americans never make any objection to paying five dollars or whatever you ask for. Most Americans are good. Some of them will step aside to let you pass on a narrow sidewalk, and there are Americans who will defend you if necessary.

But when the bad ones get drunk, they don't respect anybody. They'll start asking any woman to go with them as if she were a whore, even if she's a respectable housewife. And they start grabbing a person's ass even if she is a virgin or is married. And if they see a poor woman, many of them, at least a fourth of them, will ridicule her. But some Americans are respectful even when they're high and they like Puerto Rico because it's a gay place.

I finally had to give up the profession because there were days when I went hungry and I'd feel weak and angry all the time and without energy to do anything. I got thin as a skeleton. I couldn't go on like that. Besides, I think that prostitutes should go to work instead of earning their living by whoring. Nobody is forced to be a whore. A woman who has children to support may have to be a whore in order to earn money for them, but most whores go into the profession because they enjoy it. To my mind, it's plain laziness to get under a man for two or three dollars instead of taking a job.

When I see these women now, hanging around street corners, I feel sorry for them because they have no peace. I wish they would settle down and lead virtuous lives. Most whores could get other jobs if they wanted to, because everybody has the right to an honest job. Some of them are young women who could even work in a factory or as sales clerks.

People in general, most people, don't think it's right for a woman to take up whoring. Even the cops and the judges don't think well of the profession and they want to make an end of it. But they can't. I think they'll never be able to put an end to whoring. Suppose they tried to end it here in San Juan by arresting two or three whores. Why, by tomorrow there would be fifty more all over the place! Mary Magdalen, the saint, was once a whore and they say that's the way the profession started. If she hadn't been a whore there would be no prostitution.

CHAPTER

SIX

Fernanda

My Husbands
Fidel and Erasmo

I WAS STILL in the whoring profession when I began to live with a man named Fidel Díaz Calderón. I really didn't like him very much, he was just another man among the many I had known. But that man left his mark on me. His name is tattooed on me and there is no way it can be erased.

It happened when we were both drunk. I didn't know what he was doing, otherwise I wouldn't have let him because now I am a woman marked for life. I don't even want to remember the day it happened. When I woke up the next morning, I knew right away that something had happened to me, as though a seventh sense told me. My breasts hurt and when I looked in the mirror I saw the name "Fidel" on one breast, "Díaz" on the other and "Calderón" down below.

I told him, "You did this to me to make me even lower than I am. Now I can't hide what I am and I'll never be able to find my happiness with any man. But don't worry, I'm going to sue you this very day." I was going to do it, too, but he kneeled and begged my pardon, and as he had my name tattooed all over him, I let it go. Anyway, it wouldn't have looked good in court. God knows if they would have made me show it to them.

From then on, I have been too ashamed to let a doctor see my body, no matter what aches and pains I may have. And I told every husband I've had since, "Look, I have a man's name tattooed on me but he is dead now. Do you accept me this way or don't you?" None of them has minded, but if I could, I would have these marks removed even if it cost me a lot of money.

I was with Díaz the day he died. We were spending the week in Luquillo with his parents. On Sunday, Mother's Day, we had arrived loaded with gifts. Díaz was a street vendor of yard goods, dresses, underwear, fake jewelry and things like that, so he could buy lots of nice stuff at a discount. We were having a fine time on Tuesday, talking, joking and drinking, when Díaz asks me, "Do you have any cigarettes left?" I didn't, so he said, "Then I'll go buy some." He left the house at three o'clock and it got to be nine o'clock, ten o'clock, and Díaz hadn't come back. Eleven . . . no Fidel Díaz. By that time I was thinking, "He's loving up some woman, for sure." Not that he had ever given me any trouble that way. But he was so terribly good-looking that any woman would have been glad to get her hands on him.

By midnight I was ready to go look for him. Díaz's parents live far out in the country, a lonely place with only a few small houses, each with its storm shelter, scattered here and there. It was dark outside, dark as a wolf's mouth. My mother-in-law said, *"Muchacha,* stay indoors, you don't know how dangerous it is out there." I felt strong that night and I went, but it was no use. I didn't find him. I couldn't sleep, worrying about my man.

At six the next morning someone came knocking on the door, calling my father-in-law. *"Don* Porfirio, *don* Porfirio, get up, your son is in a terrible state at the naval base hospital." I jumped out of bed, twisted my hair into a bun, rinsed out my mouth without brushing my teeth, and I went to the hospital. They wouldn't let us in until visiting hours at two-thirty.

Díaz was unrecognizable. His limbs were hanging by shreds of flesh. He was in ruins. He had been run over by an army tow crane while he was lying asleep in the middle of the road. He had gotten drunk with a friend, and on the way home Díaz decided to sleep it off. That's the way he always acted when he was high, he didn't give a damn where he lay down to rest. His friend, who was just as drunk, went on home without a backward glance. The crane ran over Díaz and the driver didn't even notice it at the time. On the way back he saw Díaz lying there, smashed to bits. They identified him because of a bracelet I had given him. A client of mine had taken it off one night and given it to me. But I don't like to wear men's jewelry, so I gave it to Díaz and told him, "You can have the man's name rubbed off and yours put on instead."

When I went back to the hospital the next day I was met by the doctor who asked me, "Are you Fidel Díaz's wife?"

"Well," I explained, "I can't rightly say that, but I am his woman." Then I notice him make a sign to the nurse and at the same time he sticks a needle into me. After a few minutes he says, "Your husband died last night." I screamed and fell down in a dead faint. Doped as I was, that same morning I went to break the news to his parents. Three days later I was back home in Loíza Street.

Nobody there knew what had happened and the women teased me about coming home alone. "What did you do with Díaz? Where did you drop him?" they asked.

"He's dead," I said. They thought I was kidding so I said, "The hell with it. Read it in the newspaper if you don't believe me."

Altogether, I lived with Díaz for two years. He had one fault; he wouldn't let me bring my children to live with us. I had just about made up my mind to walk out on him when he had that accident. It almost seems as if God wanted to spare me the trouble.

I went back to work in the Silver Cup in La Marina. That's where I met Erasmo and we fell in love. He was working as a waiter and bartender in the same club. He was tall, thin and stoop-shouldered and his face was very wrinkled even then. He fell in love with me first and I couldn't stand the sight of him. He would tell me, "I like you," and I would say, "Go shit on your mother and go to hell. I don't like you." I insulted him because I hated him but he kept pestering me, "Come on, let's you and me go upstairs to the hotel." I always refused.

But there were times when I had no customers and no place to sleep. Then he'd say, "Sleep in my room. I promise I won't touch you." He would rent a room in the hotel and I'd sleep there. He kept his promise and let me sleep in peace. He would invite me out to dinner too. I accepted his invitations but I told him, "If you think you're going to get something from me by feeding me, you're nuts."

"Never mind," he'd answer, "I know how you hate me. But love is born of hatred, you know." Those were his very words.

Then one night the police were rounding up the whores and he said to me, "What are you going to do? Come with me."

"Let it be as God wills," said I. So we went upstairs together and I slept with him that night for free. The next few nights we did the same thing. After that, I gave him my earnings to keep safe for me because I'd go on sleeping until noon. He'd bring up my breakfast on a tray. And in spite of all that, he never asked me for money or tried to pimp for me. On the contrary, we would go shopping and we would spend all my money on clothes for me. And as long as I lived with Erasmo I never had to go to work if I didn't feel well. He was completely infatuated with me.

Men become infatuated with a woman because she has suction in her cunt. I have that attraction, see? That's why men fall in love with me and never want to leave me. I can't help it. It's the suction that holds a man. That is what happened to Erasmo.

Erasmo and I lived together for seven years. We were very happy the first two years because my children weren't living with me then. We had a room in a hotel on San Francisco Street. That was our first home. One time, when business wasn't good, Erasmo said to me, "You should have a room of your own. You know that every now and then the police raid these hotels and you have to run away." That's when he took me to La Esmeralda. I had never been there but had seen it from above in passing. Everybody talked about La Esmeralda and I would meet people who lived there. I thought, "Hell, I'd like to know it." So I said to Erasmo, "Let's take a chance. Let's go to La Esmeralda to see if we can get a little house there."

We walked all over La Esmeralda, looking for a house. *Ave María!* It was a slum but there was something about it I liked. I looked at the streets and they seemed so pretty. It was like another world. I was impressed. Finally we found a house near the beach and a man rented it to us for fourteen dollars a month. So Erasmo and I moved there. It was a big, big house. We didn't have any furniture, so Erasmo went to Pedrito Sánchez, the owner of the bar in the Silver Cup. He had practically brought up Erasmo and his foster brother Arturo, because they had both worked there since they were little boys. Sánchez's daughter sold Erasmo a bed and a bureau with a mirror. Erasmo got another old bed from the hotel and he cleaned it up. So we had a spare bed. We had several other pieces of second-hand furniture he picked up here and there. I will say this for Erasmo, he did like the house to be nice and he bought everything we needed.

La Esmeralda was different thirteen years ago when I first moved here. It is much better now. At that time you had to walk beneath the houses to get from one place to another. There even were houses built right in the water. They had to make small wooden bridges to pass from house to house. I was afraid of the big waves at first until I got used to having the sea break against the wall of my house.

In those days there was a fight or a crap game going on in every alley. And don't think anybody played for dollar bets. They bet big money then. And there was much more looseness before. Women used to walk around practically naked and joke with everybody.

Women who were in the life got into the habit of bringing *gringos* here to La Esmeralda even in the daytime. But a priest called Father Ponce stopped all that. He came and made those women behave. He would snatch the whores out of their clients' hands and send the men somewhere else. He was a real father to us, and when he was here, people in La Esmeralda went straight, see? If somebody was sick he went to see them, and if they had nothing to eat he sent food. If somebody needed a job, Father Ponce would find him one. He did a lot for the people here and he made it a better place to live. That Father was a saint.

A lot of people look down on La Esmeralda. Doctors would rather let a child die than come here. Doctors are sons of a great whore. Why, even the nurses don't want to come. They think that the people here aren't human. They think we aren't worth anything. Even the cops look down on us. That's why, when there's a fight here, the cops will say, "Let me know when they've killed two or three." When you apply for any kind of decent job, as soon as you say you're from La Esmeralda, they tell you, "Wait, wait." And you may wait till your death day, for all the good it does you. But if you go to a bar looking for work, that's different—they'll snap you up.

I've never liked horse racing but I began to bet on the races after I moved to La Esmeralda. Luis the Queer was the one who taught me to like it. One day he says to me, "Nanda, why don't you play the races? I'll take your slip over to be stamped." I told him, "Oh, but I don't know how." Then he said, "I'll teach you." He brought me a form and taught me how to fill it in. He said, "You know how to read, so you read the list of horses that are going to run and select one for each race. Or I'll choose for you if you'd rather." From then on he'd show me the lists and pick out horses for me to bet on. Every time a race was scheduled he came to me, "Nanda, aren't you going to play?" Then we'd play together.

This betting just about ruined me. Every cent I made I spent on the races and I'd pawn things to get money for more betting. It's entertaining, though, because you get interested in radio programs about the races. You tune in to hear about the points the different horses made and the changes in jockeys, and you learn which are the favorites and so on. Two dollars is the legal price to play a daily double. But you can play the daily double illegally for as little as half a dollar. And you can win as much as two hundred dollars. But I've never won much at the races.

I once won a hundred dollars playing illegal numbers. My daughter Cruz sold me the winning number herself. That happened the week my father died. When I play bingo I often win fifteen or twenty dollars, but I've never had the luck to win a lot of money. I lost more than I won. When I got really involved in a game I'd pawn everything I could lay my hands on. I've pawned and lost a watch, chains, flatirons, furniture, lots of things, just to get money to keep on betting. Gambling is a vice with me. I gamble in the hope of winning something big so I'll be able to leave something to my grandchildren. I would like to buy a house before I die and register it in their names. That's my only ambition.

When Erasmo and I came to live in La Esmeralda, my children were still staying with their father. I used to visit them every Sunday. They didn't know I was a whore at that time because when they asked questions I always told them I was a servant. They found out about me when Simplicio showed up in La Marina one day. He was only a little boy then, but he slipped away when Hortensia wasn't looking and he went all the way down to La Marina and found me. Somebody must have told him they'd seen me at the Silver Cup.

Anyway, he found me there with a *gringo*. When I saw him, I was so taken aback I changed color. But Simplicio didn't make any remarks, so I didn't say anything either. Do you know what he did say? He said, "Take me to live with you." I told him, "Don't worry, I will." Then I gave him some money and he went away. A few days later Soledad and Felícita came. They also said they wanted to live with me. At least Soledad did.

Later on I explained everything to them. I told them that I was able to buy them presents on the Day of the Kings because I earned money whoring. I thought it was better that they should hear it from me before anybody else told them. It was not Hortensia, their stepmother, who told them about me. She knew all about it but she never said a word to the children, and she would always receive me well when I went to visit them at her house.

On Sundays I'd take them to the park or to eat at La Bombonera restaurant, and whenever I was alone I'd visit them. That's why they were so fond of me and wanted to live with me. Whenever there was a hurricane warning I was the first to go get my children and take them to one of the shelters set up in the schools.

One Sunday Erasmo said I should stay home and look after the house, so I said, "All right, but in that case I would like to bring my kids to live here."

"Any time you wish," he said. "I have no objection."

First I brought Soledad, then Cruz. Then one day they broadcast hurricane warnings. I said, "Erasmo, they're announcing a hurricane and Simplicio isn't here." So I went after him. Felícita didn't want to come, but I brought Simplicio home with me.

He stayed there about a week, then Hortensia sent for him. So I told him, "It's time you went back, Simplicio." But he said, "I'm not going back. I want to stay with you." Then he cut up one of his shoes and threw it away so I couldn't take him back.

I decided to keep him and went to Hortensia to tell her so. She said, "Well, they're your children, so naturally they want to stay with you. Take Simplicio if you want to." The only one who never wanted to live with me was Felícita. She chose to stay with her stepmother.

Cruz was five years old when I took her to live with me. She was lame by then, and her godmother Elsa claims it was Hortensia, the child's stepmother, who crippled her. But that's not true, because the minute Elsa told me that story I took steps to find out what was really wrong with Cruz. I had her X-rayed, and everywhere I took her they'd tell me that her spine was straight and that she had not been made lame by a fall.

I don't know what happened at her stepmother's house to make her lame. I was living in Río Grande and they hardly ever sent me any news of the children. Cruz was born healthy but she has been ill most of her life. She used to have asthma and she'd get such bad attacks that we had to rush her to the hospital. When she was about three, she got very sick and had to be taken to the Municipal Hospital. After that she walked with a limp. We don't know what kind of illness it was.

Erasmo was a good stepfather to my children. He was hard on Simplicio, but if Simplicio grew up straight and honest, it's all due to Erasmo. Because as a boy, Simplicio was a real little hooligan and you could just see he was going to grow up bad. He would stay away from home three or four days at a time, sleeping in the streets and all. But between Erasmo and me we made a decent fellow out of him. If I had been one of those mothers who objected to having her son punished by his stepfather, God knows what would have become of the boy.

I sent Simplicio to school but he went only as far as the fourth grade. I had to take him out of school because he kept getting into *trouble* there and I was afraid I might be tempted to hit him too hard. So I told him, "It's better that you should remain ignorant." He didn't learn a thing in school anyhow. He can read a little, and he can write, printing the letters slowly.

Simplicio was a good boy but he got into a lot of mischief. He'd play hooky with Marcelo, his only friend. They were so close to each other that if one wanted to shit, the other one had to shit too. If it was time for one of them to take a bath, they both bathed. They'd go together to school, or they'd decide to play hooky and go to the beach or beg or shine shoes.

I had to go to court with Simplicio a number of times. When he played hooky he would go out smashing things. One day he broke a street light in front of the Traffic Division and was arrested. The police were after me about Simplicio all the time.

The first time they took him was on a Saturday when I went to Hortensia's house to get the money Cristóbal left for the children. Simplicio had been shining the shoes of a *gringo* when a boy came up to him and gave Simplicio some stolen masks. It was carnival time, so Simplicio accepted them and put one on. Then the cops came and arrested him.

When I got to the police station I said, "What have you done, Simplicio? You know that there are no thieves in our family."

He said to me, "Nanda, I didn't steal anything."

The belt I had on was a thin one, so I asked the cop to lend me his. Then I started to beat Simplicio as hard as I could, right there. He cried, *"Ay, Nanda, don't beat me. Look, may a car run over you and kill you right now if I robbed anyone. Don't beat me any more, Nanda, may I drop dead or may somebody stab you if I stole anything."*

Then the judge said, "Let him be. Don't beat him any more. He says he didn't steal the masks and he's swearing it by you who are his mother." They took us to the juvenile officer and she gave Simplicio some good advice. She told him that he didn't look like a thief and that he shouldn't join up with others, and that he should keep to himself.

Simplicio once ran away from home and didn't return for three days.

Then a detective knocked on the door at about six o'clock in the morning. He said that my son was begging around San Juan because I took his money away from him. That detective really had balls to say that to me! I bet he really had bigger balls than my son. And I'm telling you, Simplicio's balls are so big that they've called him "three for two" ever since he was little.

Well, I took hold of that boy and beat him nearly to death. Then I took away all his clothes. But there was a hole in the floor that we used to shit through and he got out that way. I don't know who gave him a pair of pants. I searched and searched for him all over San Juan. And I told Erasmo, "When I get hold of that boy, I'm going to tie him up. From now on, I'll just tie him up."

I saw him one afternoon at San Juan Gate. He was filthy. So I went to a boy who was hanging around there and we cooked up a trick. The boy went to Simplicio and said, "Come here, you stole a watch from me." When Simplicio came over I grabbed him. And I slapped him all the way home. Then I bought a chain with a padlock and tied him to a strong stake, driven deep into the ground. And can you believe it? The boy showed up at the place where I worked in San Juan, with his wrists still chained. I tell you, he was unbearable.

One day he asked me how much it cost to go to Cataño. I told him, "Six cents," because that's what it cost at that time. Then he started counting on his fingers. But how was I to imagine he was planning to go all the way over there? Well, he went even farther. He went to Bayamón. He was terrible. And no matter how I punished him or what Erasmo did to him, he didn't change. That's the way he was. If I hadn't kept after him he would have been the worst kind of thief, like the ones in the movies.

When he was a fairly big boy, the people from the civil defense came over to enroll him in their group. Well, a few days later they brought him back home to me because he fought with everybody there. They couldn't stand him. One night they showed a civil defense movie here in La Esmeralda. I don't know what really happened that time. I have been told that the man from the civil defense hit Simplicio. Then Simplicio grabbed a tin can and split the man's eyebrow. We had to go to trial and everything. I prayed and prayed to my saint, the Virgin of Everlasting Mercy, that Simplicio should not be sent to the juvenile detention home. But he never did anything serious, so they sent him back home to me.

After that we had a flood tide and my boy jumped into the sea to save people. He has a beautiful soul, even if I do say so myself. He got all wet and almost drowned too. Then the civil defense man came up, and imagine! —he tried to order Simplicio around. The boy got mad and said, "You know a lot and give orders, don't you? But you haven't jumped into the water to save anybody yet. I don't know anything or give any orders, but you're nice and dry and I'm all wet. I'm the one who's been saving lives here, not you."

Simplicio is very affectionate and he won't allow anybody to make fun of me in front of him, not like my daughters, who don't care what anyone says to me. Why, when he was a little bit of a boy, here in La Esmeralda, he'd say, "Make fun of everybody else if you want to, but my mother you have to respect." When I beat him, the other boys would say, "Ah, your mother beats you, why don't you hit her." Then he'd fight with them and come home crying and say, "Nanda, you know what that boy said to me? He said that when you hit me, I should hit you." I beat Simplicio a lot but he never in his life tried to hit me.

Boys are a lot more trouble to raise than girls. I would have liked to have only one child, a daughter, because you don't have to be quarreling with your husband all the time the way you do when you have many children. With only one child you have a more peaceful life. I would prefer a daughter because with a son you are always getting upset about something.

Well, now I was living with my three children, and Erasmo was supporting them. We were getting along fine. It's true I didn't love him much, but anyway, I lived with him. He would give me money to buy food according to what he earned, which wasn't an awful lot. I think he earned about twenty dollars a week and he gave me fifteen for household expenses. I stayed home all day to wash and iron, and went out peddling my wares at night, about ten o'clock, after the children were asleep. Erasmo came to bring me back every night. My being in the life never bothered him because I never gave him any cause to worry.

But we had a lot of fights. Our biggest quarrel was one night in La Marina when he called me a dirty Negro. Then I insulted him and slapped his face, and he kicked me. I said I shit on his mother and he answered that my mother was a dirty Negro. He was drunk and he knocked me down and went on kicking me with those pointed shoes he wears. I didn't have a weapon on me to defend myself, so I just hit him and socked him. I don't know where I got the strength, but I hit him hard. I've always thought that someone there, seeing me helpless on the floor, must have put something into my hand to hit him with. Whatever happened, the fact is that I cut open the flesh above his cheekbone. When he saw himself all bloody, he left me alone.

That night we came back together to La Esmeralda to sleep. He didn't say a word to me on the way, but when we got home he began to rub some ointment on me, Vicks and arnica. There were no marks on my body, though, because no matter how hard I'm hit, I never get any bruises. The only time a bruise shows on me is when I get a black eye. I didn't do a thing for Erasmo. I just left him with his pain. His eye got black and swelled up, and his legs were black and blue from my bites.

The next day his brother Arturo came and asked him, "Say, what's the matter with you?" And Erasmo answered, "Oh, the bitch I keep here bit me." Arturo said, "Good for her. You didn't have to beat her. After all, you're not her father."

Another time we had a fight and I had him arrested. I never did under-stand what that fight was about. I just know that he came and hit me over the right ear so hard that I felt as if the whole side of my head had exploded. I told him, "Wait a minute, if that's what you want I'll go call the cops." The cops were near and I had him arrested. They kept him in jail about seven days. I said to Arturo, "Tell him to fix the bail himself if he wants to go free, or he can stay in jail for all I care. I won't lift a finger to help him." So Erasmo sent for some money and bailed himself out. Then we made up and went on living together, but I had lost my love for him. When I love I love without limit, but when a man hits me I stop loving him at once.

It was about that time that a lesbian fell in love with me. I didn't pay any attention to her and what happened was Erasmo's fault because that Sunday he wouldn't take me to the movies and I had to go alone. Afterward I went to a bar in La Marina and sat at a table to read the newspaper. Then that lesbian came and snatched the newspaper from my hands. I asked her, "Why do you do this?" And she answered, "You think you're tough, don't you?" I said, "I'm not tough but I can take on the toughest." Then she socked me, and we started to fight.

Arturo was in the bar at the time. Somebody said to him, "Look, Ar-turo, your sister-in-law is fighting." Arturo was very surprised because I really beat her up. She wasn't able to hurt me at all, except for one bite she gave me. I left her all scratched and practically naked. The cops came but the owner of the bar and the boy who worked there hid me. They knew I'd never fought before and they all liked me. So the cops started taking away this other woman and she kept saying, "No. I fought with a tiny woman in there and she tore all my clothes off my back."

"Why did you fight?" the policeman asked.

"Because I've always liked that woman and she has never paid any atten-tion to me. I took the newspaper away from her to see if she'd at least talk with me. Because I like her!"

Then Arturo and some others said to her in front of the cops, "Look, that woman you're after is no lesbian. She's a woman through and through. Don't you make any mistake about that, and be careful what you do to her."

Well, she ended up fighting with the cops and they hit her and took her away. She was in jail a month. When she got out she started looking for me everywhere. She meant to cut me if I didn't accept her advances. She came to the bar with a *Gem* in her hand and another in her hair. When Erasmo saw her he sent for me and said, "Nanda, don't go down to the bar. That woman came in with a *Gem* and she's threatening to cut you up."

I said, "She is? Then I'll go down all the quicker, because I'm no coward." He insisted, "Look, you'd better not go." Erasmo has always been a sissy. He'll never stand up for anybody. I bet he was at the movies when I was having the fight.

I took my *Gem* and went to the bar. When they saw me there, the boys bought me a Coke so I could attack her with the bottle if I had to. Then she sent for me to talk with her alone. I sent word back that the one who was in need was the one who did the walking. And she was the one who needed me, not I her. Well, she never paid any more attention to me after that, but we are still enemies. She doesn't say a word to me, nor I to her, when we meet.

I think it's very ugly for two women to do it with each other. If I'd had a taste for that, I'd be sleeping with women and living off the fat of the land. Because women ran after me too, you know, and offered gifts and money and clothes. But I didn't accept them because I never did like that way of life.

I left Erasmo because he was drunk all the time and he kept after the kids. Any little thing the children did bothered him. He just didn't like them. Another reason I had for leaving him was that he embarrassed me so often. Like the time *doña* Regina, a neighbor of mine, told me that Erasmo had broken into her house one night when he was drunk. *Doña* Regina woke up and found him standing beside the bed of her daughter Noemi. That's what *doña* Regina says anyway. I don't know if it's true, but the fact is—he didn't deny it. And it seems to me that when you bring up something like that, a man tries to explain or justify himself unless it's true and there's nothing he can say.

But the real reason I left Erasmo was because of Soledad. According to what I was told, Erasmo had fallen in love with her. Soledad was nearly grown by then, and you should have seen her! At that time she was really pretty, and then she was so pleasant, so *simpática,* with everybody. You see how nice Cruz is? Well, Soledad was better than Cruz. Why, there's no comparison. People kept telling me, "Be careful. Erasmo's in love with Soledad." Then one day when I was standing at the water faucet, a boy named Pedro came up to me and said, "I've been hearing rumors."

I asked him, "What rumors?"

"Is it true that Erasmo is in love with your daughter?"

"Not that I know of. At least I haven't seen anything happen when I'm around."

Then Pedro said to me, "I like you." He was only a youth of eighteen, but I said, "Oh well, if you like me, let's do something about it. Get into me if you like me," I said.

Well, that's the way it all started, and after a time I really got involved in an affair with Pedro. I kept on living with Erasmo, but I was seeing Pedro. While Erasmo was away at work I was busy putting the horns on him. Not that I did anything with Pedro at home. No, we met outside.

Then one morning Soledad got up and called to me, "Nanda, Nanda." "What is it?" I asked.

She said, "Erasmo was standing beside my bed." That's when the fight started. Erasmo said it was a lie. He told me that my daughters talked too much and liked to make trouble. I told him, just like that, "Either you go to hell or I will. And I want you to know something, I'm putting the horns on you."

And he said, "Yes, I know. And I know you're doing it with Pedro." A short time after that quarrel we separated.

But before we separated Soledad took off with Arturo. He had been coming almost every day to visit his foster brother Erasmo. That's how Soledad and he fell in love. Erasmo had never said a word to Arturo about his coming to the house so often, but when Arturo left, Erasmo would begin to gossip behind his back. I said to Erasmo, "Look, if you don't like something Arturo does, tell him. After all, he's your brother. What's the use of telling me? The two of you are men and understand each other. Or are you in love with my daughter? Is that the trouble? You sure seem to be jealous!"

"Oh, you! You get something in your head and go on and on about it."

Soledad has never told me why she took off with Arturo. I had whipped her with a strap a few days before because she had said she shit on my mother. Then I told her teacher that Soledad couldn't go to school that day because I'd given her a beating. And I told her why. The following day Soledad was punished at school. She was in the fifth grade then and she was put back to the fourth because of what she'd said to me. The teacher had asked her to kneel down and beg my pardon, but Soledad just wouldn't do it.

Then on Friday I got it into my head to go iron clothes over on Fortaleza Street to earn some money. I knew Arturo and Soledad were sweethearts, but I didn't know about that plan of theirs. Well, while I was away she took off with him. When I got home in the afternoon and started looking for Soledad to help me with the cooking, I couldn't find her anywhere. She had already gone off. When I went to work at the Club I asked the boys at the bar, "Say, do you know where Soledad is?"

A friend of mine said, "Here, this is for you," and handed me a piece of paper. Soledad had written it to say she was going off with Arturo. She said if I sent a cop to get her she'd kill herself because she'd rather die than go back home.

I went to see her. She was in the country near Toa Alta. When we met we rushed into each other's arms. I didn't do anything more, because what else was there to do? I wanted to make her and Arturo marry, but she said she would never marry him. She never explained that to me either. A short time later my daughter Felícita ran off with a boy named Ángel. She, too, left me a little note. That was all. I never know what my daughters are up to or why. I never know.

I was still living with Erasmo at the time but I left him about fifteen days later. Pedro and Erasmo never did get around to having a fight. Erasmo wasn't very brave. Pedro was much more daring and he was much better for me because later he made an honest woman of me.

In the house next door there was a small room for rent and I went to live there with my children. Pedro helped me out. I was having an affair with him, but he paid me every time we were together. Then Pedro told me that I could go live in a room with him if I was willing. I told him I was. But the room he got was worse than the one I had because it had rats. The rats promenaded around and there were mornings when I'd wake up with my feet half chewed up by them.

Erasmo came to call on me every day while I was living with Pedro. Pedro was never in, you see, he was out working, so Erasmo would come every single day to pester me and screw around, insisting that I should go back to him. He said that he'd take me to live somewhere else, out of La Esmeralda, until finally I told him, "You're a real *cabrón,* a man who knows that his woman sleeps with another man and doesn't mind it. I put the horns on you and still you chase after me."

He said, "All right, I'll just have to be a *cabrón* then, because you're the woman I love."

But I answered, "Look, you're wasting your time, you'll get no more of me."

The first woman he took up with was a whore nicknamed Mechón. He said he took up with her to help him forget me. But he said he couldn't enjoy that woman as long as he had me on his mind. So I told him, "Well, the best thing you can do is to go abroad." He started to get ready right away. The day he went to the States he came over to say good-bye.

Erasmo

○

A Whore in the Morning Disgusts Me

THE SEVEN years of my life I spent with Nanda, I would say were not good years. She was affectionate but a man can never know what a woman is up to. If a woman shows love she may only be putting it on, and when she really loves she may hide her feelings. So how can I tell whether Nanda lived with me because she loved me or simply because I kept her well?

While she lived with me one might say that Nanda had the position of an honorable woman, because she did not need to go peddle her goods. At first she kept going to work at the Silver Cup but then I said to her, "If you live with me, stop going to the bar." After that she stayed home and all she did was read romances, eat, sleep and go to the movies. But even so, behind my back, she went and did everything on schedule, as the saying goes, not for money but because she wanted to. When I finally found out—you know, the husband is always the last one to learn about such things—I was all set to kill her, and her kids too, but my friends spoke to me and gave me good advice. If I hadn't broken up with Nanda I would be in jail today.

I didn't want Nanda to go hustling any more, because if I have a woman I don't like to share her with another man. And I don't like to take another man's wife either. This business of lying with one man after another and then coming home to the husband doesn't appeal to me. That's not my way. Like food, see? I don't like to eat anybody's leftovers and I don't like to have anybody come eat from my plate either. A woman who has four or five men in one night is a mess by the time she gets home, all sticky and slobbered over by others. A whore in the morning disgusts me.

I met Nanda at a bar about twenty years ago. At first I paid no attention to her but it seems she fell for me and was always kidding around. The poor thing was all skin and bones then. *Ay, bendito,* a smoked herring was what she looked like. She never earned much as a prostitute but you should have seen her at that time! For one thing, money isn't what she's most interested in, so far as whoring goes. For another, if she was able to make four or five dollars, she used it to buy cigarettes or to gamble at bingo, which she loved. She even liked to shoot craps.

Well, she was hard up, so one night I said, *"O.K.,* do you want to go to bed with me?" and she said yes. I had invited many of those women to sleep with me and the following morning they always went home and I would go to my room on San Francisco Street. I never dreamed that Nanda would keep on with me, but she became my first wife. She lived in my room for several months and then we moved to La Esmeralda.

I don't really know how much I loved Nanda at that time. I do know that I sought her out and was sorry when she had problems. I thought that she would allow herself to be raised up from the mud and become a good wife, willing to stay home and stick to a husband. It seemed to me that having suffered so much she could reform and become a virtuous woman. I have seen it happen. But that wasn't the case with Nanda.

During our first year together we didn't have a single quarrel. I rented a little house in La Esmeralda for fifteen dollars a month and I fixed it up so nicely that my neighbors were jealous. It bothered them that we had a radio and everything, so I had a lot of *trouble.* When I was new there, everybody wanted to fight me and later they were always borrowing from me. The second year, I bought the shack for sixty dollars, twenty dollars down and the rest in ten-dollar installments. I was making good money, so after it was all paid up I laid a concrete floor, added a porch and made other little improvements.

I worked in a bar all night. I got through at five in the morning, and unless I stopped somewhere for a few drinks, I'd get home at seven. I always brought Nanda a breaded cutlet or fried meat and she'd have a meal ready and waiting for me on the table. At that hour she'd still be asleep, and when I went to bed she'd get up. I'd sleep until four in the afternoon, then I'd get up, bathe, dress and leave. It was like being married to a Chinese woman—there wasn't much opportunity to talk or to quarrel.

Nanda is not what you would call a frigid woman. In fact, she down-right enjoys sex, and then with me she had food, drink, clothes and every-thing, so she stuck to me for quite a while and she gained weight. In the beginning she ironed my clothes and did all the housework. We would go to the movies and take trips to Toa Alta and Río Grande. We went out often. That's the way I lived during most of those seven years.

Nanda had never told me she had children until one day a hurricane was announced and she said, "I'm going to see my kids."

"You mean you have children?" I asked.

Anyway, she went and came back with her daughter Soledad. Then she heard that Simplicio was begging on Dock No. 9 and she brought him and the lame girl and finally Felícita too. Felícita didn't stay long because her *papá* came and took her away to Panama. But later Nanda's sister Migdalia lived with us for a while with her children and so did Teté, a cousin of Nanda's. Also, the sister's husband and their daughter Brunilda, and Generoso and Vir-ginia and an aunt, Amparo. All those people lived, ate and drank at my house without contributing one penny to the expenses. I was the one who worked and who paid for everything. But things were cheap then and I had credit at Chavo's store.

Nanda never was a good housekeeper. She'd fix herself up fine, but try to get her to fix up the house! Her kids were just like her that way. You had to be ordering them to wash the dishes every time and that really was a chore. Soledad, the eldest, never wanted to do a lick of work around the house, so her mother had to whip her hard. But Soledad and the rest of those kids never behaved badly to me. If I sent Soledad on an errand she always went will-ingly. But by the time she had been living with us a year you could see clearly what she was going to be in the future. I had dogs and she spent a lot of time with them and, well, several times I found her sucking their little pricks. And she'd do the same thing to her little brother Simplicio. By the time she was eleven or twelve she wanted to have a sweetheart and stay out at all hours on the beach with him. Soledad liked men from the very beginning.

I don't think Nanda did the right thing when Soledad went off with Arturo. If she had been my daughter, I would have made Arturo marry her. But she's no kin of mine, so I kept hands off. It's hard to believe that Soledad was a virgin when Arturo took her, because before that Guito was her sweet-heart and she used to go to the beach with him. But that's the least of it. After all, what's done is done and if a man finds that he has made a mistake, he should put up with it. For myself, I think an experienced woman is far better than a virgin. A woman who knows all about life can be a great help to a man. She can make a nobody into a good man; she can save him from anything, even from perdition itself. But when Arturo took Soledad to live with him, he didn't know what he was getting into.

Nanda's other daughter, Cruz, was only eight or nine when she came to live with us. She was never any problem to me because I went away and when I came back to Puerto Rico she was already married.

Simplicio was something else again, mischievous as they come. More than mischievous! He had everything he needed at home but he would go out begging with his friends. Nanda would tie him up but it did no good. When a child is going to become a hoodlum, he becomes one no matter what anybody does to prevent it. I'm bringing up my two daughters now and I realize that if they are to turn out bad they will, even if I set them up on an altar or lock them up in a convent.

I never had any objection to having all those kids in my house, although in my opinion not one of Nanda's children has a brain in his head. Nanda gave me authority to behave like a father to her kids but I never liked to do that. I hated to be whipped as a child and now that I am a man I hate to whip children. Why, even with my own daughters, if I spank them I feel it more than they do. But they have the furniture all beat up and the lamps broken—they act like savages, so I have to hit them at times.

Nanda let her kids shift for themselves. She spanked them a lot but in spite of that, well, they say that the more you beat a child, the less he respects you. There's no closeness at all in Nanda's family. When Nanda and Soledad quarrel they go around saying nasty things about each other. It's the same with Felícita and Cruz. Then, after they have been really vile to each other, they'll make up as if nothing had happened and then they'll quarrel again. They go on like that all the time. That's the kind of life and environment they've made for themselves.

In the Ríos family, each person seems to exist for himself alone. They want the rest of humanity to give and give to them so they can just take it all, enjoy it, and not give even a peanut in return. If a person isn't willing to give something for nothing they think he's bad. That's the way those people see life. Now, me, I seek out my relatives, although they have never done the same for me, and I give them money when I can afford to. I sent all of them money from New York. But the Ríos'? Oh, no. It's good I managed to get rid of them. True, the woman I have now is Nanda's cousin Adela, but she's the best one in all the family.

Nanda and I never quarreled about her kids, not once. My first big quarrel with her came after we had been married four years. I was told she was in love with a boy named Alvaro. He worked on a schooner and stole on the side. So one night I came home from work unexpectedly and caught them together. I went right up to him and told him, "Look, you'd better get out of here before I lose my temper." He left but he kept chasing her even after that. We almost had a gun battle because he came to my house at midnight to challenge me.

For six years I supported Nanda and kept her out of the life. Then, after

I threw a big party which cost me about one hundred dollars—it was a birthday party, a baptismal feast and a Mother's Day celebration all in one—and after I had given Nanda a sixty-dollar Zenith radio, I caught her out dancing with a boy named Pedro. We had a big fight and I think I slapped her in the face. She flew at me like a lioness and Simplicio ran off and told a cop I was killing his *mamá*.

When the cop came I told him, "All right, so I slapped my wife. I'm in my own house and you've no right to interfere. Besides, you don't know why I hit her in the first place." The cop said I had to go to the police station. "I'm willing to go to the end of the earth," said I. "Just wait until I get my clothes on." Nanda, to get even with me, took Soledad along, telling her to say that I had gotten into her bed naked and tried to do her damage. Soledad was a minor, so that story could really do me a lot of harm.

In the police station the cops were against me to begin with. But when I told my story, the sergeant sided with me and refused to charge me, so the marshal went and charged me on his own. They sent me to jail and I had to spend seven days in the cooler.

The week I was there, Nanda visited me every single day and brought me cigarettes. At the end of that time she went to the judge and withdrew the charges because she knew full well she had lied. So after that I was a free man again.

You know that when a man has a stepdaughter who is attractive there's always something between them, even if it's only the intention in the man's mind. But in my case it wasn't so. What Nanda and Soledad said was plain slander. But I have never borne Soledad a grudge for that, nor she me.

After our quarrel Nanda and I broke up and were separated for about two months. I stayed at the hotel and lived well during that time. Nanda sometimes slept at Pedro's house, other times she spent nights in hotels. She and Pedro were not actually living together yet, they were having an affair behind my back. He was only a young boy then and he couldn't keep her as I kept her, so she wrote me notes asking me to send her food, and I did. Then one day I grabbed her and said, "Damn it all, I didn't kick you out, you walked out on me. The whole thing was your fault, so come back now, will you?" We lived together one more year, the seventh.

We lived as before, going out frequently to the movies and so on. But it seems women get bored living the same old way with the same old husband. They like to have one man after another and go drinking with them and all that. I can't explain Nanda but I do know she has never in her life been capable of living with one man *steady*. She knows how to satisfy a man in bed, but as a wife she has nothing further to give. It seems to me that deep inside she must bear a grudge against somebody. Now, take Adela. She bears a grudge against her stepfather who, according to her, once even tried to shoot her. In Nanda's case, I don't know if she ever had a stepfather or whether she hated men or was simply a neurotic woman. But whatever it was, I couldn't put up with it. I decided to go to New York.

About two weeks before I left Puerto Rico, Nanda stood in front of my house and threw stones at it. I had taken a girl called Mechón to spend the night there and someone must have told Nanda. She challenged Mechón to fight the following morning. But I went to Nanda and said, "Damn it, this isn't your house any more. What makes you think you have the right to stone it? Take the bed and everything else in the place. I'm going to sell it." I gave her everything I had, the radio and all. Then, after I sold the house, Nanda went around telling everybody that I hadn't given her a cent. Well, I didn't. Why should I have? It was my house, not hers, and she and I had never married. She never contributed anything. All she brought me was that bunch of kids to support. And support them I did, for seven long years.

It seems to me that Nanda is like many women who live in La Esmeralda, but in a way she is different because she has real humanitarian feelings, except when she drinks too much or when she's fed up with the husband she has. Then she does things that force him to leave her. She can never stay permanently with one man, not Nanda. After two or three years, she's out hunting for a new one.

I was not a demanding husband as far as sex goes. It's the same way with my present wife; sometimes months go by without our having intercourse. I was younger when I lived with Nanda, of course, but I drank a lot and didn't eat much and when I got home drunk I just wasn't interested. Nanda never made any demands on me that way either. Well, it did happen sometimes that she'd be hot when I got home but when I'm tired, sex isn't for me. I'd just tell her, "No, not tonight. Forget it." Why should I go to all that trouble when I was tired to begin with?

What I take pride in is the fact that whenever I have lived with a woman everyone says, "*Coño*, that woman has luck, living with that man. She's well off and doesn't have to work." No woman of mine has ever had to go begging. I dress them well, give them everything. I liked having a nice home but I never felt any desire to marry. When I was young I wanted to enjoy my youth, to see the world, to have new experiences, to make up for what I had suffered as a child. Married, I couldn't have done any of that.

I have lived through many sad days. I'd be doing well for a couple of years and then everything would go wrong. Well, not really everything— clothes I've always had but there have been times when I didn't have one lousy nickel in my pocket.

When I was only two, I lost both my father and mother. I don't know what *mamá* died of, nobody ever told me. I only know that she was blond and pretty. I don't even know if my parents ever married. I use my mother's surname instead of my father's, because that's what everybody has always called me.

My *papá* died in the hospital and that is all I was ever told about his death. After that I was adopted by my uncle Marcos Acosta, the husband of my *mamá*'s sister and father of my cousin Arturo. He kept me for a time, so I consider that he's the one who brought me up and is my only close relative.

When my parents died there were three of us orphans. The youngest, a boy, died while still a child. I had a sister who was turned over to a certain Candó Caballero to be brought up. He kept her until she was twelve and he did his damage to her. Afterward she came to San Juan and fell in love with a guy there. He was a cheat and was involved in playing the races. I don't know much about it except that it seems she died from a beating he gave her. She was sixteen at the time. They came to take me to see her when she was dying, and once again after she was dead. In all I saw her about three times. I was fond of her, of course, because she was my sister, but we were waifs, both of us, and there was nothing I could do for her. I was a hanger-on too and couldn't do a thing for myself, either. I did tell the man whose blows killed her, "You just wait. Some day I'll be a grown man." But when I was sixteen he was shot and killed at Stop 21.

Well, I was alone in the world and I had to make my own way. I'd find odd jobs or go begging. I didn't like to beg. I'll do any kind of work rather than beg. My wife says I'm proud but I'm not really, it's just that I have never liked what comes easy. I like things to be difficult, that way I know what it costs to get it and I appreciate what I have. If I should take the easy way out and ask for a dollar here and a dollar there, I'd never know the real worth of money. It would be easy come, easy go. But I don't let money slip through my fingers, because I have gone through so much to get it. I don't risk my money at gambling. I neither waste it nor give it away as so many do. That's why people around here don't like me much—because I don't go paying for anybody's drinks. I just tell anyone who disapproves of me, "If I'm stingy with my money, I have a right to be—after all, it *is* mine. And if you think I'm a bad guy, that's all right too."

My uncle was unable to send me to school because he had four children of his own, and anyway, it was difficult to do so, living in the country as he did. Besides, I was nothing but an orphan he had taken into his house. He never did treat me like one of his own. And he beat me often. Once my uncle really whaled the daylights out of us, with a rope, so Arturo and I ran away to an aunt's house. But she beat me with a rope too, without my having done anything to deserve it. Arturo and I ran off to a circus but someone saw us and told our aunt.

It was then that they decided to give me away to someone else. They took me to Toa Alta and gave me to a good woman, but I had to work hard for my keep. I milked the cows, cleaned the whole place and ran lots of errands. They gave me plenty of food, but it was only rice and beans and boiled vegetables. Now whenever I can afford to eat what I like, I buy meat.

It hurt me to realize that I was a thing to be passed from hand to hand and tossed away like a scrap of paper. If I were to recount the times I went to bed hungry, or the times I slept in alleys and on the bare ground in the country, I could talk forever. So as far as schooling is concerned, I don't have any. I have learned to read a little and to do sums. Writing I don't know at all. God didn't give me an education but he had to give me something, so I learned how to make a living. Nobody taught me anything, I learned what I know by watching others. That's the way I learned to be a carpenter, a plumber and an electrician. I just look and practice. Usually you learn more from practice than theory.

But I never felt any resentment against my uncle, because all he had was the miserable wages farm laborers got at that time. It simply wasn't enough to support his children and me too. Maybe he thought I would have a better chance with the people to whom he gave me, although it sure didn't turn out that way.

I worked for the woman in Toa Alta for about three years and then went to work for her son, Pedrito Sánchez, in his rooming house in San Juan. I was only about ten years old and Pedrito's brother Chavo began to invite me to drink *pitorro*.* From the time I was a child I was used to making beer and raw rum, but I had never drunk it. When I did, I got so sick I nearly died. At first I couldn't get down the beer unless it was heavily sugared, but little by little I learned.

Pedro sold the rooming house and then I had no job or anything. I rented a tiny room to live in and set myself up in a little business of my own, selling grapefruit. I was going on eleven.

Then I got swellings all over my body, especially my hands, blisters which got infected and full of pus. I couldn't get my feet into shoes. Instead I wore sandals with wooden soles and rubber straps. I had to lean on two sticks when I walked. Every time I got into the shower and saw myself all swollen and full of festering sores I'd say to myself, "I'm sure to die of this and someone is bound to take the nickels I earned selling grapefruit."

I went to Isla Verde to stay with a friend of mine who ran a bathing beach. I sold coconuts there and even made charcoal. When I got completely over my swelling, I went back to San Juan to work in Pedrito's new bar in the Silver Cup Club. I was a little man already.

I lived a long time among women in the life but I wasn't interested in them. It is not that I have anything against women in the life. They are to be pitied, putting up with blows and worse, and having to get under a man to earn a few dollars. They do it because God, or Fate, didn't give them any

* Raw rum.

other way to earn a living. There's no denying they do terrible things and feel no shame, they dress provocatively and sleep with any man that asks them. They live an evil life but far be it from me to say they are evil women. All they're doing is earning their living. Think of all the sleepless nights they have in order to earn money! The really bad woman is the one who has a husband who supports her and feeds her well and yet she goes with another man, not for money but out of sheer viciousness.

At fifteen I still had never had a woman. Being young, with so many women around, some of them were bound to take a fancy to me. One day this woman went up to the hotel and told a waiter there, "Go get Erasmo at the bar and tell him to come up here." When I went to her room, she padlocked the door and kept me there for three days. She was a big blonde from Juncos. I was really scared of that kind of woman because she cut up people and all that. That affair with her lasted about three months. Afterward I would go to bed with one or another of them from time to time. But I have never really liked that sort of thing.

I was still very young when I caught the "white flower," that illness men get when they use a women while she has her period. But I think I got it because I stayed at the beach too much. Anyway, a white fluid kept coming out of my penis and when I urinated I would find large clots of blood in the chamber pot. A man told me to cure it with chickpea water but what finally cured me were injections of salvarsan and bismuth. Later I had syphilis too. I had it when I was called up by the Army, and there they gave me penicillin injections every day until I was cured. I wasn't inducted into the Army anyway, not because of the illness but because I'm knock-kneed. After that I was scared of catching a disease, so I was cautious about the women I took up with. If I saw they had cuts or scars I gave them a wide berth.

I knew most whores had a pimp for whom they bought shirts and things with the money they got from their customers. I didn't like to live off those women, because when they had a fight the whore would scream at her pimp, "Those clothes you have on were bought by me." She'd yell that right out in the street, no matter who could hear. Or she would cut up his clothes if she got mad. Knowing that, I never accepted a gift from the women at the bar and I was never a pimp. I just didn't like the idea.

I preferred to work for my living. But I had a lot of accidents in my work, mostly when I was young, before I met Nanda. When I was loading trucks at fifteen, someone let a heavy sack fall on me and it injured my neck. I couldn't straighten up and I didn't even have anyone to give me massages. I couldn't work for some time after that. Later, when I was a house painter, I had a bad fall and I had to walk with crutches for three months.

I received a check from the State Insurance Fund with a letter saying if I had worked during that time, would I please return it. My employer sent me a check for one dollar, so I tore it up. Why, I was paying three dollars a week just for my room rent! He kept sending me a dollar every so often, but I depended on Pedro Sánchez for my meals while I couldn't work. Pedro was a good man and gave me a helping hand. The only other help I got was from my landlord, who let me owe him the rent. Later I was in a truck accident and I've had trouble with my leg ever since. I was really badly hurt and was in the District Hospital. That time Arturo made a vow for my recovery.

I went to New York without knowing a soul there. It was a cold, foggy day and all I had besides the clothes in my suitcase was sixty dollars. But even so, I said to myself, "I'll never go back to Puerto Rico." The first thing I did was go drinking in El Barrio,* where the *hispanos* lived, because I wanted to get in with the toughs. I figured that if I stayed in New York I could be killed at any moment unless I made myself known to them. Also, I was very much afraid of the Negroes.

I lived by myself in New York for eleven years, always in furnished rooms. I worked as a cook, as a polisher, stuffing dolls in a toy factory, as a longshoremen, a house painter. I worked hard and I have always tried to earn just a little bit more each time. Of course, one must be content with what one has, because for all I know I may be even worse off in the future. Still, I don't think I'll fall any lower, at least not until I have to fall into a hole in the earth.

Getting a job in New York is very different from getting one in Puerto Rico. In Puerto Rico when you apply, they ask a lot of questions about yourself and your family, how much schooling you've had and where you come from. In New York all they ask is, "Do you know English?" If you know a little, you're hired. They pay you while you're learning the job and they give you two months, until you are able to do it on your own. In Puerto Rico nobody gives you such a chance. If you don't know your job in a week, you're out. That's why things here in my country are going from bad to worse.

To my mind, I think Puerto Rico would be better off as a state because then the poor people would have the same rights and privileges as everybody else. I learned a lot living in the States. I learned what a state is and I found out about unemployment insurance and social security and what life is like. If you work six months and earn over five hundred dollars in that time, you can collect forty dollars a month for nine months or one full year. In Puerto Rico, even if you earn eighty dollars a week on your job, to collect unemployment insurance you have to go to ten or fifteen places, and get ten or fifteen witnesses and your employers and take them to the insurance office, and then all you get is fifteen or sixteen dollars for four months. After that, nothing.

* Spanish Harlem.

Puerto Rico has grown a great deal but the situation hasn't changed. The government builds roads and more roads and the poor live as they always did. I have seen no change at all in the past twenty years. Twenty years ago La Esmeralda was no different, or rather, it was better, because more ships came to San Juan and the longshoremen were able to live better. Now the government allows those trailer-truck boats to come and twenty men's work can be done by two or three. That's the kind of thing that is killing the working class. They don't get enough wages and everything is so terribly expensive. A room you could once rent for two or three dollars now costs twenty-five or thirty. And that's the way with everything else. There's the same poverty as always, and more crime. The only way we can progress is to become a state of the Union.

The way it is now, as a commonwealth, what is Puerto Rico anyway? Suppose the United States should decide to say, "All right, we will send no more aid to Puerto Rico." Wouldn't we be worse off even than Santo Domingo then? We would. The rice grown here and the food reserves on the island wouldn't last four months. After that we'd all be starving and anyone who had a dollar would have to go around armed with a machine gun to keep from being robbed.

As for independence, it would never work out for Puerto Rico. Maybe there was a time when it would have, but not now. You just have to look and see the development in other countries during the past years. There's nothing but war. That's what's happening in Santo Domingo, Venezuela, Cuba, in Argentina after Perón left. When Trujillo was in power in Santo Domingo, people had to respect him but they had plenty to eat. Now the country has had three or four different governments since he died, and everything is going from bad to worse. If Puerto Ricans were granted independence the same thing would happen. We would have a President, and maybe his brother or this or that relative would own the government and they would hire the ones who know a lot, so then the people of Puerto Rico would be automatically dominated by two or three hundred persons. Once that happened, you wouldn't be able to say, "This man is bad," because they would clap you in jail or stand you up against a wall and shoot you. In the United States people say anything they want to, because in a democracy you can do and undo as you please. But, of course, that leads to hooliganism because everyone can do what he wants to.

Muñoz Marín, the governor, hasn't brought Puerto Rico anything, because all that is American money. Felisa Rincón, the mayoress, has done nothing. What's the good of that Communal Center she has here in La Esmeralda? What goes on there is a lot of hooliganism, young girls falling in love and learning all sorts of bad things. Why don't they set up washing machines and sewing machines and teach them to use them, instead of putting in a man who does nothing but paw over all those little girls. They pay that man over a hundred dollars a month for not doing anything, instead of giving that money to the poor.

I have watched the developments here and I find Ferré of the Republican Statehood Party the best political leader we have today. As to Muñoz Marín, I know his origins, where he came from, what he did when he started out. I knew him personally too and got to know what he was like. He, whose father was a "Liberal" and the one who got U.S. citizenship for Puerto Ricans, do you know what he did? Well, the first party Muñoz Marín joined was the Socialist, that's what they call Communism, see, and he went to the docks with their leader Santiago Iglesias. I was just a kid of fifteen then, but I remember. Muñoz Marín wanted to give the orders but Santiago Iglesias said nothing doing, *he* was the boss. So then Muñoz went and joined the Liberal Party. But as the Liberal Party did nothing he went up to the States, to a foster sister he has there. Well, when Roosevelt was in power, Mrs. Roosevelt ordered Muñoz Marín to go and make the Popular Party campaign. That's where he got his start. At that time he had an old beat-up Ford that didn't even have a running board. He used to buy a nickel's worth of cigarettes and a half of Palo Viejo rum, and he and all the big people spoke at public meetings. They were the ones who built up the Popular Party.

The trouble is, though, that Puerto Ricans are stupid. There are people in Puerto Rico who don't even know whom they are voting for. They cast their vote, shout "Long live the *Pava!*" * And then, to get a free pound of rice from City Hall they have to wait in line six months. So how can one be in favor of those people? Now my own political theory is this: If I don't work I don't eat. I don't cast my vote for anybody. When anybody asks me, "Which is your party?" I say, "I don't belong to any, because no matter who is in power, if I don't work I don't eat."

In 1959 I went to Puerto Rico on a visit to see my uncle Marcos because I have always been grateful to him. He didn't care for me, I know, but at least I'm alive, thanks to him. It was on that trip that I met Adela, who is now my woman. She lived in La Esmeralda with her sister Teté, and one day when I was pretty high, I went to see her. I told her, "Look, my child, I like you a lot." She let it pass and tried to talk about something else, but I insisted. "Don't try to change the subject. I am proposing to you." After that I took her to meet my uncle.

Adela's mother, Sofía, is dead but her *papá,* Servando, is living in Río

* The *pava* is a broad-brimmed straw hat once typical of the Puerto Rican *jíbaro,* or peasant. It appears as part of the insignia on the flag of the Popular Party. The flag is white with an image in red silhouette of the head of a *jíbaro* wearing a *pava.*

Grande. I don't know whether Sofía was his first wife or not because I never ask Adela such intimate questions. I respect her privacy.

Adela is different from Nanda. Adela has done a great deal for me. In the first place, she saw to it that I ate properly. She took good care of my clothing too, yet she asked for nothing in exchange. All she got were her meals and a place to sleep. I never took her out. But Adela has two faults. She's jealous and she likes to rule the roost. Nanda was not domineering, but Adela is if I let her. But when all her relatives were against me and told her a million things to keep her from living with me, she went right ahead. They went so far as to say I was a pimp. I, who was really scared as hell of whores! The truth is, I have been very good to her. When I first met her she was real skinny and she looked worn out. Now she's gained weight and looks like a young woman of twenty-five.

Adela is a medium and has had nerve illness and all that. How could it be otherwise, with her having to bring up all her brothers and sisters? She worked for an American woman who told her, "If you want to do something for yourself you'll have to set aside your family and live your own life." She learned the trade of *beautician* but never made a dollar because her relatives would come to her for free haircuts.

To top it all, her aunt Amparo sold the little house where Adela lived. It had belonged to Clotilde, Adela's grandmother. That lady, Amparo, came from New York to get Nanda's signature for the sale while Nanda and I were still together. Amparo didn't know who I was, but she ate at our place and stayed overnight. I advised Nanda not to sign, but she did. Well, it was none of my business, I admit, and you know that money is king. Amparo gave Nanda fifteen dollars from the sale, Adela got fifty, and the rest ten apiece. For the dough they all signed in a hurry. Amparo kept the larger part of the money and went back, leaving Adela out in the street, homeless. She had to take her three children and move to another place where she had to pay rent. Adela had three other children, but those kids were raised by Americans in the United States.

Adela went with me to New York. She got a job there with no trouble because she knows some English. If she had followed my advice she would know even more because I kept telling her, "Instead of wasting your time reading love stories and comic books, why don't you get yourself a Spanish-English dictionary and learn English? Or a history book? Something that might be useful to you when you least expect it." Well, she paid no attention to me then but now she says she plans to go to night school.

Adela is still in New York with our two little girls. I came back to Puerto Rico because the cold was bad for my leg. I'll stay until my unemployment checks stop coming, then, God willing, I'll go to New York where my woman is working and I'll marry her. That way my daughters will benefit from my social security insurance if I should die. Here in Puerto Rico they would get only a miserable pittance. I have already sent Adela the wedding rings.

When I saw Nanda again she was living with a man named Héctor. She was drinking a lot then. Had I done as she wished, I would have gone back to live with her. But I told her, "No, my child, I came here to have a good time and I'll be going back shortly. I bought a round-trip ticket."

Even if I hadn't met Adela I would never have gone back to Nanda. Oh, no! My life with her was all *trouble*. Nanda is *trouble*, not only for me but for any man.

· Fernanda

———

Life with
Pedro and Héctor

———

I WAS STILL hustling because Pedro hadn't yet told me he wanted me to give it up. Later he said he wanted us to live together honorably and he kept asking me to marry him. I always answered, "Well, if you're willing to marry me, then let's get married." He took all the necessary steps and got all the papers and everything. So I wasn't a whore for long.

The day of the wedding I bought a green dress and matching green shoes. Pedro bought himself a pair of pants and I bought him a shirt. He didn't dress formally for the wedding, you see. We went to the judge at the District Court on Cristo Street and we got married. I had a ring and everything. I was embarrassed because he was so young and I was about twenty-five or twenty-six.* Gertrudis, a friend of mine who is in New York now, was my witness. The judge himself was the other witness because we hadn't asked anybody.

I was very happy about being married. I'd never been married before, see, and I felt like a great lady. But I have never used Pedro's surname. I didn't want to. I said to myself, "Hell, why should I give up my father's and

* Actually, Fernanda was about thirty-three.

mother's names? Not me!" I'm really supposed to be called Fernanda Fuentes de Cortés. But I won't have it. I'll keep on being Fernanda Fuentes Hernández. I'm a married woman, but I won't drop my mother's name and take my husband's instead. The very thought of doing that makes me unhappy. I said, "If I do that, it means my mother has no value." It makes me so sad I want to cry.

After the wedding we met a friend of ours and he said, "Hey, Pedro, where were you?" And Pedro said, "I just got married." So the friend said, "Then we must celebrate the wedding," and he took us to drink and have a good time. He paid for the drinks and everything. All up and down La Esmeralda everybody was very happy about my getting married. Everybody there likes me. After the party we went home to bed to have a good time, for our honeymoon, see? *Ave María!* That night was phenomenal! He screwed me about ten times. We kept it up until it was nearly light. Why, we hardly got any sleep at all. We were both drunk, so you can imagine. It was as if it had been my first night, as if I'd been a virgin.

After I gave up whoring I began to work as a cook with a family in El Condado. I earned forty dollars a month, just for cooking. But I couldn't go out anywhere because I was on the job until nine o'clock at night and I didn't have the day off on Sunday. The lady of the house said I couldn't have any Sundays off and that if I did, she would cut my wages. So I told her, "Keep the wages, then. I'm getting out of here." And I did.

Then I got a job with another lady, at Stop 19. She was so stingy that if I lost a penny she wanted to deduct it from my pay. One lousy penny! She said that a penny was real money. I told her, "Keep your real money then. I'm quitting." I lasted only a month on that job.

After that I worked in so many places I don't even remember them all. Once I worked in a *laundry*. I was paid three cents apiece for washing dresses and men's shirts, and two cents apiece for undershorts. Some weeks I earned ten dollars, other weeks I earned twelve. Then I worked as a laundress at the Silver Cup Night Club where I'd practiced the profession before. They paid me twelve dollars a week. I asked for a raise but they wouldn't give me one, so I left that job too. After that I went to work at *doña* Ofelia's house. At that time she paid me twenty-five dollars a month. *Doña* Ofelia has been the best of all to me. She was rich but kind. Most rich people look down on the poor and don't help them at all.

Well, I lived with Pedro for four or five years. I liked his ways a lot because he never treated me like a whore. He treated me with great affection, as if I were a lady. And I will always be grateful to him for taking me out of the whoring profession because that was a very sad time in my life.

Pedro was good in every way, I don't deny it. He behaved like a son to my *papá,* and *papá* was crazy about him. When my cousin came to tell me my father had thrombosis and was in the hospital, we were watching a TV program at home. Pedro had a business selling breaded cutlets, and he left everything to go get my *papá* and bring him home where we could take care of him. Pedro let him have a bed all to himself and he kept the refrigerator filled with all sorts of nourishing food for *papá*—eggnog, malt beer,* grape juice, pigeons—the best of everything. We had a refrigerator, a good stove, a glassed-in china cabinet and a TV set, the first I ever owned. Pedro bought it all on credit.

While my father lived with us, I took good care of him. I wanted to show him that in me he had a daughter, even though he had never been a good father. In my house nothing was too good for him, although he never gave me anything. If he gave me four, five or six dollars every now and then, I'd take the money and put it away, because when he was broke I'd have to give it back to him. Then, as soon as he got well he went to Río Grande, to his mother's house. But he would come to see us often because he was so fond of Pedro.

All my father's relatives liked Pedro, and so we sometimes went to my grandmother's house to see them and my *papá*. Whenever I went, that old woman would beg me for things. "Your father needs this, your father needs that. Why don't you bring me a nickel's worth of chewing tobacco when you come?" She scolded and yelled at me but I just kept quiet.

My father's sister, Aunt Aurora, also lived in my grandmother's house, but I didn't get along well with her. She was an *evangelísta* and was very strict. Once when I was there alone, my aunt Aurora put up a sign which said "No Smoking." I smoked a lot and paid no more attention than if she hadn't been there. I drank a lot at that time too. "Look," she said, "when people who belong to the Religion come here, at least don't smoke or drink in front of them." She kept talking and I went outside. Then she said something, I don't remember what, and I burst out, "Go to hell, all of you." I was standing at the foot of the stairs when I said it, in case I had to get away in a hurry.

"Ah," she said, "just wait until your father comes. I'm going to tell him and then he'll beat you."

"Tell him," I yelled. "I'm leaving right now, so give me your blessing if you like. I'm going to hell, to get together with my own kind."

My father didn't know I was in the life. At least I never told him and he never saw me at it. Oh, he must have known but he never said one word to me about it. But my grandmother Fernanda used to say to me, "It's your mother's fault that you are the way you are. Because if she hadn't taken you away you would still be here with me. Now you're nothing but a tramp."

I'd get right back at her. "Tramp or not, I'm better than the whole bunch of you."

May God forgive me, but I don't like to go to Río Grande. They spied on me there, my *papá*, my aunt, my uncle, and they pestered me. They felt I

* A sweet, nutritious, nonalcoholic beverage.

snubbed them because I hardly ate there and I never stayed to sleep. One of my aunts said to me, "Fernanda, your visits here are shorter than a doctor's call. You practically have to be held here by force."

I would stay one or two days at Migdalia's house in Mameyes and then I would take a car that passed right through Río Grande without stopping. After I broke up with Pedro I almost never went to see my father's family.

Pedro was a good husband but he had one bad fault. He gambled all his money away, and I said to myself, "Ugh, that's one thing I won't put up with." It was fight, fight, day in and day out, until I told him I couldn't go on living with him any longer because of that. Besides, he didn't love my children, so how could I love him? When Soledad came from the country and slept at our house, he quarreled about that. He didn't want me to give my children anything. He didn't want my daughters to eat at my house. And when my daughter Felícita had the twins, he didn't even want her to give birth at home with me.

Felícita had fought with her husband Ángel in Culebra* and she came home to me. You know how girls are, they quarrel with their husband and right off they want to go home to Mother, no other place will do. She was pregnant then and she appeared at the house with two black eyes. She came to La Esmeralda with the intention of giving birth at my house, and she passed by the house of *doña* Yolanda, a neighbor who has a bar. Pedro was there. When he saw Felícita he said, "Look! Here's that girl coming to stay with us. Beginning tomorrow I'm going to throw away all the food in the house and not buy any more. Let them eat shit! I don't have to support a married stepdaughter. Let her husband support her." Then Pedro began to shoot craps.

I found out what Pedro had said, and when he came home I started right in quarreling. I told him, "Look here, my daughter just arrived and you said that you were going to throw away the food. You shouldn't say those things because you know I have a duty to my daughters."

Then Pedro said to me, "If she has a home with her husband, that's where she should stay."

"Well, if she came to me, maybe she plans to have her baby here."

"Oh? And where is she going to sleep?" We had a folding cot and a bed, one was for us and the other for my son, Simplicio, and his little sister Cruz.

"She can sleep in the big bed. You and I can use the small one."

"Oh, no, she's not. Not in that bed." When he said that, I was overcome by such sadness I began to cry. I didn't say a word to him and he went away. And Felícita stayed with me only one day. She came on Sunday and left on Monday. After that I really had it out with Pedro.

I said to him, "I'm going to tell you something, either you leave this

* A small island off the east coast of Puerto Rico.

house or I'll put the horns on you. It's up to you to decide if you want to be known as a *cabrón*." I said, "You'll have horns like an old he-goat and everyone will know about it. I don't care if you take me to court and accuse me of adultery. I'll bring witnesses and I know exactly what to tell the judge."

He answered, "I'm not leaving."

A few days later Soledad, my eldest daughter, had labor pains. She was pregnant with her first child, Quique. I told my husband—we hadn't made up but we were talking to each other again—"Pedro, Soledad is in labor."

He answered, "Tell her to go fuck herself."

So I told him, "You're the one who's going to be all fucked up."

Then, as Soledad was feeling so sick, I went to Papo's bar for help. Papo borrowed a friend's car right away and took us to the Municipal Hospital. Soledad was in labor, so I stayed with her all night. She had labor pains for three whole days and three nights. Arturo, her husband, stayed there too, to take care of her. But Pedro began to fight and fight and fight because he didn't want me to go. Finally Soledad had the baby and I would take food over to her every day and do whatever had to be done.

Pedro kept on pestering me and shooting craps and quarreling. The trouble with him was that he let himself be influenced by a friend of his. This friend would say to him, "Don't let any woman give you orders. When Nanda starts screwing around, take a stick to her." Pedro thought he could really go ahead and do it, but I let him know that he couldn't. When he tried to hit me, I hit him first or I would cut him up. I cut him up lots of times. He went from bad to worse until he became a drug addict, and I wasn't going to stand for that. You can imagine how I felt when he came home with his friends and asked me to go into the bedroom so they could inject themselves with drugs right there in the living room.

Well, a short time after Soledad gave birth, at the beginning of the elections, I went to a dance at Papo's place. That was Saturday, so Pedro was at his crap game. It got so that the minute he was paid he would go find a crap game. He played away the rent money and the money for the installment payments on the furniture. I tell you, he had become a crap hooligan. I said to Papo then, "This is my last day with that son of a great whore."

I started drinking and dancing with a tall Negro called Benjamín. Then Pedro came in and he snatched the beer from my hand. Benjamín stopped him short. "She was drinking that beer. Now I'll buy her another to see if you dare break that one."

Later I said to Benjamín, "You're a real he-man, a *macho*."

He tells me, "Of course I'm a *macho*."

"Then take me to bed. I'm going to sleep with you tonight." And that night I slept with him, even though I was still living with Pedro. Pedro was looking for me all over the place like a madman, and I was in bed with another man!

Next day I showed up at home and Pedro says to me, "Where were you last night?"

I said, "Nowhere. Putting the horns on you."

"Oh, you were? Now I'll have you—"

"All right, have me arrested." But he didn't do a thing. On December 1, 1956, we broke up.

I went on living with Benjamín. He was a boy from La Esmeralda who had lived in New York a long time. He had been in Puerto Rico only a few days when I met him. He had no one, he was alone in the world. At that time I lived in a little room in Papo's house. When I slept with Benjamín, we went to a hotel in Fortaleza Street. Cruz was in the country near Toa Alta, in Soledad's house, and Simplicio was with my cousin Adela. Felícita was in Culebra with her husband.

Benjamín wanted to set me up in a room of my own and everything. He offered to pay a month's rent in advance so I could get a room. But I told him, "No, don't do it. I'm only doing this in revenge." I didn't love him or feel anything for him. Nothing at all. It was a passing thing. Soon after, he went back to New York. He wrote to me but I never answered.

The night Benjamín left, I cut up Pedro. I remember it as if it had just happened. It was December 8, and I was at Papo's bar. Pedro was there too, and he was drunk. He asked me to dance. I refused, so he punched me. When he did that, I cut his neck. I just grabbed a little knife Papo had for sharpening the spurs of fighting cocks and I slashed Pedro's neck. He was taken to the hospital. The wound was serious.

The police came after me but I didn't give myself up that night. I stayed in Papo's house, and when he saw the police coming he said, "Run and hide, here they are." I hid upstairs and Papo locked me in, but the next day, Sunday, I went to give myself up to the police. Pedro had filed charges against me and the cops were already after me. I said, "Well, Papo, I'm going to give myself up because if I go running away from the police it will be worse for me in the end." So Papo went with me and on the way to the police station we met Gilberto, the cop who had been sent after me. Papo turned me over to him. I had always gotten on well with Gilberto. I'm polite to the cops and never swear at them or anything. So Gilberto said to me, "You wounded that man with a knife that's used to sharpen cocks' spurs, didn't you?"

I answered, "I sure did."

He told me, "Then I'll give you some good advice. Don't say you used a knife. Tell the judge you cut him with the ass-end of a bottle so they won't charge you with carrying a weapon."

We went to Stop 8, where the court was at that time.

I passed that day in jail very well. I met a lot of my friends there, prostitutes and all that. I told them my story and we started talking and joking, because that's the way you amuse yourself in jail. There's always something going on there. Why, look, they sing all the time. One jail song they sing goes:

Tick-tock clock	*Bota, bota, relojito*
Tick away the time.	*tus horas completas.*
I'm in for twenty years,	*Que lo mío son veinte años,*
Not for all my life.	*que no cadena perpetua.*

And there's another jail song that goes:

Through the bars of the jail	*Por las rejas de la cárcel*
Don't come to look at me.	*no me vengas a mirar.*
If you can't ease my sorrow,	*Ya que no me quitas pena*
Why can't you let me be?	*no me la vengas a dar.*

The judge set bail at one thousand dollars. Papo paid the twenty-dollar fee to have the bond posted and I was out by Monday night. For a while I slept at Papo's house and helped him out. I brought money to his business because I danced with the men and attracted customers to his bar. And if I had to go out with a customer I paid Papo for the bed. I hardly earned anything for myself because Papo was the one who owned the business. But while I lived there I didn't work in any other place.

I stayed in La Esmeralda. I rented a room for five dollars a month, and Simplicio came back from Adela's house to live with me. I kept on doing business at Papo's. That's where I met Héctor. I had really known him for years, but he had been living with Cecilia and a number of other women all that time. Well, I was in the life again, drinking and playing around and sleeping with any man who paid me, so Héctor invited me to go to bed with him. I said no and no for about a month. Then one day I accepted, I don't know why. After that he came for me every day after work and we'd go together to a hotel or to the room where he lived. That room was as dark and airless as a little mine. But after all, he paid me every time we were together.

We didn't keep this up more than a month because we started living together. He said to me, "I'm in love with you. I don't know if you love me, but I don't like this business of going to hotels to be together. It's better to have a little room." His room was tiny, but anyway, it was his own. I told him, "Let's do it then. I'll keep on paying rent for this room so Simplicio can keep it and I'll go to sleep with you in your room." And that's just what we did.

Héctor worked on the docks. When he was away at work I'd slip out and go dancing, but I never went with any other man during that time. I like to dance boleros, guarachas, mazurkas, and I like the old-fashioned songs, not the modern ones. So as soon as Héctor left, about two o'clock in the afternoon, I'd go to Papo's bar to dance and drink and have a good time. But I didn't do anything wrong. Héctor found out about it and would tell me, "Look, don't go dancing at Papo's place." I'd say, "No, I won't dance," but no sooner was he on his way to work than I was on my way to dance. We had quarrels about that.

I went to trial on February 10 for cutting up Pedro. I didn't have a lawyer, so the court appointed one to defend me. Pedro testified that I had cut him up. The judge found me guilty and fined me twenty-five dollars for assault and battery. Héctor paid the fine.

My father went to the trial, being so fond of Pedro and all. My father had never been to court before and it was the first time a relative of his was in trouble. He never should have gone, because it made him sick. It really killed him. First he lost his hearing, then he got an attack of that thrombosis again.

As soon as the trial was over, I went straight to the Río Grande hospital because my father was very ill. I spent the whole night sitting up with him. He was dying, and in his agony he gasped as if he wanted to speak. I have always thought he was asking for Pedro. My *papá* was really fond of that boy.

My father died the next day. His wake was held at my uncle's house because they didn't dare do it where his mother was living. My grandmother Fernanda was one hundred and six years old, and she didn't know my father was dead. She thought he was staying with me. The doctor had said that if we told her that her son was dead or held the wake there, then we'd have two corpses to watch over.

During the days of the wake I went to her house several times. She always asked me, "How's Rogelio?" and I answered, "Don't worry, *mamá,* I'm going to take him to San Juan." Then she'd say, "When you take him, stop by my house first." She must have found out because she died exactly one month and eighteen days later.

Soledad was a whore by the time my father died. She took up whoring because she wanted to, not because she had any need to do it. I didn't force her or even ask her to do that. I didn't know about it until she came home once with a card from the clinic. I asked her why she was carrying that card and she said, "You were a whore once for our sake, so I have the right to do the same for my children."

I was against her going into the profession but it was really up to her husband. Arturo never objected, so what could I do? When a daughter lives with a man, she's under his orders, not her mother's. Arturo stayed home while Soledad brought him money. That's why he let her go whoring. Arturo was a whore's pimp. He's been a pimp all his life.

Arturo was my favorite son-in-law because he has always been good to me. He was the only one who came to my *papá*'s funeral. Listen, my *papá* died unshaven and with his hair too long and when Arturo arrived and saw him like that he was very angry and said, "*Ave María,* it doesn't seem possible that nobody has taken the trouble to cut his hair. If I had known I would have brought a razor and shaved him at least." Arturo stayed right there until *papá* was buried.

Arturo has never failed me. He is a daring man and will take any risk, although no one would think it to see him, so small and skinny and quiet. He looks after me because he remembers the time he had to go to court and I gave him money for a lawyer to get him out on *parole* and all that. When he was out of a job I helped him too. I gave him his lunch every day. We've always gotten along, he and I. The only other son-in-law I liked was one of Soledad's husbands, Tavio, who died.

Cruz came back to La Esmeralda to live with Héctor and me. She was still going to school and had completed the sixth grade. When she was fourteen she took off with that good-for-nothing Emilio Pabón. I was always against her having anything to do with him. She lost her virginity to him just to annoy me. I never, never got along with him, because he's such a bigot. He belongs to the Popular Party and likes to criticize other people. Me, I'm a Statehood Republican. When he begins one of those discussions I get out of the way, because he likes to get the best of everybody and I have a hot temper. Some people try to get a rise out of you the way he does, saying things about the party. But he never can get me to argue about politics, because if I do I get mad.

I'm a Statehood Republican because that's what my father and mother were. I may not know much, but nobody can take that away from me. My son and daughters are Republicans, too. In the old times, when the Republican Party was in power, people had less money but they lived better than they do now. Everything was cheaper and there weren't so many illnesses. You could buy a meal for half a dollar then. Now, with five dollars you starve. Cancer and those things were unknown, because food was grown right here and was fresher and more healthful.

As I was saying, Emilio, Cruz's husband, is a good-for-nothing and I hate him. Cruz didn't go to live with him, see? He deflowered her and she went on living at home as if nothing had happened. Then Cruz told Soledad about it and Soledad told me. Right away I sent for Emilio so that he and Cruz could get married. It turned out he couldn't because he was a minor and his mother was in New York. I wrote to Cruz's father in the Army, but he paid no attention. Cristóbal never takes any interest in his children. He never even answered my letter.

When Cruz made her misstep with Emilio I didn't care a bit. On the contrary, I told her, "Now let Emilio get you a room. He was the one who dishonored you, so let him take charge of you. You can't keep on living with me, because you're not a virgin any longer. You're a woman. I'm not responsible for you now." I got after him too and told him, "You did your damage. Now you can take Cruz away from here to live somewhere else." So he took her away.

I was having a problem with Simplicio, too. For a while he was in love with his cousin Brunilda, my sister Migdalia's daughter. They would drink and kiss and all that. That girl got into it knowing they were cousins. I didn't tell Migdalia about it, because she's so dumb. She never went to school and she would have said a lot of foolish things. I told Simplicio, "Don't go putting your foot in it," because I knew Brunilda already had made a slip with a man. I didn't say anything to them at the time, but afterward I spoke privately to Simplicio. As for Brunilda, I gave her dirty looks.

I have always avoided anything like that with my cousins, out of respect. I wish you could see some of my cousins on my father's side of the family. They're dark, but most of them are terribly handsome. And I never have even said to any of them, "What a man!" I have always respected them, see? For me a cousin is like a brother, because he's a relative; his blood is my blood.

Migdalia and I didn't get along with each other for some reason I don't understand. I love her like a sister and I don't know why it is that she doesn't love me at all. Maybe it's because I have bad hair, that is, kinky hair. She has good hair. And also perhaps because my mother didn't bring her up. Say! I think that must be the reason. My mother kept me with her and brought me up, but Migdalia was brought up by my grandmother Clotilde. Then Migdalia wanted to stay in Santurce with my *mamá* for a holiday, and the way it turned out, the holiday was permanent because Migdalia stayed on. My grandmother couldn't control her. She never obeyed *mami* either, no matter how hard *mami* beat her. And some of those beatings caused real injuries.

Once *mami* went to a spiritist center to ask about Migdalia, but they said, "Don't waste any more time. That girl is not a virgin and the man who did his harm to her is married." After that, Migdalia just kept on whoring. *Mami* couldn't control her. She would beat that girl practically to death. Finally my *mamá* broke Migdalia's head and that stopped her; she went back to Río Grande and there she settled down. That's where she met Basilio. She lived with him and bore him four children. When the fourth child was born, Basilio had her sterilized. Then she took up with Federico, the man she lives with now in Mameyes. She's quieter and more settled, now that she has a job. But hardly anybody in Mameyes can stand her. She's so dumb, you see. She always quarreling with people because of her children; she makes a mountain out of a molehill.

Once Migdalia got into trouble with the public welfare office. I thought it was some kind of routine business when I got a letter from them. Then I read: "Mrs. Fernanda Fuentes, would you please inform us as to the amount of the salary you pay your sister and whether said salary is payable by the week or by the month?" That really burned me up. I wrote to Public Welfare saying

I was every bit as poor as my sister and could not possibly employ her and that I did not know what kind of mess she was in, but I didn't want to get involved in it myself. She hasn't spoken to me since.

Listen, it's Migdalia's fault that Clotilde got cancer. Migdalia hit her on the face right over the spot where she had had a molar pulled and that gave her angina, and that's what brought on the cancer. If Clotilde is beneath the earth now, it's all because of Migdalia. And they tell me that while Clotilde was laid out and Migdalia was still living with the father of her children, she showed up with another man to view the corpse. There they were, pawing at each other and all that. It was a real scandal, I'm told. I didn't go to Clotilde's funeral. I figured that if they didn't make the effort to come and get me, it was because I wasn't needed there.

Migdalia and I don't visit each other. If she should come to my house she will be well received, but I'm not going to seek her out. And if we ever should meet in the street I'll say hello to her, provided she says hello to me first. She and her family did nothing but embarrass me when they did come.

One day during the Christmas holidays they came here and a neighbor, Mario, invited us all to his house. He put a quart of rum out on the table and they kept talking and helping themselves to drinks, without even offering the man a glass of his own rum. Bold as brass, that's them. There was a bottle of whiskey there too, and Mario told them he was keeping it for a friend but they went ahead and drank it anyway. Migdalia likes her drink. She's a bigger drunkard than I am. I stop before I pass out, but not my sister.

A few days after they left I ran across Mario and he said to me, *"Ave María,* those relatives of yours really drink, don't they?" I told Héctor about it, saying, "What he really meant was that my sister has no manners and no shame." I smell out a person's real meaning a mile off, and I know how to interpret what they say. Migdalia hasn't been back here since that day.

Simplicio finally got some sense and got himself a woman. He fell in love with Flora when he was fifteen. She was living with Fontánez at the time, across the way from Cruz. I didn't know anything about Simplicio's planning to take off with that woman. He didn't say a word about it and I don't know how they arranged it or anything. I just know that they stayed at my sister's house for about five days. Then they showed up at Soledad's. They stayed there awhile and then I kept them in my house. They lived with me until Simplicio went to the States. They haven't married yet, because Simplicio has only just turned twenty-one.

Felícita was in New York and her twin boys were staying with me, and so were Simplicio and Flora, and I had a hard time finding money to feed them. When things really got tough, I'd take my *troubles* to *doña* Minerva. Minerva is black, but I tell you, that *negra's* heart is like cream, the best. She always helped me. If the twins got sick I'd fly straight to her. And when Soledad's children got sick, she made them well too. The time I had no money to buy gifts for my grandchildren on the Day of the Kings I went to her crying, and she gave me money. I say it again and again, her heart is like cream. If I had to kiss the sole of that black foot, I'd do it gladly.

But Felícita didn't help me out at all. She never sent me anything from the States, not even a letter at Christmas time, not even a post card or a Christmas card for her children. Nothing! But when she came back, she told *doña* Minerva that she had been sending me five or ten dollars every week. *Doña* Minerva always tells the truth, and that's why Felícita doesn't get along with her. *Doña* Minerva said, "I have the whole story from Nanda about how you let Mother's Day pass without sending even a card. And you sent nothing for the kids on the Day of the Kings. I saw Nanda crying her eyes out because she didn't have any money. The only thing you sent was a measly little toy revolver that they paid no attention to. And then you arrived here a few days ago without even a pin to give them." And that's the truth. Felícita came home with over seven hundred dollars and she didn't bring a single gift for the children, not so much as a pair of undershorts.

But at least, when Simplicio wrote to her in New York about wanting to go to the States, she did try to help him out. She wrote for him to come ahead if that's what he wanted, and she sent him fifteen dollars. A friend of his gave him seven dollars more, and so he reserved a ticket. Then he went to work at the docks to raise the rest of the money to pay the fare and to buy everything he needed.

I wasn't happy about Simplicio going to the States, because I was used to having him with me. But in a way I *was* happy to see him go because there's so much that's bad around here, drug addiction and all that, and Simplicio had gotten in with a very bad crowd. It was better that he go rather than do wrong here and be jailed. I couldn't help worrying, but as the saying has it, "What the eyes don't see, the heart doesn't feel."

Some of Héctor's friends had advised me not to live with him because he was a wife beater. But to tell you the truth, I was the one who used to beat him. He hit me only once and that time he gave me a black eye. That was the first and last time he ever hit me. I took a milk bottle and went at him. He put up his arm to protect his face, so I cut his arm.

Once he was drunk and I yelled at him and he got mad. He threw out all my things and hit at me with all his strength. I wouldn't have a tooth in my head if that blow had landed. When I saw what he was about I took a big can of powdered milk and threw it at him. He still has the scar. Héctor won't forget Nanda in a hurry, not with all those scars I've left to remind him!

The first time I cut Héctor, I cut him on the chest. I hadn't intended to cut the man or to hurt him in any way. I think that happened about the time of the Santa Clara hurricane. They were asking everybody to take shelter in the school building because of the storm. I was putting everything away in the house and Héctor got drunk. That's Héctor's only vice, drinking. He's too lazy to have other vices. In fact, he's so lazy, I don't see how he can work on the docks.

That day it rained a lot before the storm, and everybody started to board up their windows and I did too. I was afraid of staying in that house during a storm because it was so broken down. I said, "Héctor, help me pick up things and put them in a safe place." But he wouldn't, not he. If I wanted anything done I had to ask the neighbors. I had a husband but it was just for show. If a nail had to be hammered in, I couldn't count on Héctor. So when I asked him to help me, he just went "Ahhh" because he was already drunk, and he walked off to drink some more. I got everything ready myself and went to the shelter with Simplicio and Flora and the twins. Cruz was in Miami then, with Soledad. We got along fine at the shelter because I'd taken along a kerosene stove, and if anybody wanted to use my stove to heat milk or something, I'd let them.

About ten that night I said to Flora, "Let's go to the house to see why Héctor hasn't come around." I went out to look for him and I saw him sitting in a bar with a woman called The Snake. He was drinking and she was pawing him. Right then and there I grabbed The Snake and hit her and threw her down on the floor. Then I socked Héctor. He swung a chair, trying to hit me with it, and I grabbed another chair and threw it at him. Then he and I went home together.

I was so angry that I went up into the house and found a *Gem* and when he wasn't looking I got him with it. The only thing he said was, "You've cut me." It was a very long cut. I heard later that they had to take eighteen stitches. You can see the scar when he's in his undershirt. I wasn't arrested that time. Héctor told the cops he had interfered in a fight to defend a friend of his, and that one of the boys cut him but he didn't notice which one. I don't know why he didn't accuse me.

I went back to the shelter with the twins and lay down to sleep. I was still so blind with rage that I didn't cry and I didn't feel sorry, either. That same night, after his wound was attended to, Héctor came to see me for a while. He talked to me but I didn't say a word. After a while he gave up and went home to bed. The next day I gathered up all the things I'd taken to the shelter and went back home. Héctor was sleeping. I put the children to sleep on the big bed and left him on the cot. He had a fever but I didn't do anything for him. I didn't even prepare his breakfast. The minute Héctor got up I got busy and prepared food for myself and the children. We didn't speak to each other for one week and we slept apart.

At the end of the week the stitches were cut. But one stitch was left in and the place was bleeding. Then I spoke to him and said, "Look, they didn't take out all the stitches. Come here and let me take out that one." I took the scissors and cut the thread and pulled it out. Then I put some medicine on the bleeding spot. He didn't make a fuss and he didn't do anything to me.

People are wrong about Héctor. He was good about supporting us, I can't deny it, and he was steady and generous and takes care that his wife has everything she needs. There aren't many men like that in La Esmeralda. That's the reason why my daughters will even criticize me to defend him. But when Héctor gets drunk he's a pest, and not even God could stand him. He'll come in when you're feeling calm and peaceful, and throw the food you've kept for him in your face. And when he was drinking he had the bad habit of grabbing my cunt in front of everybody and saying that he wanted to fuck. I don't like that. He did that just because I had been a whore.

Also, he's very unfriendly. Sometimes we went out together and he wouldn't even say hello to anybody. And then people would come and tell me, "Say, what's wrong with your husband? Why should an old queer like him be so stuck up?"

Another thing that always bothered me about Héctor was that he's terribly jealous. The worst of it was he'd be jealous without any reason. One day they had a wake at Papo's house. His wife, Genoveva, came over to invite me, and Héctor was drunk, so he let me go. About three hours later he showed up, still drunk. I was standing at the door talking with Arturo and Papo. Héctor said to me in a loud voice, "What! Are these two inviting you to go fuck with them?" I was so ashamed I didn't know what to do. The next day Arturo and Papo went to Héctor, who was sober by then, and told him that they were decent people and he shouldn't act like that.

In spite of everything, I lived with Héctor for six years. At first I loved him, I won't deny it. Then he played so many dirty tricks on me that little by little I began losing all my love for him. He loves me a lot still, and he says I'm the only woman he has ever loved. If I went to him right now and told him, "Héctor, get a house for me," he'd leave that woman he has and come to live with me. Héctor is the husband I've been happiest with, not counting Junior, the one I have now.

When I was thinking about breaking up with Héctor I wrote to my son, Simplicio, who was in Philadelphia. He had asked me what I wanted for a Mother's Day present, so I told him I wanted a trip to Philadelphia to see him. I had asked Felícita to send for me and she promised to, but she returned to Puerto Rico without doing it. She is so selfish! But Simplicio is a good son and he wrote back telling me to get ready and not worry, because he wasn't Felícita. And he really did send me a ticket. I went to Philadelphia on September 23, 1962.

This was the first time I was leaving Puerto Rico, that land I loved. It was a big wrench for me. Felícita and her husband Edmundo went to see me off at the airport, and so did Cruz, who was back from Florida. One of my *compadres* went too, and three of my grandchildren, and Soledad's ex-husband, Arturo.

When I got to Philadelphia, my son and his wife came to meet me, together with a friend of theirs who had driven them over in his car. It was bitterly cold when I arrived. I hate cold weather. I thought it would kill me. Even the slightest drop in the temperature sends me to bed to keep warm. I had taken a suitcase full of freshly ironed cotton dresses, but it was so cold that all I wore were woolen slacks and *un coat*.

At first my son wouldn't let me do anything at all. He said I was here to get a rest. I didn't see any of the sights. Simplicio would take me out walking, teaching me the streets so that I'd learn my way around. I went to where he worked, to a friend's house, and to the house of his wife's sister. But I hardly went anywhere else. On Fridays, when he wasn't working, we'd go shopping for the *Christmas* presents I was going to bring to my grandchildren when I came back to Puerto Rico. What we did was buy presents for a different child each week. I kept some money for my cigarettes and things like that.

After a while I started taking care of two little girls. I earned twelve dollars a week. Simplicio's wife, Flora, had found the job for me so I could earn some money while I was there. I spent all my money filling a suitcase with toys. First, I rushed off and bought each of Felícita's twins a cowboy suit and a belt with a holster and pistol. I'd had those children for three years and they were my darlings.

You should have seen them while they were staying with me. I bought them lots of clothes and made them wear shoes all the time. I bathed them every afternoon at about three o'clock, and I never let them stray far from the house. I saved up money to pay their fare to Philadelphia and told Simplicio that I'd go back to Puerto Rico unless he sent for the twins. Simplicio said all right, send for them if I wanted to. But when I wrote to Felícita, she wrote back that she didn't give away her children. She wouldn't let me have them until I was in Puerto Rico.

You can't imagine how happy I was to go back. It was like a magnet pulling me. I didn't like living in the Americas.

Fernanda

My Teen-age Husband

WHEN I RETURNED to Puerto Rico, nobody was waiting for me at the airport. I remember I got here on the Day of the Three Kings. I had only two dollars and fifty cents and with that I took a taxi to La Esmeralda. The taxi cost two dollars, so I stopped at *doña* Yolanda's and drank fifty cents' worth of rum.

In the bar everybody came to throw their arms around me and I kissed all of them. I kidded with everybody as if I'd never been out of La Esmeralda at all. My sister Migdalia had told Cruz that I'd be too stuck up to speak to anybody, as I'd been to the States. But it wasn't so.

I said to Cruz, "What you should have told my sister is, 'You're worse than Nanda. You don't have any learning, but since you've been to the States you think you've got God by the ass.'" Migdalia tries to speak English, and the truth is, when I see two Puerto Ricans speaking English to each other, I don't like it. They only want to show off and pretend they're better than others.

I really was glad to be home. I cried all the time I was in Philadelphia because I wanted to come back. How can I help liking it here? This is my country. Puerto Rico is better than the States. Better for me, I mean. This is where my men are, and everybody here knows me and speaks my language, so we understand one another. Here we get together *en bunches* to talk or to play thirty-one or bingo—always *en bunches*. And if I get sick some neighbor will take me to the hospital. Out there, in the States, it's not like that. Neighbors live behind locked doors; everybody is locked away from everybody else, so nobody knows anybody.

I was sad, too, in Philadelphia because I had left a sweetheart back in Puerto Rico. His name is Junior. He was only seventeen then. When I went away he told me, "If you go, stay two months, no longer." But I stayed four months and eighteen days. We wrote to each other, but then somebody sent me an anonymous letter saying that Junior had a sweetheart and was planning to marry her. After that I didn't write any more letters to him.

When I got back I was crazy to see Junior, but he wasn't anywhere around. I quarreled with Héctor later that day because he hadn't met me at the airport. That hurt my feelings. And my daughters, like fools, said, "We didn't know you were coming today." I told him, "Oh, so you can't read a letter or ask somebody to read it to you!" It's true I barely know how to write, but what I write anybody can understand. I also quarreled with Zulma because I'd been told she had spent all her time in Héctor's house.

I didn't expect to see Junior and anyway the trip had made me feel ill, so I went to bed early. Later, when I met Junior, he walked right by me without speaking and I didn't speak to him, either. He didn't have any idea why I had stopped writing to him. Then one day he sent me a note by a friend asking why I had left him. I told him about the letter I had received, and I said that if he had a sweetheart I shouldn't interfere and spoil his happiness with her.

Junior said it was all a lie and asked who was the gossip who had written such a thing. He said he thought about me all the time and he had gone to the post office every day, hoping for a letter from me. He said that when no more letters came, he was desperate and cried and cried. When he heard I was coming he was happy again. We went on talking back and forth like that for almost a week more.

I lived with Héctor a little while longer, then I left him. Do you know what happened while I was away? Why, Héctor would bring Luis the Queer to the house. To my own house! People wrote me all those things while I was in Philadelphia. And it was true, all right. I know, because once Héctor didn't want to pay Luis afterward and Luis grabbed Héctor's shirt and ripped it. Later he stole a good radio Héctor had. Everybody knows that, and my children know it too, but Héctor always gave them money, so they defend him.

Before I left him, Héctor infected me with a venereal disease. I told him, "Héctor, I'm sick, because when I wash, a stink comes out, and you are the one who infected me."

"Who, me?"

"Yes, you, because of all those women you had in here."

Héctor may have infected me innocently, without knowing, because there are women who will screw with a man during their period and the menstrual blood makes the man sick without his knowing it. This happens even if she doesn't have an infection, because her pores are open down there and she's throwing off that blood, that filth that she has. Well, when she comes, all that blood flows down and the man gets sick. There are women who will even give a man their ass at that time. They tell him, "Better go in through the kitchen, they're painting the parlor red." I don't do that though; I never let any man touch me at that time of the month.

I had such a pain with that venereal that I even went to the hospital. When he realized it was true, Héctor gave me two dollars for a penicillin injection. He must have known that Zulma, and that queer he was going with, laid so many men they must surely have been infected. He just wanted to use me at the time, so he used me.

People had told me that Héctor used men as if they were women, but I never believed it. I asked Héctor himself and he said, "Who, me? Oh no, not me!" And the truth is that he behaved like a real he-man, with me. I mean, he was really and truly a *macho* in bed. So how could I believe those stories?

Héctor was not a queer. But he was a *bubarrón*. A *bubarrón* is a man who gives it to a faggot in the ass. He is the one who plays the part of the man; the faggot plays the part of a woman. But in spite of that I don't like it—this business of a man's having intercourse with another man.

Once Luis the Queer went after Junior, but Junior hates queers. Luis was so infatuated that he simply went wild when he saw Junior. One day Junior was in the poolroom when along comes Luis, throws his arms around him and says, "If you are broke I can let you have some money." Junior would have broken a chair on Luis' head if people hadn't intervened. "Why do you want to hit him?" they asked.

"Because I'm fed up with this queer," Junior answered, "He's in love with me and I don't like faggots, I like women."

Naturally I feel proud of Junior, knowing that nobody can say, "Look at him, he's a *bubarrón.*" Nobody can say that Junior has ever gone to bed with a faggot. He has always disliked that business, ever since he was a little boy. That's the reason I preferred him to Héctor.

The first time I met Junior, he was about five years old. In a manner of speaking, I helped bring him up. Marcelo, Junior's half brother, was Simplicio's best friend and practically grew up in my house. I have known Junior's parents for many years. Both of them are white. Their house was near mine and we went there to watch television.

When Junior's mother had a baby, I'd go over and help out around the house, washing dishes and all that. She had nine children; Junior is the eldest. Junior's father, Adán, had Marcelo and a lot more children with other women, because he was a ladies' man. But he has stuck to Junior's mother for more than twenty-five years. They're a couple who really got along well with each other. She doesn't spend her time gossiping out in the street. If she goes out at all it's to go shopping, and as soon as she's through, she goes right back to her house.

Junior and I began falling in love when he was in the eighth grade. At that time I started joking with him and we even kissed each other. The first day we kissed, Junior was sitting on a neighbor's fence. When I saw him looking sort of absent-minded, I went over and kissed him. I kissed him and he kissed me. Then I told him, "Don't just sit there, go home to bed." He went home, but after that we were sweethearts on the sly for about three months. There was nothing between us, see? I mean, we didn't have intercourse. Only kissing, nothing else.

One day I went alone to the movies and ran into Junior there. We held hands and all that, and he invited me to go to the movies with him again. We went often while Héctor was away at work. At that point I invited Junior to my house and I helped him climb in through the window.

I did it because of what Héctor had told me, "I don't like to live a long time with one woman." Do you know how it hurts a woman when a man says that to her? I told him, "Don't worry, you won't live long with me. You have something coming to you and it's something big. I'm going to put the horns on you. Just wait and see." It was then that I had Junior come over to the house.

Junior really knows how to lay a woman and he stays in a long time. I thought it would be a passing affair, but Junior got so infatuated, *Ave María!* He can't stand to see me talk with anybody else. He gets this angry-dog look on his face. He's really jealous. He's the most jealous of all the men I've had. But he does know how to lay a woman.

Héctor knew that I had put the horns on him and had made a *cabrón* of him. He must have known, because the story got around, but he never said anything to me about it. Not one word ever. When we separated he stayed on in the house and I moved in with Cruz. Then Héctor began trying to pick a quarrel with Junior, just acting jealous and screwing around and pestering. I kept telling him, "Look, *chico,* I'm not going to live with you any more. You know me, I love a man for a time and then I leave him. And besides, you once told me you never could stay long with one woman. I wasn't going to wait until you left me."

When Héctor got drunk he would say, "Look at your *tinayel** going by. Just look at him." One day I was drinking and I told Junior, "Come here, I

* Teen-ager.

want to talk with you." Junior got up and came to me. I was sitting with Junior when Héctor came up with a pig's head in his hands and asked me, "Want some?"

"I don't want anything. Get away from here." Héctor began to insult me and to use obscene words. He used a word I didn't like, so I just fell on him and slapped his face. Then he started kicking me and bit my shoulder. I didn't let Junior get into the fight because Héctor is stronger than Junior. Besides Junior was a minor. Héctor threatened him, that's all. And I grabbed a bottle and broke it and cut Héctor's face with it.

I don't know what happened after that because Cruz took me to the hospital, and they took Héctor to have his wounds treated too. He didn't sue me. I've cut him twice but he never took me to court. This time I accused him and we went to court. But I had my lawyer fix everything up for him. I didn't want to testify against him, nor harm him in any way.

Yet, Héctor wouldn't leave me in peace. I don't know what's the trouble with me, but when I leave a man he keeps right after me. The only way I can get a man to leave me in peace is to go live with him. But I had already lived with Héctor and I no longer loved him. He was angry because I was so happy with Junior.

Don Guillo, a spiritist, claims that it's envy that kills, not sorcery. When a person is getting along well, others begin to envy him and that's the cause of all his troubles. I wasn't feeling well, so I went to a lady spiritist in Loíza Aldea to see if I could make Héctor leave me alone. The spiritist told me that somebody had done a job on me, cast a spell, with a piece of new rope and a package that they'd tossed into the sea. She said that next door to the house where I lived, which was Héctor's daughter's place, there was a white horse tied to a post. She also told me that I had daughters and that one of them had turned her back on me.

This spiritist doesn't charge anything, you give her whatever you want to. I left her half a dollar and paid for the prayers she had given me. There were prayers to Saint Alexander, to the Guardian Angels, to the Archangel Michael and several more, but I decided not to do any of the things she told me to. I have the prayers in my purse, to protect me from my enemies. I keep them but I never recite them.

To me, God is the only spiritist. I believe only in God because He was the One who threw us into this world and only He can cure. When God sends you a mortal illness, the spiritists cannot cure you.

I am a Catholic, but I'll tell you the truth, I hardly ever go to church. I don't pray at home. The only thing I do is cross myself before going to bed and give my blessing to my children and grandchildren. But my *mamá* taught me to pray the Pater Noster and to go to church and to catechism class and all that. To me the Catholic religion is something great, something out of this world. When people die, they go first into a hole and then to Heaven, and from there the dead can help you. They let you know the winning number and then you play it without telling anybody how you got it. I believe that, but the dead have never helped me.

The last time I went to confession was when Felícita's twins lived with me. One of them got a very bad case of pneumonia, and I went down on my knees here at home and prayed to the Virgin of Everlasting Mercy. I made a vow to walk barefoot for three months and wear her habit all through the Christmas season if she would only make my grandson get well. He was terribly sick, but after my vow he started to get better the very next day. Then I did everything I said I would.

I am devoted to the Virgin of Everlasting Mercy because she was my *mamá*'s favorite saint. She grants me everything I ask for. I carry many saints' pictures in my billfold, and whenever I find anything in the street with the picture of a saint on it, I stoop and pick it up. Anything, even a broken medal. I put them away, see? But compared to the Everlasting Mercy, the others mean nothing to me.

Well, as long as Héctor kept after me, Junior and I had relations in Cruz's house, because Cruz was alone then and I went to live with her. Cruz doesn't get along with Junior because he's no "little pig." That means he's not one who hands out money. Cruz likes anybody who gives her money and she'll treat him like a king. But Junior doesn't, so she can't stand him. That's why we finally went to live in Cataño.

Another thing Cruz dislikes about Junior is that he wouldn't let me drink or dance or go anywhere. I had the habit of telling dirty jokes and using bad words, the way people do in La Esmeralda. Well, Junior forbade me to speak like that. He forbade me to do a lot of things, and in a way I'm grateful to him for that, because now I have peace of mind and I feel better. But my daughter wishes I were still in the life so I could help her more than I do.

Cruz has two children by Emilio, and when I'm working I always give her five dollars a month and also buy a little something for the children. If she needs anything she tells me, and I always get it for her at the house where I work. Or I'll ask for an advance of a couple of dollars so Cruz can buy food for lunch. When I get a dress or a pair of shoes for myself, I always buy something for Cruz's children too. I can't go home with just something for myself. I have to buy a pair of pants for Chuito and some little thing for Anita because I love Anita very much and she's very affectionate and loves me too. She makes faces to amuse me and does all sorts of cute things. *Ave María!* She acts as if I'm something great and glorious. She's crazy about me. None of my other grandchildren loves me just the way she does. When Cruz beats Anita I get into a rage and I feel like killing my daughter.

The trouble with Cruz is that she's a spendthrift. Give her fifteen dollars and in a moment they're shot; give her twenty-five, poof, they're gone. She'll buy everything the kids ask for if she has the money. She never stops to think of tomorrow's needs, nor to consider that she may not be able to provide for them. She could be better off than anybody else if she saved her money. But she doesn't economize or try to save or anything. If she gets pregnant again, she'll really be in trouble.

Soledad had an operation to keep from having more babies. That was when Toya, her youngest daughter, was born, three or four years ago. The operation hasn't changed her at all. Felícita had the same thing done and it's changed her a lot. Before the operation she took good care of her children. She was very agreeable, *simpática,* and always looked out for me. If I needed anything she'd send it to me. I tell you, everybody spoke well of Felícita before. Now she's very different. She's in the profession and not a home-loving woman at all. She doesn't bother about her dear children or about anything else. She'll go out with *gringos* and with anybody. I think all this came about because of the operation.

I think Felícita doesn't love me. She says she loves only her stepmother, who was a real mother to her. She doesn't bother about me at all. I say flatly that she's not the same daughter I had before. Felícita used to be my favorite among my children, but since she went to New Jersey and met her last husband, Edmundo Capó, she changed for the worse. She's become slovenly and acts as if nothing mattered to her any more. Now she wants to put her children in a reform school so that she can be free to come and go as she pleases and wander around like a stray animal. That is why God can't possibly help her. He never helps mothers who treat their children badly.

After all, if you bring a child into the world it's up to you to bring him up. For instance, there's no reason why I should take care of my grandchildren while their mothers are plump and red-cheeked and their fathers have themselves a good time. No, they had the children, it's up to them to care for them. If my daughters fell ill or died, that would be different, although even then, if the fathers were around I'd give the children to them. I would help in every possible way, but as for living with them, no.

Of all my children, the one I love is Soledad. She's scatterbrained and she was crazy once, but that's why I love her. Everybody loves Soledad because she's so good to her children. She has no vices of any kind, at least none that I know of. She'll smoke now and then but only when she's at a party.

Soledad hasn't always been as good as she is now. She and I were on bad terms with each other and always quarreling, but you may be sure that when she was sick I went to her. If I had been other than I am, I wouldn't have gone. My neighbor *doña* Minerva used to say, "If a daughter of mine treated me the way Soledad treats you, I wouldn't want her in my house. I wouldn't even look at her." But none of us can change the heart we have. Right?

The time Soledad hit me I cried and cried. It hurt my feelings terribly. I had scolded her and told her that she shouldn't get involved with a certain man. But she never liked to have a person give her good advice or anything like that. So she insulted me, she said terrible things and she hit me. We didn't speak to each other for a long time. But she no longer treats me like that. She is always in my heart and anything that happens to her over there in New York, I suffer here. I suffer inside and keep quiet.

Soledad is the one who's most attentive to me now. For instance, Felícita and Cruz, who live right around here, may give me something or other when they see me, but Soledad really thinks about me. She came back to Puerto Rico to spend part of *las Christmas* with me. She always does that. She may not get here in time for the Christmas Eve celebrations, but she never fails to show up for New Year's. She's the only one of my children who has ever made a point of spending New Year's Day with me.

She writes to me and says, "Go to the hospital. If you need anything, let me know. I'm always ready to help you." Yes, she takes better care of me even than the son that God gave me, or than Cruz, because I was sick in Cataño for several weeks and neither of them came to see me. After a while Cruz decided to pay me a visit, and I said to her, "That's big of you, Cruz, to come and see me after I'm well." When I really needed them, they didn't come.

A good daughter should treat her mother well and help her out until she dies. And she should do it while her mother is still alive and healthy. Because after you die, what difference does anything make? She should shield her mother from criticism, even if the mother is a bitch. A daughter should pardon her mother, you know, and she should never contradict her, no matter what. A mother has the right to advise her daughter and to yell at her. And a mother even has the right to break her daughter's neck if the daughter pays no attention. Else why bear children?

I always used to beat my children. I whipped their feet with a belt or anything that was handy, so they wouldn't go out. I brought up my children the way I was brought up myself. I never got into mischief when I was a girl but they taught me what was right, the proper time to go to bed and all that. That's the way to bring up children, scold them so they won't be rude to their elders, feed them at the right time, bathe them regularly. And punish them, beat them, so they will be respectful.

Nowadays mothers themselves give freedom to their children, that's how bad things are. Maybe children have more schooling now, but they're worse than they used to be. It's the fault of the government that there is so much juvenile delinquency now. A mother can't beat her own child any longer, because the government passed a law against it. And the worst of it is that the children know about it. So a child goes to the cops when he's whipped. Not that I ever paid any attention to that law. Not me. I told the cops, if a child of mine misbehaves, I'll beat him in front of the judge or the Virgin Mary if I have to. But here in La Esmeralda, the mothers who have never been arrested are scared of going to jail. They'd rather see their children grow up to be roughnecks.

I never know anything about my daughters' affairs. When I heard that Felícita, too, was a whore, I didn't say anything to her. I let her go her own way because she's always saying I'm a busybody and that I stick my nose into everything. So I just let my daughters do as they please. I would tell them that a whore's life isn't good enough for them, but I never speak against it because now that they are whores they are better off than I was when I was first married and didn't have a house or anything of my own.

People here in La Esmeralda can't get along with Cruz or Felícita. Felícita always did take after father. She's so presumptuous she tries to shit from higher up than her ass-hole. And that's why nobody can stand her. Why, people stop me in the street to ask, "What makes your daughter so stuck up? What's wrong with her, anyway?" I can't figure it out myself, because Felícita is as homely as anything. What does she have to be proud about? She boasts and pretends to be what she's not, and Cruz uses dirty words. Cruz doesn't know what she's doing, she's so stupid. But Soledad's different. She always got along well with everybody in La Esmeralda. When she's here, everybody seeks her out. I've been told right to my face, "The only one who has a right to be stuck up in your family is Soledad. She's the prettiest one of them, yet she's so modest. But that Felícita thinks she's something special. She thinks she's a Fourth of July."

Simplicio used to be crazy about Felícita, but since he went to live with her he really got to hate her. He'd say to me, "I'm sorry to tell you this because you're my mother, but I don't look upon Felícita as my sister." He said he wanted to kill her husband, Edmundo. I advised him to do nothing of the kind. On the contrary, I told him to treat Edmundo with courtesy. I said, "The turns of the world are great, and rolling stones are apt to collide."

Junior

---

*I'm the Best Husband
She's Had*

I MUST HAVE been destined to live with Nanda. At least it seems like that, because ever since I was a small boy she was after me. When God gives you something, nobody can take it away. I've tried to leave Nanda but I haven't been able to. I didn't want to carry on relations with her because she was living with Héctor, but she insisted and I had to go along.

I never had any problems when I was a kid. I had a happy life. I was always fooling around. When I wasn't going to San Juan with my brothers to raise a little hell, I would go drinking with friends. I was always gay. My problems started at fifteen when I began to have relations with Nanda.

Nanda and I had always been friends. I was in her house all the time. At first there wasn't anything between us, we just kidded around. I would lend her comic books and she would write on one of them, "I want you to go to bed early." Finally, one day she says to me, "Today I don't want you to go to bed early. Sit down here and wait for me."

So I sat down on the little wall there by the side of the house. Héctor wasn't home. Well, I was sitting there when she came over, took me by surprise and began kissing me.

"Cut it out, *chica*. I have to go to school tomorrow. I'm leaving," I told her.

"No, you are not going," she said. And that's how we began.

We hadn't started to have relations yet when I got the chicken pox. One day my head began to hurt and I felt feverish, but I thought it was just a headache. Nanda said to me, "Let's go to the movies," and as I liked to go to the movies with her, I went. There, in the theater, she began putting her hands on me. The next day I woke up with a rash. She would come to the house to see me all the time and bring me comic books, and we have kept up together ever since. It's three years now that I have been having relations with her.

A few months after we started, Nanda told me her son had sent for her. She said she wouldn't go on account of me, but she had to because they had sent her the ticket and all. Besides, Héctor was behaving like a son of a great whore and she was ready to leave him.

When Nanda went to the States, a fag named Luis who lived near by told Héctor about Nanda and me. Luis was in love with me but I didn't give him a tumble. He took advantage of Nanda being away to go with Héctor, and you know, he slept with him and all.

Nanda wrote me only two letters while she was away, because she got word that I had a sweetheart and was about to get married. It was a lie. I didn't have any girl friend or anything. I was waiting for her all the time. I amused myself at night by playing dominoes.

Nanda was due back on a Sunday, the Day of the Kings. I went home, got dressed up in my one and only suit, and then took off to the house of my friend Muñiz. I didn't speak to Nanda because she hadn't written to me. Every time I saw her I would walk off in another direction. One day I was standing on the roof, dressed only in my undershirt and pants, waiting for a friend of mine, when Nanda walked by and said, "How I hate you!" I let it go at that and just went inside. After that she kept coming around but I didn't talk to her.

One night at about nine o'clock I came home from playing dominoes and I heard a whistle. It was Nanda at the window. Héctor was at work.

"I have to talk to you," she said.

"All right, let's talk." And we did.

"Why don't you want to see me any more?" she asked.

Because of so and so and so, I told her.

"But they told me you had a sweetheart—" she answered. Then she invited me to the movies and after that we began having relations again, always trying to keep Héctor from finding out. I was careful not to do anything that might make Héctor suspect us. I wanted him to think that we had broken up.

I don't know much about Héctor except that he used to quarrel with

Nanda and mistreat her. He abused her and beat her all the time. And another thing. You can see how neat she keeps the house, with the beds made and everything. Well, when he came home drunk, he would mess up the big bed and then the small one, and with the door wide open and him all naked, he would grab hold of her ass in front of everybody. I saw it myself. He would do it all the time.

Héctor doesn't know how to do anything around the house. My brother Marcelo was the one who did everything. He was living with them, and Nanda practically brought him up. He installed all the electric wiring, and he made the two corner tables and all the shelves in the house. Héctor was jealous of Marcelo because Nanda was nice to him. But Héctor couldn't even hammer a nail.

Héctor would go out drinking some place and people would take his money away from him. Then he would come home and accuse Nanda of stealing it, and he would beat her up. She began to drink because he behaved like that, and while she was drunk she cut him up a few times. Finally she left him and went to live with Cruz.

Even though Héctor and Nanda had broken up, he didn't want her to go with another man. I was told that Héctor was out to get me, so I bought myself a revolver. One day I was playing *volleyball* when Nanda called me. We went to a friend's house, and while we were standing there with our arms around each other, talking, Héctor passed by, carrying a pig's head. When he saw us he threw that pig's head at Nanda, and then jumped on her and tried to hit her.

I threw the ball at him and stepped in to defend her. I was getting the best of Héctor when Cruz came and hit me with a piece of pipe. "All right," I said, and let go. Nanda picked up a piece of glass and cut Héctor with it. I plunged in again and Cruz hit me with the pipe a second time. She pretended she was trying to hit Héctor and got me instead, but I realized that she was doing it on purpose and I said to myself, "She's not on my side." I left for home, where I took a bath and changed my clothes. When I came back, Nanda and Héctor were both in jail. Nanda got out the same night and Héctor went to the hospital.

Cruz talked about me afterward, saying that I didn't defend Nanda. How could I defend her if they were going to take sides against me, too? Cruz is one way to you to your face and another way behind your back. She was the same when we were in school together. She never liked me because I wouldn't let Nanda drink or anything, or go out much. Right now, though, Cruz is on good terms with me, talks to me and everything. That only happens when she needs me for something, but all the same, if I have to help her, I do.

For a while Nanda was having relations with me and also with a foreman on the docks by the name of Tony the Dutchman. The thing was that neither she nor I was working and you know how it is, a woman needs things. She just had him to get money to buy what she wanted, her clothes and so on, to support herself. I didn't say a word to her. They never went to a hotel or anything. But the minute I got work I told her, "Now, either you leave him or you leave me." We fought and fought over it until Cruz wanted to call the cops, but Nanda stopped her.

Well, one day I warned Tony. I grabbed him and swung him around and said to him, "See this gun? I am going to empty it right into you if I catch you down here again."

"Why?" he asks me.

I told him about my relations with Nanda. Then I told Nanda I had to talk to her and we went to the beach. First she started trying to raise hell with me, but I said to her, "You've been going too far, making a horse's ass out of me." And I shot past her face twice, just to scare her. She covered her head and ran. But she kept going out with Tony anyway. They were drinking together and going out and having fun, and I was sick of it. Water can wear down a stone. I told her for the second time, "Either you leave him or you leave me." I kept insisting until she finally left him.

That's when I decided once and for all to go and live with Nanda. I said to her, "If I live with you and find out that you are doing something bad, be careful, because I'll go to jail but you'll go to the cemetery." I warned her. And she knows how I get when I drink.

It took us two months to find a house. Every payday I put aside some money toward it. I was working with *papi,* making thirty-five dollars a week. I asked my sister-in-law, Cecilia, Marcelo's wife, to look around for a room for me. There was one for twenty dollars a month, but somebody got it ahead of me. When I finally found the room over in Cataño, I didn't have the money for the security, but the next day I hocked my two watches and one of Nanda's. A week later I had them out again. That's how I am. I got twenty-six dollars for them and the rent was sixteen dollars, so I had ten dollars left for food for the rest of the week. I had to do the moving myself. I was going back and forth on the ferry, for a whole week.

When I was planning to set up a house with Nanda, nobody knew about it in La Esmeralda except Cruz. Nanda was still living at Crucita's house then. Soledad's little girl Catín was living there too. Every time we sat down to talk over plans for our own place, Cruz would send Catín over to listen and Nanda would say to me, "Don't talk any more, here is Catín." Do you know the only place that I could talk to Nanda in private? On the steps near Bonilla's store. And then I would have to send Cruz and the kids to the movies. "Here," I would say, "take this five dollars and everybody go."

Mami and *papi* found out about Nanda and me on account of Cruz. I would go to my house every day and they didn't know anything about what was going on, but Cruz took care of that. She went and told *mami* and spread it around.

One day *mami* came and asked me if it was true and I told her it was. "I am in love with Nanda," I said, "and I intend to live with her, whether you like it or not. I am a man all the way through." Believe me, I told her right out. "Marcelo and Jimmy could do it, why not me?"

After that, when I had the room all set up, *papi* talked to me again. "Is it true that you are going to set up a place with Nanda?" he asked.

"I am not going to. I already have," I told him. "I don't intend to live with her. I already do." They kept bawling me out and trying to make me leave her but I never would. They really wanted me to drop her. I never back down, never.

They kept saying that she was an old woman for me, that she used to hustle when she was younger. I don't care about that. It's past. That she doesn't do it now is the important thing. It was over fifteen years ago when she used to do that, and Nanda is forty now.

After we lived together awhile, I began taking Nanda to my parents' house. She didn't want to go until I said to her, "Don't worry. Sooner or later they'll realize that you aren't what you used to be any more." We kept going, until now anybody can see that *mami* likes Nanda. Nanda eats there and everything. *Papi* likes her, too.

Adán, my *papá,* is a hard-working man. He is fifty-eight and he has been working since he was thirteen. *Papi* had twenty-one children in all, not counting those who died. They say there are seven women in the world for every man, besides the ones you might pick up later. But all kidding aside, *papi* has had more than seven, it seems to me. Those are things that are outside a person's control. It isn't that you want them to happen, it's fate.

Both my parents have always been very good to me. I remember that I nursed until I was five and then I was on the bottle for another five years. I used to spend a lot of time at the beach when I was little, most of the time with my brothers. Jimmy, Marcelo and I used to hang around together. Marcelo is the eldest. I was always horsing around in La Esmeralda, carrying on with the girls, shooting pool, playing the machine in Papo's bar. Every night I'd go around and throw stones at the guys playing dominoes and knock over garbage cans in the street. And we would rap on doors or I would go to San Juan Gate and play on the swings. I was practically never at home.

I was a sleepwalker and I talked in my sleep when I was a kid. A neighbor of ours, *doña* Angela, who was a spiritist, cured me of that defect. I was also a medium and spoke to the dead nearly every night.

When I was a kid I used to wash the dishes, sweep, wash and iron, scrub floors and everything. Or I would pay a quarter or half a dollar to one of my sisters to do it for me. I also worked in the house, helping *papi* put in sockets and I helped fix the floor and the walls. When *papi* bought the house it was a wreck, and we pitched in and fixed it up. I was the one who painted it every year, with my other brother.

My elder brothers were loafers, because they spent all their time in the streets begging money from people and getting into mischief. When our parents bought clothes for us, Marcelo would sell his shoes and go barefoot. He'd sell the new clothes and toys and everything. Jimmy too. Then they'd go around saying they never got anything.

Marcelo has played me dirty a few times, but after all, that's between brothers. Once he stole my ring, which cost forty dollars. If it had been anybody else I would have killed him, but he is my brother and brothers shouldn't fight. One thing about him, though, he never tried to make my wife or any of my girl friends. And we used to have a lot of good times together. We would go all over, drinking and dancing. I used to be a scrapper and a curser, ready for a fight. I have been drinking since I was fourteen or fifteen, but they didn't know it at home. I go crazy when I'm drinking.

I used to go to the Catholic church when I was small, but I haven't gone since my First Communion when I was fourteen. I believe in God and respect the church, so that's why I don't go. Let's suppose that I went to confession and all that, and then for some reason or other when I left the church I had to use bad language. I have heard fellows shitting on God right after they have stepped out of church. It's better not to go.

I was eighteen when I left school. I was in second-year high school. *Papi* was sick, Marcelo was out of a job, and Jimmy was in jail. So I decided to work to help them out until *papi* could go back to work. When he did, I went back to school. I left school for good when I went to live with Nanda.

I have always worked. I like to. During vacations I worked with *papi*. I made over eighty dollars. When I was thirteen and fourteen, I worked for two months doing odd jobs around. Every week I would give five dollars to *papi* and *mami* and buy clothes for myself. I had one hundred and twenty-five dollars saved up in the house, and I went and spent it all on clothes for them and for myself. I kept fifteen dollars to have fun with. Before I went with Nanda I always had ten or twenty dollars on me. You always saw me well dressed. You could never find me with my pants torn or anything like that.

I manage to get along. When I'm out of a job I don't bother trying to collect unemployment because I don't like to waste my time. I went there once, but first they sent me upstairs, then they sent me downstairs, and when they told me to go upstairs again I said, "No, man, that's it. Give me back my card, I'm leaving." It's not worth it for what they give you—fifteen dollars. And you have to report in every week. It's a nuisance.

Nanda and I were happy when we went to live together in Cataño, but we began to have fights, which started over nothing . . . nothing. We had our first fight the day the moving was finished and we kept fighting as long as we lived there. Twice I packed up to leave. The first time we quarreled, I saw a pack of Pall Mall cigarettes on the bed and wanted to know whose it was.

"It belongs to a *macho* who was here with me and he left it behind," Nanda answered.

"Watch out the way you talk," I told her.

Then she started in with me. "Who do you think you are, ordering me around? Nothing in this house is yours."

But Nanda never gave me one cent to pay for that house. I bought everything in it except the stove, everything, out of the money that I earned each week.

So I said that time, "I want all my things packed when I get home from work today."

"Are you really going to leave?" she wanted to know.

"I can't stay with you any more. I am your husband and you have to respect me." But I didn't leave, because my friend Muñiz was with me and he wouldn't let me.

Nanda and I kept on fighting about little things like that, because I tell her something and she raises a row. I can't say a word to her because everything makes her mad. Imagine, the second time we fought was because we were playing parchesi! Instead of shooting for my brother Marcelo, she defends him and goes after me. I kept playing, but then I got mad and let her have it in the face with the board. She took the board, broke it and began raising hell. "All right," I said, and I packed my things and got dressed. Marcelo was on his way to San Juan and I said to him, "Wait a minute, I want you to help me carry my things."

"No, stay here," he said.

"I am leaving even if you won't help me," I answered. But Nanda came over to me and wouldn't let me go. The two of them kept it up until it was midnight and too late for me to leave.

Finally Nanda and I moved back to La Esmeralda, and the same day, Sunday, we had a fight. The thing is that she wants to dominate me. I have told her many times she has a terrible temper and is an awful nag besides, and I haven't got such a good temper myself. But I have never laid a hand on her. When we were sweethearts I beat her, but not now. I haven't touched her since we've been living together.

She picks fights with me, but she'd better not raise her hand to me, though, because that's something I won't allow. One night when we got into a fight she picked up the clock and was going to throw it at me, but I said to her, "If you hit me with that, I am not going to just stand there and take it. And the day you try to cut me, I swear you'll die. Because I am not going to just let it go at that. I'm not Héctor or Pedro."

Nanda only cuts people when she is drunk, so I told her, "The day you drink even a beer, you are not going to see me around here again." Besides, the doctor forbade her to drink.

People don't know that Nanda and I have fights, and the next day we make up. Felícita and Cruz are trying to get us to break up but they are going to have a hard job with me. A hard job, because I told Nanda, "I am not going to leave unless you do something that really hurts me. If I leave you it will be because I want to, and not because somebody else wants me to."

I'll tell you something. When Nanda got sick I came home straight from work every day. If I wasn't working, you'd see me in the house at ten o'clock at the latest. Why? To be with her. If it was one in the morning and she was hungry, I'd run out, and even if I had to go to town in Cataño to get food, I would do it. While she was sick I would sweep, and wash the dishes, and do everything in the house.

Once I went for a month without shaving or cutting my hair because of a vow I made for Nanda when she got those pains. I have made a lot of sacrifices for her that another young man like me wouldn't have made. I'll tell you something. I never took any of my other sweethearts seriously. I could take them or leave them and it didn't mean a thing. It's different with her because I love her.

Whenever I get paid I give Nanda money. Or I say to her, "Nanda, let's go shopping." And we go and I buy all her clothes for her. I always bought her presents and took her to the movies, too. I used to buy her *panties* and whatever she needed even when I wasn't living with her.

I never refuse Nanda anything. When we went to live over there, in Cataño, she couldn't sleep for the heat and so I said to her, "Don't worry, I'll find a way to get a fan." It took a long time but I finally got one. It's not too good but it does make a breeze.

"I'd like to have a television," she says to me. But I tell her, "Wait until I'm finished paying off what we've already got." I owe eighty-something on the bed, one hundred and ten dollars on the refrigerator, and fifty-something on the record player I gave *mami*. That's nearly four hundred dollars I owe and I can't pay it all at once.

She doesn't push me, though, and she doesn't mind if I give my mother things. On the contrary, she says I should. One time all I had was thirteen dollars. Nanda came and took five dollars and gave them to *mami* because I didn't want to. She always gives money to *mami*, two or three dollars, whatever she can spare.

The age difference between Nanda and me doesn't bother me, because love doesn't depend on age. Look, I have seen young fellows, younger than me, with women up to eighty years old. Women without money, so you can't say that was the reason. One boy here can't be more than twenty or twenty-one, tops, and God knows how old the wife is. Not only that, but she hustles.

And do you think he leaves her? They get along fine and have three or four little kids. They really live happily. Love doesn't depend on age.

Look, I'll tell you something. I'd rather take up with an old woman than live with a virgin. We haven't had any children yet, though. I tell Nanda, "The day you get pregnant and get rid of the baby, I swear to you we are through." Just last night I said it to her. When I asked her why we weren't having any children, she said, "Because we are always fighting. What if I get pregnant and you go off and leave me?"

So I told her, "Even though you don't have any children with me, and you aren't pregnant, I am not going to leave you. If I wanted to leave you I would have done it when we were living in Cataño." But God and the Virgin willing, I think we can be happy together. That's what I keep telling her. I say, "Nanda, what I want is to be happy with you."

What I would like for the future would be to have a house of my own and live in it with Nanda. It wouldn't matter where. If they could at least give me the lumber at election time, I'd build it myself even if it takes me one or two months. The minute I figure out how a thing should be done, I get to work on it and do it, and it comes out fine. I want to give myself *el sport* of being the only one of Nanda's husbands who set up a private house for her. I want to be the one. Nanda has had bad luck with her husbands. And I say, even though people don't believe it, the best husband she has had, in my opinion, is me.

Fernanda

I'm Still Young

I AM HAPPY with Junior. He treats me better than any of my other men. When I get sick he suffers more than I. I'm in a terrible state as far as health goes. Sometimes when I wake up I don't feel like doing anything. When I come home from work in the restaurant I just go limp. The lady I work for drives me crazy. When those women come there for lunch, I feel like throwing the whole lot of them out in the street. Can you imagine what it's like, all of them asking for something at the same time? They don't give me any peace.

My nerves often trouble me. On my job, for instance, when that *bunche* comes in, my stomach nerves are the first to act up and then my hands shake and I drop things. When I get a nervous spell I want to vomit but I can't. I've had a stomach ache since New Year's Eve. Felícita told me I had a fit that night. I only know that I began to think about Simplicio, who was far away, and it made me sad. I must have fainted. It makes me sad to have my children so far away, especially on New Year's Eve.

Soledad was here for the New Year and she acted like a dog to me. I had this pain in the mouth of my stomach and she and Felícita went off and left me alone with Junior and the children. I invited Soledad to my house in Cataño and she said no, that she was going to San Juan. She came to my house only once during the days she was here. I practically never saw her face. I sent her food and left the worst for myself. And then I had to go looking for her to spend New Year's Eve with her. It was half past twelve and

I with my pain and she still hadn't come. And later she wrote from New York saying that I acted like a bitch to her. On the contrary, if we are going to really look at it, she was the one who behaved like a bitch.

What happened was that she was jealous because I sent a little picture of myself to Simplicio and not to her. That's her complaint. That's why I want to take another photo to send her so she and Simplicio won't be quarreling with each other. She is always the one who starts trouble. She knows that when she comes here I am always right with her, as she's my daughter, and as she was that way with her nerves, crazy and all that. I want to love her more, I *should* love her more, see?

I've had that pain in my stomach before and it went away, but since New Year's Eve it's been worse. This illness I have worries Junior terribly. When I'm in pain, Junior says he wishes he could draw the pain out of me by taking it into himself. He wishes he could cure me of any illness I get by catching it himself. He gets the medicines the doctors prescribe for me and he brings me my food. He won't let me do a thing as long as I'm sick. If I ask him to bring me something or do anything for me, he never objects, not even when he's already gone to bed. He gets up and does it.

Sometimes I tell him, "Junior, I want to shit but I don't feel like going to the toilet." Then he'll go get the chamber pot and when I'm through he throws away the mess himself. When I'm menstruating, Junior will go himself to buy me some Tampax. When I want to wash, I call Junior and tell him, "Bring me the Tampax and my *panties* and wash me." And he himself washes my private parts and all that.

None of the other men I've had ever treated me with such affection. If I tell him, "*Ay,* Junior, how tired my body is!" he'll say to me, "Well, lie down and get some rest." When I tell him, "I'd like to read this or that," he'll get it for me if he has the money. He buys me comic books and magazines so I can amuse myself. Whenever I ask to go someplace he never refuses me, he just takes me there. When there are good films he takes me to the movies; if not, we go to look at the shop windows in San Juan. He is not ashamed to go out with me, in spite of the age difference. I've had five husbands, but the only one that goes everywhere with me is Junior. I was unlucky with the other men I've had.

A little while ago I got the idea of selling flavored gelatins and soft drinks here at home, and Junior has already made a sign, which he put up outside the house. I'm going to quit my job and keep myself busy making gelatin and Kool-Aid. I will live an easier life that way, just washing Junior's clothes and the dishes and lying down when I'm tired.

I see to it that Junior is clean. I always have his undershorts and undershirts nicely ironed and kept in separate piles and his clothes pressed so he can get what he needs at any time. In the year he's been living with me he can't say that he has ever had to use a wrinkled handkerchief. If his trousers are ripped or torn, I mend them. If a button is missing from a shirt, I sew it on. I'm attentive to his needs, you see. I always have clothes ready for him, just to show his family. I feel very proud of that and so does he. He stands there and looks and looks at the clothes hanging there.

I keep the house nice and neat for him too. When he comes home and lies down, I tell him, "If you lie down on the bed, be sure to make it up again after you get up. When you take off your shoes, put them away in the proper place." I won't allow him to scatter his things around.

On Saturdays I let him sleep late. I pull down that curtain, shut the door and don't turn on the radio or anything—there is deep silence. I even go outdoors so that he can get all the sleep he wants. Sometimes he wakes up as late as eleven. Sometimes, so that he'll sleep longer, I even stay in bed myself.

But once in a while I'll tell him, "Junior, there's work to do around the house tomorrow, we have to do the cleaning, and I need such and such." That day he gets up early. Like the day he made the clothes rack for me. We changed the bed around and everything. During the week he eats at his *mamá*'s house and only comes here to read and rest.

Junior was always a good boy and behaved well with his *mamá* and *papá*. He never got into trouble the way his brothers Jimmy and Marcelo did. Jimmy is in jail now. That boy was bad since he was a child. It was his destiny to be a thief, because he always liked to steal. Now he's a junkie too, and he steals to buy drugs. He's bad through and through.

Marcelo is still my son Simplicio's best friend. They never forget each other. Marcelo is living now with my *comadre* Cecilia, who is Soledad's godmother of Holy Water. She is a good woman and has a heart of gold and I'm grateful to her for the help she's given me. But she has one defect; she's a born troublemaker. If I say anything about Junior's mother, Cecilia will go right back and tell her about it. Then she comes back here to tell me what Junior's mother said. She's always doing things like that. I haven't come right out and told her off, only because she's my *comadre*. When she comes to visit me I greet her, oh, so cordially. It's *"comadre* this" and *"comadre* that." After the greetings are over, though, I sit down to read while she talks, and I think, "Dear God, why did you give me this woman for a *comadre?"*

To me the *compadre* relationship is a great thing. Its greatness comes from God and it is something to be respected, venerated and treated lovingly, see? I have only three godchildren and I respect all their parents, who are my *compadres*. I respect them so much that I am ashamed to look them in the face.

My *compadres* are like my relatives, because as the old saying goes, "A *compadre* is one's father." If one should die, the godfather and godmother are there to take over and bring up the child. Some people don't know how to treat their *compadres* with respect any more. One of my *compadres* has a *comadre* that he's been living with for years. To me it's shameless for them to be lovers. They even have had children together. It is the biggest sin in the whole world. That is the only case here in La Esmeralda.

Junior's parents are the only real in-laws I have ever had except for Erasmo's *papá,* and I want them to like me. I told Junior that, little by little, I was going to steal back their affection. Before I went with Junior, they had always been nice to me. Now that I'm working, I am going to help them out with money when they need it. And when his mother gives birth to the next baby, I'll buy a chicken to make broth for her. I'll behave real well and help her in the house. I'll win them over that way.

A while back I missed my period for two months and it turned out that I was pregnant. Then Junior said, "I've already been looking at maternity clothes for you. I won't buy you a smock but a real maternity dress and low shoes. Also I'm going to make you quit working. Any day now I'm going to make you begin to get fat around the middle." So he gave me a lot of advice, "Take care of yourself. Don't do anything that might harm you and don't go taking any drinks." What he meant was that I shouldn't do anything that might make me miscarry. He's crazy to have a son of his own and he doesn't want to take any risks.

I talked about it with *doña* Zoila, the sister of the gentleman I work for. She prescribed rue, avocado-tree shoots and other plants. She also told me to take a laxative of castor oil in black malt beer. I never got to take that laxative. I don't know if it was the rue and all those plants that did it or if I strained myself lugging a tub. I really think it was that plant infusion I drank, but I didn't say a word to Junior about having taken it.

I had told him I was going to abort and he must have kept on thinking about it because that night he started screaming in his sleep, "Oh, my God, she killed him, she killed him!" He stroked my belly without waking up. I shook him, saying, "What's the matter?" Then he stared at me. "Nothing. Nothing's the matter." When I told him my blood had begun to flow he looked as if he was terribly shocked.

I don't know what future I may have with Junior but now I think I ought to have another baby because of him. I'm forty years old, but I can still have fifty more babies if I want to. Other women my age have had babies, what would be so strange about my having one? I'm still young!

PART II

SOLEDAD

Days with Soledad
in New York

Rosa hurried along Eagle Avenue toward Soledad's house. It was almost nine o'clock and Soledad and her daughters had to be at the Public Health unit by nine-thirty. Rosa had agreed to go along as interpreter. Soledad lived in a four-story tenement in a Puerto Rican neighborhood in the Bronx. Her narrow, ground-floor railroad apartment consisted of a small living room in the front, a kitchen and bathroom in the rear, and two windowless bedrooms between. The living-room window, close to the street, was covered by a screen of heavy chicken wire. In the summertime when the window was kept open and the Venetian blind pulled up, passers-by could easily look into the apartment and Soledad could carry on conversations with her friends outside.

This April morning* the blinds were closed. Rosa entered the tenement hallway, went directly to the kitchen door in the back, and knocked. Soledad's sister-in-law, Flora, a short, thin, pleasant-faced woman of about thirty, opened the door. "Good morning, Rosa," she said with a smile. "I'm coming along too, to see if they'll take the stitches out of Gabi's head."

* 1964.

Gabriel, Felícita's seven-year-old son, had come from Puerto Rico a few days earlier to stay with his uncle Simplicio and Flora. The day he left Puerto Rico, Gabriel had fallen and cut his head, and the cut had required nine stitches.

Rosa sat down at the kitchen table. Although the kitchen was clean and cheerful-looking, she saw several cockroaches crawling on the walls and over the sink. On one side of the crowded room were a china cabinet, a large four-burner gas stove, and a table and three chairs. On the outer wall a combination sink and washtub was partially blocked by the refrigerator, making the washtub inaccessible. Soledad often washed clothes in the bathtub. The kitchen walls had just been painted a bright green. They were decorated with religious calendars, plastic flowers, a fancy match holder, a plaster plaque of brightly colored fruit, and a new set of aluminum pans. Fresh red-and-white curtains hung at the window. The linoleum, although worn, was scrubbed clean. On a shelf above the kitchen door stood an improvised altar for Saint Expedito, who brings luck to gamblers. On the altar, before a small straw cross, Soledad kept as an offering a glass of rum, cigarettes, coins, dice, playing cards, and bread and butter.

"Hello, Rosa, I'm almost ready," Soledad called from the far bedroom. "Just wait till I get shoes on these little bitches."

In a few minutes Soledad appeared with her three daughters and her nephew Gabriel. Soledad was an attractive, full-bodied mulatto woman, about five feet four inches in height. She had a broad face with high cheekbones, deep-set dark eyes and a short, slightly flat nose. Her hair, normally brown and kinky, had been straightened and tinted a coppery hue. Today she had it done up in two buns behind her ears.

"Well, let's go or we'll be late and then heaven knows when we'll get out," she said. "Those people fill out forms like the devil."

The three women walked together while the children, dressed in inexpensive though clean clothes and new shoes, skipped on ahead. Catín, Soledad's adopted daughter, was eight and a half years old. She was olive-skinned, with straight brown hair and large brown eyes. Her thin body and plain face had a pinched, sickly look and she walked with a limp because one leg was shorter than the other. Six-year-old Sarita, the prettiest of the sisters, was a slender, small-boned child, with blue eyes, white skin and abundant light-brown hair. Toya, who was only four years old but looked older and larger than Sarita, was an attractive, dark-skinned, robust child with a round face, bright black eyes and tightly curled black hair. Gabriel, also dark-skinned, with closely cropped black kinky hair and several front teeth missing, was dressed in a new gray wool suit, red plaid vest, white shirt and black shoes—the outfit he had worn on the plane.

"Oh, my God, I wonder what they'll tell me at the Health Bureau," Soledad said as they walked along. "If Catín is sick, I'm going to write my mother such a letter! She was the one in charge and she abandoned the child to go off with that *teenager*. She loves her husband more than her grand-child. But she'd better look out. If you harm a child you pay dearly for it. I wonder what came over my mother to take up with that *teenager*."

"He works, doesn't he?" Flora answered. "He gives her what she needs. That's what counts. Nothing else matters. Well, who am I to talk? When I first saw Simplicio he was a tiny boy, and now he's my husband."

"But, Flora, how can you compare your marriage to my mother's?" Soledad protested. "The difference between you and Simplicio isn't so great."

"Well, everyone to his own taste," Flora replied. "Isn't that right?"

"Yes, everyone to his taste, but wait until that kid grows up," Soledad said cynically. "He's bound to meet some young girl and then a kick in the ass is all Nanda can expect. He'll get rid of her. As for me, I've always said I like old men. When I break up with a man, I don't want him to be able to call me 'old hag.' Let him look at himself and see who's younger."

They arrived at the Public Health unit and were told by the receptionist to take the elevator to the second floor.

"Oh no, I won't go up in that!" Soledad protested. "Suppose it gets stuck between floors? I'm always dreaming that I'm in an elevator that keeps going up and down, up and down. Or else up and up without stopping."

"Oh, come on, Soledad!" Flora said, and they all crowded into the ele-vator.

They were given turn number 7 and sat down to wait. *"Ay,* I don't like to come to the doctor," Soledad said. "I wonder why I get so scared?"

To pass the time, Soledad began to tease Gabi. "What's the matter with you? You're trembling."

"I was born trembly," the boy answered.

"Ah, you're scared," Soledad said, taking his hand in hers. "That must mean you ran away from something in Puerto Rico. You've got a woman down there, haven't you? Whose wife did you steal, eh?"

"I didn't, Aunt Soledad, really I didn't do anything."

"Yes, you must have seduced some girl. We'll have to send you back to Puerto Rico."

"I won't go back," the boy said, looking worried. "I was hungry there, and everybody beat me, Cruz, Fela, and all of them. I won't go back."

"All right, you can stay here and be my pimp," Soledad said. "You love me, *papito,* don't you?" And she kissed him.

The boy wiped away the kiss. "I won't. I won't be your pimp."

"Oh, yes, you're going to be my man," Soledad insisted, pressing his little hand on her stomach.

"Don't be so fresh with him," Flora said. "He might begin to get fresh himself."

"Oh, when will we get out of here?" Soledad said impatiently. "I can't bear waiting." She fell silent for a few moments. Then she said, "You know, I made a vow to go on my knees from my house to Saint Peter's church if Catín comes out of this well. I wouldn't stop at the greatest sacrifice for my daughter. If He died nailed to the cross for His children, there's nothing wrong in my going to Saint Peter's on my knees. If I had money I'd have Catín treated by good doctors. I'd give my life for that child."

"Did I tell you what Nanda said when I wrote her that Catín was sick?" Flora asked.

"Yes. How could Nanda say that Catín got sick because I beat her! What wickedness! I never beat that child. If a person got sick from beatings, I'd be dead by now. Nanda gave me enough of those."

Finally Soledad's turn came. A tall Negro woman in a navy-blue uniform handed her paper jackets, saying, "Here, put these on the children." Then she began to fill out a form for Soledad, beginning with her name and address.

"And how many children have you?"

"Four."

"Names?"

Soledad gave the children's names, explaining that her son, Quique, was in Puerto Rico with his father.

"How come this little girl's last name is Alvarado?"

"Because she isn't my own daughter. I adopted her," Soledad answered.

"Well, I'd better put them all down as Ríos," the woman said. "What's your husband's name?"

"My husband is dead."

"What did he die of?"

"In an accident." Soledad answered the woman's questions rather sullenly. "What busybodies these people are!" she said in an aside to Rosa. "You'd think I was being jailed for murder."

The attendant asked if Soledad was getting welfare aid. Soledad replied that she was not. "Don't you know you qualify for it?"

"Forget it," Soledad said shortly. "As long as I can work to support my children, I don't want *welfare*. Not the way they treat you."

"Have the children been in contact with anyone who had tuberculosis?" the woman asked.

"Well, yes, with a cousin of mine in Puerto Rico a long time ago. But it was the school doctor who told me to bring the children here." The attendant went out and a doctor came in to give the children the tuberculin test. He then sent them to an adjoining room for chest X-rays, telling them to come back for the results a week later, on Friday.

Before they left the Health Bureau, Soledad spoke to the attendant who had filled out their forms. "Could you take care of my nephew? All he needs is to have these stitches cut."

"No, not here," the woman answered. "You'll have to take him to a hospital for that."

"But we can pay," Soledad said.

"No, we can't do it here," the woman repeated impatiently, waving them out.

"What sons of the great whore they are, all of them! They should have a bomb dropped on them," Soledad exclaimed. "Look," she said when they were outside, "I'm going to cut Gabi's stitches myself. I just know they won't do it at the hospital either. They don't want to take care of him."

Sarita, skipping ahead, stopped in front of a chewing-gum vending machine. "*Mami,* give me a penny," she begged.

"A knife in your back is what you'll get," snapped her mother. "Let's go over to Third Avenue. I have to pawn my ring because I'm flat broke. That stupid husband of mine hasn't sent me a thing. I guess he expects me to live on air."

At the pawnshop Soledad stood admiring her ring while the proprietor waited on other customers.

When it was Soledad's turn, she held out her ring.

"How much do you want for it?" the pawnbroker asked.

"Seven."

"Four."

"All right. Give it to me and let's get it over with." She took the bills and the ticket and put them in her purse. "Let's go to the stationery store and buy some stamps," she said.

Inside the store some small religious pictures caught Soledad's eye. "Say, how much do these cost?"

"Thirty-five cents each."

"I'm going to buy one for Fernanda," she said. "You know, she's writing to me again. It's a miracle. The wings of her heart must have started fluttering." She chose a picture and wrote on the back of it, "Nanda, I am sending you this Saint Anthony so that he will get you lots of sweethearts. Save him as a keepsake from your daughter Soledad."

Leaving the store, she said to Rosa, "Saint Anthony gets sweethearts for you if you stand him on his head. But he's a bad saint. They say the men you get through him always beat you. I'm so unlucky with men, damn it! There hasn't been one good one except for Tavio, and he died. Good things never last."

They passed a Chinese woman and her two children. "Sainted Virgin, that woman looks like the devil's own mother!" Soledad said. "I wouldn't bear a baby to a Chinaman even if they tied me up. They say Chinese men are good husbands and all that, but they're so ugly!"

"I have to go home and cook Simplicio's dinner," Flora said abruptly. She took Gabriel by the hand and turned to leave.

"Yes, go along and take good care of your husband," Soledad called mockingly after her. Then she said to Rosa, *"Ay,* let's go to the park awhile so the children can get some sun. They're always shut up in the house."

When they reached the park Soledad broke into a run and raced the children to the swings. She picked each one up, set them on the swings and began pushing them. Then, smiling, she stopped Toya's swinging in order to hug the child. "This is *mami's* littlest girl. *Mami's* little Toya. Come, give me a real lover's kiss on the mouth like in the movies." Toya kissed her mother full on the mouth.

"Ummm, good!" Soledad said, licking her lips.

She went to Sarita, who was in the next swing. "Get down, get down!" Holding the child in her arms, she pulled down her panties and kissed her buttocks. Then she touched the little girl's vagina. "And who does this little kitchen belong to?"

"Don't be so fresh, *mami,"* the little girl said, squirming free.

Soledad ran to Catín and hugged and kissed her. *"Ay,* this daughter is almost a young lady already."

"Mami, swing me on your lap," Catín said.

Soledad sat down on a swing and took Catín on her lap. As they swung, Soledad looked childishly happy; she laughed aloud like a little girl. After a time Catín slipped from her lap and ran with her sisters to the slides. Soledad began to swing high. When she tired of it she abruptly jumped from the swing and announced, "We're going now."

Outside the house they met Rosalía, an old, stout Negro woman who was a friend and neighbor. She was dressed in black as usual.

"Hello, my darling! How are you?" Soledad called, running up to hug and kiss the woman.

"Keep off, sugar, you aren't my husband," Rosalía said good-naturedly.

"You know you're my darling," Soledad answered as she hurried into the house. She unlocked the kitchen door and went straight to the bathroom. When Rosa and the girls came into the kitchen, they heard her urinating. "I can't hold my urine very long," she said when she came out. "They must have hurt my bladder when they operated on me."

Soledad went to her bedroom and threw herself face down on the big double bed. Because she seemed tired, Rosa tried to keep the girls in the kitchen, but after a few minutes they went to stand quietly beside the bed, looking at their mother with anxious faces. The room was very small and the bedroom set almost completely filled it. Between the bed and the matching dresser there was a space of only sixteen inches, and here the girls lined up. The foot of the bed was so close to the chest of drawers that the two bottom drawers could not be opened more than three inches. There was no closet;

clothes were hung from hooks on the wall. Over the bookcase headboard, a shelf held several suitcases and cartons. Underneath the shelf behind a short plastic curtain, a bar had been suspended to hold more clothing.

On top of the chest Soledad had arranged a number of religious objects to form an altar. In the center were statuettes of Jesus, the Sacred Heart, Saint Felícita, the Virgin of Carmen, and the dark-faced Saint Martin of Porres. Around these figures were two candles in candleholders, a vase of artificial flowers, a small crucifix, a paperweight with the figure of Jesus, a gold ceramic incense burner, a bottle of French perfume and three gracefully draped rosaries. On the wall above the chest were eight religious pictures: the Virgin, Saint Martha, Saint Michael Archangel, the African Saint Barbara, the Heart of Jesus, the Child with the Torch, the Three Virtues—Faith, Hope and Charity—and a large Brazilian picture showing the Virgin as the Queen of the Sea who cast down stars that turned to roses.

Two prayer books lay open on the altar, one opened to "Prayers to the Guardian Angels," the other, a spiritist gospel, opened to "Instructions of the Spirits: In Gratitude for Children and Family Bonds." A glass of water to "catch evil spirits" stood next to the books. Each week Soledad poured the old water down the toilet and refilled the glass.

After watching her mother for several minutes, Catín said timidly, "What's the matter, *mami?*" Toya, who often demanded caresses, said, *"Mami,* please give me a kiss."

Soledad opened her eyes and said crossly, "Oh, go away and leave me alone! I'm all right." Seeing Rosa, she sat up and added, "I'll have to go to the old man. No matter how I stretch them, four dollars won't be enough for the whole week. Oh, I'm all screwed up!"

Suddenly she gathered the children into her arms. "But look at the treasures I have. Aren't my little girls pretty? There's just one thing missing, and that's my son, my only male child. I gave him my tits until he was five years old. Oh, Rosa, you don't know how much a mother loves her children! Look, want to see how beautiful Quique was when he was a baby?"

She got out a photograph album from a suitcase under the bed. Leafing through the album, she showed Rosa pictures of Quique at different ages. Then she came to some pictures of Octavio, her dead husband. In one photograph which had the words "My Heart Is Yours" inscribed on it, he was shown leaning against a counter. In another he and Soledad were together, she in a maternity dress and he proudly touching her stomach. On other pages Octavio's death was recorded. One showed his coffin covered with flowers; there were other photos of the grave. Soledad began to cry, silently at first. She shut the album, flung herself on the bed and sobbed, not caring who heard her. The children, who had wandered off to play, came running in.

"Mami, what's the matter? Why are you crying?"

Soledad drew Toya into her arms. "Come here, my little Toya. Where's your *papá?"*

"They killed him. They shot him dead."

"Yes, they did, they shot him dead." Soledad let the child go and turned to Rosa. "I loved that man and I still do," she said. "He was so affectionate, so nice to me. What a thing to happen! He's buried in the cemetery at La Esmeralda. We used to go there to talk and we'd play hide and seek and cowboys and Indians. He'd pretend to shoot me and I'd drop on the ground and then he'd pick me up."

Soledad fell silent for a moment, then stood up and freshened her make-up before the mirror. "Come out with me to call El Polaco," she said to Rosa. "I'll see if he asks me to go over. I just have to get hold of some money." The two women went to a telephone in a nearby store. Soledad dialed a number and then said engagingly. "Hello, lover, how are you? . . . Well, I was wondering about you, too. . . . You don't say! But that's no problem because I'll make it go down in no time at all. I'll be right over, *O.K.?* See you, darling."

Soledad hung up, and she and Rosa hurried back to the apartment. "Do me a favor, Rosa, and stay with the children? I'll just wash up and leave and come right back with some money." The children asked where she was going and she told them she had to buy something in El Barrio. She reminded Catín to tidy up the house and she warned all the girls that they must behave well. When she was gone, the children went back to playing with her old pocketbooks and shoes.

Rosa began to make the beds, and the three girls helped her. Catín tidied the jumble of cosmetics on Soledad's dresser—the small-sized jars and tubes of creams and pomades, the make-up lotion, hair spray, wave set, deodorant, nail polish, powder and perfumes, almost all of the Avon brand. There were also two large eau de cologne bottles and a small bottle of Lanvin perfume. A cracker tin held hair curlers and bobby pins, and a cardboard box was filled with several lipsticks, pins, jewelry, buttons, combs and odds and ends. There were several paperback books, love stories in Spanish and two in English that a neighbor had given to Soledad.

When the bedrooms were neat, Rosa and the girls washed the breakfast dishes and made lunch. Rosa fried some pork chops and bananas, setting aside enough for Soledad. After lunch Rosa lay down on the bed to rest and the girls crowded around her, hugging her and demanding to be kissed.

Rosa was teaching them the English alphabet when Soledad returned at two o'clock. She had been gone an hour and a half.

She came into the bedroom, gave the children some cookies she had bought and sent them to the kitchen, saying, "Don't come in here until I say so." She lit the two candles and knelt with bowed head in front of the altar for several minutes. She did this whenever she was unfaithful to her husband. As there were no prayers in either of her prayer books for a situation like this, she just remained silent until she felt better. When she left the bedroom to go to the kitchen to eat her lunch, her face was serious but she seemed calm.

"*Mami,* where have you been?" Catín asked.

"Don't ask questions. What a little busybody you are!"

"But what were you doing, *mami?*" Sarita said.

"Nothing. It's none of your business. Run away and play."

When the children had gone to the living room to watch television, Soledad said to Rosa, "Look, I got my fifteen dollars. It only takes a little while, because he comes right away."

Someone knocked on the kitchen door and Soledad opened it to Rosalía. "Hello, my love. You can't live without me, eh? What's new?"

"Oh, go to hell," Rosalía answered.

"Don't say that. I want you to take good care of your you-know-what, because it belongs to me."

"And since when have you become a lesbian, you shameless hussy?" Rosalía said, laughing. "Aren't you ashamed of yourself? How's your husband?"

"With a stiff prick, I suppose, since I'm not there to give him anything."

"Have some respect, dirty mouth!"

"*Ay,* Rosalía, that's the way we talk in La Esmeralda. You talk even worse, because you're from Loíza Aldea, where people aren't civilized yet."

"Now look," Rosalía said, "I came here forty years ago. I've never been back to Puerto Rico and I never will go back. Not even when I die. I want to be buried here where it's cold so the worms won't eat me."

"I want to die in my own country. Me buried here? Oh no!"

"Do you know how much it costs to ship a body to Puerto Rico? About fifteen hundred dollars."

"Don't be a damn fool," Soledad said. "Do you think I'd let myself die here? What an idea! The minute I feel even a little bit sick, I'll fly right back to Puerto Rico."

"I don't even remember what Puerto Rico's like. To tell you the truth, I don't even like to eat green bananas."

"Why, you shameless creature! You don't deserve to live. To think that a countrywoman from Loíza Aldea shouldn't like green bananas! There's nothing better than a dish of fresh-cut green bananas boiled with codfish. Oh, well, let's skip it. Want some coffee? Some soup? A banana?"

"No, no."

"Well then, eat shit if that's what you want. Toya, come over here. Don't you want to make *caca?* Rosalía feels like eating some shit."

"All kidding aside, I don't like to eat in anybody else's house," Rosalía said. "Not since I visited some people and found a gob of phlegm in the kitchen sink. I haven't eaten outside my own house since then."

"*Ave María!* Don't be so finicky. Water cleans anything."

"Oh no, I can't stand dirty habits, like people brushing their teeth over the kitchen sink. Listen, that girl of yours, the dark one, is getting fresh. She won't pay any attention to me any more."

"Tell Benedicto," Soledad said indifferently. "He's the one that spoils her. If I spank Toya, Benedicto practically eats me alive. He'd let her throw the doors out of the windows if she wanted to. But if Sarita, the white one, does anything at all, he spanks her right away. Do you think it's because of Toya's color that he likes her better? She's dark like him."

"That's what it is. You see, a white person sooner or later is going to call a Negro '*nigger.*' You mark my words. A white person will always throw your color up to you. Well, I have to go now. I'm waiting for my son and he's due to show up any minute."

"Oh, drop it, Rosalía," Soledad said. "Do you think that boy is still a baby? He must be twenty-eight years old. He's off some place screwing a girl. Or do you put out for him yourself?"

"Damn it, Soledad, have a little more respect for my son!" Rosalía said in real annoyance. "I love that boy like he was God, girl."

"All right, you love him like God, *chica,* but for God's sake, let loose of him," Soledad answered.

A few minutes after Rosalía had gone there was another knock on the door, and Soledad opened it this time to Elfredo, a white-skinned, baby-faced, dark-haired young man. He was a numbers runner and Soledad bought a number from him almost every day. Today she asked for three numbers, paying fifteen cents each.

After she had finished her business with Elfredo, Soledad suggested that they go into the living room. She sent the children back to the kitchen and sat down with Elfredo on a bulky black sofa in front of the window. Rosa took a large blue chair in the opposite corner. This chair stood in front of the living-room door, which Soledad kept permanently locked. An orange chair in another corner was occupied by a life-sized doll dressed in black and yellow tulle. A false fireplace covered almost the entire left-hand wall; on the mantel was a profusion of photographs, ceramic figurines of a lion and a panther, a little boat in a stemmed glass, a set of toy animals and, in the center, an African voodoo doll which Benedicto had brought from Brazil. The plaster doll had two faces, a black one on one side and a brown one on the other. Soledad turned the faces around each week. She had more faith in this doll, she said, than in her two black saints. A coffee table that stood in front of the fireplace held a crocheted doily, a set of glass ashtrays shaped like butterflies, and various inexpensive ceramic objects. End tables holding similar objects

stood beside each of the big chairs. On one of the end tables there was also a
record player; a stack of records was piled on the shelf beneath. A television
set occupied a corner between the coffee table and the sofa. The walls also
were decorated with objects, a cheap tapestry of "The Last Supper," artificial
flowers, ceramic plaques, small pictures, some tiny straw hats, and two necklaces of multicolored plastic fruit with bracelets to match. On the window sill,
partly hidden by the cretonne drapes, stood a green plant, some artificial
flowers in a brightly painted vase, and a ceramic figure of a naked woman
sitting on a beer barrel. A washable gray rug covered the small space in the
center of the floor.

The television set was still turned on and they all watched a scene in
which a young girl was contemplating suicide because her father had been
killed for selling stolen goods and she was left alone and penniless.

"Dope! Idiot!" Soledad said, switching off the set impatiently. "How can
she think of killing herself? She shouldn't be such a coward. You have to face
whatever life brings. Hell, some people shit on themselves over every little
thing that happens to them. I say put a good face to bad times. No trouble
lasts a hundred years."

Elfredo looked at Soledad admiringly and said, "You know, Soledad, I
wouldn't mind getting married to you."

"How can you say such a thing to me? And with all those sweethearts.
Really, how can you? I have four children."

"That's nothing. If you love the hen, you love her chicks."

"You know very well that I have a husband."

"Yes, and I know something else, too. I know you aren't happy with him."
He moved closer to Soledad on the sofa. "Come on, give me a kiss."

Soledad leaned back to avoid him but he kissed her on her closed lips
anyway.

"I have to go now," he said. "It's getting late and I have to turn in these
numbers. But I'll be back tomorrow and I'll be much hotter then."

"It's time for me to leave too," Rosa said. "Will you walk me to the bus,
Elfredo?"

They went through the two darkened bedrooms. There was a strong
stench of urine from the children's bed. "Those girls are real pissers," Soledad
said. "I'll have to change their sheet tomorrow."

In the kitchen, the children were coloring pictures on the floor. Soledad
said good-bye to Rosa and Elfredo and double-locked the door behind them.

Three Months Later

ONE FRIDAY EVENING in August, Rosa came again to visit Soledad. She found Soledad, Rosalía, Benedicto and a neighbor, Moisés, sitting around the kitchen table drinking whiskey.

"Hello, I'm glad you've come," Soledad said.

"What do you think, I just got home yesterday and I have to ship out again tomorrow," Benedicto said. *"Negra,* show Rosa the gift I brought you."

Benedicto was a handsome, stocky, brown-skinned, kinky-haired man of about forty. He had a small, natty mustache and was wearing well-cut trousers, a good sport shirt and new shoes.

Soledad went to her bedroom and brought out a pretty red bedspread, also a straw purse and several bottles of perfume.

"He brought a lot of things but he forgot the wine tonic I need for my health," Soledad remarked.

"I did buy it for you, *negra,*" Benedicto said. "What happened is that it fell and broke when I went through customs. And two bottles of whiskey along with it."

"You think I'm dope enough to believe that? Ah, go to hell and leave me alone. I'm hopping mad today. You low-down drunk, you're going to end up an *atómico."**

"Look, Soledad, I've had a few drinks today but that doesn't make me a drunk. You know I can hold my liquor."

"Just listen to the poor bastard. He dares to deny he's a drunk. When I got home from work yesterday, I found him in that chair dead to the world. Who was drinking with you? You told me somebody took the bottle of whiskey and thirty dollars you had."

"I was with my cousin Ramón and my son."

"That goes to show they only bother to look you up when you have rum or money. The bastards!"

"It must have been Ramón who took the things," Benedicto said. "My son wouldn't do such a thing. When he needs anything he comes to me and says, '*Papi,* give me money to do this or that.' And I pull the money out of my belly if I have to so as to give it to him."

"Your son's an overgrown sissy and he has a job of his own. Why should he be asking you for money? And why should you hand it over when he does?"

"I don't mind. I have a duty toward him and toward everybody at home.

* Alcoholic.

That responsibility fell on my shoulders when I was a boy and I've had it ever since."

"You don't say! And when have you ever given your family anything? All you care about is chasing after whores."

"I really must speak up," Rosalía said. "Beni was my next-door neighbor for a long time and I know he supported his family."

"*Negra,* don't be so critical of the other women," Benedicto said. "Remember where I met you?"

"All right, you met me in a *bar*. But you know how you had to keep after me until you got me. I wasn't like the rest of them. True or false?"

"Oh, *negra,* I don't know what you do to me that I can't live without you," Benedicto said, taking hold of Soledad's hand.

Soledad jerked it away. "You're always saying you love me, but you almost let me starve this time. You sent me only fifteen dollars while you were gone. And much good that did me because I couldn't cash the money order."

"But, *negra,* I wrote telling you to buy on credit and that I'd give you money when I got back."

"Like hell you wrote me," Soledad said indignantly. "In the twenty-five days you were away I only got one letter. Were you too broke to buy stamps? Or were your hands too full of shit to write?"

"I swear I wrote you. I wrote three times. Something must be happening to the mail here. Come on, Moisés, take one more drink to kill the bottle." Both men took a long swallow.

Soledad opened two cans of vegetable soup and put the contents in a saucepan to heat. When the soup was ready, she called the children and gave them each a bowl. Sarita and Catín took their bowls back to the living room. Toya sat down on the kitchen floor and gobbled her soup as if she were very hungry. When she had finished, Benedicto took her up in his arms.

"Did *mami* feed you well while I was away? How did she behave? Did any men come here?" he asked.

"Stop, stop! I'd better go before there's a fight," Rosalía said. "Look at the way this man is teaching the child to be a tattletale. *Cristiano,* you shouldn't teach children things like that. And then people complain when their children turn out to be delinquents."

"No, Rosalía, don't leave," Soledad said, throwing her arms around her friend. "You know that you're my *mamá* and I love you very much."

"Those are the rumors that are going around," Rosalía said, disengaging herself. "But the minute your fat old mother shows up here, you'll give me two swift kicks in the ass."

"Oh, Rosalía, don't say such things, you hurt my feelings. When my *mamá* comes, you're the first person I'll take her to see. And I'll tell her, 'Look, this is Rosalía and she's been more of a mother to me than you ever were.' "

"Stop pawing me, child. All right. I'll stay a little longer."

"Listen, Soledad, when I got here yesterday, the first thing I did was to ask for you," Benedicto said. "They told me you were out working. Then I asked for the children because I had a little bracelet for each of them. And do you know what Catín did? She ran away and hid and wouldn't take the bracelet. I don't like rude, sassy children around. So let's just send that kid back to Puerto Rico."

"That kid's going to stay right here," Soledad said angrily. "I'm her mother and she stays with me. Where the hell could she go in Puerto Rico? Just today I got a letter from Fernanda saying that Felícita has gotten to be a rich bitch and doesn't even look after her own children. As for that Crucita, forget it. So this kid's going to die wherever I die. And listen, you, you were asking who came or didn't come to this house. Well, I'll tell you, you idiot. Every lover I ever had or will have comes here. Somebody has to satisfy me if you don't."

Benedicto replied, "As far as I can tell, I can still get a good hard-on."

"Oh, you do?" Soledad said, laughing now. "You get a hard-on, do you?"

Benedicto got up unsteadily from his chair and grabbed her. "You know I have a great big prick just for you," he said and began to open his fly. "I'm a man who has his balls in the right place. See? Let's go into the parlor so you can get a taste of it."

He passed his hands roughly over his wife's breasts, then turned her around so that she had her back to him, and kissed her neck. Soledad pushed back against him so hard that he fell down on his chair.

"Say, you two, how fresh can you get!" Rosalía said. "You're bold as brass. Aren't you ashamed of yourselves?"

"Oh, well, it's all in the family," Soledad answered. "Besides, we haven't done anything bad."

"No, not at all, you shameless good-for-nothing! Look, when I was young there was nothing I loved better than to play with that thing men pee with. But I didn't get fresh like you."

"Well, you'll still do," Benedicto said, touching her hips. "What a luscious babe!"

"Don't be fresh. You know I'm like a mother to you."

"There's no doubt about it, Rosalía," Benedicto went on, "you still have some juicy bits."

"Shut up, you dirty mouth," Rosalía answered. "My lovers have already told me that. Do you know I have an Italian sweetheart? But we don't do *that*, nothing doing. If Enrico heard me, he'd tear out my hair. But you two know I don't mean it. I don't give a thought to all that any more. It's all ancient history to me."

"Benedicto, where's your jacket?" Soledad asked.

"It's right there, Soledad."

"No, it isn't. As soon as I came home I looked for your things and I didn't find it."

"Then I must have left it over at *mamá*'s."

"At *mamá*'s," Soledad said, mimicking him. "Are you sure you didn't lose it in the fight?"

"Oh, so they've already told you I had a fight."

"Of course. I can find out about you just as easily as you can find out about me. You're making a monkey of yourself, fighting and trying to find out what I've been doing."

"I had to fight," Benedicto said defensively. "They called me a queer in front of my son. I couldn't stand for that."

"They beat you up for being drunk, that's what happened," Soledad said.

"Beni, where did you sail on this trip?" Rosalía asked, trying to keep the peace.

"Well, I went to Italy, Spain, and to an island near Spain where they make a lot of dolls. When I go there again, I'll get one for Soledad."

Soledad went into the children's bedroom to see if they were all right. They had fallen asleep on top of their bed and she covered them with a bedspread before going back to the kitchen. "You're always saying you'll bring me something," she said tartly to Benedicto.

"Look, I've been here since three o'clock and I haven't had a bite to eat," Benedicto said. "Cook something for me, will you, Soledad?"

"No, I won't! I've already made dinner and I'm not going to begin cooking for you at this hour of the night. I'm tired and I got up early this morning to go to work."

"Don't go to work then."

"Oh no? And who's going to pay for all the extras. You?"

"Well, if you won't cook for me, I'll have to go out to eat," Benedicto said.

"No, sir, you aren't going anywhere," Rosalía said. "I'll cook your dinner."

She found some hamburger in the refrigerator and made meat balls and French fried potatoes. While Benedicto was eating, Simplicio arrived. "See the kind of wife I have?" Benedicto complained. "Her husband returns after twenty-five days at sea and she won't even cook his dinner. But never mind, I can give as good as I get. How's Flora?"

"She's all right. She's home," Simplicio replied.

"He always leaves her alone so he can go out whoring," Soledad said. "Someday Flora's going to catch you and go back to Puerto Rico. Then you'll really be in trouble."

"Flora looks as skinny as a skeleton lately," Rosalía said.

"That's because this damn fool makes her suffer so much," said Soledad. "He spends every weekend with some woman or other."

"It's not true. I don't make her suffer at all. She's always been like that," Simplicio said. "She never weighed more than a hundred pounds. How could I make her suffer when she's my saint? To me she's the Virgin Mary. That woman is wife and mother to me."

"All right, keep on chasing after other women," his sister told him. "When you catch a woman's disease I'll be the first to tell Flora not to let you screw her."

"Let him take his pleasure, that's what he's a man for," Rosalía said. "These days, women want to rule the men. In the old times a man could leave his wife for a month and go do what he pleased. And when he returned she had to smile and take him back. I'll tell you something. A man who lived next door to us brought his mistress home to help his wife with the housework. Well, the two women lived under one roof as happy as could be."

"That wouldn't work with me," Soledad said. "If I don't satisfy a man, let him leave me and get himself another woman. I won't stand for my man having a mistress. That's the reason why I'll never get mixed up with a married man. In the first place, I wouldn't do anything that I wouldn't like to have done to me. And in the second place, I don't want to be some man's toy, to play second fiddle."

There was a knock on the door and a fat, rather short young Negro girl entered. She lived across the street.

"Hello, Sylvia. What's new, chicken?" Benedicto said. "You look very nice. Want a drink?"

"If I have another, I'll fall down," the girl answered. "I'm high already."

She went to sit on the radiator near the window. Simplicio sat down beside her. "*Ave María,* what a tiny waist you have, girl." He put his arm around her.

"I've looked in the mirror and I know what my waist is like. So you needn't say that again," Sylvia replied flirtatiously.

"Soledad, hand me a cigarette and give me the wallet from my coat pocket," Simplicio said.

Soledad looked in the pockets. "It isn't here," she said. "You must have lost it screwing down there on the grass." Although she spoke to Simplicio she looked fixedly at Sylvia.

"Oh, don't say such things," Sylvia giggled. "It makes me feel funny right away." She got up to leave. Simplicio remained seated on the radiator.

"Simplicio, don't be so rude," his sister scolded. "Go with Sylvia down to the sidewalk at least." They went out. Simplicio returned almost at once.

Soledad turned on him. "Simplicio, have a little shame. Take your whores to hell if you want to, but don't bring them here. Next time you do that, I'm going straight to Flora and tell her. What would she think of me if she knew?"

"I didn't bring that girl here," Simplicio said. "Hand me my jacket. I want to see if I can find my wallet."

While Simplicio was searching in his pockets, Rosalía looked him over from head to foot. "Look, son," she said. "I'm going to tell you something, but don't get mad. You dress in bad taste, the way the street boys dress. Look at that little black hat and the way you tip it sideways. And that striped jacket, that gray cha-cha shirt and black pants tied at the ankle. And you're wearing sandals instead of shoes. Respectable men don't dress like that."

"Look, Rosalía, I wear what's in fashion," the young man replied. "Damn it, I lost my wallet with all my papers and everything. Well, maybe somebody will find it and mail it back to me."

"There isn't any post office in the grass, sonny," Soledad said with heavy sarcasm.

"Oh, skip it, Soledad. Say, lend me two dollars, will you?"

"Do you think I'm a millionaire? You know I have four children to support. You don't have even one, yet you're always whining."

"Oh, stop it, and give me something."

"My cunt is what I'll give you," his sister said. "Here, want it? Take it."

"*Maricona!*" Simplicio said.

"Listen, you'd better shut up before I bash your face in. Men are nothing but sons of the great whore. And my brother is the biggest bastard of them all."

A puppy that had been sleeping near the radiator woke up and began to bark. "I don't want any dogs in here," Benedicto said. "So you can take this one back where you got him."

"I'm not going to take him back," Soledad said. "He was a present to the girls and they're crazy about him. Besides, I'm the one who cleans up his shit, not you. Right now he's whining to go out, but I'll bet you wouldn't take him."

"I've never gotten along very well with dogs," Benedicto answered.

Soledad went out with the dog. When she came back she said to Benedicto, "Nilsa wants to know if you'll give her a drink."

"When have I ever refused anybody a drink? Tell her to come on in."

Moisés, a dark-skinned man of medium height, with boyish features and large, expressive eyes, raised his head at the mention of his wife's name. He had been sitting quietly with his head lowered, half listening to the conversation. Now he said, "*Ay,* I can't stand that wife of mine anymore! I'm going to leave her one of these days." He took another drink from Benedicto's bottle. "Now she doesn't want my children around. Nobody can imagine what I have to put up with from *her* children. That dope-addict son of hers is driving me crazy."

"Don't get mad now, but I tell you you're a damn fool," Benedicto said. "How can you allow that boy to kick you out of your own house?"

"Oh, I don't count for anything there," Moisés said, "I have to sleep on the floor so her son can sleep comfortably in the bed. And look what the woman has done to me. I worked in a factory for eight years, but when I hurt my hand I had to stay home until it got well. So she went there and told them about it and they gave her a job. And now I don't dare show my face there. God knows what terrible things she has told them about me. Now I'm not worth anything at home because she has the job, not me. What I can earn doing odd jobs here and there can't begin to measure up to her wages."

"I repeat that you're acting like a damn fool," Benedicto said. "The first thing I'd do if I were you would be to get her out of that job. That would really screw things up for her."

Nilsa pushed open the door. She swayed tipsily as she came in. She was a short slender woman of about fifty, with long brown hair hanging about her wrinkled face. She wore round, black-rimmed glasses and was dressed in a cotton housecoat.

"Hello, Nilsa, feeling gay?" Benedicto said.

"Sure I am," the woman answered. She sat down on the radiator. "A person should enjoy life. After you're dead, what difference does it make? *Ay le lo le, ay le lo lai,*" she sang. She looked at her husband. "I'm going to split that man's skull. I'm just like my son, the one who's in jail in Puerto Rico. I don't care what I do or what happens to me. I can't stand this lazy, fucking bastard."

Nilsa's son called from outside the apartment, *"Mamá,* come on home and go to sleep. Don't kick up a row in somebody else's house."

"Ah, go to hell. Go shit on your mother."

"Did you hear that?" Moisés said. "And then she expects her son to respect her. Listen, you, respect your son's beard. He's a grown man already."

"I don't respect even your pubic hairs, because you're a lazy good-for-nothing who doesn't support his wife."

"Soledad, give me five dollars to buy beer," Benedicto said. "The whiskey's all gone."

"What! Are you crazy? Don't you dare ask me."

"Yes, I will. Give me three at least."

"Not even one, you drunken bastard. We have so much money, don't we? You give me such a lot!"

"Didn't I just give you a hundred and fifty dollars? What do you expect, anyway?"

"That you shouldn't take them away again. With that money I have to pay the insurance, the furniture store, two months I owe for milk, buy food, get the TV set out of the *pawnshop,* and I don't know what else."

"There must be about two hundred dollars under the pillow," Benedicto said. "I put the money some place but I can't remember where."

"I've already looked all over the house for it. That money isn't here. Two hundred turds is what you must have left. God knows where you lost that money, you idiot."

Nilsa's son called to her. *"Mamá,* the baby woke up and you're not here. All you care about is drinking beer. Come on home. Remember, you promised my brother to take care of the baby."

"Oh, the baby! Well, I'm going," Nilsa said, getting up. "Come on, Moisés, we're going." Moisés didn't move. "I said we're going," Nilsa said. "Come on, you walk ahead."

"You do this to me in front of other people?"

"Yes, in front of other people. So what?"

"But is that an order?"

"Yes, it's an order. Come on, I said let's go."

"Well, if it's an order, I'll go," Moisés said, getting up. They went out, Moisés walking ahead as Nilsa had commanded.

"Ave María, what that woman has done to him!" Rosalía said. "It's terrible. She must have boiled his coffee in ass-water."

"It's just that he's a damn fool," Soledad said, putting down the Spanish language newspaper she had been reading.

"Soledad, give me two dollars," Benedicto said.

"Give that man the money so he'll stop bothering," Rosalía said. "Remember, he's going away tomorrow."

"All right, I'll give them to you, but only because Rosalía asked me to." Soledad went into the bedroom for her purse. Simplicio offered to go buy the beer.

"Have one, Rosalía," Benedicto said when Simplicio came back with several cans.

"No, thanks. I just stayed on to make you two behave. Now I have to go. My son will be home soon and I want to be there before he comes. How can I, a woman, get home later than the man who wears the pants? I kid around and all that but I respect my son."

When the beer was all gone Simplicio got up to leave. "If Flora won't let you in, come back here," his sister said.

Simplicio and Rosalía left together.

In the children's bedroom Toya began to cry because her ear ached. Soledad warmed a bottle of milk and went to the little girl, but Toya refused it and went on crying. "My little Toya, come here," Soledad said, taking the child in her arms. "Your ear hurts you, doesn't it? Come, let's go to the bathroom and I'll cure you. But stop crying, because it makes me nervous and if you make me nervous I'll hit you."

When Toya had urinated into a little chamber pot, Soledad carefully put some urine and then a wad of cotton into the child's ear. She carried Toya back to the smelly bed, gave her the bottle and rocked the mattress up and down until Toya went to sleep.

Soon they all prepared to go to sleep. Benedicto went to bed. Soledad put a clean sheet and blankets on the couch in the living room for Rosa and handed her a nightgown. Both women began to undress. Soledad noticed Rosa looking at the scars on her back. On the left side the skin was puckered and there was a thick ugly scar from the shoulder to the waist. Two other, narrower scars began at the right shoulder and ended midway, at the ribs.

"Yes, just look at my back," Soledad said. "I got this thing on my left side when my stepmother's sister burned me. That's why I love her so much. Every time I undress I remember, and I curse Hortensia and her whole family. And these scars my first husband Arturo gave me." With that, Soledad went into the bedroom to join Benedicto.

For a while there was silence. Then Soledad spoke. "Why do you have to go and get drunk when you know you won't be good for anything? Get off me. I'm not going to stay awake all night waiting for you to come. What do you think I am, an animal?"

There was silence again. A little later Benedicto got up and went to the bathroom. "Soledad, you get this dog out of here," he exclaimed angrily as he returned to the bedroom. "Look, I got shit all over my foot. You get rid of him before I come back."

Soledad did not answer.

At about three in the morning Toya woke up. *"Mami,"* she cried. "Give me some milk."

"Yes, my love," Soledad mumbled, still half asleep. She went to the kitchen and warmed some milk. On her way back she picked up the child and brought her into her own bed.

An hour or so later Sarita awoke and called, *"Mami,* I'm cold."

"All right," Soledad yelled, out of patience now. "Get in here with us too. You bitches aren't going to let us get any sleep tonight."

Soledad

————

Nobody Loved Me

————

THEY SAY that things were better in olden times. I wish I had lived centuries ago when life was more peaceful. People had no worries then and children behaved; aunts and uncles looked out for their nieces and nephews; godparents took care of their godchildren. But now all that has changed. We are living in a time when nobody cares about anybody.

Even the poor no longer help each other. In the old times, if a neighbor needed a bowl of broth somebody would prepare it and take it to him. Who would do that nowadays? Now the poor care only about keeping what they have and grabbing somebody else's share too. Even country people have changed. You know how generous they used to be, always giving you a vegetable or something. Now you have to buy it from them. You find selfishness everywhere. The time when we helped each other is ancient history, as the saying goes.

And the envy that exists among the poor! If you have two dresses, they wish you had only one and they begrudge you that. They even cast their dirty spells to take your husband away from you. If you happen to have a small farm or a little shack, they'd like to see you lose it and become a pauper. Little do they care that you sacrificed your whole life to get it.

Nothing like that ever happened to me, thank God, because I've never had anything to lose. No house or farm or anything. If I have a husband and another woman wants him, let her have him. If a man leaves you because of a spell, only God's power can bring him back. I'd let him go. After all, there's always another man waiting.

Some of us are born poor and some rich. I am poor, but when I come across somebody who's been luckier than I it doesn't bother me, because that was his destiny. But just because you're poor, the rich think you aren't worth anything and despise you. Suppose I live near a rich woman. And suppose her little girls want to play with mine. That rich woman would come and shoo off my children because she doesn't want hers to be friends with mine. Who the hell does she think she is? It's not right, because we're all children of God and each life is a world of its own. That's God's divine truth. But when have you seen a rich person get together with a poor one? When? That only happens in fairy tales where a princess marries a shepherd. That was in the olden times and this is 1964.

I hate the rich. When I was a child, I never played with rich children. I only worked for some fucking Arabs. They were well off and they treated me like a servant. They squeezed me dry. I worked from noon until nine at night and all day Saturday. I had to scrub the whole house, and help with the cooking and washing and ironing. All that for fifteen dollars a month. Is that justice? You tell me. That's the main problem in these times. The rich want to be even richer, and instead of helping the poor, they would like to see us lower still.

I have rich relatives on my father's side of the family. My father owns a house and a car, and here I am a pauper. He worked and sacrificed, it's true, but God only knows what dishonest tricks he played to get all that. Do you believe that he bought a house and a car on the salary he earns? I'll tell you how he got them, by starving his children's bellies, that's how. Because the government sent him money for us and he let his wife keep it. So you see, our own father stole from us. And God only knows how many corpses he robbed when he was killing people over in Korea. There's no telling what he did, but that's between him and God.

I'll tell you frankly, my father didn't love me. He never treated me like a daughter or paid any attention to me. He had enough money to help me but he didn't when I needed it most. If he had been a good father I wouldn't be what I am now.

The truth is, I never had any affection from anybody. I never had a loving home. My grandmother died when I was a child. I had no one to love me, neither my *papá* nor my *mamá,* nor my grandmother, nor my great-grandmother, nor my grandfather. And such is my bad luck that even my husband doesn't love me. I have never been happy with any man. The only love I've had was what I've given myself.

I don't care about affection any more nor about any kind of love. What I want is money. I have three daughters and love and affection aren't going to support them. Yes, I've looked for love but when I got it everything went wrong.

You know how it is when you are young and inexperienced and ignorant. A man comes and says, "I adore you," and promises villas and castles. He screws you two or three times and then to hell with you. At the time Sarita was born, when I left my husband Arturo, I was the worst flirt in the world. Whenever an American came along I'd go wild. *"Honey, honey,"* he'd say and then he'd fuck me. The following day he wouldn't even recognize me.

Little by little I learned. I've gotten so I can see at a glance what a man will give and what he won't. And the ones that look most respectable, teachers, doctors and politicians, are the worst of the lot. They go around looking as if butter wouldn't melt in their mouths. Those are the important ones, so what can you expect of the bums around here? If they see a hen owl pass by they say, "Hi, beautiful." For a man, anything in skirts is beautiful. Why should I believe I'm pretty merely because men tell me so? There aren't any beautiful girls in my family. I go by what I can see with my own eyes. When I look in the mirror I say to myself, "How can they call me beautiful when I'm so homely?" If I were beautiful I'd be in Hollywood.

Men often call me a gold digger. They say. "You're a frigid woman with a lump of ice for a heart."

"Because I make you pay?" I ask. "If I spent the whole night screwing for free with you until I got calluses on my cunt, then I'd be simply wonderful, eh?" Yes, life has taught me a great deal.

Can you imagine what it's like to fall in love and think the man loves you for yourself only to realize that all he's interested in is having his pleasure with you and then send you packing? And then to humiliate you by refusing to give you a dollar when you ask for it! Most men want women to support them. That's why I'd just as soon there were no men in my life. What for? For a bit of screwing? I can do it to myself with my own fingers.

What I feel toward men now is a desire for revenge. If Benedicto and I break up I'll never marry again. I'm twenty-five and I'd marry again only if I could find a man to spend all the rest of my life with. But I've never yet come across a perfect man, and that's what I want. A man who doesn't drink or smoke, who has no vices of any kind, who's attached to his wife, his children, and his home. A man who won't cheat on me because he knows that if he's unfaithful to me I'll be unfaithful to him. But the man who will have no woman except his wife hasn't been born yet. I've never known a man who doesn't have a mistress on the side.

I don't think any other woman feels the way I do about men. I wouldn't care if there were no men in the world. What do I need a man for? Don't I have a big, strong brother to protect me? Tomorrow it will be ten days since Benedicto left. Have I missed him? Have I been wishing he was here to screw me? No, I feel happy and contented and free as a bird. When I live alone I get plump. The minute I hook up with a man I become just skin and bones. I only do it for my daughters' sake.

It isn't love that I get from a man any more, it's the pleasure. But I want it over quickly. That's the way for a woman to live. If she takes a man, she should take one who'll climb on top of her and leave money when he goes. Because a woman is unhappy from the time she's a child. A girl who sees her *papá* abandon her *mamá,* who's been neglected, who has had to live with a stepmother. That's what I call having an unhappy life. And if she's unlucky with men, too, it's better for her to live alone.

When I was little—until I was six—my *papá* and *mamá* lived a normal life together. My memories of that time are happy ones. My *mamá* was busy with the younger children and never bothered me. I spent the day running around, climbing trees and eating nuts and mangoes. I was free and never had to wash the dishes or do anything. The ones who gave me most attention were my father and my grandmother. My *papá* would come home from work looking for me and when he found me dirty he would spank me and then my grandmother would scold him for hitting me so hard. She always defended me. He would wash me at the fountain but I'd soon get dirty again. He worked as a delivery boy then and he made his deliveries on a bicycle. He would sit me on the back of the bike and take me with him. He always took me and I was very happy.

My grandma Luisa loved me very much. I remember her well and I can even describe her. She was taller than Nanda and not so dark. She had long straight black Indian hair and she had false teeth. She worked for some rich people in El Condado and would take me with her. I would play in a pine grove while she did the washing and ironing. Once a horse was killed on the beach and I went out just in *panties* to watch. They thought I was lost and everybody was looking for me. When I got back my grandma grabbed me and hit me. She tied my hands together and hung me up and burned my feet so that I'd never go out alone again. When she put that burning paper to me I screamed to high heaven.

My mother and father got along pretty well, but of course they had quarrels. Once Nanda cut open *papito*'s head with a spoon because he ran around with women. And he and my uncles Sergio and Pablo would go to a *cafetín* to play dominoes. Then he became a soldier, you know, and was gone a lot. Nanda was always a little crazy and she liked gambling and spent all the money he sent her. When he came home she'd quarrel with him. Once he hit her but my grandma didn't allow that and she threw a pot of boiling fish at him. It scarred the left side of his face. His skin is so fair you can hardly notice it, but he's had trouble with his left eye ever since.

Later my grandma got a *pasmo* from ironing and going out into the cold afterward and they had to take out her guts. They left her only two and one of them burst and she died. I saw her in her casket but they sent me on an errand so I wouldn't be there when they went to the cemetery to bury her. Oh, if my grandmother hadn't died we wouldn't have turned out the way we did! Nanda would never have left *papito* and he would not have married Hortensia.

I was about seven when my *papá* went away to French Guiana. When he came back my *mamá* was pregnant by another man, a boxer called Gregorio the Grass. So my *papá* hit her and they broke up. He took Cruz, Simplicio and Felícita to my uncle Pablo's house at Stop 27 and he left me with my *mamá*.

A month later he married Hortensia Rivera, who lived next door. She stole my *papá* from Nanda. She was married with a veil and crown like a virgin but I think they had been lovers before. I once saw them kissing out in the back near the toilet. I told my *mamá* but she said it was a lie.

Hortensia was tall, skinny and white and she had good hair, but her face was that of a daughter of a great whore. Her relatives were a low-down lot. It was her *mamá* who put Hortensia under my *papá*. Of course! Because he was a soldier and in those days a soldier was a good catch.

Well, Fernanda had a little girl but Gregorio was killed, so she gave the baby away, with ink and paper, to a family named Maldonado. I don't know where they live now. The little girl is called Alba Nidia and she's about seventeen years old. I've seen her several times and she looks like Cruz and Nanda. Her hair is not really bad like mine but it's not good either. And she's quite dark but pretty.

I'm the only person in the whole family who gives her a thought. I've never heard Cruz, Felícita or Simplicio speak of her. Fernanda never mentions her, as if she'd never had her at all. I will always remember Alba Nidia because I like to keep my relatives and my dear ones in mind.

After the boxer died, Fernanda and I went to live in Río Grande for a while. We lived in Aunt Sofía's house, a big four-room shack, with my cousins Adela, Teté, Ester, Lydia, Delia and Chango, and with Nanda's grandmother Clotilde. It was a big family and my life there was good. I was happy but I missed my *mamá* because she was always going away. Aunt Sofía was the one who took me to school. I was with my cousins most of the time. When we came home from school in the afternoon we played in the back yard and knocked coconuts down from the trees. Then we'd go to the graveyard to get berries and almonds. Once Clotilde gave us a terrible beating because we went to the graveyard instead of to school. She sent us back to get some tamarind twigs and then, when we were undressed and ready for bed, she whipped us so hard with those twigs that our bodies were swollen for days.

I met my great-grandmother Fernandita, too. She had olive-colored eyes and good hair but she was a bad woman. She didn't like Nanda or Luisa and said they were both whores. All that woman was interested in was money. That's why she kept Rogelio away from Nanda. Rogelio was Nanda's father. He was colored and he drank a lot but he was good. He never hurt our feelings or hit us and he didn't approve of Fernanda's beating us. But he never interfered, as if nothing made any difference to him. Fernanda says her *papá* never gave her anything, but I know that when he came to San Juan he brought her money and gifts. When he had money Fernanda was fond of him, but when he was broke she'd begin to complain about him. What Fernanda likes about people is their money. My grandfather had a stroke and lost his voice, and my *mamá* never went to see him until he was already dying. But I felt his death deeply.

From Río Grande, Nanda took me to Stop 26 in Santurce to her *comadre* Gilda's house. Many colored people lived there in shacks. There were lots of sandy open spaces and I ran loose all day with other children. Fernanda put me in the first grade all over again. I lived there about two years and then Hortensia came to see us and to ask if I wanted to go live with her. I said I would rather stay with my *mamá*. But Fernanda said I had to go with Hortensia and that I'd be better off there because my *papá* didn't send her enough money to take care of me. So I went.

That's when I really began to suffer, because my stepmother treated me very badly. She called me bad names and she'd beat me with a broomstick until it broke. Once she saw Crucita shitting. Cruz was just a baby, but my stepmother grabbed a stick and hit her across her little hip. It seems that the blow put Crucita's hip out of joint because when she started to walk she limped. That blow crippled her. When my *papá* came home, Hortensia told him that Cruz had fallen down. I had seen what really happened but I had to keep it to myself. I couldn't tell the truth to my *papá* because he wouldn't have believed me. He didn't believe anything I said.

When my *papá* was around, Hortensia was not so bad, but the minute he went away everything was quite different. She didn't buy us clothes and she never took us anywhere. She kept us locked in. When her relatives came to visit she'd give them the best of everything. They would eat in the dining room, but we got the leftovers and had to eat sitting on the floor under the kitchen table. Once Hortensia's sister, Blanca Iris, brought a man into the house. I said I'd tell my *papá* as soon as he came home, so she pushed me down on top of the hot stove. A pot of boiling beans spilled and burned me. My whole back was scarred. All of my stepmother's relatives hit us and my *papá* didn't try to stop them.

My uncle Pablo had bought a house at Stop 22. At first he lived there with my aunt Elsa. Then she put the horns on him and took off with another man, and Uncle Pablo went to California. He was an elderly man who suffered from asthma. When he left, he turned the house over to my *papá*.

The house was yellow and had four rooms and a little kitchen. The yard had coconut palms, and breadfruit and almond trees. Behind the house you could see a mangrove swamp. There was a bridge over the swamp, then more swamp and more mud. It stank and there were crabs there and everything. To go from Uncle Pablo's to Uncle Simón's house we had to cross the swamp and I fell in about three times.

We slept in the dining room. My stepmother had a bedroom set but we slept huddled up together on a *caucho*.* We ached all over, because four children can't sleep on one small cot. Then, if we wet the bed, she'd hit us. Once she set fire to a piece of paper and passed it back and forth, near our legs, saying she was going to burn us because we wet the bed. We screamed and screamed. She made us lie down on the floor, on the bare boards, without a blanket or anything, and we had to sleep there the rest of the night. Then she beat us the next morning when we got up. She did it because she didn't want us to wet the bed, but you know, it wasn't our fault. We were only children and it was so cold there with only one blanket to cover us. All I could think was, "I wish I was grown-up, because then if she did such things to me I would kill her!" Simplicio would tell her, "Just you wait until I'm big. You won't dare beat me then."

We had to go out and beg all over the neighborhood to get enough to eat. Simplicio would get up at six in the morning. Carrying Crucita piggyback, he would go to a place near Stop 20 to beg or shine shoes. He wouldn't get home before ten at night, and then both he and Crucita got a tremendous beating. Being the eldest, I would intervene, and Hortensia would beat me nearly to death. When my *papá* came home, Hortensia would complain that she was trying to bring us up right but that we didn't respect her.

The government sent my *papá* a check for a hundred and twenty-five dollars every month. My stepmother got all that money and she never bought us even a pair of *panties*. I owned one dress, one pair of shoes and socks, and one pair of *panties*. I didn't have an extra pair to wear while I washed those. I had to comb my own hair and the other children's and wash our clothes. My stepmother wouldn't even delouse us.

My *papá* never made a move to protect us. He treated me like a slave. He would hit me with the buckle end of his belt, and with his foot. He made welts all over my back. Whenever he beat me they had to give me arnica. And all this was my stepmother's fault. She kept telling him that I didn't obey her and that I took money from her. She didn't give us any, so when she cashed the check my *papá* sent, I'd sneak some money and buy candy with it. That's the way I lived with her and my *papá*.

When I was eight years old my teeth began hurting me. They were full of holes and they hurt so much that I couldn't sleep. For three weeks they hurt me day and night. Finally I went to see my *mamá* about it and she told me to go to the city hospital. So I went and I got an *appointment*.

Nanda didn't bother to go with me and I went alone and they took out my four front teeth. I got nervous when they gave me the injection, and later when they pulled the teeth I felt everything. It hurt and I screamed. They took out those teeth in cold blood.

From the hospital I went to María del Carmen's house. She's my step-

* A folding cot.

mother's sister. I went there because I would be better off there. She treated me very well and washed my mouth with hot water and gave me soup to eat and didn't make me do any work the way my stepmother would. I was in tremendous pain and my mouth bled until the next day.

After that I didn't dare speak to anyone because I was ashamed. I was a little girl and I was practically toothless! And that was what they nicknamed me until I was nineteen. Toothless One!

One day my *mamá* sent for me. She had to do that because Hortensia wouldn't allow her in the house. My *mamá* asked me whether I wanted to come and live with her. She was living in La Esmeralda with *don* Erasmo then and she had a place for me. Hortensia was still treating us badly and I was always, always hungry, so I said yes to my *mamá*. I was about nine then.

When I told Hortensia she said, "Look, if you leave, don't ever come back here." I answered that I wouldn't because she treated me like a slave, and besides, I was going to my own *mamá* who had borne me.

La Esmeralda seemed strange to me because I had never seen the open sea. I liked it. The house stood on stilts, and when the tide came in you could hear the water lapping underneath. It was a comfortable house.

My *papá* sent Fernanda fifteen dollars a month for me. Fernanda bought me clothes and shoes and treated me well at first. She took me to the movies and everywhere. I knew she was hustling, because *doña* Clarita, a neighbor, told me. My stepmother had told me too. And you know, one begins to notice things. I saw Fernanda go out every day and I asked her about it, and she told me she was working. But sometimes men came home with her and she sent me to the other room, and that's how I began to learn about sex. Once I spied on her. As I was still innocent then, I said, "Nanda, why do these men come here and why do you lie down with them?"

She said, "Oh, I have to do it so I can support all of you."

That made me sad. I thought, "*Ay, coño*, my *mamá* is with *don* Erasmo and with other men too." Who wouldn't be ashamed to know that her mother was doing something bad? I asked her why she didn't get a job, but no, she wouldn't.

I never blamed my *mamá* for what she did. On the contrary, I felt sorry for her. I wished I was big and could go to work so she wouldn't have to do that. I would have liked to sacrifice myself for her rather than have her sacrifice for me. But in a way, if she had really sacrificed so much for us, she would have tried to set us a good example.

I was happy with my *mamá* but sometimes I felt sad too. You see, I had never lived with a stepfather. A stepmother, yes. But a stepfather? One way or another, one never feels safe. You understand? I never did like *don* Erasmo. Fernanda had met him in the *bar* called El Black Magic, the one that's called the Silver Cup now. Erasmo was a *chulo*, a pimp. He had a job but he also lived off my *mamá*. He never bought me even a pair of shoes. He couldn't deny me food, though, because my *papá* sent money regularly, and anyway, Nanda bought the food on credit. She also used the money to help Erasmo buy a house.

Simplicio was seven or eight years old when I went to my stepmother's house to bring him to my *mamá*'s house to visit. Then he didn't want to leave. After a while we went to get Crucita too. My stepmother said, "I had the trouble of bringing up those children and now they want to go and leave me."

Felícita was the only one who didn't come to live with *mamá*. My stepmother filled her head full of ideas, and so Felícita said my *mamá* didn't take good care of us and was colored besides. I was angry with Felícita because she ought not to look down on her own mother. People get punished for things like that. As for me, so long as someone is of my race and is Puerto Rican, his color isn't important to me. We should be united and get along with each other and help each other to live. Why should a person's color bother me? Especially my mother's? If she were as dark as charcoal, I still would take care of her and never look down on her. Yet Fernanda likes Felícita more than me. She likes Simplicio most of all and she pays more attention to Cruz's and Felícita's children than to mine.

To tell the truth, Fernanda didn't take very good care of us. Well, sometimes she did and sometimes she didn't. There were times when she got a meal for us at a restaurant and then left us alone, or she'd give us fifty cents or a dollar in the morning and would go away for the whole day.

She brought us up any old way. She never took me to church. I went with my friends. I went to learn the catechism and would have made my First Communion but she wouldn't let me. She never cared if we had a future or a career or anything. And as you can see, none of us has anything. We are nobodies.

My *mamá* didn't want me to play or go outdoors. She didn't let me do anything. It was my nature always to be playing and I think that I've never changed. I still like to tell dirty jokes and use bad words because I've heard them ever since I was a little girl. In La Esmeralda people tell those jokes or curse as calmly as they might eat a plate of rice and beans. When Fernanda was away I spent all my time playing. I never played tricks on other children and I never was rude to anybody, but if my stepfather or somebody complained about me, my *mamá* hit me.

She beat me all the time. Sometimes she even beat me with the flat of a machete. One day she sent me to my *papá*'s house to get the fifteen dollars he always sent her. On the way back it rained, so I changed one of the bills to take a taxi from Santurce to San Juan. And because of that she hit me with a can full of nails and broke a bottle over my head. All because I'd spent fifty cents on taxi fare. And anyway, it was our money, not hers.

She's the kind that hits and doesn't regret it. But when I was really naughty she never punished me, which goes to show you. Sometimes I went down to the beach to play with the boys or I would play hooky and spend all day wandering around, and she didn't beat me.

I felt rage and resentment against her because she beat me without cause. I had a terrible temper. I used to have tantrums and bang my head against the floor. I think there has never been a worse-tempered little girl than I was. I wanted to grow up so I could get away from my home. That was my dream.

Then when I grew up, my stepfather began to get fresh with me. Sometimes when he was drunk, he crawled into my bed. I would wake up to find him touching me or passing his hands over my body. But when I told my *mamá* she called me a liar and hit me. She insisted Erasmo didn't do those things, but it was true. When she went out and left us, I'd go to *doña* Clarita's house to sleep. I was scared to sleep in the house with my stepfather, see?

I was out in the street most of the time. When Erasmo fought with Fernanda we would all leave. He'd kick her out and she'd rent another room. After a while they'd make up and we'd move back. Sometimes our stepfather said mean things to us and we answered back. Once *don* Erasmo beat Simplicio and me black and blue with the inner tube of a tire. I was going to tell the police, but *mamá* said if I accused Erasmo she'd say he beat me because I was a tramp and didn't respect him and that he only wanted to correct me.

I felt bad because my *mamá* sided with her husband. She's been like that with all of her husbands. She was always for them and against us.

Fernanda wasn't the kind of mother I am. I stay with my children all day long and go out only at night. She went out in the daytime and at night too. She'd get dressed up and go to Papo's *bar* in La Esmeralda and drink and dance there before she went hustling. I'd peek in and see her acting real fresh while she danced. I'd leave because I didn't like the way she was behaving.

It also bothered me to hear her blaspheme. It seems that from the moment anyone descends to La Esmeralda, one must also bring down God and the saints by cursing them. My mother says of God, "That Cuckold, that Fag. I shit on Him." I leave when she talks like that. I say to her, "I know I'm no saint but I don't blaspheme against God."

When I was almost twelve years old I got that job with the Arab family. They wanted a little girl to help them with the housework. I went to school in the morning, and at noon I went to clean their house. It had about twelve bedrooms, two living rooms, a big kitchen and a long hall. I never got through before nine or ten at night. Then I went home to wash dishes and fetch water to fill the barrel. I had to work just as hard at my *mamá's* house as at my stepmother's. I washed and ironed the clothes, scrubbed the floor and cleaned. If I didn't, my *mamá* beat me and my stepfather did too. The next day I'd get up at seven to go to school. Sometimes I had to go without breakfast because *mamá* didn't make any. When I got home at noon she hadn't made any lunch either.

At that time my *mamá* gave up the life she had been leading and got a job at a *laundry*. I dropped out of school after finishing second grade and spent part of the day at the *laundry* and part at the Arabs' house. I never went back to school again.

I was working when I became a *señorita* and felt the blood come down for the first time. My *mamá* hadn't explained anything to me. That's the way she was, a careless mother. When I saw that bloodstain I imagined something terrible had happened. I thought my stepfather must have dishonored me. So I called to a girl friend to come over and I asked her what she thought. She explained it to me and told me that I was now a *señorita*.

And so life went on. I had two or three sweethearts, but nothing serious. I don't remember the name of the boy who gave me my first kiss. It happened at a movie. I had gone to the Royal, a movie theater in San Juan. They were showing a Maria Antonieta Pons picture. That shows you how long ago it happened. I went to sit upstairs. A boy who was sitting there put his arm around me and I let him. After a while he began to squeeze me. Then he kissed me. When he did that, he put his tongue into my mouth and some of his saliva along with it. He asked me to open my mouth and give him my tongue. I did it because I didn't know any better then. Ugh, it was disgusting as all hell. I was so disgusted my stomach was upset. I had to spit afterward and I felt dirty. One gets germs that way. I still don't like that kissing with the tongue. I have to be drunk before I kiss a man like that.

For a while I had a little sweetheart named Pichi, a country boy from Manatí, very nice and good-looking. He came to La Esmeralda to stay with his brother.

The boys of San Juan are very knowing. Country boys are clever too, but when a girl from San Juan falls in love with a country boy, she finds that he's shy and that he treats girls with delicacy and politeness. San Juan boys think nothing of grabbing your tits, sticking their fingers in your cunt or taking hold of your ass. Pichi kissed me and hugged me and all, but he was so nice about it, it was as if he were caressing a flower. As if he were plucking a rosebud and putting it in a glass of water and wishing it would never unfold. That's the way he treated me. Naturally I liked that.

But when my *mamá* found out that we were going steady she talked to him. She told him I was ignorant and a dirty pig. She said I left blood-stained *panties* strewn all over and she called me a whore even though I was still a virgin. My own *mamá!* She shamed me so much that I never went out with that boy again.

I don't know why Fernanda had to do that. If she didn't want me to go steady, she should have explained why to me. She might have said, "Look, you're too young to fall in love. You're ignorant of life. You don't know anything yet. Wait until you're a little older before you take a sweetheart." And she should have given the boy good advice—not talked to him like that.

Then I met Arturo. He was my stepfather's brother and he used to visit at *mamá*'s house. I was a child still and he was much older. He wasn't at all good-looking but he was always well dressed. I liked the smell of the lotion he used. He bought me clothes and he gave me money. He offered it and I, well, I took it. He would give me five or ten dollars, depending on how much he had in his pocket. But it wasn't because he gave me money that I liked Arturo so much. No, I was beside myself with love for him.

Arturo already had a wife, Elisa, and a child, Chiripa, but he didn't live with them. He lived in San Juan in the San Fernando Hotel, where he worked. When my stepfather found out that his brother was in love with me, he began to put ideas into *mamá*'s head. He convinced her that Arturo was a pimp and wanted me only to hustle for him. So then my *mamá* was opposed to our being sweethearts.

Once Arturo was going to Bayamón and he asked Fernanda to let Cruz and Simplicio and me go with him. Fernanda gave us permission and we went. But my stepfather was such a bastard that after we had gone, he persuaded Fernanda to follow us. We were standing high on a hill when Arturo came up behind me and put his arms around me and said, "Look over there. You can see all the way to San Juan." Just then Fernanda sneaked up behind us and beat me with a sugar cane stalk. She said I was a dirty slut and took me back to San Juan.

Arturo courted me for less than two months. On the night of May 27 Fernanda beat me in front of him again and he asked me if I wanted to go away with him. I said yes. My *mamá* and my stepfather had to be out of the house by six in the morning to get to their jobs. The next day I waited until they had gone, packed all my things and went off with Arturo.

Soledad

————

Life with Arturo

————

ARTURO'S *papá,* Marcos, lived near Toa Alta and we went to his house. He greeted us with the words, "Arturo, do you realize what you've done?" Arturo said that he had brought his bride home. His *papá* went off to his daughter Purísima's house, as he did every morning, but before leaving, he repeated, "Arturo, do you really know what you've done?"

After his *papá* left, Arturo wanted to take off my clothes. I didn't want him to, so he tore them off by force. By then I was frightened and already sorry I'd gone with him. Then Arturo took off his own clothes. I was surprised to see how big his thing was. I'd never seen a naked man before. He tried to talk to me and to explain what it was all about, but I burst out crying. Then he grabbed me hard and held me down on the bed. That's when it happened. I let out a holy yell that shook the house. It hurt me terribly. I thought to myself, "I'm a woman now." Arturo did it again that night and again it hurt. But he kissed me and stroked me all over before doing it. By the third day I liked it.

On that day my *mamá* came to the house and asked me if I wanted to marry him. I said I didn't. Arturo yelled from the bathroom, "We're going to get married." I said, "I'm not marrying anybody." I don't like to be tied down. One can love without ever getting married. God only knows what would have happened if I had married Arturo. Maybe I wouldn't have been able to get a divorce. Some of my friends have married and have been very unhappy. No, *hombre,* no. That's not for me. The day I get tired of a man I walk out and

leave him. That way I'm not obligated to him in any way. Most people in La
Esmeralda are like that. One never knows what life will bring so it's better to
stay unmarried.

We lived together and I began to see Arturo doing things I didn't like
and I fell out of love with him. I even got to hate him. Arturo had other
women and he gambled away every cent he had. He went to the Feast of the
Patron Saint in Toa Alta and lost the fifteen dollars he'd earned. And he beat
me. But I'm no fool, I always hit back.

We had our first fight very soon. Arturo was jealous of me for no reason
at all. There I was living deep in the country and never saw anybody. How
could I have done anything to make him jealous? Nobody ever came to see
me. Even my family came only about once a month. The one who came most
often was Simplicio, but what could I talk about with him? He was a mere
child. I wanted to see my *mamá*. I wished she'd stay longer when she came.
She'd get there at noon and by three o'clock she was ready to leave.

I didn't like the country. It was hardly a lively place and nothing was
there, no stores or movies, no radio, no electricity. And Arturo made my life
miserable. He'd go to San Juan to work at three in the afternoon and come
back the next day at ten in the morning, and I had to stay there by myself with
no one to talk to. Part of the time I was afraid. We had no neighbors near by.
The landscape was pretty, but I was bored every single day. I had to go to bed
by five in the evening. Catch me going to live in the country again!

Marcos' house was small. It was all one big room, with a little kitchen
outside. The walls were made of reeds. I had to do the wash for Arturo and his
father in the river and bring water from a well which was far from the house. I
also got a job at the farm where Arturo sometimes worked. Nobody forced me
to, but I wanted to earn some money of my own and save a little. I started
at ten in the morning and I earned three measly dollars a week for all that hard
work.

Arturo's father was a very good man and treated me well. We had many
talks together and he always gave me good advice. Arturo is very fond of his
father. That old man is the light of his eyes. Arturo has a sister and he's fond
enough of her, but he doesn't love her the way he loves his father. He's more
or less a Catholic, and Purísima belongs to the Evangelist religion. She's
greedy and self-centered and is always asking for things. She wouldn't even
give alms to a beggar. She and her husband own a farm and they sell all their
sugar cane to the government mill there. You get good money for that, yet she
was always whining about how poor they were. She claimed her children had
to go barefoot to school. I'd say, "With that farm of yours you can't get your
children shoes?"

Purísima wanted me to join her religion. But I've been a Catholic all my
life and I couldn't change over that easily. She kept telling me about Jesus
Christ's Second Coming and all that. I'd answer, "I don't know what Jesus

Christ is like. He's never come to me to tell me He's coming to earth again."

In some ways the Evangelists lead a better life than we do. They don't smoke, drink or dance. But they're evil-minded gossips and they criticize and spy on other people. They're worse than Catholics that way. We don't care what anybody else does.

The only church I believe in is the Apostolic Roman Catholic Church. It's true that I hardly ever go to church. That's because I don't like to go to Mass and then come back home to criticize and gossip about others. I consider myself a better Catholic than the ones who go to church and take communion every day and are always with the priest. I believe in God and say my prayers at home and keep my saints, and I don't say a single blasphemous word. My home is my religion.

The saint whom I pray to most often and ask favors from is Saint Martha. When I'm in a tight spot I pray for her help, but to myself, not out loud. I don't know anything about Saint Martha's life, but she's the saint of my devotion and she has performed miracles for me. For instance, a while ago I had a sick headache that was driving me crazy. I went to the hospital, I went to doctors, I went here and there, and nothing helped. I went to a spiritist and she helped me a little, but the pain in my head was so bad I couldn't even bend down. Well, one day I went and stood in front of my little altar and said, "Saint Martha, for the sake of whatever you love most, take care of me. If you're going to take this pain from me, take it away. If you're going to send me anything else, send it soon." And all my pain left me.

Arturo never admitted it, but I knew that even though he worked he was a pimp, because he lived with whores. In that way he was like his brother *don* Erasmo. Arturo had a *comadre* called Gregoria, and he and that *comadre* had an affair, which was a big sin. I knew too that Arturo kept a room in the San Fernando Hotel, and I thought he might have another woman because he had changed toward me. We were hardly ever intimate any more. One day I went to San Juan and found him in his room with a woman. I saw her hug him and kiss him and all that. I thought it over and decided to leave the country and go live with him in San Juan. We got a room in La Esmeralda and were happy there for a while. By this time I had been married three years and still didn't have a baby. I went to the hospital for a checkup but I never did find out what the trouble was.

Aracelis Cotto lived next door to me and she bore a baby girl, Catalina. Aracelis was crazy and spent all her time wandering around. Her husband mistreated that baby even when she was only a few days old. The child wasn't his, you see. When I saw how badly they were treating the baby, I asked Aracelis to give her to me. At first Aracelis said no, but I went to her house every day and took care of Catín and played with her. The child was terribly skinny because they didn't feed her enough. Once all they had for her was a can of milk that had gone sour. Her little hands were raw and sore and she had no hair on her head.

One day when the child was not yet forty days old Aracelis left the baby under the public water faucet. A friend came and told me, "You'd better go get that baby, Soledad. Her mother threw her out." I went to Aracelis and asked her again, "Will you give me the baby?" "All right," she said. "Take her." So I gathered up all her diapers and little shirts and a coat *doña* Clarita gave me, and I took Catín home with me. I had some baby things that I'd bought myself and I dressed her in them. When Arturo got home the next day, he took one look at the baby and said, "Get that kid out of here. Give her away to somebody."

"If she goes, I go," I answered. He quarreled with me about the child every single day after that. But I wouldn't give up Catín.

Then the baby got sick. I took her to have the sign of the cross made over her but it did no good, so I took her to the hospital. I had to be at the hospital at six in the morning and stay with that child until nine or ten at night every single day. When they had to feed her through her veins, I stayed at the hospital for three or four days. I went hungry during that time because nobody, not my sisters or *mamá* or anybody, bothered to bring me any food. Even my own husband didn't take the trouble.

A month after I had adopted the baby, I got pregnant. That made me happy but I wouldn't part with Catín. I loved that baby from the day I saw her.

During the first two months of my pregnancy I was so sick I threw up everything I ate or drank and my belly swelled enormously. Arturo behaved very badly. I had to quarrel with him over every piece of the layette I wanted to buy before he'd give me money for it. It was my first child. But it wasn't his first child and you know what men are like.

By then my *mamá* wasn't living with Erasmo. She was already married to Pedro. That man had been my sweetheart once but Fernanda kept telling me he was a tramp and not good enough for me, and she told him she'd beat him up if he kept going with me. Fernanda took up with Pedro when she left Erasmo. When I heard about it I didn't feel anything at all. Anyway, I seldom went to my *mamá*'s house or even spoke to her during the three or four years that she and Pedro were together.

One time I hit Pedro. You see, I had gone to their house and he said nasty things to me. He said that I went to Crucita's house to sponge off her and that I was lazy and never did a lick of work. I answered that he was a gossip and as much of a woman as I was. So he slapped me and I tangled with him. I would have killed him if I could. Then Fernanda, instead of separating us, started beating me with a stick. I grabbed her by the hair but I didn't hit her. She says I did but it's not true. I never in my life hit my *mamá*. It hurts your feelings when your own mother attacks you for a man who's nothing to you, a man she meets today who may leave her tomorrow. One feels those things. I felt it in my very soul.

While I was pregnant with Quique I washed and ironed for whores. They paid me a dollar or two, and with what Arturo gave me I bought baby shirts and bootees. When Quique was born he didn't have much but at least he had something. My cousin Adela helped me too. She brought me baby clothes an American family gave her. I'm a person who's grateful for anything people give me.

I knew the baby would be a boy. They say you can't tell but I knew the signs. For one thing my belly got terribly big and it was pointed. If it's a girl you have a small, round belly. I also had a lot of sickness right at the beginning.

When I was a little more than eight months pregnant, the baby, Catín, began to stand up. That's when I noticed that one of her little legs was shorter than the other. Then, big as my belly was, I had to carry her back and forth between the hospital and our house. They told me to take her to the Center for Handicapped Children. I had to leave her there three days. When I went to get her they had put her leg in a plaster cast. They said her hip was out of joint somehow, and it still is. That's the same trouble Crucita has.

When I took the baby back home and her mother, Aracelis, saw her with her leg in a cast, she went around telling everybody that I was the one who had hurt the child and that she was going to take Catín back. I told her, "If you take Catín, I'll return her to you dead. I'd rather see her dead than have anybody take her away from me." One night Catín's real father came to my house to take her away. I picked her up, ran out of the house and hid so they couldn't find us.

When I was pregnant with Quique, Arturo kept saying the baby wasn't his. He denied Quique because we had quarreled and had been separated for a little while. I took my things and went with Catín to a friend's house, where I spent about four days. I just walked around La Esmeralda during that time, but Arturo spied on me jealously.

Now, Arturo's not a passionate man. When he had a free day we had intercourse once, and that was that. And he never caressed me, kissed me or excited me any more. He had his women and was indifferent to me. So I became as cold as he. What pleasure can one feel with a man like that? One gets disillusioned with life, you know. You have to treat people the way they treat you. I won't lower myself to plead with a man so that he can boast about it later.

But we made up and that's when I got pregnant. Then he said that I had come back to him after getting pregnant in the streets. He said the baby would be black because I had made friends with Negroes. "After it's born you'll be able to tell whether it's yours or not," I said.

On Catín's first birthday my labor pains started. Again, Arturo didn't treat me right. Not with that baby nor with the others. He went to sleep. My cousin Adela was the one who took me to the hospital. Nobody else did anything for me.

I was in labor for four days and just about to go crazy. I didn't know anything about childbirth. I cried and cried. The doctors kept telling me that it was nothing and that I should take it easy and not cry like that. Finally they gave me an injection. Then, on the last day at about ten o'clock at night, they took me into the labor room. They had to cut me and take the baby out with forceps. They had to take nineteen stitches afterward. The baby weighed eight pounds six ounces. He was fat, beautiful, fair-skinned. He didn't look newborn.

After three days, when they told me I could go home, my *mamá* came to see me at last. Nobody at all had come around to ask for me in all that time. I went home in an ambulance.

Nanda had taken care of Catín for me while I was in the hospital, but I had to get up to clean the house and wash clothes almost as soon as I got home. The place was a mess. Catín's dirty diapers were piled up in a washtub. I couldn't stay in bed for forty days because nobody offered to help me, not even to wash a single diaper. Cruz was little then and so was Simplicio. Felícita was with my *papá*. And you know how it is with two small children!

Arturo still refused to recognize the baby as his own, even though Quique had blue eyes and light hair. The truth is that while I lived with Arturo I had no other man. Then people began to say that the child looked exactly like him. After nine days Arturo finally did accept the baby because I told him I was going to take the case to court. Soon Arturo was crazy about the boy. Arturo certainly is a big bastard, but I stuck with him anyway.

In spite of Arturo and in spite of the pain I suffered, the day I had my first baby was the happiest of my life because now I had somebody to think about, to take care of, somebody I was willing to make any sacrifice for. When you have your first child you feel such joy, such happiness!

I didn't want Quique to be bottle-fed, he being my first, so I fed him at my breast. He nursed until he was five years old. All my babies nursed, but Quique was the one who sucked me dry. But as long as it's for my children, I'll do anything.

We stayed on in La Esmeralda until the tidal wave. That time the sea frightened me! I had never seen it so furious before. I had seen it rise but never like that time, when it swept away two hundred houses. My house was one of them. We had to move to the Llorens Torres Housing Development.

I didn't like living in the *caserío*. You had to pay for the electricity, gas and water. I had three unfurnished rooms and I had to furnish them myself. The apartment didn't have anything in it except a small two-burner stove and some shelves. The walls were plastered and there was running water, but even so I didn't like it. It was so far away from a store that I had to take a bus when

I went shopping. The only place you could buy was from a co-op and the prices there were sky-high. And they wouldn't even give credit.

To my way of thinking, the government hasn't made any improvement for poor people with its public housing. In La Esmeralda I paid eight dollars for rent, and eleven in the *caserío*. Three dollars' difference to start with. Then social workers came to investigate, and if you bought new furniture or a refrigerator or any little thing, they raised the rent. Then you had to be careful not to get the place dirty. If you broke the stove you had to pay for it. If you scratched the paint on the wall you had to paint it over. And how can you live in a place where you aren't even allowed to yell now and then? But lots of people from La Esmeralda moved there and they behaved the same as always, yelling and talking dirty.

I stayed only a month in the *caserío* because Arturo didn't want to pay the rent. I was flat broke and all I had to move out was a bed. I was pregnant again, so we went back to the country with the children. Arturo gave me a bad life there. On Saturdays, when he got paid, he went off and gambled, and by the time he came home he was cleaned out. I had to depend on whatever money his *papá* could give me. Arturo beat me too and tore up my clothes and threw them away. I got to hate him more and more. He never let me go out. He spied on me. If he saw me talking to another man, that man must be my sweetheart. He'd say I was a dirty, low-down, two-bit whore. I was fed up with his bad treatment.

So I said, "All right. I'm going back to San Juan." Then and there I packed up all my clothes and the children's and I left him. He followed me and begged me to come back to him. But once I leave a man or he leaves me, it's over, and that's that.

Arturo

If I Could Lock Her in a Cage

I HAVE KNOWN Soledad ever since she was a little girl. Fernanda used to send her to me for haircuts. She was a kid with terribly kinky hair, like a great ball of wire. She tore up all her girlhood pictures because of it. I didn't need a comb to cut that hair, it stood straight up of its own accord. It was like a thicket. As I cut it I would pull down on the hair to straighten it. One day I gave her a haircut that was so short she even cursed my mother when she left. I was trying to get her to shed that hair and grow good hair. Yes indeed, the hair she now has grew straighter because I forced it to. When she started getting good hair, she never even thanked me.

My foster brother, Erasmo, introduced me to Fernanda. I had seen her before in a *bar* and had noticed her because, you know, she's a fairly good-looking woman. Erasmo was living with her then. Simplicio, Cruz and Soledad all slept in the same room with Fernanda and Erasmo.

What I didn't like was the way Fernanda kept that house. I don't like to see a house in a mess when I know there's a woman living in it. But I guess Fernanda couldn't manage because she worked nights and was tired and sleepy.

And then the kids were running around and pulling and throwing and generally making a mess of things. Fernanda just let it stay the way it was.

Soledad said that when she went to live with her mother it was like moving from hell to hell. It seems that the mother had lost some of her affection for her children after living away from them all that time. I have seen parents mistreat their children, but no one to compare with Fernanda. Of course I won't deny that children brought up in a neighborhood like that are devils and sometimes a parent will hit out with whatever is handy. But Soledad wasn't spanked with the hand, she was beaten with sticks, struck with planks. It was a terrible thing. I know because I saw it.

I was thirty when I became interested in Soledad, and she was thirteen. I liked her but the main thing was that she should like me. It seemed to me that it was mutual, because even when I was living with another woman Soledad was always hanging around. I got her easy, without any trouble at all. She told her *mamá* about it right away. It has always been my custom to let a girl's parents know as soon as I get engaged to their daughter. That way a man is safer and so is the girl. Her *mamá* accepted it because she knew me. Then we sent a letter to her father in Panama. He wrote back saying that the girl was too young.

I went with Erasmo to a spiritist at Stop 25. He asked me, "Do you know what a flying fish is?"

"Well, I don't, but your question gives me an idea of what it must be."

He said, "I like to speak with people who understand me. Well, that girl you are going with now is going to bring you a lot of trouble." Soledad and I were sweethearts then. We weren't yet living together. Then the spiritist said that I would go to jail because of her and that she would lead a disastrous life once she was out of my hands. He said she would spend some time in an insane asylum and finally she would take her own life. "She thinks she's a sort of queen, superior to everybody else. She likes to order people around," he said. That man told me incredible things. When he mentioned the flying fish, he meant to warn me not to be involved with Soledad. I paid no attention to him. I wanted to see for myself. But most of what that man said has come true.

When Soledad's father wouldn't give us permission to marry, we went on being sweethearts until one day Fernanda beat Soledad terribly. Soledad gathered up her clothes and came to where I worked. I told her to go home. I didn't want her there, because I knew her father and I didn't want him to imagine anything bad. "Parents are always right," I said to her. But she wouldn't go back because the truth is, they did mistreat her. I had to protect her. And I did, the best way I knew how, by making her my wife.

We went to live at my *papá*'s house in the country. He already knew Soledad and made her very welcome. As for her, she had adored *papá* from the time she was a little girl. He treated her as one of the family. And from the day I took off with Soledad I have never brought another woman to my father's home.

We went to the church on the Baldorioty plaza but they wouldn't marry us. The priest told us that he wasn't allowed to marry so young a girl unless she was pregnant. I said, "Let's leave it then until she wants to get married." But later on she refused. She said, "Why bother about getting married when we can live together just the same without marrying?" But of course, a couple isn't married unless they've gone through with the ceremony.

For a time we lived on my *papá*'s farm. I cut sugar cane and also worked for my *papá*. We planted *yautía*,* sweet potatoes, tobacco, corn and beans. We had some animals too, goats, pigs and a few cows. Soledad learned to help with them and finally she even got a job in the fields. She and I had only a few arguments and they weren't important. I, being the wiser, tolerated her. It wasn't until after we had separated that I realized how hard she had been to put up with.

I gave Soledad's family what help I could. Cruz lived with us for a while. I don't know Felícita very well. She has lived apart from the rest of that family. She's always been a gay and affectionate girl, friendly with everybody.

I know Simplicio well. Everybody was always very fond of him. To my way of thinking, Simplicio hasn't suffered much because he's healthy and well developed physically. Fernanda beat him now and then, but she treated him well and was always generous with him. He never was disrespectful to his mother. That's really something, a boy brought up in La Esmeralda and yet respectful to his mother!

There aren't many people in the world I've liked as much as my mothers-in-law. I adored them so much, I was always happy as long as I was with one of them. You see, I felt that they were like my own *mamá*.

Fernanda was always good to me. Her strong temper showed only when she was angry or when she had problems with somebody. She was good as long as you didn't cross her. If you did, she was your enemy for sure. As a mother she was always ready to lend a helping hand.

I always thought Fernanda was a sincere woman. She proved to me that she was. But this business of selling her body! It seems to me a woman who does that puts herself in an unfavorable light. A woman ought not to be for sale. I've never liked to buy that, I don't know why. Nanda used to press herself against me closer than my own wife did, but it was meant in a friendly way. It seemed she regarded me as highly as I regarded her. If she went out and burned the whole world, I would still think she was good.

·   ·   ·

* An edible root (*Xanthosoma sagittafolium*) which resembles the elephant's-ear, or taro.

My *mamá* died when I was about six years old. Oh, she was lovely, one of those really beautiful women with fair skin and blue eyes. Her hair fell down to her knees. They called her "The Virgin" because her given name was Virginia and that's what she looked like. When she had been dead for about four years, my *papá* took another woman into the house. The little woman was quite pleasant. Really, she was just a young girl herself. But it seems that those quiet people hide their real nature. When my old man went out to work she took advantage of us. My eldest brother was fifteen and pretty grown up by then. She made him have intercourse with her. She did the same with the rest of us kids. I wasn't quite ten years old.

One day we children were playing and that woman came and hit my little sister on the head with a stick. She cut her scalp and the blood streamed out. Then my brother struck the woman a terrific blow. When my *papá* came home that evening, she was still unconscious. My little sister was covered with blood, and the rest of us were too. We had tried to help my sister and we had carried the woman inside but we didn't know what to do. "What's going on here?" my father asked. We told him and he sent the woman away. He never again got a stepmother for us.

I was always having accidents. When I was ten or eleven I rolled down a steep hill inside a tire and lost consciousness. Another time I fell off a horse and had to be carried home. But the worst time was when I was in an accident with a truck. I lost a lot of blood, because when they finally got me to a hospital there was no doctor on duty. They sent me to a first-aid station but we didn't find anybody there either. With all the delay I got a fever from the injury and I was sick for a long time. I was out of school for five months.

I went to the fifth grade in school. When I was fourteen, I quit for good to help my *papá* on the farm. But before the year was over I went to live in San Juan because my friend Obdulio advised me to. That boy had great powers. He warned me I would get into trouble in the country when I least expected it and I trusted him, so I went to San Juan. I lived first with my brother, then with my uncle.

I worked in Johnny's *bar* for a while, then as an attendant in a dance club, and then in the *bar* again. I earned money but I was a spendthrift. After all, it was easy money. Yes, I drank and danced and went to every party. I started going to places where women in the life were. I was so young they practically ate me alive. They passed me from hand to hand. When one let go another grabbed me, as in the game of *pase y pase*.

That very year I took my first woman. Her name was Santa Isabel. I lived with her eleven months and fourteen days. I left her because she went to a dance at her aunt's house in San Juan without asking my permission. After that I had a brief affair with a little black girl. She was still in school and it was all on the sly, a secret love. Then there was Pura, the one I lived with for the shortest time. She was a very good girl, that Pura. She was the best of them all because she was so meek. Afterward I had another woman but I don't know what became of her. She just disappeared. According to a girl friend of hers, she was pregnant at the time.

I went on living a gay life until I met Elisa Torres, a Guayanilla girl, and fell in love with her. I started living with her in 1942, and in 1943 Chiripa was born. I was proud when I knew I was going to be a father. And when I went to the maternity ward at the hospital in Santurce to see him, he was the most beautiful baby there. I was filled with happiness to see how all the world admired my son.

For some reason my wife got into the habit of cursing all day long. It puzzled me. I thought maybe she was going crazy, because what else could it be? I told her to do things properly, but she was about four years older than I was so she wouldn't listen. She went on like that until I, thinking anything could happen, packed up the baby's clothes and took the child to my *papá*'s house. Then my *papá* got gored by an ox and was left crippled, so I had to help him as much as possible and I couldn't leave the baby with him.

I moved with the baby into a house near the airport and set up a gambling place. Lots of people came to play the numbers and card games like thirty-one and so I managed. I stayed on there until they tore down my house to make the new airport.

Little old Pedrito Sánchez asked me to come to San Juan to work for him at the *bar,* so I did. I waited on customers during rush hours. We had some unpleasantness with the police there. There were certain agents who wanted every business to give them a cut secretly. When we wouldn't do it, they made vicious and unjust charges against us. Among other things I was charged three times for assault and battery against policemen. There wasn't a word of truth in it! It was such a slander that the judge himself said so in court. He said it was unbelievable that I, a mere child, could have assaulted and battered those policemen. "Not even if he were a wild beast," said the judge. "Those are all lies and you should never have preferred such charges." A lawyer from the Labor Department defended me without a fee. I was found not guilty of every charge against me.

Later one of the toughest police agents asked us to give him twenty dollars a week. We refused, and so there were times when, at three o'clock in the morning, twenty cops came to the place, woke us up, broke down the doors and arrested our women. We were supposed to plead guilty and pay a three-dollar fine. I always pleaded not guilty. One time the judge found me guilty anyway. That was the same judge that put Muñoz Marín and all of Tugwell's Cabinet in jail once so what would you expect? The Republicans were in power then. Anyone capable of voting for a party like the Republicans, may God forgive me, doesn't deserve His mercy.

·   ·   ·

While Soledad and I were living on the farm, I went to San Juan to take a job in the San Fernando Hotel. I waited on customers as I had done before, and sometimes I did a little barbering. Soledad and I were getting along all right. As a woman Soledad is the kind that can satisfy a man. She'll do anything to give him pleasure. She's an affectionate woman and an amorous one. She's a good girl, good in every way.

We didn't have many arguments then. In the first place, Soledad was never jealous of other women on my account. She and I are not jealous people. If I live with a woman, she knows I'm her husband, so if she does anything she shouldn't, that's her problem. She's harming herself, not me. And of course I didn't suspect anything about Soledad because out there in the country we lived in peace and quiet.

Oh, we did have our little clashes but never anything serious. Soledad was pretty strong-willed, so she had to be tamed by force to see if she'd toe the line, see? But it wasn't a war between us. Many times when she came looking for trouble I'd say, "Oh, stop this nonsense. It doesn't look well to get into an argument over every little thing." I didn't enjoy fighting with my wife.

We went on living at my *papá*'s house until Fernanda wanted us to come to live in La Esmeralda. I didn't want to, because I didn't like it there. I never have liked it. It's not because the people who live there are bad or anything but because it's unsanitary. During a dry spell the smell of the place is sickening. I can't imagine how people thrive and grow fat there. At first, after we had moved there, I felt worse with every day that passed. We lived in a room for which we paid six dollars' rent a month. It was terribly uncomfortable. Our big bed took up almost all the space. There was no toilet or running water. I had to go to endless trouble. Whenever I wanted to take a bath or even go to the toilet, I had to go to San Juan. And I was used to having a few comforts!

In 1954 I had a problem with a man in San Juan and he became my enemy. He tried everything to get me in trouble. Finally I found out he was even trying to get to my job. I decided to get rid of him and I went home for my gun. Soledad kept it under the mattress, but when I asked her for it she wouldn't give it to me. "You'll only get yourself in trouble," she said. I pushed her over on the bed and reached under the mattress. Just as I got hold of the gun she jumped on me and tried to take it away from me. It went off and the bullet creased one of her fingers. She said, "Now I'm really going to get the cops," and she did. She told them the gun was mine but it so happened that it wasn't registered. Well, I'd always been curious to know what it's like in jail, so I didn't mind too much when the judge gave me six months.

I made friends with all the prisoners. I have no complaints against any of them. They were all really good, and they respected me. Why, most of them addressed me as *usted*. I've never regretted my stay in jail, because I learned a lot. After one has seen so many braggarts parading down the street thinking they are better than anybody else and making a show of bravery, one finds out in jail that most of them are nothing but fakes. I learned the lion is not as fierce as he's painted.

In prison you are allowed to have three visitors. I put down Soledad, Nanda and my son. His grandmother raised him and he's a fine boy. He's in the *Army* now. I didn't put down any of my own relatives. My *papá* was too old and my sister was an Evangelist—and to have her come to jail! Not that it's anything bad, but I would have felt very sorry for her. Soledad came to visit me often. We didn't have a child at that time. Then she got a job as washerwoman in the same hotel where I worked. That was her *mamá*'s job but Nanda turned it over to Soledad.

I was put to work in the prison barber shop. You know, I have liked to cut hair ever since I was nine years old. I hadn't been there long before we barbers went on a sort of strike. It was on account of one of the prisoners who hit a little Negro barber. Bullies, that's what some people are. They beat up somebody for any little thing just because they're stronger. So I said, "All right, let's stop working." It was not exactly to strike, but to get some respect for the barbers. With a pair of scissors in his hand a barber can easily take revenge, see? I was afraid that one of the barbers might lose his head and commit a crime before my very eyes.

We were called to a hearing in the warden's office and I learned at least one thing in jail, that prison laws are pretty fair. The warden asked what had happened and the rest of the men made excuses. But I, never having been in jail before, said, "Well, the thing is, you can't attack a barber, because barbers are dangerous. If a man socks me or knocks out my teeth, I can easily stab him with my scissors or slit his throat with my razor." I just told him the truth and the truth is a daughter of God. So then the warden gave an order that nobody was to attack a barber and the problem was solved. He asked us if we wanted to go on working and I answered, "It will be a pleasure."

All the time I was in jail, the Ríos family was very nice to me. They thought a lot of me, see? especially Fernanda. And I thought a lot of her too. But the day I got out of jail nobody was waiting for me. I don't know why, because they all knew when I was coming out.

I'm pretty sure that Soledad was unfaithful to me while I was in jail. I myself used to go to La Marina, in front of the penitentiary, to take advantage of just such situations. Women who go to visit their husbands in jail are usually easy to get. A young woman on her own for six months is capable of anything, husband or no husband. I've never said anything about this to anyone, but Soledad must have been unfaithful because there was a lot of talk about her at the time. I didn't hear it then, of course. I was told about it later on. If I'd known it the day I left jail, everything would be different now because we wouldn't have had all those children. Well, it could have been worse. If she had gotten pregnant by another man, that would really have been bad.

I did notice that she seemed strange that day. But she explained that it was only because she felt so sorry for me and I don't know what all. I said to her, "Well, look, we've already been living apart for six months. Why don't we just go on like that, each alone?" She burst into tears and said she didn't want to, so we got together again.

When I got out of jail I was offered my old job at the hotel. Soledad got a job as a maid at a hotel in Santurce. She was plump when she started but the longer she worked the skinnier she got. And she changed toward me. Because she had a job she thought that she could give the orders. So when I saw her getting thin I said, "Quit that job. I can support us both."

When Soledad got pregnant for the first time, we already had Catín. That child's *mamá* was a crazy kind of girl. She set up housekeeping with a boy, and every time they quarreled the baby landed on the floor. Catín turned out to be lame. Instead of operating on the leg the doctor put it in a cast, which seemed to me a very ordinary kind of treatment. He told Soledad he couldn't guarantee that the child would be cured. I left the cast on for two or three days, then seeing that it hadn't done a bit of good, I took it off myself. And to this day the child is lame. I think her condition is an act of nature. Only a miracle could cure her.

When Quique was born I was very impressed to see how gay and happy my wife was with her baby boy and Catín. I was full of admiration at the fine care she took of them. She has always been very good with children from the time she herself was only a little girl. It's a gift she has, a very nice quality.

Soledad was pregnant with Sarita when our marriage finally broke up. I know Soledad has a quick temper, but what reason could she have had for objecting to my giving my nephew a haircut? I was supposed to trim his hair because he was going to the clinic that day. Soledad didn't want me to leave the house. She seemed dreadfully upset! I tried to soothe her: "Now look, I'll come back right away, the minute I finish cutting his hair. I don't want my old man to have to come as far as this. With both him and the boy sick, they might feel faint or have an accident." When she saw me getting my tools together she fell on me like a fury. "I don't want you to go," she yelled. In that situation all I could say was, "All right, if you want to live with me you'll have to act like a decent person. If not, it's no go. That attitude isn't going to get you anywhere."

Cruz was visiting us that day, and it seemed that every time she came, Soledad would begin to act up. That's what made me think that Cruz brought a message from somebody to Soledad. I never mentioned my suspicions but I had them just the same. The truth is that little girl, Crucita, would betray half the people in town and act as if she hadn't done a thing. She's one of those women who's always carrying tales from one person to another. That's where all the foolish little upsets between Soledad and me must have got started. I had tried to get her away from her family for that reason. If she had only followed my advice! But in spite of everything I've been the one to bear the consequences because I've always had to help Soledad out of tight spots. Thank God I've been able to do it.

When Soledad and I broke up she went to the Welfare for aid. She didn't have to do that. I gave her money for the children, and I made arrangements to let her have groceries on credit. If anything else came up I was willing to pay for that, too. Yet she accused me of deserting my children. I went to the welfare people too, the very same day she did, and they stopped the investigation of the case at once.

I had to go to court, though, and they told me that I'd been charged with nonsupport of my son, Quique. "That's not true," I said. "And if there's money to support my son there's money for the little girl, Catín, who if anything belongs even more to us, because she came to us first."

"This isn't the kind of man who would abandon his children," the judge said and threw the case out of court. But my wife, who let herself be influenced by other people, went next to the Institute of Family Relations. When I showed up there they had a long paper full of Soledad's accusations against me. She claimed I had beaten her up in the street, and I don't know what all. It was terrible! When the lawyer read me all that I said, "That woman's nuts. If I'd done anything like that, she wouldn't come to you about it, would she? She'd have filed charges in court. Besides, I'm not that kind of person. If I had to beat my wife, I'd do it at home behind closed doors without any witnesses." Then the lawyer crossed out all that stuff.

There's no doubt that at times Soledad was more or less out of her head for a week or two. When we still lived in the country she had some kind of brain trouble that lasted about two weeks. I watched her closely and suspected something was wrong. With the children, for instance, sometimes she'd eat a piece of fruit or some other snack and wouldn't offer them any. She'd have a kind of blank stare on her face as if she didn't know what she was doing. And she didn't. I'm sure of that, because when she was in her right mind she wouldn't have dreamed of eating a tidbit in front of the children and not offering them any. No good mother would. And Soledad is a model mother because she adores her children.

Naturally I worry that something might happen to the children when she's like that. God and the Virgin grant it may never come! If Soledad should want to come back to me sometime, well, it would take God speaking to me in a dream to make me agree to it. I would only risk it if I had a cage to lock her up in. But I do admire her in spite of everything.

One day I realized she just wasn't all there when she knocked a man down in Tanca Street. I was walking a few steps behind her when it happened. The man had stuck out his arm a little to make room between them as they passed each other. Soledad turned around and slapped him so hard that he fell.

I stood there and watched him in case he tried to hit her back. But he only said, "*Ave María,* what a boxer!" Soledad was a strong girl and she got even stronger in the country, where she had plenty of good nourishing food. That girl gained nine pounds in twenty-one days. It was unbelievable!

There was another thing she did that I learned only lately. I had taught Soledad to use my pistol because we were living in the country and she was often alone. I said to her, "You'll have this in the house in case anyone comes looking for trouble. If you find yourself in danger, don't hesitate to shoot. You have a right to defend yourself."

Well, it was Soledad who made the danger. She'd get on a horse and ride over to my sister's or my niece's house and threaten them with the gun. She didn't say one word but just sat there and pointed the gun. It was all in play, but people have lost their lives from jokes like that. And my niece never told me until now! I said to her, "*Caramba,* you sure took your time telling me. What were you waiting for? For the gun to go off accidentally and kill one of you? If I'd known I'd have taken a hammer and smashed that pistol."

As long as we lived together Soledad behaved well. She was always pleasant to my relatives and they loved her because of her very ignorance and because even then she was a woman who could deal with any emergency. And she was a good wife. So I just can't explain why at times she acted as if she was half crazy. It wasn't as if she had been ill-fed as a child. I used to go to Fernanda's house and there always was plenty of food. There was even food to waste because sometimes the children had eaten at some neighbor's house. As long as one has friendly neighbors, eating is no problem.

I never caught Soledad with another man while she was living with me. But when she was pregnant with Sarita after we had separated, I went to her house one day because a hurricane was coming and I wanted to take the children to a safe place. When she didn't answer my knock I felt pretty sure she had a man in the room. That made no difference to me because I had already utterly forgotten her. All I cared about was the children. Soledad opened a small window to talk to me and that's when I saw the man standing behind her. When I saw him I said, "You bring those children to me, Soledad, or I'll break down the door."

"Oh no," she said, "you can't!"

"I can and I will, because those children need me to protect them." As I said that I walked toward the door and then the man came out and I struck out at him with a knife. "It's your fault," I said. "Those children would be safe in the school already." He ran off before I could strike again and then Soledad came out, locked the door, and ran after him. I looked for Fernanda to see if she would turn the children over to me, but she was nowhere to be found. I went back to San Juan, and on Norzagaray Street I came face to face with Soledad. I grabbed hold of her blouse, and when she tried to slip away the blouse tore from top to bottom and Soledad had nothing on underneath. So there I was with Soledad naked from the waist up. Just then a police patrol came by. Soledad called out, "Help! This man is attacking me."

"I'm not attacking her. All I'm trying to do is get her to let me take my children out of La Esmeralda. The hurricane warnings are out and this woman has left them there alone."

The cop turned to her, "You get those children out of there at once. If you don't, I'll have to arrest you."

At that Soledad went with me to get the children. Once we were inside the school building I said to her, "Now you can go look for that man. The children are safe here. At least if anything happens to them, it will happen to me too."

When Soledad gave birth to Sarita she had been back in San Juan for some time, doing as she pleased with her life. She seemed to be quite happy and not miss me at all. Yet when the baby was born I had to stand by her because no one else bothered about her, not even her own family. I helped her as much as I could until the baby was about two months old.

I was living in La Marina at the time and one night, on a sudden impulse, I walked over to La Esmeralda. As I passed by Soledad's house I noticed that the door was padlocked on the outside and I heard the baby crying inside. I went on to Papo's *bar* and Soledad was there dancing. Her *mamá* was there too and several other women. I went up to Soledad and told her the baby was screaming her head off. "What are you doing to those children?" I said. "If you're going to abandon them like this, at least leave the door unlocked so that somebody can go in and help them."

Well, the next day I went there again and found Sarita in a terrible state. Alone and with nobody to feed her, the child was starving. She looked as if she was already dead. I said to Soledad, "Well, next time you lock up the place, stay away two or three days. By then Sarita should be dead and you'll be free of the trouble of raising another baby." That made her cry. Then she looked very thoughtful. I told her that she had to take Sarita to a doctor at once. She agreed, and she took not only Sarita but Catín and Quique too.

Before that it had been her custom to take the children everywhere she went. It was the wickedness in La Esmeralda that caused her to lock the children in when she was invited to go out at night. I told her that if she didn't take better care of them, I would bring them to my sister. She knows I would never abandon them.

The things that happen! Soledad began to go out with many different men. Once she even came with a man to the hotel where I worked and I had to wait on them! I wasn't at all surprised because I already knew about her goings-on, but just the same I knew Soledad didn't really enjoy being a whore because she's a one-man woman. Yes sir, a one-man woman.

She finally settled down with Octavio, the one who was killed. After her baby Toya was born, Soledad went to the clinic to be sterilized. They sent for me and said, "We want you to sign here because you're her husband."

"I'm not her husband."

"She wrote your name down here as her husband."

"You don't say! Well, isn't that sweet!"

The nurse said, "Well, you can do her a favor, can't you?" They took me to see Soledad and she begged me to sign for her because she didn't want any more children.

I thought it over. "Well," I said to myself, "better this than to keep on throwing children into the world to suffer. The best thing for Puerto Rico would be to sterilize all the women to keep so many vermin from being born. As it is, things are going from bad to worse." So I told her I'd sign, but if anything went wrong she wasn't to blame me. The operation really did affect Soledad's health because she was always sickly afterward.

Imagine what a problem I had while Soledad was in the clinic. I had Catín and Quique and Sarita with me, and Toya was sick in another hospital. I had to earn a couple of dollars to feed the ones at home, visit Toya at the hospital, and go now and then to see Soledad. I went to see her against my will, but I had to find out how she was and give her news of Toya. *Ave María,* it was enough to drive anyone crazy! If at least I had had enough money, but I was out of a job. And I had to leave the children alone while I went out looking for work. My trade as a barber wasn't a steady job. You have to wait for a client to appear. And it wasn't very profitable in a poor neighborhood.

I was keeping all four of the children. Sometimes I had them all in bed with me. I enjoyed seeing them playing on the bed, especially that little dark-skinned Toya. All the rest would drop off to sleep and Toya would still be sitting there sucking her bottle. "Go to sleep, baby, go to sleep, Toya," I'd say. She'd shake her head and say, "Ah, ah."

Soledad was supposed to pay me for keeping them, but if she managed to hustle up four or five dollars she spent most of it on herself. I was the one who supported them. I was always able to make a dollar or two cutting hair, but that wasn't enough to feed four children.

I wanted to go back to the country with the children but Soledad wouldn't hear of it. She was making a mess of her life. I know women through and through. As soon as they leave one man they grab another. And that way, grabbing and leaving, everything goes wrong. When they do get a good man, they don't want him.

Ever since I separated from Soledad I have lived alone rather than go around looking for another woman. Nowadays women are more powerful than men. Once a man gets married, his wife's the boss. And if a man is poor he doesn't have much chance of getting a younger girl. I can make friends with any girl. That part is easy. But I can't forget that I'm old enough to be her father and that it's my responsibility to make some sort of home for her. I can't ask her to live in the same poverty she has known at home. And now that I'm out of a job I'm in a really bad situation. When I do manage to earn two or three dollars I have to think first of my son, who may need a pair of pants or a shirt or shoes. You have to use your common sense, right? As it is, it's a miracle I'm still alive at forty-four. Having been poor all my life, I never could make any real progress. For me, everything has turned out a failure.

Soledad

——

Alone in San Juan

——

THERE I WAS, all alone in San Juan with my big belly! I had left Arturo and had no one to cater to my cravings. A pregnant woman always craves something or other, you see. I would be dying for a melon or a mango and I wouldn't have a nickel to buy them. You know how it is in Puerto Rico. Sometimes you don't have a red cent and there's nobody to give it to you. I was living with my *mamá* and Héctor but that didn't help much. When it was a matter of my cravings I wasn't ashamed to ask because if I didn't eat what I wanted, the baby would suffer. So now and then I'd say, "Nanda, make some soup, will you?" But would she make it for me? She would not. It was always, "I'll cook something that Héctor likes." So I had to eat whatever she gave me.

I was still living in the country when Nanda took up with Héctor. He set her up in a house and bought everything to go with it. Héctor was good. Nanda won't find another man like him anywhere. That *teenager* she lives with now will never give her as much as Héctor did. She was well off with him but she cut him up. That was a nasty, vicious thing to do. Nanda does things like that because she's never come across a man who can keep her in line.

My sister Felícita was living with my *mamá* by then. I really can't explain how it came about, because Felícita was Hortensia's favorite. My stepmother always treated her well and they took her everywhere, to Panama, Trinidad, the Gulf of Mexico and all the places where my *papá* was sent. He never took me to any of those places. It was always Felícita.

When Felícita came to live with Fernanda, she was a *señorita* already. She was in love with Ángel Cubero. He was tall and his hair was sort of kinky and bad, but his skin was light. He drank like nobody's business. He did nothing but chase women and have a good time and fritter away his money. He was flush today and broke tomorrow. But he was good to Felícita. He bought her food, paid the rent, and kept up all his payments. He was nice to me, too. I don't know why Felícita and Cubero broke up. I think he was the only good husband she ever had.

Felícita is a bitch if I ever saw one. Any little thing makes her mad. Felícita has never had a brain in her head. When she left Cubero she'd lock up the twins as soon as they fell asleep. Then she'd go off to dance until dawn. She just wanted a good time. I believe she first thought of going whoring about then, because she'd ask me, "How do you go about becoming a prostitute?" I'd say, "What are you thinking of? Get yourself a job."

Felícita controlled herself and didn't become a whore then, but she lived with Nicolás and after him she lived with Rosario. Rosario used to beat her because she went out to have a good time, and she worked spells on him, at twenty-five dollars a spell. "You're crazy," I told her. "Do you think you're going to keep him that way? Let a man love when it comes from his heart. If you make him love you by casting spells he'll turn against you sooner or later."

Cruz does that too and the spiritists eat up what little money she has. I can't find it in myself to give money to some bitch who does nothing but sit in front of a table all day long. I don't believe in mediums who charge a fee. It's a gift of God and one shouldn't charge for God's gifts. When God gave the power to Saint Matthew, Saint Peter, Judas, Saint Martin of Porres and a couple of other saints, did they go around charging a fee? Were they paid for helping the poor, for lifting up weak sinners and making them good? Of course not!

Most of those people only know a little bit about spiritism, anyway. What they practice is evil and comes from the Devil. I won't let anything evil come near me. Anyone who tries to put a spell on me is only screwing himself, because I just wash it away with herbs. You put the herbs in water and then wash the floor from the kitchen to the door. You have to be sure to wash toward the outside of the house in order to get all the evil out. And you have to do it with faith. But you shouldn't do it on Tuesdays or Fridays.

When a woman is casting spells on her husband, I just wish he'd kill her! If a man leaves a woman it means he's tired of her, and if she holds him against his will he's capable of anything, even of killing her. Why do you think Emilio beats Cruz? Because she's holding him against his will, that's why. And she's the one that's getting hurt by it. He keeps getting her pregnant while that other little woman he has stays pink and plump.

Cruz's tongue is sharp as a razor. That little beak of hers can set the four corners of La Esmeralda on fire! Oh, she's a rattle-brained chatterer! The trouble with Cruz is that she's a tramp. She's been a shameless flirt ever since she was a child. She was noisy, restless and talkative, and always hot in the pants and falling for the men. If I had a boy friend she'd try to take him away from me. And I, being one of those people who don't need to have things spelled out, would step aside and give her the right of way.

She's the only one who makes any sacrifices in our family, according to her. "Oh, you're Saint Martin of Porres," I told her. "You're the most self-sacrificing person in the world. Nobody else has ever suffered. You've suffered because you wanted to. You brought it on yourself." Emilio used to tear the clothes off her back and beat her even when they were sweethearts. Even so, she chased after him and cast spells to hold him and she still does. Yet she put the horns on him while they were still living together. She had an affair with a numbers vendor. She may be small, but her heart has room for more men than an apartment house. Naturally Emilio beat her. He had good reason to.

Cruz would run home to us, but later on she'd tell Emilio everything we had said about him. The time he kicked her in the belly when she was pregnant, I went and told his aunt *doña* Minerva. Cruz said, "It's none of her business what he does. Maybe you think he likes you? Maybe you want him to fuck you? Well, let him." I jumped up and grabbed a knife. I could have killed that bitch. Lucky she ran out before I could catch her!

We kept telling her, "Cruz, if it isn't working out right, leave him." But no. She liked him even if he was a beast and a bastard. He would corner her and fuck her standing up as if she'd been a whore. When a man does that to a woman it means he doesn't give a damn about her. At the beach, on the sand, anywhere, he screwed her. What can you do with a sister like that?

After a while my *mamá* began to get notions and she nagged me about going to bed at six o'clock. I never went to bed that early when I was a *señorita,* and she wanted me to do it now! And she kept hinting things. If I sat down for a minute outside the house, she'd ask me if I was watching for men or if I had hot pants. One night she even locked me out with Catín and Quique. She wanted to control me in everything. But once a daughter is a grown woman who's had a husband of her own, her mother has no right to do that. I had already lost what I had to lose, so what was the point of all that preaching?

Besides nagging me, Fernanda complained about Quique. He cried, he was in her way, I was in her way. One day she told me to leave her house and I went. A boy called Lipe got me a dark little room to live in. Then my *mamá* said I was a whore and a slob and that I had left Arturo only because I wanted to run around. Once she beat me, pregnant as I was, because of an argument we had with Lipe and my cousin Darío. She bit my finger and hit me with a pot. She yelled that I let myself be laid just to see the white stuff run.

I said, "If I'm a whore you know why. You taught me to be one." That shut her up. But she went around telling everybody that I was worthless and that I wasn't even her daughter. That really hurt.

Lipe didn't live with me or help me. He got me that little room because I was disgusted with my *mamá* and her house. After I moved I often went hungry. If I ate one day I had to fast the next. I wanted to kill myself. I was willing to do anything, but there's not much work a pregnant woman can do. I went to Margarita's house to take care of her baby, to wash dishes or to iron, and she would give me food for my children. She was good to me then, but we aren't friends any more because a little later she got jealous. She went around saying that I was making love to Mario, her husband. It's a lie! Every time he gave me a compliment or invited me out I put him off. I told him, "No, because I respect your wife."

When I was really desperate I'd go to the men who hung out at Papo's *bar*. "Listen," I'd say. "Let me have a dollar. I know you got paid today and I haven't had a thing to eat." None of them could give me a whole dollar, naturally, but each would give a quarter or a little more. They gave it to be nice. I was ashamed, of course, but when a woman has children she's often forced to do that, and worse things too. I went to the Public Welfare but I couldn't live for a month on the thirteen dollars they gave me. We ate up that amount in a week. After two months of public welfare I gave it up.

When Sarita was born I almost died. My pains started on a Sunday and I had them all that day and all night. I didn't want to go to the hospital because there was no one to take care of Catín and Quique. I had pains all day Monday too. By five o'clock I couldn't bear it any longer, so I took a hot bath. A neighbor woman came in to massage my belly. Then a lot of people crowded into the house. They didn't come to do me a favor but because they were curious. To see how I was doing, they said. To get a look at my cunt, say I. Finally I told *mamá* to lock the door and not to let anybody come in. She put an ironing board under me. I'd had all I could take of pain by the time the midwife got there. At eight o'clock sharp I had my baby. Sarita was born plump and pretty. I felt very happy then, the way you always feel when you've just had a baby.

Right after the baby was born I wanted a cup of chocolate. I asked Fernanda to make me some but she didn't. She and the midwife both went home. A woman is weak after having had a baby. What she needs then is some good strong broth. So what do you think Fernanda did? The next day she showed up with a plate of white rice and fried meat for me. I couldn't eat that, so I sent out for a quarter of a pound of dried codfish and tomato sauce and I got up and cooked some soup for myself.

I bought food on credit at Muriente's until I was strong enough to be up and around. I ate, but even so I was skinny. Sarita took the breast for three months. After that she got some sort of tumors and boils because I had taken quinine pills while I was pregnant, to cause an abortion. I had to keep taking her to the hospital for a month or two until she got well.

That was a bad time for me. I owed rent for eight months. I really suffered. My relatives were near by but I had to go hungry. I couldn't say, "Now I'll go to my *mamá* or to my sister and get a plate of rice." When they cooked it seemed they'd rather feed a stranger than a relative. I couldn't count on anything or anybody.

Then I almost committed a terrible sin. I swear I have repented a thousand times and I ask God to forgive me for what I planned to do. You see, my cousin Adela was working for an American family then. She had given them her twins and she spoke to them about taking my baby too. At first I said yes. People kept telling me that Sarita would be better off with the American couple, and after all she didn't have a surname because Arturo wouldn't recognize her. Then I stopped to think, "What! Give away my daughter?"

Doña Minerva advised me, "Don't give your children away. Even a bitch barks when they take away her puppies." She asked me how I could take in somebody else's baby and then give away my own. So I changed my mind. I remembered how my *mamá* gave away a daughter and has never seen her since. I was overcome with remorse. It was as if something inside me, like the voice of my soul, cried out, "No!" I think it was Divine Providence that guided me at that time. Do you know what it is to have a child and abandon it, as so many mothers do? Can they ever hope for God's forgiveness? Never!

So the next time Adela came, I told her I'd decided to keep Sarita. And I said, "Even if I have to eat dirt I won't give my daughter to anybody."

About three months after Sarita was born, I spoke about my problems to a girl called Luz Celeste. She said, "I'm going to take you to a place where you can earn money by hustling. That way you can pay the rent and give your children what they need." So one night I fixed myself up, left my children alone and went with Luz Celeste. That was my first night. We went to the Silver Cup, a big place with its name in neon letters that flash on and off and lots of tables and low lights. There was a hotel on the third floor.

That night, being new, I couldn't find any customers. I felt embarrassed, sitting off in a corner by myself. Then Luz Celeste herself brought a man over to me and told him I was new to the life. He took me upstairs. He asked me why I had decided to become a whore. I said that I had three small children and no husband and I couldn't find a job. I had to earn a living somehow, didn't I? He sat on the bed then and talked to me. He was Italian, but he spoke to me in Spanish.

It was very strange. He gave me twenty dollars and he didn't even touch me. I felt grateful. That doesn't happen very often, you know. I didn't go with anybody else that night. The owner of the *bar* said, "Listen, if you want to stay here you have to drink and go with the men, because that's the kind of business I have." I explained that it was my first day and would he please let me go home. He agreed and I went home, alone and on foot. It must have been about three o'clock and it was a long way from La Marina to La Esmeralda.

The next day I bought clothes and food for my children and even had some money left over. My *mamá* found out about me right away. She said, "Now you've got what you wanted, haven't you? To go around being laid. You dirty hunk of a whore! You good-for-nothing scum!" I told her, "That's what you taught me to be. It's your fault, yours and my *papá*'s, that I've been driven to this."

That night Luz Celeste gave me a dress and made up my face. I went with an American, who, by chance, took me to the very hotel where Arturo worked. And Arturo liked it fine, I guess. At least he didn't say anything to me. You might say that it was Arturo who forced me into the life, because that night he could have objected.

When we got to the room I sat down on the bed. I didn't understand English but I knew the American was telling me to take off my clothes. He unbuttoned my dress. I was awfully nervous and I wanted to get out. He grabbed my arm to stop me and I yelled for the houseboy. The boy told me that if the man had already paid I had to stay. Then the American took off my dress and I stood there in my half-slip and *bra*. He told me to take those off too but I said no. I took off my shoes and *panties* and lay down.

After it was over I went to the bathroom to take a bath. I said to myself that I'd never go with another man again. When I got dressed I went to talk to Luz Celeste. I said, "I'm going home now and I'm never coming back."

"If you go," Luz Celeste said, "they won't ever let you come back. And you know how hard it is to get a job in San Juan." The other girls also advised me to stay. They said the work was pleasant after you got used to it. They gave me a drink and I stayed.

After that, I worked a five-day week. I stayed home on Tuesdays and Wednesdays. Now I had money. I wasn't ambitious; I didn't try to make fifty or a hundred dollars in one night. As long as I had five dollars in my pocket, enough to buy food and milk, I was satisfied. If Fernanda had been the way a mother should be and had said to me, "I'll help you so you can get what you need," I would never have done what I did.

You suffer a lot in the life. Can you imagine how ashamed you are to take off all your clothes in front of men who are strangers, for a miserable five-dollar bill? Some of them even beat you and take back the five dollars. Can you imagine what it is to be forced to do that kind of work every day? After I'd had two or three drinks I was able to forget. Then I'd dance and be gay and have a good time.

Liquor makes me sick but after a few drinks you forget about morality and about being shy. Morality is the shame you feel. If you feel ashamed you can't do a thing.

I never had a pimp. Sometimes I suffered because of it, but I always said that my children were my only pimps. They were the only ones who could get a dollar out of me. No man ever made a living out of my skirts. I'd never help any lazy, useless man fill his belly or grow his balls at my expense. Never!

People talk against prostitutes but no one should do that, because there's a whore in heaven whose name is Magdalen. She was the first whore in the world and God forgave her. So we too have the right to be forgiven. I was a whore in order to support my children. What I'm against are whores who do it to support their lovers. I'd like to put women like that in jail and never let them out.

Some whores think a lot of themselves. But I believe that when a woman is a whore she has nothing to be proud of. I don't deny that I was a whore but I was discreet about it. The cops never caught me, thank God, because I didn't disturb the peace. Nobody could have told that I was a whore. I went out with men only at night. I never wore dresses that were too close-fitting and I didn't wear tight pants the way Felícita does. I went out after dark and by dawn I was back home.

With men I went straight to the point, came to an agreement and did what I had to do, and that's all. I didn't ride in a car with a man the way lots of other women did. I'd say, "I don't need to take rides in cars. If you want to be with me there's a hotel upstairs." That business of going out to dinner with a man and then have him do goodness knows what! That's not for me.

I paid to have my children taken care of. Arturo offered to do it if I paid him, and I, being ignorant, accepted. He took the money but he still mistreated me and said nasty things, so I got to hate him even more.

At that time lots of Americans from the *Navy* came to the *bar* and I tried to learn English. I could say "Come in" or "I am sorry." When they asked me what I wanted I said *rum,* Coca-Cola, *beer* or whiskey. Puerto Ricans order for you and usually it's beer. Puerto Ricans were not for me, because they're too greedy. Once they mount you there's no getting them off. They squeeze you dry for the measly five dollars. With an American you don't have to take all your clothes off, just your *panties,* and he doesn't even take off his pants. With Puerto Ricans you have to strip naked, kiss him, give him your breasts. I don't like to kiss off a man or to have him suck my tits.

Many men wanted to give it to me from behind but that I wouldn't do. I never let any man have my ass. If you do it once, they get used to it and never again want to screw your cunt. It seems men get more pleasure that way. I would give my ass to a man only if I felt sure we never would break up in all our lives.

I never stayed more than five minutes with a man. I'd tell him, "For five dollars you can't expect me to bring the stars down from heaven. If you want to stay longer you have to pay more." I always asked them to pay me in advance. Thank God, I never had to quarrel to get my fee. Just the same, I sometimes didn't have a dollar to my name because you can go for weeks on end without a customer. That happened when the ships were all away. Then there were too few customers for so many women. And after you've worked for a while you get shopworn. The men always look for the new girls who keep coming in.

There's no comradeship of any kind in the life. Look at Luz Celeste, for instance. She was the one who took me there in the first place, but our friendship broke up because she was brazen when it came to money. You know, when you sit down at a table with a man, other women will sit near by and make signs to him, trying to get him to go with them. As for me, I don't fight over a man if it's only a matter of money. It was just as easy for me to get a new customer as it was for another woman to take away the one I had. I worked for money, not to get a man for keeps. A customer spends one night with you and tomorrow God knows where he is. I never fought. Anyhow, I was luckier than the other girls. I usually went home with fifteen or twenty dollars.

Some women were infatuated with the American *sailors*. They're the kind who screw for art's sake. They went with the Americans because they were handsome. I never went for a man's beauty. It was his dollars I was after. When the Americans said, "Come with me for free," I'd answer, "Bitches give what they have to dogs for nothing." You should have heard them yell!

The Americans didn't ask for me especially, but even so I preferred them to Puerto Ricans. For one thing, Americans treat their wives better than Puerto Ricans do. If an American man has an affair, his wife never finds it out. They're very reserved, not like the vulgar Puerto Rican men who blab everything. Americans are more affectionate, more helpful, and easier to get along with. When you lie with an American he treats you like a goddess, as if you were his wife. They don't ask anything of you. They go directly where they're supposed to go.

One night I met Allen. He was a tall, strong, fair-skinned American. He worked as a diver repairing ships and he earned good money. He was just like the other Americans. When we did it together we hardly talked at all. He stayed with me all night and went back to his ship the next morning.

At that time my brother Simplicio was working for *don* Camacho, the owner of the Silver Cup Club. I was the one who got him the job. Simplicio is the one I've always got along with best in the family. I didn't know much English, so I'd tell Simplicio what I wanted to say and he would tell Allen. Simplicio knew English because he had spent a lot of time at La Marina when he was small. He used to dive for coins off the Cataño ferry.

Allen told Simplicio that he wanted to marry me in a year's time when he got his discharge. But I've always had a suspicious mind. I don't believe in gay-colored birds because for me they always turn out to be black. For me fairies turn into witches. I told him to forget about it for the present and we'd just be friends. I said too that what I did was for hard cash, not for promises.

While Allen was away at sea I made other friends. I've always had good friends. I know how to get along with people. I may not have much schooling, I don't have a doctor's degree or anything like that, but I have experience. And I've been in places where one's supposed to behave like a decent person. I never got any training from Fernanda. It's something I picked up myself.

Fernanda behaved, may God forgive me, like a savage! I used to take decent men to my home, not two- or three-dollar customers but rich men from the Condado, and my *mamá* would turn her back on them. She'd walk away as though I'd brought a dog home. And she's never changed.

Well, Allen loved me and didn't much like what he saw at my *mamá*'s house. He told me he'd get me out of there and set me up in a house of my own. I agreed, because all I wanted was to stop working at the *bar*. By chance Arturo was living in two rooms in La Esmeralda and he gave them to me so I could move in with the American. Allen bought me thirty dollars' worth of food at one time. He paid the rent, bought me a bed, a wardrobe, a crib for the baby, a stove and a kitchen cabinet. I had no worries with him. He was fond of my children, but he did object to my nursing Quique so long. He said Americans didn't do that. I told him I wasn't an American and I brought up my children my way.

I couldn't love Allen, of course, because I didn't know English. I was fond of him for the things he gave me, but he was cold. Most Americans are. He didn't want intercourse often. But did he drink! Floods! I was faithful to him as long as we were together. Why shouldn't I, when I had things so good?

All the time I was with Allen, Arturo kept pestering me as if he were still my husband. He was always following me around and screwing things up for me. If he saw me talking to another man, right away he thought that fellow must be my lover or my pimp. Arturo has always lived off whores. Now he wanted to force himself on me as my pimp. I said no. What he wanted was just plain dirty. His being the father of my children only made it worse.

One day I was talking to a boy, and Arturo came up and insulted me. He called me a dirty cock-sucker and things like that. I spoke back to him and he socked me. Then Marciano and Adela grabbed me and held me. That's when Arturo tried to cut my face but got me in the back instead. If Adela and Marciano hadn't held me he couldn't have cut my back. That's one thing for which I have to thank them. If Arturo had cut my face I would have killed him. As it was, I only broke his head.

I didn't call the cops because Fernanda didn't want me to. Her *papá*, Rogelio, was staying with her at the time and he said he'd never been to court in his life and never wanted to go. So I went to the first-aid station. There they stuck a Band-Aid on me and asked who had cut me. I said someone had jumped out behind me and I hadn't seen who it was. But I'll always bear a grudge against Arturo for that. If I had a *revolver* I'd empty it out on him. Inside, I bear a grudge against all men.

Allen asked me about the cut. I didn't want anything tragic to happen, so I just told him I'd been in a fight. About that time Allen shipped out. For over a month he didn't write or send me money and I stayed shut up in the house. The only place I went to was Papo's *bar*.

Genoveva, Papo's wife, was good to me and she was fond of my children. But Papo was a son of a bitch and a stool pigeon. He liked to shoot craps and bet on the cockfights and he had lots of women.

Papo would call the cops for any little thing. He had my cousin Darío jailed for no reason at all. Darío touched a glass jar at Papo's place one day and the jar happened to fall and break. Papo called the police and told them Darío had smashed the jar in order to cut him up. Darío ran off to the beach but the cops caught up with him. Then, instead of arresting him, they beat him with their sticks and left him lying under a house half conscious. His sister Virginia and I crawled under and got him out, and took him to the first-aid station.

Later on Papo changed and became a nice guy. He had a tiny little *bar* with only two tables. Women used to go there just to dance and drink, not for anything else. If they did pick up a man there they'd have to go either to her house or to his because there's no place for that kind of thing in La Esmeralda. Some women rent a bed but their rooms are dirty and without a toilet.

The men who came to Papo's *bar* were mostly longshoremen and fellows who work on the little boats that take produce and other things up and down the coast. I wouldn't go with any of them. They're dirty and smell like pigs. Papo liked to have me come to his place because he said I attracted customers. He used to give me ten or fifteen dollars just to come around and dance with the men.

One day at Papo's *bar* I met a boy by the name of Octavio. When he first came in I noticed that he gave me the eye. He began to talk to me. Pretty soon he grabbed my arm and kissed me by force. I danced with him and later, when I was ready to leave, he saw me home. Lying in bed, I got to thinking about him and felt love for him. I was in love but I thought, "I have this American. How can I get rid of him?" Allen still hadn't written to me. I owed two months' rent and installments on the furniture. Finally, Allen showed up drunk. I told him to go away because I didn't want to live with him any longer. He said that was all right with him and he left.

Soledad

Life with Octavio

AT THE END of the year 1958, Octavio and I started living together. Tavio was tall, with dark skin, gray-green eyes and good wavy hair. He was very handsome and I loved him. He had only one fault. He was a thief. Because of that I was never at peace. When he went out I'd say, "Look here, Tavio, don't steal. That's bad. And if they arrest you the police will beat you up." He told me not to nag him and promised to give up stealing as soon as we had a child.

Aside from the stealing he gave me a good life. He loved me and he never beat me or treated me badly in any way. He was fond of my children. I never lacked anything as long as I lived with him. He didn't work but in spite of that he always managed to get our food every day. He paid the rent and the installments on my furniture and he bought me anything I asked for.

He was good-tempered, the kind of person who never gets angry. When we had a quarrel he would laugh about it afterward. He made a joke of everything. He was always happy, always singing. He wasn't bad. He just stole because he liked to have nice things. I loved him very, very much, probably because he treated me so nicely. We're like animals, you know. Where we get good treatment that's where we stay. He gave me affection, he took care of me, he worried about me. If I got sick he watched over me.

Another thing he did was get me a set of false teeth. When I was with Arturo, I had had four more teeth pulled because they were hurting me, so I really was almost toothless. I was ashamed to speak or to laugh when I went out with men because they would see the empty spaces in my mouth. Octavio wanted me to look more elegant and prettier, to look like a somebody. Arturo and my *mamá* never bothered themselves about it but Tavio took me to a friend of his who made teeth and he paid 55 pesos for a bridge with a gold tooth in front.

I shall always be grateful to him for that. I've never found a man like him since. He was hot and sweet and affectionate. There was a world of difference between him and Arturo.

When I met Tavio, he'd gotten out of jail only a few days before and I knew all about it. That's why I say that when you're going to fall in love with somebody you fall in love no matter what. Tavio never told me much about his business. But he did tell me all about his family. His mother Petra had treated him very badly. She didn't love him although he was the eldest. When his father was dying, Petra took a sweetheart so the old man died knowing that his wife was putting the horns on him. She even refused to cook for him, nor did she give Tavio good advice or take care of him or give him food. Petra had another son named Bernardo and he had the same vice as Tavio. The two of them stole everything they could lay their hands on. All that matterd to Petra was that her sons should bring her plenty of money. She didn't care how they got it. She never said to Tavio, "Look, you shouldn't do that. Go straight, son, now that you have a good wife."

My own *mamá* didn't like Tavio because he was a thief and had a gang that wouldn't stop at anything. They were capable of knifing anybody. And Tavio was like that too. One member of the gang, The Panther, had escaped from jail and was hiding out at our place. I let him stay. I wasn't worried about the cops. I can talk back to them if I have to. Two or three times some detectives showed up looking for Tavio, and once they even wanted to get into the house.

"You can come in here when you bring a search warrant," I told them. "Without that you can't come in." And I stood at the door blocking their way. "You're bold as brass, you sons of the great whore. Tavio isn't here. And you couldn't come in even if he was. So what do you say to that?"

"Come to the station with us," they said.

"All right, let's go," I said. "We'll see who comes off best, you or me." They didn't insist on going in after that. They knew very well that I was right.

One time I went with Tavio and the gang when they were out stealing. The Panther, Pico, El Mulato and Tavio were the ones who went that day. They robbed a department store in Río Piedras. The boys had looked the place over three days before and made a floor plan. They had gone in and walked all around the store. One of them bought a chain and then they walked out through a different door. So they had already decided how they were going to get out.

We went there at about noon. They had less than half an hour to rob the place. I knocked on the inside door. Nobody answered, the place was empty. Then the boys broke the glass pane on the door and went in. I was carrying a large purse and Tavio took it and filled it with stuff. I waited outside. I saw a detective squad car stop at the corner and I tapped on the store window. That was the sign we had agreed on in case anything suspicious happened. After the squad car drove on, the others came out and we took a taxi to La Esmeralda. We got rid of the stolen cameras and jewels in a town a long way from San Juan. We went there that very same day so nobody would catch on. Tavio had friends there. He kept two or three of the things for me. The stuff was worth five thousand dollars and he got four thousand for it. He kept fifteen hundred dollars for himself and the others shared the rest. Tavio gave me a thousand dollars out of his share.

Later that day we passed by the store and it was full of cops and detectives. I stopped and asked, "What happened here?"

"Twelve thousand dollars' worth of stuff was stolen," I was told. And that's what the newspaper said the next day too.

They never found out who did it. The boys didn't leave a clue. There were no fingerprints because they wore gloves. I wasn't a bit afraid because it had all been planned.

Let me tell you something, most of the characters who go stealing don't know how to do it right. When they break into a house, suppose there are people in it? The first thing you have to do if you want to rob a place is knock on the door, the way Tavio always did. If nobody answered, he went back the next day. He'd pretend he was a salesman or something. The third day, he went back and knocked again. If there was no answer that time, then he broke in. But how many have been killed because they go, *pra, pra,* and break into a house without taking any precautions at all?

None of my relatives ever knew that Tavio had anything to do with that robbery. Tavio wanted me to go with him to rob another place in Río Piedras, but I didn't have anybody to take care of my children. I couldn't ask Fernanda because I didn't dare tell her about it so I decided not to go.

When Tavio robbed a rich person I felt nothing but pleasure. The rich are sons of a great whore and they take plenty away from us. Robbing the poor is something else again. Tavio didn't steal from the poor. He never robbed a single person here in La Esmeralda. And what he stole from the rich he shared with the poor. He went to the large food stores and brought things for me, for *doña* Minerva, *doña* Lucelia, my *mamá,* Felícita, and everybody in the neighborhood. Everybody really appreciated him then.

I don't repent having gone with Tavio when he robbed. Why should I? I never repent after I do something. But I would never do it again because a thief's life is not an easy one. You're always anxious and watching out for the cops and the detectives. If they catch you they beat you. And then you have to put up one thousand, three thousand, five thousand dollars for bail. I don't even want to think of it. All the money we got from that robbery was spent on bail because Tavio was arrested four times. The cops caught him easily because they already knew him.

In May I got pregnant. When I told Tavio he was so happy he went wild, buying *baby* clothes, taking care of me, getting me everything I wanted. I was really happy with Tavio, but there's a saying that good things never last. When I was five months pregnant they killed him.

That day he was planning to go to Río Piedras with a fellow called Angie. Angie didn't show up. Instead, Pico came to ask Tavio to go with him and break into a store. They had already robbed that store once, and if you steal somewhere you should wait several months at least before going back to the same place. So I told Tavio, "Don't go, please don't go." He said, "I'll go this time. When you give birth to my child I'll stop doing these things."

He left that night at about eleven o'clock. I was still begging him not to go because I had a presentiment that he would be killed. I told him so, but he didn't believe in those things. Five days before, I had dreamed that he had been killed.

"Watch out, Tavio," I had told him. "They're going to kill you."

"Oh, you! Always dreaming nonsense!"

"It's not nonsense. They're going to kill you and it's going to be soon. Please be careful."

That was five days before his death! Even before that, I had dreamed several times that I was walking along when someone came up to me and said, "Listen, they shot Tavio." I would start back to find him and then always at that point I'd wake up. I had other dreams that he had fallen down a precipice and gotten killed running away from the cops.

When Tavio didn't come back that night I went to Pico's house at about six o'clock in the morning. Pico told me what had happened. Tavio had gone in first and it seems the proprietor must have been waiting for them and he fired. The very first bullet caught Tavio in the chest. "I got scared and ran back home," Pico said.

When I heard the story I screamed and cried like a madwoman. Then I went to my *mamá*'s house to tell her what had happened. From there I went to Tavio's aunt's house and she took me to the hospital. A detective came to me there and I asked him about Tavio. He said, "Oh, he's the thief who was killed like a dog." When he said that, I fell on him and hammered him with my fists. I was pregnant with Toya and I fainted. I tell you, I went mad.

When I came to, his aunt had gone to claim the body. I rushed out of the emergency ward to the morgue. They didn't want to let me in, but I forced my way in by pushing ahead through the doorway with my pregnant belly. When I got inside I looked and looked everywhere but I couldn't find Tavio. Suddenly off to one side I saw a body with a mole and my initials on his thigh.

They had opened him up. They'd taken his brains out and put them on top of his chest. His throat was cut to the bone, from the jaw to chest. One of his thighs had been cut open too. When I saw him like that I went to him and cradled him in my arms. I went mad, mad, mad. For a month I didn't even know who I was.

That was the saddest day of my life. There have been many sad days for me, but none so unhappy as that one. I think it's even sadder to lose a husband than to lose a child, God protect mine! The only man I ever loved, and to have that happen to him! I wanted to die too. I wished the earth would open up and swallow me. I was about to bear his first child and he leaves me like that, five months pregnant. Who wouldn't want to die? We didn't even have a full year together.

I think there's no justice in Puerto Rico, because no justice was done in the case of Tavio's death. They didn't do anything to the man who killed him. Of course not, because he was a rich businessman. They didn't even punish him for having killed Tavio with a gun he didn't have a license for. He was tried and acquitted. They even congratulated him. I admit they were right in a way. Tavio was a thief and it's not right to steal from somebody who works himself to death to earn his money. But there should be justice the other way around too, even if the proprietor killed in self-defense. Because he was rich he went free. A poor man would have gone straight to jail.

But God is just. Maybe the world's justice won't do anything but you can always count on God's justice. If I should harm someone, for instance, that person shouldn't do anything. He should just say, "Never mind, I'll leave that in God's hands." And in time, you may be sure, I'll pay for it. God punishes without sticks or whips. Early or late, no matter how much time has passed or how safe the evildoer feels, a person who does a wrong always has to pay.

On the day of Tavio's funeral the house was filled with people. Lots of people came, because they really loved him. Hardly any of his own friends came, but our friends did. I paid for the funeral. It cost me nearly five hundred dollars. I paid for the singing with Tavio's own money. They took him to San José Church because that's near the graveyard.

Fernanda went with me. We carried him up to the Boulevard, down Sol Street, and then back up to San José. I wanted to do all that so that he would receive the Holy Apostles' and God's blessing. I think that helped him some. Not a lot, because he had sinned so much, being a thief. I don't think that's bad but it seems to me God must think it is.

On that very day his *mamá* and his aunt came over to quarrel with me. They quarreled right there in the presence of his corpse. They had come to get his things because they thought he'd left me a pile of money. I told them that all he had left me were debts. Right after his death, when I was out of my mind with grief, most of the jewelry had been stolen. The only thing left was a set of table silver, which I still keep in its box.

Since Tavio's family didn't get anything, they wouldn't even go to the funeral. I paid for a headstone and for the rosaries. His mother and aunt didn't come to the rosaries either or to the prayers on the anniversaries of his death. After the funeral I went on a big drunk. I have a weak head for liquor so it only takes two or three beers to make me drunk. I drank with the girls to forget, but it didn't help. I even smoked a marijuana cigarette. I thought of the life I'd had with him and how it had all come to an end. That time they had to carry me home.

Well, now I was alone, a woman with three children and another on the way. I went by myself to look for a job at the Municipal Hospital and I filled in the application blanks for a nurse's aid. You don't really need to know much for that job. And what did they tell me? "You have to have a certain number of years in school as well as experience."

"Some people working here have never been to school," I answered. "They don't even know how to sign their names." The truth is that one of them is a cousin of a city official and two others are relatives of that politician in La Esmeralda. So I said, "You're all bribed here. Ha, if I were one of those fanatic *Populares* who spend twenty-four hours a day at City Hall, they'd give me a job. I've seen it happen."

I went to the lady mayor, *doña* Fela, and explained the situation to her. I told her that my husband had been killed and all. Then I asked her to give me some blanks so I could get a nurse's aid job at the hospital. I got a paper to take to the hospital but it all came to nothing. What am I supposed to do with a paper, wipe my ass? I tore it up and never went back again. That was the only time I asked the mayor for help and I didn't get it. If I'd spent all my time at City Hall licking her boots, then there would have been work for me. But I didn't, so no job.

I went to ask for more help from *el welfare*. Everybody was asking for something there, so I thought I would too. I wanted something from them in return for all they've soaked me for. Nobody can make me believe that when tomato sauce goes up from eight cents to ten, some of that isn't finding its way into the governor's wallet.

The *welfare* people investigate even your ass before they give you a miserable pittance. After the shame of going to them and being asked all sorts of questions, they send you a measly eighteen dollars a month, for a mother with three children. I can't live on eighteen dollars. I explained that to them, and what did they say, the sons of the great whore? That they couldn't do more for me.

I wrote a letter to the governor of Puerto Rico and told him my problem. I told him I had no one to turn to and I asked him to help me get a job or help out with money because what *el welfare* gave me wasn't enough. He never answered my letter. That's the governor of Puerto Rico for you! On election day, when he wants people's votes, he'll give even his ass if he's asked for it. But meanwhile, nothing doing unless you have connections in the government. The only connections we poor people have is the connection of our mouths with a plate of rice and beans.

I won't have anything to do with politics. I don't even like to hear about it. I belong to no party because when we get a new governor he will be the same as this one, if not worse. They said they were bringing free electricity to the poor. Then we found we had to pay for it. We have to pay for running water too. That's not what I call progress. I think it's robbery.

This governor we have, what has he done? He's built hotels for tourists—but we're not tourists, we're Puerto Ricans. He's built houses and made the streets pretty; but you can't eat those. What he should do is improve the slums. He should give houses to the really poor people. But all he knows is how to make the roads run on the ground and the buildings rise up in the air. We want the kind of progress that means you can get a job.

Now, with elections coming on, Muñoz Marín is giving away little plots of land to people so he can say he did something for them. But what was he doing before? If the Governor's Mansion had been blown to bits that time it was bombed by the Nationalists, I'd have been glad.

Take this business of employment. If a Cuban and a Puerto Rican apply for the same job in Puerto Rico, the Cuban is hired and to hell with the Puerto Rican. I tried to get a job in the overalls factory in Cataño and in the shoe factory. Oh, I went to so many places! "Experience?" they'd ask. "How many years? How old are you? Where are you working now?" You can't get a job unless you already have one or unless you have experience. But the place to get experience is on the job. You aren't born knowing.

That's why so many young men use junk and there's so much delinquency in Puerto Rico. The government doesn't do anything about that. All they do is persecute the numbers runners, who are earning an honest living. And they arrest people for taking one little shot of rum.

Well, I went on trying but I couldn't find a job. I wrote to my father in Virginia telling him about my problems and he didn't even bother to answer. If he had been a good, loving father he would have said, "Don't worry, daughter, I'll pay your rent and help you out as best I can." Even twelve dollars a week is a lot of money in Puerto Rico. With his salary he could have sent me twenty-five and that would have been enough. Why didn't he do it? He had the money.

Since nobody would help me, I went back to my old job at the Silver Cup. That's when, pregnant as I was, *don* Camacho fell in love with me.

I went out with men but not so much as before. When I was in my eighth month of pregnancy *don* Camacho told me I'd better not go out at all. He kept on giving me money until I had my baby.

On Sunday, January 15, 1960, my daughter Victoria Vásquez was born in the Municipal Hospital. It was a very easy birth. My pregnancy had been good because Tavio had given me everything I craved. But the baby was born sick and full of sores. She had syphilis and looked like a mangy dog.

Tavio had that illness. He infected the baby and then Toya infected me. Tavio had told me about it, but only after we were already living together. I said it didn't matter. I didn't know then what it was and, really, I still don't. When I went with men I always went to the clinic and had blood tests and everything. And I always asked the men to use *condoms* or I wouldn't let them do it.

I don't bear any grudge against Tavio because of my illness. After all, I got cured. If it had been incurable I would hold it against him. I had to go to the clinic for penicillin and streptomycin injections for almost fifteen days. I felt weak, very weak, and I was thin, thin, thin. The baby had to have treatments at the hospital for almost a year.

Don Camacho kept helping me. He told me that if I didn't want to have any more children he would give me the money for an operation. It cost ninety dollars. I thought I'd better do it because I wasn't living steadily with one man, and this business of having a child by every man you sleep with isn't a good idea. It looks bad. And I would have had to keep on having abortions. If it hadn't been for *don* Camacho, God knows how many children I'd have by now. I'm very grateful to him for what he did.

After I left the hospital, some of the stitches inside broke and I had a hernia. They had to operate again. That cost *don* Camacho another seventy-five dollars. He took good care of me but we quarreled and I left him and started going with Americans again. Then I went back to old man Camacho. In spite of everything, he gave me more than the Americans did.

Don Camacho was just the same as he'd been before. Whatever I asked for he gave me. He paid off the furniture store; he bought a baby carriage for Toya; he got me a sewing machine, a set of furniture, and a crib. He gave my little girls necklaces and rings. Actually, he kept me like a rich society lady.

Then he bought a small *bar* and I worked there. He wanted to get me out of the life and to keep my mind occupied. I took care of the business for him. In a way, his intentions were good. I didn't love him, because he was a married man, and the time was bound to come when he'd give me a kick in the ass, send me on my way and go back to his wife. Later on he'd get another mistress. That's why I say a man can have his pleasure with me so long as he pleases my pocketbook. None of that mush about "I'm yours and you're mine."

But that old man didn't satisfy me sexually. He was over sixty and I didn't feel any thrill with him. He didn't get up much pressure, see? And I felt as if nothing was happening. And he was so jealous. Once he tried to kill me because of an Italian friend of mine, Luigi.

The Italian called me and I went to sit with him. When I got up to get him a whiskey, *don* Camacho came over, grabbed my dress and tore it from top to bottom. Then he dragged me up the steps by the hair. We tangled with each other up there. He socked me and I hit him back. Then he took out the revolver he always carried and said, "I'm going to shoot you."

"Shoot me if you're man enough," I said. "What do you think that'll do for you?"

"You have a terrible temper," he said. "Nobody can control you."

"That's right," I answered. "Only God can control me and that's because He's more powerful than anybody. So be quiet and don't threaten me with that revolver if you don't want me to grab it and kill you."

He put the revolver away and went downstairs. But first he said, "I'll buy you another dress tomorrow."

"No, thank you. I'll buy one myself, and now I'm going home."

He begged me to stay. He always padlocked my room on the outside and he did it now. I couldn't escape because the room was on the third floor of the building. So I went to sleep. At about three o'clock in the morning he brought me a fried pork chop, fried plantains and some lettuce. "I don't want anything except to get away from here," I said.

"Well, you aren't leaving." He came and lay down beside me but I turned my back on him. After a while he got up and left and I went back to sleep. The next morning I found a note and fifty dollars he'd left for me. He wrote that he was very sorry and hoped I'd forgive him.

Later, he told me he was going to take a pleasure trip to New York with his wife. I'd had the idea for a long time that I'd like to go to New York. After Tavio died it was as if I had no joy in living. I wasn't able to forget him. He was always in my mind. I thought it would help me if I went to New York. I told all this to *don* Camacho and he said, "When I come back I'll send you there."

I began to get ready to go to New York. My brother was already in the States, in Salem, New Jersey, and so was Felícita. I wrote my sister asking her to let me stay at her home with my children. She said yes, but you know how a person can say "Yes" in such a way that you know they're thinking "No." But I went anyway. *Don* Camacho gave me money for my children too. I sold my furniture and everything I had. I told *don* Camacho that if I liked it in the States I'd stay there. If I didn't, he was to send my fare to come back. Simplicio's wife, Flora, was still in Puerto Rico, so I asked her if she wanted to go with me to help take care of my children while I worked. She said she did, so *don* Camacho gave me money for her too.

Soledad

To New York

WE LEFT FOR New York at eleven-thirty in the morning in an Eastern Airlines plane. It was my first airplane trip. Only *mamá,* Cruz and a girl named Hilda came to see us off. Nobody else. The trip took over eight hours because fog delayed us. I was airsick and it seemed to me the flight would never end. I was scared to death and with four children to look after!

When I got off the plane I was soaked through with the kids' piss. I looked around and saw my brother. Felícita hadn't come. But Simplicio had come because his wife was with me. If not, he wouldn't have come, either. *Don* Camacho had given me two hundred dollars cash, so I paid the bus fare, thirty dollars, to Salem. The trip took six hours and I was feeling so sick that I couldn't see straight. All I wanted was to flop down on a bed. We got there at about half past twelve. Felícita came out and hugged me. She looked very happy, as if she really was glad to see us. She said, "*Ave María,* and with four children! You're crazy."

I'll leave if I don't like it here," I told her. "If I like it, I'll stay. As soon as I can, I'll look for a place to live."

Felícita lived in a small one-story house. It wasn't made of wood but of some kind of material they use in New York. It had a living room, a bedroom, bathroom, a small porch and a back yard. It was a very pretty little house. Fela's husband, Edmundo, was in the hospital. He had had an accident at the graveyard where he worked. Three boarders came to the house to eat and one of them, Lorenzo, also slept there. Sleeping in that house were Felícita, her children Tany and Mundito, Simplicio, Flora, Catín, Sarita, Toya, Quique, myself, *don* Lorenzo and, later, Edmundo. Felícita and Flora slept on the bed and I slept on the floor with all the children.

The first day, Fela was very attentive to us. She gave us food and was very pleasant. But I'm a person who studies people and keeps her mouth shut. I wondered how long it would last.

I came to America on Sunday, and on Tuesday I was already working. Uncle Simón's wife, Iris, got me the job. She spoke to her brother about me and he knew of a job picking vegetables. He took me there in his car. It was a completely new experience to me, because I'd never worked on a farm like that before. Those fields were so big it would take a whole day just to walk across them. The plants are low, like lettuce, so you had to work bent over. I worked from eight in the morning until six in the evening. At the end of three days I had earned twenty-five dollars. I gave Flora eight dollars for looking after the children and I gave Felícita ten. That left only seven for me. I bought a crib for Toya.

Then Felícita's husband, Edmundo, came home from the hospital and began complaining about the children. He said they were a nuisance, a bunch of crybabies. Well, one of Felícita's boarders was a boy named Eddy. He liked me and I liked him too. We fell in love, but not deeply. Eddy asked me for dates and I went to the movies with him.

One day he and I went to the beach. When we got back Felícita had put Toya's crib outside. I asked her why, and she answered that the crib was in the way. What she meant was that my children and I were in the way. Now she wasn't cooking meals except when she felt like it. Eddy noticed how she treated me and asked me if I would go off with him. That was thirteen days after I had arrived from Puerto Rico. I said yes, not because I loved him but to have a place where I could take my children and live in peace. That boy really did me a favor, taking me out of my sister's house. He found a place in Bridgeboro and we moved there.

Felícita's tongue started to wag about how I went with a man I hardly knew. That's my sister Felícita for you. I asked Flora if she was coming with me to take care of my children. She said she was staying with Felícita. So I said, "You're just plain ungrateful. But you'll pay for it. I'll get even with you, never fear."

Flora is very *cheapy*. She won't do you a favor no matter how bad off you are. She's a hard and selfish woman. When she and Simplicio were in trouble with Flora's husband, Fontánez, I was the one who took the risk of letting them stay with me, even though I was pregnant with Toya, because Fernanda wouldn't have Flora in the house. She didn't want to go looking for trouble, she said. Later, when Fontánez had calmed down and my *mamá* saw how Flora helped around the house and took care of my children, she said to Flora,

"Look here, the only thanks you'll ever get for staying with Soledad is to have her kick you out some day. Better come stay with me. You'll live well and do whatever you please." So one day Flora packed up her things and left.

Simplicio is a good brother in his way but his wife has him under her thumb. All the women in her family like to rule their men. Flora would hand over Heaven to her relatives if she could, but she doesn't want one of us to borrow five dollars from Simplicio. She'll say, "You people think we're millionaires." If one of her brothers or sisters asks for five dollars she'll take the money out of her gizzard if she has to. That's not right. It should be all for one and one for all. But when Simplicio is working Flora takes his money away from him. She has done awful things to him, like call him a "dirty Negro." I feel for him because Flora's skin is light but she has big blubber lips. She's Simplicio's wife, so I don't say anything. I don't interfere in their life. If they kill each other, let them.

I went to work in Bridgeboro picking tomatoes. Eddy worked there too and acted as my interpreter. I had to get up at six o'clock, leave the children with the woman who took care of them, and be on the job by seven. Whichever of us got home first in the evening cooked dinner. I washed our clothes at the *laundry*. Eddy took me there and showed me what coins to use. He never once beat me and we never had a quarrel either. I knew that he liked women but he never told me anything about his life.

There weren't many jobs in Bridgeboro, so after a month we went back to Salem. I got a job packing in a canning factory. Felícita wanted a job too, but they wouldn't hire her because she had worked there before and one day had just walked out. I made ninety to a hundred dollars a week there. *Don* Camacho was sending me about twenty-five dollars every month. I paid twenty-five each week to a lady to take care of my children and twenty dollars a week rent. Felícita had moved out and we were living in her little house.

After a while the lady couldn't come any more to look after the kids, so Felícita took over. One day she didn't feel like staying with them and just walked off and left them all alone. The neighbors must have called the cops because a detective came to get me at the factory. He even wanted to take me to court. I explained that I had left the children with my sister, so he let me off. He caught up with her at the railroad station but didn't do anything to her. She got mad at me and hardly spoke to me for a while. I got somebody else for the children but later Felícita took them back again.

Finally I quarreled with Eddy because I found out he had a wife in Puerto Rico. I discovered it from a letter and he admitted it. I told him I couldn't live with a married man. He insisted that I stay with him, because he didn't love his wife. I said, "All right. But if you keep on living with me you have to put up with anything that happens, because I don't love you."

· · ·

After about eight months in New Jersey I decided to go back to Puerto Rico. Things hadn't turned out the way I had expected. I had planned to make a home in the States, but my family didn't understand me and set themselves against me. I wrote my *papá* to send me half the fare but he didn't answer. So *don* Camacho sent me the money. Eddy went to Florida and I went to Puerto Rico. Felícita left for Puerto Rico the same day I did, on an earlier plane.

When we got back to San Juan, *don* Camacho sent for me and asked me what I wanted to do next. I said I wanted to go to Florida. Eddy had told me that if I came, he could get me a job there. So after a short visit in Puerto Rico, I left for Florida. *Don* Camacho paid my fare. I left Catín and Quique with Nanda.

For about a month I worked packing tomatoes. I had my little house there with Eddy, and my two girls with me, and I was doing well. Then they wrote me that Catín was very sick. I had to go and get her, so Eddy paid my fare. I brought Catín back with me, but Quique stayed with his *papá*. Cruz had broken up with Emilio by then, so I brought her and her baby, Anita, too. She was to look after the children.

I had written Eddy to meet me at the airport, but when I arrived Eddy's brother was there. He said, "Say, look, I have to tell you something. Eddy's wife came and he's living with her."

While I was away Eddy had sent for her to come to Florida. First they lived in the very house he and I had lived in. I went to the house, but Eddy and his wife had taken practically everything away. They were living in a shack at a *farmer*'s place.

Eddy didn't come to see me that day or the next. The third day he showed up, very affectionate, as though nothing had happened. "Look," he said, "my wife's been having fits and all that. And the spirits told her I shouldn't go to meet you because if I did I'd be killed in the car." That's what she was up to, scaring him to keep him away from me. A spirit, she said. Liar! He told me, "I'll go on paying the rent but I won't be able to come here as I used to. I'm with her now."

I said, "You know that the evil we do on earth we pay for on earth. You've done me a wrong. You should have told me what was going on before I wasted my time coming back to this mess. But never mind. I'll get even."

I arrived on a Saturday, and on Sunday I got sick with a strong vaginal pain. A colored neighbor got me a car, and Eddy's cousin, a boy called Jorge Luis took me to the hospital. I was in the hospital for five days and Eddy never once visited me. Not that I expected him to, since he was with his wife. Cruz was with my children. I had given her money for expenses and all that, but even so I suffered thinking about them.

A week after I got home, Jorge Luis asked me if I would let him sleep at my place. I told him to stay because we were all alone there. But then he fell in love with me and we began to live together. He was twenty-four years old and not very good-looking. He was dark-skinned, thick-lipped and rather fat, but I needed a man to help me. I went on working and so did he. I was picking *las stróberi*.

I didn't know anything about Jorge Luis' family and I didn't want to. I saw his sister only twice. The second time it was because she wanted an abortion. She asked me to find someone who would take the baby out of her when she was already five months gone. She wanted to get rid of it because she and her husband were always quarreling. I didn't know anyone, so I took it out myself.

The way to do it is to stick a rubber tube or a syringe into the neck of the womb and then irrigate the womb with a solution of castile soap. Afterward you pull out the syringe. Half an hour later the blood comes. Then there are pains and more pains. Finally the woman aborts. I gave the girl the irrigation, then I went home. She could have died but it would have been her own damn fault. I didn't tell her to do it.

I didn't like Jorge Luis, even though he satisfied me. He was a skirt-chaser, with women all over the place, and he was dirty. In the factory he was always making love to Negro girls. I pretended not to notice but I can't bear a man who does that. Once he spent all his money drinking and he wanted me to give him some of my money. I refused. Then we had a fight that was the daddy of all fights. He hit me on the head and I threw a kettleful of boiling water on him and it burned his face and arm. He grabbed a knife. Cruz tried to interfere, but much good that did. After all, she's a cripple. "All right, cut me," I said. And I stood there facing him. He turned around and went out. They had to take him to the hospital.

Because of that quarrel they arrested both of us. They let me go because he had hit me first. They fined him fifteen dollars. He couldn't pay, so he had to spend three days in jail. His friends told me to get him out, and one of them gave me the money. So I went and got him out. His face and arm were badly burned. I took him back home and I stayed there with him.

About a month after getting out of jail Jorge Luis caught a cold and stayed home from work. When he got paid, he bought some groceries and kept the rest of the money. He took half of the fifty dollars we had saved and then he told me he was leaving for New York. That's why I feel about men the way I do. They're always playing dirty tricks on me. I just told him, "All right. Go."

He left on a Sunday, and on Monday I went to work. That night, about eight o'clock, I got dizzy and felt myself falling. After that I blacked out. I'd gone crazy, see? They took me to a sanatorium for crazy people and drug addicts. I was there nineteen days. When I came to my senses, I found myself tied hand and foot and locked up. They even tied me to the bed at night. My mind felt strange. I prayed to Saint Martha to help me. I vowed that I would pay for a Mass for her and hear it through on my knees. She answered my prayer. I still owe her that Mass and some day I'll do it.

I wasn't treated very well in that sanatorium. They didn't beat me but they gave us hardly any food at all. Then we had to be in bed by seven and the nurses were mean to us. For instance, when I got angry and wanted to leave my room, they tied me up. And they pumped me full of drugs so I'd sleep all the time. That was the only treatment they gave me. A doctor came to see me every other day. He could tell I wasn't crazy and it was only my nerves. He told me they were taking steps to send me back to Puerto Rico.

A month later I did go back. Cruz stayed on in Florida with her baby, Anita, waiting until I sent for her. *El welfare* paid half my fare and I paid the other half. I had written to my mother that I was coming, but when I got there nobody was at the airport to meet me. I took a taxi to La Esmeralda and the first person I saw was Arturo playing dominoes. He was glad to see me. He took the children home and then went with me to Fernanda's house. She was drinking beer. When she saw me she began to cry, but it was all hypocrisy.

That night *don* Camacho sent a car for me and I went to his *bar*. Felícita's husband, Edmundo, had gotten a job there and had told *don* Camacho everything I had done in New Jersey and made me out to be a whore. But *don* Camacho said I could still count on him whenever I needed anything, and he wanted to keep going with me. I said no thanks. I slept sometimes at my *mamá*'s house and sometimes at Felícita's. Fela had already bought a house in La Esmeralda. When Edmundo saw me he didn't let on about anything. He greeted me like the hypocrite he was, and Felícita did too.

Arturo behaved very well. He took care of my children and told me not to worry and to take it easy. He helped me. But not Fernanda or anybody else. Nobody took me to a doctor or to a spiritist. Once I went to the Psychiatric Hospital in the District Medical Center in Río Piedras. I went all by myself and I waited from early morning until the afternoon. Then, since nobody paid any attention to me, I went home and I never went back. I kept on getting nervous spells, but I made an effort to control myself and little by little I became calmer.

I started looking for work but couldn't find any. I was bored and lonely, with nothing to do. So I went hustling at a *bar* on San José Street. Then I began to put money in the bank. I stayed at Fernanda's house and gave her money for food, but she didn't cook or save my meals for me unless she felt like it. Sometimes I had to eat in San Juan or else I gave money to Arturo to buy food for me and the children.

Jorge Luis wrote to me and begged my pardon for treating me as he had. He said he had repented and a lot more lies. He asked me to come to New York. I didn't answer that letter, but he kept on insisting, so finally I told him

I'd come when he sent me the fare. Two months later he sent it. I got Sarita and Toya ready, and on June 22, 1962, I went to New York. I left Quique with Arturo and Catín with my *mamá*.

Jorge Luis came to meet me at the airport and received me very nicely. He had a *furnished room* in the Bronx, for which he paid sixteen dollars a week. He was working and I started to work too. My first job was making purses. I worked as an *operator,* at forty-three dollars a week.

The boss was Italian, a very rude, quick-tempered man. He got angry over every little thing. As long as you worked well everything was *O.K.* But when a piece of work didn't come out quite right, as sometimes happened, he would lose his temper and yell. I have weak nerves and couldn't take it. That's why I quit after about a month. I wasn't going to kill myself working for forty-three dollars.

I didn't have a single friend in that place. I don't like to strike up friendships with the other employees when I work in a factory. Besides, there's no comradeship among workers in this country. Most of the Americans would like to keep all the jobs for themselves, so they won't co-operate with a Spanish person. I didn't know the work well and I had to ask how to do things, where to hook on the thread, and so on. They never had the courtesy to explain. They'd just say, "I don't know. Ask the boss." Even the Puerto Rican women were like that. Once I asked a girl named Feliciana how to turn a purse.

"I'm sorry," she said, "but I can't leave my work to help you. You have to learn by yourself. The rest of us can't attend you new ones."

I said, "You don't have to make such a big thing of it. I just asked you a simple question." After that I was never very friendly with any of them. They were all stuck up. And I don't take, so I won't have to give, understand?

Then, on August 11, 1962, I got sick again. Jorge Luis and I had quarreled over some money he took. I told him to give it back to me to buy food. He said he wouldn't, and went off. I went to my cousin Chango's. I got a sort of nervous *shock* there because Chango told me Jorge Luis had a mistress called Yvette. I fell down and my cousin took me to the hospital. Then, according to Chango, he went to Jorge Luis and told him I was sick and Jorge Luis answered, "I can't go to her. I have to work tomorrow."

They sent me to Bellevue Hospital because they thought I was crazy again. It seems I attacked some nurses and all five of them hit me. A keeper came and twisted my arm. You can see this bone sticking out here. It's still dislocated. They tied me up in a strait jacket and filled me with all sorts of drugs. I didn't know what was going on, I didn't recognize anything or anybody.

But just because a person is nervous and falls in a fit, is that any reason to send her to a crazy house? If they send someone like me, in full possession of her four senses, to a place for crazy people, what can you expect? It's impossible to talk to those people. You say one thing and they start talking about something else. They can't keep anything in their minds, you see. And then they laugh!

When I got out of the hospital, my cousin Chango signed the papers and took me to my room. There I found that Jorge Luis had taken the TV set and his clothes and had gone off somewhere. I was still full of drugs. When I tried to get up I'd fall down. I hardly ate at all because I didn't have money to buy food. The lady downstairs fed my little girls, and Chango took care of them during the day.

I realized later that Jorge Luis had taken up with Yvette because she had bought him a car. The next time he came I said to him, "Well, so you sold yourself. I'm young and she's old, but she has money. So go to her." He kept quarreling and trying to force himself on me but I said no.

One day I went to Jorge Luis' house and tried to smash up his car. I was angry at him for what he'd done to me, see? Then he came to my house to beat me up. When he started to hit me I grabbed a knife to stab him. He yelled for the police. The boys downstairs called, "Kill him, Soledad, we'll be your witnesses." At that he got into his car and drove off.

About a week later he got drunk and came to see me. He had parked his car badly and a cop came up to tell him so. He hit the cop and got himself arrested. They also tore up his driving license because it had some words scratched out. He wrote asking me to come get him out of jail. Of course I wouldn't. I went over to Yvette's place and I told her, "I don't fight over a man. Here's the key to Jorge Luis' car. You drive to the jail and get him out." She took the key and gave the car to another lover. She never even went to the jail to visit Jorge Luis. On the day of the trial I got a telegram from the police asking me to go see him. I told them that I wasn't his wife. I didn't go, and I've never seen him again. He was sentenced to six months in jail.

By then I was already eight weeks behind with the rent. They sent me a dispossess notice. Then a boy called Diego went room-hunting with me. We found a little furnished room and Diego paid the deposit. He had a wife, but he paid for the room on condition that I give him certain favors. He also bought me some food. Sick as I was, without a job and with two children, I was satisfied. My *mamá* never wrote to me, nor did the rest of my relatives. My *mamá* was in Pennsylvania then with Simplicio, but neither she nor Simplicio wrote.

I have relatives in New York but they were no help at all. I have many cousins on my father's side who were born in the States, but they all speak English and we don't keep up any kind of family relationship. One day I called up Aunt María del Carmen, whom I had not seen for sixteen years. I got her telephone number from Uncle Simón. She said, "Well, if you plan to call on me, come early because I have to go out." What did that mean? Clearly, that she didn't want me to come. So I didn't go and I've never phoned her since. I tore up the slip with her telephone number.

On my mother's side, Aunt Amparo is here in New York. She's the mother of my cousins Darío, Virginia, Beatriz, José and Delia. I also have my cousin Chango and his brother, Generoso. Chango is the best of my cousins. We fight all the time but he has been good to me. When his wife was here she took care of my little girls. Afterward they separated because she put the horns on him. I don't really know much about Chango's life because he has spent most of it in New York. I don't know much about anybody's life because I don't bother about it. I only care about what happens to me.

I lived with Diego for a while but I felt no love for the man and one night I told him so. I said I was going to break with him and get myself a job. He said that was all right and left.

I had trouble finding a job, so I applied to *welfare*. I figured that on *relief* I should get about a hundred dollars a month for rent and food. In Puerto Rico, all I got was eighteen dollars. But *welfare* wouldn't accept my case. They said they couldn't help me because I hadn't established residence and because I had no place where I could buy on credit. That's the way they are. Yet you see women all the time who hide their husbands or lovers from *welfare* so they can get help from them. And you see women having one child after another with never a husband in sight, but they get their weekly check all the same. In fact, every time a baby comes they get a larger check.

Just compare my case to Juanita's. She's a friend of mine who took care of the kids for me for a while. She had five children. Her husband pretended to leave her so she could go to *welfare*. They sent her *relief* checks for over a hundred dollars. And do you know what she did with that money? She spent it all on her husband. She bought meat for him and gave only rice and beans to her children. I never saw those kids neat or well cared for. He spent every single night at her house and gave her another baby. So *welfare* increased her check! That just goes to show you how unfair they are.

Well, there I was, alone and unable to find work or get on *relief* and already owing rent. I decided to speak to my cousin Virginia about my problem. Virginia is a hustler, and her husband, Moncho, is a pimp. She has to earn money because he doesn't work. All he does is stay in the house and pace the floor. He's crazy because he drinks a lot. Right now he's in an insane asylum, but even so she has to support him. He's a weakling. She's stronger than he and she's older, yet he beats her and everything. She's afraid of him. She's a fool, that's what she is.

Moncho got me a job in a *bar* owned by an Italian. I worked from six at night to two in the morning, Friday, Saturday and Sunday, and I earned thirty dollars.

The *bars* here are different from those in Puerto Rico. In Puerto Rico if you go into a *bar* they know you're a whore. Here women go in just to get a drink and nobody criticizes them. I was happy at this job.

I always went out with old men that Virginia got for me, and they gave me ten or fifteen dollars. Once I had an old man who did nothing except lick my cunt. That's all he did every single day. I had another old man who could really bear down hard with his tongue. He would do it from back to front and front to back. That just made me wild in bed. Then he'd open me up and put his tongue inside and go "shashashasha" with such a movement in there that I would flow like a cow. He swallowed all that too. It has lots of vitamin A, you know.

But one can't help being afraid that they might bite you down there because they take it in their mouth. And sometimes they blow into you and inflate your ovaries. That gives you such a pain you wish you were dead. You have to be careful, see? But when they put their tongue way in there, *ay,* it's wonderful. Mostly Americans do it. I don't know how they got to like it so much.

I'd been working a month at that *bar* when one night Benedicto walked in. He was a seaman. He looked like a man in San Juan called Mario, so when I was serving him I said, "Say, are you Mario?"

"No, I'm not Mario."

"Well, you look like Mario." Then we began to talk. He invited me to have a drink and I accepted. Then he said, "Would you like to go dancing tomorrow?" He must have thought, "This one is an easy mark. I'll fuck her once and send her packing." But nobody can do that to me. So I said, "I'm working here for my daughters' sake and I don't go out dancing with anybody." He said, "Well, tomorrow we'll go out as a couple. First we'll dance and then we'll have dinner and after dinner—you know!" He insisted so much that finally I said I would go.

But I didn't go. I stood him up. I was home all day that Sunday with my daughters. When I went to work on Wednesday he was waiting for me. "That was a nice thing to do, wasn't it?" he said. We got to talking again and he said, "I want to visit you in your house."

"Sorry, it's no," I answered.

But he went and talked with my cousin Virginia. He gave her two or three dollars. And Virginia, who would sell the mother who bore her, gave him my address. The next day, as I was standing outside my house talking to the landlord, I saw Benedicto strolling down the street. I was surprised. He was the last person I expected to see around there. Benedicto said, "May I come into your house?"

"Of course."

My girls were asleep. "Are these your daughters?" he asked. "I didn't believe you had children."

I said, "If I had no children I wouldn't be doing what I do. I would find myself a good man who would give me all I need, and relax. But there isn't a man in a thousand who'd want to take on a woman with children."

"Yes, I know," he answered. Then he said, "Let's go eat." I hadn't eaten that day because I couldn't stretch what I earned to cover all my expenses. The room rent was fourteen dollars and I had to pay for the care of the children. Sometimes I went to bed hungry. So I went out to dinner with Benedicto and that night Benedicto stayed with me. The next morning he gave me ten dollars and said, "I'll be seeing you."

At the *bar* that night he said, "I want to talk to you. I'd like to make a home for you. You quit working here and come live with me. I'll give you everything you need and you can get yourself a more decent job." But I went on working right where I was for a while. I never believe right off what a man tells me. I watch him. So I said, "All right, I'll think it over."

Benedicto came to my house and stayed with me every other day. One day he brought over a few of his clothes. The next time he brought a few more, until finally he moved in with me. He paid the rent and he gave me money for the children's food. Then I stopped working at the *bar*.

Soledad

———

Life with Benedicto

———

AT FIRST BENEDICTO was very nice. He told me about his life and all the hard knocks he'd had. His *mamá* never loved him. His *papá* abandoned her when she was pregnant with Beni, so she took it out on him. Later she left Beni with her sister and went to New York. She married again and had several children with Benedicto's stepfather. Beni went hungry in Puerto Rico until he was big, and his mother never gave him a thought. Now that he's a seaman and makes good money, she wants to tie him to her. He gives her five or ten dollars once in a while but she says he never gives her anything. She's a no-good, shameless old woman.

Benedicto had a wife who put the horns on him, but that was because he did to her what he later did to me. He's had a pile of sweethearts. He has seven or eight kids with different women. He had one woman who hustled for him. If she earned sixty dollars she gave it all to him, but he beat her every day. He liked to live off whores.

Benedicto is one of those men who begins to behave badly as soon as he's caught a woman. The very first time he shipped out he didn't send me any money. He didn't care whether I ate or not. The rent went unpaid for three weeks.

I would go to my cousin Virginia to get food for my daughters. But one day she said, "I haven't got enough to feed you. Do you think I have to support you and your daughters?"

"All right," I answered and left. Do you know what I did then? I went to a *bar* called Romance Boricano, where a lot of Puerto Ricans go. A little old man asked me to go with him and he paid me fifteen dollars. Then that old man fell in love with me and I still go to see him. He's called El Polaco. He speaks a little Spanish and a little English, so we get along. He's not terribly old, about sixty-eight, but I don't feel anything with him.

I go to his place almost every week. He likes to cook for me. I phone him and say I'll be there at such and such a time, and when I get there a meal is ready. The man is so clean you could eat off the floor of his apartment. He treats me well, depending on the state of his wallet and his feelings. Sometimes he gives me fifteen dollars, sometimes twenty. I take two or three drinks with him, we go to bed and do it once, quickly.

El Polaco has lived alone for many, many years. He talks to me about his wife and his daughter. They live in Poland. It seems his wife had a nephew whom she liked and she put the horns on her husband. So he went to Argentina, where he got work as a mason and earned good money. He told me he had decided never to marry again because of his daughter.

But he's nuts about me. This *jacket* I have is a gift from him and he has given me things for the children too. He doesn't know I have a husband. Now he's peeved at me because he wants me to come and live with him. But I think the difference in our ages would be a problem. I know, because I had that trouble before with *don* Camacho. If I could keep up with my expenses I wouldn't go to him at all.

Benedicto doesn't know that I sometimes go hustling. He's never asked me. At first he used to question my little girls but then he stopped. I don't know what he thinks I do for money to pay the furniture installments, the rent, food and bus fare. The thought must cross his mind sometimes. "How does Soledad get money for all that?" But he doesn't really care whether I eat or not, whether I'm sick or well. When he leaves he gives me only twenty-five or maybe thirty dollars, and he expects it to last until he comes home. He'll write, "I can't send you money because I'm not too well off myself." But it's a lie. He has women in all the ports and spends his money drinking and gambling.

A neighbor of mine, Tití, got me a job in a zipper factory. I earned forty-six dollars a week. The work was easy and *el boss* was friendly and didn't hurry us too much. The employees were nice too. There were both Americans and Puerto Ricans on our floor. But then I got sick and lost the job. I had a vaginal infection and had to go to the hospital. My fever went up to 108 degrees and they put me in an alcohol-and-ice bath to bring it down. They took care of me, all right, but I had an argument with a colored woman who called me a bitch. I answered that the whoring mother who bore her was more of a bitch than I was. You see, they put colored Americans in the ward where I was and I didn't talk to one of them, except the woman who insulted me.

·   ·   ·

I don't like the black people here because they're all sons of a great whore. They throw their weight around, and boast and think they're better than anybody else. If they could have their way, they'd control the whole of New York. You hear talk of racial prejudices, of the slavery in which Negroes live, but it's all their own fault. Abraham Lincoln was the one who freed the Negroes, and do you know who killed him? A Negro! Yes, he was a Negro, though he looked white. It happens sometimes.

For all I care, they can take away all the colored people. The women are whores and the men are so foul-mouthed they'll yell dirty words at you even if you're with your husband. If you're alone they'll say, "Hey, give me your little cunt, give me your ass." That's what the Negroes here are like. I'm a Negro myself, but I'm a Puerto Rican Negro. I'm not one of the same race as they are. Negroes here are bullies, they don't fight one against one but in gangs. There are Puerto Rican gangs, too, I don't deny it. I'm not going to try to cover the sky with my hand because it can't be done. I tell the truth about things. There are Puerto Rican gangs, American gangs, and gangs of Negroes. My cousin José belongs to a gang, the Indians. There are Puerto Ricans and colored Americans mixed up in that gang, but the Negroes are the worst.

The Italians don't get along with Puerto Ricans either. As soon as they see a Puerto Rican they begin to insult him and they don't want us in their neighborhood. I don't know why they're against us. I'd like to find out. They say it's our fault but that's not so. Naturally, if an Italian hits me first, I'll knock him out. One can't allow those things. But that's how the trouble starts.

I wish I had power in this country. The first thing I'd do would be to end the persecution of the Puerto Ricans. I'd put an end to the landlords who want to squeeze the last drop of juice from us, charging high rents for tiny apartments and rooms. And I'd impose strict discipline in the schools and wipe out those gangs of Italians and Negroes that defame the Puerto Ricans. And I'd stop all the bad vocabulary they use against us.

A Puerto Rican up here has a hard time finding a job and a safe place to live. If you're a Puerto Rican you can apply in twenty thousand places without getting a job. You can't get a job in a hospital or in the big department stores. But go to the factories, the cheap, ratty ones, and there you find Puerto Ricans, earning miserable wages. In the best places you find only Americans, never a Puerto Rican. That's why there's so much delinquency and crime among us.

In this country everyone lives his own life and takes the other fellow's dollar if he can. Whoever gets a chance to steal something, steals it. If they see anyone who is weak and old and has trouble crossing a street, they steal his bundle and run instead of helping him. They steal wallets from little old men. And they have no respect for anybody. Any young squirt will tell an old person to go to hell.

You see little girls, eleven to thirteen years old, smooching with men, smoking and using junk. You see those kids pregnant and having babies by the time they're twelve. And why? Because their mothers pay no attention to them. There should be a law about that. The time will come when you won't be able to step outside because someone might kill you in the street. Then all they'll say is that the killer was crazy and they'll send him to an insane asylum. I tell you, this country, New York, is plain rotten.

The public schools here hardly teach anything at all. Nowadays the pupils hit the teachers. With women teachers, what else can you expect? Then they waste time in exercises, games and cultivation. Why teach them to cultivate? This isn't a tropical country. Even in Puerto Rico this business of cultivating the land doesn't get you anywhere. And what good are games and exercises? Playing is not studying. Teach them to type, I say. I'd like to send my little girls to a parochial school, where they'd be taught good things.

I went to school in New York two years ago. I enrolled in an English course but there was so much kidding around that you can imagine what we learned! We got there at seven and they gave us half an hour to smoke. By eight-thirty the class was over. Is that a class? And what did they teach us? First-grade stuff! I quit.

I'd like to be a *beautician* or a nurse. All my life I've dreamed about being a nurse. But even if I had a nursing degree right now they wouldn't hire me at a hospital here, because I don't know English. That's an injustice. There should be hospitals here with Spanish-speaking staffs. North Americans go to Puerto Rico without knowing a word of Spanish and get jobs right away. So why can't we get a job without knowing English? You need English here to get any kind of a job, even to sweep floors.

I say that I shouldn't have to know English because I'm a Puerto Rican, not an American. It's not our fault we don't know English. The whole burden shouldn't fall on us. Everyone speaks his own language and has his place. There's room for all. And let me tell you, if a Puerto Rican child learns only English it's because his mother wants to show off. But all she does is create problems for her children because people say, "Look at that kid. He's Puerto Rican and he thinks he's an American." I wouldn't want my children to forget their Spanish. If they came home from school saying, "*Mami,* whatcha-maycallit," in English, it would be a problem for me. My children learned Spanish from me and speak Spanish, and they'd better not start speaking English to me because I'd kill them.

A month after I got out of the hospital I went looking for work. I'd leave in the morning at seven and sometimes I wouldn't get home till four in the afternoon. I'd get lost on the *subways*. Once I took a train that didn't stop in the Bronx at all. It went around behind Brooklyn and I got lost three times. I went up and down taking the same train. Finally I asked a Puerto Rican and he took me to the right platform.

To get a job here, you really have to suffer and to spend money. I'd see a "Vacancy" sign, but by the time I applied the vacancy was filled. Sometimes they told me, "Wait here," and after I'd waited for a whole hour they'd come out and say, "No work today." I even tried to buy a job. I saw an ad in the paper. "Experienced girls needed to work as *operators*. Go to such and such an agency." So I went and gave them ten dollars and got a job, finishing and packing *baby* clothes. I earned forty-six dollars there, forty-three after deductions. But I got fired in two weeks so the agency could sell that job to somebody else, see? It's a *racket*.

While I was working at that place I had a problem with a girl from Ecuador. She didn't like Spanish-speaking people. One day when I had to sit beside her she said, "Oh, Latins are all a bunch of *bushie.*" That means, they're shit-eaters. Well, I said that the Ecuadorians were worse shit-eaters than we were, and that the people in her country were still uncivilized because they live where the sun hits the very middle of the earth. And I told her we Puerto Ricans were better off than she because we had flags to spare. I meant that we have both the American and the Puerto Rican flags. We could give her one and still have one left. We're not expatriates like her. And we didn't have to pay for passports to come here. I really told her off.

After I lost the job I got another one as a sewing-machine *operator*. It was *piecework,* and to earn fifty dollars a week you had to sew about twenty-six dozen a day. But I didn't hurry myself because I don't like to be pushed.

You can't get a factory job in Puerto Rico that pays fifty dollars a week. I only worked in one factory there, making *panties,* but the most I earned was twenty-five dollars. And it's hard to find a job there. You need a recommendation from somebody to get one at all. Then if you're sick and have to stay away, they fire you. There aren't many factories in San Juan. I never met anyone in La Esmeralda who worked in a factory.

But life here is very rushed. In the morning you have to run to catch the bus. You have to run to get on the *subway,* to get off, to get to work from the station. At twelve you have to rush through lunch because you're only allowed half an hour. *Ay, bendito,* what can you do with half an hour? It takes fifteen minutes to go down in an elevator and another fifteen to go up. In Puerto Rico they give you a whole hour.

I swear that I'm not afraid of any *boss*. If a *boss* curses me or pushes me around I give it right back to him. Let him fire me if he wants to! I won't starve. Once I was working in a shoe factory and a girl named Carmen took some pairs of *Medium* size shoes and sewed them *Small*. When I went to check my work I saw she had thrown two or three pieces of hers in with mine. The *boss* blamed me and said I was stupid. I said he was the stupid one, he and his whole family, and I told him I was an employee, not a slave, because slavery had been abolished long ago. He said I shouldn't answer back and I said, "If you speak to me like that I'll answer back. I don't take that kind of thing from anybody. Not from my own mother."

He told me to punch the clock and get out. I told him I'd punch out when I finished my day's work at four-fifteen and not a minute earlier. And that's what I did. But before I left I proved to him that Carmen had been the one who had done the bad work. Then he asked me to forgive him. "I forgive the dead, not the living," I told him. None of the other girls dared talk to the *boss* like that.

I got sick again, and then for a month I went the rounds looking for work. I got a job making pens. The *foreman* was a Puerto Rican named Willie. He was a good-for-nothing, dirty dog! We had to work from eight in the morning to nine at night. And it was rush, rush, rush, all day long. He didn't let you take a minute off even for a cup of coffee or to go to the toilet. And he said horrible things to the employees. He shit on their mothers and called them dirty whores. And if a girl didn't allow him to paw her she got fired.

I liked to kid around and joke with the girls there. We talked about the funny things that happened to us in the *subway*. You know, most of the time you have to ride standing up and there are a lot of people crowded around you. A girl called Milán stood up in the *subway* once and when she got to the factory she found semen on her *coat*. And once I was standing in the train, not thinking of anything in particular, and an old man began to rub his penis against my behind. I've had to slap two or three men's faces for playing dirty tricks on me. Another girl thought she was holding her purse when she got off the train, but all she had in her hand was the handle.

On December 30 I went to my brother's house in Pennsylvania. Fernanda was staying there at the time. Right after work, not even changing my clothes, I took my two little girls and went by bus. It was about eleven o'clock at night when I got there. My *mamá* hugged me. I saw the New Year out with her. On January 2 I went back to New York.

Benedicto and I lived in my little room until we moved to Fox Street in May, 1963. I bought furniture on credit. I made a *down payment* of one hundred and fifty dollars. I bought a living-room set with three end tables, a bedroom set and a breakfast set. The whole thing cost eight hundred dollars. I still owe four hundred. I'm paying five dollars a week. My husband helped me, but not much. All he paid was fifty dollars. I was able to make the *down payment* because I belonged to an Association and I got one hundred and ten dollars from that. This is the way the Association works. A number of people who work in a factory—twelve, say—get together. Every week each of them puts ten dollars into the kitty. You make twelve slips of paper, one for each member. Each draws his slip by turn, one every week. The slip on top shows who gets the kitty that week. In that way everyone gets the whole amount when his turn comes.

Juanita Castro was taking care of my children at that time. She's the one who lives on *welfare* and has five children. Now she's going to have the sixth. Her husband is twenty-three years old and she's thirty-five. Juanita had *parties* at her house every Saturday and I went to them. That was all the social life I had. Juanita invited me because the two of us were in business together. I gave her a certain amount of money, and she bought beer and whiskey and resold it at her *parties*.

Juanita's *parties* were for queers and lesbians. Women had a lesbian for a partner and men went with a fag. The pansy had to pay a man to go with him. I'm sorry for effeminate men. They think they're women but they never can be as we are. You should have seen them dressed as women, with their false breasts, tight dresses, wigs and painted eyebrows. No one could have believed they were men. Some of my friends have been lesbians, but that is a vice that I pity, too. Once in La Esmeralda I was bathing with a girl friend and she kissed my cunt. I let her do it. Why not, if she liked it? And do you know, you feel just the same when a woman does it. But I never have been tempted by them.

Someone told Benedicto about Juanita and once he got drunk and said to me, "So you go to *parties!*"

"Wait a minute, Benedicto," I said. "Do you ever bother about what goes on here? When you come home after a trip, all you care about is going away again. I did help give a couple of *parties* at Juanita's house but don't think I went there to meet men. It's for business. I have to go out and get more money. I simply don't earn enough."

"How much do you make from that?" Benedicto asked. At times he is kind of sharp.

"I can't tell you because I don't know myself. Sometimes we sell and sometimes we don't."

Then Benedicto said, "Well, you're not going back there."

"How can you expect me not to go? I have a stake in that business. I have to see how much money we take in."

"At least you aren't going to dance at that place."

I said, "I never do dance there." I did, of course, but I wasn't going to tell him that.

Benedicto finally made me break off my friendship with Juanita. He said she was a madam. I told him, "Listen, Juanita hasn't put me under a man yet. When I want to I can get a man by myself. I don't need a go-between. Besides, Juanita is taking care of my kids. So please leave me alone." Juanita went on taking care of my daughters, but not long after that we moved.

On June 1, 1963, Benedicto shipped out to Brazil. All the time he was gone, he didn't send me a penny and then I lost my job. On top of that, my brother and his wife came to New York and moved in with me. They didn't have any money either. So to pay for all the expenses, I went out with men, friends of mine, and they each gave me ten or fifteen dollars.

I looked for work, and when I found it I rented a room for Simplicio and Flora. I gave them money to buy food and I got Simplicio a job too. I was paying Flora twelve dollars for looking after my children, but all the thanks I got for my help was that they played a dirty trick on me. When a perfect stranger offered Flora twenty dollars to take care of some children she accepted the job and left me in the lurch.

Simplicio is the only one of the family who hasn't changed toward me. We have our arguments and quarrels but we're very close to each other. Simplicio is twenty-two years old but he still acts like a child in some ways. He plays like a little boy. He buys toy cars, trains and boats, and other playthings. He fills up the tub, gets into it and plays with his boats. When he was a kid he never had a chance to play like other children, you see. He wears *teenager* clothes, shiny pants halfway up his calf, brightly colored shirts and shoes with pointed toes. I don't like his way of dressing and I tell him so. He's a grown man and he should dress like one.

When Benedicto got back from Brazil he had only five hundred dollars on him. He had drunk up all the rest. For about two months he stayed ashore and collected *employment*. Of course he drank that up too. Then he got himself a mistress. He stayed away for five days and came home with a kiss mark on his neck and lipstick all over him. That was the time I went at him with a pair of scissors and tried to kill him like a dog. I cut that little thing on top of his penis. He's full of scars I made. And that was when I completely lost my love for him. I began to pack my clothes. Benedicto said, "All right, if you go, leave me the apartment."

"That's what you'd like, isn't it?" I said. "If I go I'm taking everything with me." Why should I leave the furniture that I had to work to pay for? There were times when I'd let my children go hungry to pay an installment. I wouldn't think of leaving everything for another woman to enjoy! So we went on living together. But now when he goes to sea he can write or not write just as he pleases. It's all the same to me.

I know I won't last with Benedicto much longer. He stayed in Brazil two months and a half without sending me a penny. Yet he expected me to be faithful to him. Who the hell would be faithful to a man like him? I didn't take such behavior from Arturo, who is the father of two of my children and I won't take it from him. It isn't that he was so terribly good-looking or a representative of the government of Puerto Rico or something. He's just a shitting sailor, a Negro with nostrils big enough to let a transport through.

I haven't left Benedicto yet because I have to get even with him first for everything he's done to me and because I don't want him to have the apartment and the furniture. I'm defending my rights. As long as I live with him he has to support me. But Benedicto is a man who mounts a woman and then wants to do it again and again. I don't like that. Once a week is enough for me. Having intercourse too often makes a person go blind and weakens his brain. After working hard all day, must I have him on top of me all night long? Let him find himself another woman, since he can't go three days without screwing. I know him through and through. Look at the way we've practically killed each other and yet he's always on top of me. The man is too passionate and his prick is as big as a water pipe. If he didn't wear a jock it would hang down to the floor. That's why so many women are crazy about him. But I'm afraid of that man. If Benedicto had his way he'd pierce me clear through.

I'm not jealous of Benedicto any more, but this business of a man's coming home after two days or four days with kiss marks and with his prick raw from so many cunts! How can a woman feel like coming when the man's crotch is messy with white stuff and his pubic hairs are sticky and matted! That's the way it was with Benedicto. When he came and took off his clothes to jump on me, can you picture it? That prick, black to begin with, with the white scar where I cut him with the scissors, and then the white crust of semen all over it. What I felt was disgust.

Benedicto never caught a venereal disease that I know of. The day he comes home with a venereal I'll split his skinned prick in two. I'll kill him. I don't risk my body and my cunt. I take the best care of them. That's the reason I don't screw with just anybody. My clients are hand-picked by me. I'm no lady, but my men are clean little old men, the kind that put their little pricks into one of those rubber bags before we screw.

When I started living with Benedicto he told me he didn't want to have any children with me. Now he says he wants a child. So now I'm taking revenge on him. I tell him I'm pregnant and he believes it. Then when he comes back from a trip I say, "Oh, I had an abortion. I stuck the rubber tube in me and that did it." I really have had three abortions and he knows it, so he believes that too. It makes him furious. Then I say, "Why, what are you mad about? I'm surprised at you. After all, you told me you didn't want a child with me. Right?" I never told him about my operation. He thinks the scar is from something else. That just goes to show you that men aren't nearly as clever as they think they are.

The only good thing about Benedicto is that he's fond of my daughters and doesn't mistreat them. He also asked me to quit working at the *bar,* so even if I don't love him, I stay out of gratitude. Maybe he feels the same way about me. He said once that he stayed with me just to have someone to live with. But lately he behaved very badly. He drew out all the money we had in the bank. The account was in both our names and we had three hundred and sixteen dollars. I told him, "You can't do that, because that money belongs to two people. I put money into that account too." He said he needed it but he spent every last cent of it on drink.

I like to have money in the bank. It has always been my idea to have some money saved for an emergency or to meet any problem that might arise. In Puerto Rico I had about three hundred dollars in the bank. Here I never had anything until now. I was happy the first time I went to the bank and I kept adding a little at a time to the account. Benedicto helped sometimes but now that it's all gone I am discouraged.

Then Benedicto got involved with a girl from Ecuador. One night he said to me, "Go to the movies and I'll come and get you." I went but I got out early, and so I walked to Third Avenue and asked Julio, a friend of mine, if he had seen Benedicto around.

"Benedicto? He's in the house on the corner."

"Well," I said, "that's where I'm going." I didn't know what floor he was on, so I left the children downstairs and walked up. When I got to the top floor I heard him talking. I knocked on the door and asked the lady who opened it, "Is Benedicto in there?"

"Yes." I just walked in. And there I found him with that Ecuadorian woman. Before, he had insisted that he wasn't involved with any woman and that it was all in my imagination. "Don't worry, I'll catch you," I said, and I did.

I fought with him right there, with as much courage as any man. Whenever I fight with Benedicto I use my fists. He has to bash me on the head to knock me down. I think I was born to be a man, no kidding. But if I'd been made with a cock instead of a cunt someone would have killed me by now because I have a terrible temper. I'm always ready to pick a quarrel and to stand up and fight.

When I was through with Benedicto, I took on the Ecuadorian woman. I went at her with my teeth and bit her face. I had a small knife on me but someone snatched it out of my hand.

After the fight I went home with the children. The next day Beni told me he was leaving. I said, "All right, if you want to go, go. I'm not holding you. An honest, decent man like you shouldn't be living with the likes of me. There are your things and the suitcase." But he didn't go. He stayed and drank. He drank day after day, and all the time he cursed me. A week later he shipped out. He left me five dollars to live on while he was away on a twelve-day trip. When he returned he had fifty dollars on him. Instead of coming here he bought other people rum and he took gifts over to that woman.

Benedicto

No Fault of Mine

I HAD JUST separated from my wife, América, and was living alone in a furnished room in New York when I met Soledad. One afternoon as I was leaving the dock (I was working on the S.S. *Libertad*), a friend of mine asked me to go to a *bar* for a few drinks. We took a bus, and as we got off I said in a loud voice to my friend, "Look at that pretty girl." Soledad heard me and smiled. We kept on walking and entered the *bar* and so did she. It was fate. I started courting her right away.

I have always given thought to the future. And what kind of future can a man expect, living alone in a big city like New York? A man needs a woman to do for him, keep his clothes looking nice, take care of him and all that. And I had observed Soledad's good qualities, see? She lived alone with her little girls and worked to support them and pay the rent. She was clean and neat and she was skillful and experienced in everything that needs to be done around the house. I could see how well she treated her children, and many other good things about her.

I knew that other women of the life get married and have children and live in such a way that no one could point a finger at them. They are now honest women. And remembering all the troubles I've had and the mistakes I've made, I thought, "Who knows, maybe if I make a home with her everything will change. Maybe we can be happy together." And so I decided to live with her.

Our honeymoon lasted only about fourteen days because I was recalled to the ship. I sailed off for Europe and was away for forty-seven days. When I returned I brought money, so we decided to set up an apartment, on Fox Street in the Bronx.

For the first seven months or so it was pure heaven. Every time I came home Soledad fussed over me. It was her for me and me for her. We went out dancing. I took Soledad to meet my family. For a time I stayed on land, but even then I managed to earn something to support her.

Soledad was the first to be disillusioned, but through no fault of mine. Everything went well until I went on a three-and-a-half-month voyage to Brazil. When I signed my papers the inspector wouldn't accept Soledad as my dependent because we weren't married. I explained to her why she couldn't receive the sixty-five-dollar fortnightly allotment to which a seaman's wife is entitled. I agreed to send her money every time the ship touched port. But everything went wrong, because at the time Brazil was in a state of revolutionary chaos and they didn't permit any money to leave the country. I couldn't send Soledad one penny.

I did write to her, at least eight letters in those three and a half months, explaining everything. But she didn't believe me. She still thinks I didn't send her money because I squandered it on women or drink. I haven't been able to convince her in spite of the fact that I returned with some eleven hundred dollars I had saved. And I wasn't drunk the day I came back, either. I was dead sober. I gave her a hundred and fifty dollars and bought a TV set for a hundred and fifty-four, cash. After that I paid off most of her debts. The rest of my money went for food and other household expenses.

There are many good things about Soledad. She's a hard-working woman and a great helper to any man she lives with. There are no limits to what she will do. If you are sick she takes good care of you. She has her husband's clothes ready when he needs them. Of all the women I have had, I can say without hypocrisy that none can compare with Soledad. She is also a terribly passionate woman, and when a man desires her he desires her passionately.

Soledad's defects are due mostly to her lack of schooling, and to the fact that the people among whom she grew up did her more harm than good. She goes to a lot of trouble for the sake of her relatives, although the last thing they do is bother to be nice to her. She was brought up in a low kind of place among a low kind of people. And from what I hear, that holds for the places where she has worked too. I don't mean here in New York but before, in Puerto Rico. After all, once a woman goes to work at a *bar,* what can you expect? No matter how you look at it, that kind of thing is a defect in a woman. I learned all about her from Soledad herself. She has been quite open with me. Many of the things she went through before I met her would never have happened if I had known her earlier. What she needs most is a relative, or somebody, to give her advice and help her spiritually because she makes totally unnecessary mistakes.

The worst things about Soledad, as I said before, come from her lack of social opportunities. She doesn't even know how to express herself properly. Even when we are on the best of terms, I don't take her among friends who know how to behave, people who are decent, respectably married couples, because I never know when she's going to do something shocking. She's a terribly jealous woman.

Her temper is the only complaint I have against her. She can't stand to see me go anywhere. I have women friends whom I have known since we were children together. We like to kid around and go to the same *parties*. They are people for whom I have a certain regard, as they have for me. Well, if I happen to meet one of these women when I'm out with Soledad, I have to refrain from greeting her. Because if I do, Soledad makes a scene, screaming, "Who is that whore you said hello to?" She embarrasses me terribly.

We have a neighbor, Nilsa, whom I have known for many years, and her husband is also my friend. Soledad often says to me, "Oh, I know that woman goes to bed with you for a couple of dollars while I'm away at work." Yet I have never done anything of the kind with Nilsa. Besides, you have only to look at her—she's had four operations and she's as blind as a bat. I'll say this for Nilsa, though, she goes out of her way to do anybody a favor. The truth is the truth.

I remind Soledad that if you spit upward the spit falls on you, and if you speak ill of others you harm only yourself. Because now that Soledad is sick, after all the dreadful things Soledad has said about Nilsa, look at the great favor Nilsa is doing her, taking care of the children.

There is a lack of understanding between Soledad and me. She wants to boss me. She is headstrong and so am I. At times I have had no choice but to slap her good, because a man can't allow himself to be dominated by a woman. There should be proper respect and good mutual understanding in order to have a good marriage. Sometimes she'll say, "I will do this or that." But if I stand firm she doesn't do it. At least not as long as I'm home. But when I'm away on a trip she does whatever she pleases.

Money, that's what we quarrel mostly about. Because I can't leave her much money when I go away. I leave her whatever I can afford, sometimes a hundred, sometimes eighty, forty, twenty, whatever I have. Add that to the sixty she earns and she should be able to do all right. But when I come back she hasn't paid anything, not even the rent, and yet she's broke. Then I look around to see what she bought with the money and all I find is dozens of dresses and loads of *junk*. She has good taste but the money can be better used in other ways. Right now we have one perfectly unnecessary debt. I brought her a wrist watch and then she went and bought another one on credit for eighty-five dollars. Why two watches? What's she going to do with them? The one I gave her is much better than the one she bought.

I try to explain to her, "Soledad, that's not the way . . ." That's why I quarrel with her. I'm so fed up, I'm thinking of leaving. I didn't use to drink so much. When we lived on Fox Street I'd take a drink now and then, but not like I do now. I'm not even so terribly fond of liquor, but lately, every time I get back from a trip I come home a little high. And I keep on drinking because Soledad objects to every little thing I do. Actually, the idea of drinking too much scares me, but I'm a little weak-willed. I don't know why I do it. I'm not a mental alcoholic or anything like that.

I have always liked to dress well and to have some nice jewelry. In my good times, I've had as many as fifteen suits, many of them made to measure, about ten pairs of shoes, and hats made to order at eighteen dollars apiece. I would like to be not necessarily a millionaire but fairly well off, for my family's sake as well as my own. Right now I have two watches and three pretty good rings in hock. One of the watches is worth two hundred dollars. The other one is worth about a hundred and twenty-five. Soledad has a wrist watch of her own in hock, a chain I gave her, a ring, her sewing machine and a radio-victrola. I left some money with her and she spent it all and then pawned the TV set. We owe the *pawnshop* about four hundred dollars, counting the interest.

Soledad gives me material help. But spiritually speaking, she doesn't help me as she should. I have six children. They used to come to visit me, and I sent Soledad out to get clothes and things for them. But lately she has a very strange attitude. I can't explain it. She doesn't want my children to come. "No, don't bring those kids here," she tells me. That's what hurts me most, see? After all, I have taken on the support of her children and she should realize I care for my own too. And she should allow them to visit me at our home.

I know that Soledad loves me but I can't understand her manner of loving. "Is it selfishness?" I ask myself. No, not if that means being selfish about money. But selfishness in love, maybe? That is, not wanting to give me up, being determined that I must stay here with her. I go on searching for an answer but none satisfies me. Is it a sort of revenge she wants? "No," I say to myself, "what have I ever done to her to make her feel vengeful?" I can't find an explanation.

I had a happy childhood in spite of the fact that I grew up without a mother's love. According to what I have heard from my relatives, my parents married and had twin boys who died. At the same time, my *papá* had another woman, let's call a spade a spade, a mistress, with whom he had a daughter. When that girl was born my *mamá* was already pregnant with me. I believe my *papá* walked out on her and went to live with the other woman. When I was born it seems that my mother was resentful at being abandoned. She blamed me for it, for everything, even for having been born. I've been told that I look a great deal like my *papá* except that his coloring is rather Indian. My *papá*'s relatives tell me that he liked to dress in white, and was always going out to dances and chasing after women. And it must be true, because no two of his thirteen children had the same mother. I was three or four years old when my *papá* left my *mamá* for good. That very same day I was sent to my aunt Socorro's.

I remember the day *mamá* sailed for the States. Everything she wore was brown, her dress, her purse, her high-heeled shoes with pointed toes. I went to see her off. She cried and I cried, and her niece who had brought me cried too. I watched the ship pull away from the dock and followed it with my eyes until it sailed out of sight behind the promontory of El Morro. I remember that so clearly. Such things are etched in one's memory forever, don't you think? A child's feelings are so intense!

My aunt Socorro was an elderly woman, very tall, about five feet eleven inches. She was always at the service of the rest of the family. Maybe it was the fate God assigned to her because she never had a husband. She was the eldest of eleven, and as her younger brothers and sisters got married she would take charge of their children. She and her sister, Joaquina Fermín, brought up almost all of the children in the family.

My aunt had bought a big house with a peaked, four-sided roof. The house was big enough for eighteen or nineteen people and was high enough on its stilts so that animals could be kept underneath. The house was in Puerta de Tierra at Stop 9, facing the docks. We had a view of the bay and of the ships that came and went.

My aunt's work was washing and ironing, and the first clothes she saw to were ours. It happened that all of us boys wore about the same size clothes and shoes, so we changed around and shared our things. There was never any question of "this is mine, so you can't have it." We grew up as a very united family. We were lucky that way.

The situation at our home was a bit tight. Sometimes I had to go to school with no breakfast but a cup of coffee. If there was nothing to eat when I got home at noon, I went back to school with an empty stomach without a word of protest. But I was always happy.

My family, all of them, have always been Catholics. I was baptized at Saint Augustine Church in Puerta de Tierra, a church only a block away from us. I went to Mass there, and there I made my First Communion. Although I am a Catholic, I also have another religion, a religion of my own, spiritism. It is a gift God has granted me, although I don't exercise it as I should. Spiritism is mentioned in the Bible just as Catholicism is.

My aunt who brought me up also had spiritual powers. They had religious or spiritist meetings at our house. The mediums, seven or eight of them, sit around a table laid with a white cloth, with a lighted candle in the middle.

The group around the table does all the work. The others who are inexperienced come because they want to find out something or be cured of an illness.
They sit in an outside circle, not at the table. One person presides. He is the
one who leads the prayers before they start to work on something. Each person at the table is supposed to have a guiding spirit that passes through his
brain. After the initial prayers, the session is declared open. Then any one of
the mediums studies the problem of some person, with the second sight
granted to him by his spirits, and he explains to the person what he has seen.
He tells everything. If he finds the person is possessed by an evil spirit, they all
work on it and try to cure him.

These things disturbed me when I was a child because often at a meeting
someone would start jumping or screaming. When that happened I was really
scared. One night there was a meeting at home and they told me to sit down in
the outer circle. Then, after the opening prayer, the president said that any
person who saw something, who received any "evidence," as they call it,
should speak up. As usual a bowl of water was placed on the table, and I saw
a tree trunk rising from it and a policeman leaning against it. I could only see
him from the waist up. I told them what I saw and then the leader and the rest
followed my cue.

According to them, the policeman had been killed and his soul was crying
out for spiritual aid, for prayers and all the rest. He had chosen me and clung
to me because I was a child, the youngest, weakest person there. I was asked
to stand up. When I did, the spirit started to speak through somebody else. I
don't remember what he said. I have only a vague memory of the spirit's
speaking. After he stopped they prayed over me, because it was this spirit that
made me get into mischief.

I have a healing guide, a kind of doctor that gives me the mental strength
to combat spirits. Once a little girl was brought to one of our meetings, which
were held every Friday night. We all heard the evidence, but the fluids of the
case came to me and I worked on the problem. It seemed the child had intesti-
nal parasites. Before my guide possessed me, I noticed that the girl's body
gave off a smell of rottenness. I don't remember what I did. But the others told
me that after the Being took possession of me, I passed my hand above the
girl's stomach without actually touching her. The girl was cured, see? and her
mamá shook hands with me. A month or so later, when I met her, she told me
that the child was feeling quite well.

But I wasn't interested in those things. What I really liked was to have a
good time dancing, and sports like baseball and swimming. I was young then.
By the time I reached the sixth grade, I had fallen in love several times. These
were boyish little affairs without evil thoughts or intentions.

When I was in the seventh grade I caught a venereal disease. It happened
because after work I went with my friend to Stop 27, just across Martin Peña
Bridge, where we could find whores. They gave the sickness to me and to

Feliciano as well. He was the son of the company's paymaster. Feliciano didn't dare tell his father what had happened, so the infection spread until it affected his lungs and he died.

But I could speak freely to my *mamá* Socorro, so I told her my trouble and she spoke to my uncle about it. He took me to a lady who told me to buy a fresh coconut, open it without spilling the water, put in some chickpeas and pieces of charcoal, and close it again. After that I had to bury it, being very careful that nothing spilled out, and leave it overnight. The next morning I dug it up and drank it. I went through the whole business three times and I got cured.

I was almost through the eighth grade when I made a bad mistake. I fell in love with Nina, my first wife. It was *teenage* stuff.

My aunt had planned for me to continue my schooling, but with Nina expecting, it just wasn't possible. My aunt was one of those old-fashioned people and she said, "What one owes, one pays. You have to marry the girl." Nina and I only managed to finish the eighth grade. We were the same age, seventeen. We got married at the home of a judge at Stop 18. We went all by ourselves. Not even our parents went with us. There was no wedding celebration or anything. I was simply paying off a debt.

At that time, jobs were not so easy to get as now. Even with a diploma it was hard to get a job as a *clerk* or anything. My uncle Emeterio suggested, "Come to work at the docks with us." The pay was on a piecework basis. During the sugar-cane harvest I always earned enough to buy the day's food for the whole family, seven dollars some days, six, nine. I liked that kind of arrangement because I could work when I pleased. The day I felt like going to a dance or a movie, I went. I got no pay for those days but neither did I have to go to work unless I wanted to.

My wife and I didn't live together long. One time, at a dance, she cut me but it was a mere scratch. She's a good person, see? But she had her temper. That night we were at a dance near home, and to tell the truth, there was a girl. Nina pulled out her *Gem* blade and tried to cut me. She didn't aim at my face, she aimed low and cut my hand. Another time, when I came home after working thirty-six hours, I asked my wife to prepare an herb bath with bay rum but Nina wanted to go to the movies. She insisted and insisted and finally I slapped her face.

It is a custom of us Puerto Rican men not to let ourselves be put at a disadvantage, not to be weaker than one's wife. I said, "If that's the way it is, you and I can't go on living together. I'll pack my things and go back to my folks and you stay here with your family." Her only answer to that was, "You hit me, and now I'm going to have you arrested." She brought the police and they charged me. The case was settled with the help of my uncle who worked with Judge Báez. My wife and I have been separated since then.

When my son was born I was very happy and went to see him right away.

As soon as Nina left the hospital I went to her house with a chicken for broth for her. Nina never objected to my seeing the boy. Both families were fond of the child and he was brought up in both our houses.

Shortly after I left my wife I was drafted into the *Army*, but they rejected me, I don't know why. At that time practically everybody was migrating to the United States because there were lots of job opportunities there. I wrote to my real *mamá* that I wanted to come, and she wrote back saying that she would send money for my fare within a week. But I had savings of my own, so I bought a ticket.

My aunt didn't want me to go and began to cry. "But, *mamá*," I said, "I want to look for more opportunity." Then she understood and everything was all right. We sailed on October 15, 1944.

My *mamá* and my sisters were very happy to see me. I didn't even know my sisters. I had no *coat* and my *mamá* was waiting for me with one over her arm. But our greetings did not have the warmth you'd expect from a mother and son meeting for the first time in so many years, no embraces, nothing like that.

My sisters were very nice to me and a great help whenever I needed them. If I had to go some place they did most of the talking for me. The only thing that bothered me was that my *mamá* didn't treat me as she treated her other children. The first night I was with her I went to help myself to some milk in the refrigerator. My *mamá* snatched the bottle away from me and said that my sister Sasa was the only one who had a right to do that.

My second *mamá* and I wrote to each other often. When I got a letter from her my first *mamá* would open it. She wanted to see what I had said about her, because I used to write about her treatment of me. I was only eighteen and my *mamá*'s behavior hurt me so that I often wept. She really didn't act as if I was her son. And yet, her husband Genio, my stepfather, a Dominican, couldn't have been nicer to me if I had been his own. He often gave me good advice. If I'd ask him for Heaven, Heaven is what he'd bring me.

I already knew English when I came here. I learned to speak it in Puerto Rico. I had every chance to learn because everyone at home spoke it. But I didn't like New York. I still don't, although there are some good things here. The drinking water is always cold, milk is pure and you have lots of money to spend. For the rest, it isn't as good as people think. Everything here has to be done in a hurry, I don't know why. In Puerto Rico, if you have to go some place, you go, but you take your time about it. Here you have to do things fast because that's what's expected of you. There is no tranquillity, only rush, rush, rush.

Another bad thing about the United States is that in some places, especially in the South, there is racial prejudice and discrimination. There are laws forbidding a Negro to marry a white woman. If they marry, both go to jail. I have seen white boys from one of the Southern states make friends with a Negro shipmate. As long as they are in foreign lands they will go out together, drink together and everything. But once they land in some seaport in the South, say, Norfolk, all that changes. Because if the cops catch the white boy and the black together, they nab them both. So they each have to go their different ways, although they may have been as close as flesh and fingernails.

When I came to New York everything was rationed, sugar, rice, everything. So my *mamá* sent me to get a ration card. My cousin Gino, the one who had written suggesting I come here, went with me. He spoke the language much better than I, so he did all the talking. I noticed the girl there was writing down everything in a questionnaire. She asked my nationality and my cousin answered "Puerto Rican," but she wrote down "Negro." My cousin protested, "No, no, no, not Negro, Puerto Rican." She gave him a look but she erased "Negro" and wrote down "Puerto Rican." It was my first experience of that kind up here.

I got a job at the Stuyvesant Hotel. I earned about a hundred and twenty-five dollars a week there. You see, my *overtime* pay amounted to more than my regular wages. I stayed there a month. It was on a Saturday that I met my friend Marlon who said to me, "Say, they are making out papers for sailors. Come with me and sign up." Marlon took me to the union and I got a job.

So I went to sea on a ship bound for France. Marlon and I worked in the ship's *laundry,* ironing the passengers' clothes. We earned fair wages. On our first trip, which lasted twenty-eight days, we made six hundred and eighty dollars. They paid us a bonus on top of the salary because we sailed in the danger areas where we might be blown up by mines. We made five trips, one after another. It was too hot working in the laundry, so I finally left that ship for another. There were lots of jobs on ships at that time.

When I first sailed, the war was almost over. But there was lots of contraband and we made money that way. We could get as many cigarettes as we wished from the canteen aboard. We paid ninety-four cents for a carton, which we could sell later for as much as five dollars. I had a hundred cartons when we landed, so I tripled my money. We laid in a good store of chocolate bars, clothes and so on, to barter for whatever we wanted, souvenirs and gifts for the folks back home. Marlon and I later began to take sewing needles and needles for record players to sell in Europe.

On one trip we made about fifteen hundred dollars each. Then we went to Paris for three days and we had a pretty good time. I got into a bit of trouble there. Five of us went to a hotel, one of the biggest in town. Each of us brought along a girl to spend the night. The whole group gathered in my room, where there happened to be some liquor. We didn't know who it belonged to but we drank it and had quite a *party,* drinking and kidding around. Then each went to his own room and my girl and I went to bed.

It was about three o'clock when I heard someone knocking. I opened the door and there stood a well-dressed middle-aged lady who screamed when she saw me. I shut the door again and the girl got out of bed. A few minutes later the lady was back with the desk *clerk* and a couple of MP's. *"What is this man doing in my room?"* she asked the *clerk.* The MP's wanted to arrest me. "But this room was assigned to me by the *clerk,"* I told them and showed them the receipt. Well, after that it was the *clerk* who was in trouble, not me. It turned out that the lady was the wife of a general in the U. S. Armed Forces; she had come from Germany for a holiday in Paris. I had bribed the *clerk* to give me a room and he had given me hers!

Everywhere in Europe I saw what the war had done. When we carried garbage out of the ship, a crowd of children and old men rushed up and scrabbled in it looking for something to eat. There was a woman of thirty-five or so, still young, who gathered up the coffee grinds. And people would sell anything for a bar of chocolate or an orange. Everything was scarce. You could exchange a couple of cartons of cigarettes for a diamond ring. The women would sell themselves for food. I knew one who would do it for a pack of cigarettes, a box of Chiclets or a chocolate bar. They'd give anything for chocolate. They were starving, and chocolate gives the body energy, that's why they prized it so highly. One man took some of us to his house and tried to sell us his wife for chocolate and cigarettes.

That's how poor people were right after the war. And there were no young people. Almost everybody between the ages of twelve and thirty had been killed. On the streets you saw only old men and women or small children. That's the reason why I hope the United States doesn't get into war again. People who have never been out of this country don't know what war is.

All the time I was sailing, I had a sweetheart named Helen. I met her through my cousin Julián. She was a social worker, a little older than I was, and she used to take me along when she was calling on people. We rented a room where we could be together when I was on shore and we went on like that for two years. I never gave her any money. When we went out, sometimes I paid, sometimes she did. I met a lot of people and learned a lot through her. Then a boy who had been her sweetheart before came back from the *Army,* and she just walked out on me and got married.

Sometime later I met Cándida at a friend's house. We fell in love and all that. She was not a virgin but had never married. She was about twenty-three years old then, about my age. She was dark. Her hair was bad but the kind that can take a hairdo. We dated and then we began to live together.

When we had lived together for a year she got pregnant. We had a son, Ricardo. We were doing fine. She had a job in a *coat* factory and I went to sea. Then she got pregnant again, when Ricardo was about a year old. We had our second boy, Beni.

Our married life was pretty good, she satisfied me sexually and I her. I drank then, I always have, but not as I've been doing lately. She never complained about my drinking or about money either. She never fought with me about other women either, because she never found out when I had a mistress.

Ours was a very good marriage until Cándida's sister Petrona came from Puerto Rico with her husband and five kids and moved in on us. The apartment was too small for so many people. And then a cousin came and moved in too. That's when there began to be trouble. Petrona was the eldest of the family and she started throwing her weight around, giving orders to her sister, telling us what to do.

Once I gave Cándida five hundred dollars to save for me. When I got back to port it was Sunday, which meant we didn't get paid until the following day. That didn't worry me a bit. I thought, "There must be plenty of money at home." But when I asked Cándida how much money she had left, she confessed she didn't have any. "And what about the five hundred dollars I asked you to keep for me?"

"Oh, I lent it to my sister. Petrona wanted to buy an electric refrigerator."

"And didn't you stop to think that you and I have two children? Why did they borrow from you? If she had been ill and needed it, I wouldn't say a word. But for something like that . . . !" Well, the long and the short of it was, we had a quarrel. In the midst of it she gave me a crack on the head with the mop handle. So I went at her and beat her good. Petrona and her husband tried to interfere, so I hit them too. And that's the way we broke up our home.

All things considered, Cándida has always been a good woman. When I have no money to send for the kids, she never takes me to court. When I am working *steady* I send them money every month. She doesn't have a job any more because by now she has six or seven children, counting my two boys.

Then I ran into Janette, a girl I'd known in Puerto Rico. Janette is white and comes from a fairly good family. We were very happy together for a long time.

Once when she was longing to see her mother, I sent her on a trip to Puerto Rico for Mother's Day. While she was gone the wife of one of my cousins wrote her that I was taking women to our apartment. It was a lie but Janette believed it and she took poison. She was in the hospital in a coma for seventeen days but she had the good luck to survive. During that time Janette's first husband went to visit her frequently and helped her a lot. He was very decent to her, considering that they were divorced. And so they were reconciled and remarried.

When I was about thirty-six I met América at my sister's house. They worked in the same place. América and I were attracted to each other. She was a fair-skinned girl, with brown hair and eyes. She lived in New York with her *mamá* and spoke English pretty well. Whenever I came back from a trip I called her up and we went out somewhere. Finally we decided to live together. We furnished an apartment and lived together for six years.

While I lived with América I also had an American colored girl called Ida Lou Jennings. That woman helped me a lot, both spiritually and materially. She was a *clerk* and worked in the same office as my sister Sasa. Ida Lou was separated from her husband, but still married to him. And then she found out that he had committed bigamy with her. He told Ida that he often had to work at night, but what he did those nights was to go to sleep with the other woman. In the daytime he came to Ida Lou but hardly had time to be with her. So she had more opportunity to do it with me. She used to help me out. Every week she gave me fifteen or twenty dollars. At that time she became pregnant. We have a six-year-old daughter called Juanita. She goes to a parochial school on Long Island and plays the violin. I saw the child about two months ago. Ida pays some relatives to take care of her. When Ida needs money she calls me.

América and I separated because of her brother-in-law. He wore my clothes. He was a highly educated boy, had gone to college and all that, but I guess he was hard up. When he first came here he couldn't find a job. I don't know why it was, but he wore my clothes. Aside from that, we were too crowded with fourteen people in a four-room apartment. And América always took her family's side, although I was the one who supported the whole bunch of them. So, what with one thing and another, we finally had to separate.

América and I had two children, Guiso, who is almost eight now, and Avilda, who will soon be seven. I go to see them from time to time. In a way I am sorry América and I separated, because I would like to be with my children and have them grow up at my side.

When she found herself alone, América applied for *welfare* and they took me to court. I was sending money, but according to *welfare,* it wasn't enough. So we agreed that I would send them twenty dollars a month and *welfare* would supply the rest.

I'm not perfect, nobody in this world is perfect, but to my way of thinking, I have been a good father to all my children. The son I have with my first wife is now twenty-one. He lives with my *mamá* and always seeks me out. He's working as a dental technician and studying electronics here in the Bronx. I have helped all of my children, in one way or another. But to give them moral and spiritual support, to live with their mothers and to bring them up with me, that I have not been able to do. Not because I haven't wanted to, but because of the things that have happened to me.

I have been all over in my travels. I have seen Ireland, Denmark, Japan, China, India and the Philippines, Spain and Portugal. In the past few years I've been going mostly to the Latin American countries. Of course I know all of the countries of the Caribbean and many in South America, too. Brazil and Argentina are the most interesting to me.

I belong to the National Maritime Union. Not so long ago, a sailor would work from six in the morning to nine at night and would earn only fifty dollars a week. Now all that is changed. We get hired through the union, and wages are according to the kind of work. Take a waiter, for instance. He earns about three hundred dollars a month, not counting *overtime*. Saturdays and Sundays are paid at double the rate, and there will usually be extra hours of work besides.

Union members are covered by a ten-thousand-dollar life insurance and we get a lot of medical help besides. If I have to go to the hospital I get free care, plus forty dollars a month as long as I'm laid up. Then there's a clinic for ordinary treatment. And my wife and children have the same hospitalization rights I have. When I first went to sea, my shipmates were people who didn't care what they did. They didn't bother to dress properly when on land or anything. There was no comradeship aboard. Each one did his job and that's all. But all that has changed because of the union. Now there is better understanding among men. We have three meetings during every trip. Committees are formed to teach us how to express ourselves, politically and socially, among our working companions and so on.

Under a clause in our contracts, we may retire after twenty years of work, no matter what age we are. I still have two years, two months to go before retiring. When that time comes I have two choices: to retire altogether or to work at something else. I am also allowed to take two trips a year, even after I begin receiving my pension, as long as my total earnings in those trips are not more than three thousand five hundred dollars a year. For all this, we have the union to thank.

Three years ago I got word that my aunt Socorro, my second *mamá,* was very sick. I went to Puerto Rico as soon as I could and found her on her deathbed. I went to the hospital every evening and stayed with her from five to seven. I am grateful to that first wife of mine, Nina, for all she did for my *mamá.* Nina is a nurse now, and she gave my *mamá* medicines and the injections she needed. Of course it was necessary for me to see Nina, so after all those years we finally spoke with each other. She introduced me to everybody as the father of her son. We talked as if we were meeting for the first time!

My aunt Socorro died a virgin, at the age of ninety-six. As long as she lived she never lacked for anything because the children she had raised helped her all of her life. After she got sick I signed her name for an *allotment* of seventy-five dollars twice a month for her support. And with the help of the union I had bought her another house, which cost four hundred dollars.

I was proud to be there beside her at the hour of her death. Yes, because everything I am now, I owe to her. She was the *mamá* who brought me up and gave me all the love and education it was in her power to give.

Frankly, I don't know what to do about Soledad. I can't walk out on her, now that she's sick and needs me. I have always tried to have a happy home, and with Soledad I made every possible effort. Any other man who had to go through the things she's made me go through would have left her long ago.

In regard to sex, I think she's *oversexed*. She's a very strong woman in that respect, too strong. It isn't that she's younger than me. She can't tire me out! Because if you stop to think of it, maybe we are both the same that way. And we have another thing in common, which very few married couples do: when I'm excited I ask her and she never refuses me. And when she asks me I never refuse her. We are doing all right in that way!

The worst thing about Soledad is her jealousy. Of all my women, the only ones that Soledad knows personally are Janette and Cándida. But the one she's really jealous of is Janette. So much so, that the mere mention of Janette's name makes her angry. I can't understand it, because Janette is married now. The only reason I can think of is that I have told Soledad how good Janette has been to my family and to my second *mamá*. What Soledad doesn't know is that Janette used to help me out, because one thing Soledad has never called me is "pimp." "I don't like to live off a woman's ass," I have told her. When I go to bed with a woman I put my money at the head of the bed. "Give it to me," I say. "I can pay for it."

Once Soledad got terribly jealous because I stayed away from the house for two days. It happened this way. By accident I ran into a girl named Georgina whom I've known since were children. Before I met Soledad, she and I had had relations but nothing serious, see? At that time she wasn't in the life. Well, Georgina and I went into a *bar* to have a few drinks and then we decided to get a bottle and go to her apartment with another couple. Some more people came in and we had a *party*. When the *party* was over and we were left alone, Georgina started to caress me, biting and so on, but I didn't make love to her. When I left her, about five the next afternoon, I went over to Simplicio's house. At eight o'clock Soledad showed up. She had been looking for me all over the place. She asks me, "Where have you been?"

"In Ponce," say I. That's a saying of mine when she or one of the kids wants to know where I'm going. It means that it's none of their business. I was leaning back and she comes up to me and grabs me by the tie, trying to choke me. Then that passed and we went on home. When we got there, I undressed and went to bed. She got in beside me and started to caress me. I, being half drunk, forgot Georgina's bite, and took off my undershirt. Then she saw the mark . . . *Ay!* That woman jumped on me like . . . I can't think of anything to compare with it. Then she leaped out of bed like a wild animal, grabbed the scissors and screamed, "I'm going to cut off your prick. If it isn't mine it's nobody's!" And she really tried to! But she only pinched it some and left it sore, naturally. She was just pretending.

Once I bit her because of an unpleasant habit she has of attacking me as if she were a man. I forgot what we were arguing about that day, but at some point she got so mad she grabbed me by the testicles and squeezed them roughly. I bit her shoulder as hard as I could. It was the only way to make her let go. She still has the marks of my teeth on her shoulder. After it was over she showed me the marks and I rubbed on some Mentholatum.

I don't like to hit her hard because I'm afraid of hurting her. If I socked her like I would a man, I'd harm her for sure. Once on my return from a trip I found her looking haggard and far too thin. When I asked her what the trouble was, she wouldn't answer. Then she started saying rude things to me, so I just slapped her in the face. I was sitting on the edge of the bed and she was combing her hair. When I slapped her she jumped on me. She always keeps a bayonet she found in Pennsylvania. Well, she went and got it and tried to kill me with it. I grabbed her hand, and in the struggle she cut herself. She said it was nothing, so I went on out. When I came back, her hands were all bound up. She had cut a tendon.

Twice she has bitten me. The first time, a man had come to the house to bring a box of women's bathing suits and she handed him some money. After the man left I asked her who he was and to whom the money belonged. Then she told me that she was selling bathing suits for him and he paid her for it. "But who is he?" I insisted.

"He's the elevator operator at the place where I work." Those suits were stolen from the bathing-suit factory there and the elevator operator was the fence. And he turned the goods over to Soledad so she'd be the one to sell them. I was furious. She doesn't have to sell stolen bathing suits. That set us off, and in the middle of the quarrel she sank her teeth into me and wouldn't let go until I put my hands around her neck and started to choke her.

I can't describe Soledad—I think no dictionary has the words for her. Really, she's just too . . . For one thing, she's far too restless. It's not the kind of restlessness that keeps a person on the go and makes them active. No, it's the kind that makes her suddenly explode. And I just can't describe what Soledad is like when she's in a rage. She'll yell, "Get out of here! I don't love you, go on, get out!" But it's all over in a moment. I tell her, "You want me to leave? Well, good-bye." And no sooner does she see me going out the door than she grabs me and says, "You aren't going anywhere. Don't you dare leave this place."

I did leave her once. I had to wait until she was out of the house to sneak out my clothes. And then she tried to poison herself with some pills. She had money, a hundred and sixty dollars or so, and she spent about thirty dollars in four days chasing all over town in taxis, trying to find me.

When Soledad and I first got together, she told me she was pregnant.

Then I went off on a trip, and when I came back Soledad was sick. She had tried to abort the baby and thought she had, but actually it was still inside her, dead. She had to go to the hospital and get cleaned out. I am absolutely against abortion. To my mind a woman who provokes an abortion has committed a crime. I look at it this way, where six can eat, so can seven, and where seven eat, eight can eat.

The doctor told Soledad she couldn't have any more children. But I think she's about three months pregnant right now. I surely would like to have a child with Soledad.

Soledad

—————

I'm Ready for Anything

—————

WELL, FINALLY I got another job in the purse factory where I work now. I got that job by myself, looking around and asking. I went to the place one morning and the elevator operator told me they were hiring girls on the eighth floor. I went up and spoke to Fonso, the *foreman.* He told me to wait. Ten minutes later he called me. My first job there was putting on hinges. Then Fonso asked me if I could sew. I said yes, and he put me to sewing ornaments on the purses. After that I sewed in the *linings* and then I made *handles.* I worked on the floor, turning purses; I worked on *covers* and I worked in shipping.

None of those jobs is hard, but they have to be learned and you're supposed to be quick at them. Thank God, I manage to do anything they set me to. I have some intelligence, I'm not so dumb, see? And the *boss,* Fonso, was very fond of me. He appreciated me and treated me very well. He yelled at me now and then and he didn't want us to talk or to eat at the tables, but he was good.

Then one day I got a nervous *shock.* It's a kind of epileptic fit, because I fall down and later I can't remember anything about it. It was on account of Benedicto and worrying about all those problems. Fonso sent me home and told me to rest for a week. He always let me go home early when I asked him to. Then he got fired, I can't imagine why. He was so good. He gave me the address of the place where he works now and I'm telling you, if I ever get *lay off* here I'm going to work with him. They hired another *foreman,* an old man. That old man! He thinks we are slaves. One morning he sent me to work at the *stapling machine,* where I had never worked before.

"All right," I said. "Where shall I go? To the *stapling machine* or to the floor? I'm only one person, not twenty. I'll work anywhere, as long as I'm asked nicely." I said that because he had yelled at me. "I know you're the *foreman,*" I answered, "and I'm an employee here. But I'm not your personal slave. I'm a Puerto Rican and you're an American, but that doesn't mean you can come screwing around. Give me *lay off* and I'll go to the union and tell them."

Then the union man came up to me. "What's wrong?" he asked.

"This man insulted me," I explained. "He keeps making me rush from one job to another. My card isn't for working on the floor, nor for pasting, nor for the *stapling machine.* My card says I'm an *operator,* but he doesn't have me working one machine, he has me working everywhere."

The *foreman* explained that work was *slow* and so forth and so on. He hasn't spoken to me since. The other day I noticed him watching me and I stood up hoping he would fire me. I don't want to work there any more because if I do, I'm going to smash his face or hit him with something. If he fired me I could stay home and collect *employment.*

I wanted to get away from that job for another reason too. I went to a spiritist and she told me that someone at the factory was "working" on me to make me go mad and leave my job and break up my home. I knew it before she ever told me, because the spirits tell me things as in a dream. A distant relative of Benedicto's, a sort of cousin, worked there, and the bitch kept needling me. She wanted to provoke me so I'd have a fight with her and lose my job. Think of that! But no matter who tries to harm me, I put everything in the hands of God, because my soul is clean. I don't like to harm anybody and I return good for evil. But I was afraid I'd sock Benedicto's cousin or cut her to ribbons with a *Gem.* She knew I have a terrible temper. I thought I'd better quit the job because I didn't want to land in jail.

There wasn't any problem getting another job, because I had *social security.* When you go get a job, the first thing they ask about is *social security.* I got my card a long time ago, in Puerto Rico, because I had heard about needing *social security* to get a job. I was living with Arturo then. I just thought I'd better have it, because I like to be ready for anything. That's why I always have my papers in order. One person with foresight is worth twenty without.

One day I went to the ship to see Benedicto off. I was sitting there when I heard someone say, "The President was killed." I was amazed but I didn't want to believe it, so I walked away. A bit farther on someone told me, "Listen, President Kennedy was murdered," and I saw how people were milling around. As soon as I got home I turned on the television and the radio. I didn't cry, but it would have been better if I had because I couldn't eat. I was very upset. The next day Eustaquia, a friend of mine at the factory, invited me to go to Washington and we went. I felt it as deeply as if it had been something that happened to me. There were hordes of people there. I was overcome with emotion. If Muñoz Marín had died, frankly, I wouldn't have felt anything compared to what I felt about Kennedy.

I had thirty-five dollars and I spent all of it on the trip to Washington. We went by bus with my two little girls. We didn't sleep a wink. When we got there we walked to the White House to see if they would let us in to look at him. But they didn't, because there were too many people ahead of us. I walked and looked at everything. I had never been to Washington before. I was very moved. They buried him the next Monday. We saw the funeral. We stayed there all day. Nobody slept. We went to a hotel but the first night I couldn't sleep. It was terribly cold in Washington and the children caught colds. On the third day we came home.

I still feel it. You know, a President like that . . . I had a lot of faith in him because he did many things to end racial prejudice which neither President Eisenhower nor Roosevelt was able to do. He helped Puerto Rico get ahead and he helped us *hispanos* get the same minimum wage as other workers. So far, this Johnson doesn't make a good impression on me.

That same year I wanted to go to Puerto Rico. I had had a dream in which I saw Catín looking skinny and my family in a bad way. I would write home asking about everybody but they never told me anything. I kept thinking, maybe Catín really is sick, maybe she's having a hard time. Something is wrong back home. So I got myself laid off from work and Ben gave me the round-trip fare for me and Sarita and Toya, because he was sailing to San Juan too. And he told me to bring Catín back with me. I wrote to my *mamá* to tell her I was coming. At that time I didn't know Fernanda was living with Junior. I also wrote to Arturo and he immediately answered me. He sent a letter to Toya and another to Sarita, which I read aloud to them:

"My most esteemed daughter of my heart,

"Every time I look at your picture I weep, because you have won my heart entirely. You don't know how much I love you but, baby, I love you a lot. But do you understand why I love you so? It's so you'll be good to your *mami*. Take good care of her. And don't quarrel with your sister. She is good too and I also love her very much. God bless you. Quique and Catín send you lots of kisses.

"Your *papi*, who adores you,

"Arturo"

"My beautiful and beloved daughter Sarita,

"You cannot imagine how happy it makes me to know you will soon be here. Listen, the orange and grapefruit trees are loaded down with fruit. How you will enjoy it! Everybody is already looking forward to your arrival as if you were a little princess. And you know, it's true, because you are the most beautiful little princess in the world. Quique and Catín send you many kisses. Behave yourself now.

"Your *papá*, who loves you,

"Arturo"

The girls were crazy to see Arturo and Quique and Catín again. I was too, and even more to see my *mamá*.

Ben's ship sailed on December 21 and my plane took off on the twenty-third, at eleven-thirty. Flight 290 it was. I took some pills somebody gave me and I slept all the way over. I always take sleeping medicine when I fly, otherwise I get scared, and airsick too. I didn't feel a thing during that flight.

We got there at four-thirty in the morning on December 24, the same day Ben's ship was due to dock. Not a soul had come to meet me at the airport. There I was, at that hour, all alone, with two children and loaded down with packages.

I got a taxi and went to La Esmeralda. Three dollars it cost me, and twenty dollars was my whole capital. Twenty dollars! When we got to La Esmeralda, we went in the wrong way. I didn't know where Fernanda lived, or Cruz. A boy I knew carried my suitcases and I carried my little girls. We went down the alley past Padilla's house. I knocked on the door of the house in front of the public water faucet—I thought Fernanda was still living there with Héctor. When no one answered, I went to *doña* Minerva's house and greeted her. She was already up at that hour.

Doña Minerva has always been very good to me. After Sarita was born I lived next door to her for about three years. She earned her living slaughtering hogs, making cakes, and from the rent I paid her. Her daughter worked in a clinic. Minerva used to quarrel with me all the time but I didn't pay any attention to that. She'd call me a whore, a bitch, daughter of your mother. I just said, "You're crazy. The trouble with you is that you need a man." Then I would walk away and after a while she made friends with me again. She quarreled like that with everybody. But she always said that I was the only one she got along with. And she took care of my daughters too, of Toya especially. She was always good to Octavio. One day she saw him running from the cops and she took him into her house and hid him under the bed. Later he got away through the back door. And when I was late with the rent she'd say, "Never mind, it's all right." See what I mean?

She never had any children except Mónica, and another daughter who died. Mónica is the apple of her eye. And you know, sometimes that made me feel jealous, because I always wished my *mamá* would act that way with me. In La Esmeralda it isn't usual for parents to be affectionate to their children. They don't seem to bother about them at all, and let them do as they please.

Doña Minerva was the one who told me that Fernanda was living in Cataño with Junior. When I heard that, my stomach turned right over. But what was there to do? Lots of things like that have happened to me and I've just had to take them. I just said, "And where does Felícita live? And Crucita?"

"Crucita lives up here, a bit further on, and Fela is in one of Papo's houses." We talked awhile. She asked me how my kids were and so on. Small talk. Pretty soon Cruz came and we embraced, hypocritically, because they're all hypocrites. She brought Catín at that hour—*bendito,* poor baby. That little girl was so skinny that when I looked at her the tears came to my eyes. And you should have seen the way they kept her ragged and barefoot. I had often sent five or six dollars for her, and Fernanda took it for herself. That child was a bundle of bare bones. I couldn't help crying. The dress I had sent for her birthday was covered, simply covered with I don't know how many days' mold. A pair of ragged sneakers were her only shoes. I had to buy her two pairs of shoes while I was down there.

I went to Puerto Rico loaded down with things for Cruz and her little girl. And what did Cruz say? "Oh, used clothes? I don't want that junk."

"You're an ungrateful bitch," I told her. "You're never thankful to people who try to do something for you." Because I'm willing to bet she said that we never helped her, nor gave her anything. Felícita gave Cruz money when she went out with men, but Cruz talked scandal about Fela, and about my *mamá* and me, too. I know she did. All her life Cruz has been a busybody. She could put you to sleep with her gossip. She told people that I was taking on men up here and that I never sent a penny to Catín. But what care did she give the child, eh? Someday I'm going to sock her hard and then she'll be done for. She's small and won't be able to fight back.

Cruz took me to Felícita's house. Fela had just got in from work at that hour. She left her children alone at night and never got home before dawn. She seemed very thin and haggard to me. We embraced and she said, "The other night I dreamed that you were coming. Think of it!"

"Really?" said I, and we got to talking.

I may complain about the things Fela did to me, but as for her leaving her children alone to go earn a dollar or two, I never criticize her for that. Nobody can judge her for those things. I have had to do them myself. She has a right to do as she damn well pleases, but I will admit she's sort of careless. You know her girl Evita? It was I who cured her of worms, which had made her belly all swollen. And before I left, I cut off her hair and poured a bottle of Flit over her head to get rid of the lice. Felícita doesn't pay any attention to those things. When I was in the life I looked after my children as a mother should.

I love Fela as a sister and I'm sorry for her. I wish I could do something for her in spite of the fact that no one in my family has ever done anything for me. I don't bear them a grudge for that. To have a family is to have problems, many problems. Felícita could have been better off now if only she had wanted to. Edmundo gave Felícita everything she needed but he's the kind of a man who claims it all belongs to him. If a man came to me with that story I'd tell him to stick it all up his ass and I'd clear out. And that's exactly what Fela did.

I pity Fela for her sufferings and her ignorance, the way she goes out with a man, not caring whether he pays her or not. She falls in love right away and takes those damn fool Americans seriously. And I know that she's had an affair with *don* Camacho. Oh, I don't care about that old man. When I leave somebody, I don't want to ever talk about him any more; I even get to hate him. But it hurt me, just the same, because Fela is my own sister. And after that, Felícita had an affair with a boy, Martín, who had been my sweetheart. My sisters know I would never go to bed with any man with whom they had been intimate. Yet, they do it to me.

Well, at six o'clock in the morning I went to *doña* Ofelia's house, where my *mamá* worked. Fernanda was there and she hugged me and we talked awhile. I found her looking thin and run-down. She spoke to me about her husband right away and I said, "Do you realize he's a *teenager?*" I only meant to make it clear that he was much younger than she, understand?

She asked me about Simplicio and I told her he was well. "And Flora?"

"I don't speak to the bitch," I said. She asked about Aunt Amparo and so on, and then I said I was going. "I'm leaving now because I'm expecting Ben. I'll come back later." I took a taxi and went to Dock No. 14. There they told me the ship wouldn't get in until Wednesday because it had been delayed.

Fernanda took me to her house in Cataño. The house was real pretty. She had furniture, a small bed, a table and a refrigerator, but there was nothing in the refrigerator. *Doña* Ofelia had given Fernanda most of the furniture. It wasn't Junior who got it for her. Now, with Junior, she had to work to pay the rent and everything. With Héctor my *mamá* didn't have to work and she never skipped a meal, because he always managed to dig up a dollar or two. He never bought just one pound of pork chops or chicken, he'd get three or four pounds at one time and give us all food. Think of that!

Héctor was the only good stepfather we've ever had. He was never rude to any of us. He never made a pass at us girls. And he was lots of fun, too. He often joked with us. If I asked him for a dollar or anything, he always gave it to me. Why, if Fernanda would have asked Héctor to bring down a star from the sky and he couldn't, he'd have had an imitation star made for her. And look at the trick she played on him, taking off with that little *bum,* Junior.

"This place is full of mosquitoes, the kind that buzz and dive like jets," Fernanda said. Well, I'm an intelligent woman and I can take a hint. So since Fernanda didn't show any pleasure in my company nor any intention of inviting me to stay, I didn't ask her. I left around eight-thirty at night, and Fernanda didn't care enough to say, "Junior, take her as far as the road, she has a long way to go." We went by ourselves, Gabriel, Angelito, Sarita, Catín, Toya and I, and we got lost. We got to La Esmeralda late and my sisters hadn't saved a bit of food for us.

I changed my clothes and sat down in front of Cruz's house. It was Christmas Eve but nobody had any dinner for me. I hadn't eaten a thing all day long. I was flat broke. I got into conversation with old Cayetano, our neighbor. He's a good old man. He went out with Felícita sometimes. I said, "Cayetano, lend me twenty dollars. I'll pay you back tomorrow."

Cayetano promised, "I'll have it for you in the morning." I stayed there talking with him until eleven that night. Then I went looking for Cruz and found her drinking at a *bar.*

"Come on, Crucita," I said, "let's go to bed. I'm tired and sleepy. I haven't had any rest today." She was so tipsy she fell down and then she said I had pushed her. I had to put her under the faucet to sober her up. Fernanda also went on one hell of a binge that night. I was the one who should have gone partying and I was the only one who didn't. What a Christmas Eve I had! Imagine, I hadn't had a bite of bread or a drop of coffee all day.

So I put Crucita to bed and lay down myself. As soon as I climbed into the bed, it tipped and made me slide off the other side. I swear I didn't sleep a wink that night. The place stank of kerosene, I don't know why, and it was crawling with enormous cockroaches and with rats. I screamed because I thought the rats were going to bite me. At five in the morning I was up and under the shower but that didn't make me feel any better.

While I was getting dressed my ex-boy friend Martín showed up. I had met him at the Río Piedras Penitentiary when I went to visit my cousin Darío. Martín was from Bayamón. He was in jail because he found his wife with her lover and had killed him. He spared his wife. She got out alive so she could laugh at him.

He and I fell in love while he was still in jail. Then one day he was let out on a pass and he came to my house with Darío. Could that man screw! After being so long in jail . . . well, you can imagine! He hadn't even got his prick well up inside me when all his milk came out. He really emptied himself. *Ay, dear God* . . . what a prick he had! When that man threw himself on top of me he was like a sloop in a hurricane on the high seas. He kissed me from the tip of my toes to the top of my head. *Ave María!* it was kiss, kiss, kiss and screw, screw, screw. And he came so fast, just like that! We went on together for a long time. When I came up here to New York he wrote to me now and then. I stopped going to see him because I found out that another woman was visiting him in jail. And then when he got out of jail, he went and stayed with my sister. I heard all about it, up in the States.

"I heard you were in Puerto Rico," he said, "so I came right over." Imagine him coming to see me at six o'clock in the morning!

"Listen you," I said to him. "I don't want to have anything to do with a dirty bastard like you."

"But what have I done?"

"I know you slept with my sister. And besides, I have a husband now."

"No, no, that's a lie," he said. "Your sister's a dirty bitch."

"Don't drag my sister into this," I yelled at him. "She's not a dirty bitch. You're the one that's dirty and repulsive." Because really, he was ugly. He looked like a chimpanzee. He started to say something but I walked out and left him with the words in his mouth.

I phoned customs to ask when Benedicto's ship was due. "It docked at six," they said. I waited around until nine and then went down to the dock. I waited, *ay,* dear God! I waited and waited. Finally Benedicto turned up, reeling drunk. We went back to the ship to get some cigarettes, a bottle of perfume, and a bottle of cognac for my *mamá.* Then we went to Puerto Nuevo, to the house of a certain Auntie Janette, a former mistress of Benedicto's. He took me to see her because I asked him to. I wanted to prove to him that I no longer felt any love for him, understand? When your husband takes you to his ex-mistress and you don't react, what can the man think?

When she saw Benedicto she said hello, and he gave her the bottle of perfume. They talked of this and that while I sat on a rocker. They talked and I rocked. When I said, "Let's go," he had to leave.

We took a taxi to Villa Palmeras, to the house of a lady called *doña* Neticia. She's a spiritist and Benedicto sometimes went there. As soon as she saw Benedicto she bubbled over, "Oh, Beni, Benito," and went on chattering to him. I just sat there without saying a word.

Benedicto asked her to work a spell for him, so we went into another room. They made me preside that day, God forgive me. I sat in the middle, with Benedicto and *doña* Neticia on either side. *Doña* Neticia talked and Benedicto prayed until a spirit took possession of her. I don't know what she said because the last thing I remember was that I jumped up and threw myself down at the altar. I don't know what happened afterward. When I came to, my knees were skinned.

Benedicto says I worked for that woman and for him too. She told me that in her opinion I was one of the best young mediums she had ever seen. It's bad luck to mention the protectors one has, but she said to me, "A gypsy came. You dress like a gypsy at times, don't you?" And I realized that it's true, I really do. She also said, "You are under the protection of an Indian. You like Indian things, isn't that so?"

"I don't know," I answered. My Indian protection must take the form of perfume because sometimes when I am just sitting, not doing anything, I smell this wonderful fragrance, like the best of perfumes. Then she told me about a little African Negro, which is the "Congo" idol I have. And also I have Faith, Hope and Charity. That makes four very good protectors.

Doña Neticia said I had one evil influence and she wanted to help me get rid of it, but I didn't let her. I'd rather not get too involved in spiritism. I'm not one to stir things up because, as the saying goes, the more you stir up shit, the worse it stinks.

We went back to Crucita's house and Fernanda was there. I said, "Nanda, this is my husband."

"Yes, it's a pleasure," she said to Benedicto. Then Junior burst out, "Come on, I shit on God, let's get out of here!" And Fernanda hurried after him without a word to any of us. She didn't say good-bye to Ben or me or invite us to her house or anything. I shit on the lot of them! If I could have gotten a seat on a plane I would have left that very day.

I swear to you that was the unhappiest day of my life. Every single day I spent back home was unhappy. Benedicto was drunk when we walked down Tanca Street. I was so ashamed. You know how it is. That street was full of prostitutes, and if they see you walking around with a drunk they think you're a whore yourself. Another drunkard brushed against me and Benedicto was bent on fighting with him. And then Benedicto had to go try to flag a taxi right in Tetuan Street, where all the whores and Americans hang out. There was Benedicto, right in the middle of the street as if he were the governor. I could feel the pounds melt off me by the minute. Some Americans went by and stared at me. I just stood there, hanging my head.

Finally I stopped a taxi and told the driver, "Look, I'll pay whatever you say but please take us to Dock Fourteen." When we got there the driver and I had to help Benedicto go aboard. That night at ten, sitting on Crucita's stoop, I saw the ship go by. Then I went to bed. That was on Christmas Day.

On Thursday, Felícita with her five children and I with Catín, Sarita, Toya, and Crucita's daughter, Anita, went to Toa Alta to see Quique. There were so many of us that we hired a car.

I was very happy to see my son. He was seven years old and was nice and plump, and he called me *mamá* and all that. I sat out in the yard and talked to him. I said, "Quique, do you want a tit?"

"Yes," he said. I bared my breast and he was about to take it but his *papá* wouldn't let him. Later I asked Arturo to keep the girls with him because there was no place for them to stay in San Juan. I told him what Fernanda had done and he said I could leave them, so I gave him some money.

Felícita and I went back to San Juan because it was getting dark and we had to put Fela's kids and Anita to bed. I changed into a black dress and went to the place on Luna Street where my sister worked. Felícita introduced me to Harry, an American boy, and he fell for me. We got to talking, he bought me a few drinks, and we went to bed together. After that I went to Cruz's house and went to sleep.

On New Year's Eve I wore a green dress. Felícita didn't go to work, although she was supposed to. We got dressed and went to meet some boys she knew. Her friend Tommy was there with two more boys, whose names I don't know. We went to the Normandie Hotel, where American tourists go. There were only five of us, but one shot of whiskey apiece cost us twelve dollars. Twelve dollars for five shots of whiskey! We danced two or three times. When it got to be eleven I said, "Let's go. I want to see the year out with my *mamá*." So we went down to La Esmeralda.

Ay, the pain one feels after being in a nice hotel and walking by the Caribe Hilton, seeing so many pretty things and then having to go back to La Esmeralda! Such terrible poverty, so much dirt, garbage scattered everywhere! They live in separate worlds, the poor and the rich. I'll never go back to La Esmeralda, may the dear God forgive me! I may go back for a visit, but not to live there with my children. Never again.

Well, we went to Felícita's house and my *mamá* was there, so I did see the year out with her as I wanted to. My *mamá* was indifferent to me, but when we began to talk about Simplicio she got hysterical. I left and went back to San Juan because I was so mad at her.

We danced until four in the morning and then I went back to sleep at Fela's house. I earned fifty dollars that night and I saved every cent of it. Next morning I went to the country to get my children. Arturo brought the girls to me and Toya began to cry because she wanted to stay with him. I asked Quique if he would like to come with me but he said he wanted to stay with his father, so I left him. A son always loves his father more.

Felícita's friend Tommy had given me his picture and asked me to write to him. I said nothing doing, that I esteemed him as a friend but that I had a husband. But he did write me just the same and Benedicto found one of the letters. He gave me two black eyes because of that. My face was so swollen, I couldn't go out for two weeks. But I cut him up. I cut him in the back behind the shoulder. It's true I did go with Tommy, and I went with old Cayetano, too, for money. Money, that's all I care about. What else could I do? Benedicto had paid my fare but he didn't give me any money to live on. And I had to bring Catín back with me. I went with the Americans to bring the kid over.

Before I left Puerto Rico I had a dream about the place at Stop 26 where I used to live with my *mamá*. I often dream about that shack, I don't know why. And there was Santiago's store where we used to buy. I saw a girl crying and I asked her, "Don't you know me?"

She said, "Oh, you're Cristóbal's daughter."

"Yes," and then a little farther on I asked, "Haven't you seen *papito?*"

"No, your *papá* isn't here but your stepmother is." But when I walked past my stepmother she paid no attention to me. María del Carmen, her sister, called out to me, "Why don't you go to your *mamá?*" Then I told her, weeping all the while, everything my *mamá* had done to me, how she neglected my daughters, how she paid more attention to her husband than to me.

I woke up crying. I have to forgive my *mamá* because it's not up to me to punish her. Only God can punish. I'd have to divide myself into a thousand pieces to punish all the people who have done bad things to me. But I was hurt, terribly hurt, and I'll never forget it. That was my pleasure trip to Puerto Rico.

Catín

I Love My Mamá

I SPEAK God's truth. I am just a little girl, nine years old, and don't know much but I do know that I love Arturo, Grandma, Crucita and *mami* very much. *Mami* is good and gives me love. She says all the time, "I have my children. I am not alone. I don't abandon my children." That's why, when I grow up, I want to be a doctor or a chambermaid. So when I work and earn money, I'll put it in the bank and give *mami* the bank book so she can take out what she wants. Then I'll send for Arturo and Quique and I'll buy *mami* furniture and everything. This furniture we have is no good.

I'd like to be happy like other girls and have a *papá* so that when *mami* gets sick she can run and tell him. I love my *mamá* and will never leave her alone. And neither will she leave me.

I am a good girl. I am clean, I sweep, I do everything, and I behave myself. I mind others, obey my *teacher* and all that. I don't ask my *mamá* to buy me things. I say to *mami* in a nice way, *"Mami,* are you going to buy me that dress?" If she can't, then she doesn't buy it. The nuns say that's how you have to be to be good.

The boys say I am pretty, that I have pretty hair, but I think I am ugly. What I would like now is to get this leg of mine cured.

Benedicto said to me, "Don't you worry. One of these days we're going to take you to the hospital and have you fixed up." *Mami* says so, too. But I am afraid of the doctor and I don't want to miss school. So, what I do is go to church a lot so I'll be cured.

The thing is, I am a coward. I'm afraid of the hospital. I'd rather stay home. I'm afraid they will stick a needle in me and open me with a knife. The only way they will ever be able to catch me and give me an injection is if they get me when I am asleep. They told me they were going to take X-rays and I got so nervous you could hear my teeth chattering. Toya came over right away and said, "Did they cut your leg?" I was afraid I was going to die and then they would pull out all my guts. That's what they do in the hospital. They cover you with a sheet and put you in a coffin and bury you. Nobody ever sees you again after you are buried.

I cry when *mami* gets an attack and goes to the hospital, because I have to stay with the children. That Toya doesn't obey me and begins pestering me. *Mami* tells her to do something and she doesn't do it. When she behaves badly I smack her in the face. *Mami* doesn't want me to hit her, but I do it so she won't be calling me nasty names. I'm tired of taking care of the children and it makes me mad.

If my cousin Gabriel stays over it's even worse. If *mami* leaves a sausage, Gabi and Toya eat the whole thing. They eat all the bread, and when *mami* comes home I am the one who gets all the blame. That's why I smack Gabi in the face, too. That child is a big rascal. When I go to his house he doesn't want me to touch anything. Auntie Flora says to him, "Whatever is here is for everybody, not just for you."

That boy! One day I dreamed that Auntie died and Uncle wanted the things in the house for himself and he brought his girl friend Leila there. But I told Leila no, she couldn't have the things. Then, right away Gabi came and said, "Flora told me that nobody was going to get those things."

And so I said to him, "Look, Gabi, you get out of here! Those things are not yours. Auntie told me way back to take care of them." That child is always butting in.

What I would like is to go back to Puerto Rico. I am going to tell *mami* that when school is over we should leave. They don't cure her here and the doctors are making her nervous. In Puerto Rico they will cure her. Then she could go back to work. She can't do that here because she is in the hospital so much. She says that when I am a big girl and she is working, she is going to buy us real pretty clothes.

My own mother is bad. She has about a hundred children. She gives some away and the others she neglects. She dresses herself up real pretty but the children go around the house with shit in their pants.

They say that a man who lived with my *mamá* was my *papá* and that he gave her a beating for mistreating me and so she threw me against the drainpipe and broke my leg. That's why *mami* asked her for me. *Mami* wanted me and asked her for my clothes and took me to a hospital. She says that she alone is my *mamá* and Arturo is my *papá*.

I remember that we were living in the country with Arturo. *Mami* and Arturo used to fight there. He would hit her hard because she didn't listen to him. That was why we left and went to La Esmeralda. Arturo was paying for the room but one day *mami* began to fight with him and she picked up a knife and went after him. We took it away from her. Arturo left but he came back a few days later.

Then *mami* went to work in *don* Camacho's *bar*. She worked selling, collecting the money and serving the tables. She sold rum. She worked and paid the rent and Arturo took care of us. He would get up at one to go to the store and he brought us *lunch*. Then he would go for Quique and let him play in the street. *Mami* continued in the life and she would leave us with Arturo.

I remember *mami*'s dead husband, Tavio. He was very good to me. He gave me a very pretty dress. He was very strong, taller than *mami*, and he could jump the fence without hurting himself or anything. But one day he went out with his friend to get some things for *mami* . . . a lot of things all of gold . . . Then when he was coming out, they were waiting for him and they shot him. I think he used to go out to steal, because that's what *mami* said.

That's when *mami*'s attacks first began. She loved him very much, just like Arturo. The funeral was real pretty. We still have some pictures of the funeral.

Afterward *don* Camacho used to come to La Esmeralda, but I didn't know him well because he would be in the living room in Grandma's house. What I know is that *don* Camacho was an old man with a house and a wife. But he was real rich and had *bars* on every street.

Simplicio began to work for *don* Camacho, too, because he got married to Flora. I knew Flora when she lived with Fontánez. I used to go there, but Fontánez didn't like me because I would come to tell Flora that Uncle wanted to talk to her.

I remember once I saw Simplicio giving Alvaro's wife some beer and I went and told Grandma. Fernanda and Flora went over there and started a big fight! Alvaro's wife hid because Auntie was going to kill her. Then Uncle took a bat and was going to beat me, but *mami* came and started to fight with him.

After that *don* Camacho paid the fares for all of us to go to New Jersey— Simplicio, too. We went to live with Felícita, who was with Edmundo then. Edmundo made a lot of faces over that. He always had a long face. Simplicio, Flora, Felícita and all the children were living there, except Felícita's twins, Angelito and Gabi, who stayed with Grandma in Puerto Rico.

One day in Fela's house I went through the bedroom and Fela was naked and so was Edmundo. Fela began laughing and I said to her, "You shameless thing," and I went out. I told *mami* but she didn't say anything. And then

Felícita made fun of *mami.* So we did it back at her and Quique said, "I have to defend her, she is our *mamá.*"

Mami took a room and we began living in that other house. It was a real big one and *mami* worked there. She kept on working and began to live with Eddy. He was all right. But I hate all the husbands *mami* takes and I don't call them *"papá"* or anything. Once he started to fight with *mami* and she went and burned him.

On my birthday they made a *party.* That was when *mami* went crazy. The day of my *party* there was such a fight that *mami* was screaming. She gets very nervous. She was very pretty that day and they knocked her earrings off. There was a nice glass door there and they smashed it and everything else. *Mami* was biting the man, so he hit her and Cruz grabbed a knife. *Mami* got nervous and began screaming, "Get out of here or I'll kill you!" And she nearly did. Well, he left.

They took my *mami* to the hospital in a car and left her there. The thing is she can't stand it if she gets hit in the head very many times and she was in the crazy house for two months. They took everything away from her in the crazy house, her watch and all.

Eddy used to go to see her, and Crucita, too. We used to peek in and see her through the *window.* The *window* was all barred up, because she threw out everything they gave her.

We stayed with Crucita, who was good to us. At lunchtime she fried us eggs and gave us potatoes with sweet sauce, and for dinner she made soups and everything. Crucita wasn't working outside, as there was a man by the name of Jorge Luis who was in love with her and bought her everything.

Crucita wanted to go back to Puerto Rico and abandon us. She had her ticket and money. Then they got a ticket for *mami,* too, while she was in the hospital, and Crucita got tickets for us and we all went to Puerto Rico.

Grandma was glad to see us. She was living with Héctor when this happened. Grandma made a special vow and that was why *mami* got cured. So then *mami* began working for *don* Camacho again. He gave her money and *mami* rented a room.

Arturo used to take care of us. He is really nice and I love him and he loves me. I had a lovely photo of him, and Emilio, Crucita's husband, tore it up. He thought it was some sweetheart of Crucita's.

Then, I don't know, but when *mami* came here to New York she left me behind. She said she didn't have the fare for me but only for Sarita and Toya and I had to stay but that she would come for me later. Quique didn't go either, because he didn't want to.

Well, so I stayed. In the daytime I was at Nanda's house. It was good there because Héctor was nice to me. He worked and bought the food and she would cook a great big potful for everybody. She would give some to Arturo and to Eufemia, the next-door neighbor. I ate a lot, but Grandma always gave me plenty. One day she took one of those short sticks and beat me with it because a neighbor had hit me and I had scratched her. I wasn't going to let that woman get away with it. I hit right back. So they came and told Grandma. I got sick with a fever. I would get asthma and I was always catching cold. That's why I am so skinny.

Fernanda didn't pay any attention to me at that time because she was in love with Junior. That is why I hate Junior. I don't like him; I love Héctor. When Héctor went to work, Fernanda would open the *window* and begin whistling. "Who are you whistling to?" I would say to her.

"Junior," she answered.

"What if Héctor catches you?" I'd ask her.

On *Thanksgiving,* Héctor bought Nanda a roast turkey, and he gave it to her and said, "For you, *negra.*" And would you believe it, but that afternoon when he came back from work he found Junior and Fernanda kissing. So Junior left and I went to his house and said to him, "Why don't you go away?"

Crucita went and said to him, "Junior, why don't you go away? Can't you see she loves Héctor more? Because when she's broke Héctor gives her money."

I slept with Arturo and Quique. I didn't stay at Fernanda's because when she got drunk there was no living with her. She would put on pants and begin dancing and carrying on and Crucita pulling at her to try to make her stop. There was no living with her when she was like that.

Arturo lived alone. He says he doesn't marry because *mami* is his wife. He didn't dare bring many women around because of Quique and me. I would knock on the door real loud and say, "Arturo, let me in. It's nighttime." When he didn't open, I would go looking for Quique and he would come back with me and say, *"Papi,* open up, it's me and Catín. It's raining." It wasn't really but he said it just so he would let me in. If he didn't open, Quique would climb over the house and go in through a *window.*

One time I had to throw that drunk Pucha out of there. I said to her, "You get out of this house. You don't live here and can't give orders." I got her out but she gave me a slap, a real hard one. Crucita heard and came right over. I was crying and she spoke real nasty to Pucha. Pucha is a fresh one and that is why Crucita insulted her and bawled her out.

Finally Nanda left Héctor. It happened on a day when we were eating at Crucita's house. Arturo was very warm and Quique was sweating, so we moved to the bench outside to eat. Héctor came and caught Nanda and Junior kissing and said, "What a fine thing this is!" So right then and there Nanda pulled out a *Gem* she had, broke it into pieces and cut Héctor. Arturo jumped in and held her to stop the fight. They were going to send Nanda to jail but Héctor didn't want that. I kept quiet because there were a lot of people around.

Arturo left for the country and we went to live in Crucita's house. *Bendito,* but Crucita didn't have money. She had so many things to pay for and the sick baby to take care of. The little house was so small.

Then Crucita lived with Alejandro. He was good. He bought Crucita a bed and I slept in it with her. When he came off the ship he would give everything to Crucita and tell her to go and pay the grocery bill and buy whatever she wanted. It was fine, except that Emilio still loved her and always kept spying on her. He came to Crucita's at night to fight. "Why do you open the door for him?" I asked her. "He threatens you with a gun but that's nothing to you. If I were you I wouldn't open the door."

Crucita is lame. They are going to send her to New York to see if she can't be cured, but she doesn't want to leave the children with anybody. I feel sorry for her and would like to see her again. She was really nice and would play with us and everything. I would call Angelito and Quique and tell them to get together a gang because Crucita was waiting to play with us. So we would go there and she would tell us all to line up to play hide-and-seek or whoever-touches-this-wins. I'd run and run and win.

Once a fight started because Quique called me cripple, even though he doesn't like it when they say that to Crucita. A kid was saying it to her and Quique punched him in the mouth. Angelito held the boy and Quique punched him. Crucita said, "If he calls me cripple again he better get away because my nephew will beat him up."

But Quique teased me by calling me cripple. He likes cats and has a lot of them. So I told him that if he called me cripple again I would throw out his cats and he said, *"O.K.,* I won't call you cripple any more."

Crucita was the one who bought things for me. *Mami* sent Fernanda money but I never saw any of it. Fernanda wanted it for Junior. Crucita put me in school and I liked it very much. I was going into the second grade, and Felícita was still saying I didn't know how to write, that Gabi was the one who knew. But I was good in school. The *teachers* hit me only once. Crucita would fix up my clothes to go to school and so did my Grandma. Nanda would buy me my uniforms. Once she said to me, "Catín, go and pawn this chain for me. You have to go to school tomorrow and you have no shoes."

It was a Saturday and Arturo had not come for me that day. Arturo came for me on Saturdays and brought me back on Sunday. When I was going to pawn the chain, Emilio went to Crucita's house to beat Grandma. Emilio owned a gun and he had traded it with Héctor for a knife. "You're a no-good *bum,"* Nanda said to Emilio and he hit her. I put down the money I got for the chain and went for Auntie. I knocked and knocked, and in a minute the police were there and they caught Emilio with that long knife he had. Arturo and nearly everybody came to see. Crucita did, too.

What happened was that Héctor gave Emilio the knife to kill Junior.

Héctor didn't want to get into *trouble,* so he sent Emilio. And Emilio said, "All right, if I get into *trouble,* you will too. I know you're a good man, Héctor. You treat my children good." So Emilio was looking for Junior. But Junior went running home and Héctor said, "I'll get even for this sliced-up face of mine. That's how she is, my *negra!"*

Look how nice Héctor is. He told Nanda about the job at *doña* Ofelia's. Otherwise Nanda wouldn't have gotten it. Sometimes I used to go over there to help Nanda serve the tables, and wash the dishes and scrub. After Nanda served all the people and everything, we would shut the door tight and sit down to eat ourselves. Then we would clean off the tables and all that.

I can say that Crucita never beat me. But Fernanda did. When I got home from school, Crucita would send me to wash Chuito's diapers. I liked doing it. And she would fix my clothes for me and all so that I would be neat and clean. Crucita loves children, but just imagine, Emilio nearly took her little girl away from her!

Once there was a real big fight in Papo's place. What happened was that Gladys came to Cruz's house once and Alejandro fell in love with her, but Gladys is a coward and doesn't fight fair. Luckily, Fela and a friend mixed in and defended Cruz. You see, Gladys was carrying on with Alejandro.

"I knew Alejandro before you did," Crucita told her. "We knew him before anybody here. If you think you're going to get him, you better beat it right now."

The next day Auntie Fela went out on the street singing, and when she passed by on the side where Gladys' house is, they tried to hit her with a bottle. Auntie Fela fought back, though. They took a punch at her but she ducked, and it hit a friend of Auntie Fela's, but he grabbed her and held her back. Then Crucita got in it and said, "Drop that bottle! I know my husband is in there. You can have him!"

And that is how life went along there.

Felícita spent all her time picking up men, and she would say to me, "Put the children to bed for me and I'll give you money." She didn't pay Crucita anything for taking care of the children at night and that was why Crucita got angry. Because she can't work much on account of being lame. She was always fighting with her sister because Fela neglected the children. Cruz spoke real rough to her. "Great whore, why don't you attend to your children," she would say. Taking care of those children of Felícita's was killing me. I was so skinny that I hardly had any strength to do anything. And I was so nervous I couldn't even pick up Chuito because I was afraid I would drop him. Then one day when I was coming out of church with a lot of people around, Felícita got hold of me and slapped me. She always does things like that so people will talk about us.

Arturo and his son once wanted to take me to the country. Chiripa is

Arturo's son and he has a little girl who looks like Sarita, and a very pretty wife. I said yes, yes, I wanted to go. Because there is a rowboat there that belongs to him and a long bridge. I ride in the boat and jump in the river. Arturo made a little playhouse for us and we used to climb up on top of it. At this hour he would be having us ride horseback or be bathing us in the river or playing with us. He is very good. I would like *mami* and Arturo to get together again, but she doesn't want to.

So that is how things were when I was sleeping one day in Crucita's house. At about one in the morning there was a knock on the door and it was *mami.* She hugged me right away. I didn't see Sarita but I heard her talking English: *"Mami, come over here,"* and *"Mami, your friend." Mami* didn't know any English, though.

Mami stayed at Crucita's house. She went to visit Héctor and when she saw his cut-up face, she got furious. "How did that happen?" she wanted to know.

"Your *mamá.* But that's nothing, she's my *negra,*" he told her. Then Leonor, the wife he has now, came out and gave him a shove. So Héctor kicked her and she hit Gabi. *Mami* said to her, "Leonor, if you beat that child, you are going to get into *trouble,* because he is my nephew. If you touch him, you are going to have to settle with me."

The next day *mami* asked me what Cruz said about her. "Nothing," I told her. "Cruz said you got attacks of hot pants."

"Oh, that's nothing. Don't pay any attention."

I told *mami* I wanted to go back with her, that I was tired of Puerto Rico and didn't want to live there. I said I was dying because Grandma hit me all the time, and I couldn't hold out much longer. *Mami* told me it was a good thing she came to see me. So then I told Cruz and she said, "Don't go. You're in school. Soledad will come again next year and you can leave with her then."

I said to her, "No, I'm leaving. I have to learn English. I must learn!"

"Write me," Crucita said. I would but I don't know her address.

The trip was all a blank. I got airsick. When I came to, they were saying, "Fasten your seat belts. We are about to land." I asked *mami* where we were going, but she didn't say anything.

When we came out Benedicto was there, but I didn't recognize him. I kept looking him over because Toya called him *papi.*

"Toya, don't be calling him *papi.* That's not your *papá,*" I told her. Toya's real *papá* is Tavio.

"Yes, he is my *papá,*" she said.

When we got to the house I asked *mami,* "Mami, who is he?"

"That's my husband," she said.

"Husband? Oh. I'm going out, *mami.* I can't take that," I told her. So I went outside and ate a piece of cake.

I cried all the time when I first came to New York. It was the beginning of the cold weather and I didn't like it. I missed Arturo and kept calling for him. At night I couldn't sleep. I missed Chuito, too.

Benedicto never did anything to me. But it's that I hate all the husbands *mami* ever had. And he beats *mami*. He stays out all night and they fight over that a lot. *Mami* gets furious and beats him. One time he was going to punch *mami*, and she ducked and he hit his fist on a drawer. Then he said to her, "*Ay*, Soledad, fix up my hand for me."

"Drop dead!" she told him.

I loved that. *Mami* had got the better of him. I hate Benedicto because he says that if I keep on hanging out in the street he is going to send me back to Puerto Rico. That is why, when he is around, I lock myself in the bathroom and don't come out. The thing is, he beats *mami* and drives her crazy. He punches her so hard he knocks her against the wall.

I keep saying to *mami*, "Let's go to Puerto Rico to Arturo. Leave Benedicto, because one of these days he's going to hit you and kill you." But she doesn't listen to me. So let her stay with him!

When I am big, I am going to say to Benedicto, "How much money do you want to leave my *mami?*" Then I'll send for Arturo and Quique. If Arturo is around when Benedicto tries to take advantage of *mami* or if he grabs us and smashes us against the floor, he won't get away with it.

I don't know why, but once there was *trouble* and *mami* sent me over to Uncle Simplicio's house. I slept on the *caucho* there and Flora took me to Delancey Street. I put on shorts and washed the bathroom and scrubbed and washed dishes for her. Then, when Flora began to work, I came back home. But now, since Gabriel is there, they don't want me. I say to him, "Uncle, can I go for the *weekend?*" But he won't let me. When Gabriel isn't here, though, he does want me. That's the thing. Now when he wants to take me home, I tell him I won't go with him. "You want Gabriel?" I say to him. "Then stick with your Gabriel."

I beat Gabriel because he hits me. If he hits me, I am not just going to take it. He is a very nice-looking boy and thinks he is *Superman*. The only difference is, everybody loves *Superman* and I hate Gabriel. Uncle is always buying him a *coat* and everything, and telling me what a good boy he is. He never stops talking about it. He took him to Pennsylvania twice already but he wouldn't take me. It doesn't matter though, because *mami* is going to take me any day now.

Uncle is no saint. He doesn't gamble because he knows they might arrest him. He drinks, though, and has girls. He is in love with the girl from across the street. "Let's you and me kiss," he says to her. "Catín, cover your eyes. Cover your eyes." And he goes chasing her around the table. I know he tries to make love to that little girl. Then she gets mad and says, "If *papá* knew you were trying to kiss me . . . I am going to tell my *papá*." Simplicio is no saint, even though he tries to make people think he is.

I don't like to play with anybody, just *mami*. We jump rope, but *mami* comes home late from work. I don't have many girl friends. Those friends of mine just give a person *trouble*.

One day they said that *mami* is a whore. I answered right back, "Isn't your *mamá* one, too? She picks up men and takes money from them."

Right away, Aida says to me, "No, she never does that."

"Oh no, never!" I said to her. "Wait till she sends you outside with the *baby* so she can get the money from the men. But don't worry, I'm going to tell *mami* now."

So I went and told her, *"Mami,* Aida says you're a whore and pick up men." *Mami* went to Aida's *mamá* and said to her, "Say, tell Aida I'm not a whore." Then she went and locked herself in the house and right away she got an attack. She can't have bad things happen to her because she gets that way and can't speak or breathe. She throws herself on the floor and bites her tongue. She wants to bite it off.

They say that *mami* goes to men's houses but *mami* says, "Nobody can say anything about me because I do it so my children can eat."

I feel sorry for *mami*. I wish she wasn't in *trouble* with anybody. Let her not talk to Rosalía because that old woman has a longer tongue than I. Rosalía is the one to blame for everything that happens because she introduces men to my *mami* and then gets her into *trouble*. I think she told Benedicto that *mami* was in love with Elfredo.

One day I went looking for *mami* and they told me, "Your *mamá* is at Elfredo's house."

I acted innocent and said, "Who is Elfredo? I don't know him." I was afraid on account of Benedicto because they fell in love in his house behind his back. Elfredo says he doesn't beat women and I like men like that. Elfredo brought us records and played them. Benedicto came and saw them so I took and gave them back to Elfredo. "Here, Elfredo," I said, "take them so *mami* won't have *trouble.*"

Right now we have to take advantage because Benedicto has a lot of money. He came back from the ship with it. I am going to tell *mami* to ask him to get the *television* out of the *punchoff* so that when I come home from school I can sit on the couch and take a rest watching *television.*

Yesterday I told *mami* that Benedicto was talking English to Rosalía. They just said a few words but I went and told *mami* because she gets mad when he speaks English. My *mamá* hates English. So she said, "Listen, go tell Benedicto to come here."

When Benedicto came he said about me, "That child should have her tongue cut off. One of these days she's going to get us all put in jail."

Elfredo and *mami* kept seeing each other, but *mami* wanted him to give her money and buy her things whether he wanted to or not. He would say to her, "Wait a moment! Take it easy, daughter, I haven't collected yet."

One time *mami* slapped Elfredo because she saw him with a woman. Then she got very nervous and had an attack. Elfredo stopped coming around to the house and I said, "Elfredo got married." *Mami* told me he was not married and to stop coming around with gossip.

The thing is that Elfredo knew that *mami* was in love with the Colombian and I think Benedicto did, too. It's Rosalía's fault, because she told *mami* that this Colombian was nice and so he gave *mami* the eye and invited us to the movies.

I gave *mami* a dirty look and later I said to her, *"Mami,* is that man going to the movies with me? I won't go. You know I don't like Colombians."

When *mami* is in love she acts different. She stays out in the street. I think she is going to stop going with men because she has these attacks. If she is going to have bad times with men, she better leave them. Oh, my Lord! I want her to leave them.

Imagine, that Colombian left *mami* in the lurch. Every few minutes *mami* would tell me to go see if he was coming. And I would answer, *"Oh, mami!* I'm not your servant. I'm not going to be on the lookout for him. I wish all Colombians would drop dead." So she grabbed me and hit me. She gave me two slaps in the face in front of Uncle.

Mami was even going to poison herself on account of him. She was lying back on the couch when she called me and said, "Catín, bring me a glass of water. I am going to take these pills to poison myself."

I gave her the water and ran out yelling and crying. When I came back she didn't open her eyes any more or answer, or anything. They called the ambulance and took her away. We stayed with the lady next door but they brought *mami* back right away and she was well.

I am afraid that if Benedicto comes back there is going to be *trouble* here. Rosalía might tell him about *mami* and the Colombian. The thing is that they lie down in *mami*'s bed and we get into the bed in the other room. I have seen them kissing. Yes, that's the truth. If Benedicto goes after *mami* and hits her, I am not going to talk to any of them again.

What I would like to see is Uncle beat up Benedicto. If the police came he could say, "This man began beating my sister and I just defended her." And he could bring *mami* as a witness and nothing would happen.

Mami put me in school now, and it's better there. I can learn English. I love to talk English. After I know how, I can talk in English and she won't know what I am saying.

I have been here for a long time already and so I am forgetting Spanish. English is what comes into my head. In school, I want to say *"Ven acá"* and what comes out is "Come on." *Mami* says that if I learn to talk English she'll beat me. But I tell her I would love to learn English. I start talking to Sarita and *mami* says to me, "Listen, you shut that mouth. You are not going to talk English around here." She gets very mad.

So I tell her, "But, *mami,* I have to learn to talk English, because if I don't I'll get left back in school."

Mami says, "I hate the Americans but not the ones who speak Spanish."

Mami didn't want to buy me a notebook I needed for school. I began to cry but then I stopped. She just left and didn't even listen to me. That's why they give me F. And at home the kids throw my things around and I can't find anything. Now I can't find my pencil case.

The schools are better here. They mistreat you in the schools in Puerto Rico. Mrs. Guerra, my teacher in Puerto Rico, was a bully and made me kneel down and all. If you come late here they leave you alone, but in Puerto Rico you have to go to the stupid *principal.* They grab the children by the hair there and they don't let you play. They tell you to go to the bathroom and come right back. Not here. Here they let you play a lot and the *lunches* are better. They give fresh milk and all kinds of fruit. That's why I like school better here.

But the children here are worse than the ones in Puerto Rico. They bully me. They muss my hair and one girl scratched me and Sarita and didn't let us eat. But that doesn't matter. If that girl hits me I hit her back. I have two good hands and I can hit back. But believe me, I used to be afraid. When I got home I told my mother and she said not to be such a dummy . . . that whoever hit me, I should hit back. Since that time I don't let anybody hit me any more.

When I grow up I am going to get even with all of them. I want to go back to Puerto Rico, but only after I know English so as not to talk Spanish to anybody. Not even to *mami.* I will talk to her in English. I'll call her *"Mother."* As I won't know much Spanish, I will take somebody with me and I will pay their fare just for them to speak Spanish for me. And so, I'll tell this friend of mine who speaks Spanish, "Tell my grandma to leave Junior because Junior won't do her any good."

Then I'll go to Héctor's and I'll tell him, "Don't worry, Héctor." Héctor knows English. He is a *merchant marine* and the *merchant marine* know a lot of English. So I will be able to talk to Héctor and he will understand. I will say to him, "Don't you worry, Héctor. One of these days, Grandma is going to leave Junior and go back to you. *Mami* is coming over here to fix it up."

I am going to tell Junior's *mamá,* too, "Now look, *doña* Celestina, tell your son to go look for somebody else, and that Nanda is not young. So let Junior leave her, because I can't keep on spending money to be coming here." Maybe Celestina will tell him, because she used to hate Nanda.

Oh, how Grandma will cry when I get hold of her and say, "When we were little, you didn't want to take care of us. Now you can't be with Simplicio because he is with me in New York."

And if Simplicio is there, I'll say to him, "Listen, Simplicio, tell your *mamá* to forget about me. I didn't come to see her. I just came to see Crucita."

And then I'll go to Crucita's and I'll say, "Crucita, do you remember how it used to be? Sure you remember. You don't know English, Crucita, but come to New York and I will help you take care of the children. Come on. You'll live with *mami*. You know, I'll give you a room for yourself and for Anita and Chuito."

Benedicto has to fix up this house and not keep it like a dump. We have money in the bank. This is a good house. When *mami* fixes it up it is as pretty as it can be. The bad thing is that the neighbors don't let you sleep and those children turn the place upside down. That Toya has her bed all rotted out with pee and that makes *mami* mad.

Oh, my Lord! If only *mami* wouldn't get any more of those attacks. She gets the attacks more on account of Benedicto than anything else. It's because he wants to use her like she was a servant. "Soledad, put my shoes on for me. Soledad, my shirt. Soledad, go buy me this." He orders her and orders her and *mami* can't walk much. And how they fight! One day *mami* was going out and Benedicto had to go somewhere too. So *mami* told him, "I'll be back when you are, because I'm not going to be shut in the house here by myself."

So he said to her, "Who gives the orders? You or me?"

"Me," *mami* said to him, "because you are not my husband any more."

So he grabbed her and punched her and *mami* pulled a knife and was going to stick him with it but he held her off. *Mami* nearly killed me because he grabbed me and shoved me in between the two of them. He tried to cover himself with Sarita, too. He hates us both. *Mami* would have killed him if he hadn't covered himself with us. Then Benedicto tried to get the knife away from her and tried to bend her hand until finally the knife stuck in his finger. "I cut my own self," he said.

I called him a liar and Toya called him a fairy, a son of a whore, and all kinds of bad things. I felt like taking that cover off the knife and sticking it through his head. It is a strong thing and if you stick it into somebody he dies. I wanted to stick it into him, but I got into bed all nervous and shaking.

This is the last time he is going to hit her, because if he does it again, I am going to stick a knife into him so he can't take advantage of *mami* any more. Men are bad, all of them. There isn't a single good one. That's why, when I grow up, I am not going to get married. I am going to be a nun. That way you can be alone and work and earn a lot of money.

Nearly every week we go to the Pee House. That's what they call the movie theater, because everybody pees on the floor. It's down Eagle Avenue and it's cheap. All it costs is a quarter. We go in at one o'clock and don't get back sometimes until ten when the pictures are good.

Oh, how I like going to the movies with *mami!* Because *mami* likes the funny pictures and enjoys herself. She laughs the most at Cuquita. He is a man who dresses up like a woman. He puts on a dress and a wig and ribbons and he looks like a fat woman and he dances real nice.

I liked the one we saw about Zorro. It was real good. Antonio Aguilar was in it and Antonio Aguilar's brother. He played Zorro. He had daughters and when they grew up they could ride horses and everything. So they grabbed the bad men, the rich ones, and took their money away and gave it to the good ones, you know, the poor people . . . the ones who send their children to school dirty and all that. I feel sorry for them. Then after that the father, Zorro, got old and they shot him with an arrow, but the daughters saved him.

When I grow up I would like to be one of the Zorros so when I go back to Puerto Rico I can put on the Zorro clothes and get a horse and begin helping the poor people and kill the rich ones. They have to get what's coming to them, and I will kill the crooks too.

Soledad

——

What the Hell!

——

WHEN WE lived on Fox Street the government took over about six blocks to put up some buildings. Our house was one that was going to be torn down. It was a private house, nice and clean, but the government said it had to go. Hardly any *hispanos* lived there. It was on a better street than this one, twice as good. They came to investigate us before we went to Puerto Rico and offered us one hundred dollars per room. We were supposed to move within six months.

The six months passed and Benedicto hadn't made any effort to get another place. The Cuban gentleman downstairs moved out, the people upstairs did too. We were the only ones left in the place. When Benedicto went off on his trips I was there by myself. Was I scared!

Finally Ben stayed on shore for a while and looked and looked until he found this place where we live now. I was working then. Ben borrowed two hundred dollars from a cousin of his to pay the deposit and the rent. A friend of Ben's who had a second-hand car, together with Ben's brother and his first cousin, moved all our things. I had to pawn my sewing machine to get the twenty-five dollars it cost us to move, because Benedicto didn't have a cent. The machine is still in the *pawnshop*.

We moved here in April, 1964. I like it here on Eagle Avenue, although the rooms are very small. We paid sixty-five dollars for the house on Fox

Street but we didn't have to pay for electricity or anything. Here I pay sixty-nine dollars and seventy-nine cents, and the electricity besides.

I didn't know anybody in the neighborhood when I moved here. One of my neighbors is called Nilsa. Her husband, Moisés Pagán, is her second husband. They don't pay rent, because they're the building superintendent. They also take care of my children. Aside from that, it seems like they don't do anything. At least, neither of them goes to work. Nilsa has two sons. Both of them have been in jail, Gardo for dope peddling and robbery, the other one, Berto, got out of jail just the other day. Besides her two sons, Nilsa's two granddaughters and her mother-in-law are staying with them. I don't go to their house much. They used to be always asking for things, "Give me this, give me that," until I stopped it by saying, "I gave and gave, now it's your turn to give me something." They haven't asked me for anything since then.

The only friend I have here is Rosalía. I met her a short while ago. Benedicto introduced us. She's a very close friend of Ben's; she's known him since he was born. She's a widow and lives alone with her son. I'm fond of her because she's good and has been nice to me. If I need a dollar she gives it to me, although she's very, very poor. Her son supports her and he's pretty old himself. Rosalía's only fault is that she's a troublemaker and a gossip.

I'd like to have more friends. Not just anybody, but friends who are somebody. I'd like to know people who are a bit above me, see? People who live comfortably and have good connections, people with a better social position than mine. Because, you know, sometimes you have a friend who will act fresh and make off-color jokes in the street, acting like a tramp. I don't deny I'm a bit of a tramp myself, but I don't go looking for another one like me. Understand?

I don't get along any too well with Benedicto's family. They can't stand me because he found me in a *bar*. They say I only care for him because of his money. According to them, he gives it all to me. People think a *merchant marine* is rolling in money, but we don't have anything because he drinks it all up.

All of Ben's family are a bunch of hypocrites. When Ben is screwed up, none of them give him anything. They flock around when he's flush, but when he's broke you don't see hide nor hair of them. That's what my relatives do, too. My cousin Virginia comes to me when she's in a fix but when she has money she tells everybody, "Oh, my family never gives me a thing. My cousin Soledad is stingy." That makes me mad as hell. What does she expect? For me to let her have my apartment? Eh? I have my needs too. I am humanitarian but I don't carry it to extremes.

I met Elfredo a month after we had moved here. The man in charge of the lottery sent him to get the lottery numbers here and to put Benedicto and me on his list. I like gambling, I've been doing it ever since I opened my eyes on the world. I learned it from my *mamá*. I have even sold lottery books at the place where I worked. I took a book with ten dollars' worth of tickets. Then I turned in seven-fifty and kept two-fifty for myself.

I have faith in gambling but I don't have much luck. Once I won with number 316 and another time with 220. In Puerto Rico I hit it almost every year, but not here. Unlucky at games and unlucky in love, that's me. I'm lucky when I go gadding about, when I'm in the prostitution game. But when I want to live in peace and quiet, like now, I don't have any luck at all.

I've always been lucky with the horses, though. In Puerto Rico I used to go to the race track on Sundays and Fridays and Wednesdays. Once I went with my *papá* and between the two of us we won fourteen dollars. We used to play the daily double, the illegal one. Sometimes I won fifty, sixty dollars, like that. I went alone and played alone. Afterward I would find myself a man to escort me and we would go to San Juan.

Elfredo, the *bolita* banker, would come to the house every day. Benedicto was the one who spoke to him a lot, but when Benedicto left, Elfredo would come and sit down and start talking. He was about nineteen, a country boy from Puerto Rico. He kept coming to the house for about a month without saying a word about love. I was attracted but I didn't say anything.

Then one night he came, drunk probably, because he told me he liked me. He spoke very respectfully and I said I would think it over. Three days later he came and asked me for an answer. I said yes.

See, I loved him at first but then I didn't, not a bit. He was a mere boy and didn't know how to be intimate with women. He was cold, nervous, scared, and I . . . well, I didn't much like it. I told him so.

The first time we were together I went to his room and we talked and drank. Then I took off my clothes, he took off his clothes and we lay on the bed. He wanted to kiss me and I told him I didn't like to be kissed on the lips. Then he wanted to suck my tits and I told him not to. He asked me why and I said no. Well, then when we started to get intimate, I noticed he didn't move or anything, I was the one who had to move. I had to do all the work. I said to him, "Oh no, I don't like this. You don't know how to move. You don't do the things a man does when he is with a woman."

"I don't know how," he tells me.

"Why do you take a woman then? You're nothing but a kid. You don't know anything yet." He had told me that he'd had women, but I said, "I don't think you've seen even one pubic hair in your whole life." Ha, ha, it made him mad, my saying that.

At first I didn't charge him anything, but later on I asked him for money and he gave it to me. I stayed away from him for two weeks, then I went back. After that he bought me a little *jacket*. I sent it to Felícita. He bought me stockings too, and other things. Then two weeks later I went back again. I was kind of angry that second time because he had told *doña* Ana Delia that I was too old for him, that compared to him I was an old woman. *Doña* Ana Delia told me and I said to her, "Is that right? Well, don't worry, I'll get even with him. He'll be sorry he ever said that."

So we went to the room and I took off my clothes and we lay down. He began to kiss me and I let him and I began to kiss him too and to caress and excite him until the man went wild. Then I got up and left without saying a word. I stayed at home after that and the man kept hanging around. He said he would take off with me and promised to take my children too and, well, he promised a thousand things. But I'm no dope. I didn't love him. He was too young for me and bound to be disillusioned sooner or later.

Then one day I saw him with a woman. I don't know who she was. When he realized I saw him, he made tracks to his aunt's house. I followed him and slapped him twice. He claimed he wasn't talking with her at all, so I slapped his face again. His eyes filled with tears but he didn't do anything. His brother snapped, "You don't have to go hit him," and I answered, "I'll hit you too if you try to butt in." Then I went home. Benedicto was there and he asked me, "What's the matter with you?"

"Nothing," I said.

What I felt for Elfredo was only an infatuation and that's something that is soon undone. Benedicto doesn't give me the affection I crave. He is so crude, he doesn't know how to win over a woman, see? He doesn't care what happens to me, how I feel. All he cares for is drinking and keeping himself alive. As he doesn't give me what I need, I have to look for it somewhere else, no matter what happens to me.

I like a man who spoils me and makes a lot of fuss over me, no? Not one who treats me brutally. I think a man who doesn't know how to treat a woman is a savage, that's what he is. I wanted love from Elfredo but he didn't know how.

Some time after meeting Elfredo, I met the Colombian. He reminds me of Tavio, especially the eyes. He's very affectionate with me, treats me like the departed one did. They are so alike I'm amazed. He's a seaman and a friend of Rosalía's. I went to her house and she introduced me. After that, he spoke to me and everything. Then we went and stayed at a hotel in New York. He really is a man, that one. Oh, there's something about him that would turn the head of any woman. He knows how to treat a woman with courtesy. Well, I fell in love with him.

He asked me to live with him. He wanted to know if I had a husband and I told him I did not. He said, "Who pays the rent on your apartment, then?"

"I pay it. Don't ask any more questions, I don't like prying." Then he made two more trips and came here. He gave me money and sent me things. This radio was a gift from him, this dress, too, and this fur blanket. In his letters, he claimed to be single, but a friend of his told me that he had a wife and three children, and his wife was expecting. When I heard that I said to myself, "Liar!" When he comes back, I'll tell him, "Sorry, but I'm through. I don't want to have anything to do with you again." I don't like men who lie to me.

The only love I trust is the love between a mother and her children. Men come and go; only a child's love is sure, especially when he's small. But children grow up and marry and leave you, so the only real love is mother love, which lasts forever. When you bear a child you have to be very close to God and the saints, because you risk your life. Nobody knows whether you'll live or die. You resign yourself to whatever may come. I love my children because they are the children of my soul, of my heart, and because I carried them for nine months and suffered to bear them.

The greatest deed I ever did in my life, the only good thing I have done, was to adopt my daughter Catín. I've done so many bad things, I don't know which is the worst, but I'm proud of what I've done for her. She got no love from her father or her mother, she's never known any love but mine and I love her as if she were my own.

My mother never felt any love for me and I never had that feeling of love for Fernanda that people have for their mothers. I won't ever make my children suffer as my *mamá* made me suffer so they'll never be tempted to do anything bad. I never beat my children the way she did. When I beat them I do it in the normal way, with a strap or whatever is handy, but I never cut them or break their heads.

I have no intention of bringing up my daughters as she brought me up. If I did we'd have a bunch of whores in the family, the grandmother, the aunts, the granddaughters. If my girls turn out to be the way I am, the way their grandmother was, what will happen? They will go on having kids and bringing them up the same way.

There are so many things I was never taught. I was never given an education and that is something I want to give my daughters. And I want to see that they go to school and do their work. Not the way it was with me. If I played hooky, nobody cared. When they're a little older I'll watch over them to make sure that there won't be any getting together with tramps. That's another thing nobody ever did for me.

I want my girls to be well behaved. When I see them playing with boys, I hit them. If I hear them say dirty words, I hit them. I won't have them answer back to a grownup either. I tell them, "If a lady calls you 'bitch,' don't you answer 'bitch.' Come and tell me and I will go to her, woman to woman, and fix her up." I'll smash her face if I have to, or anybody else's for that matter, but children should respect older people. Never laugh at the aged, it is bad to make fun of the helpless. When Catín sees a crippled person she always laughs. I tell her, "Don't laugh. You're a cripple yourself." I don't like to see them do improper things or make dirty jokes or anything like that. I want to bring them up to take the straight path.

Girls should also be taught to wash dishes, cook, wash and iron clothes. And I won't stand for that business of little girls acting like young ladies, painting their faces and manicuring their nails. They can use make-up when they reach the proper age. On *weekends* I'll let them go to the movies but not to dances. And my girls won't wear close-fitting dresses or plunging necklines. That's how girls get snatched away and if any girl of mine sets her fancy on a fourteen-dollar dress that I can't afford, I won't buy it. Let her wear what she has. Because if a girl has new clothes all the time, when she grows up she may even become a whore in order to get money for new dresses. My girls must wear what they have and eat what I am able to set before them. If God helps me and my luck improves, *O.K.* But as long as we're poor, we'll live like poor people.

I wouldn't like to see my daughters be what I was. I wouldn't want my son to become a pimp, either. No, I don't want him to live off women. I wouldn't like it a bit. And as long as I can prevent it, I will. I tell my daughters, "When you have a career and are somebody, get yourselves a good man, not a tramp who wants to live off you. Often a man is not what he seems. He may come to you, mild as a lamb, yet be poisonous as a snake whose poison is hidden in the tip of its tail."

Look, I give the impression of being tough, but really, I'm not. I have my feelings and I can suffer for another person. I pity the weak, the poor. I would like to help the needy. I once took a woman named Luisa Villanueva and her little girl into my house because they had no place to live. I sheltered her, she ate with me, she wore my clothes and shoes. But she paid me back with evil. After she left she began to gossip and criticize. When I see a homeless child in the street, I wish I had a house or something, some way of helping him. But you know, I think if I did have it, maybe I wouldn't help him after all. I've noticed that when people get rich, they forget.

Look at me. Right now I'm thinking, thinking about myself, about how I'm twenty-five and already a sick woman. By the time I'm thirty years old, I won't be good for anything. I've lost my teeth, I already have high blood pressure, my nerves are shot, any little thing startles me. Last night while I was mopping the floor, I blacked out and had to sit down. And I tire easily. After I walk awhile, my back and my chest hurt. I cough a lot and sometimes I bring up blood. But I don't even bother to go to the hospital any more. I don't like to go to the public hospital, and in the private ones you have to pay for everything. There's even a charge for pissing. If they take out a few drops of blood, you have to pay them although it's your own blood. *Ay*, no. I'll stay home. I have borne many troubles and I can bear many more.

I wrote to my *mamá* but she didn't answer. I wrote to Arturo and a letter from him arrived a few days later. As always, he offered to help me.

Dear Soledad,

This is in answer to your amiable little letter. My heart always over-flows with happiness when I get news of you and of my darling daughters. Soledad, according to the facts you set down in your letter, your health is not good and you have problems regarding the children. You know that the government or the Red Cross can bring you and the girls here and that you all have a sacred home in my humble dwelling. I am sure that together we can make everything come out all right. I hope you keep your head and do things right so that everything can be arranged and, God willing, you may all be able to come here where you can have the nourishing food you need. That way, you will soon be well again. With you here I will find a way to provide for you and our blessed children. Remember, Sole-dad, one doesn't have to get panicky about being ill. Sickness comes from God and God takes it away in due time. I hope you don't lose your courage. My little house is ready and waiting for your arrival. Every night, before going to sleep, I pray for you, as I have done ever since our home was broken up. I have never filled your place because I have not stopped hoping for your return. It doesn't matter how or why you come back, as long as you come, because together we should care for the children who are our treasure and whom we are so proud to have raised. They are what really matters to us. Don't worry. Do as I tell you and let me know what happens. Hug and kiss my lovely little daughters for me. Your darling Quique sends you one sweet hug.

Always your

Arturo

He offered me a home but it is not the home I want. I will never go back to Arturo again. If I were alone, I would go to far-off places, I would go all over the world, far, far away where I wouldn't have relatives or know any-body. When a rich person gets sick they usually send him on a trip, isn't that so? That is what I'd like to do but I have no money so I'll stay right here in the Americas with my daughters. And if I get sick, they'll put me in an ambulance and lock me up in a hospital. If I die, what the hell, let them bury me.

You can't get away from death. I might fall dead here and now. I might stand up, bump against something, and *pam!* I'm dead. Death perches behind your ear, as the saying goes. I'm not afraid to die, no, but they do say that what you have done on earth you have to pay for on earth. If God intends for me to die, I pray that He grant me a quick death.

When I die, I don't want any display of luxury at my funeral, a thousand-dollar coffin, a hundred dollars' worth of wreaths. I want luxury now while I'm still alive. If anyone means to spend money for my funeral, I'd rather have that money now because I need it for my daughters. After I'm dead, the hell with it, let them dump me in a hole in the ground. I won't feel it.

I want to be buried in Puerto Rico because that's my country. Even if I do live in New York, I never forget my country. I wouldn't change it for the world. That's where I was born and that's where I want to be buried. I don't want to die here because if no one claims the body, it's sent—know where?— to the Women's Jail. To a hospital they have there, where they make experiments. They cut you up, they break your arms and legs and then they bury you.

I want my body given to the School of Tropical Medicine in Puerto Rico, but not to anybody here. Let them take their own pricks and make experiments with them. If somebody's going to use my body, let it be Puerto Rican doctors in Puerto Rico. At least they are *hispanos*. But not here. Shit! I don't care what happens here. I'm only interested in what goes on in my own country, in what happens to Puerto Ricans who belong to my race. Nobody else matters to me.

PART III

FELÍCITA

A Day with Felicita
in San Juan*

FELÍCITA'S apartment was west of Fernanda's and slightly higher on the steep embankment in a tangle of green-roofed houses. This section was reached by a narrow, winding alley which began at the corner of *doña* Yolanda's bar on the blue-tinged cobblestone plaza. The houses along the alley were crowded close to each other, but occasionally, on the seaward side, there was a break through which one could see the blue ocean below.

The alleyway was only about two hundred yards long, but it was La Esmeralda in miniature. Longshoremen, bartenders, small tradesmen, prostitutes and women on relief lived there. Halfway between the bar and Felícita's house, the alley abruptly widened into a small paved area, where a dripping public water faucet was attached to an old brick wall covered with moss, and lines of laundry hung across the open space.

Some friends and relatives of the Ríos family also lived along the alley. Just west of the little open area stood the home of Gerardo, one of Felícita's lovers, who lived there with his wife and their four children. Gerardo often visited Felícita when he and his wife were quarreling. He had given Felícita a

* This day was observed in February, 1964, before Gabriel went to New York.

[271]

number of expensive gifts, including a wrist watch and a new stove. Fernanda's ex-husband, Héctor, lived next door to Gerardo. Both men worked on the docks.

Across the street was the house of *doña* Minerva, the aunt of Cruz Ríos' ex-husband. She was a short, stout Negro woman who smoked cigars and was highly regarded in the neighborhood for her kindness and her knowledge of home remedies. Another friend of the Ríos family, *doña* Lucelia, lived in the bottom half of this house.

To the west of *doña* Minerva's house, the alley detoured around a low yellow shack set on a whitewashed concrete base. Alejandro, Cruz's former husband in free union, lived there with his wife Gladys. Arturo, Soledad's former husband, rented a one-room house next door.

At the southern end of the detour was Papo's bar. It rested against the side of the embankment and was reached by a steep flight of steps. Papo had bought the bar and several houses with the compensation money he had received for an accident on the docks. His wife, Genoveva, did most of the work while he spent the profits in gambling and cockfights. Genoveva had been a prostitute in her youth; to increase the bar's business she had become a procuress, furnishing women for the men who came to the bar and renting them her own room. She also sold *bolita* tickets and was a moneylender. Miné, a friend of Felícita's, lived next door to the bar. Miné and her husband, Herminio, fought constantly; often Herminio beat her up in front of the neighbors.

Felícita's apartment was just off the alley in a large wooden building set on a concrete base which was patchy with moss and sea plants. Because of the steep incline, the south side of the building rested on the ground, while the north side, where Felícita had her rooms, was fifteen feet above another narrow alley. The building had once been painted green but now the paint was faded. The peaked roof was covered with the ubiquitous green tar paper given to the community by the mayoress.

There were three apartments in the building. Felícita and her neighbors, Florida and Wilfredo, lived on one level, sharing a common porch and toilet; the other tenant lived in relative privacy below, in an apartment which opened onto a lower alleyway. In La Esmeralda, a ground-floor or basement apartment like this one is known as "The Mine."

When Rosa arrived at Felícita's house at about seven-thirty in the morning, the neighbors, Florida and Wilfredo and their two children, already had their door open and were drinking their morning coffee. Felícita was still asleep but her front door, which opened in the middle like shutters, was standing ajar as it usually was because her children were constantly running in and out. The narrow, covered porch with its high cement balustrade provided some privacy even when the door was wide open.

Felícita's front room, about nine square feet, was bright and clean. New checkered linoleum covered the floor and the walls had been freshly painted blue with a pink trim. Felícita had painted them herself. Blue flowered curtains hung at the little window and the door to the bedroom. Four new wicker chairs and a small cot furnished the room. Felícita had bought the furniture and the linoleum on credit for a total of forty-four dollars.

Rosa pushed back the curtain and looked into Felícita's bedroom. Felícita was lying on her back, sleeping, with her knees drawn up and one hand resting on her forehead. A thin white coverlet revealed the contours of her slender body; her small breasts hardly seemed those of a grown woman with five children. The large, new-looking double bed with its brown metal headboard almost completely filled the room. The only other furniture in it was a wooden crate which served as a dressing table, and a worn, dirty child's mattress which lay beside the bed on the unpainted floor. Clothes, covered with a large towel and a sheet of plastic, hung on a pole across one corner; shoes were arranged on another pole in the opposite corner. Cardboard boxes, children's shoes and paper bags filled with clothing were lying about. The walls of the bedroom, which had not been painted, were quite dingy. The dirty white ceiling was thick with cobwebs and the room was full of flies. There was no window but an open doorway led to an outside balcony.

Rosa tiptoed through the room and went out onto the balcony. This balcony, which was roofed, served as the kitchen and as the sleeping place for Felícita's eldest children, her seven-year-old twins, Gabi and Angelito. On the left end, as one entered, a makeshift wall of plywood gave some protection to a two-burner kerosene stove which stood on a table against it. At the opposite end another table, covered with red-flowered plastic, held a pan full of dirty dishes. From a waist-high railing, odd pieces of beaverboard and plywood had been tacked to form another flimsy wall. The balcony was as much open as covered, however, and whenever it rained, the floor became drenched.

Rosa leaned against the railing, enjoying the fresh ocean breeze. In the alley below, a woman was gathering up a pile of trash. Evidently mistaking Rosa for someone from the Department of Public Welfare, the woman screamed up at her, "Why didn't you come before when the whole alley was covered? Lots of people come here to talk but they never do anything. They should come to clean out all the trash. Two days ago my daughter and I swept here and today it's filthy again."

"I'm not from Welfare, but you're right," Rosa called down to her. "They ought to come and clean the streets."

"Nobody around here cares how filthy it gets. Nobody ever cleans but me," the woman replied.

Rosa went back to the living room to wait for Felícita to wake up. She pulled a chair closer to the door to escape the overpowering odor of urine from the children's cot. This did not help much because of the foul-smelling toilet at Felícita's end of the porch. Neither Felícita nor Florida bothered much about keeping it clean. Because of leaky plumbing, the floor was usually covered with two inches of water and the toilet flushed automatically every few minutes. A pile of sodden newspapers and cardboard boxes stood just outside the toilet door.

Felícita had been living for over a year in this apartment, paying twelve dollars a month rent. On the whole she was satisfied with it, even though it had no electricity and no running water except for an erratic faucet in the toilet which often gave no water at all. When that happened, she or her children had to carry water from the public tap.

Rosa heard a baby crying and a neighbor, *doña* Bertha, came in carrying Felícita's youngest child, Evita. The baby was wearing a green dress, with nothing on underneath. The woman handed the child to Rosa and went out. Evita's sobs disturbed Felícita enough so that she turned over on her side and the coverlet fell off. She was naked except for a pair of transparent nylon panties.

Felícita's other four children came in. A moment or two later Felícita sat up abruptly, jumped out of bed and rushed out of the room toward the toilet. When she saw Rosa she stopped short, exclaiming, *"Ay, bendito!* Angelito, get me my clothes. Hurry up now."

Angelito handed her some clothes and Felícita went into the toilet. She came out wearing a shabby dress of coffee-colored lace, her hair uncombed. Despite her disheveled appearance, she seemed self-assured and sophisticated. She was a pretty, slim mulatto girl of twenty-three with a small and graceful body. Her dark hair was touched with red highlights; two gold-capped teeth showed in the front of her mouth.

Felícita sat down on the cot and took Evita on her lap. The other four children crowded around her. They were good-looking children, although their faces and hands and clothing were dirty. Gabi was wearing only black trousers, and Angelito only blue jeans. Tany, a pretty, dark child with a full, round face and frizzy hair, had on a pink-checked dress that fitted her well. Three-year-old Mundo was entirely naked. All the children were barefoot.

"Ay, bendito, I'm so tired," Felícita complained. "These savages never let me sleep."

After a few moments she set the baby on the floor and began to make up the cot.

"That's a pretty bedspread," Rosa said.

"Ah," Felícita answered, "I bought that bedspread three years ago from a *comadre* of mine when I was living with Edmundo. She sold it to me for eight dollars. Only three months ago I had six bedspreads, all paid for, but now I have only two because of what these children do to my things."

"Mami," Mundo said, "give me some bread, *mami."*

Felícita looked at him angrily but said nothing.

"Mami, give me a penny," Angelito begged.

Without answering, Felícita picked up a photograph to show Rosa. It was of Felícita dancing with a big American Marine at the bar where she worked. In the picture she was wearing an attractive dress and her hair was curled and combed. "I bought this dress at Franklin's in San Juan," she said. "I get the children's things there too, because it's the best place to buy."

Angelito pulled at her skirt. *"Mami, mami,* a penny."

"What is it, child? Leave me alone and don't bother me. Please!"

Evita began crying again. Felícita picked her up and kissed her. "I think this one has fever," she said. "Tany, run to *doña* Minerva's house and ask her to come over and give Evita a massage to get rid of her cramps. Bless her, my poor little girl. I don't like to give my children physics." Tany went out with Gabi.

"Angelito, go and tell Cruz, if she has milk of magnesia to send it over. But first find me the baby's bottle and rinse it out good." Seeing "Corporal" Pepito in the alley, she called to him, "Go to the store for me, will you, Pepito? I'll write down what I want." "Corporal" Pepito did odd jobs and ran errands for a living in this part of La Esmeralda. She ordered a large can of milk, ten cents' worth of cheese, the same of crackers, a chocolate bar, a box of Fab, and Clorox.

Felícita went into her bedroom, leaving Evita, who was now crying desperately. Taking the baby in her arms, Rosa went and stood by the bedroom door. Felícita pushed the children's reeking mattress under the bed and kicked their shoes into a corner. She made the bed, covering it with a red spread which had been given to her by Cayetano, an old man who lived near by. Picking up a broom, she started to sweep the floor. In a moment she let the broom fall and went to the crate dressing table to arrange the cloth that hung down over it. She worked until the folds were perfectly even. She transferred a jar of cold cream and a can of hair spray to a little shelf nailed above her bed. Here she kept some of her cosmetics and anything else she wanted out of the children's reach—the medicines she received free from the public dispensary, brilliantine, a jar of Noxzema, a bottle of Massengill douche powder, and a bottle of Lydia E. Pinkham's Vegetable Compound which she took every day to "keep my womb clean."

Also on the shelf were a coin purse, a bunch of letters, a notebook, a pair of stockings, a box of Tampax, a pencil, a needle and thread, a leather jewelry box full of costume jewelry, and a bottle of perfume.

The perfume had been blended especially for Felícita by a woman on San José Street to bring her luck in attracting men. Felícita believed it worked because, as she told Rosa, "One night I didn't have a single peso and I put on a little bit of this perfume and suddenly I earned fifteen dollars. And I paid only five dollars for this bottle!"

Felícita picked up the broom again and swept the floor, not bothering to move a pile of dirty clothes that lay beside the dressing table. Before she had finished, "Corporal" Pepito came back with the things he had bought, and Tany and Gabi returned to say that *doña* Minerva couldn't come that day because they were tiling her floor. She would come tomorrow. Felícita went to the little balcony kitchen to heat some milk for the baby. "Gabi, the matches," she said.

"I don't know," Gabi answered.

"And the coffee pot. Where is it?"

"The coffee pot? Let's see, Tany had it."

Rosa gave Felícita a match and she lit the kerosene stove. Immediately there was a strong smell of kerosene. She gave the warmed milk to the baby who seized the bottle and sucked it avidly. She had obviously been crying from hunger. Mundo climbed on the cot, snatched the bottle from Evita, and drank greedily until his mother forced him to give it back to the baby. "He's hungry, too," Felícita said, smiling.

"*Mami,* look at that penny," Gabi said. "I was the one who found it and Mundo took it."

"No, no. It's mine. *I* found it."

"Oh, my God!" Felícita said. "Look for another penny. The floor's full of them. Don't cry, Gabi. Crying for money! A grown man like you?"

Gabi, still crying, said, "And since when don't grown men like money?"

"But grown men work to earn it."

"But it's mine. I found it."

"It's not. It's mine," Mundo said, raising his arms in a threatening gesture. Although he was younger than Gabi, he seemed unafraid of his elder brother.

Gabi pointed to his brother's penis. "*That's* yours, all right. That's what's yours, see?"

"I'll punch you in the face."

Felícita laughed and handed a quarter to Gabi. "Go buy another can of milk and you can have the penny that's left over."

"Oh God, I'm all tired out from doing so many things," Gabi said.

"You haven't done a thing, how can you be tired? Go on, hurry!"

Felícita sat down and spilled the contents of an old purse onto the cot. She had three purses, a new one of red plastic, another, quite new, of plastic with a brightly colored design, and this old black one of cloth with pink and white flowers. Felícita stored cosmetics and other things in her purses. She used cosmetics sparingly but always bought what she needed. On the bed now were three lipsticks, a compact, a small box of rouge, an eyebrow pencil, two combs, a hairbrush, a bottle of nail polish, a nail file, Tangee Miracle Makeup, candy wrappers, an old letter, chewing gum, a coin purse, a small snapshot of a Hawaiian boy, three pairs of earrings, and a large bottle of Ambush cologne, by Dana.

Gabi came back from the store and threw the can of milk on a chair.

"Now you can have the penny. Do you want *thith* one, or *thith* one?" Felícita said teasingly, imitating his lisp.

The boy stamped his foot and yelled, "I don't talk like that, *mami.*" He ran out of the house in a rage, but in a minute he was back again. He picked up the snapshot of the Hawaiian. *"Mami,* who is that?" he asked.

"That's the man who was here last night, don't you remember?"

"Ugh," Gabi said in disgust. "He's the one who pushed me off the bed onto the floor. And he's from the *Navy* like the others. They give me a pain in the ass." Gabi lay down on the cot but sprang up at once, "Oof! This stinks like the devil." Tany laughed and he hit her on the head.

"You know why *you* don't complain of the stink?" Felícita said to Tany. "Because you're a pig, that's why."

Felícita went out to the toilet to wash her face and arms. The little room was low, with a roof of wood and walls of damp cement. The toilet had no seat. In one corner lay some wet, crumpled-up newspapers; in another corner stood a broom which Felícita had recently bought for fifty cents. Near the door a dripping faucet, the only source of water for the tenants, stuck out from the cement wall. Cobwebs hung from the ceiling, and the door had no lock.

When Felícita came back into the living room, she showed Rosa a cheap gold-colored ring and bracelet. The ring had a large sparkling stone in it. "Say, Rosa," she said, "is this a diamond?"

"No," Rosa said, "that's a fake. Did anyone tell you it was a real diamond?"

"Well, it's just . . . well, this *sailor* I danced with last night said he'd paid a hundred and fifty dollars for it. I lent him my ring, and he gave me this as guarantee that he would return it."

"It's too bad. I'm afraid he cheated you."

"But I have his address, and if he doesn't give me back my ring, I'll give it to the police. They'll find him right away, eh?" Felícita picked the dirt from under the fingernails of one hand with a nail of the other. "You know, I work in La Torre now, from five in the afternoon until three in the morning. Imagine, I only earn thirty dollars a week and no tips! The customers are mostly Americans, and they don't tip. *Ave Maria,* and now that thief got my ring. Tany, look at that dress, eh, child? Look how dirty it is." Tany hung her head.

Mundo and Evita had been playing in a large cardboard box set on the cot, pretending it was a car. Evita leaned out of the box farther and farther until she fell headfirst with a thud on the floor. Felícita lifted her up and set her back on the bed without attempting to soothe her, even though the child was crying. Felícita picked up a newspaper lying on the floor and began to read TV listings to Gabi. "Look at this program, and this one," she said. "Oh, this one should be good!" Gabi was happy at being singled out for this kind of attention and began to sing, "Look here, dark girl, don't go to work because now we're going to fuck—"

"*Mami,* milk," Mundo said.

"Stop pestering me, child. All I can think of now is my ring. If that man doesn't show up today, I'll report him. With that photograph, they'll find him fast." Felícita finally went to the balcony kitchen to prepare chocolate milk and crackers for the children's breakfast.

"This stove," she said to Rosa, "used to belong to Gerardo, a man who was interested in me. I had already bought a large stove for nine-fifty cash, but it was too big for here so I gave it to Cruz. Then I asked Gerardo for one and he gave me this one, new, as a present because he liked me and I cooked for him. And Cruz gave me the table to put the stove on."

Beside the stove were several glasses and one of Cruz's plates, for Cruz frequently sent cooked food to Felícita. A small narrow shelf above the stove served as storage space for the things Felícita managed to stock, a bottle of Ovaltine, a can of Carnation evaporated milk, an onion, a bottle of malt beer, an empty grape juice bottle, a small box of Ivory soap, a bottle of rubbing alcohol, an almost empty bottle of rum, the smallest size box of Ace soap flakes, a bottle of Clorox, and a metal-framed mirror. Like Cruz, Felícita made small purchases of food daily, but, unlike her sister Cruz, she received no supplies from the Public Welfare. She spent about ninety dollars a month on food, and yet her children did not regularly eat nourishing meals. She herself was given supper free at the bar where she worked.

Near the stove, hanging on nails, were a cloth coffee strainer, two large frying pans (one of them given to her by her stepfather, Héctor), a large saucepan, and two round metal casseroles. Felícita's dishes consisted of eight plates, two plastic bowls and one cup; she had six tablespoons and two forks. Her only knife had disappeared and now she borrowed one from a neighbor. On the table were a bottle of cod-liver oil and a can of Ajax cleanser.

Felícita kept some prized kitchen equipment on a shelf underneath the stove. These were a set of aluminum cooking pots which she had bought when she lived in New Jersey with Edmundo. "It cost me fifty-four dollars," she said, "but at that time there were a lot of pieces in the set. Now these children have thrown most of them off the balcony. I bought the set from a door-to-door salesman and Edmundo and I both helped with the payments because I was earning money then."

Felícita's children often broke dishes and glasses or threw them from the balcony into the alley below. "I had to buy new ones about four times a year so now I buy plastic ones. At least they can't break those." Felícita indicated a long thick candle which lay on the edge of the stove. "That's Saint Martha's candle that I light every day. I paid seventy-five cents for it and it burns for a week. I light it to free me from evil."

Angelito came in from ouside. *"Mami,"* he said, *"doña* Bertha says to send her the dollar to play the numbers."

"Tell her I don't even have enough money to buy food," Felícita said.

"No money for breakfast or for shit," Angelito said.

Felícita laughed and went to look through her lottery slips. "Look, Gabi, there's a number missing. Ah, no, here it is. Give them all back to *doña* Bertha and tell her not to bother me any more." The boy went out with the slips, but in a moment *doña* Bertha, the agent for the numbers game, came in herself. "Look, child," she said, "take these because they might be the ones that will hit. You can pay me the dollar later." Felícita took back the slips.

Tany had been eating crackers and Evita stretched out her hand for one. "Don't be mean, Tany," Felícita said. "Give her a bite, *Ave María!* just one little bite." Tany answered, *"Mami,* I want my breakfast."

"There's nothing but chocolate, hear?"

"All right, give me chocolate."

Felícita gave the little girl some chocolate milk in a tin can and Tany began to gulp it down as fast as she could. Mundo begged for some, but Felícita turned on him angrily. "You all have to pull in your belts, see? But especially you, Mundito, because your father doesn't give me any money." She was referring to Edmundo Capó, her third husband.

Suddenly Evita began to scream. She lay on the floor kicking and screaming. Felícita tried to quiet her, saying, "There, there, Evita. Don't cry, Evita," but the baby screamed as though in a fury.

"Oh, my God!" Felícita burst out. "I wish it was five o'clock so I could go to work and get away from this house! Tany, go to Bonilla's and see if they'll let me charge some food for lunch. Oh God! God! I feel like running out and shooting somebody." She gave some chocolate milk to Evita, and the baby stopped crying.

"You know," Felícita said to Rosa, "Ángel, my first husband, says he's going to take the twins off my hands, and Edmundo is going to take Mundito and Evita. Tany will stay with me because her father won't recognize her as his. Ah, then I'll be happy. You know, I've been operated on and can't have any more children. It's Tany I feel the most toward because her father denies her. *Ave María!* If I should hit at numbers today! Those hundred dollars would solve a lot of problems."

Felícita watched Gabi dawdle over his chocolate. "Come on and get finished so Angelito can use the cup. Then go throw the papers from the toilet out on the beach."

"I won't do it. They stink. Besides, I don't shit here."

Gabi wasn't drinking fast enough to suit Felícita and she struck him on the mouth. Blood trickled from his lip and the boy began to cry.

"I don't care," Felícita said to Rosa. "This Gabi is the worst boy in La Esmeralda. Stop screwing around, boy, or I'll get a knife and put it through you. Now go ask Héctor to lend me his washtub. Go on, run, and I'll give you a penny."

"The tub has shit in it."

"That doesn't matter, I'll rinse it out."

Gabi was soon back to say that Héctor didn't have a washtub. "Then go tell Cruz to lend me a washtub so I can soak the clothes in Clorox."

Pucha, one of Felícita's neighbors, came in. She wore a flowered bathrobe, and her bare feet were swollen. She was a drunkard who often lay sprawled in the alleys or doorways. She sometimes asked Felícita for a nickel for a drink, and Felícita would give her the money when she could, to be rid of her. Pucha claimed to be able to foresee the future, and Felícita could not quite disbelieve her. Now Felícita said, "Pucha, what you told me yesterday came out like you said. It happened to me."

"You see? And you didn't believe me."

"I believe you."

"I have something else to tell you."

"Come on, tell me right now. It makes me nervous when somebody says he's going to tell me something and then doesn't."

"I don't like to in front of the children."

Felícia shooed the children out of the room. When they were gone Pucha said, "Here's the thing. There's a fat colored woman who's going to do something bad to you tomorrow. This woman says she's going to cut your face. And you're going to have an argument with a man. He's coming here tonight. You shouldn't go out. He's after you."

"And what do I have to do so as not to let that happen?"

"I'll tell you on Friday. You'll have to say the Prayer of the Just Judge."

"So my face is going to be cut right here in my house?"

"Yes, right here."

"Then I'm going to Loíza Aldea tomorrow." Loíza Aldea was a Negro town famous for its spiritists. "Take care of the children for me, will you, when I go there? *Doña* Hegla, Cuco's *mamá,* that's the old bat who's coming here to fight me."

"I don't know, but it's a dark-complexioned lady. And I'll be doing some things in your favor tomorrow. Now, let's have a nickel so I can get myself a drink."

"Nothing doing. I haven't got a nickel." But Felícita handed a nickel to Pucha, saying, "Wash these plates for me, Pucha, will you?"

"I will later. Now I'm leaving. I'm dying for a shot."

Felícita began sweeping again, under the bed and in the corners. Along with trash she swept up papers, rags, a pair of sneakers, socks and a notebook. She picked up the useful objects and swept the rest onto a piece of paper which she rolled up and wrapped in another piece of paper. This bundle she simply tossed out of the window into the alleyway below. When Rosa asked her about it, she said she had always done this, and no one had yet complained about being hit.

Felícita said, "You know? The other day we pulled a tapeworm out of Angelito. It looked like a tiny little thing, so I took a piece of paper and started to pull it out. I pulled and pulled, and my goodness, it was as long as my arm and it was pregnant."

Shaking a small rug over the balcony railing, Felícita began to sing a popular song. She broke off to ask Rosa for a match. Then she set a short white candle on a saucer and lit it.

"Why did you light the candle?" Rosa asked.

"It's for Saint Expedito, the one who spends his time in corners. He is one of the bad ones, see? On Mondays you blow smoke into every corner of the house. Then you put out a glass of water or a shot of rum. This saint comes and drinks it and that gives you good luck."

She began singing softly, "I wish I were a tiny fish, a tiny swimming fish." Suddenly she lay down on the cot and stretched her arms over her head, "Oh, dear God! Help me to solve my problems."

Tany had come back to say that Bonilla wanted a list of the things Felícita needed. Felícita sat up to write the list. Tany hit Evita's stomach to make her laugh. Angelito came in saying he wanted his breakfast.

"You want some chocolate?"

"No, I don't want any chocolate."

"What, then? A beefsteak with fried plantains?"

"No, because you don't have any steak."

"Oh, I asked just in case. I was going to tell you to get a job in the dockyards if you want a steak. Hey, who's using my broom? Go see, and if it's Tany, sock her. No, wait, I'll go." Felícita jumped up and went out to the porch. "Look," she said, "you don't buy the brooms around here! *Maricona!* Hand it over!" Felícita struck Tany and the child burst out crying. Felícita came back into the front room to finish the list. Gabi had come in while she was gone. She noticed a piece of adhesive tape on his knee and said, "Listen, who put that tape on you?"

"I went to the dispensary. *Mami,* give me a penny."

Felícita looked fixedly at Gabi. For some time she looked straight at him, with a harsh, disdainful expression on her face. Gabi looked back at her, then at Rosa, then again at his mother. Finally his glance wavered and he hung his head and left the room. Almost immediately there was the sound of a blow outside, and Tany cried out, "You sissy! You queer!" Gabi had hit her.

Evita climbed into her mother's lap and tried to bite Felícita's breasts. Felícita pretended to be asleep, then opened her eyes in mock surprise and laughed. Mundo came in and he, too, climbed into his mother's lap. He was holding a piece of cardboard and a magazine illustration. "Where did you get that junk? Throw it away, and hurry, hurry!" Mundo didn't move until Felícita stood up. Then he ran out the door.

Felícita lay face down on the cot. The long zipper of her dress was open and her back was bare to the waist. She paid no attention to the flies that settled on her legs. Gabi came in again and Felícita sat up to hand him the grocery list. "Hurry and go to Bonilla's with this, queer."

Gabi flushed with anger. "Ah, don't call me such names!" he said and threw himself down on the floor and began to cry.

"Hey, hurry up. I still have to sleep three more hours. You aren't going to school today."

The boy said between sobs, "Yes, I am, I am so going."

"No. You haven't got any shirts ready. Well, all right. You can tell your teacher I haven't got electricity and can't have your clothes ironed all the time."

Gabi was ambivalent about school. At times he insisted on going and said that someday he would be a doctor. Other times he flatly refused to go. On the days when he and his twin, Angelito, did go to school they were dressed alike, usually in short navy-blue pants, white shirts, socks and sneakers. They seldom wore undershirts or undershorts. Perhaps because they were of school age, the twins were the best dressed of Felícita's children; she had spent seventy-five dollars on their clothes over the past nine months. They each had four sports shirts and four white shirts, eight T-shirts, seven pairs of pants, a pair of Levis, one pair each of shoes and sneakers, four undershorts and six pairs of socks. Only three items of clothing had been gifts. Fernanda had bought each of them a pair of pants and a sweater when they lived with her over a year before, and the Sisters of Charity had given them a shirt apiece.

Felícita sat down in a rocker, took Evita on her lap and began to sing,

> "The thin woman moves well, din, don, dan,
>   She swings her hips well—"

The other children clapped their hands in time to the rhythm and began to dance around. "Gabi, go on to the store. Hurry up!" Gabi went out angrily. Felícita sang,

> "The last time I slept with you,
>   I bit your balls and sucked your navel.

"Keep still, Evita, let's see if I can't catch the lice on that dome of yours." She began to pick lice from the child's hair.

Gabi came in again. In spite of the heat, he had put on an old, thick sweater. "Tourist, tourist, here comes the tourist," Felícita said mockingly.

"I'm not a tourist. I don't work in a ship. Why do you call me a tourist?"

Felícita continued to tease him. *"Ave María!* You'll catch pneumonia, it's snowing so hard."

Angelito tried to take off Gabi's sweater, and Gabi hit him. Angelito began to cry. "Oh my, listen to that foghorn!" Felícita said. Angelito cried harder and hit back at Gabi. Now the twins were fighting in earnest, punching hard enough to hurt each other, with Felícita an amused spectator. When Angelito punched Gabi so hard on the ribs that he collapsed to his knees, crying, she said, "When one of you gets killed, let me know. I'll get a shovel to scrape up the remains off the floor. Angelito, go get some kerosene." Angelito angrily refused.

"Ave María! He cries like a worn-out foghorn. Gabi, when are you going to win a fight, you sissy? Even Mundito can beat you. You don't know how to use your fists. Ah, you're the champion!"

Gabi was still on his knees, clinging to the edge of the cot, but he said in a rage, "Champion? Champion, fuck! This is the champion." He made a lewd gesture with two fingers.

Felícita said, "Oh Lord, listen to him, Mundito. Gabi says this is the champion," and she repeated the gesture Gabi had made. "Careful now, Gabi, Mundo is going to hit you."

"Come on, then," Gabi said to Mundo. "Come on, and I'll break your neck."

"Listen to that, Mundito," Felícita said. "He says he's going to break your neck." At that Mundo flung a notebook at Gabi, and Gabi jumped up and began to chase his brother.

Cruz came in lugging a washtub. "Why doesn't he leave him alone?" she said.

"Oh, those two fight all the time," Felícita answered.

"But I'll get even with you," Cruz said to Mundo. "Do you know what he did? He came to my house, belted Anita one, and ran away."

"Ave María! That boy is a devil," Felícita said, and both women laughed.

"Look," Cruz said, "when I woke up, those boys were already running around in the alley near my house. And you still fast asleep, lost to the world. You don't look after your children, Felícita."

In response, Felícita smilingly lifted up the skirt of her dress. Through her transparent panties, one could see the pubic hair. Her children all laughed.

Mundo went out to the kitchen balcony. Cruz followed him. "Mundito, leave that alone!" she said. "Look, Felícita, he's eating spoiled food." Rosa went to investigate and saw the dirty scraps of food, cooked many days ago, that the child was eating out of a pan. Felícita looked into the kitchen and made a gesture of indifference.

"I came to get my crinoline petticoat," Cruz said, picking it up from the bed. "And now I've got to go. It's past ten already."

Cruz went out, but in a moment she called, "Hey, Felícita, look at Evita! She's going ahead of me."

Felícita called back from the door, "Listen, take her awhile, will you?"

"Oh, sure, you want her to shit all over my floor."

"Take her, for God's sake, she's already shit. You should see the lump of shit she dropped. I'll send you over a slice so you can see." But Cruz went off without the child. Felícita turned back into the room. "Gabi, go get the kerosene."

"No," Gabi said, "I'm tired of doing all the work. It's always me. I'm fed up."

Felícita raised the broom threateningly, and Gabi grabbed the empty kerosene bottle and ran out. Felícita ran out on the porch after him. Safe down in the alley, Gabi stopped and shouted, "I'm not going. I'm not."

Felícita re-entered the room laughing. *"Ave María!* Why pay attention to them?" she said to Rosa. "They make me so furious I could die, but they stay cool as anything. It's better to ignore them." Mundo showed his hands, which were sticky with chewing gum. "No, I won't take that off," Felícita said. "I'm not the one who stuck it there. Pull it off yourself."

She began to sing again,

"Look, don't put in your finger,
Put in a broom instead . . ."

She went to the lighted candle on the kitchen table, picked up the tallow drippings and rolled them into a ball. "Here," she said to Mundo, "go sell it. Hurry up. Go sell it." The child took the tallow ball eagerly and went out. Felícita laughed at the trick she had played on him.

Felícita sat down in one of the rocking chairs, but a moment later she went down to the alleyway to talk to her friend Miné, who was washing clothes. "Miné, I'm going to wash too," she said. "If I finish early I'll help you."

"I hope you can because I have a terrible headache."

"The thing is, you haven't had coffee. Go buy some and I'll fix it for you."

Miné was soon back with the coffee. Felícita prepared some for her and served it in the only cup. As she drank Miné said, "I told that woman my husband is living with to make him stay at her house and not come to mine to eat or bring me his clothes to wash and iron. All that crap will stop, because I'm going to get myself another man. Just wait until I find one. Herminio doesn't want me to talk to anybody, and now I'm going to screw the bastard."

After Miné had left, Felícita sprinkled some Fab in Cruz's washtub and poured some Clorox into a pail that Miné had brought her. She planned to bleach some of the clothes. "I'm lazy, you know," she said. "If I had gotten up early I would have all these clothes washed by now. It's ten o'clock already." Ordinarily, Felícita washed clothes in a laundromat on Luna Street in San Juan and had them ironed by a neighbor or by Cruz. She went to the toilet for water and put clothes into both the tub and the pail to soak. Then she went back to the living room and threw herself face down on the cot.

Mundo was rocking back and forth as hard as he could in one of the rocking chairs. "Stop that! Mundo, I said stop!" The boy came over to his mother and pinched her eyelids. "My God! Don't do that to me! Mundo, stop it!" Felícita struck the boy hard and he ran out of the room. Evita went to her mother and kissed her on the lips. This made Felícita laugh. She leaned over the cot and put her face close to Evita's. "Do you have shit on your ass, eh?" She lifted up the back of the child's skirt. Evita imitated her, lifting up her own skirt in back, and Rosa saw flies on the baby's buttocks. Evita kissed Felícita on the neck.

Felícita hummed briefly, then said to Rosa, "Cuco said he's going to tell his mother that he's staying overnight at a friend's house so he can come here and sleep with me. The other night he told me he loved me very much and that I should look for a room. He said he'd help me out with the rent, but that I should find a place away from here. The thing is, his foster brother lives near by, you can see the house from here, and he doesn't want us to have relations. Cuco isn't even twenty yet, so the minute that queer of a brother of his sees us together he runs to tell their *mamá* and she comes around raising hell."

Felícita went out to the balcony to wash the clothes. A neighbor called to Felícita from the porch to say that Evita was playing with the Clorox. "Evita knows what she's doing," Felícita said. "You're no jerk, are you, Evita?"

She began to sing as she put things away in her kitchen. A man walking by in the alley said, *"Ave María!* But you are handy at your work!"

"Shut your mouth, you hunk of a queer," Felícita answered. "The only thing you men want from a woman is for her to put out for you." She continued to sing and then said to Rosa, "You know something? This is the first time I've ever had relations with a boy as young as Cuco. We've known each other since he was a little kid. Imagine that! He came here one day and asked me if it was true that I was single and I told him I was. So we began to dance the twist and I touched his thing with my ass. He told me he wanted me to be his, and I answered that I didn't like *teenagers*. For days after that he kept begging me to have relations, and then last week when he asked me again, I went with him."

Junior, Fernanda's young husband, and his brother appeared at the door. They seemed surprised to see Rosa, but after a moment they paid no further attention to her. "Listen, Felícita," Junior said, "I've been offered a real bargain, a twenty-one-jewel watch for forty dollars and an eighteen-carat-gold ring thrown in for seventy-five dollars. And only fifty dollars down. What do you think of that?"

Felícita said, "Well, go ahead and buy them." Felícita liked jewelry and had once bought herself a religious chain and a gold ring for sixty-five dollars.

"No," Junior said. "You see, I have the money but if I spend it I'll be broke, and I don't like to be broke. So why should I spend it?"

Felícita said, "Tell me what brought you here. You hardly ever come to see us, you know."

"Oh, I just came to see if there was any work down here," Junior answered. "That's why I came. But there isn't any, so we're going now."

When they had gone, Felícita turned to Rosa. "Let's go to my *comadre* Lucelia's and see if she'll let me hang up my clothes on her lines," she said. "Mine aren't long enough."

Doña Lucelia was sitting in the doorway of her apartment. When Felícita made her request, Lucelia answered, "Of course. When did I ever refuse you?" Felícita went home to finish the washing. *"Ay,* but I'm already tired," she said to Rosa as they walked, "and my wrist hurts. On Friday I'm going to *el welfare* to see if they won't help me out." She sang a few bars of a song and then said, "You know, that boy Cuco really knows how to thrill a woman. If the woman wants it twice, he's right there. He didn't know how to do it in certain positions, but I taught him. You know something? Any woman in the life would work for him, but I don't let him know that."

The first batch of clothes was ready to be hung when Felícita discovered she had no clothespins. "We'll buy a quarter's worth at Bonilla's," Felícita told Rosa. The store was filled with people, but as he waited on her, Bonilla said to Felícita, "Look at that ass! It's still good enough." Felícita answered belligerently, "Come on. Give me the clothespins and have some respect. Don't be so low-down."

After they had hung out the clothes at *doña* Lucelia's, the two women strolled down the alley. Felícita said, *"Ay!* I have a pain in the back. I hope I'm not getting the curse, because Cuco is coming today and we haven't done anything for two days. You know, I showed him how to do it with the woman's legs around the man's neck? I've only done it twice in my life. The first time was with a boy named Rosario, and now with Cuco and that's all. You can't do it with every man because some are so big they hurt you. I learned these low-down tricks from the other women. I'd hear them talk about them and then I'd try them. I read sexology books too."

As they rested in the wicker chairs a neighbor called from the alleyway below, "Felícita, Evita's been shitting down here." Felícita called back, "Don't worry, I'll clean it up." She went out with a piece of paper, picked up the excrement and threw it farther down the alley. Then she carried Evita into the toilet and washed her off under the faucet. Evita began to cry and for a few minutes Felícita played with her, first singing to her and then dancing her around the room until Evita was laughing. "Now, here goes the second batch of clothes," Felícita said and went out to the balcony.

Gabi and Angelito came in with the groceries. Felícita took a large can of malt beer and poured it into five smaller cans, one for each of the children who were now clamoring to be first. Felícita began to sing,

"Skinny Eva, we'll make her dance,
I want to make her tremble,
I want to make her shake."

All the children started dancing so vigorously that the house itself shook. Tany was dancing out on the porch. Felícita stopped singing and called, "Who's the mule I hear out there?" and the children stopped dancing. Tany pulled Mundo down on the floor, saying, "I'm going to grab his balls. Here, here, give me your balls." The little boy laughed, but Felícita said, "I'm going to cook now. Get out or I'll tend to all of you later, you hear?" The children disappeared, running off in different directions.

Felícita again borrowed a match from Rosa to light the stove. She washed an aluminum pan under the faucet in the toilet, and set it on the stove with water in it. She went to a neighbor's to borrow a knife, came back, and began peeling vegetables. "I don't like to borrow things, because the people here are tricky. They will borrow but they won't lend." Mundo came into the house and stood near her, masturbating. Although Felícita had once told Rosa that she punished her children for this because they might "injure" themselves if their hands were dirty, now she only said, *"Compai,* what a cock, eh? What a cock!" She crushed some garlic in an unwashed mortar and started picking over the rice. She dropped the cut vegetables into the pan on the stove and went back to washing clothes again.

Felícita used a washboard, and as she scrubbed and wrung out the clothes she talked to Rosa. "You know, as far as the neighbors here go, I haven't got a single really good one. They are all two-faced hypocrites. They are nice to your face but behind your back they knife you. My own sister Cruz insults me because she doesn't want me to bring men here. *Chica!* She came around on Sunday, and because I was with a man she yelled at him and then didn't miss telling a soul that I was here with a man. But I never get anything from her or from any of the rest of them."

Gabi came in. *"Mami,* give me a penny."

"Say, do you kids think I'm a millionaire?" Gabi picked up a small empty bottle. "Leave that there. I need it."

"What for?"

"It's none of your business what I want it for. Gabi, go to Bonilla's and get codfish. Hurry, now, *maricón!"*

Felícita filled another aluminum pan with water, leaving the toilet door open when she returned to the balcony. The strong odor from the toilet came into the living room. Felícita washed the rice and put it in the pan to cook.

"At one time I gave Gabi to Lucelia," she said, "but she gave him back to me because she said she didn't want to have an ungrateful child. The thing was, she asked him who he was going to give his money to when he grew up and went to work, and the boy didn't know any better, so he said he was going to give it to me. What a dope of a woman! She had just taken him and she wanted him to say right then that he was going to give his money to her."

Tany ran in. Felícita seized her by the front of her dress with one hand and lifted her other hand as though to strike the girl. She spoke angrily through clenched teeth. "Look! Look! See how dirty that dress is. I feel like punching you. Take that dress off. You aren't the one who's going to wash it." She gave the child a push with her foot, and Tany began to cry. The child had no clean dress to change into and she didn't know what to do. She had very few clothes, only three dresses, a pair of shoes and one pair of socks, all bought by Felícita.

Mundo came in and began playing with a plantain skin. To make him stop, Felícita hit him on the head with the flat of the knife blade. *"Mami,"* Mundo said, "Miné says send back her knife because she needs it."

"Tell her that I'll return the knife right away as soon as I'm through with it. Hurry up! Tell her."

All the children had come in because it had begun to rain. Hungry, they crowded around Felícita on the narrow kitchen-balcony, sniffing the cooking food. Suddenly, intensely annoyed, Felícita took the broom and drove them out of the house. In the brief silence that followed, Rosa heard the sputter of hot lard and the scraping of a spoon as Felícita stirred the rice. "To hell with you!" Felícita muttered, waving her hands to drive off a swarm of flies. "Doing work like this is the very devil, Rosa. Because I work at night, I feel all drained out. Look at all the dirty clothes I had. I have to change the sheets on my bed all the time, too, because the children climb on them with their dirty feet. A few months ago I had to buy six sheets at a dollar eighty-three apiece in the Boston Discount House because the sheets I bought a year back were ruined. But my bed is very comfortable. The other night I stayed in a hotel and the bed there sank down in the middle and I woke up the next morning with pains in my kidneys.

"Cuco gets a pain in the back and asks me if it could be because we did it too much. He had never done it so much before. I told him it was probably from some draft he caught at work. I said it couldn't be from that because then it would affect the brain. We'd do it seven times in one night and I'd get up the next day hotter than ever. I guess I have *sufón*. That's something that drives all men wild, according to the book on sex. It's something like extra flesh coming out of the womb. When the man puts his thing inside, it keeps closing down on it until it fits just right and as it is very tight it gives him extra pleasure. I'll tell you something. Sometimes I get so hot it makes me cry if I'm not satisfied. I would do it every day if I didn't have the children."

Felícita began to prepare the codfish. She went back and forth between the balcony and the toilet carrying pans of water. Catín, Soledad's foster daughter, came in, dressed for school. She was wearing her school uniform, a blue jumper with a white blouse, ankle socks and blue sneakers. Her hair was combed and braided, and she looked clean and neat. "Fela," she said, "Cruz says can you lend her your umbrella?"

"Bendito, tell her I forgot to bring it home yesterday. If not, I'd lend it to her. *Ay, mi madre!* I was sure I had a can of tomato sauce here."

"Yes, *mami,*" Tany said. "I saw it there."

But Felícita couldn't find the can. "Angelito, run to Bonilla's and tell him to send me a can of tomato sauce." Angelito was reluctant to go out. "Hurry up, you lazy lump," Felícita said. "Hurry now! They had to resemble their father somehow. And here, Gabi. Throw out this dirty water." Gabi started toward the toilet with a greasy pan filled to the brim with water and scraps of food. Mundo pushed him from behind and Gabi, afraid of spilling the water, called to his mother. When she ignored him he placed the pan on a chair and then pushed Mundo down on the cot. The little boy jumped wildly up and down on it until Felícita slapped his bare behind and pushed him off.

Felícita was singing another popular song, "I went out one night when you weren't there—" Angelito returned with the tomato sauce, then began to play with Mundo. He separated the little boy's buttocks and called to Tany, "Here, Tany. Suck it. It tastes good." Angelito looked closely at his brother's anus and said "Ugh!"

"I won't suck it," Tany said. "You suck your own cock."

In the meantime Felícita was washing pans and dishes in a big kettle. She rubbed the pans with a dirty rag and cleansing powder. Tany had sat down on the porch. Felícita needed to pass by and pushed the child out of the way with her foot. "Get up. Get up," she said. Evita was lying on the porch floor near the doorway of the neighbor's apartment. Two boys came out and stepped over the baby. "Just look at that," she said in a fury. "They walk over Evita to bring her bad luck."

Through the small window in the living room, Rosa saw a Navy ship bearing toward the harbor. Felícita also saw it from the balcony. *"Ave María!"* she said. "Can you see what its number is?" But since neither she nor Rosa could make out the ship's number, Felícita began to set out the plates. The rice was almost ready, and as she stirred it she sang,

> "When I'm away from you,
> There is something in my heart that says,
> Don't let her out alone,
> Or she will fall in love behind your back."

Angelito, Gabi and Mundo were rolling around on the floor, tussling with each other. Angelito pushed Mundo against Gabi with such force that Gabi's head struck against the door jamb. Gabi howled. It was a minute or so before Felícita said sarcastically, "Oh, isn't it too bad that you hit your head. So what am I supposed to do? Start crying too? Let's make it a duet." Gabi cried even louder.

Felícita began handing out plates of food; there were plantains, yams and yautía with codfish and avocado, and rice. She served Rosa first, then her children from the oldest to the youngest, and herself last. The children sat on the kitchen floor, their legs outspread, and began to eat with their fingers. Felícita and Rosa sat in the living room. Miné came in as they ate, and Felícita got up to serve her some food. Miné's husband earned comparatively good wages at the docks, but he supported his other women and children, and Miné and her five children often did not get enough to eat. Soon Pucha came weaving into the house. She asked for the parcel she had left there and Felícita gave her a large paper bag full of clothes. The woman helped herself to some food and sat down on the floor to eat. The moment she was through eating she left, and Miné soon followed.

While eating, the twins began to fight. This time Gabi was trying to hit Angelito. Felícita said mockingly, "Oh, ho, ho, ho! Angelito has a size forty-four head. He needs a great big hat, ho!" Felícita stooped to look into his face. Angelito hit out at her with his fist, but Felícita quickly moved away. "Take that fist and punch your own balls with it," she said. The boy began to cry. Mundo asked for more to eat, and Felícita gave it to him. At this, Angelito stopped crying. "And what'll we do for food tonight, eh?" he asked.

"You and your big mouth, that's what we'll eat," Felícita answered.

"Mami," Angelito asked, "aren't you going to work today?"

"Yes, I am. Why do you ask? Do you want me to stay home from work?"

"I do want you to go to work," the boy said. "I want you to go and not bother me any more."

"Oh! Well, I'm saving money to pay my fare to New York, and when I go I'll leave you with your father. You're too fresh for me."

Felícita began eating the leftover rice from the pan. "My goodness," she said, "I hardly eat at all. I must be sick," and laughed at herself. "Angelito, go for a fruit juice for Evita and a Pepsi-Cola. Go on, hurry!" Felícita took Evita on her knees and fed her some of the rice. When Angelito came back, she divided the juice and the Pepsi-Cola among the children and herself. It had stopped raining and all the children except Evita went down to the beach to play. Felícita set Evita on the floor and swept up the rice the children had scattered over the balcony floor. A popular trio, Los Panchos, could be heard singing on a neighbor's radio, and Felícita sang along with them. "Now, I'm going to take a shower," she announced. "But first a bottle for Evita so she'll stay quiet." She washed a bottle, filled it with milk, settled Evita on the cot and gave her the bottle. Evita was naked and lay on the bed with her legs stretched wide apart.

Felícita took a piece of an old towel hanging from a nail in her bedroom and went into the toilet, leaving Rosa alone with the baby. Rosa looked around the living room. It was quite bare despite Felícita's attempts to make it attractive. On the wall beside the bedroom door hung a large glass-covered picture of Saint Judas Thaddaeus, with an inscription in luminous painted letters, "God Bless Our Home." The frame, marked "Made in Japan," was ornamented with metallic butterflies. Felícita had bought the picture for eight dollars from a street vendor in La Esmeralda, paying one dollar down and the rest in small weekly payments. Over the picture hung a red plastic rose which she had brought with her from New Jersey.

Tacked to the wall above the cot by the window was a large calendar with a color photograph of a jet plane of the Iberia airline. Fernanda had brought this calendar with her when she lived for a short while with Felícita. Also on the wall, another calendar, the kind with a small sheet for each day, advertised the Banco Popular. Recently Felícita had asked one of the twins to tear off a page, and he had torn off the sheets for a whole month instead. Felícita had been furious and said she was going to try to reattach the sheets. A snapshot of Tavio, Soledad's deceased husband, had been tacked to the wall by Fernanda and left there when she moved out.

Mundo was yelling, "Fela, Fela, I want water."

"Go get it in the kitchen," Felícita called from the toilet where she was taking her shower.

"*Mami, mami,* it hurts, it hurts," Tany was crying.

"Oh, it hurts, does it? Well, tell it to stop."

"*Mami,* water."

"Well, wait until I get out and stop bothering me."

Felícita came out from her shower dressed in the same dress she had worn all day. She had washed her panties and now hung them on the clothes line on the front porch, taking down a pink pair which she put on in the bedroom. "Tany," she called, "see if you can find my curlers under the bed. *Ay!* I can't think of a thing except those dirty dishes, and there isn't anything I like to do less. I'm dying to go to Salinas and tell that daughter of a great whore, that woman of my husband's, what I think of her. She's crazy for my husband to divorce me. When I go to Salinas, I'm going to wear the best clothes I can buy. I want to look elegant because I don't like to be laughed at. That's what they did. They laughed at me when they found out I was hustling. I'm going to get some lovely, shiny shoes I saw at the González Shops for seven ninety-nine."

Someone spoke harshly out on the porch. "Look at that! You'll have to clean it up." Felícita hurried out. Tany was splashing water from a pail onto the cement floor. Apparently Evita had wandered out there and had had a bowel movement in front of the neighbor's door. Felícita went for more water and the broom and swept the excrement from the porch into the alleyway.

"Ave María!" she said to *doña* Bertha who was passing by. "This Evita! She's been up since four-thirty this morning and hasn't slept a wink since. I'm the same way. I lie down for only about four hours. I get through working at three-thirty in the morning, and just as I'm falling asleep, those kids start screwing around. I have to begin to struggle with them at that hour." Felícita took Evita to the toilet and bathed her buttocks.

"Ay, I don't feel like washing any more," Felícita said, but she went out on the balcony to finish the clothes. She began singing a happy little tune. *"Chica,"* she said to Rosa, "Cuco likes to see me in those light-colored *bikini panties.* I wore them the other night and he gave me a squeezing like you never could imagine."

Mundo was crying for a penny and Evita began to cry too. Felícita burst out in exasperation, *"Ay!* These children are driving me crazy. Thank the Lord I've had the operation and can never have another one." She gave Evita water in her bottle to quiet her, but Mundo went on crying, this time for milk. "You'll have to wait," Felícita said, "because Evita is using the bottle. So wait or keep on yelling, whichever you want."

"Corporal" Pepito came to the door, drunk, and with his eyes half closed. He tried to speak in English to Mundo, but the words were unintelligible. Although Felícita was glad enough to see him when she wanted him to run an errand, she said now, "Look, I don't want any drunken fairies around here, so get going." She had finished washing the clothes and went to the porch to pour the dirty water into the alleyway. She hung the clothes on the clothes line on the porch. Those that had been soaking in Clorox in the pail she wrung out and left damp in the tub. *"Ay!* I don't feel like cleaning the floor of the balcony where I had the washtub." Nevertheless she took the broom and swept away the water that had spilled over.

Back in the living room, Felícita played with Evita, tickling her on the ribs and stomach. Then she looked closely at a pimple on the baby's forehead. She held Evita between her legs and bent the child's head back saying, "Wait, wait, I want to get at that." She squeezed the pimple as hard as she could until bloody pus oozed out. This she wiped away with the rag she had used to dry herself in the shower. "Wait, child, the root isn't out yet. *Ave María,* my pretty baby, my pretty baby." Evita cried desperately as Felícita squeezed down on the pimple again; she tried to cover her forehead with her hands but Angelito stepped up and held down her hands. At last only blood came out.

"Tany, call Gabi. I'm going to get his pimple out too." When Gabi came in Felícita said, "Crouch down so I can get at that pimple of yours." Gabi was surprised. "There?" he asked. The pimple was on the tip of his nose. "Well, aren't you a man? Let's see your balls." When Felícita pressed down on the pimple, Gabi began to cry. *"Ave María!"* Felícita said. "Look at that root!" She wiped the blood from Gabi's nose with the same rag she had used for Evita. "Keep quiet! There's still some stuff to squeeze out. My Lord, how you like to cry! Evita's a girl, and she didn't cry as much as you do." Felícita examined the other children. Their bodies were covered with insect bites and scabs and scars, but she found no more pimples to squeeze. Angelito had recently had a very large boil on his mouth, and his lip was still a little out of shape.

Mundo, still naked, climbed up on the cot. "Ah, what an ugly ass! What a black ass-hole, eh?" Gabi stopped crying in order to laugh at his brother. Felícita repeated, "What an ugly ass-hole. It looks like a brown eye."

Felícita began cleaning the toilet. As she pulled out a large can of soiled paper she said, "After I take a shit, I wash my ass. These papers are from the people next door. Damn these La Esmeralda houses where you have to share a toilet, and damn the filthy people too. Those people next door would leave the shit right on the porch if they dared." She tried to clean the toilet bowl but gave up. *"Ave María!* The crust on this toilet won't come off. And this is the hour of the day when practically everybody is using water and we hardly get any down here." It was early afternoon.

She went out to collect the washing from *doña* Lucelia's line. Someone had already taken down one of her sheets. Felícita said, "Lucky it's dry or they would hear me swearing up in San Juan." While she folded the rest of the laundry she looked down toward the beach. "Say, let's go see the corpse. We'll have time if we hurry. A girl was killed by her husband out of jealousy. I didn't know her but that's what they tell me. They say she won't be buried until her *papá* comes home from sea on Sunday. He's in the *merchant marine.*"

Felícita took the laundry back to her apartment and deposited it on a chair in the living room. She heaped the clothes from her own line on top of the others. *"Ay,* now that we're going to see the corpse, I feel like going to the toilet. There isn't any toilet paper. Let me go get a rag." She was in the toilet for several minutes. When she came back, she went down below her house to throw out the garbage. Then she put the folded sheets in a carton, straightened her bedspread, and got dressed. She put on a tight black dress which was cut extremely low both front and back and had shoulder straps. She hastily made up her face and combed her hair, remarking that she would have to do it all over again when she went to work.

Before leaving, Felícita said, "Tany, don't upset the house now. I'll be right back."

The two women walked through several crooked alleys and along the beach for a short distance. The tide was high and the water reached far under the houses. Felícita asked everyone they met where the corpse was. They walked through other alleys that were filthy and swarming with flies. Finally they found the two-room house in one of the worst sections of the slum. Inside the house, against a wall, stood a gray coffin with a lighted candle set on each corner. The dead girl was dressed in white. Four wreaths had been placed alongside the casket. Ribbons attached to them said, "Remembrances from your neighbors in La Esmeralda," "Remembrances from your parents," "Remembrances from your grandparents" and "Remembrances from Florentine and wife." A memory album was completely filled.

Benches had been set up for visitors in both rooms, on the balcony and beside the stairs. Because of the time of day, some of these were now empty. A tall, thin woman in a black skirt and a white blouse told Felícita and Rosa that so many people had been there the night before that the house had almost collapsed.

Felícita asked what had caused the girl's death. A Negro woman answered her. "Well, daughter, when you're going to die, anything at all will carry you off."

"No," the thin woman interrupted, "she had liver trouble. We noticed that she was getting thinner and thinner every day, but she was in love and when you're in love you get thin, so we blamed it on that. Then one morning she woke up with such a pain she couldn't stand up and her urine was all blood. When the ambulance came, we carried her down in our arms. The doctor at the hospital prescribed some pills, but when we gave them to her she died. They say it was an intoxication."

"You could sue the hospital," Felícita said.

The Negro woman answered, "Ay, my daughter, that's silly. A person doesn't die until God wills it. Look, one time I was very sick and the doctor put me on a terrible diet. I hardly ate anything because the things on my diet were so expensive I couldn't buy them. So the lady of the house where I worked said to me, 'Look, we poor people can't be following diets and all that crap. Eat anything, even boiled rocks, if that's what they offer you.' So that's what I did and here I am. What the hell! If you're going to die anyhow, it might as well be with a full stomach."

Another woman said, "Oh no, no! God helps those who help themselves. The thing is that people wait until the last minute to see the doctor. Me, as soon as I get a little headache, I'm off to the hospital. I don't like any of those five-minute examinations, either. I want X-rays and all that."

The Negro woman said, "What luck this dead child had! *Don* Reyes got her a twenty-five-dollar grave in the cemetery free."

Still another woman said, "Those cemetery plots are so expensive. I've rented one for my brother for five years, and I pay three dollars a week."

"Let them bury me any place. After all, I won't know where I am," a young girl said.

"Child, you don't know what you're talking about," the Negro woman answered.

Outside, on the balcony, a girl dressed in black with a rosary around her neck stood off by herself. Someone asked who she was, and the Negro woman answered, "That's the sister of the deceased. She arrived yesterday from New

York with her mother. The thing is, the dead girl was brought up by her grand-parents. This sister is white."

Felícita and Rosa started to walk home. Felícita seemed in good spirits and sang snatches of songs until they came to Cruz's house. Cruz and Fernanda were standing on the front steps. Felícita asked, "Cruz, how is Chuito?" Cruz's baby son was in the hospital with bronchitis. "He's better," Cruz said. "I'm going there now to give him titty. Want to come along?"

"No, child, I have to go to work."

Fernanda asked, "How are you getting on with Cuco?"

"Couldn't be better. The one I don't like is his *mamá*. She came down here the other day."

"Did she say anything to you?" Fernanda asked.

"Not to me, to him. She shouted that I was driving him crazy and that he hardly ate any more and that when he went home he only stared at the clock. So I told him to leave because I didn't like men who let their *mamás* run their lives for them."

"Word is going around that I'm pregnant," Fernanda said. "I'm going to tell them all to keep their noses out of what doesn't concern them."

"Well, you have a husband. I hear that Erasmo is hanging around the docks again."

"Naturally, since they fired him from his job. And where have the two of you been?" Fernanda asked.

"To see a dead girl who died of her liver."

"Liver, my eye!" Cruz said. "I listen to the news on KVM, and they say that she was two months pregnant, and that her boy friend gave her such a beating that the baby died inside of her and then she died on account of it. In the hospital, too. They say that her parents are the only ones who believe she was a *señorita*."

"Well, it was her own business and now she's dead," Felícita said. "She's screwed for good. But that was the best thing she could have done, to at least have tried it before she died. Well, I have to go."

A little way down the alley Felícita stopped to call to her mother, "How many months pregnant did you say you were, Fernanda?"

"Only two, daughter," Fernanda called back.

An old woman walking in the alley stopped and stared at Fernanda. Fernanda stared back. "Look at the way that old bat is looking at me," she said, laughing.

At home Felícita said, "And now I've got to get some sleep." At that moment they heard heavy blows against the house, as though someone were pounding with a lead pipe. Felícita ran to the window and saw a woman in the alley below. "Hey, *Loca,*" she yelled, "stop that! You already broke one of my ornaments once."

The woman was shrieking, "Damn the mother of whores. Damn the devil's mother. Damn all the whores around here."

"Blah, blah, blah!" Felícita said. "It's the madwoman," she explained to Rosa. "She's really crazy, you know." Felícita filled a tin can with water to be ready to pour it down on *Loca* when she came directly under the balcony, but *Loca* had gone in another direction.

Felícita lay down on the bed, saying to Evita, "Damn it all, leave me alone, baby! Let me rest. I have to go to work." The twins came rushing in. "Fela, Fela, Tany's throwing tin cans down on us."

"Did she hit you?" Felícita asked, opening her eyes.

"Of course she did. She hit us," they said in unison.

"Tany, come in here. Now go out on the balcony and keep quiet. I want to sleep, understand?"

For a time there was relative peace. Mundo sat on the floor eating some of the leftover rice. Evita was on the floor also. Mundo repeatedly pointed to her genitals and laughed. Tany stood at the table, washing the tin cans. She washed them very carefully in the same water that her mother had used since noon. Felícita slept soundly, her arms stretched above her head. It was very hot in the house, and in the silence, the sound of the sea breakers was louder than ever.

About half an hour later Cruz came in with a bundle of clean clothes. "Fela. Fela! Is she here?"

"Yes, she's sleeping," Rosa said.

Cruz went into the bedroom and shook Felícita's buttocks to wake her. "Hey, you, here's your clothes." Tany brought her the pan of rice, and Cruz ate several spoonfuls of it and then left. "Now I'm going to lock the door to see if I can get some sleep," Felícita said. "Get out, all of you, except you, Rosa."

Pucha, the drunkard, who had been there earlier, walked up onto the porch and went into the toilet. Tany shouted from the porch, "Look at Pucha. She went into the toilet." Felícita got up and went to look. "What's going on here? Hey, you, get out of there."

"You goddamn bitch, leave me alone," Pucha said. "Damn it! This isn't your house."

"I don't own the house, but you can't come screwing around here. Come on out!"

Pucha emerged, shouting, *"Ave María!* I'll come whenever I please."

Felícita went back to the bedroom and tried to sleep, but Tany and Gabi were fighting on the balcony. She got up quietly, took the broom and hit both of them on the head with the broomstick. Tany cried but Gabi laughed. Evita was weeping, and Felícita finally picked her up and threw her roughly on the bed. "Gabi, bring me water in Evita's bottle. Hurry up!" When he brought it she tasted it to see if it had been sweetened. Evita sucked at it and began to grow drowsy. When she had finished the bottle, she put her thumb in her mouth and went to sleep. "Now get out, the rest of you, or I'll kill you." The children disappeared and Felícita went back to sleep.

When Felícita awoke almost a half-hour later, she began to get ready to go to work. She searched for her hairbrush and at last found it on the ledge over the balcony door. This ledge was a storage space for Felícita's purses, for miscellaneous items and for books. It held three children's books, which her children never read, and a thick volume of spiritist doctrine entitled *The Gospel According to Spiritism* by Alan Kardel. Felícita's husband Edmundo had bought the book, and she used to read passages aloud to him, from whatever prayers the spiritist had recommended.

Felícita cleaned her face thoroughly with cream. *"Ave María!"* she said. "If that American comes and returns my ring tonight, he's more than decent. I hope to God he comes. That was the ring my *papá* gave me, see?" She colored her lips before a small mirror, used the eyebrow pencil to darken her eyebrows, and painted a little beauty spot above her left eyebrow. She put on the Marine's ring and bracelet, and a pair of black high-heeled shoes. Now she was ready to choose a dress.

To Felícita her most valued possessions were her dresses. Before she had started to work in bars, Felícita had worn a dress for about a year, paying on the average about seven dollars for each. Later, however, she needed a better and larger wardrobe and she began buying a new dress every two weeks.

With obvious pleasure, Felícita held up dress after dress for Rosa to see, giving her a running account of each one. "The Filipino gave me this dress the day before he left for New York. He paid five ninety-nine in Franklin's. In December I wanted a lot of new clothes because of all the Christmas fiestas, so I bought this dress for seventeen dollars in Lerner's." It was a green dress, cut low in the back, with a matching stole. "And I wanted to buy a new dress for Mother's Day because nobody had given me anything. The one I liked at Franklin's cost twenty-five dollars so I decided to buy the same material and have one made. Two yards of Dacron material cost ten dollars and the sewing was three, so the dress only cost me thirteen dollars. I was also happy that day because I bought my *mamá* a present."

Felícita showed Rosa a white dress trimmed with blue flowers. "I bought this in Lerner's for six ninety-nine and I wore it for the first time when Walker came back from New York. He thought the dress was beautiful, and he liked my new black shoes with little straps. I felt very proud because I'd had my hair done in a beauty parlor where they fixed my eyebrows too, and I had put on a lot of make-up.

"Because I know so many men, I keep on buying clothes. I dress to please their taste, and they like the way I look. I know that the special days for the Americans to take me out are Fridays and Saturdays, so those are the days I wear new dresses. They've taken me to the Miramar Hotel and to the Condado Beach Hotel. Last New Year's Eve I bought a new nylon dress for fifteen dollars because I was going to the Normandie. And I've gone to the Americana near the airport."

Felícita slipped on a dress of light green with blue and yellow flowers and dark-green leaves. Rosa thought she looked very pretty and smart. Just then Evita woke up and began to cry. Felícita gave a tin can to Gabi, who had come home, and told him to go to Cruz's and get some milk for Evita. "Tell her I'm late for work and can't wait to fix a bottle," she said. Gabi was soon back. "Cruz says she's too busy. She says to fix the bottle yourself."

"All right, leave it there. I'll make it. Now for some perfume." She applied perfume on her ears, neck and wrists, then went to the kitchen to prepare Evita's bottle. Angelito came in and watched her.

"Mami," he said, "why do you make yourself so pretty to go there?"

"Ah, you say I'm pretty. Do you think I'm pretty, son?"

"You are now. And does he work with you?" Angelito pointed to the picture of the Marine dancing with Felícita.

"Yes, he works with me. Now, look, all of you. Eat all the food in the kitchen. There's codfish left and some vegetables." Evita, crying, toddled after her mother as Felícita went to the front door. "And Tany, please, hold this child and don't let her follow me."

Felícita slipped out, leaving her children with Rosa. On other days, she left them alone.

Felícita

My Mother Was a Prostitute

WHEN I WAS a child my stepmother told me that my *mamá* was a prostitute but I didn't believe her. I said I wanted to see my *mamá,* to know her, and my stepmother would say that there was no reason for me to see that bitch because she was no mother, the way she treated us. She said that my *mamá* didn't want to cook for us and that she went out with men, carrying on and drinking and leaving us dirty and alone at all hours of the night.

I didn't care what my stepmother said. I was sad because my *mamá* and *papá* were living apart and the only thing I wished was that they'd get together again so they could be a good example to us.

My stepmother mistreated us kids and didn't want to cook for us or send us to school. According to my godmother, Hortensia would throw our bread and food to us on the floor. She didn't want to buy us clothes, and would beat us if we sat down in the living room. Once Crucita was crying and Hortensia went and grabbed her and threw her to the floor and that's why she is lame. But my stepmother says it was meningitis that made Cruz a cripple.

My *madrina,* Elsa, the only godmother I know, loved me very much. She was the wife of my uncle Pablo, my *padrino.* People told me she was better to me than my stepmother, because she bought me clothes and shoes, and when I went to her house she caressed me and gave me whatever I needed. Once she denounced Hortensia to the Red Cross and they came to investigate to see if we could be sent to a boarding school. I wanted to go but my sister Soledad opposed it. The Red Cross came two or three times but never found my step-mother at home. They decided to leave it up to the eldest child, and Soledad said that we didn't want to go.

Soledad was the one who had fought the most with my stepmother. I remember once that one of Hortensia's cousins was taking a bath and Soledad spied on him through a hole. I told my stepmother and Soledad came and punched me in the stomach. Then my stepmother fell upon her and beat her black and blue. So my sister said she shit on my stepmother's mother and my stepmother gave her a punch in the mouth.

Once when my *papá* was not in Puerto Rico, my *mamá* came to the house, greeted my stepmother and said she wanted to see Soledad. My step-mother was frightened because people said my *mamá* carried a *Gem* in her mouth. So Nanda took Soledad out for a walk and didn't bring her back.

My stepmother didn't really want to have us, anyway, and she kept say-ing, "Oh, if that woman would only come and take all of you." Then my *mamá* came and won over my brother and, after that, Cruz. Finally I was the only one left with my stepmother. Hortensia didn't want me to go because she said my *mamá* would set me a bad example.

Hortensia had two sons by my *papá*. They were Mariano and Thomas. I got on only with Thomas. Besides being a well-behaved boy, he is very kind-hearted, and whatever you tell him he sympathizes with you. He is always ready to help, and when we come to his house he pays attention to us. But not Mariano, not him! He has always been indifferent because he is white.

When my *papá* was in Panama, he sent for Hortensia. She left us children with her sister, María del Carmen, who made me help her with everything. I couldn't even reach the sink then, and I had to stand on a bench to scrub the pots. After two months my stepmother came and took me to Panama so that I could help her in her house. I was six or seven years old then.

In Panama my stepmother was mean to me. When I got home from school, she would have coffee and things ready for her boys but nothing for me. She didn't want me to play with anybody or to have friends. She wanted me just to stay in the house. If she saw me talking to a girl friend, she would spank me. I told her that when I got back to Puerto Rico I was going to stay with my *mamá*. She said that was a good idea because I was going to be a whore just like my *mamá* was.

Oh, that stepmother of mine! When I think of her! She always acted differently when my father was around. She made him think she loved me, although she wasn't fond of me at all. She kept cursing me out when he wasn't there. She would grab bread crusts and throw them at me, and she would scrub me with a floor brush because she said I didn't bathe myself right. *Ave María!* She made my whole back red!

Hortensia didn't want my *papá* to like me. I was his daughter by his first marriage and, well, he loved me. But my stepmother would tell him things to make him stop being nice to me. When I asked my father for money for ice cream she would tell him not to give me anything and would send her children to the movies while she kept me at home to clean her shoes. She told me not to call my father *papito* because I was big already. I would sit on his lap and he would kiss me and she didn't like that because she said he cared more for me than for her children.

I loved my *papá* very much. He would give me anything I asked for. And if I got sick, he looked after me and took me to the hospital and he himself would prepare the remedies. He always saw to it that I studied, that I went to church, and that I kept my clothes washed and ironed, and he gave me permission to play softball on the team at the Y.

My *papá* is old now, and thin. He is forty-six, but at that time he was big, with pink and white skin. He liked to tell stories about his life; not to us, but I overheard conversations. He says he went through only the second grade but that he knows more than many who have gone to the university. He knows a lot about life, true stories about people. He is a fine man, my *papá,* but he was not very happy with my *mamá* or with my stepmother either, although he always did what she told him to.

I guess my *papá* was in love with Hortensia because it's seventeen years that they've been together now. My *papá* has treated her well. Probably he is grateful to her for at least bringing up his children. He set up a home for her, bought her furniture, and bought her a house right off, something he never did for my *mamá.* He bought another house, in Puerto Nuevo, that cost him thirty-eight hundred dollars but he gave it to a friend for eighty dollars one day when he had a fight with Hortensia and got drunk.

Papá behaved very well with Hortensia, even though he liked to run around with women, and once she wanted to divorce him. At first, when he cashed his pay check he wouldn't give any of it to her, but later he turned all his money over to her, as if she had him tied up.

She did as she pleased in the house. There were times when she would even beat him! What happened was that my father had a girl friend and he'd come home drunk. One day Hortensia got hold of him and was going to throw him down a staircase with seventy-three steps. I had to go out and yell for the neighbors, because he couldn't get up and she was on top of him. She broke a chair over him and he couldn't get out of bed for a week. That's how forward she was with him.

It seems to me she must have put some kind of a spell on my *papá* because she kept going to the spiritist. She had herbs all over the place, and crosses, lighted candles, saints and prayers and such. And she burned a lot of incense in the house, to hold him in check.

Even before I was developed, there were times when I had desires. I would get a feeling like a tickling, and it made me want a man. I don't even know how to explain it. When I got that feeling I would pour lots of hot water on my parts and sit in the water and I would feel so good. The next day I would have the desire again and I would open the faucet and let the hot water run until it was steaming. Then I would get under the water and I would think of a movie actor or some man and I'd stay there that way. After a while I would remember my *papá* and my stepmother and I'd get ashamed and say to myself, "Oh Lord, why do I do these things?"

When I played I would make a cigarette from a poppy pod and put it in my mouth. Then I would take off my clothes and wrap myself in a towel, leaving it open at the side. I would put a flower in my hair and go stand on the street corners, smoking and making believe I was a prostitute.

When I was about seven, I began to have the ambition to be a singer. It started when I went to some children's radio programs which were held every Saturday morning. One Saturday my stepmother gave me permission to go and I won the first prize. They gave me five dollars, a pen set and a theater ticket. The next time, I sang "Te seguiré" and "Piel Canela" and I won second prize. After that I didn't get permission to go any more, but I always listened to the program and I kept saying that when I grew up I was going to be a singer or an actress. But as my stepmother never allowed me to practice, I had to forget it. People still say I have a good voice for singing.

I used to go to church every Sunday to learn the catechism. The Mother of the Sisters of Charity gave us classes. She saw that I learned quickly, so she made me recite the catechism to the children while she watched from her desk. I taught in Sunday School and I carried the saints and all those things to my house. But in the primary school I behaved very badly. The teacher would have me watch over the children and I would throw erasers at them. One day the *Missy* left the room and I got into a fist fight with a girl. The teacher came back and punished us with a failure, but the grades on my card were good.

When I was about ten years old, everybody had graduated except me, because graduation is from fifth to sixth grade and I didn't go through fifth. I skipped from the fourth to the sixth. Well, there was going to be a graduation dance at the school and I wanted to go but my stepmother insisted I shouldn't. I had only a pair of old, torn moccasins that I had worn most of the year. Finally she said I could go to the dance if I wore her old shoes. So I did. I felt very embarrassed. Everybody wearing pretty shoes and me with those old slippers. How I hated her for that! Especially since she had gotten paid at that time. That woman loves to save money. She'd rather not eat so she can save money for luxuries. I couldn't dance, anyway, because she came for me right away. The only thing I said was that when I grew up I would get even with her for everything she did to me. But I have never done anything to her, not even been disrespectful.

My stepmother always showed the bad side of her nature toward me and that made me sad. Sometimes, when the Day of the Kings came around, she would say, *"Ay,* I'm not going to give you any presents because you're a woman now." But there always was a present for me. She would buy about ten cents' worth of candy and put it under my bed. When I got up in the morning I would eat the candy. Then I would tear a rag and put up two nails and make a hammock for my doll. I would swing her and give her milk. Then I would pour some water on the hammock to make believe she wet herself, and I would take her and clean her and wash her diapers and hang them out to dry.

When I was twelve, we came back here to Puerto Rico because my step-mother's father was very ill. We stayed for six months and then returned to Panama. The boat had to stop at Trinidad. This was February 18, 1952.

I was in our stateroom when I felt a pain in front and in back, and I told this to a boy who was on guard in the hallway. When I turned around he said to me, "Look, I know what's wrong with you." My skirt was all stained with blood but he told me not to feel ashamed, that it was nothing, and that I should take a rest. Then he asked me whether I was a *señorita.* I told him I didn't know what he meant and he explained it to me. He said, "From today on, you are a *señorita."*

No one found out I was a *señorita* until three months later. I didn't dare tell my stepmother, because she was always saying that as soon as I was a *señorita* I was going to get me a man. So I kept it from her. I would wear *panties,* lots of *panties,* which I washed. But one time I forgot a pair in the bathroom. She saw the stains and told my father and I felt very ashamed.

Now that I was a *señorita,* I would say to myself, "I have grown out of my childhood and soon I'll be able to get married." I always thought of getting married in a veil and crown. But I was never able to do it because of my stepmother's mean character. I thought of having a home, and of wearing a wedding ring on my finger like the other girls. I wanted a pretty gown and a cake with a lot of layers. I wanted to marry a boy from the *Army,* not a civilian, because civilians only cut sugar cane. That was the thing that occupied my mind. I would say, "I'm going to marry a general."

I wanted to have a bedroom set like my stepmother, a living-room set, and things of good quality. And I wanted to learn to drive so I could buy a car and take out my family. I dreamed that I was going to the opera all the time, not to the movies, only to fancy places. I imagined how I would look in pretty dresses.

I lost one year of school because of the six months we'd spent in Puerto Rico. When I was back in Panama I was thirteen and I was kept in the same sixth grade. I was still in school when a boy fell in love with me. He was a bus driver, a young fellow, and we didn't get to make love or anything. He only told me he wanted to be my boy friend. He was married but that didn't stop me. My stepmother found out and told my father. He didn't do anything, so she took a switch and peeled it clean and beat me on the lungs with it and then had me kneel for two hours on a kitchen grater.

At about fourteen, I came back to Puerto Rico. Everything looked very different to me. I spoke Panama style and didn't understand lots of things that were said to me.

My stepmother and a lot of other people told me that my mother was having relations with a lot of men. Well, one day I met this girl who is a half sister of ours. Her name is Alba Nidia. She looked a lot like Crucita and their hair was exactly the same. I said to her, "Look, child, you're my little sister."

"That's a lie," she said, and spat in my face. She never knew our *mamá*, because when she was only six days old Fernanda gave her away, with pen and paper, to some people who lived at Stop 21. The child's true father was killed, and nothing would make *mamá* accept her little daughter after that. Nanda never mentioned that child to us, but we knew of her through our stepmother.

One day Hortensia told me that she would be going to Baltimore because the *Army* was sending my father there and that she would leave me with her sister María del Carmen at Stop 26. So she went off and left me to fend for myself.

María del Carmen made me do a lot of work once again. She sold bootleg rum and had dealings with men. She made me bury the rum under the house, then dig it up later and sell it. Afterward she used to say that I refused to help her and that all I was interested in was running around.

While I was there, María del Carmen was in love with a young boy. She was an old woman and I was a *señorita* so he would give me the eye and come over and talk to me. Well, she got jealous and one day she went after me saying that I was taking away her sweetheart and that she didn't want me living there any longer. She said I was going to be a whore just like my *mamá* and she threw me out of the house. So I went to live with her daughter, Lourdes.

Lourdes was married to a man by the name of Mon, who was under a thirty-five-year parole for having killed an old woman in New York years and years ago. He also raped some little girls. He coaxed them up to his room with candy and abused them there. As for me, he tried to grab my breasts, and when I didn't want to, he forced me and kissed me. He bought and sold stolen goods and the police finally caught up with him and arrested him.

I had to do all the work in Lourdes' house, clean, wash clothes, run errands, take care of the baby. Sometimes all she gave me for breakfast was a glass of milk and a slice of cake. And when she didn't cook I had to get food for her at her mother's house in Santurce. She never let me go out and she was far too fond of beating me. Sometimes I went without a bite until six o'clock at night. I was very skinny and had to work hard, and so I was thinking about going to my *mamá*'s house. I had it in mind for quite a while.

My *mamá* lived in La Esmeralda with my sister Cruz and my brother. My other sister, Soledad, lived in La Esmeralda too. While I was in Panama she had married an old guy by the name of Arturo.

Soledad was nice to me. She told me what to do when I had my period. She tore up sheets, folded them and gave them to me. Later I learned to use *Kotex*. She told me to dress myself nicely so that the boys would admire me. She put make-up on me and took me to the movies, where she introduced me to a lot of her friends.

She said to me, "Go and stay with Nanda, because Nanda will let you go to lots of places, and if not, come here and I'll take you to dances. And look, I have lots of friends who'll take you to the beach."

So one day I left Lourdes' house and went to my *mamá*'s. I told her, "Nanda, I am going to stay with you because Lourdes is treating me badly and I don't want to stay there any more." Then my *mamá* said, "Well, you are my daughter. I will accept you. Stay here."

I stayed with her for four months. The first few days she was very nice to me. I felt very happy. I liked La Esmeralda. The house was poorer than my father's, but I felt good because my *mamá* never hit me. She used to scold me and throw me out of the house, but she never hit me.

My *mamá* was living with a man called Erasmo, a fellow she had met at the Silver Cup. Erasmo is Arturo's foster brother, and he was a real drunkard. Erasmo hardly liked to have anybody at all visit the house. Once he tried to hug Soledad. Just think, I had gone to the beach, and when I came back I saw them lying on the bed. I don't know what happened. I went out at once. I can't tell whether or not there was anything between them. My sister sure let him get familiar. But afterward she took off with Arturo. Erasmo used to wink at me, too, but I'd just give him a dirty look. He never had a chance with me. Maybe the reason my *mamá* left him was that he made passes at her daughters.

I don't know how Fernanda met Pedro, but one night she went to the movies with him, leaving Erasmo at home. Next day she came back to get her clothes and we went to live with Pedro.

Pedro, my second stepfather, was the best. Whatever I asked for he would give me. If I didn't feel like eating, he would send out for something especially appetizing for me. I could ask him for anything, a nickel, a quarter, and he'd give it to me right away without a complaint. That boy was very nice to me.

In the beginning I was afraid to be in La Esmeralda because it was very dark, because you had to go underneath other houses to get to your own.

Pedro and my *mamá* would stay awake to play tricks on me. Sometimes she would stay inside the house and send him out through the window to knock on the door. When I went out to open it there would be nobody there, then suddenly he would stick his head through the open window and I'd run. One day my *mamá* said to me, "Now look, you keep your mouth shut, because if you talk at night the dead come and stick their fingers in your mouth." Well, I began to talk and talk and talk and Pedro came and stuck his finger in my mouth and I thought it was the dead and I began to scream.

They scared me practically every day. One night when I was in bed, after the light was turned out, I saw what looked like a man in the doorway and began to scream and scream. Pedro got up like a crazy man. There was a post in the room that divided the wall and he thought it was a man hiding there and punched it with his fist. His hand was so swollen the next morning he couldn't go to work.

But my mother didn't really care for me. The truth of the matter is that she has never treated me well. She didn't fix my clothes and she wanted the house to be nice and clean when she got home from work. She didn't want to see me with people, with friends or anything, and she didn't want me to go out or to have a boy friend.

She always made soup and I would say to her, "*Ay,* Nanda, I don't like soup." She would answer, "All right, if you don't like soup, eat shit. I cook what I like and what my husband likes."

My *mamá* is tough. I never did see her soft side, and I have no idea why she is like that. I guess she didn't suffer at all on account of us because she threw us out into the world. She didn't have to make any sacrifices for us because my stepmother was the one who brought us up. I love her because she is my mother, but I repeat, she has never had affection for me as a daughter. Because I was with my *papá* for so long, she lost this feeling. The child she loves most is my brother Simplicio. Her other favorite is Cruz, because Crucita has always been with her.

I don't know what to say about my *mamá* because one moment she is very contented with a person and the next moment she is angry. But my *mamá* never has hit me. I never gave her reason to, eh?

My *mamá* took me to Río Grande one day, to meet my grandfather Rogelio for the first time. As we were going along the road I saw a man with green eyes and she says to me, "Look, that's my *papá*." I greeted him but I didn't feel as if he was a relative. I would say to him, "Listen, sir," and he'd correct me, "No, call me *papá*. I'm your grandfather." Little by little I felt more at ease with him until finally I did call him *papá*.

Rogelio was well off. He owned his home, a two-story cement house with tile floors and Venetian blinds at the windows. He had a bedroom set, a living-room set and TV. He was a good man. He spent a lot of time with us. If he went out he always invited us to go along. He bought us fruit and everything we wanted. He took us dancing too. I remember dancing with him, about four years later, in La Esmeralda. I never saw him again after that. I left for New York and there I got the news that he had died.

I don't know much about my mother's life and I don't try to find out, since she is so indifferent to me. One day she and I went bathing together and I saw tattoo marks on her body. One was a name, "Fidel Díaz," and the other said, "I love you."

"What is that, Nanda?" I asked.

"Oh," she said, "it's the mark of my pimp."

"And what does 'pimp' mean?"

"A man I'm supporting because he has treated me right."

And I said, "Oh, my God!" She was getting dressed and I asked her, "Nanda, where are you going?"

"To fuck sailors, to get bills out of them."

"Oh, then you hustle?"

"Yes, I've been hustling for years. Since I left you kids."

As my mother belonged to the profession she would bring men to the house. Sometimes, not often, she slept with them there. She usually came home to drink with them and then they would go to a hotel. At times they would be in bed and fool around before leaving for San Juan. And when she came home drunk and saw me talking to my friends she would tell me I had to get out of the house, and this made me feel bad. I had an aversion toward women of the profession, and I would ask her why she didn't get out of that life. She said it was the easiest way to get money. I cannot be ashamed of what my mother did because she did it to defend herself. And she isn't the first woman in the world to do it. I cannot judge her because that's the way her life turned out. But at that time I didn't like it.

One day she took me to the place where she picked up men so that I would know about it and could get acquainted with her friends. I was about fourteen and it was my first visit to a *bar*. The men whistled at me a lot. I hated the people there. I saw women with scars on their faces, prostitutes. When a woman has her face cut, that means she is a prostitute. They said to my mother that I was very stuck up. My *mamá* said to me, "Now look, you can be friends with these people."

"No, not me," I told her. "I'm not going to make friends with those whores." I hated those people.

I left Fernanda's house and went to live with my sister Soledad for four months. We got along fine, even though she sometimes had fits of temper. My mother didn't get along with Soledad because Soledad had no respect for her. One day Fernanda said something and my sister hit her with her fist. So my mother went and beat Soledad with an electric wire. Then Soledad, who is as strong as a man, grabbed Pedro and threw him to the floor a couple of times. He is a little fellow. She took the wire away from my mother and beat her with it.

Soledad brought men to the house when her husband, Arturo, was at work. For a while she was in love with Reinaldo the Negro. One day Arturo left as if to go to work but he turned right around and came back home. There he found my sister sitting on Reinaldo's lap letting him suck her breasts. When Arturo saw that, he took a swing at her. She got Arturo's revolver, but before she could shoot he grabbed her hand; the gun went off and the bullet hit her in the finger. She still has the scar. Then Arturo pulled a knife and sliced her twice with a "cow's tongue," a switch blade. Well, they put him in jail because she told the judge that he was the one who fired the shot. They gave him six months, and while he was there she and I went to live at Lourdes' house and she ran around with other men.

Felícita

The Fathers
of My Children

I WAS GOING to Fort Brooke to have my teeth fixed, and one day I saw a soldier, about twenty-six years old, standing at the window. He was white and tall and he looked at me and asked if I would like to come and visit him. I said I would. He was Ángel Cubero, the father of my twins.

I spoke to Soledad, and we both went to Fort Brooke the next Sunday. When we arrived some boys came to the little window and they said to my sister, "Say, do you want to visit with us?" Right off, Soledad said, "Sure, let's go." She went off with a boy and I visited Ángel. He gave me a piece of cake and asked if I would come back again the next day and I said I would.

I kept visiting Ángel for nearly a month. Soledad and I went there on Sundays and then Ángel and I became sweethearts. He told me that if I wanted he would speak to my parents. I agreed. He wrote to his *mamá* telling her that he had a girl he was going to bring back.

I was completely innocent then. Imagine, the first time Ángel asked me for a kiss I gave him one on the forehead! "Look," he said, "what I want is for you to give me a tongue kiss." I told him I didn't know what to do. "Like this,"

he said. "The movements I do with your tongue, you do with mine." So I did what he wanted and that was the first love kiss he gave me.

The only thing he told me about his life was that he had had a girl friend and she left him for somebody else. He kept telling me about the places he had been to and that he had fooled around with women, but that I would be the first one he ever lived with under the same roof.

We were sweethearts and Ángel came to my house. I was living with *mamá* and Pedro then. But they didn't accept him. Pedro didn't want me to have a boy friend and he kept a piece of pipe around, saying it was going to be used to soften up Ángel. Pedro was very fond of me, but neither he nor *mamá* wanted me to keep company, so he fought with Ángel all the time.

My *mamá* spent her time playing dice. She would leave the cabaret good and drunk, then go to a *bar* near her house and not come home until she was falling down. Then she would say that if I had a boy friend I would have to get out of the house, that she would have to talk to that son of a bitch of a father of mine, that, God willing, he would get killed in the *Army*.

My *mamá* took a dislike to Ángel from the minute she saw him. She didn't want him to ask for my hand or anything, but I kept going with him and she kept throwing me out of the house. People told her that he was a pimp for whores in La Esmeralda and that he had a wife and four children from whom he was hiding. It was a lie. He was from Culebra and didn't even know where La Esmeralda was until I showed him.

A girl always has one friend who acts as a go-between for her and that friend of mine was Marcolina. She was very good to me and would carry messages from him, or tell me, "Look, Ángel is waiting for you in such and such a place." He would give me money to buy whatever I needed because my *mamá* didn't give me anything. He was the one who bought me all my clothes. I needed *panties* and other things that a *señorita* has to have and which Fernanda wouldn't buy because she said I was raised by my *papá* and he could take care of me.

The boy saw the kind of treatment I was getting and asked me whether I wanted to go away with him. So one day after Fernanda went to work, I left. I was fourteen.

I told my elder sister that *mamá* was mistreating me badly and that I couldn't go on living like that. Soledad began to cry when she heard this. Then I went to Cruz and said, "Look, Crucita, I'm going to buy a tube of toothpaste. Wait here for me." So I took a dime and went off to a friend's house where I had everything ready, and Ángel and I left from there for Culebra. Some tube of toothpaste!

We went from San Juan to Río Piedras by taxi and then took a *público* from Río Piedras to Fajardo. At Fajardo we took a launch to Culebra. We left San Juan at eight o'clock in the morning and got to Culebra at four in the afternoon.

I got dizzy on the way and had to lie down on the seat. I woke up when the boat got to Culebra. I was imagining to myself, "Oh God, now that I've gone with this man, maybe he is going to take me off to some cane field, suitcase and all, and strangle me."

He behaved himself on the way and didn't even try to kiss me or do anything else. He told me he was going to marry me, that he wanted to make me happy, and that he had a house ready for me. But we never married. He refused to, afterward. His *mamá* didn't want me to live with him because he was white, and me, I'm colored. On the way he told me not to worry, that his *mamá* was poor and old and very good and that she was expecting me. But these were all lies. It all turned out different.

When I got there I saw that his mother was not expecting me. They lived like rich people. They owned the house and it was made of cement and had all the luxuries inside, a good living-room set, a dining-room set, bedroom sets, a kitchen with bottled gas, everything. And his mother was a young woman.

I took a bath and changed my clothes. Then his *mamá* served us food and we ate. A little later, about seven in the evening, we went to a dance hall. Ángel began to drink and drink until he got so drunk he couldn't even stand up. He drank to celebrate with his friends and to introduce me to all of them.

We got home about one-thirty in the morning. His mother had the bed fixed for us. Everything was all ready. Ángel had a separate small house for himself and me, quite a distance away but in the same yard.

Well, that same night my period came. I was so tight, he couldn't have relations with me, although he tried. He was supposed to be back at camp on Monday but he waited three days to see if my period would stop. He went back on the fourth day and they gave him a month's punishment for being late. He couldn't come home until the month was up. And so I passed as a *señora* all those weeks, although I was still a virgin.

That month Ángel's mother treated me wonderfully. She cooked, his sister washed and ironed for me, I didn't have to lift a finger the whole time. But I didn't dare set foot out of the house. Ángel's *mamá* asked me all about myself, where I'd been, what my mother was like and whether she had money, what my family was like. And I told her all about them.

When the month was up, Ángel came home. He tried to get into me and with the first thrust I fell off the bed. I had my legs down and he said, "No, raise them up." When I put them up he got into me and I screamed and fell to the floor. He got in but he couldn't break it because it was so tight. Even now when I don't have relations with a man for some time I close up tight. I don't know why. Ángel wanted me to see a doctor to open me up a little but I didn't go.

On the second day we screwed four times. I didn't like it then but on the third day it was wonderful. After that we did it every day before breakfast, at lunchtime and all through the night. We did it standing up, sitting down and lying sideways. He said, "Oh, my kidneys hurt." I said, "Don't worry, tomorrow you'll sleep late and I'll give you your breakfast in bed."

I wanted to do it very much, lots and lots and lots. He'd get tired sometimes, you know what I mean? Because I really tortured him. When I wanted it, he would say, "*Ay,* I don't feel well." But that didn't make any difference to me.

"You're on your honeymoon now, kid," I told him.

He got thirty days' leave to celebrate his honeymoon. He behaved as nicely as could be during those first days, but then he kept getting drunk and hitting me and fighting with his *mamá* until she hated me. She hated her son and she hated me. She had gone to New York and when she came back she was spoiled. She began to say that I was a Negro, that my family was a disgrace and that she didn't want her son to marry me. What was behind it all was that she was afraid she would lose her *army* allotment if we married. That made all the difference. She began to ignore me completely and to fight with him. Then he began to quarrel with me, and I kept getting it from both sides.

She kept throwing it up to me that my *mamá* was a whore. My *papá* had told Ángel what my mother was and he told his *mami*. And, like a fool, I had told him, too. I was only fourteen years old, and whatever anybody asked me, I answered. His *mamá* said, "I don't like to have anybody around whose relatives cut up people and go to jail. My family has always been a decent one."

Ángel kept mistreating me. Every month when he collected his pay, he would say, "I'll be right back." And when he got back he would be practically without a cent. I had to steal the money from him to get the things I needed, because he drank it all up. If I asked him any questions about it, he would beat me. He and his mother never stopped picking on me. I had no relatives there or anything, so everybody took advantage of me.

After four months I got pregnant. It happened when we were at my sister's house in La Esmeralda. Ángel had spent one day drinking beer and I drank a couple of beers myself. Then we had relations five times, one right after the other, and I got pregnant. He had prayed for me to become pregnant, but when it happened he became awfully mean. He started hitting me all over my body. He'd even kick me in the belly and knock me to the floor.

One week he had collected five hundred dollars because his *army* check had been delayed. Well, he went out drinking and fooling around with some women and came home looking knocked out and with lipstick all over him. I asked him for money to buy a layette but he told me he didn't have any.

"Sure," I said, "you spent it all on those whores."

"Shut your mouth," he told me.

"No. Kill me if you want but I am going to go on talking. If you stuck a knife in me right now, I don't think I'd bleed."

"So you're looking for a fight, you daughter of a great whore."

"You're a bigger son of a bitch!"

When I said that he came over and gave me a kick that knocked me into an open dresser drawer. Then he picked me up in the air by one arm and one leg and dumped me into a chamber pot full of piss. He was a very strong man. He weighed 174 pounds and I was just a skinny little thing. But I fought back and we broke a table and a mirror. It was really something!

We fought all the time. Every week it was the same story with his pay check. One day we got into an argument and he threw me out of the house. I went to my mother's in the morning, but the next day I was back in Culebra again. I came back because when I greeted Pedro he barely looked at me. He stayed away from the house all the time I was there and that made me feel bad. I didn't say anything, I just got my things together and went home. My husband was sad while I was gone, but as soon as I got back he felt better.

I was nine months pregnant by then but I scrubbed my house every day. Ángel told me not to go out any more because I might give birth any day. But I didn't like to be alone. One morning he went out with some friends and said he would be right back. I waited until ten o'clock that night but there was no sign of him. I didn't get any pains, but I had a premonition that I would.

I didn't sleep at all that night. When I got out of bed the next day, I felt something running down my thighs. *"Ay,* look at this, Ángel," I said, "water is coming out of me."

"No," he answered, "it's piss. Go to the hospital, maybe your bladder is punctured."

I put some *Kotex* on and told him, "I'm going to lie down. Maybe it has something to do with my giving birth."

"No. Straighten up the house and wash the dishes. I'm going out to buy a fish for you to cook."

I put a basin under me with my legs apart and my belly hanging over it with the water dripping out while I washed the dishes. In spite of everything, I straightened up the house, but then I couldn't do any more.

I called in a neighbor, because Ángel's *mamá* had stopped speaking to me. My neighbor said, "Oh Lord, yes, you're going to give birth." I began to cry. I sent for my husband's *mamá* but she wouldn't come. The woman called an ambulance for me. When it arrived, Ángel's *mamá* finally came. *"Ay,"* she said hypocritically, "why didn't you send for me?"

When my husband came to see me at the hospital, I was in the labor room. I told him, "Ángel, there are fifty dollars inside the stuffing of our mattress. Go get it in case I have a hard time and need to buy some medicine. Bring it to me here."

"All right," he said.

I asked, "Why are you all dressed up?"

"I'm going to celebrate the happy arrival of my son."

"But I haven't had the baby yet." He left anyhow. He got the fifty dollars and drank it up.

That night there was a raging hurricane when my labor pains started. All the hospital lights went out, they had to use gas lanterns. The graduate *nurses* weren't there, nor was the doctor. Someone went to fetch them, but meanwhile the doctor's wife and two *nurses'* aides attended me.

Angelito came first, without any trouble. When Gabi was being born, I felt as if something was holding him back. He was coming down with one of his hands stuck out. I cried out that I couldn't bear it any more. I had two attacks of eclampsia. I had to have oxygen and blood transfusions and there was no money to pay for them. If a woman has three attacks of eclampsia, one after the other, the third one kills her. One side of my body felt dead. I had a knot in my throat and I couldn't breathe. I practically had no blood pressure at all.

The *nurses* sent the ambulance at once to get my husband. When it came back without having found him, they notified the police. They tried to get my mother-in-law but she couldn't come because there was nobody to stay with the little girls. So, not being able to find anyone, they sent for the mayor of Culebra, who came at once. He told them that if the baby didn't come soon, they'd have to take me to Fajardo because I couldn't live through the birth. But thanks to God and the Virgin, they gave me oxygen, and with a great deal of effort they managed to take out the baby. Gabi was born with one of his little arms completely black.

At the break of day they went to tell Ángel that I had borne him twins. He couldn't believe it. He dressed and went to the hospital to see his children. When he arrived the doctor scolded him. The doctor himself had already been bawled out by the mayor. While I was having all that trouble, Ángel was out dancing and the doctor was at the movies with his mistress. The doctor lost his job at the hospital, too, because he hadn't been there to attend such a serious case.

When Ángel saw me, he asked, "*Ay,* how do you feel?"

"I couldn't feel better," I said, and as soon as the words came out of my mouth I passed out cold.

I knew I was going to have twins because I went to the clinic every month and they had taken an X-ray and had told me. As it was my first big belly, I didn't even feel heavy, and I rode a bicycle, went roller-skating, played ball and jumped rope. People said, "Look at her, she's going to have that baby ahead of time." I didn't feel a thing, just nice and light. I think that exercise must have been the cause of my attacks. It must have done me harm.

As Ángel had spent the fifty dollars I had saved, when I came back to the house I didn't have any money, not even enough to make a cup of broth. So his mother killed a chicken I was raising, made me some broth and gave it to me. I had bought a few baby things, just about enough for one child.

My husband felt guilty and said to me, "*Ay,* I am going to straighten myself out. I have children now." But right after that, he began to behave worse than before. He was always drunk and quarrelsome. One day his *mamá* told him not to fight so much and to stop mistreating me. He called her an old whore and tried to hit her. One of his sisters threw a shoe at him and cut his lip. He was about to strike his sister, so his mother hit him. Then he hit his own mother right back. He was bad, bad as they come. Because of this, he now has heart trouble, high blood pressure and the chest sickness, too.

He continued to beat me and he told me to get out of the house because he didn't want to have any part of me or of the boys. They were tiny babies, one weighed three pounds and the other four. Little bits of things. I had to put a pillow under them to be able to pick them up to nurse them. I would sit in the middle of the bed, cross my legs, put a pillow in my lap and give them the breast, one on each side. I gave them the breast for eleven months. The two of them would cry at the same time, and whatever one did, the other did. They would both get sick at the same time too, so I had to carry them both. It was a terrible thing.

Then Ángel's mother went to New York again. He started ruining himself, drinking, and beating me every day. And I had to take care of that little sister of his. I had to mind the other house as well as look after my own.

Cruz came to visit me at Culebra after the two children were born. But she lost her taste for visiting me because Ángel chased the two of us with a knife. He came home drunk that day and it happened that I told Cruz a joke. Then Cruz cracked one back at me, about an old woman who farted so loudly she killed three chickens. I burst out laughing and so did Cruz, but he thought we were laughing at him, and he slapped me. So I threw a cup at him, and he pulled a knife and went after us. We ran out of the house and got away from him.

Finally, one day when he began drinking, I told him that if he kept it up, I was going to leave. He said that I should go ahead, because I wanted to go back to San Juan and be a whore just like my mother. I began preparing everything in the house and getting things together to leave for San Juan. When he came home and found everything packed, he said, "Oh, so that's what you want, is it?" and he gave me a push. This started a fight and he beat me up, giving me a black eye to take back to San Juan. I had no money so I asked my *compadre* Félix to lend me ten dollars.

My *compadre* was very nice, especially when Ángel was being mean. Félix gave me the money and said, "Here, take it and go, because your husband is giving you a bad time. Don't worry about paying me back."

So after living with Ángel for two years I went back to San Juan with the children. He had no word of me for a long time, and when he realized that I was right he asked me to come back, but I didn't want to. For three months he sent me seventy-five dollars a month. Later he sent fifty, then only ten.

. . .

I went to live in La Esmeralda with my *mamá*. "What you have to do now is get yourself a room," she said. So from the money I had left over, I rented a room for five and a half dollars. And that's where I lived. Sometimes she would send me food for the children and sometimes Cruz would give me money for milk. That's how I managed to keep going.

When I moved back to San Juan, Cruz already had a sweetheart. She and Emilio had fallen in love with each other when I was living in Culebra. *"Ave María,* there's such a good-looking young fellow over at *doña* Minerva's house. I'll introduce him to you," she said. *"Ay,* how I like that boy."

"Well, fall in love if you want to. You're old enough," I told her. She was about fourteen years old at the time.

One day she came to me and said, "Look, Fela, I'm going to my god-mother's house."

"Why?" I asked.

"Because Emilio did his damage to me."

I went and told Soledad about it, and she burst into tears. None of us liked Emilio because he was so abusive of Cruz. When I saw Soledad cry, I got sentimental and began to cry too. "Oh, dear God, Crucita," I said. "How could you have done such a thing with a man who beats you even before you are married?"

She always answered, "That's nothing. What matters is that I love him."

Soledad and I gave her good advice but she wouldn't listen. She said the trouble with us was that we had gotten men of our own and now we didn't want her to have one. So she and Emilio got married.

Soledad was still with Arturo then, but they had many fights and she would often leave him. She would come to my house and I always took her in. Arturo didn't want me to but she had always been good to me, so I would let her in. One day Arturo got hold of me in the street and hit me because of this. She would go back to him after two or three days, but in a little while she'd get angry again and would leave.

I don't know exactly when Soledad began to hustle but she has always liked it. It was my *mamá's* fault because if she had at least given us a good example, if she had hit my sister when she saw her with a boy friend— But instead of punishing her, what my mother did was hand her the brilliantine and send her to the movies. There the girl began to flirt and was passed from one boy to another for so long that she joined the profession.

Soledad has always had luck with men, she has had some awfully good ones. She is the best-looking one in the family, nice and tall, with a good figure. But she was always getting into fights with her husbands and deceiving them. That is what her life has been, taking husbands and getting rid of them.

One day I saw a boy coming down to La Esmeralda. As he passed by close to me, I said, "What lovely blue eyes." He stopped, looked me up and down, burst out laughing, and went on to Papo's *bar*. When he came by later I tossed him the same compliment. The next morning, when I was at my sister's house, there he was. He was Soledad's new husband.

He was a very nice boy. His name was Octavio. He would bring all sorts of things to my sister. He gave her a lot of jewelry, all gold. *Ay,* and he was the one who gave me *un coat* for my trip to New York. He helped me in every way. He would give me gold earrings and anything else I needed and was very nice to all of us. He was very good to Soledad and to everybody. But my sister was not nice to him. She has had many chances with good men but has never known how to take advantage of them. She fought with him all the time and would get jealous over any little thing—unjustly, because he never went out with any other woman. Tavio was a good man. He was by far the best husband Soledad ever had.

He would have gotten knifed by Soledad one time if not for me. I put my hand in the way and still have the scar where I was cut. Soledad pulled a knife on him because she was angry and had told him she didn't want to live with him any more. She wanted him to get out of the house and had asked me to tell him to come for his clothes. I saw her groping around inside her skirt, and at first I thought she was just holding it because it was unbuttoned. When Tavio came she tried to sneak behind him, but I stuck out my hand and said, "Watch out, Tavio, she's going to kill you." We got into a free-for-all which ended when she pulled off his pants in front of everybody.

After he left she went and jumped into the sea. I jumped in to save her, but I started to drown and it took a whole bunch of people to pull us out. She was purple because she had swallowed her tongue. After that she went home and broke all the dishes. Later that night we went looking for Tavio, but when he saw her coming he thought she was after him again and he took off. Finally she spoke to him and asked him to come back to the house and promised that she wouldn't fight with him any more. So he did and he brought all his things to her house. But she behaved badly, because when he went out she would go with other men.

One day they arrested Tavio, for no fault of his own because he hadn't done anything. When he was taken away in the patrol wagon, I took Soledad's arm and she began to tremble. Her whole body shook and her face got red. Then she fell in a fit, foaming at the mouth and trembling. She opened her mouth and her tongue went back in as if she were trying to swallow it. They rubbed ice on her and fanned her. They also put a little piece of wood in her mouth. Then I grasped her middle finger and held it hard. We worked on her like that for five minutes or so. When the fit was over she began to scream. She had another attack when Tavio was shot.

At that time I had a friend by the name of Zulma. She's in jail in Vega Alta right now. I knew Zulma when I first came to La Esmeralda, because she was in the profession then and used to go around a lot with my *mamá.* They went out together to pick up Americans. Well, Zulma tried to make friends with me and kept at it until finally I gave in. She had a fight once with a woman, Crazy Carmen, because Carmen fell in love with her and invited her up to a hotel. Zulma wouldn't go, so Carmen cut her face, her breast, her ass and her belly. They had to take Zulma to the hospital and give her a transfusion. "Rival Knifes Girl Friend" is the way it came out in the newspaper, but they weren't rivals. Carmen just likes other women. They put her in jail for one year. When Zulma got out of the hospital she kept knocking around. She began taking drugs and now she's an addict.

One day Zulma invited me to Papo's *bar* and she said, "Let's go to San Juan. I'll introduce you to a friend of mine." We went and she introduced me to a boy by the name of Nicolás Nieves, who looked as nice as could be. He was so well dressed, and from the way he behaved, it seemed to me he must come from good people. Well, we were talking and conversing. Then Zulma said to me, "Look, this boy has no wife and he would like to get next to you."

I told him I had children but he said that he didn't care, because if he loved me he would love my children, too. He said that he wanted to live with me and that he would support me and the children. I was only sixteen then and very ignorant. I fell for any little thing people told me. I really didn't know anything and on top of that I had to worry about feeding the two boys. Lots of times I gave them sugar water because I didn't have money for milk. So I let myself get tied up with Nicolás. After a week I had relations with him. It wasn't that I was crazy in love with him. What I had with Nicolás was only an affair. I enjoyed being with him because, after all, I'm a woman and have sensations. Besides, he kissed my neck and caressed me. My husband never did that.

Nicolás used to tell me that he wanted me to bear him a little girl. And, not having one myself, I said I'd like that too. I had planned for us to live together under one roof. But as it turned out, my *mamá* didn't like him and she quarreled a lot with him. One day I said to her that I was going to the movies and I offered her two dollars to take care of the twins. I returned with Nicolás at ten-thirty. Fernanda was waiting for me on the stairway to La Esmeralda. "Look at you, hot pants," she said. "What the hell are you doing with that dirty bastard, knowing I don't want you to go out with him?"

"Why, didn't you yourself tell me to go ahead and go to the movies?"

"Ah, but I thought you were going with another kind of man, not with that dirty Negro."

"But, Nanda, why do you say that to me?"

"Because I never have liked the looks of that man. I have known him a long time, longer than you have."

"All right, but you shouldn't insult me as you did and embarrass me in front of him."

And she said, "Ah, go to hell, both of you. And as for you, young man, get out of my sight before I get one of my ideas."

From that time on, she tongue-lashed him whenever she saw him, but he never answered back. Fernanda went so far as to threaten to cut him. When she said anything to him, he simply hung his head.

Fernanda stopped speaking to me for a whole month because I was with Nicolás. She said, "Until you leave that man, you and I won't be on speaking terms." Sometimes I sent her a dish of food I had cooked and she always threw it away. One day Nicolás bought some cigarettes for her and she threw them away in front of him and slammed the door in his face. But after he had left, she went down and picked up the pack of cigarettes. And she smoked them too.

Nicolás and I were together so often that I got pregnant right away. When he found out I was pregnant he told me he was married and would have to break off with me. He kept seeing me for a while but didn't help me. I took Quinine No. 50 and No. 80 and tea of sage and *ruda*. I also gave myself douches of Lifebuoy soap and of different kinds of plants the girls told me about. I went to the hospital and they prescribed a medicine with iron in it. Bitter as gall it was. I was told not to take too much of that or I might miscarry. But I took half a bottle and even so the pregnancy went on.

I was three months pregnant when Nicolás abandoned me. He claimed I was carrying another man's child. That hurt me so much I got sick and had to go to the hospital. I cried all the time. I couldn't touch my food and that gave me a weakness of the womb. Nicolás knew that my mother had taken me to the Municipal Hospital but he didn't visit me there. I was hospitalized for six days. After I got out I kept on having headaches and dizzy spells, and so I didn't take very good care of the children. Sometimes I got up and went over to a friend's to talk. Two and three hours went by before I returned home. I thought of having a talk with Nicolás' wife. But I decided not to. After all, she was married and had a better right to him than I did.

Then, a week later, I met Rosario. He lives in La Esmeralda and is a dock worker. Practically the only time you see him is when he is in the street drinking. But he is a good boy and he said to me, "Don't worry, I'll help you out, and the children, too." He gave me fifteen dollars and bought the baby's layette.

When I had the baby they had to give me serum and blood transfusions. All the time I was in the hospital Rosario would bring Nanda money for food for the twins. My mother did take care of them, but all she did was feed them and then leave them alone in the house.

Etanislá is my favorite child, and Nicolás said she wasn't his! After about two weeks, when the little girl's features began to form nicely, people asked him why he didn't go to see her, because her face was a copy of his. He didn't come to the house but asked for her, so I sent her to him. As soon as he saw

Tany he burst out crying, because she does resemble him. The very next day
he accepted her as his and gave me five dollars. The next week he gave me three
more and that was the last.

I kept on fighting and fighting to keep afloat. I was in bad shape, very bad
shape, and decided to go to New York. So I sent word to my father, who was
in Virginia, that if he didn't want his daughter to become a prostitute he'd
better help me find some way to get to New York. So he said he would, and the
first week he sent me fourteen dollars and then twenty after that. Rosario
helped me buy the ticket but I had to have relations with him to get it. Well,
finally I went, when the little girl was seven months old. I was seventeen or
eighteen, I don't remember exactly.

I decided to take only Etanislá with me. I asked my *mamá* if she wouldn't
keep the twins and she said she didn't want to. One day after she'd had a
couple of beers I said to her, "Keep them, Nanda, and let me see if I can't
manage to make a go of it over there. If I do, I'll send for you and the
children." She said "All right." It was the only favor she ever did me and it was
because the twins got money from Ángel through the Veterans Administration.
The first check was for one hundred and twenty-five dollars, for some back
money the Administration owed. After that they sent twenty-eight dollars a
month. When the money stopped coming in, Fernanda stopped taking care of
the children and gave them back to me.

She did take good care of them, I must say, for the two years she had
them. They didn't much like being with Fernanda, though, because she often
beat them black and blue with sticks. That is why they now respect my mother
and not me. If she says to them, "Go away," they get out at once. She doesn't
need to beat them any more to make them mind.

The twins were only two and a half years old when I left them. I felt
terrible about it, but what could I do? I couldn't take them with me because I
myself didn't know where I was going. Besides, I only had money enough to
pay my own fare.

I went to Virginia to live with my *papá* and stepmother. On the plane I
imagined myself in the States, struggling through the snow, surrounded by
luxurious buildings, like in the movies. I dreamed that I was going to be rich.
"I'll work and get money together and find my happiness there." That's what I
told myself and that's why I went.

As soon as I arrived in New York I got a boy who worked in the airport to
help me. He went with me to buy the ticket to Washington and carried the
baby and all my bundles. A lot of people were nice to me because I was all
alone with a little baby, and it was my first trip.

I got to Washington at eleven o'clock at night. My father wasn't there and
I had no money left, so I went to the office and with my little bit of English I
made the girl understand my problem. I didn't know where Virginia was, but I
had my father's address. I thought I was going to give a taxi driver two dollars

like you do here in Puerto Rico, but he said that not even fifteen would be enough. So they began to call my father on the loudspeaker, saying, *"Señor Ríos, Señor Ríos,* your daughter Felícita Ríos is here, please come to *el Pan American."*

My father had been in the airport all the time. What happened was that it is so big he couldn't find us. They kept calling on the loudspeaker for about two hours. My father said that he heard the call and kept looking and looking like crazy for me all over the Washington airport. The more he heard them calling his name on the loudspeaker the more nervous he got, until he found me. He was as happy as could be when he finally saw me.

It was snowing in Virginia when we arrived, the first snow I had ever seen. My father immediately offered me food and gave the baby milk. My stepmother was nice to me, but all she said when she saw me was, *"Ay,* how skinny and dark you are!"

"But, child," I said to her, "I just came from Puerto Rico and the sun there is terrific now."

Hortensia behaved well for a couple of days. After that I had to wash and wax and polish the floors. I had to clean the Venetian blinds and the furniture, cook and iron for her. The baby had begun to crawl and would grab Hortensia's little figurines. She broke one and my stepmother hit her so hard that her little leg swelled up.

Then my stepmother began saying things to me. One day she let me know that a spiritist had told her I was a witch. I was putting on some cologne and she says to me, "Oh, pfui, that stinks of witchcraft."

Then *papito* said to Hortensia, "Oh, don't go believing in sorcery. You're always getting sick because you believe in crazy things." That's the way my stepmother was and still is to this day.

When Hortensia began to treat me badly I decided to go to my uncle Simón's house in New Jersey to work and save money for my fare back to Puerto Rico. I left Tany with my *papá.* This was after living in Virginia for five months.

My father's brother, Uncle Simón, had a wife and four children in Salem, New Jersey. They live well. They own a two-story house and have sets of furniture in the living room, dining room and bedroom. They also have a very pretty, well-equipped kitchen.

In Puerto Rico my uncle had sold candy off a pushcart. He lived at Stop 26, and his house was built right in the mud. If they ate a chicken there, they couldn't afford to discard even the neck and feet. In the States they'll take nothing but the breast and the drumsticks. The rest they throw away.

When I saw my uncle he had almost forgotten how to speak Spanish. My cousins, his daughters, spoke only English. They had a dance at their house when we got there and they played only English reords. They didn't have a single Spanish one. When I explained to them that I only knew Spanish, they turned to the other girls and spoke to them. And I, hearing them chatter in a language I didn't much understand, turned my back on them and didn't pay any attention to what they said. I remembered how miserably poor they had been in Puerto Rico, and I felt very uncomfortable seeing them try to act as if they were better than other people.

What I'd like to do to people who show off talking English! If I could be governor of Puerto Rico or the mayor of New York for five or ten minutes I'd take a pistol and I'd shoot every Puerto Rican who has forgotten Spanish.

It's a disgrace, and it makes me uncomfortable to hear a Puerto Rican talk in such a ridiculous way. The modern *teenagers,* for instance, are speaking a brand of English nobody can make head or tail of. They'll play an American record and exclaim, *"Ave María,* that's really *cool!"* but if you ask them what the words mean, they have to shut up because all they can understand about that record is the name of the singer.

I'll speak English to an American if I have to, but forget my own language? Never! Latins should speak their native tongue at home. Those who don't, can't love their own father and mother. If they want to give up their language they shouldn't call themselves Puerto Ricans.

The family doesn't count there in New York. Money is behind whatever anybody does. I got a job in a canning factory belonging to Italians and was supposed to give my uncle twenty dollars a week. That was just for food alone. I bought my own clothes and shoes, and washed my clothes. If I didn't give my uncle the twenty dollars a week on the day I was supposed to, he would go around with a sour look on his face. He was never nice to me.

The only ones who were nice to me were the neighbors and Iris, my uncle's wife. She would take me along with her wherever she went. You see, she was in love with a fifteen-year-old boy, he couldn't have been any older, and she put the horns on my uncle. She would say to me, "Look, go tell so and so to come over here to do an errand for me." And I would go and tell him.

My uncle's friends let him know Iris was putting the horns on him. But so what! He had two Negro women and didn't want to have relations with her! Months would go by and he wouldn't come home, so she fell in love with that boy. She would go to dances and everywhere with him.

My uncle said that I was the one who was influencing his wife and he kept scolding me until he finally drove me out of the house. He embarrassed me in front of people by saying all kinds of things about me. One day some friends were at the house and one of them asked who I was. "Aah, she's the no-good daughter of a no-good whore!" He told them I wasn't really his niece. I started to cry and told him not to worry, that I was going to leave his house. So he said, "That's what you should do. Get out of here." But I went on living there because I had no place to go and I didn't know anyone but him.

Felícita

The Man I Married

I MET MY HUSBAND Edmundo at my uncle's house. Edmundo is a little darker than I and his hair is wavy. He looks Spanish, is short and thin, and was about twenty-four years old then. He was a friend of my uncle's and he came to a dance in the house. I was bringing coffee to the guests in the living room when he said to me, "Miss or Mrs.—may I know your name?"

"Well, my name is Felícita Ríos."

"Are you related to Simón?"

"Yes, I am."

"I wish we could be something to each other some day," he said.

"Look, *señor,* I didn't come here to have affairs, I came to work. I don't want anything to do with any man, because I have been through so much that now I hate them all."

"Ah, but I'm going to put a magic spell on you to make you come to me. You appealed to me the minute I saw you there in the kitchen fixing the coffee and you're going to be mine."

"You're making a big mistake," I told him. "As far as I'm concerned I piss on you spell-makers."

"Oh, Virgin, what a way to put it."

"What about it? I'm a Puerto Rican and so are you. You're no foreigner."

Well, there we were arguing back and forth until finally he asked me to dance. After the first one, he wanted to dance all the rest of the numbers with me.

He came to my uncle's house the next day and every single day after that, to see me. Sometimes he would come with his shoes untied and he'd ask me to tie them for him, and I would. And he kept calling me on the telephone until finally he won me over.

One day Edmundo said, "You don't happen to know of a house for rent around here, do you?"

"There is one right next door to the church," I answered.

"All right, then, go see the man there and give him this money," he said and he handed me twenty dollars for a week's rent. I went and gave it to the man and closed the deal. The house was *furnished*. Edmundo bought a blanket which he asked me to keep for him and then he went to the store and spent fifty dollars on things to fill up the icebox. How was I supposed to know it was all for me? He didn't tell me it was. Then he said to me, "Take your cousins, so your uncle won't say anything, and go fix up the house. Clean it up for me."

I went alone, but had no evil ideas at all in mind. When I got there, he grabbed me. I tried to push him off, a woman is always supposed to, you know, but he got the better of me and kissed me. Then he said, "Look, I'll call for you at your uncle's on Saturday and we'll go dancing." I agreed. So I bought new clothes and spent twenty-five dollars on a pair of shoes. After all, I was going dancing with my boy friend.

When Saturday night came around, there we all were with our hair up in curlers getting ready to go. When my uncle saw this, he began to shout, "Nobody is leaving this house tonight, not even the Mother of God! Anybody who goes through that door is going to get her neck broken!" So I hung my dress up in the closet and we all went upstairs to take the curlers out of our hair. When Edmundo arrived, he asked, "Aren't you coming to the dance?"

"No," I told him, "my uncle doesn't want us to."

"All right then," he said, "let's go down the street and buy ice cream."

It turned out to be some ice cream! That same night we began to live together. I went off with Edmundo just a week after we met. My uncle stopped speaking to me for three whole months.

The first time I had relations with Edmundo, he was worried because he thought I had lied to him and that I was really a virgin. It had been a long time for me and when he tried to get inside me, he couldn't. "Are you sure you aren't a virgin?" he said.

"Yes, I'm sure," I told him.

"No," he insisted, "you are a virgin and you want to get me into a jam."

"No, *chico,* I'm a woman. I have a little daughter but she's in Virginia. I couldn't bring her with me because my uncle is strict."

We kept at it for over half an hour until finally he was able to get in and then when he saw there was no blood or anything, he said, "All right, now I believe you." We knocked off about seven pieces that night—yum, yum, yum, delicious! And every day after that it was one after another. Sometimes we would go into the bathroom, fill the tub and do it right there in the water. And then, after that, under the shower, "chicken style."

We enjoyed ourselves very much in the beginning, but then after a while I got sick of it, we did it so much. We really went at it seriously at first, and then afterward there were days when we only did it once, because I got pregnant. I swelled up inside and it hurt me and it wasn't much fun.

My first house in New Jersey was very pretty. After that we moved twice. All three houses were nicer than the ones in Puerto Rico, because I had a set of furniture and a carpet for the living room. There were big curtains to cover the glass windows, and I had a dining-room set and a lamp. There was a separate room for the children. Edmundo gave me a washing machine, and later on he got himself a car. I had everything I needed.

Edmundo earned sixty-four dollars a week in the winter working at the graveyard. He paid the rent, bought the groceries and gave me spending money. In summer he got a job at the canning factory. He gave me money for the groceries and he often went shopping with me too. When we didn't go to the movies, he would take me to the beach. And he gave me driving lessons. But I didn't learn much because his car was a '49 model Cadillac and it was too heavy for me.

Edmundo was a member of the Sacred Name of Jesus. That's why he married me. We got married, there in New Jersey, both in the Catholic church and before a judge. Before I got married I had to make my First Communion. I got scared when they put that stuff into my mouth. The week before, I had to go to confession. I told the priest, "This is the first time I have confessed."

"Confess, then, my daughter," he said, "and tell me your sins."

"Well, Father, I have committed adultery, I have wished my husband dead, I beat my children often, I like married men." Just like that I said it. After all, I couldn't see him and he couldn't see me.

He asked me, "What else?"

"Father, when I was a child I sneaked money from my stepmother and when she went out I went to the neighbors. When I lived with my *mamá,* I was always falling for the boys. I didn't obey her and I took stuff from the refrigerator without permission. One day, in a store, I saw a little pearly clip I liked. I put it in my hair and walked off without paying for it." I said lots more things that I've forgotten now. He asked me, see? So I answered. He talked a lot to me. He kept saying, "My daughter, you shouldn't do that, the Lord—"

I answered, "Yes, Father, I'll never do that again." When I finished he blessed me without giving me any more advice. It had taken me about an hour to confess. My knees hurt from kneeling so long.

Edmundo worked and I would help him out sometimes, taking care of children. Then he began putting money in the bank, saving and saving. He worked in a box factory—making boxes for apples, I think—until he had an accident and hurt a kidney and was in the hospital for a month and a half. When that happened I got four people together that I gave meals to. I had to get up at two in the morning to make their lunches and then I had to have dinner ready at five in the afternoon when they came from work. I couldn't sleep because I was worried about getting up at two in the morning to cook for the boarders. I couldn't rest in the daytime either, because I was washing and ironing and doing the other household chores. At six in the evening I was in the hospital visiting my husband and bringing him food. I did this for a month and a half and made ninety-five dollars a week, but got even skinnier than I am now. It was at this time that Soledad and her children came from Puerto Rico and lived in my house for a while.

When Edmundo came out of the hospital, he went back to work. I went back to the factory again for two weeks. I worked on the *labor machine* making piccalilli, soup and spaghetti. Every year in the summertime they hire a lot of women. I made one hundred and two dollars the first week and ninety-four the second week. They pay like that because there is a lot of work in the summer, from seven in the morning till eight at night, and that's a lot of hours! But you can make a lot of money. Edmundo bought his car, paid for the license and paid off our debts with that money.

But being pregnant, I had a bad belly and the smell of the tomato sauce at the factory made me sick. I couldn't work any more and Edmundo wanted me to keep on working. He claimed that the money he earned wasn't enough. He'd burst out, "Ah, you're the only woman who doesn't work." I told him I didn't go because I knew I couldn't do it and I wasn't going to kill myself. And right there we began to quarrel. Every time he spoke about that business of me getting a job I got mad and swore at him. Then he wanted me, with my sick belly, to get up at two in the morning and cook for him. I, who threw up if I even smelled food. So we quarreled and he kicked me out of the house.

Finally I said, "All right, I'll take care of children to help you out a bit." And I went, on my own, to our next-door neighbor and asked her to let me take care of her children. She told me she'd be delighted. There were four children and I took care of them while she worked. She and her husband paid me sixty dollars a week. Then they left, and I got thirty dollars for taking care of two other children. I was with them from seven in the morning to eight at night. I had to bathe and dress them and wash their diapers. I kept this job for seven months, until winter.

I had about three hundred dollars in the bank in New Jersey. The account was in my name. Edmundo was getting money from *el Employment*, you know, and he didn't want them to go thinking he had any money. This was before we moved to New York.

While I was pregnant my husband treated me well. The day the pains began I didn't say anything to him. I just went ahead and got the dinner ready early, bathed, put up my hair, fixed my eyebrows, and put a little cream on my face for when I went to the hospital. Then I made myself a strong cup of ginger tea with milk and drank it good and hot. The pains were getting worse and finally I said to Edmundo, "*Ay,* I'm feeling sharp pains." He didn't wait for another word but ran out to look for a taxi. There were no taxis at that late hour and they took me to the hospital in a police car.

They weren't sure I was going to pull through. They had to give me four quarts of blood and three of serum, because I was left without blood. When I went in to give birth, my pulse was so fast that I just emptied out. The blood smothered the baby and they had to massage him to revive him. When Edmundo heard about what was going on, he wouldn't leave the hospital. That man stayed at the hospital for six days without eating or shaving. He suffered very, very much. He would come in the morning, afternoon and evening, and bring me breakfast, lunch and dinner from the house. And he would always bring me a present, his hands were never empty when he came.

We were getting along wonderfully then, but afterward he began to go with other women and to mistreat me. He would stay out all night and one day he chased me with a gun. And he'd bring his women to the house, telling me they were just friends. But a next-door neighbor explained to me that they were women he was going with because she had seen them at the movies and dancing at the club. So there we were, fighting again and everything.

In August, 1961, I went with Tany and Mundito to Puerto Rico for two weeks to see my *mamá,* and six months later Edmundo and I were back in Puerto Rico for good. Edmundo didn't want to live in the United States any more. I had been with him there for nearly two years but we decided to go back and buy a house with the money they gave him for his accident.

We arrived in San Juan at seven in the morning and left for Salinas at two that afternoon. Edmundo was eager to visit his relatives, whom he had not seen for many years. We got to Salinas in the evening. That was the first time I had even been there. We took Tany and Mundito. The twins were still with my *mamá.*

Edmundo's relatives are terribly poor. They are farm laborers. The houses they live in are made of zinc. They don't pay rent, because the owner of the farm provides houses for all the workers. Edmundo's family used to own some land but they sold most of it and they completely neglected what little they kept.

Edmundo's relatives were very nice to me during that first visit. They offered me coffee, and when I told them that I never drank coffee they made chocolate for me. They asked me what I wanted for dinner. I said I'd like a dish of tubers because I hadn't had any in a long time. They couldn't get any, but they killed a chicken instead, to make soup for us. We had arrived at seven and they were still cooking at nine.

They asked me about my family and I told them we were very poor and that my father was in the *Army*. I was well dressed, so when they first saw me, they thought I must come from a rich family. We returned to San Juan the next day.

We had saved nine hundred dollars in New York and Edmundo bought a wooden house in La Esmeralda for five hundred and twenty-five. So now we had property, a house of our own. I thought it was very pretty inside. It had a refrigerator, a living-room set, curtains, figurines and a radio. Edmundo bought everything *cash* except the bed, which he bought on the installment plan.

He was out of work, so I said, "I'm going to take you to a place where you can get a job." I took him to the Silver Cup, where Soledad had worked. *Don* Camacho was the owner then and he hired Edmundo at once as a waiter. He started out earning twenty-five dollars a week. Then he was made bartender at thirty-five. It was really more because of the tips. Sometimes he earned as much as twenty-four or sixteen dollars a night.

Edmundo gave me everything I needed, but at the same time he treated me badly. He kept insulting me because of my sister Soledad. How could he live with me, he would say, while she was a prostitute? And if my sister was a prostitute, what was I? But no sooner did he begin to work at the Silver Cup than he fell in love with a prostitute there.

I didn't know about it at the time, though. Every day I would have a clean white shirt ready for him because he always came home with red spots on his shirt. He told me it was the red coloring they put in the Tom Collinses. One day he came home with a bite mark on his neck. She must have been one of those women who climb all over a man.

I had fixed him some chicken broth, and brought it to him in bed. "Here, baby," I said. Then I noticed the mark. "What is that mark you have on your neck?" "Oh, that's where I got hit by a piece of plaster Johnny threw at me." I gave him a look fit to kill. I felt like throwing the plate in his face but I knew he kept a knife under the mattress.

Then he sent for my *mamá* and told her, "Look, Nanda, Fela wants to know if this is a bite."

My *mamá* said, "No, it's from a piece of ice, because one day I got hit in the thigh with one and that's the mark it made."

I left everything in peace for the time being, but the next day the big fight started. If my husband had behaved right with me, I wouldn't have gone through his pockets and his wallet. I often found contraceptives in that wallet of his. This time I found the wallet damp and with a lump in it. Well, I found her watch and chain and the key to her house. The next morning I asked him, "Say, Mundo, whose are these?"

"Oh," he answered, "somebody gave them to me to hold."

"You don't say?" I said.

Edmundo and I had a terrific fight. I tried to kill him. I punched him in the nose and drew blood. He couldn't handle me alone because my nerves were so unstrung that I got strength from I don't know where. He had to punch me in the jaw and knock me out cold to get the better of me. When I woke up I was in bed, with him fanning me. Well, he had a nervous attack then and told me everything. He admitted that he had the woman. Her name was Pupa.

I knew Pupa. She is shorter and slimmer than I am. She's fair-skinned and has a face like a doll. I took Edmundo's knife and went straight to the Silver Cup Club, ready to kill her or be killed, but they wouldn't let her come out and face up to me.

I fought with Edmundo about her, over and over again. He worked at the Silver Cup for eight months and the laundresses there told me he was with Pupa all that time. To win him over, she said she'd work for him and that he shouldn't knock himself out working for me and my children. She said she would do whatever he wanted. If she had to suck it for him, she would, and if he wanted to do it in the ass, she'd let him. What happened then was that he wanted me to do the same and I wouldn't. So he kept saying, "Oh, but Pupa will do whatever I ask her."

My answer to that was, *"O.K., but she's a whore and I'm not."* After being with her, naturally he came home tired and went to sleep. Sometimes three or four weeks passed without us having relations. If he didn't want to, I didn't insist. I didn't try to do anything about it because I didn't think I was going to lose him.

I was pregnant with Eva María at that time and I felt sick and upset all the time. The first time I had a seizure, I was combing my hair, getting ready to go to San Juan. As I looked in the mirror my face stared back at me, disfigured. A monster's face. Then I felt some force pushing me out of the house. I dashed out and ran and ran. When I came to, I was back home and the house was crowded with people. According to them, I tried to jump into the sea. My head and face were swollen. My whole body was covered with welts.

I was nervous most of the time. It's nerves, isn't it, when one can't have a fight or get into an argument without feeling like killing the other person or cutting him up?

One day a man came to my house and said, "Your little boy broke off a piece of concrete."

"It's strange," I said, "that such a small boy should be strong enough to do that."

"Well, you should beat him for it." the man said, "or I'll smash your face."

"All right, let's have it out, you as a man who wears pants and I as a woman with *panties*. If you don't believe it, look." And with that I lifted my skirt and showed him. "I'll prove to you that I'm a better man than you are and you're nothing but a woman."

"Ah, I don't fight women," he said.

"Well, I dare you to hurt my little boy and see what happens." He slapped the child's bottom and I jumped on him and slapped him twice. Then I took a stick and hit him over the head. Several people had to come pull me away because I wouldn't stop. I meant to beat him unconscious with that stick. I screamed and screamed. People tell me my eyes look as if they'll come right out of my head when I am that way.

Before I gave birth I told my husband I wanted to be sterilized after the baby was born. But he said that when a woman was sterilized, she put the horns on her husband and the marriage broke up. I insisted, so he said, "I trust to the great power of God that he will grant me a little girl so I can have a pair, a boy and a girl. And if it works out like that, I'll have you operated."

As luck would have it, it turned out to be a girl and so, after she was born, he said to me, "On Monday, go for your blood tests and get the money together for your operation." He decided it was all right because I was not yet twenty-two and I already had five children, and I was dreadfully sick every time I got pregnant. So I saved the money out of what he gave me for the house. He would give me fifteen dollars for expenses, and I would spend ten or eleven and save the rest. Little by little, I saved up twenty-five dollars, and he gave his signature and I was operated. They told me to wait six months, but who's going to wait that long? I was having relations with Edmundo two weeks after the operation and I didn't get a hernia or anything. After I was sterilized, I enjoyed sex much more. Before, I accepted my husband when he wanted me, simply because he was my husband but I didn't get as much pleasure then. Now it's different. When I go to bed with a man, I wish he'd never get up. I want to keep on doing it. My sensations are more acute. Some women lose their desire when they are sterilized and they can't please their husband as they should. Thank God and the Virgin that didn't happen to me.

As a man my husband was weak, because if he didn't do it right away, he lost the desire. There were times when we were going to do it but the baby would cry and I had to get up. By the time I got through giving her milk, he was lying on his side and I was left high and dry. I would try to get him to do it, but he would say, "*Ay*, I'm sleepy." So I would leave him alone, but I'd spend the whole next day fighting with him.

Well, Edmundo and I kept fighting until finally he decided to move to Salinas to see if it would change our life any. He sold our house for five hundred dollars, losing twenty-five dollars on the sale. And after he had painted it, too!

We got to Salinas at noon but our things hadn't arrived yet. By six o'clock it was very dark and there were no lights in the house. My husband went to town and asked if anybody had seen the *truck* that was bringing our furniture.

Then he walked over to the highway and found that the *truck* had hit a car, and the paint was chipped off our refrigerator and everything else. Edmundo had to pay thirty-five dollars to bail out the driver. It was almost nine before they started to unload the furniture, with only a *frarlai** to see by because we had no electricity there yet. That night we had to sleep on the floor because we couldn't set up the bed. It was very dark and terribly cold. This was in October, 1962.

We had brought only one bed because there wasn't enough room in the *truck*. We left the twins' *caucho* in San Juan. I took the twins to Salinas with us because Fernanda had gone to Philadelphia to stay with Simplicio. When she came back to Puerto Rico she fell hard for Junior and didn't say anything about wanting the twins. So I kept them.

Edmundo's relatives came to call on us that morning and one of his brothers gave us a bed. We made a room for the boys in the back and used another room for ourselves. We had a front room, dining room and kitchen. That was all. We couldn't find a house to buy. Edmundo poured his money into that place until finally we found ourselves with no money and no house of our own.

I started living as the people there lived. I washed the clothes in the brook. The first time, I poured Fab into the water and the girls laughed and laughed. Nobody used detergent there, just big bars of soap. And they scrubbed the clothes on top of a stone. The pebbles in that stream shine like gold. I gathered a lot of them to keep in the parlor.

Everybody asked me, "Where do you come from?" And when I told them they said, "Think of it! Here's one from the capital." None of those people have ever been to San Juan. The only one who's been to San Juan is Edmundo and he came because I brought him.

Salinas is pretty but I cried all the time I was there. There weren't any lights along the road, only in the houses. I wanted to go back to San Juan because there everything is lighted up and the streets are full of people. In Salinas all we had at night was the sound of the frogs and the dampness of the earth. The people there go to bed at seven; chickens at six and the people at seven. Against my will it was, but I lay down early every night and closed my eyes. Edmundo would stay talking until eight or nine at his brother Poncio's place, two houses down the road.

* Flashlight.

On Christmas Eve, the first I spent in Salinas, everyone invited us to share in the fun of keeping the "vows" they had made. They went from house to house, singing and eating and drinking to keep their vows. A group of girls and men went together, as they had to walk long distances. Houses in that part of the country are few and far between. We would tell jokes as we walked along and we'd scare each other with stories of the headless man who was supposed to haunt the place.

In Salinas, people roast a pig and buy all sorts of things for Christmas Eve dinner. I made fried cakes and rice pudding at home. Then we invited a few people over to dance. All the guests had left by one or two in the morning and we went to bed. But at about three o'clock a group of people serenaded our house. In Salinas they sing and say a prayer for the people of the house and then the hosts open the door and let them in.

The first time we spent the Day of the Three Kings there, my husband had no money. He hadn't been able to work much because it rained so often. When he did work, he earned five dollars a day. Sometimes I worked too, gathering coffee. I scrambled uphill with my basket and picked the ripe beans off the ground. Sometimes I gathered half a sackful. We were paid ninety cents for each *almud,* or small basket of coffee. I took some of the coffee home and I put it outside to dry in the daytime. After about three days it was completely dry. I hulled it by beating it with a stick. After that I put it in a basin to pick over and clean out the chaff. I did everything the way I saw my neighbors do it. Then I put the coffee in a large paper sack and sent it to town to be sold. With that money, my husband bought presents for the children on the Day of the Kings.

I was well off and had every comfort at home. My only trouble was that I had a quarrelsome husband. He quarreled as much as ever while we were in the country and he beat me. It wasn't jealousy, because I never left the house. I don't know what it was, a kind of madness. It's only when Edmundo is sober that he's so unpleasant. When he's drinking, he's a good guy. He was even worse in Salinas than in San Juan, because he beat my little girl Tany, too, and mistreated the twins. He made those little boys go out into the fields with him to dig yams and carry them down to the house on their backs. I didn't like the way he overworked them. When I asked him not to beat the children, he'd say they could get out because, after all, they were not his children and he didn't have to support them. He often said he wished he had stayed with Pupa, because at least she worked to support him.

He made me get up at two in the morning to prepare his breakfast and make a dinner for him to take to work. If I overslept until two-thirty or three in the morning, he'd quarrel with me and wouldn't let me make his breakfast. He was always sharpening his *perrillo,* as they call a machete in Salinas, and saying he was getting it ready for me and the boys. I got to be really scared of him.

He was always throwing me out of the house, too, just as he'd done in New York. I had warned him then, saying, "You know that I have no one to go to here, but once we are back in Puerto Rico, if you do the least little thing to me, I'll leave you. When you feel happiest with me, that's the day I'm going to leave you." He'd just answer, "What you should do is get the hell out of here now." He said this to me three or four times.

The day he didn't kick me out was the day I left him.

That Sunday he went to the farm and brought me oranges, grapefruit and a whole sackful of vegetables. He filled up the refrigerator with all kinds of soft drinks, fruit juices and other things. I cleaned the house from top to bottom that day. I gave him breakfast in bed and fed him his oatmeal with my own hands. Then I watched him go. As soon as he was out of sight, I got myself and the children ready. I had already packed the suitcases and hidden them under the bed. He didn't know anything about my plans but I had given him fair warning. I'd told him that the day I saw him most pleased with me, I would leave. And so I did.

Edmundo says that when he was halfway to the fields he suddenly felt like turning back. He had a feeling something was going to happen because he had never seen me so attentive before. But something seemed to keep him from turning, so he went on. According to him, if he had gone back and found me while I was waiting for a car, he would have chopped off my head with his machete. But he didn't catch up with me.

I returned with the children to San Juan and went to Cruz's house. Alejandro, the lover she had, was no longer with her, so I stayed there. I wrote to Edmundo telling him the children needed money. He sent me ten dollars every two weeks. One day he came to San Juan to fetch me back but I wouldn't go. He came two more times, trying to get me back, but I wouldn't go.

The last time he came I got the biggest scare of my life. That day I'd gone to the Saint John's Day celebrations with the children. I had a place of my own by then but Edmundo went to Cruz's house and asked for me. She told him where I had gone and he got there before I did. I was scared because I wasn't expecting to see him.

"Let's go to San Juan. I want to speak to you," he said to me. I noticed that he looked pale and nervous. It was dark when we got home, but I saw the butt of a revolver under his belt. He stopped outside the house to say something and he began to pull out the gun slowly as he spoke. I dashed up the stairs and locked myself in Cruz's house. My sister really told Edmundo off. She said that as he had stopped sending me money, he had no right to interfere in my life. My *mamá* insulted him too and threatened to call the cops.

Edmundo decided to go away and stay away. He went to Connecticut. He didn't tell me he was going, but he wrote me a letter after he got there. He sent money for about four weeks after that. I sent him three letters but they were all returned by the post office. The court couldn't trace him because I didn't have his exact address. Later on he explained that he had stopped writing because he was sick.

I loved Edmundo very much. He's the only man I ever really loved and I still think of him now and then. I have reason to be grateful to him, even if he wasn't the most manly man I've known. He was good to me when I was sick, but then, I was good to him, too, when he was in the hospital. When I have a man, I respect him. I don't go out of the house without his permission. I keep the house clean and in order, and his clothes pressed, and I have his meals ready on time. Whatever I have been, I can claim respect as a woman who is a homebody.

I decided never to live with Edmundo again and he didn't want me any more either. Whenever he tried to get me back it seemed to me that what he wanted was to get even with me. But I didn't let him, so he wasn't able to. Once I leave a man, I don't want him to pester me any more. When I love, I love with my whole heart. I love blindly, I live as in a dream. And I'm jealous even if a fly approaches the man I love. But when a man fails me in anything, even if it's only once, I hate him. I hate him and hate him and I'd rather see him dead. That's why all three men I've had have ended up the same way. And all of them have wanted me back. Everybody here in La Esmeralda can bear witness to that. But I just stopped loving them.

Edmundo

Everything Is Finished for Me

I NEVER had luck with women. Maybe it is because Our Lord hasn't given me my mate for life yet. It could be, couldn't it? Or perhaps it is a punishment for something I did—a test. The Bible says, "God helps those who help themselves." According to that system He should have helped me because I have certainly done my part.

I was about twenty-two years old when I met Felícita. I happened to be in New York at the time, in the state of New Jersey. The name of the town is Salem. One day my brother says to me, "Let's go to Simón's house," and we got in the car and went. When we got there I saw this girl, and at first sight, like they say—

I was pouring some beer when she sat down on the couch. It was one of those with a wide arm, and as the room was full of people I sat down right there on the arm of the couch. She was eating peanuts and I said to her, kidding, "I would like to have some of those." Quick as a flash she dumps her peanuts into my hand.

One day after that I was passing in front of her house in the car and Felícita waved to me and made me stop. She asked me to take her to a dance but I didn't know whether she was kidding or not. "I'll take you," I told her.

I went to *el bosso* where I work and made up some story about how I had to go to New York. That way I could get the day off, keep the appointment with the girl and bring her back to her house.

Well, I bought two tickets, one for her and one for me, but the girl never showed up. I went to her house and said to her, "You should have told me you weren't going to come. Then I wouldn't have had to let my *bosso* down. I told him I was going to New York and if anything happens they'll go looking for me there."

"I didn't go because my uncle wouldn't let the other girls come along," she told me.

Being a person who likes things open and aboveboard, I said to her, "Now look, you got me in bad on account of this, so what do you say? Are you coming with me?"

"Oh, did I?" she says. "Well, no."

I kept insisting so she asked Iris, her uncle's wife. I had lived around there all my life and Iris knew the kind of person I was. She said I was a nice boy, so I took Felícita to the dance.

Well, we liked each other and in time we began to fall in love. I was working in a *diner* and the girl would call me up on the telephone. Sometimes I would neglect what I was doing to talk to her.

She told me she had three children but I said that didn't matter. If you take a risk you have to go all the way, win or lose. The way I looked at it, if I could take her in, I could take the children. So she accepted my proposition.

Before that she wrote to her *papá*. He answered that she should wait until he could meet me. But the girl didn't wait, and when he got her answer she was already living with me.

I made forty-five dollars a week then. The first thing I would do when I got paid was pay the rent, twenty-two fifty a week. The house had a bedroom, living room, dining room and bathroom. Everything was included. All I had to pay for was food and rent.

A month after we got together she went and got her little girl from her father's in Virginia. Tany was just beginning to walk when Fela brought her to the house. I didn't have any children yet, so I treated that little Negro baby better than if she were my own daughter. I am the only father she knows. When her *mamá* says to her now, "I am going to send you to your father in San Juan," meaning her real father, Nicolás, she answers, "No, my *pai* is in Salinas, my *pai* is Mundo." I consider her the same as my personal, legitimate child.

During the first few months Felícita couldn't do enough for me. It was a real honeymoon. I had a lot of confidence in her because I went to work knowing very well I was leaving behind a woman alone, you know what I mean? I worked nights as assistant cook in a *diner,* so I would not be back until five in the morning. I'd leave again the next day at four in the afternoon.

Finally Felícita decided she wanted to work. I said to her, "Look, even though I don't make much, it pays my expenses." But she insisted and she worked for a week, when she got pregnant. After she got the *mala barriga,* bad belly, as they call it, she couldn't do any work around the kitchen and everything stank. I took her to the doctor and he prescribed some pills. The little bottle had six pills in it, I think, and it cost me two forty-five. After that she was able to do things and could sleep, but doped up. Finally, I said to her, "Don't take the medicine today, and go to bed and see if you can sleep or not." She slept as peacefully as a child, thank God! After that, I threw away the pills because it was a drug and could harm her.

Her belly kept growing bigger and bigger and I put her into the welfare hospital for treatment. They took care of the expenses until she gave birth. She got very sick when the baby was born and I ran to call the nurse. They had to give her four quarts of blood. I asked the nurse whether she came out of it all right and she said yes.

I was crazy happy when I saw my first son and all that. It seemed to me like I had the greatest thing in the world. Before I could see Fela, they brought me a whole outfit to put on, white pants, shirt, a cap, and a mask for my mouth. I spoke to her but she didn't know who I was. She was drugged.

I came back the next day and asked her how she was and she answered, "Pretty good, except I feel a little drunk." I told her that they had the baby in an incubator. I went again that night to see the baby, but he looked awfully dark to me and I said to myself, "I don't think that baby is mine. I wonder if it is." I could see through the glass that he had a lot of hair and it was very dark.

They kept Felícita in the hospital for three or four days, and then I took her home. I did everything in the house so that she wouldn't hurt herself. I even washed and cooked and mopped so she wouldn't have to do anything but take care of the baby. I tried to make it easy for her. I still gave her little girl Tany the same love I would give my own daughter. For me there was no difference between the two.

Before I started living with Felícita, I belonged to the Holy Name Church there. Felícita was my *concubine,* as they say, so I went and talked to the priest.

"Father," I said, "I can't go on belonging to the church, because I have committed a sin."

"How?"

I told him.

"You have to get married, then."

Well, I had been living with Felícita and studying her. A year and a half after the baby was born, I said to myself, *"Caramba,* I have a good wife, even though she is new at it and all that. She takes care of things for me, not always the way I would like, but *anyway,* she deserves my help and I am going to give her my name because I don't want to leave the church."

So I say to her, "Fela, you know that I belong to this religion and I am living in sin. Are you willing to marry me? I don't have anything to say against you and I don't believe you have anything against me."

"Well," she said, "I would not have thought of getting married, see? But, as long as you have the idea, well, *O.K.,* let's get married."

The wedding didn't cost me a cent. I didn't have to spend money on preparing Felícita or anything like that. The godparents of marriage were a couple from right around there. They belonged to the church, too. And the priest said to me, "Now, you go into my office and I'll marry you. The idea is to get you out of your situation, not for you to spend money." So we got married and everything went along just fine until now. If I had realized what was going to happen to me, possibly I wouldn't have gotten married.

Things kept changing, with me trying to be patient. Soon after the wedding I had an accident at work. I moved the wrong way, lifting something, and it was as if something broke in my back. I was in the hospital for thirty-three days with weights on my legs and a band around my waist. I couldn't move at all and had to do everything right there in my bed. I got to thinking about how my wife needed my love and what would happen to my children. The more I thought, the sicker I got. Felícita didn't have anybody with her and I was leaving her alone. So, sick as I was, I said to the doctor, "I want you to discharge me so I can go back to work. I am paying rent right along and I have a wife and children who have to eat."

"Don't worry about it," he told me. "You'll get paid for all this time."

"But I haven't been paid anything yet and I have to have money. I am going to work, come what may."

So the doctor said, "All right, if you can walk I'll give you the paper and you can go."

And so he gave me the paper and I took it to *el bosso.* When *el bosso* asked me how I was, I told him not very good but that I wanted to work. He had consideration and he gave me a very light job where I didn't have to move around at all. So I kept on working.

A little while later *el bosso* asked me, "What would you do with fifty dollars?" This was the pay I got for one week.

I said, "I would pay my rent, buy food for my wife and children, and some milk and extras. I owe the furniture store, so I would pay them too."

So he says to me, *"Negro,* how are you going to do it with fifty dollars?"

"Well, I stretch out my leg as far as the blanket reaches," I told him. "If I owe twenty dollars in one place, I pay off at least fifteen and that's how I keep covering." Because I was really in a jam with debts.

Then he smiled and said, "Now, what you have here is two hundred and twenty-four dollars for the days you were in the hospital." A saint had come to help me!

I owed *el bosso* money I had borrowed to buy Felícita a ticket to Puerto Rico. She wanted to see Fernanda because she had been away a long time. "All right," I told her. "Take the children with you, though, because I can't look after them." I got them tickets and they went. Felícita was with her *mamá* for two weeks so Fernanda could get to know her grandchild and all that. I had never met Fernanda, but I did know Simplicio, Flora and Soledad. They were sleeping and eating at our house with Soledad's three children and all.

A month after Felícita came back from Puerto Rico, I received a letter from the State Fund saying I had to go to court for a hearing. "But I didn't kill anybody or fight," I said to myself, "why do I have to go to court?"

In the court I had an interpreter who explained to me that the letter was about a cash settlement for the accident I had, and they wanted to know whether I was in agreement with the amount or if I wanted to get a lawyer and fight the case, see? The settlement was for eight hundred and eighty dollars. They were giving me that, plus the two hundred and twenty-four dollars I got before.

I thought it over. If I accepted, I could go back to Puerto Rico and buy a house for my wife and children. If I didn't, I would have to get a lawyer and God knows how much he would charge, two or three hundred dollars at least, and I might end up with less. So I decided to accept.

"You are thinking straight," the lawyer told me. "The check for eight hundred and eighty dollars will arrive within two weeks."

When I told Felícita that I intended to go back to Puerto Rico, she said, "Ah, but I just got back from there."

"Yes, child," I told her, "you went, but I haven't been there for four years and I would like to see my family. Let's go. I'll buy a house there and get a job."

Well, I sent all the packages I had in the house by air cargo and Fernanda received them. Then Felícita and I arrived with the kids. We went straight out to the house, and that was when I first met Fernanda and Cruz and everybody.

I did not like the atmosphere in La Esmeralda. The people there use very bad language. Where I came from, you never heard a bad word from a little boy or girl. Everybody lived in peace and co-operation. You could lie down to take a nap at noon and you would be able to sleep as if it were the middle of the night. Nobody bothered anybody. But in La Esmeralda I couldn't lie down and be at peace. To be so sleepy and not be able to sleep on account of all that racket and noise! And every time I heard those words, they would lift me up in the air, turn me around and drop me down again. I had never heard words like that in all my life, from the women, girls, boys, old ladies, everybody! I would put my hands over my ears and say, *"Ay,* my mother!"

Felícita told me that the owner of the Silver Cup was a good friend of hers. She introduced us and I went to work. I didn't know anything about what went on there, as I had never worked at that kind of thing before. I went into it like a newborn child. I didn't have a minute's peace because of the terrible language I heard there. But I got used to it.

I started in at twenty-two dollars, as a waiter in the main room. When *el bosso* saw how I could work, he moved me to the *bar* and raised me to thirty-five dollars.

When I was working as a waiter that place really got jammed. Every time I tried to serve a table I had to be begging pardon and pushing past people when I brought the drinks. Well, when the women turned their heads to let me go by they would smear lipstick all over my white shirt, and so my wife got jealous. That's what happened and I said, "Listen, don't fight with me, because you have no reason to. Besides, if I make enemies out of those women it's bad for me and bad for the business."

One day one of the women, that Pupa, says to me, "Here, take this key, my watch and my medallion and leave them at the *bar* for me." I was busy and somebody called me at that moment, so I stuck them in my pocket. I kept on working and forgot about it. Finally Pupa was good and drunk, and she says to me, "Let's go to the hotel when I get off."

"No, I can't," I told her. "Find somebody else to go with you because I have a wife and children. I'm working here, it's true, but not because I am interested in any of the women."

So she says to me, "You're a cock-sucker"—excuse me for the expression.

When she called me that, I said, "All right, even though I have a wife, I'll show you I'm not. I'll prove to you I am a man. I'll go with you, but I don't want anybody to know because it might make trouble for me. It might even cause a separation from my wife."

I forgot to give her the things she left with me and I didn't remember until I went to light a cigarette on the stairs near the house and felt them in my pocket. I said to myself, "Oh, my mother! Look what I've done. I was supposed to leave these things at the bar!" I turned back, but by the time I got there the *bar* was closed. I put the things in a special compartment in my wallet so Felícita wouldn't find them.

I took a bath and went to bed. The next morning around nine o'clock Felícita got up and brought me water and my breakfast in bed. She kept looking at me as she handed it to me. I didn't know it, but that woman, Pupa, trying to make herself irresistible, had even made a kiss mark on my neck and Felícita saw it. She was very angry and that must have made her more malicious, because she went through my wallet and found all those things. She really raised a row with me then, and I couldn't answer her because she was right. I know I did the wrong thing.

I found out later that she went down to the *bar* looking for the other woman. At first she didn't want to give me back the things she found in my wallet, but then she broke them and handed them back to me like that. When I gave them to Pupa, she was very annoyed. "Listen," I said to her, "I had a lot of *trouble* and it was your fault."

"Look at this," she said. "The watch is broken, too!"

"You're lucky she didn't break your head for you," I told her.

I never beat Felícita except one time when I had to. We were living right here in La Esmeralda. I remember it as if it was yesterday.

"Fela, I want a little black coffee," I said to her, but she started arguing with me. She kept quarreling and quarreling, but I didn't answer because I knew that one word leads to another. I just acted deaf and she got so mad she jumped up from the bed and flew at my face with her nails and teeth and cut me all up.

"What's the idea? What's wrong with you?" I asked her and went for the alcohol to put on my face. In twenty-nine years I have never raised these hands of mine against anybody, but my face isn't to be handled like that, either. When I took a look in the mirror and saw my face all scratched up, the blood rushed to my head and I had to slap her. She kept coming after me like a wild animal and I said to her, "Calm down, Felícita, because I don't want to have to hit you again. You asked for it and had it coming."

Just then somebody arrived from a furniture store to collect for some pictures. I took out the money to pay the boy. I was talking to him with my back to Felícita when that woman came and hit me in the face. That mortified me and I lost my head. I lifted her up in the air and slammed her to the floor. That quieted her down. I was so furious that the boy with the pictures even said, *"Bendito,* don't do that. Look at her."

"But you see the problem," I said.

"I know. She did wrong."

"If she hadn't I wouldn't have punished her, because that is not my way." I had a mother, and it would have made me sad if my father had laid a hand on her. It really would. But sometimes a woman looks for it and you have to punish her.

Still, I kept on being nice to Felícita and treating her with consideration. After Evita was born, when Fela spoke to me about having an operation, I agreed in good faith. She gets seriously sick with each birth, and I wanted to spare her the shock of nearly dying or being left disabled after another delivery. She had five already, *anyway,* and it would look ridiculous for a girl of twenty or twenty-two to have more. By the time she got to be thirty or thirty-five she would be buried in children. I signed for her and she was operated on in the hospital the very same day. Three days later I brought her home. I paid only twenty-five dollars, because the government helped.

After the operation I realized that Felícita did not have the same pleasure with me. The husband more or less knows, and it was as if she was doing something she disliked. She didn't have a quarter of the life she had before. I thought about it myself and afterward talked to her, and she admitted that she was doing it now, *anyway,* because it was her duty, but that she didn't enjoy it. That meant that she had lost her love for me. So, I said, "Well, my girl, I don't compel you to do it. You know that. I don't force you."

As she still used to get together with me, I took her to the doctor and he certified that she had a vaginal infection. I never had a venereal disease myself, never. Every time I took her to the doctor it was a question of medicines and pills.

I kept on working and struggling and struggling until I finally decided to move to Salinas. Felícita agreed. We went to Salinas to avoid trouble and to live quietly. Our quarrel was all over with, but Felícita got even angrier and worse-tempered there. She was not the same toward me. She didn't show any of the affection she had before. But I didn't complain or beat her. I would come home calmly. If she was at home, fine, if she wasn't, fine too. Nobody ever heard me complaining and I have the whole neighborhood there as my witnesses.

It seems that once when she went to San Juan a woman there told her something. All I know is that when she came back it was terrible. That night she said to me, "I met somebody whose name was Ileana and she explained that whole business about you and Pupa."

"Forget about it, girl," I told her. "I want to live quietly in peace with you. That's why I moved here."

But the woman had that burned into her brain and kept harping and harping on it until finally she left me. One day when I came back from the fields at four in the afternoon, she was gone. Without saying a word to me, she had packed up and left.

"Well," I said to myself, "all I cared for most in the world is gone—my wife and my children." I told myself that she did what she did because of what she heard about Pupa. So I went down to the court and told the judge what had happened. When he asked me what I wanted to do, I said to him, "You are the one who decides that. You are the justice. You decide."

"All right," he answered, "if you want to press charges, accuse her." And he gave me a paper to take to the police station. I was all nervous when I got there. The policeman told me to sit down outside and he would take care of me as soon as he was free. I lit a cigarette and took a good look at the paper the judge gave me. It said, "Warrant for Arrest. Bond: $300." And then I began to think about how I had a mother and maybe Fela would not be able to travel or pay the fine and all that.

So I took the warrant and went to San Juan. My family didn't want me to go because they didn't know what trouble I might get into. But I told them not to worry.

I went to Felícita's house and at twelve o'clock sharp I marched into the kitchen, where she was preparing lunch for the children. When she saw me she turned white. "Don't get scared," I told her. "I didn't come to fight with you. All I want is for you to get my children ready. I am taking them with me." But the woman did not move because she thought I was only fooling. "Hurry up, I have to get back to Salinas and I want to be there early."

Then she said I couldn't do anything to her as far as abandonment of the children is concerned because she had brought them with her.

"I would like to know the reason why you left the house," I told her. "You know I didn't throw you out or beat you. I didn't keep you like a rich man, but for a poor man I gave you whatever you needed. As long as you lived with me you had a roof over your head and you never went to bed hungry. You never stepped out on the street without good clothes on your back and good shoes on your feet."

And then she comes out with it. "I don't know why. I don't know the reason myself."

"Well, I would like to know why, or else I might get some wrong idea." I was imagining that she might have done something wrong and then picked up and left before I found out.

I told her that I was not accusing her of abandoning the children but of abandoning the home, and I handed her the paper the judge gave me. After looking at it, she says to me, "I'll give you the children but only on condition that I have the right to see them."

I told her that she was the mother and they were her children and I was not going to stop her from seeing them. I also said that I wanted to take them with me so they could grow up in a better atmosphere than what they would have in La Esmeralda. Well, she accepted my proposal and I took Mundito and Evita.

About a week after I had them there in Salinas, the older one picked up a photograph of Felícita and he kept looking at it and saying, "Look—*mami. Mami, mami.*" He was calling her. And every time he saw the photograph, he would keep repeating the same thing over and over. At night when I came home and was putting them to bed he would say, *"Papi—"*

"Yes, baby."

"Mami—?"

"Don't worry. She's coming."

And that's the way I had it for a whole week. It was a struggle for me all alone, although my sister-in-law Matilde helped me out with them.

Finally I decided to take the children back to Felícita, because I didn't want them to be getting sick on me, especially the older one, who missed her so much. And since she was the mother, it was easier for her to take care of them, right?

Once when I came from Salinas to see the children and bring money, it got too late for me to go back and so, as I had worked at the Silver Cup bar, I figured I would stop by there and then sleep over at a hotel.

All the friends I used to work with said hello. "Mundo, how are you?" they asked.

"So-so—"

"And how's life over there?"

"Everything is all right."

"*Caramba,* I'm awfully sorry!"

"About what?"

"Well, you are such a nice guy, a peaceful man, a poor man who kept his wife like a queen on what he earned, as far as it went. And the way she threw it around and showed off. I bet she never went hungry when she was with you. *Caramba,* you were terrific to your wife. You haven't divorced her, have you?"

"No, I haven't."

"Well, you'd better find a way to do it, because that woman comes around here and takes out *tickets* to go upstairs with men."

When I heard that, it hit me very hard because Felícita bears my name even though she doesn't use it, and we are still married.

It made me feel really ashamed that she, knowing that I used to work there and still had my friends and working companions at the place, went there, when she could have gone to other places. I suppose she did it purposely so that they would tell me once and for all.

This happened in 1963, on March 26. I have been working on the divorce since then, for about a year now. I had a sweetheart. I really needed her. I have to have a wife. I was going with this girl seriously, with intentions of marrying. I said to her, "I can't get married by Church because you know I am already married as a Catholic." We could get married by the judge, though, if Felícita ever gives me a divorce. That would be better because I cannot afford any more sins, can I?

About a month and a half ago my wife came around with the children and left them at the house. They are my children and how could I not accept them? I was working, and a *compadre* of mine came out and said to me, "*Compadre,* your wife just came with the children and she is going to give you the divorce."

I hurried over and there she was. I greeted her just the way people are supposed to be greeted, without doing anything special. Then I picked up my children and kissed and petted them, put them on my shoulder and played with them for a while. My sister-in-law said to Felícita, "*Comadre,* why don't you stay with Mundo?"

"You can stay," I said, "but then I would have to move out. You abandoned everything because you didn't love me. Now I can't accept you any more."

I thought she would stay at my brother's, but later she said, "I am going to sleep over at Edmundo's." I was embarrassed because the whole town knew all about her already and this girl I was engaged to was watching.

But my *comadre* says to me, "She's your wife. As long as she lived here with you she was honorable. Besides, she's the mother of your children." It was true. She had behaved herself all the time she was with me and I am not going to deny it. And even though she has done what she has done, I still love her.

Fela helped me bring the children over to my house. After I put them to bed she says to me, "Come on, lie down." I couldn't bring myself to do it because I was so embarrassed at having to get together with her after what she had been doing. But I slept with her anyway and I was really embarrassed to have to do it.

I was forced into it, like when somebody sticks a gun in your ribs and says, "Do it." It was very strange and I said to myself, *"Caray,* it's over a year since we have been separated, and now to be coming around expecting the same pleasure and enjoyment!"

Well, a man is a man! In spite of everything I found her exciting, even better than before. And she got pleasure out of it, too, but not much.

The next day I told her, "Get up early and go to my sister-in-law's house so nobody will see you leave. I don't want *trouble."*

She got up but then she said to me, "I would like to have some of that fried bread that they make here."

"Is it a long time since you've eaten it?"

"Since I left here."

"Ah, then you should have some. I'll fix it for you myself."

So with all the calm in the world I got to work and prepared it to satisfy her whim. She had breakfast and then we went to town together to see the lawyer. He was charging me sixty dollars for the divorce.

The lawyer said to us in front of the judge, "Is this a divorce by mutual consent and with no objections by either party?"

I said, "Yes. We came together of our own free will, we got married of our free will, and now we are getting divorced the same way."

Then the lawyer asked Felícita, "When can you come and sign?"

"I'm coming to Salinas next Tuesday."

Well, Tuesday came and she didn't show up. Saturday came, and the following Wednesday and Thursday, and no sign of her. I figured I would wait until the next Tuesday but she didn't appear then either. The children were with me for a month and two days without her coming to see them. That was a real case of abandonment, because I had no woman to look after those children. Mother or not, Felícita didn't seem to care that she left her children in Salinas.

During the day my *comadre* looked after them for me and I took care of them at night. I had to be in at seven o'clock and at that hour it is still light. Imagine a man who likes to go out at night and have a little fun, having to be in the house at seven! That's how it was until I took the children back to San Juan.

As for that girl I was going with, well, I had to leave her, even though she was as fine as they come. I told her, "I can't talk about marriage now, because, number one, I haven't been divorced and, number two, I am not so sure my wife is going to give it to me. I may have to be alone forever. The only way I will be able to get a girl is to find one who will say, 'Well, even though this man cannot get married, I'll go with him because he needs me. Look, my girl, let's break up. I'll go where you won't be able to see me and I won't be able to see you, so there won't be any problems."

I packed my clothes and left Salinas. I told my family I was going to Bayamón, but my idea was to go where Fela was. I don't know how to explain it or how I could be willing to do it, but I would take her back again. I still feel a little love for her. Maybe because I have two children with her. I would be crazy with happiness if she said to me, "Get a house, Mundo. I'm going to stop working and just take care of your children." That would probably reconcile me with her. But she is the one who doesn't want to.

Fernanda is practically on my side. Thank God and the Virgin, Fernanda has always been the same to me ever since I have known her. I never had any trouble with her at all or with Felícita's family. The only problem is Felícita. "You know, Nanda," I'd say to her, "even though Fela did what she did, I'm going to put a proposal to her. If she accepts, I'll get a house and live with her and bring up my children with a father's warmth. They should know what it means to have a father and a mother. Understand? Maybe one of these days Fela will catch a sickness, God forbid. She loses her nights with the bad life she leads and that could affect her one of these days."

Fernanda answered, "I have already told her that. I told her, 'Fela, think it over!' You should look for a house and she should go there to live." But Felícita doesn't want to.

Felícita loved me, but on account of that Pupa, from that time until now, her feelings for me have faded and gone. Felícita is just the same as always. She hasn't changed, although she dresses differently. Now she has to fix herself up for everybody to admire her, do you know what I mean? As far as her having gone into the life is concerned, the thing that bothers me is that she is the *mamá* of my children.

During the time Felícita lived with me and had the warmth of my affection, she was a good mother to our children, although it was her *mamá* who brought up the twins. Let us say that Felícita was not the kind of mother who says, "I will go through tortures for my children," or the kind who will stay up nights for her children. Felícita was never that kind of mother.

I have really studied Felícita and I know how she is. She seems to me to be intelligent, like her father. I imagine she is the most intelligent of all the children. I consider her very clever, and besides, she has an education. Another thing about her is that she is very stubborn and will kill herself proving she is right. I don't think she has the same ability as I do, but as far as her mind is concerned she is very capable. She reads well and she can write a letter good enough to go to the governor. You can understand everything she writes down. The same in English as in Spanish. She was with her father all the time, talking to Americans and all, so it is much easier for her. It is very hard for me, as I had only been in school one year when my father died, so I couldn't get an education. Even now I can hardly sign my own name. I learned to do it after I was grown-up. When a child's *papá* and *mamá* die, his education doesn't get attended to the way it would if they were alive.

When my *papá* died, my *mamá* had no help from anywhere and didn't work, so she had to take another husband. I loved my stepfather as if he were my father. His name was Modesto Vargas. When I was eight or nine years old I said to myself, "I take care of things around the house, like getting the water and the firewood and all that, so why can't I go out and earn a few dollars and help them out, or at least pay for my own clothes and shoes?"

I spoke to my stepfather and asked his permission. I began earning half a dollar for eight hours of work, helping out a family. Every time I got paid I would go home and say, "Here, *mamá,* so much for you, so much for Modesto," and the rest went into a little bank I had. Well, that is how I kept on struggling and struggling.

My mother had high blood pressure from a tooth that had been pulled, and the doctor said she should have a calm life and not get into fits of anger or be frightened or anything like that. Well, something finally made such a strong impression on her that it caused her death. That was in 1952, on April 11.

I was seventeen years old then. From that time on, I have gone through a lot of hard times and suffering.

In 1956 I went to New York for two months. I heard that things were very good there and you could make money, but I didn't like the atmosphere. I couldn't get used to it. The language is so different and that made it very hard for me. I said to myself, "I'm going back to Puerto Rico, where I can ask for whatever I want and everybody understands me." So I did farm work and saved up some money for two months and then I flew home.

Even knowing how I suffered that time in New York, I went back in '57. I figured I would get used to it little by little. I went back in '57 and in '58. I was there a year. A brother of mine had gone there, too, before I did. It was a long time since he had written or anything, and I happened to run into him. He made me come to his home right away and I did.

At the end of the year I thought to myself, *"Caramba,* my nephews and brothers and sisters are in Puerto Rico and I haven't been back for a year. I want to go and see them even if I come back here later." So I went to Salinas from New York, with the idea of coming back. Well, I had trouble there with a girl. It was my luck that she was sort of a relative. I saw this kid and she was real pretty and I said to myself, *"Caray,* maybe I've got something here." But there are always people in the family who open a person's eyes. "She was a nice girl," they told me, "but such and such happened to her, and she has this little girl." It was a child of deception, as the saying goes. A married man deceived her and gave her a baby. So I took up with her and after a while she wanted me to come to the house. Her *mamá* was separated from her *papá*, who was a relative of mine. Well, I spoke to the *mamá* and she accepted me because she knew me.

Then I said to the girl, "I'm going to let your *papá* know." He was delighted. "Better you than some outsider," he said. The girl's *mamá* was very sick and the girl was the one who looked after her, so I said to the *mamá,* "Maybe you think I want to take your daughter away from here and leave you alone, but I wouldn't do such a thing to you."

And she said to me, *"Ay,* my son, but if God takes me away, I want to leave her in good hands. If you, a poor man, could marry her, it would make it easier for me to go." Well, because she asked me, I was going to do her the favor of marrying her daughter.

When I knew the girl well, I spoke to the priest. He issued the banns and I paid him five dollars for it. We were supposed to get married on Easter Sunday. One week before the wedding, the girl was ironing my clothes and getting them all ready for me. As she stood there, two tears came rolling down her cheeks. "What's wrong, child?" I asked her.

"Nothing," she said.

Then two more tears came out of her eyes. "But you have some *trouble,* child. Tell me what is wrong with you."

"All right, I'll tell you. Drink your coffee, then I will tell you."

I drank the coffee and she came over and sat down. I lighted a cigarette. Her eyes were pouring tears.

"Well, daughter, tell me what it is that pains you."

"Look, Edmundo, there is just one thing. You will have to forgive me for what I am going to say. It hurts me deep down in my heart and I beg a thousand pardons of you but I'm going to ask you to do me a favor and take away all these things you bought and look for another girl to marry you because I have changed my mind."

"What is the trouble?" I wanted to know.

"I changed my mind about getting married."

"But, my girl, you know very well I didn't force you into anything. I didn't put a gun to your head or a knife to your chest to make you love me. And I'm not going to do it to make you marry me, even though I have gotten myself involved, spent all I had and now none of it is worth anything to me because I am not going to use it. I won't bear a grudge against you for it, though. It's better for you to break off with me now than for us to get married and have you regret it in the future."

Every day I keep asking the Lord to give me more strength and more will and more courage to bear up under all the things that are grinding me down. My life is a novel. If you take a good look at it, it's like a novel.

And now, on top of all I have been through, to get more knocks and end up like this! Felícita refuses to accept any kind of proposal that I make to her. After she leaves a man, she says, it is impossible for her to go back to him. But then, her life is very different from mine. Hers is the gay life, no attachments or responsibility. And that is not for me. My life is, eat and sleep and work in peace.

Still and all, to get divorced now would cost me a lot of money. But we must get divorced because I have been traveling from here to New York and from New York back here again, and airplanes have accidents, you know. It might be my luck to die and then she would live off what happened to me, from the insurance, right? And if it comes down to that, there is never some person lacking to slip in with some kind of story or other, and marry her to get the benefit of what is mine. There would be four getting the benefit, or God knows how many more. Felícita should at least enjoy it alone with my two children, but she won't. And that is the problem of why I want to get a divorce.

Since I have been alone, I don't seem to be able to get anywhere. Everything is finishing up for me, as the saying goes, even my taste for getting pleasure out of life, for going out. I have gotten so I don't enjoy anything.

Felícita

I'll Do Anything for My Children

I HAD NO money because my husband didn't send me any. Soledad was in New York and Cruz was as poor as I, so I couldn't get any help from them. I would go to where my *mamá* worked to ask her for leftover food and half a dollar or so for milk.

I practically went begging for about two weeks. I would often ask people for money for the children's breakfast. If the boys at Papo's *bar* invited me for a beer, I always said, "No. Give me the twenty cents instead."

I began seeing my friend Zulma again, and she helped me out. She was already using dope, though, and those addicts get sick or go crazy if they stop. I have seen Zulma scratching herself and vomiting, hardly able to stand up. She was using heroin, and she smoked marijuana too. One day they caught her red-handed and arrested her. She had the hypodermic, the bottle cap and the powder on her, so now she's in the Women's Jail at Vega Alta. She has two children, but they have been with her husband ever since she left him.

Zulma, the addict, helped me out when she could, but my own *mamá* often denied me money, even when she had it. One day Nanda told me that if I wanted money, there was plenty to be earned in La Marina, especially since the sailors were in. That day happened to be payday and sailors are free spenders, she said. I told my *mamá* that I would never do what she suggested. Time passed and my children got sick. I went to my *mamá* again to ask for money. This time she said she had money, but not for me because she had to spend it on her husband. I asked her then, "What do you think, Nanda, shall I go down to La Marina tonight?"

I had thought of going down before because I saw that the women who were whores dressed well and had all kinds of luxuries and I wanted those things too. But I wanted advice from someone who might at least point out some other way. But Fernanda said, "Well, go ahead. There's good money to be made there. I was in the life for a long time and I made quite a bit of money. All you have to do is get ready, put the children to bed and wait until they fall asleep. Then you lock them in with a padlock. You can go out hustling this very night." She told me too that *gringos* paid pretty well and that some old men would pay quite a bit of money when they knew it was a woman's first time as a whore.

It made me feel uncomfortable that my *mamá* should give me such advice. In fact, I didn't go to La Marina that night, nor for many nights after that. But none of my children's fathers ever sent money. When my children got sick again, I got ready that same night. I told Cruz, "Edmundo doesn't send me any money, so I'm going out." She didn't argue but said, "Go if you want to, but be careful nobody cuts up your face and be sure you get home early." I put the children to bed and prayed to the Guardian Angel to shed his light on them. I left them locked in with Cruz and went to the Silver Cup to find customers.

Nena, a friend of mine who goes hustling at the Silver Cup too, promised to meet me so we could go there together. On the way she told me, "What you have to do is tell *don* Camacho that you are going to the clinic on Monday. Then, if some man invites you, dance with him and ask him to buy you a drink." She was real nice to me!

When we got to the Silver Cup, I sat at a table to talk with her and some other girls. We started to drink because *don* Camacho paid for the first round. I asked him for permission to go upstairs and he said it was all right. So I sat down at the *bar* and a man said to me, "You're a beginner, aren't you?"

"Yes, I am."

"Ah, then let's go upstairs. I'll pay you three dollars."

"No. I need the money because my children are sick. Just because I'm new I'm not making any celebration for three miserable dollars."

Well, things were like that until two o'clock that morning. Nobody came, or rather, nobody asked me. They could see I was new and looked like a little girl. In fact, they told me I was too young to be hustling in a place like that. Then a Puerto Rican soldier, just arrived from Germany, came in and asked if he could buy me a drink. I accepted and he asked what I would charge for going out with him. When I told him ten dollars he said it was too much. I explained, "But this is the first time I'm going to go out with a man in this way. I'm new at this."

"Are you sure?"

Don Camacho assured him that he was my very first customer. Then he offered me nine dollars and I accepted.

I felt ashamed as I went up, because the cashier knew my mother from the times she went hustling at the Silver Cup. When we got to the room, I told the man that if he wanted me to get in bed with him, he'd have to put out the light. He didn't want to do that, but I told him, "If you don't you'll lose your nine dollars because when I go down I'll tell the owner you had intercourse with me and refused to pay."

"Yes, I can see you're really new at this. But you're very cagey too."

"Well, turn out the light." I insisted so much that he finally did. He wanted to undress me but I didn't let him. I never strip naked in front of a man.

It made me feel sick to be with him because that man was so white. Ugly as all get-out. After that I drew a Negro, and he was so black. *Ave María!* Horrible-looking. But I was doing this for my children. So I shut my eyes, put out the light and went through with it. I did it without love. I wasn't serious about any of them. But one makes a show of loving them, all because of money, see? And some of the men believe it! A whore tells a man, "Be sure to come back tomorrow, *papito*. You did it so well." But it's a lie. That's what you say until the money is safely in your hand. After that, the hell with them! There are some men who'll come back to a woman and pay the same as the first time, but usually they try to beat down the price. They pay less and less until they wind up being her pimp and getting money from her.

Well, the same night I took another man, the third, and he gave me ten dollars. That made twenty-nine so far. The next one gave me eight. So I made my bit of money. At about four o'clock I walked all the way home by myself. Dawn was breaking and taxis are few and far between at that hour.

I rented a room for myself with the thirty-seven dollars I earned that night. We weren't comfortable in Cruz's house and I had to look for something better, although I liked it there because Cruz helped me. When I went out she looked after the children. But I had to sleep on the floor with my three little ones. Cruz slept in her big bed, with her little girl and with our *mamá*. Catín and the twins slept on a cot. We got along very well. Cruz cooked, I did the housework and *mamá* washed the dishes. But the house had only one room and it was always in a mess because there was no place to put things. Cruz kept saying that the house was too small, that it was too full of relatives and children, and that that was no way to live. So I decided to move, and Genoveva, Papo's wife, found two rooms for me in one of the houses she rented out. It looked comfortable, so I paid twelve dollars in advance for the first month's rent. The first day, I washed the rooms from top to bottom. They were very dirty. I didn't have a stove, nor any pots and pans, so I talked to Héctor and he gave me some kitchen utensils and a stove.

The bed Cruz had was the one that Alejandro had bought for her on a weekly installment plan. After he took off with Gladys, he left Crucita with the debt. She got a letter from the store saying that the payments were more than a month behind. The bed cost one hundred and forty dollars and Alejandro had paid only fifteen. Cruz didn't want to return the bed to the store, so she asked me if I wanted to pay the balance and keep the bed for myself. I really needed it, so as a favor to her, I had the account put in my name.

I painted the front room myself before we moved. Cruz, a boy and I did the moving. The boy brought *el matre* and I carried the head and foot boards of the bed. Cruz lugged a small tub full of clothes. Each of the twins carried a small suitcase, and Nanda took a box full of baby clothes. I also bought a big box of bedclothes. That was all I had. Cruz gave me a table and Héctor gave me another, so I had two tables. First I got everything straightened up. Then I borrowed a hammer and some nails and went to work. I put up shelves and nailed up the curtains. After everything was done, I gave a half a dollar for beer to the young man who had helped me.

I was very happy in my own house. I could get up when I pleased and make my own breakfast and buy food from a restaurant. I kept on going out with men. I bought a set of furniture for the parlor, but I couldn't keep up the payments, so they took it back. That embarrassed me because when people asked, "Where is your furniture?" I had to tell them, "Well, the store took it back." But little by little I bought what I needed.

The bathroom that I shared with another family was on the porch. It was always dirty. If I didn't clean it, nobody did. It bothered me when people found my house in a mess. Sometimes I didn't have time to clean it and visitors would find it dirty. That really made me ashamed.

My place was divided from my neighbors' by a thin board wall, and we could hear everything that went on in each other's house. My neighbors were Florida and Wilfredo. Florida was older and had three children by another man. Wilfredo was scared of her. I had a lot of fun when they quarreled. I'd go on the porch to watch. If Florida was cooking rice, she'd scoop it out and throw it at him by spoonfuls, and he'd scuttle away as fast as he could and dive under the bed. Then she'd go and pull him out by the pants. Wilfredo always wore very wide shorts. Florida would pull the clothes off him and then she'd grab one of his legs and whirl him all around the room. And he'd keep begging, "Oh, *mamita,* leave me alone, *mamita.*" Everybody would gather around to watch.

Sometimes when he felt like screwing her, he'd say, "Come, *mamita,* get between the sheets." And she'd answer, "I will not, you queer. Go away, and don't bother me. Your mouth stinks like it was full of shit."

He'd insist, "Oh, come on, *mamita*—"

"No, your balls are full of ticks. You never wash them. They stink."

Then they'd really begin to quarrel. "Your mother is the one that stinks, you daughter of a great whore."

"You're the one who's a son of a great whore."

At that point I'd blow out the candles, climb up on the bed and peek over the partition. I could see him there, stark naked, with no ass and a big belly and his little bitty balls hanging down, and his prick erect. He'd start begging again, "But look, *mamita,* can't you see I'm hot?"

"Go fuck Pucha. She's the kind of woman you should screw." She'd throw a glass at him and he'd grab her by the neck. When he grabbed her she'd start screeching like a mouse. And they'd wind up doing it after all. People talked a lot about Wilfredo and Florida because their daughter and her sweetheart shared the bed with them. And before she had the sweetheart, the daughter always slept in the same bed with her parents.

For my part, I don't make any noise, so nobody knows what's going on. Or if they do, well, let them suffer.

The people I meet at work often ask me where I live, and when I answer, "La Esmeralda," they say, *"Ave María!* That's a terrible place!" But it used to be worse. When I first came to live there, the place was full of whores. There were lots of fights, too. And many of the houses were right at the edge of the sea. Everything is different now. There are fewer fights and fewer whores. It's much more peaceful than it used to be.

Father Ponce did a lot to improve the place. When that priest first came here, people from La Esmeralda were going to church just to joke and have a good time, and drunks used the church as a place to drink. Father Ponce would say, "Inside the church, I'm the priest. But out here, I'm a man like any other." He'd take off his cloak, cross himself and punch any man or woman in the face. Once he scolded my friend Zulma because she had treated a little old woman disrespectfully and Zulma answered, "Shut up, you sissy priest." He just hauled off and hit her in the face. Often he would take off his cloak and challenge everybody to fight. That's why we all were so fond of him. More people went to church when he was here.

The Catholic church helps people. If you ask for clothes they'll give you some. Medicines too. At a municipal hospital they'll prescribe something and tell you to buy it yourself, but if you take the prescription to the cathedral, *las sisters* will give you the medicine free. After a flood tide, the priests and nuns come to La Esmeralda with food and shoes and clothing for the people. And they come to take the children to church. Protestants don't do any of those things, except take the children to church on Sundays.

Life in La Esmeralda can be very hard but it has its good side too. It's very gay during the Christmas season. Every family throws a party. It's an amusing place to live. There are drunks everywhere, dancing around and acting funny. You can often see naked people bathing at the beach too. And cops chasing robbers. With such a good *show* on the street, who needs the movies?

Still, the first thing I'd do if I won a big lottery prize would be to get a house somewhere else. I'd like to move with my children to a suburb or a housing development, some place with a very different atmosphere. If I could afford to pay thirty dollars a month for an apartment in San Juan, I'd leave La Esmeralda, although in some ways I like it. Here I pay only twelve dollars a month and there are still times when I simply can't make ends meet.

At the Silver Cup I made good money the first night, but after that I earned very little, ten dollars or so a night. Business dropped off and they had to close the hotel because the cops were going around arresting the women. They never arrested me, though. When business is slow, the girls sit around killing time and asking the people who go there to give them money, "Say, buy me a drink or give me a quarter." Then the girls will start horsing around and they'll press close and rub against each other. They'll lift their skirts and dance together. Or they'll sit around and gossip about the men.

After the girls told me about certain men, I would avoid them. Once my friend Zoraida said, "I went with an Italian and he took me to a hotel. He bought a bottle of champagne there and after I'd bathed he poured it all over me. Then he put me on the bed and began to lick me. Those men don't screw. They just lick." I asked the Italian about that and he said it was true, that was what he liked.

I have never, thanks be to God and the Virgin, had to deal with brutes. My customers have been decent people who treated me with respect and consideration. I have never done the "69" with any man, not even my husband. The "69" means that you lie head-to-foot and suck each other. I've had it done to me but I've never done it myself. An American did it to me once. I liked it; it gives more pleasure. But one night a man offered me fifteen dollars to suck his cock and I refused. I told him I didn't do that. Then he gave me five dollars just for letting him kiss me.

What men like the most is to go in through the ass because it's tighter than in front. If a woman wants to fascinate a man, let her give him her ass and see what happens. That's how whores hold their pimps. You see, after a woman has had babies the vagina has already been opened and it opens more. But the tissues of your behind are tight. And that's what a man wants, something tight. I have tried it in the ass and it gives me more pleasure. That way, a man can make better use of a woman. It hurts at first. But if the man uses Vaseline, once it's in it's really good.

I went to the *bars,* but I didn't have any deep friendships with any of the other women who went there. I'd sit alone at my table, and if anyone smiled at me I'd smile back. I didn't start any conversations because those women are treacherous. They get very friendly and tell each other their most intimate secrets. Then they start gossiping about each other. That's the way quarrels start and you get to cutting up people and having to spend your life in court.

My *mamá* says I'm stuck up because I don't like to go to some places down in La Esmeralda or have anything to do with people there. She also says I'm stuck up because I have a pair of shoes to match every dress. She says I spend every cent I get on clothes for myself and my children to make people think I'm better off than I really am.

I always tell her that I like tile better than tar. By tar, I mean a place like La Esmeralda. And by tile, a place like San Juan, where you can live in a painted house with nicely furnished rooms. In San Juan it's easier to bring up children well, among decent people, and to find good neighbors who don't talk the way people do in La Esmeralda. In San Juan people keep their houses clean. You clean your part of the house and everybody else cleans theirs. That's what I mean when I say that I like tile better than tar.

People say that gay women are no good and that they are whores because they want to be. The neighbors won't have anything to do with a woman if they know she's in the profession. But I can't understand it. *Don* Luis, who lives near me, won't let his wife speak to me. He always shows his contempt and talks about how whores do all sorts of things and then go sit on respectable people's beds. Wilfredo, too, can barely stand to have me talk with his wife or go to his house or sit on his chairs. He believes that I must have an infection because I go out with men, and he's afraid that if I visit them I'll infect them or that I'll advise his wife to become a whore too.

You can't imagine how low people are. Just because they have been lucky enough to find their happiness, they treat whores terribly. You should hear those women with husbands, gossiping about whores. They'll say, "Imagine the condition her cunt must be in," and so on. If they see you're sort of thin they'll say at once, "Oh, that woman surely takes drugs." People think that if one is a whore one smokes marijuana, takes heroin and steals. They get those three kinds of life mixed up.

But I'm telling you, I'd rather be with twenty thousand whores than with one honest woman. Because whores know more about life. Suppose I'm going down the street with a whore and someone starts to attack me. The whore, being used to blows, would come to my defense. But if I was with a housewife, an honest woman, her thoughts would be about herself and her own danger. She'd be afraid of losing her husband or getting cut up, so she'd run the minute she saw *trouble.*

As far as I can see, all the women here cheat on their husbands and no Puerto Rican ever has only one wife. There are women who throw themselves at other men, and if a man is offered beefsteak, he doesn't turn it down. Everybody who comes to La Esmeralda gets ruined, even if he comes from the other end of the world. There is a kind of fever here that everybody catches. They say, "Ah, if that one does it, I will, too." But when I had a husband, I didn't even dare leave my house. After all, the man provides everything and if he is there when you need him, you are satisfied. But if you have a man and he's no good to you, what's the use of it? What else can you do but look further?

I don't think of myself as a prostitute. I have done what I've done for the sake of my children. But nobody takes that into account. Let me tell you, I will do anything for my children. I don't care what people say because I don't ask anybody for anything, not even a bite of food. It's true that I go out with many men. But that's not like going to a *bar* every day or going to Luna Street to pick up customers. That's one thing I don't have to do. I have my workdays and I'll go out with the same man for a week, and the money he pays me will be enough for that week. And I take care of myself so that I won't get an infection. I go to the clinic in Cataño, where we are well treated.

There are some women who want to be whores from their earliest youth, even from childhood, I think. They do it for love of the art. They may have good opportunities and yet refuse to leave the life, because they really like it. But all I ever think of is my children and the bit of food I'm earning for them. I hope that someday I'll find a good man who will take me out of this life. I keep dreaming that some boy, a foreigner, or even an old man whose eyelashes are gone, will come along and offer me and my children a home.

Once a spiritist told me that a married man was going to fall in love with me, and as I wouldn't pay any attention to him, he was going to cut my face. The spiritist prepared some essence with my name hidden in it, to protect me against evil and to wipe all such things out of his mind. It cost six dollars. I was to keep it in my *brassière* all the time, but I lost it.

In order to make you dominate a man, the spiritist writes his first and last names on two pieces of paper and then drips some strong essence, like "come-with-me" essence, on them. She puts your name and your rival's name on top and folds it tight with those drops of perfume. She wraps all this in a piece of plastic and sews it with a needle and white thread. She makes some passes over it, then you take it and put it in your shoe or under your pillow.

You can also dominate a man with Saint Martha's or Saint Napoleon's prayer. You buy a red candle and the prayer of the Seven Restless Spirits, to make him uneasy outside the house and come back to you. You say the prayer backward three times, light the candle from the bottom, say the first and last name of the person, stamp on the floor three times in the name of the woman. Then take a string and cut it into nine pieces. Take one by the end, another by the middle and one by the other end, and throw them out of the house while saying the prayer. Do this for nine days.

There are many things like that and others which I have to look into more carefully. Some of this kind of work has turned out well for me. When Edmundo kept coming to my house, I bought mercury to make him go away. I threw it outside and that's why he left and has never come back.

Another way to make a person go away is to buy "flying powder." You put it in the person's doorway on a Tuesday or Friday, saying as you scatter it, "This isn't powder I'm throwing, it is explosive to blow such and such a woman out of this place." You have to mention her name and surname. And that makes her go.

I hardly ever ask the Virgin for anything. Saint Judas Thaddaeus is my favorite saint. He grants everything I ask him. I light a lamp for him, pray a Pater Noster or an Ave Maria and he grants my wish. But one must pray with faith.

I never have revelations, ever, but I do have some healing powers. The other day, for instance, when I was at Cruz's house, she had a bad headache. I stood behind her and got goose flesh. I felt a sort of pressure inside me, too. I made a few gestures over her head but it wasn't really me doing it. Later she told me that I had shaken her very hard and almost tossed her out of the door. That frightened her, and she said, "Wait, wait, Fela." Her words scared away whatever it was that had possessed me and I got such a headache that I had to go home. I lost my powers after that.

I finally quit working at the Silver Cup because I had to go there every single day and stay from eight at night until four in the morning. If one of the girls got there late, at nine, say, *don* Camacho wouldn't let her go upstairs. It was a kind of slavery. He made you show up every day but he never helped you out when business was bad.

Some nights I'd stay until dawn without making a cent. I had to stay up all night and then take care of the children the next day because I had nobody to look after them. I would leave them alone, locked in, and not get home until four or five in the morning. I got very thin. I decided I couldn't go on like that.

Besides, I don't like to go out with men every night. If I made twenty dollars in one night, that was enough for the next two or three days. When I was broke I'd go out again. But *don* Camacho told me, "If you don't obey my orders and come here every night, the rest of the women are going to resent it. Then I'll have a strike on my hands."

So I said to myself, "May it be God's desire! I'm leaving the Silver Cup." Before I left, *don* Camacho invited me to go out. That was after he had separated from my sister. Anyway, he paid me. I went out with him once and we were together just a short while. He paid me fifteen dollars.

Next I worked at a *bar* called the Golden Circle. It belongs to a Cuban and he offered to pay me twenty-five dollars a week. There I fixed the drinks and served them to the customers. If anybody asked me to dance, I danced. Some of the Cuban boys there explained to me that they had had plenty of money in Cuba. They had gambling houses and cabarets all over the place but Fidel Castro took it all. They had money put away and they made a plan to come up here. But Fidel Castro found out and he had them put in jail. The

guards threw them out on the street one night in order to kill them, this fellow
said, because that's what they do in Cuba. But the boys escaped to the base in
Guantánamo and then came here.

This Cuban is a spiritist. He told me that if I wanted luck, every Monday
I should do what he used to do in Cuba. He takes lots of tobacco smoke and
blows it in the doorway, and then he goes and puts a shot of rum there for a
saint, I forget which. I did this, and when I thought it was more or less time I
looked at the rum in the glass. It still had rum in it, but I imagined the saint
had drunk some. The Cuban told me that that was the moment I should ask
for whatever I wanted, and I would get it.

This Cuban was in love with me. He had been in Puerto Rico only eighteen days and he said to me, "I like you because I like all women, but I like you
even more because I see how decent you are. You haven't accepted me, but
I'm going back to Cuba to fight and if I come out alive you're going to belong
to me."

I didn't like him. The Cubans here are all pimps. They think they can do
everything here that they did in Cuba. I know because of another who was in
love with me. He worked in a gambling house and he would say to me all the
time, "Listen, you don't have any money you can give me, do you?"

"Well, I don't know anything about pimps," I told him. "I'm a Puerto
Rican and I don't want to even hear the name of Fidel Castro or of any Cubans. And from the things you tell me, I don't want to know you or the name
of the blessed mother who gave birth to you!" Then he tried to kiss me and I
gave him such a slap I cut his lip open.

"You're the first woman in the world who ever did that to me," he said.

"You're a slimy bunch. We Puerto Rican women hit first and ask questions later."

At the Golden Circle I met a lot of American sailors. I am skinny, ugly
and colored but I get along very well with Americans. All those snapshots in
my purse are pictures of Americans who slept with me once, then stayed with
me until they had to leave Puerto Rico.

One night when the Americans came in from Panama I could have made
about fifty dollars, but I didn't feel like going out with anybody. The men had
made a lot of money in Panama and they had all been two months without a
woman. The U.S. was going to declare war on Panama and so all the time they
were there, waiting to see whether or not there would be a war, they weren't
allowed out on a pass. When they got to Puerto Rico they were savage. They
had a lot of money and a lot of lust. But there are times when I just don't want
to go out.

I'll tell you one thing, I am a Puerto Rican but I'd rather put up with fifty
thousand Americans than one Puerto Rican. The Puerto Rican takes a drink
and feels like big stuff. He'll come over and proposition a woman, and if she
pays no attention he'll even cut her or hit her.

One night a Puerto Rican slapped a girl friend of mine who wouldn't dance with him. He said that we took care of the Americans and not the Puerto Ricans. But what does he expect? God forgive me, but it seems to me that Puerto Rican men are stupid. I think they're a lost breed. When a Puerto Rican courts a girl he swears he'll treat her well and work to get whatever she needs for the home. But as soon as the girl gives in to him, she suffers the consequences. Because right away he falls for another girl. He treats his wife badly and prefers any other woman to her. And Puerto Rican men slap women around. That's the reason why I don't want to marry any more Puerto Ricans. I have failed three times with Puerto Rican husbands.

American men are affectionate and more considerate of women sexually. They like to please and satisfy a woman and they pay well. And from what I saw in the States, they are good to their wives. An American will help his wife do the housework when she's sick. And you should see how he takes care of her when she's pregnant. That's when a Puerto Rican hates his wife most. I have seen that with my own eyes.

My *mamá* has different ideas. She can't stand American men and says they are bad. When she was in the life, Americans mistreated whores. It happened to some of her friends and I think to her too. They'd make a monkey of her, because after they had her they wouldn't pay up. So it bothers my *mamá* that I go out with Americans, and she claims that I like them so much that I don't charge them. One day we were going down to La Esmeralda together when two Americans passed by. I said, "Oh Lord, how cute! I feel so proud when I go down the street with one of them."

"You're telling me!" my *mamá* said. "Why, the way you get hot pants with Americans, I bet you do it with them for free. I'll put my neck under a cleaver if you don't!"

I told her, "Maybe *you* did it for free once." She didn't say one more word.

Felícita

Whoring Is Not My Line

I WOULD like Puerto Rico to change. I want it to become a state. My *mamá*
and *papá* have always favored the Statehood Party and I do too because I've
seen how well people live in New York. If Puerto Rico should become an independent republic, with all the delinquency we have here now, people would be
strung up on posts along the streets and everybody would be dead.

I hate Nationalists, *Independentistas,* and Communists. They're all the
same. I never talk with any of them. I can't. I don't get along with the governor, Muñoz Marín, either, and I don't like his Popular Party. A lot of people
around San Juan are saying that some of the big shots in the Popular Party,
Muñoz Marín himself, and even the mayoress, Felisa, are half-Communist.
I've heard businessmen in San Juan say so, and the man in charge of Joe's
place, where I've worked, told me he'd heard it too. All I know about the
Popular Party is what I've heard, and I feel that Muñoz Marín offered us the
world on a silver platter before he reached the throne. But what does he do
now that he's in power?

My *mamá* has always spoken well to me of Ferré, the candidate of the
Republican Statehood Party. She says that there aren't any others like him.

When a person needs something, that man goes at once to help, even though people have never paid a lot of attention to him. He's not like Muñoz Marín, who won't see you unless you write him a card first, and sometimes not even then, because he pays attention only to rich people and the *Populares*.

Ferré paid the plane fare for anybody who wanted to come from New York to vote for him, but many came and gave their votes to the Popular Party instead. It was Ferré, and not Muñoz Marín, who brought running water to every house in La Esmeralda. We used to have a single public water faucet for the whole neighborhood, and it just gave a thin little stream of water, so that if you put a can under it at nine in the morning it would be only half full at one in the afternoon. Ferré had plumbing laid to get water to every house and paid for it out of his own pocket. Ferré gave wood to the people to fix their houses and to build new ones.

I don't remember exactly when it was that I first saw Ferré. I think it was during the election the year before last. He had promised to come to La Esmeralda on a certain day and he came right on time. He came in shirt sleeves and shabby old shoes. He went around the neighborhood of Bonilla's grocery, all the way down to the beach. The beach was full of garbage and stuff and people kept saying, "Come walk up here on the cement." He answered, "No, I'm going this way. These people here are poor, just like me. I feel for them because I know they need help. I hope this year you'll vote for me so that I can keep all my promises. If I don't, may I lose the next election!"

Truly, people felt so happy during that meeting. Everyone shouted as he spoke. During the campaign Soledad and I, Fernanda, Cruz, Cruz's husband and some others, went with a group of forty or fifty people through all the streets of San Juan playing and singing *bombas*.* There were a lot of *Popular* flags out then, but when the *Populares* tried to form a group like ours they weren't able to. Almost every Friday, Saturday and Sunday our groups gave dances at the Republican Statehood Committee headquarters and organized meetings to elect the president of the Party for each neighborhood. One night, as we were passing City Hall, we saw a parked car with a *Popular* flag on it. My sister Soledad tore off the flag and wore it like a diaper. "Look," she yelled, "this is for the *Populares*." The police couldn't do a thing because, after all, it was only a group of merrymakers, *Estadistas* against the *Populares*. At election time everybody can do as they please.

Ferré promised that if he won he would build a public housing development for the poor, but not on the outskirts of the city like those of Muñoz Marín. Ferré would build houses right here in La Esmeralda so that people can live near their relatives and in their own neighborhood.

If I were governor I'd let all the poor people stay where they are. I would give wood to everybody, or at least to the ones who live at the edge of the sea, so that they could repair their houses. All the houses there have rotten boards. I

* Popular songs and dances, presumably of African origin.

would see that people get enough water. I hardly get any at all where I live. I would give electricity to those who don't have any. And I would fill the holes in the alley pavements and fix the roads. That's all I'd do, because that's all that needs to be done around here.

Muñoz Marín hadn't come down to La Esmeralda in about eight years, in spite of all the suffering here. And then he showed up about fifteen days ago, just because it's election year. I saw him when he was here but I didn't speak to him because I feel nothing but hatred for him. He didn't hold a meeting but only visited his *Populares* here. He didn't go down to the beach the way Ferré did to mess up his shoes with the shit there. Ferré is my man. He gave a big dinner with loads of food. The *Populares* just gave us sweetened water, so to speak. They are going to fix all the streets and they have set up a dispensary and the doctor is coming, I think, the week after next. They have even put public TV sets in La Esmeralda. And that is something we *never* had here. They have put benches around too. But I say, as soon as the elections are over, they'll tear all those things down. Even the doctor won't come any more. Because that's what's happened in other elections.

The mayoress of San Juan, *doña* Felisa Rincón, takes care of the *Populares* members only and not of the others. Thank God I've never had to ask the city for a handout. This year, for the Day of the Three Kings, she gave the *comisario* of La Esmeralda tickets to distribute for toys for the children of the poor. All the *Populares* got tickets, I saw that with my own eyes, but the people who were in need did *not* get any. I didn't get any toys for my children because I am not a *Popular*. My next-door neighbor didn't get any and neither did the woman who lives right below me, because it is known that they are not *Populares*. On December 22, the day the toys were to be distributed, Felisa Rincón came here. I went with Cruz and another girl. Felisa was crying, the hypocrite, because President Kennedy had died. And she said there wouldn't be any music that day. I, for my part, didn't applaud her. I merely laughed and said that she was just putting on a show in front of Wagner, the governor of New York, who was with her.

Doña Felisa said that Kennedy would have brought peace to the whole world, that we had lost a hero, and a lot of other things. Just then Cruz farted. So we started to joke about it. The people around us were hopping mad because we never stopped kidding all the time Felisa was speaking. I don't get along with that old woman because she only takes care of her own.

On December 23, 1963, at four o'clock in the morning, I had just gone to bed when someone came knocking at my door as if they wanted to break it down. I sent Angelito to answer, and who should be outside but my sister Soledad. Her first words were, *"Ave María,* child, how skinny you are. Put on the light."

"We don't have electric lights in this house, just candles," I explained.

But I couldn't find a candle either, so we all went outside. Even the children got up and we went walking around the streets of La Esmeralda, waking up everybody and shouting at the top of our voices that Soledad was back from New York. She had come to see the year out with our *mamá*. Her husband came too, but he was on a ship and only stayed two hours.

Soledad had told me that Benedicto was very good, but that he was also jealous and a terrible pest when he was drunk. When he arrived, *mamá* didn't pay any attention to him at all. She wasn't fond of him, and when she saw him she just said "Hi" and walked on.

In New York, Soledad had a job in a factory and she never hustled there. But that night, after Ben's ship left, she went to work with me. We spent New Year's Eve with three Americans. We had met them at the Golden Circle and they invited us to get another girl like us, not too dark, so that we could all have a good time together. But I couldn't find another girl, so the third American had to go off by himself.

I had never been to the Normandie before. What a wonderful way to start the New Year! *Ave María!* I felt so proud, dancing to refined music in such an elegant ballroom. And the boys danced in a refined way too. The dress I had on was very pretty and so were my shoes. When I sat down at the little table, one of the boys would pull out my chair and then push it back for me. They treated me like a *blanquita,* a society girl.* When they asked me where I lived, I said, "In San Juan." I didn't mention La Esmeralda. We had a few drinks but they were so expensive that I asked the boys to take us somewhere else.

We went to the Cave, where they charged three dollars just to get in. So we went to Joe's, and there we drank and danced and kissed and enjoyed ourselves until ten-thirty. Soledad decided to go to the house to get a bottle of cognac and her partner wanted to go with her. I told her that La Esmeralda was *off limits* for sailors, so she left the American waiting in the taxi up on the Boulevard. But she took her time and he got mad. He came back to us and said, "I wanted to meet your mother but your sister didn't want to take me." I explained that we didn't live in a nice house, so she didn't want to take him there.

"Well, if it has a roof to keep out the rain, I don't care what it looks like," he said. "I want to spend New Year's Day with you and your mother."

So I gave in and took him and my partner down to my house to meet my mother and have a few drinks and wait for midnight. It was dark because we had no candles, but I said I wasn't turning on the lights because the children were asleep. Light was coming in from Florida's house, so my American said it was all right.

At the stroke of twelve, as I was hugging the American, my mother fell to the floor in a fit. First she began to cry. Then she let out a scream and fell. She

* *Blanquita* is literally the diminutive for "white woman," but is used to indicate a person who is well-to-do or of high status.

lay there, stiff and straight. I fanned her, and then my sister and I put her to bed until she got over it. I was so embarrassed. I explained to the American that my mother always had a fit on New Year's Eve if my brother wasn't home to see out the year with her.

As soon as the fit wore off, my *mamá* went to Cruz's to wish her a Happy New Year, and we followed, each carrying a glass full of cognac. Cruz's house was a mess. The dishes were dirty, the beds unmade, the chairs upside down, the clothes scattered all over the floor, and her little girl was banging on a wash basin. I made a sign to Soledad not to invite the boys in, but they had already gone up and started to play with Crucita's baby.

Then the four of us went to dance at my cousin's house for a while, but the Americans wanted to see the New Year's Eve celebration in New York. They kept saying, "Let's go some place where we can watch TV, no matter what it costs."

We took a taxi to Stop 8 to look for a hotel, but we couldn't find one with TV. We wandered around until nearly five o'clock in the morning and my American was running out of money. He'd spent about ninety dollars altogether, because they'd fleeced him at the *bars* and the taxi drivers had cheated him too. Finally we went to a hotel near the *base* and rented a double room.

Oh Lord! This isn't funny, but I have to laugh when I think of it. The man told them they could have a *double room* for eight dollars. We went up. It turned out to be a room with one double bed! So we took turns. First I went in for a while with my American. Then we put on our clothes and went out so my sister could use the room. Everything worked out fine. Then we decided to put *el matre** on the floor. I slept on it with my American and my sister slept on the bed with the other American. There we were, all together in one room. After a while I had to go to the toilet. And when I put on the light, there was the other American kissing my sister's cunt. He said, "Never mind, leave the light on." The next day I kidded them about it. We had a wonderful time.

We made a date to meet at *Joe's Place* at about nine in the morning to spend the day together. The boys were broke by then, so my sister and I paid for the food and the drinks.

Before he went back to his ship, the American showed me a snapshot of his mother and the house where he lived. It was such a pretty house that I was embarrassed and passed the picture to my sister right away. Soledad took it and stared. I called the boy *liar man* because he told me that he didn't live well. He laughed at that. I snatched the picture from my sister and handed it back to him. I was ashamed, remembering the mess Cruz's house was in when we took them there, and even though my house was in order, I was ashamed of not having electricity or any kind of luxury there. They had wanted to watch TV and we didn't have a set.

Here in Puerto Rico practically nobody lives well. It's not like the States.

* Mattress.

They have to have good houses there because it's so cold. But it isn't cold here, so one has to live in a wooden shack gnawed to pieces by termites.

I quit my job at the Golden Circle because although the owner had offered me twenty-five dollars a week, he never paid more than twelve or eighteen. My shift was from four in the afternoon till midnight, but he wanted me to stay until four or five in the morning, and he objected because I never worked more than nine hours a day.

I get so exhausted when I work at night. I have to keep opening the refrigerator, waiting on clients, going back and forth all the time. I don't have any energy left to work around the house. When I don't have a job but just go out with men I have a chance to rest because I get home earlier. You don't get tired if you take on two or three men for five minutes each. I've never had more than four men in one night.

I can't work in the daytime unless I can make enough to pay someone to look after the children. Wages are miserably low here in Puerto Rico. Even in a factory the most you can get, if you are a very good worker, is twenty-two dollars a week. And you'd have to spend at least fifteen to pay a woman to look after your children and buy their food. After all, there are five children. So, is one to work so hard for just seven dollars a week? I'd rather not work at all. And I can hardly ever get anyone to stay with my children at night. In La Esmeralda people won't do anything for you, not even if you offer to pay and put the money in their hands. That was another reason I quit my job.

I went to work in *Joe's Place,* but I quit after five months because I had to stay there all night too. He made us work too hard. That man wanted us to sweep the floor and help him clean up until dawn. He paid twenty-five dollars a week, but it wasn't worth it.

So I was out of a job again and the children had no shoes or anything. I even owed two months' rent. In fact, Genoveva, the owner of the house, said she'd evict me if I didn't pay up. Ángel had stopped sending me money for the twins, so in June I went to court. I told the sergeant I wanted to sue my husband for the children's support. He wanted to know the last time Ángel had sent money, how much he had been sending before, if the children were legitimate, where Ángel lived, and a lot of other things. I answered all his questions. Right away they sent a letter to Ángel, and within a week they arrested him.

When Ángel arrived, he told me he was very surprised. He didn't know that the Veterans Administration had stopped sending me money. I wanted to give him the two boys, but he said he couldn't help me out because his wife was pregnant and he himself was sick and couldn't work. He explained all this in court and the lady judge herself spoke up for him. Since his own allowance from the Administration had been cut, he couldn't take any money out of that to send me. And so the case ended.

Then I went to *Welfare* to ask for help. But they said, "You look healthy.

You should get a job and leave the children in the care of a relative. We can't do anything for you now. But come back later if you still need help."

I asked them to send my children to a boarding school reformatory because they wouldn't go to school. I'd send them off in the morning, and they'd never get there. They never obey me. Angelito has even tried to hit me. I told all that to the people at the school and at the *Welfare*.

Finally they said they would send me thirty dollars a month, but as long as I was getting it, I couldn't work. That wasn't enough for the children and me. They told me, "All right, we'll see. We'll come to visit you." They came to my house once and never came back. I said to myself that I wouldn't bother them any more. But one of these days I'm going to the newspapers to make a complaint. I'll tell *El Imparcial* that I want to give *el Welfare* a thousand thanks for all the attention they paid me. They help the ones who don't need it, but I, the mother of five and without a husband, had to sacrifice myself and leave my children alone at night to go to work.

I struggled and struggled for my children, and all for nothing. I thought to myself, "I'm already a grown woman and can't allow myself to die yet. Maybe I'll find my future in New York." I thought that if I could leave the other children with their fathers I could take Tany with me. I decided to take the twins to Culebra to hand them over to Ángel but I found that he was really too sick to take them. Then I took the two little ones, Mundito and Evita, to Salinas to see if Edmundo would keep them.

Edmundo told me he hadn't come to San Juan to see me, because I was in the life. He said, "I felt terrible when I heard you were hustling at the same place where I once worked. I used to speak so well of you."

But then he asked me if I was willing to go back to him. He had a house all to himself, with a dining-room set and a living-room set, but I wouldn't, because I didn't love him any longer. Sometimes I even felt myself hating him. I didn't want to spend that night in his house, but his brother's place is very small. I think they have only two beds for six or seven children. Edmundo wanted me to stay with him in case the children cried. "I can't look after them," he said, "because I have to go to work in the morning." So I stayed.

I didn't try to get him to make love to me but he wanted to, so I did it, without desire and without coming. He liked it, though, and when we were through he said, *"Ay,* some little machine you have there!" But I told him that I didn't want to see him ever again.

I was willing to divorce him any time. He'd had two women since we separated and I didn't mind at all. Once I even wrote to his sweetheart for him. He can't write and he asked me to do it. I began the letter "My unforgettable darling," and then went on to say, as if I were Edmundo, "Well, my little girl, don't worry too much, because I started work on Saturday. I am saving money for a divorce so that I can marry you. I want you to be a good girl because if you are, I'm going to bring you to San Juan when we get married. I hope you will keep the promise you made to me." Edmundo didn't tell me what the promise was. At the bottom I wrote, "From the one who loves you and will never forget you, Edmundo Capó." I wrote all that myself! That shows how little I cared.

Well, Edmundo took the children, but he returned them a week later because they got the measles and he had nobody to stay with them. I got mad when I saw him. I kissed the children but I didn't pay any attention to him. He greeted me, but stayed out on the porch for a while before he dared come in.

The next day, Sunday, he came to my house and changed his clothes, and when I got to work at six o'clock there he was, sitting at the *bar* drinking. He had refused to give me half a dollar for stockings that very afternoon but he handed me a dollar to pay for his drink. I said, "Look, Edmundo, I'm going to keep the rest for the children's milk." He said, "No, take only a quarter instead." He explained that he was keeping the other quarter to buy himself a beer. Yet he spent a total of six dollars for beer that day, not counting the nickels he dropped in the juke box or the twenty cents' tip he gave me.

He got home before I did. I went to look at the children and there he was, snuggling down on my bed. "Lie down here," he said.

"No, thanks. I'll go lie on the sofa." I told him that we would treat each other like brother and sister. I took off my clothes and lay down.

He wanted to get in with me but I stuck out my leg and tripped him. He said, "How mean you are and I love you so much."

"But I don't love you."

"You're really fresh," he says. "How dare you tell me you don't love me, right to my face like that? You shouldn't say those things to a man. If I wasn't the kind of man I am and if I had a gun here, I'd kill you right now."

I said, "Why should I tell you I love you when I don't? What I'm telling you is the truth, and Our Lord Jesus Christ died for the truth. I don't love you and I won't have anything to do with you." He took his suitcase and went away. I had to lend him five dollars so he could go. The children stayed with me.

For a while Edmundo sent me ten dollars a month and then . . . nothing. He is in Connecticut now, working in the fields, I think. His girl friend is living in Salinas. He says that when he gets back from the U.S. he will take his two children from me.

So I couldn't count on either Edmundo or Ángel to take their children. But when Tany's father, Nicolás, learned that I was talking of going to New York, he begged me to leave Tany with him so that she wouldn't have to live there among strangers. He said I could have the child back when he died. I told him that he couldn't interfere in Tany's life because he'd never done a thing for her. So that year, for the very first time, he sent her *un baby* set on the Day of the Kings, a doll with diapers and soap, in a small box which wasn't even wrapped. He gave it to his sister-in-law to bring to the house. I don't know what I ever saw in that man but I do know that I'll never give Tany to him.

I couldn't expect any help from my father this time, but when the *Army* sent him back from France I went to visit him. No one was at home, so I waited there until about eleven-thirty. While I was standing at the bus stop, *papá* and Hortensia came by in a taxi. My *papá* looked at me a moment and said, "How skinny you are, girl. You look like a broomstick." He didn't know I was a whore.

I laughed and said, "What can I do? I thought I was very fat."

My stepmother gave me a sour look and screwed up her mouth. I was wearing a tight *jersey* dress which was open at one seam. So she said, "Why did you come in that torn dress?"

"It stretched a little and opened up on me."

"I have a little chain for the baby," my *papá* said and he gave it to me. It was made of copper and must have cost about twenty-nine cents. The baby broke it right away.

Then I told my father, "I was hungry, so I scraped the bottom of the pot."

He said, "Look, why don't you take a piece of cabbage home with you?"

He comes from France after three years and offers me a piece of cabbage! "That's a good one!" I said. It wouldn't have been so bad if he had given me a present at least. But a piece of plain cabbage! I'm going to tell everybody about it.

I always, always loved my *papá* very much. But he lets my stepmother boss him around and when he dies we are not going to get a thing because whatever they own is in her name. The *Army* used to give us an allowance, but she had it turned over to her children and they cut us off.

So all my father had to say to me was that I looked like a broomstick and did I want a piece of cabbage. I didn't say anything to them, but when I was leaving, my *papá* seemed to know how I felt because he said, "Well, good-bye, and come again on Sunday." But I didn't go back. Why should I? Just to have a bad time? Besides, my stepmother doesn't like us to come to the house, and whenever we do, she follows us around with a *mop,* cleaning up behind us. If we come with the children she gives us a dirty look, and all the time she's mopping up wherever we set foot, and spraying Flit.

When we wanted to see our father we always had to go to his house. He came down to La Esmeralda only once, to offer to take us to visit the commanding officer. But he never came back. He stood us up. And when I went in his car I always had to sit in the back seat, never in the front.

The trouble with my stepmother is that she puts on a lot of airs and wants to be better than everybody else. But I must say that when you need something, she will help you. I care the same for my stepmother as for my mother. Fernanda has a bad temper, worse than my stepmother's, and she won't let me borrow anything from her. The other day she refused to lend me a pair of slippers. She said her husband didn't want her to lend things. I have lots of clothes but no house slippers, so I really needed them. But no matter what I ask for, Fernanda refuses to lend it.

I have suffered, you know, because I haven't had the good fortune to have the mother's love I need. Some mothers at least care enough about their daughters to visit them. Fernanda has been to Cruz's house twice but never to mine. She doesn't give a thought to me or to my children. When I was sick in bed for two weeks she didn't come to my house once. Cruz came one day and Gladys, the one who went off with Crucita's lover, also took care of me when I was in all that pain. My period hadn't come, so I took things to bring it on and I had pain and hemorrhaging.

My *mamá* enjoys life. She goes to the movies almost every day and she has a good time with that lover of hers. Whenever there's a *fiesta* she's there. But if I say, "Nanda, please take care of the baby while I go to the hospital," she says, "Ah, that boy cries too much!" But if it's Cruz, she'll say, "All right, don't be long." She has never, never stayed with my children so I could go out and have a good time.

When I went hustling, I had to leave my children locked in at home. I used to leave them with Cruz but the next day she would insult me and want to know what made me so late. She'd say that I took better care of my boy friends than I did of my children and I would answer, "I have to, because they're the ones who give me cash."

She was angry because I took men to my house. One day she went and told everybody in the neighborhood about finding me with a man. The way she talks about me and insults the men I am with, no one would think she was a whore herself. She was, though. She went hustling at Papo's *bar,* with Alejandro and anybody else she could find there. Let her need ten or fifteen dollars and to Papo's *bar* she'd go. Papo's wife, Genoveva, was her pal.

Cruz is bad-tempered, but she's good and I love her. She usually does whatever I ask her to do. And I've been good to her, too, because when she had her quarrels with Emilio I always took her into my house. If I got sick she'd look after me and the kids. If she needed money for food I'd give it to her. And if she wanted any little thing for her children, I'd get it for her if I could afford it. I didn't pay her a salary but we helped each other. But she was better off than I was. Besides *welfare,* her husband gave her money for the children. And she's always running to the *comisario* for help. She had electricity in her house and could wash and iron there. I didn't have any of those conveniences and I had five children. Nobody, not even *el Welfare,* gave me a hand. And Cruz sold lottery tickets but she never kept any for herself. She never thinks of taking a chance so that she'll win something. She doesn't think that way. All she worries about is the next day and no further.

I'm different from Cruz. She'll suck up to anybody but I'm never one to make advances. If someone doesn't speak to me first, I don't speak to him. But I'm always willing to help a person in need. If someone needs his ass wiped, I'm glad to wipe it. But as for lowering myself just because someone thinks he's better than I am—never. Not me.

Fernanda always claimed that I neglect my children and let them run wild in the streets. I'd tell her, "If my children were neglected they wouldn't be alive. They'd have starved long ago."

"Oh, sure," she'd say. "It's the neighbors who take care of them."

"Yes, because I don't have a single relative who would lift a finger to help me, even if I paid him."

"Well, you don't deserve it."

Then I'd just tell her that every cat's kitten hunts mice.

My *mamá* is very unfair to speak of me the way she does. I'm affectionate with my children. I love them because they're growing up without a father. I work hard for them and I suffer for them too. Christmas time is the worst because they expect new clothes and toys for the holidays and I begin to think about what I can do, with no money and owing rent and payments on the furniture. Many people are sad at that time of year.

The year Edmundo left me, I couldn't buy any presents for my kids. I started to cry right in the *bar*. A boy asked me what was the matter, and I told him.

"How many children do you have?" he asked me.

"Five."

"Listen, stop worrying. I have seven, and last year I had no money for presents either. So I stole some." But when I need something, I'd rather pray. I ask God for what I need and pray an Our Father or a Hail Mary.

What I'd like most for my children is for them to study and see if they can't make something of themselves. Not something very big, because I can't afford to send them to college. But I hope they at least finish high school and have a trade so that they can get good jobs. And I'd like my daughters to be virgins and marry with a veil and crown. I want them to be decent people, better than I am. One should always live with hope. But as long as I stay in Puerto Rico, I don't see how I can get ahead.

I worry about my situation, about not having a husband. There are times when I can't even buy milk for the children. When I get hungry—*Ave María!*—I get very nervous and can't stand to have anyone talk to me. I get very weak too, and my stomach aches and I get cold all over. I can't stand being hungry. It makes me lose my temper and snap at people. But I bear it as best I can and drink sugar water to make it go away.

I get fed up, but what can I do? Sometimes I feel like killing the children and then setting fire to myself. I have really thought of that and have almost done it too. One day I grabbed a knife, meaning to run it through Angelito. My nerves are bad and he was giving me a hard time. I asked him to do some little thing and he raised his hand to me and said, "Shit, who are you to be sending me on errands?"

"Look here, you damn brat," I yelled, but then I controlled myself.

When I really get angry I punish those kids with fury. I do that because I want them to be well brought up. I beat them when they won't go to school, but when I punish them they stick out their tongues at me. The truth is, I don't punish them the way a mother should, because when they yell at me and don't obey, I feel myself getting tense all over. I lose my self-control when they jump about and start fighting each other. The little one hits the big one and the big one hits back. Then they make such an uproar that I don't know what to do. They begin to turn the house upside-down and say dirty words. That really makes me wild. I grab one of them and punish him. Sometimes I'll slap their faces. Other times I'll take a strap and whip them on the legs or on the hands. I'll even hit them with the broomstick. But never hard enough to cause a dangerous injury.

I have told my boys to hit back when other children hit them, and if they don't, I beat them. Because it's up to me to develop their character. I don't beat them often, only about once a week when I've had all I can take.

Angelito is a serious-minded boy, even though he's only seven. He doesn't like noisy play and doesn't often get into mischief. He's usually obedient, too. When he gets new clothes he doesn't mind taking them off if he has to. He folds them up and hangs them up in a corner of the house. But he can be troublesome because of his terrible temper. If I send him on an errand he'll sit in a corner and sulk and won't budge unless I scold or offer him money. When I hit him he calls me names and says, "Puñeta, leave me alone," or "Watch out or I'll throw stones at you." He has never shown much affection for me. Only once, that I remember. That day I was sick and I asked him to rub some bay rum on me and he did. His teacher tells me that he's very studious. The twins won't study at home, but they know their lessons in school.

Angelito's favorite game is playing cowboy. Every year, the only thing he wants on the Day of the Kings is a cowboy pistol with a holster. He's hardly ever at home. He spends all his time out in the street. He comes home for meals and at bedtime. When we have visitors, though, all the kids stay in the house instead of going out and minding their own business. I think that when there are guests, children shouldn't interrupt to complain of one another and they shouldn't cry about every little thing. They should at least wait until the grownups give them a chance to speak. I'm always telling them, "When we have visitors, go lie down if you have a pain or don't feel well. And if you need something, wait until the visitors leave."

Gabriel, the other twin, wishes he were a girl. He likes to wear my *panties* and *brassière*. I took him to the hospital and they found that his little balls haven't come down. They said he'll need an operation. Gabi is sort of vain. If he could have his way, he'd get new clothes every day. When I buy him new clothes he never wants to take them off. He likes to keep his shoes shiny and gives his little friends pennies for shining them. He spends a lot of time combing his hair. Once I didn't buy the children new clothes for the Day of the Kings because I thought they could use the ones they had worn only once, on Christmas Eve. Well, Gabi didn't want to get dressed at all if he couldn't have new clothes like the other boys.

Gabi is brighter than Angelito in school. He can read well, add, and write his name. Sometimes when I take him to a store he'll read the price tags for other people.

I don't know what my kids think of me because I've never asked them if they love me or anything like that. Gabi says that when he grows up he'll buy me a house and work to support me. And Angelito also says that he'll give me money when he works.

But Tany shows more affection for me than they do. Of all my children, I love her best. I ask her if she loves her *papá* and she says no, only her *mami*. She's always playing that she's taking lice out of my hair. The twins push her around and hit her, and all she does is cry. When she finally makes up her mind to bite them or something like that, it's because she's had all she can take. Usually she lets herself be pushed around by everybody, even though she's almost five years old. Her presents for the Day of the Kings have all been stolen by now. She lets her friends cart them all away. She's a real little dope.

Mundo likes to play a lot. But he cries all the time and begs me for money. He's not even three and he already takes money out of my purse. Just now, when I went out, he asked me to light a cigarette for him. If he sees me drinking beer he'll beg for some. He really likes it, too. Mundito is very troublesome, and in spite of being the youngest boy, he's always fighting. When he decides to hit somebody, it always has to be a bigger boy. I don't know what to do with that child because he's going to have his father's temper.

There isn't much I can say about Evita because she's still a baby. She just sits in a corner sucking her thumb and pulling her ear. When she's hungry she points to the bottle. That baby hardly gives me any trouble at all.

One time the twins wanted to watch TV and I told them, "All right, but let's go home and use the new TV set I just bought." They ran all the way home. When they got there they were mad at me because I had fooled them. There was no TV set at all. There was only a wooden box I had covered with a cloth. They began to cry, so I said, "Do you want me to play with you?" I gave them a nickel for two rolls of caps and I told them to get their pistols. Then they hid behind the box and started shooting. Gabi kept saying, "*Ay, they killed me.*" Every time Evita heard a shot she would point to the box. The neighbors across the way laughed and laughed at our goings-on.

It makes me sad that the children call for their father so often. The other day the baby kept saying, "*Papá, papá,*" and pointing outside every time she said it. That kind of thing makes me very sad. And so does the thought that I might get sick for a long time and have no one to support my children. My family would take care of them but that's not the same as their own mother. When I'm working I buy them anything that catches their eye. If I could at least find somebody to take care of those kids I would look for a better job, because whoring is not my line.

Gabriel

———

I Walk Alone

———

I LOVE FELÍCITA very much because she borned me, but I wish she behaved herself. I want her to be good, not to run around with men like she does and to pay more attention to her children than to the fellows she goes with. She used to live with Rosario, who beat her a lot. He didn't beat me, though. If he had I would have taken a stick to him. I'd have taken a club and bashed his head in.

Sometimes when I'm alone, Felícita comes to me and says, "Listen, you, don't you dare go saying I have a man or I'll slap your mouth hard enough to make the blood come." When she says that, I always answer, "And why do you spend all your time with men instead of taking care of your children? You better pay some attention to us because if you don't I'm going to go live with Fernanda."

I think my *mamá* doesn't love us. When children are left alone all the time, it means their *mamá* doesn't love them. Isn't that right? Look, she would get up and go away and when I asked her, "Where are you going?" she answered, "To hunt goats."

"What! You really mean it? If you are going to hunt goats you'll have to take the children along. Those kids are badder than the devil and I'm not going to look after them for you. If you go out, you'll have to take us all with you."

Then Felícita left Rosario and went to New York, so Fernanda took me to live with her. It was swell, living with Fernanda; she's nice. She used to buy us *tennis shoes* and lots of other things. She gave us toys for the Day of the Three Kings and put up a Christmas tree. That was when I met Héctor. He was nice too; he gave me nickels. He was crazy about me. You know what he said to me? He said, "I love you so much I don't ever want to lose you." He took me to parks, he took me to the merry-go-round, he took me to the beach. One day I went to the beach all by myself. "I'll go play at the water's edge," says I. I put *un tubo* around me and floated way off deep. My cousin Darío brought me back ashore. He had to carry me piggyback.

When I was with Nanda, Simplicio and his wife, Flora, lived there too and Héctor never said anything about it. I remember that they arrested Simplicio one day. They took him away in a patrol car. He was crazy. I didn't know what it was all about, only that they were all saying that it wasn't right, that it wasn't possible for them to arrest him. Then Nanda said, "Let's go to court." So we went to court to talk, just Nanda, Flora and I.

The court is big and full of people. Every little while I'd want to get up and go. The judge had a beard and a mustache and policemen standing beside him. The judge began: "How did it happen?" I felt like speaking up too, but I kept my mouth shut because you have to tell a judge the truth. If you don't, they shut you up in a jail. Then we went home and they put my uncle in a jail but he got out right away.

Afterward Felícita came back and took us to live with her, but she has never taken care of us. What she did was leave us at Crucita's house and give her money to buy malt beer for us.

You know, Cruz sometimes plays dirty tricks on me. She locks me up and makes me work but I don't always sleep there, I sleep at Fela's house. Sometimes Cruz bolts the door so that the kids can't go out. When she does that I take something to cover myself with and I go to sleep in a car that's parked beside the house. It's better out there. Like last night, Cruz didn't put a diaper on her baby girl and I rolled over in my sleep and got her shit all over me. And then Cruz quarrels with me because she thinks I'm the one that shits on the bed. But I don't do that. I help clean up the house.

What happens is that Felícita works in a *bar* giving people things and all that. She leaves home at about five in the afternoon and comes back at midnight. We have to stay in the house all by ourselves but that's all right. I myself told her to get a job because she doesn't have a husband to give her money.

One day it got to be two in the morning and Felícita hadn't come home. I was scared, real scared, so I got up and started searching for her. Suddenly I hear "click, click, click," Felícita's heels. I shouted "Boo!" Boy, did she jump! "Well, what are you up to now?" I ask her. "Here it is two o'clock and you still out with that American. I don't want him coming here any more."

But then Fernanda comes to me and says, "That man is Fela's husband. Didn't you know it?"

"I don't care," says I. "I don't want him here."

Edmundo, the husband she used to have, behaved real well. He worked in a coffee plantation doing all kinds of work with a machete. He had us kids with him, in a room in Salinas. The house we lived in was little, like an ant, and the sink was broken. There were woods near the house and we used to go there to get firewood, yams, bananas and all that. Sometimes I pulled off a banana and ate it. When we got home, Felícita put firewood in a stone hearth and she'd light the wood with a match and cook there.

Ah, how I liked the country! There were rivers where I could bathe and everything was nice and clean. And I knew a pretty girl with white skin and black hair who lived there. Her name was Carmen Rosa. I whistled when she went by, because I was in love with her. She was my sweetheart.

Edmundo wasn't bad, he behaved well. But one day Felícita said, "I'm going to visit my *mamá.*" Edmundo had given her five dollars to buy food but she used it to pay the fare to San Juan, without even asking his permission. A few days later Edmundo showed up at La Esmeralda hopping mad, and said he never wanted to see Felícita anymore. That was just what Felícita wanted, so then they broke up and she went and got herself a room at Papo's and moved in there with all us kids.

Well, so now Felícita doesn't have a husband any more. She has to hustle to get money for breakfast. She usually prepares our breakfast herself. But sometimes she doesn't have money and then I take a nickel and get myself some bread and butter and coffee.

One bad thing Felícita does is to bring men to the house. She's always going out with Cuco. And she often asks me, "Have you seen Cuco?" I always answer, "No." Because, you know, when Cuco goes to the house he gets into bed with Fela and they do bad things. I say to him, "If you can sleep in my *mamá*'s bed, I can too." Then they pull the sheet up over my face. I can't breathe like that, so I soon pull it off and catch them screwing. So I cover my eyes with my hand and move to the couch.

There's another American she also takes home to screw. I cover my face when they are at it but I peek at them through my fingers. They begin to play in the bed and after a while they start jumping. Then I know what's coming— oops! they throw me down on the floor. I pick myself up and go to sleep on *el caucho.* Then they have the bed all to themselves. Sometimes it comes over me all of a sudden, "How terrible—Felícita doing bad things." But nobody dares tell me anything like that about her. Besides, I'm always alone.

One night I had gone to bed when I heard men laughing in my house. When I see what they are up to I try to make them go away. I pull the man's legs to make him fall, Puerto Rican or American, it's all the same to me. Then I take a piece of charcoal and paint my face black as I can. I put on a pair of old gloves and take a stick to carry over my shoulder. I think maybe they'll get scared and run away, seeing me like that. I wish Felícita would stop doing the things she does with men. Those things are bad and God will punish her.

I don't even like to have her do it with Cayetano, who gives her five dollars every time she goes to his house. Cayetano is a long, skinny old man who has lots of money. One day he bought thirty dollars' worth of food for Felícita. I don't know where all the money comes from. Maybe he gets it from a cave, or from the bank. The thing is, he gives me money too, quarters. And pomade for the hair and for the face. Last year, the Three Kings left presents for me at his house: balls, a machine gun, *un revolver*. They left *un revolver* for Mundito and a tea set for Tany. Angelito got a holster and Evita a doll that said "Eeeee."

The trouble with Cayetano is that when Felícita doesn't go to him, he gets mad and comes and complains to me about her. "I'm angry with you," he says. "I don't want to see that tramp in my house ever again." But that's a lie, he's never stopped being interested in her. When he gets to talking like that, I always tell him, "I don't know anything about that. You and Fela solve your own problems. I'm fed up. Some day I'm going to sneak out when you aren't looking and never come back again."

Cayetano wants Crucita to go to him too but Crucita won't. She never has done anything like that.

When I see a ship coming I say to Felícita, "Look, see what's coming? A *gringo* ship. Just the thing for you." That makes her laugh. "All right, tell me when it comes in, maybe one of my Americans is on it." When she says that, I run out into the street and play until I tire myself out. That way I can't see the ship come in.

An ugly, thick-lipped American called Walker comes in one of those ships. He comes to our house and goes to bed there and everything. "Look," I say to him, "I don't like you, so there." He's mean to me, you know. Sometimes he curses me out and other times he scares me.

There's a picture of him and Fela with their arms around each other. I'll have to tell Fela to get rid of that picture. If Edmundo should ever come to the house and see it, he'll chop Felícita's head off with his machete.

Felícita was going to take Angelito and me to our *papá* Cubero* and leave us with him because he stopped sending money to buy us clothes and shoes. Someone told him something bad about Felícita and the money stopped coming. Felícita went to court so they would make Cubero take us, but he didn't want us either.

Cubero is my *papá* and sometimes I think I would like to stay with him. But no, he doesn't like children. Besides, I won't go there to stay because his house looks like a worm and the roof is all black. He lives way off, in Culebra, where it's as cold as the inside of a refrigerator and muddy all over. The mud is deep and your feet sink into it with every step.

I didn't want her to, but Felícita took us to Culebra anyway. There Cu-

* The surname of Ángel, the twins' father.

bero's old mother asked me, "Would you like a cup of coffee?" I said no and began to cry. When I looked up I saw Cubero beside me, sitting on a horse. He picked me up and set me on the horse, to take my picture. His wife was there, a skinny woman, but fat around the middle because she's going to have a baby. She's bad. Sometimes she laughs and then you can see where her teeth are missing. They had a little girl there called Etanislá, just like my sister Tany.

It turned out we all had to go back home with Fela because Cubero had the chest sickness and couldn't keep us. It got to be almost five o'clock, time for the ferry to start back to Fajardo, and Cubero's *mai* bawled him out because he hadn't given us money for the fare. So he finally gave Felícita five dollars, which is what it cost.

We got back to La Esmeralda and I was mad as hell because of what Felícita had done. I don't want them to do that to us. I stayed out in the street until it was dark. Then I got hungry and went over to Crucita's for a malt beer.

That night I said to myself, "Oh, if I could ever have some peace!" I lay down on the floor and fell fast asleep. Suddenly I woke up because something was going boom, boom. "What can that be?" I asked myself. "Could the door be banging like that?" Then I looked outside and saw Nanda and Héctor fighting. "Listen!" I jumped up fast and yelled at them, "Don't fight!" Then I ran out. I thought, "Well, they had to fight someday. But this fight is something people will talk about because Nanda and Héctor are really hitting each other hard." Héctor was all bloody where Nanda had scratched him with her long fingernails. Right in the middle of the fight, a cop walks by and sees them.

I said to myself, "I'll go watch from upstairs in Crucita's house. I'll pretend not to know about this so they won't make me tell." Cruz was already watching when I got there. She's a busybody and a troublemaker. She is like a news sheet, spreading gossip and making trouble. Crucita is *El Recreo* and Catín is *El Imparcial*.

The cop hit Héctor on the knees with his club. That made me real mad. "Just you wait," I thought. I felt like going to court with them but they didn't take me that time. I wanted to tell the judge the truth, that neither of them should be arrested because it was the fault of both. Héctor started the fight but it was because he caught Nanda kissing Junior.

Those cops! They are the real bad ones. Bullies, that's what they are. When I see a cop I feel like snatching away his club and bashing him over the head with it. They are like the undertow, because the undertow carries people away and so do the cops, only the cops are worse.

All cops are bad but the worst one in the world is right here in La Esmeralda—Gilberto. When people are shooting craps, Gilberto grabs the money and runs off with it. I yell to him, "Go on, take the money and buy yourself a beer."

Sometimes he hits me with his club and I insult him. "Look here, Mustache," I tell him. "You're bad. I'm scared of you." He hits people. One day they brought a man down and Gilberto snapped the handcuffs on him. I have caught him doing all those things.

Well, the day of the fight, late in the morning, I see Héctor around there and ask him, "What happened in court? Say, what's the matter with you, fighting like that? Don't you know they can lock you up in jail and then you won't have anybody to get you out?" It's expensive to get someone out of jail. It costs a hundred dollars.

Felícita wants me to go to school. But sometimes she sends me there at one, knowing that it's too late, or at nine, which is too early. I don't like school because it's so big. And the bell rings so early it makes me mad because I know I can't get out again until five. Sometimes the teacher hits me right on top of those infected boils I have, thinking I have done something bad. I never do anything bad. I just sit there quietly without saying a word. All they do at school is study and read books, and I can hardly read at all. I would like to learn but I don't know how.

When I get out of school in the afternoon, the boys yell "Pansy!" at me. "Come on, let me wipe your ass," they'll say. Once I grabbed one of them by the ear and *pum, pum, pum,* I punched him. "Do you think I'm a dope?" I asked him. "Go ahead, come on and find out!" They call me "queer" and "pansy" and I answer back, "Your fucking mother, you pansy!" I fight them with my fists. I yell at them, "Come on, come on and see if I'm a dope, you bastards!"

I'm not really a pansy, you know. It's just that I have to wear girl's shoes. Felícita bought them for Tany but they were too big for her so she gave them to me. And now I have to wear them because I have no others. Then, too, Felícita kids around with me as if I were a grown-up young man. A queer goes by our house sometimes and Felícita tells me I'm going to marry him. That makes me feel like socking her one. But no, I can't fight with my own mother. Besides, she's bigger than me and throws chairs.

Felícita prepares our dinner herself. Then she leaves it there and goes to bed. After we eat, we go outside to play so our noise won't bother her. She has to go to work, you see. Then she gets up and begins to say I take money from her purse when she isn't looking. "I don't do those things," I tell her. "Only grown men who are thieves do them."

She beats us for any little thing. One day she made me bleed, she hit me so hard with a stick. She thought I had socked Tany but it was the other way around. Tany had hit me and had bitten my ear. I cried a lot that time, not because my feelings were hurt but because I was so mad.

I don't love my brothers and sisters. Angelito, well, he's my twin and is just like me, but Catín used to say that Felícita loved him more than me. When she said that I'd answer, "Well, what can I do? But if she loves Angelito, how can she help loving his twin?" Angelito has "bad" hair and thick lips. He and I used to go out together and defend each other. One day I was fighting four boys and Angelito came up and gave one of them a black eye. I socked another one so hard that he bled. But then Angelito and I separated—he would go one way and I another. But when I got something he claimed it had to be for both. If I got myself a girl, Angelito would say, "She's my sweetheart." One day we fought and I made one of his eyes all puffy. We fought all the time.

With Tany I don't get along at all. She sleeps with me and wets the bed. I don't like her, she's a dirty pig. She shits, she pees and she steals Fela's money. One day she found some coins and took them. When Fela asked her, "Where's the change for that dollar?" Tany said, "I don't know. I didn't take anything. I gave them to Nanda." Fela asked Nanda and Nanda said that was a lie. Then Fela beat Tany but she says she loves that kid a lot. She says Tany is the one she'll always keep because her *papá* is dead.

I don't like my other brother, Mundito, either, that goes without saying. He's bad as they come. If he wants a penny, you have to give it to him, whether you want to or not. When I'm eating, he sits there and stares at me. And he won't let me sleep. With Felícita away, drinking beer and then coming home so drunk and sleepy that I have to take her shoes off because she isn't sober enough to do it herself, I'm the one who gets screwed. I say to Mundito, "Look here, if you don't let me sleep, with your shitting and yelling, I'll beat you up." He steals Fela's money too. He once took a dollar from Fela's purse and lost it. She beat him up for that. And then she tells me to watch Mundito. "Listen," I say to her, "I'm not supposed to be the watchman around here. Take your purse with you. Don't leave it lying around if you don't want your money stolen."

The only one I love a little bit is Evita. She shits in bed too but she's the baby. I saw her being born. It was on a Friday. Fela was lying in bed, with the curtain drawn so nobody could look. A nurse-doctor came to take care of her and put on some gloves of the kind that don't make any noise. I was out on the porch when they called me to see my new baby sister. I looked at her a long time. She was crying. They slap newborn babies, you know, to make them cry. Sometimes I take care of Evita, a little bit.

But for all of that, I still don't want to live with Felícita because of the things she does. I'd rather live alone and work on the docks, as Héctor did when he left Nanda and was all by himself.

Lucelia lives near us. Sometimes I go to see her and ask her blessing, because she's my godmother. I treat her with respect because she can't walk and had to be taken to the hospital. Crucita took her. One day Felícita gave me away to Lucelia—she told me to go live with my godmother. I went, but Lucelia likes to use her fists. Once she socked me so hard that I still have the mark. That night I watched for a lady from Santo Domingo, who is Fela's friend. When she passed by, I ran to her and had her take me back home. I would rather live with Fela because Lucelia beat me too much and wanted to keep me under her thumb. Sometimes I don't like being alive.

I went back to Felícita's but there the next-door neighbors keep you awake. They start fighting and end up screwing. Florida calls her husband "you big queer" and he answers "you dirty, kinky-haired sow!" Then the light goes on and Florida yells, "You damn fool, can't you let me sleep in peace." They go on and on, quarreling like that. One night I yelled out, "I shit on both your mothers." That shut them up all right!

I don't like the house where I live because its always full of children's shit. I keep cleaning up the place but it's often in a mess. Who would ever visit such a place, anyway? The toilet is always smeared with shit, too, because the neighbors use it. They climb up on it and get it all dirty and then they blame it on us. That's why I go to the beach to shit, so they won't blame me.

I don't like La Esmeralda either, because the other kids won't play with me. They act as if they hated me, throwing stones and tin cans at me. They claim it's because I play tricks on them when I'm really staying at home quietly.

There's one good thing, I haven't gone hungry too often. Lots of the people around will give me something to eat. There's *don* Luis. I always get food when I go to his house. Bertha, *don* Luis' wife, feeds me too. So do a lot of other people. I go there to watch TV and they give me dinner.

When I'm hungry and no one gives me anything to eat, I go buy a malt beer before going to bed. If I have no money, I hang around a little longer to see if someone will offer me food. If not, I go to Crucita's house. But if Felícita hasn't given Cruz money to buy malt beer that day, I go hungry, because Cruz doesn't have any money herself. She never takes men to her house, not even Cayetano, who hardly counts at all.

When I'm hungry I get mad. I don't say anything about it and I get into bed. But then I begin to cry and pick quarrels. Oh, how I wish *don* Luis were my *papá!* Then he would give me lots of food and I would grow big like him.

I would like to work, but I enjoy playing too. I play horsie: you hold on to something and go running and yelling, "Hee, haw, haw, horsie." I would love to have a swing. I asked the Kings for one, but they don't come until you fall asleep, so I didn't get to see them and tell them. And just think! On the eve of the Three Kings, real late at night, I was almost asleep when I see Mundito get up. Then he goes and shits on the floor. I saw him but I just let him do it. Felícita comes and says the Kings had an upset stomach. "That doesn't matter," I tell her. I had gotten some grass, the good green kind, for the Kings' camels and I wasn't worried. I fell asleep and when I woke up the Kings had left me a set of holsters. I was real happy that day.

I like to go to church. I go every Sunday, to that one on Tetuan Street. The captain* is there and a Dominican woman. We can paint there, with crayons or brushes. I draw a lot when I go there. And they give us food, too, ice cream and lots of things. I also go to Father Ponce's church. *Don* Luis and Bertha often pray to God there, together with the Sisters of Charity and Father Ponce. They help one to get into Heaven. You need a lot of help to get there and sometimes you have to help your friends get there, too. They put something white in your mouth and then it disappears. You aren't supposed to swallow it.

I know a prayer, the one you say before going to sleep. It goes like this, "Holy Mary, Mother of God, pray for us now and at the hour of our death. Amen." I learned it hearing people say it when someone dies. Did you know that when someone dies he comes back as a monster? I have seen that on TV, in *The Premiere of the Beyond,* and in the movies. People pray for the dead and go to church to keep the monsters from coming back. Felícita never goes to church because she doesn't have a man who's died.

God is good to me. He's always following me around to see if I can go to Heaven. Christ is good. He comes from Heaven. Sometimes I dream I am there with him, as an angel. It's so nice to see myself in Heaven.

Felícita told me she was going to send me to New York to live in Simplicio's house. He wanted me there. In New York, I can go to school and learn English to speak with Americans. Then I can get a job as a cook or get a job at the docks and earn lots of money. That way, when people are broke I can give them money for food. I won't give Felícita any because she has a job, nor Nanda either because she spends her time with drunks. I don't like that. Sometimes those people go naked or they wear torn pants and such.

I want to grow up so they'll quit screwing me. Grownups are big bullies. When I'm grown-up I can lift weights and drive cars because by then I will be earning money. And then I can get married. I'll find me a grown-up girl so I can be a real man and have sons and daughters. I'll have a job and give her money so she can make our dinner. When I get home from work I'll hand her the money and kiss her. If she gets sick I will send her to a doctor. When she's going to have a baby I'll take good care of her. And we will never quarrel or anything.

I told everybody I was going to New York and it was true. Felícita bought all new clothes for me. She brought me a suitcase and it was packed and ready.

On Sunday we were supposed to go. I said, *"O.K.,* I'm leaving." By seven I was all dressed. Héctor was still asleep when I left La Esmeralda.

I got to the airport at around nine. Nanda, my *mamá* and Crucita went to see me off. Angelito went too, and Chuito, the black one. When I said good-

* The chaplain.

bye, I kissed Fernanda and Felícita and said to them, "Your blessing." Then I was sorry for them because they were crying. Fela looked sad. But I wasn't sad, I was happy. "Have a nice trip," Fernanda said, "and hug Simplicio and Flora tight for me."

I was thinking, "Maybe I'll never go back again, so at Christmas and for Mother's Day I am going to send Nanda perfume and powder, the kinds that smell a lot. Or maybe Uncle can save enough money to bring Nanda up to New York for Christmas."

Well, the plane took off at about ten and we didn't see each other any more. The plane was so full that it looked as if it would fall down. I wasn't a bit scared because I wasn't alone. An American was taking care of me. And when we landed I'd be with Simplicio and Flora.

I arrived at twelve. Oh, I felt happy! I didn't know what New York was like. In Puerto Rico the trees were full of leaves, all green and pretty. Here, they looked dried up, as if they had been through a hurricane. I asked Aunt Soledad about it and she said, "Oh no, it's because of the cold."

"Ah . . ." I said, "then it's all right."

We took a bus, which cost a lot of money—eight dollars. Eight dollars to get in! Then we had to get off and take a taxi for five dollars and finally change to another bus, which charged six and took us all the way to Uncle's place. When we got there we cooked and unpacked my suitcase.

I feel very happy here with Uncle and Flora. They treat me well. Here I dream that this is a royal palace and I'm the prince and that's why they love me so much. But Felícita told me before I came, "Be careful what you say about me up there." She thought I was going to tell everybody that she spends her time hanging around *bars* and leaves us all alone. But I said to her, "Oh no, I won't say anything. I'll tell lies there." I had forgotten all about it when she sends a letter here saying that at home I used to run off to the beach and never paid any attention to her. And she wrote too. "Goodness knows what he says about me up there."

She was scared, you see, because she was living with an American. She thought I was going to tell that up here. But all I did was tell Soledad, "When you write, tell that rat I'm not saying anything bad about her. Tell her too, I'm never going back to Puerto Rico until I grow up and that I'm going to school already."

What I'd like is for Uncle and Aunt to have a baby in the house. I soon outgrow my shoes and if they had a little boy, he could wear them. I wish Angelito were here with me. Felícita just has to send him because we are twins and if we aren't together we miss each other. I'd like to have lots of sisters too . . . nice sisters who would write to me. So that when I'm grown-up they'll be my family. But the trouble is that if Fela goes and has a lot more children, there won't be anybody to help her support them and then I won't be able to buy food for all of them.

Flora has a job at a factory. She sent for her sister Irene. She's not related to Uncle at all, but he paid her fare over so that she could come take care of me. One hundred dollars it cost us.

I took all my things out of my suitcase so Irene could use it and I put my stuff in an old suitcase. I even went to meet Irene at the airport. And after all I did for her, you should hear the way she insults me now. She tells me to go to hell, but I get right back at her. I say, "Go to hell yourself! I have more right to be here because I got here before you did. You shouldn't curse me like that because I'm not bad. I'm a good boy. If I were bad, I would have kicked you out of here already."

She slept in my bed and I'd say to her, "You'd better lie with your head to the footboard and I'll lie with my head up." Then, after I fell asleep, she'd take my pillow away from me. What a witch!

They said someone had to go with me the day I enrolled in school, so she took me there. Then she went and said I was in first grade. I said, "No, I am in *second grade.*" She didn't do anything right. And on top of everything, she beat me. She hit my fingers and made my nails black. She even cut me up. You see, I play with her and then she gets mad and hits me. "I'm older than you. You're just a little pile of shit," says she.

"You're a bigger pile of shit than me," I answer. "You don't know how to take care of little boys. From now on, I'll take care of myself."

I don't know why she acted like that. Maybe she hated me. The fact is, she took off with her sweetheart, Pío. He's skinny as a lead pipe, ugly as they come and snaggle-toothed. And is he fresh!

They went off just like that. Now I take care of myself and I like it much better. I don't need anybody to look after me.

I like going to school here because this place is new to me. The school would be really good if they spoke Spanish as well as English. I don't like to be spoken to in English because I don't understand it. People speak English in such a way that one can't understand anything. I tell the teacher, *"I don't speak English."* If she gives me a paper and I don't understand what's written on it, I say, *"Teacher, I don't know."* She gives me low marks because I don't know anything. There's one *teacher* who knows Spanish, but even she teaches in English. All, all of them teach in English.

The kids are bad as the devil. They push me. There are all kinds of kids there, Americans, Chinese, Puerto Ricans, Negroes. Those Negroes hide so they can stick out their leg and trip you up when you pass by. The Chinese pull my ears. There's a real mean kid called Buffelman who grabs my little ass. So, you see, I don't have any friends in school.

There's a little girl called Karen, I wasn't doing anything bad to her, just touching her under the table, when she suddenly kicked me in the ribs with the heel of her shoe. I don't know how to speak with her because I don't know

English. Then I called a little boy and told him, "Say something to her." You know what he did? He burst out laughing, "Haw, haw." I waited until school let out at three, then I really got hold of him. I hit him so hard, he bled. *Teacher* didn't see us. I never fight in front of her, because if I did she'd take me to the office.

I like it here, no matter if I don't know English. I speak English just anyhow, but now people understand what I say. I can ask to leave the room in English and then I go to the *toilet*. I repeat whatever I hear the other kids say and that way I learn quickly. I hear something today and keep repeating so by tomorrow I'll have learned it. A *gato* here is a "cat"; the *mesa* is called "table." This morning I wrote, "Today is Monday" in English. "Monday" means *lunes*. They call the *ventana*, "window," and the *casa*, "home." Isn't it true that I am beginning to learn?

In the afternoon I usually go with Simplicio to his girl friend Leila's house. She lives way off in Brooklyn. You have to take *el Lexington*. When we get there we find all of them drinking. I would have liked to stay outside. I didn't want to see what went on in there.

Leila was in love with Uncle. One day they were kissing and everything over at Soledad's house. I say to myself, "What the devil is this?" Then she and Simplicio went out together and left me at Soledad's. The rest of us went over to see Flora and they told her that Uncle had stopped at a bar. But that was a big lie. I told Flora the truth. "They are lying to you. Uncle is with Leila. So now you know." Flora said she was going to throw a stone in Simplicio's eyes and pull out all of Leila's teeth. When Simplicio stays out late at night, until seven or nine or even two in the morning, Flora curses him out. On Fridays he gets home at five in the morning. He can do it because he's a grown man.

I wish I were a grown man too. I dreamed that I was twenty years old. I bought myself *un apartament*, I bought *furnitura* with a mirror. The bathroom was next to the bed. I lived with Carmen Rosa and got up early to go to work. I gave money to Fela's kids so they could get themselves some clothes. And I bought Fela a stove and furniture and a dining-room set and a record player.

Then it was Saturday and I went out to buy the food, *corn flakes* and oatmeal, meat and milk, chicken, canned spaghetti, sausage, bread, sugar, laundry soap—well, everything. After that, I went to pay the furniture store. And when my wife was sick I did the cooking. I was always good to her. I'm telling you, though, if she does anything to me, I'll have a fight with her. You know what women are when a man is all screwed up and doesn't have a house and lots of things. That is when they walk out on him. Yes, that's what makes wives leave their husbands. Well, if my wife does that to me, then I'll really beat her.

In my dream I walked and walked until I met some people. I asked them the way to the Bronx and they told me to turn and keep walking until I came to a hill. So I kept on going until I got to Soledad's house but nobody was home. I went into several *bars*. In one of them I played pool. A man came and bumped against me. I said to him, "No, no, I don't want to fight," because he had *un revolver*. But I had a knife, so the other man gave up. I was big already.

Felícita

Will You Marry Me?

I WAS STILL working at *Joe's Place* when I met an American by the name of Walker. I came to work at about six and there was a small group of Americans sitting in a booth. The first one I saw as I came in was this Walker, but I paid no attention to him. I was wearing a dress that fitted me scandalously, so he touched me and said, *"Hey, you, skinny* with a big ass."

"Oh yeah? Fresh thing!" I said to him. "We'll see about that." I walked into the *bar* and we didn't speak any more. I could see in the mirror that he kept watching me. I came over to wait on the table and he couldn't take his eyes off me. Then he asked me why I was so serious and I told him not for any special reason, that that's the way I am.

The next day he arrived earlier and began talking to me. He spoke in English. Well, that night we danced and he bought drinks for me. Then he asked if I was married and I told him that I was and I wasn't. I had to say that because some Americans think if you're not married you are a virgin. I said, "I have no husband but I have five children." He didn't believe me.

Then he took a piece of paper and made a drawing of me. He drew the glass I was holding in my hand, the cigarette and everything. He could draw very nicely. He told me to keep the picture as a remembrance.

He kept playing records. He invited me to dance, and during the first number he hugged me tight and kissed me. I told him not to, because if others saw him kissing me they would want to do the same.

Then he said, "I can see that you are not the same as the other girls who work in *bars*. I would like to meet your *mamá* and make friends with your family because it is going to be serious between you and me."

"All right. Come by early tomorrow and we'll do it."

The next day was a Sunday. I met him at nine in the morning and took him to the place where my mother works. I went around with him until two the next morning, and he didn't make a pass at me or invite me to a hotel or anything. All we did was kiss and talk. I was expecting him to suggest something to me, but he didn't. He behaved very well. He bought me drinks and meals and gave me whatever I wanted. But I didn't let him spend too much money on me, because I don't like to take advantage of men like that.

Later he said, "I have clothes that I'm going to take to *el laundry*."

And I said, "No, bring them to me, I'll iron them for you." He said I was the first woman who had ever done that for him, that not even his mother had. Then he told me he wanted to marry me. I said he couldn't because I had five children. He thought about that for a while and said, "That isn't so, because I tell you I love you and it doesn't matter to me what you have. You are poor and my family has money, but that is not going to stand in the way of our happiness." So I told him that was fine.

About a week later I asked him if he wanted to come to my house and he said he did. He kept looking at the place and at my children. He could see that even though it was a poor house it was nice and clean. He asked if I was really the mother of all of the children and I said yes. He was standing up all this time, so I asked him to sit. He did, and he kept looking at me.

"Say something," I said.

"The only thing I can tell you is that I'm nervous about losing my day off today."

"Don't worry. I'll press something for you so you can change into civilian clothes." Then I invited him into my room where my bed is and he said that he didn't want to go in because there might be somebody in the kitchen. I explained to him that I had asked him to come to the house just so he could see that I lived alone with my children. I told him to sit on the bed and then asked him if he wasn't going to kiss me. He said that the children were right there, but I told him that didn't matter. So we kissed, and I pulled him back onto the bed, but he got embarrassed. I told him he had nothing to be embarrassed about, that he was a man and I was a woman. I kissed him, and that made him lower his eyes.

I went out on the balcony and called him to look at the beach, which he said was very pretty. Then I went inside and lay down on the bed. He gave me a smack on the behind and I gave him a push and we began wrestling on the bed. Then I began kissing him and he kissed me, too, but shyly. So I asked him what was the matter, didn't he love me? He said he felt shy because it was his first time with me and he wanted to know what I intended to do with the kids.

He was nervous on account of the children being there. I told him I would send them to buy candy, so he gave each child a quarter. Then I began kissing him again, and he started to sweat and his eyes got very red and little. He said, "Ay, how you can kiss!"

"Whatever I have is yours," I told him.

"Do you really mean it?" And a little while later he said, "Fela, I love you very much. I hate having to go to New York, although I must, but if you wait for me, I'll be back. And to prove it to you, I'm going to leave my clothes here." Then he said, "Get dressed and we'll go to the movies."

"No, I want to spend the time here with you." I kissed him on the neck and it made him shiver, so then I kissed him over and over again. I pulled him back on top of me in the bed. I rubbed against him and he squeezed me tight. He asked me what I thought of him and, "What do you think of what we are doing now?"

"Nothing," I said and then I told him that I was going to take a bath. Afterward I came back wearing a tiny *bikini,* the only kind of *panties* I like. He kept looking at me and said, "What a big behind you have."

"Do you like it?" I asked, and he dropped his eyes. Then I said, "Take off your shirt," and he did. "Take off your undershirt." He did. When I told him to take his shoes off, he did. Then I said, "And what are you waiting for? Take off your pants." I had to tell him, he was very shy. He took them off and lay down in his shorts. I said to him, "What's the idea? Are you going to lie in bed in shorts? Nothing doing, here you have to go naked. Take them off." Well, when he was naked I began kissing and caressing him. I kissed him on the nipples, a sexual thing, and so he did the same to me. He asked me what I thought of that and I said, "What I think, my boy, is that you are hot and so am I."

"Fela, I love you very much," he said, "and I want to have *un baby* with you."

I told him that I would give him one. So we began embracing and kissing each other and all of a sudden, bang, bang, one of the children was back, knocking on the door. I went swearing to the door, but smiled at the child and gave him a quarter to buy more candy and he got lost.

Walker closed his eyes and squeezed me very tight and I embraced him. He told me that he would never forget the experience he was going to have with me that day. We did it three times in a row. We knocked off four pieces, *ayyy!* nice hot ones. Well, he didn't want to pull out of me and he asked me how come I was so tight. He told me that he went with a Dominican girl one time and she was so big he nearly fell in. Then he said he loved me and that he didn't want to get up out of bed. I told him, "I have to go to work, *chico!*" And he said that he had spent the happiest day of his life with me.

Then I asked him a question. I wanted to know why, since he was such a good-looking man, he hadn't fallen in love with some girl. He explained that he had had a bad experience with his sweetheart in New York and that after he had bought her everything, she went off with somebody else. He told me that he had written to his parents about me and was waiting for an answer, but that even if they were against it, he would stick to me.

I told him not to tell his mother about my work, because my past life has been what it has been not because I wanted it that way, but because of my children. I told him that I didn't want to have problems with his family. They were rich and I was poor. I'm almost colored and he was such a good-looking person. I told him if he couldn't make me happy, I'd stay right here in Puerto Rico. But Walker wouldn't hear of it. He told me that his father has a house in Manhattan but that he, Walker, had a house of his own, with a washing machine and everything in it, because he always intended to get married but the *Navy* didn't give him a chance. He said that he was the boss in his own house and that no one could tell him whom to love or not to love. "It would be better for us to go to New York," he told me, "because I have a house and a sure job there. Here I haven't got either." And that was where we left it.

When Walker was with me, he never looked at another girl. He was mine. He didn't want me to dance with other men. And he kissed and caressed me no matter where we were. He was nice to my children, and he got along well with my *mamá*. But the time came when he had to leave.

I got to love him a lot. He told me he loved me very much and asked me not to forget him, ever. I once had myself photographed for him in a transparent *bikini* and another time in my *bra*. He said that as long as he had my photographs and I had his to look at, we would be in love with each other.

I didn't know if he was telling me the truth or not. I wanted to share my future with him because I could see he was a good boy. But I have a thing with men—I don't believe a word they tell me. I never let on. I agree to everything, but deep in my heart I just don't believe in men.

Here are some of the letters I wrote to Walker while he was away. A friend of mine helped me write them in English.

December 1, 1963

My dear,

I resiebed three letters from you yesterday every day that I resiebe your letters you fill me with joy and happiness because we both of us love each other.

Darling about the surprise you tell me about I think it must be a wedding ring say you already changed the date when you return tell me are you getting tired of my already first you said the 28th and now the 29 please don't keep putting it off and making wait longer.

Well about my job I'll tell you that I quareled with Joe and dont
have a job we eat a little something my sister always sends when she
cooks and thats how we pass the day. I owe the house rent and I
dont know what to do because I have so many problems dear Ill try
to get a job before you come well I'm going to remind you of something too that I dont like your telling anybody about the things that
happen between you and me you told Zoraida that I was drunk that
you dont like me to do that in front of you because then it must be
worse behind your back. I want you to know that since you left I am
not drinking any kind of liqor because I like to respect you and if I
did it that time it was to forget the moment of parting from you well
forgive the bad things I have put in this letter and I hope you understand me. Darling if god granted us the hapiness of having a child
we would be even happier. I want to have one of yours because you
deserve it, well I dont write much the way you do in your letters
because you Know I cant write in english so good bye until I get
yours. With nothing more to say from one who wishes to see you
more than to rite to you your love

Felícita

Since Walker wanted to have a baby, I regretted that operation to close
my tubes. I never told him about it. He saw my scar but I said it was from
appendicitis. I can always have the tubes opened when I want to have babies
again. After all, they can transfer a liver from one person to another. Science
is so great!

I wrote Walker a letter telling him that the doctor had said I seemed to be
pregnant because he found some clots of blood, and I said that I got dizzy and
had stomach upsets every day. He didn't answer that letter. I didn't hear any
more from him until he wrote saying that his mother had died. I answered
right away.

January 28, 1964

Dear Walker,

I am very sorry about what happende to your mother well I
kept thinking that you had forgoten me. Darling I hoped to meet
your mama but I didnt have that hapines dont worry about me for I
always was waiting for some reply from you I looked at your picture
all the time I want you to sent word to me does the boat come in
that last week of february? I want to go meet you I have some tikets
reserved for me and the children to go to the Bronx with my sister I
mean to go in march. Darling when I reseibed your letter I reseibed
the bigest surprise of my life.

Well I hope you send me word if youre coming the last week of february.

with lots of love

Felícita

February 12, 1964

Dear Walker,

I reseibed your letter where you say you havnt reseibed my letters well the minute I reseibe your letters I anser them I dont know what the trouble is the leter I sent has a snapshot of me. Tell me if you reseibed that leter. Darling I am working at La Torre which is a better place than Joe's. But they don't pay me as well. Darling I know how much you want a baby but I want it even more. Well I was pregnant but I lost it on the 6th of January. I had much sufering when you stopped riting and one nite it was raining it was about 2 oclock in the morning and I fell down the stairs where you and I used to go down remember? My love how I suffered and with nobody to help me but never mind we will soon make another baby. Walker I wish you would send me some mony for the fares I want to go soon to be with you and take an apartment. Darling I want to leave on the date I said in my last leter if you send me the mony I will send you some of my things to keep for me untill I get there. Darling dont have another woman untill I get there I want you to be good and hot when I get there so we can have a good time like that first night do you remember? Well my little love Anser soon With nothing more to say

Yours

Felícita

While Walker was gone, I met a Filipino who fell in love with me and asked me to marry him. So there I was, with two men who had promised to marry me. But both were away at sea and I was still living all alone in La Esmeralda with my children.

I couldn't decide which man to wait for, so one morning I got up very early and went to Loíza Aldea to see *doña* Magdalena. I sat down and the lady asked me what I needed. I took out a picture of Walker and one of Amadeo and said, "These two men have promised to marry me. But I want you to tell me which of the two I should accept."

Then she told me, "Look, that Walker is only making a fool of you. He has a love in every port and he laughs at them all. Besides, he has a wife in New York, a blond woman with short hair, blue eyes. He's just amusing himself with you." Then she looked at the other picture. "When I see this man, Amadeo, I notice that he's sort of winking one eye, that's a sign of victory. Maybe you can get something out of him. Now, I'm going to give you a prescription for some prayers and some baths. Do these things at home and then come back to me."

I felt very sad that day I returned home. I had gone hoping that maybe she could tell me something good about Walker. But she told me he was married, so I just decided to forget him. But I couldn't help thinking about what he had done to me and how he'd made me suffer. Still, I felt better in a way because I know many people who have gone to *doña* Magdalena and everything has come out for them just the way she said.

The next Monday I went back to Loíza Aldea. I got up at five o'clock, sent for some food and prepared the children's breakfast. I straightened up the house, washed the dishes, got ready to leave. On the way I stopped at Cruz's and asked her to watch out for the children. I gave her a dollar to buy food for lunch and I left for *doña* Magdalena's.

When I arrived I told her, *"Señora,* whenever I come here, I get a sort of pain."

She answered, "You didn't have to tell me that. I could have told you before you even sat down. I'll tell you what it is." And she asked me who "Rosita" was, and "Edmundo" and "Pilar." I told her that Edmundo was my husband and Rosita my next-door neighbor. Pilar was the woman who lived with Edmundo. Then she said, "Well, look, between them, Pilar and Rosita did a job on your womb so that you couldn't ever take a man and would always have pain and bleeding, because they didn't want you to marry."

My pain was very bad by then. So she began to work me over. She caught my pain and she shook and trembled in her chair. *"Ay,* now you've made me sick," she said, "but anyway, I'll get rid of it and you can go home cured." After she took the pain out of me, I don't know why, but I felt very happy.

She prescribed some baths for me and something to drink. I made myself a hot bath with these herbs and it took away my pain at once, and the lump I had in there. After that I kept on bleeding for a few days. *Doña* Magdalena told me that I'd bleed until I was quite cleaned out. She prescribed a bottle of Lydia E. Pinkham and black beer with warm oil to drink. Now, thank God, I am well.

One Saturday I was still asleep when my *mamá* called me. "Felícita, get up! Your food and drink's about to arrive."

I looked outside and saw two ships coming into port. "Fernanda, my heart tells me that the second ship is Walker's!" You could hardly make it out, it was so far away. I kept saying, "Nanda, that's S.S. *223.* Nanda, it's *223!"* until I could see it clearly. Oh, but it made me happy to see that ship!

"Go on, get ready," Fernanda says, "so you can go meet him."

"No, no. I'll wait until he comes to see me."

Then a third ship, a small white one, came in, right behind Walker's. It was my sister who said, "Hey, maybe that ship behind Walker's is Amadeo's." I couldn't tell whether it was or not, but I said, "Oh no! Amadeo has gone to New York."

Well, I got ready. I went to the beauty parlor and got myself a hairdo. Then I put on some lovely shoes and a dress—everything brand new. As I was going down the sidewalk I saw two Americans. I had a tight feeling in my chest and a sudden impulse to run toward them as fast as I could. I saw Walker smiling at me. I ran, with half-closed eyes, to hug him. Just as I was about to throw my arms around him, that Filipino appeared right behind him! I don't know where he came from. I made my decision quickly. I went right past Walker and hugged Amadeo.

Walker just stood there, staring at me. I went on kissing the Filipino right in front of him. Then Amadeo and I went to *Joe's Place*, where I used to work, and Walker followed us there. He said, "Felícita . . ." I pretended not to hear him. Then he said, "Would you like a drink?"

"No. No thanks. I'm here with this boy who is going to marry me." I meant Amadeo. Walker started playing records and downing double rums with anisette until he got sick and collapsed on the table. His friends rubbed his head with ice and massaged him until he came to. Then he said to me, "Fela, let's get photographed." I lifted my head and they took our picture right then. Walker said, "Let's dance."

"Let's," I said.

The Filipino didn't realize what was going on, because I was paying more attention to him than to Walker. I went up to him and kissed him and petted him but with Walker I sort of kept my distance.

"Let's get out of here," the Filipino said. "Let's go eat some place."

"No, not yet. Let's wait awhile," I said. "I'm not hungry. Come on, Amadeo, let's dance." While we were dancing Amadeo kissed me and said, "Oh, I want to marry you this year." Walker was sitting there hearing every word so I said to Amadeo, "Hurry up. Let's go to my house. I'm sleepy." Walker looked at me and I smiled and winked at him. After a while, when Amadeo wasn't watching, I slipped out. Walker followed me and asked, "Felícita, are you mad at me?"

"No, I'm not mad at you." We went to the *bar* on the corner and watched *el show*. He started to kiss me and I bit him real hard. He kissed me again and we kissed and kissed. "Do you remember the first time?" he asked me.

"Yes. And I remember the last time too."

"Why are you so indifferent to me?"

"I don't know, I don't understand English." Then I said to him, "How I hate you for making me suffer. You knew how much I loved you and how often I wrote to you. And yet you stopped answering my letters. Now I can tell you that in my heart I hate you. Tomorrow I want my pictures back and I'll return yours. I hope we never meet again."

He didn't say a word. He got up and rushed down the street and tore down a street sign. The shore patrol saw him and made him put the sign back. After that he came and said to me, "Fela, I don't know how to be angry with you. Come, let's drink until they drag me away."

At a quarter of two I went back to *Joe's Place* to get my purse. The girl there whispered to me, "Be careful. The Filipino is still here." He had been sitting there, alone, for more than two hours, waiting for me. "Take your purse and go quickly," she advised me. I did and went back to Walker.

"Are you really getting married?" Walker asked me.

"Why, yes, of course. The man is good to me. He gives me money and he even gives some to my mother. So naturally I'll marry him."

"All right," he says, and he went off to his ship.

It seems that Amadeo stayed at Joe's until five in the morning, waiting for me, but I went straight home as soon as Walker had gone. I hardly slept at all that night. The next morning at eight I set off for the *base* to look for Amadeo, but his ship was at the Alcoa dock and I didn't have enough money to pay the fare over. I only had one-fifty with me because I'd spent most of my money. So, since Amadeo wasn't there, I decided to see Walker instead. I told the taxi driver, "All right, leave me at the *Army Terminal.*"

When I got there, Walker was in his working clothes and looked embarrassed when he saw me. "What are you doing here?" he asked.

"Are you angry with me?"

"No, but listen, will you wait for me? I'm off at twelve."

I waited for Walker in the hot sun. Then we went to my house and he said hello to my *mamá*. She prepared some soup for him and he ate it and thanked her and told her it was very good. I lent him a pair of pants that Amadeo had given to Fernanda's husband. That struck me funny and I said to Fernanda, "Say, suppose Amadeo shows up and says, "Isn't it enough that you're putting the horns on me? Do you have to lend my clothes to your lover too?" My *mamá* laughed out loud. "One of these days some man is going to kill you," she said.

Walker asked what we were talking about and I answered, "Nothing. I was just telling Fernanda what a nice boy you are." He listens very hard to what people say but he doesn't know much Spanish.

After a while I bathed the kids and sent them out and locked the door. And then he screwed me for the first time in six months. He was not affectionate the way he used to be. He kissed me and then got on top of me, just like that, very indifferently. Then he asked me, "What about the bambino you mentioned?" I said that I didn't want to talk about it.

The children started knocking on the door before he had even finished screwing once. So we hurried it up. But we stayed in bed awhile for the second time around. We started kissing and all that to warm up. And then, while we were hugging each other, a girl I knew called in that Amadeo was on his way. And I was in bed with Walker! I didn't have time to dress, so I went out as I was, in my nightgown, and said, "Why, hello, Amadeo, how are you?"

"Pretty well. Where is Tany?" He's very fond of her. So I called the child and he kissed her. Then he says to me, "Come, child. Come, darling, let's go inside."

"Oh no, we can't. My husband's in there."

"Your husband by marriage?"

I said yes, so he went away.

When I went back in the room I burst into tears from sheer nervousness. Walker asked me what the trouble was and started caressing me. "Oh, Walker, I have so many problems. Put on your clothes, because we have to get out of here in a hurry." After we left I told him that the Filipino kept bothering me and that I didn't love the man. Then I said, "Listen, he's sure to be waiting for me at *Joe's Place,* and I don't want him to see me with you, so you go to the La Torre *bar* and have a beer. After you've been there about fifteen minutes, come over to Joe's and pretend you haven't been with me."

I was wearing a beautiful dress that night.

When I went into Joe's, the Filipino was there and I sat down with him. Right off he says, "Have a double Cuba Libre." I drank it down without stopping to take a breath.

At about five o'clock, when I had just started dancing with the Filipino, Walker showed up. He just stood there and looked at me. I went to him and said, "I have to report to work around seven. And I want to eat first, so I'm going in a few minutes." We went out together and as we passed La Torre, the owner came out and said, "I've been waiting here to tell you you're out of a job." What made the old guy mad was that Amadeo had cashed a two-hundred-and-seventy-five-dollar check at the *bar* the night before, and he thought that I had been out with Amadeo spending that money at somebody else's *bar.*

"All right," said I, and kept on walking.

After dinner I left Walker, and I went back and said, "Well, if I don't have any more work here, pay me what you owe me."

And he said, "Come in and get to work." So I went in.

Amadeo was sitting at the *bar,* dead drunk. He just said, *"Ay,* let's dance," but no sooner had we started dancing than he said, "Oh, I can't, I can't wait any longer. Let's go to the hotel." So we did, Amadeo and I.

We only stayed about twenty minutes. Amadeo told me, "I like you a hell of a lot because you have a good pussy."

"Really? Well, why don't you take it with you to New York?"

Then Amadeo said he wanted to go home with me. He waited for me to finish work and we went to my house and screwed twice more. He's pretty good at it. Well, so-so. Before he left he said, "Heck, I don't know, I'd like to stay but I'd lose the most for the least. I'd lose my job, I mean. I'm going, but I promise I'll be back." That's what they all say, you know. And that's the end of the story. I never saw him again.

The next day two *sailors, un army, un civil* and nineteen *Marinos* came to La Torre. I entertained them all and Walker just looked at me. I danced with each in turn and they all applauded me at the end of the dance. It was a very gay and noisy table. And Walker sat there, staring. He was furious with me. I kept putting on records and I pretended not to notice him. He had to get his drinks from the *bar* himself because I wouldn't serve him.

He sat there and looked at me. Then I said to him in English, *"I hate you!"* He made a gesture, but I went on, *"You know why you like me? Because I go with you for nothing."* That made him angry, terribly angry. He gulped down his drink and threw the ice on the floor. I said a lot of other things. I told him he was a *fucking sailor* and that *sailors* were *no good.* I said, *"I like Marines, not sailors. Sailors* are shit to me."

When I stopped, he handed me a five-dollar bill and said, "Bring me two Cuba Libres." I took the bill but didn't get him the drinks. I was cool as anything. Walker said again, "I want two Cuba Libres." I didn't move. Then he says, "Chavela, get me two Cuba Libres," and she went and got them for him. I handed her Walker's bill and she gave me four-twenty in change. I kept the four dollars and threw the twenty cents in his face. Walker said, "Give me that money, Felícita. Give it to me. I'm really mad."

That was all the money he had, those four dollars. I crushed them and threw them at him. "Take your *fucky* four dollars." He took them and drank the rest of his Cuba Libre and went out with Chavela. He did it to make me jealous. I burst out laughing as they left, and said, *"Bendito,* poor thing, he'll have to be satisfied with dry bread instead of cheese from now on."

I didn't really love Walker anyway. I felt a sort of weight in my chest, though, a feeling of sentiment, you know. But that only lasted one day. The next morning I felt fine.

I still wanted to go to New York, but I decided to just wait and see if I'd win in the lottery and get the money that way. I deposited forty dollars toward the fare but after that I didn't pay any more. I didn't have any money left. Everything I got from Walker or earned working I spent on clothes, shoes and so on. I never did know how to save.

There was an old man, a Mexican named Pepe, who wanted me to live with him. He said he would put everything he owned in my name. He had a small *bar* in partnership with another man. He gave me several necklaces and then he asked me to be his wife. He said he loved me and wanted me, but not until we were living together under one roof.

I thought Pepe was a good man but I didn't like him. He was about sixty years old. And he had fits sometimes that made him lose consciousness and look like a corpse. That scared me. "Oh no," I thought, "I'd rather be alone." Still, I got into the habit of going to have a few drinks with him every night after work.

Then one night at work I saw a man who had known me when I worked at the Silver Cup. He was with an older friend, a Greek captain, and he introduced us and told the captain that I was a good girl. The captain took me to Pepe's *bar* to have some drinks. That was really funny, because Pepe had said he wanted to talk with me that night, and when I went into the *bar* he took me by the hand right away and tried to kiss my cheek. Then I kissed the old captain in plain sight of Pepe, and Pepe started to cough. I wound up going to a hotel with the Greek. I don't know why, but it makes me happy to see men get jealous.

The Greek captain looked even older than Pepe. His face was wrinkled and he had grandchildren already. The first night I had intercourse with him, he wanted to bathe me. He began to soap me over and over. After I was well soaped, he started to kiss every part of my body. He kissed the sole of my foot and said it was a custom in his country to do that when a man was about to have intercourse with a woman. He looked me over from head to foot and was beginning to get excited. After he had a strong erection, he soaped me once more and carried me to the bed. Then, wet as I was, we started to have intercourse.

It gave me a lot of pleasure and I guess I really did it well, too, because he paid me twenty dollars and he came back for me the next two nights. I don't know, I'm lucky that way.

I planned to use the money the captain gave me to get Gabi some clothes. Because I was going to send him to New York to Simplicio for a while. I bought everything he needed and packed his little suitcase. That made me very happy.

It was around this time that I first met Georgie. The night after he arrived in Puerto Rico from Florida, he was walking by the La Torre *bar,* where I worked, and stopped to look in. He said to his friend Mike, who was a Spaniard, "This looks like a quiet place. I'm going to have a few drinks and then go to bed."

The *bartender* was off that night and I was behind the *bar*. There were four girls sitting there when he came over and ordered a drink. He offered to buy them all drinks and they accepted. While I was mixing them, I could see in the mirror that he was pointing at me and saying something to his friend, who laughed.

Then he asked the girls how much they charged for going up to the hotel. "You know something?" he said. "I like the girl at the *bar* and she is the one I am going to take out." He came over and held my hands and kissed me on the forehead. Then he pulled out a roll of twenties and the girls began climbing all over him, saying, "Ahhh, take me, take me!"

He had about three more drinks that first night and he left me a twenty-cent tip. "How do you like that!" I said. "He loves me so much he leaves me twenty cents."

"Don't worry about it. Later I'll give you more," he answered.

That week he came around just to drink and talk to me. Then one night we went to a hotel in San Juan. We had relations just one time that night. He kissed me and told me that I was a good girl and had behaved right toward him and not demanded anything, and he wanted to keep on seeing me. He gave me ten dollars just for the one hour. I took the money, very satisfied.

We went out again the following week, and he treated me well. He took me to dinner and told me that he was going to give me a present and that if I behaved he would take me away from my job. I said, *"Ave María,* this rooster sure pecks fast."

He was getting fond of me. The second time we were together, he gave me twenty dollars and a bottle of perfume and he said, "Look, Felícita, I'm getting a house. Will you come and live with me?"

"Well," I said, "you know I have children and can't just abandon my home."

"Don't worry about that. I'll pay somebody to take care of them for you. And I'll pay your rent besides, so if you have trouble with me some day you can go back."

"All right. As long as it's like that, I'll go with you."

So he and his friend, Mike, took a house together. Georgie was an engineer and Mike was his assistant. They paid three hundred and fifty dollars a month for rent. It was a fine house, made of wood and tile, with Miami *windows,* and it was right on the beach in El Condado. It had a kitchen with bottled gas and hot water and a lovely bathroom, all tiled. Mike took Paula, the dark-skinned girl, who worked at the same *bar,* and Georgie brought me.

I was still working at the *bar* and every day Georgie would say that he wanted me to leave but I thought he was just kidding. "Look, Fela," he said, "I don't want you to work there because of those *sailors.* If you go with them they will make you sick."

"But I don't go out with anybody, Georgie."

Then one day Georgie says to me, "Let's go to La Esmeralda and get the kids and have them spend a week with us." So I went and brought back all the children except Angelito, who was with Cruz. They stayed for two weeks. Georgie was very nice to the children. When he came home from work in the afternoon he would take them to the beach and go swimming with them. Georgie knew I couldn't swim, but one time I sat on his shoulders and he swam into the deep part and dumped me off. I sank to the bottom and he had to dive down and pull me out. After that, I was afraid to go into the water with him.

He kept insisting that I leave work, but I wouldn't. Georgie would give me money, but it wasn't enough. He gave me fifty dollars a week but out of that I had to buy the food we ate, which cost twenty, and I had to give ten to the boys who took care of the house, and ten to Lucelia, who was watching the children for me in La Esmeralda, and then there was the children's food. And sometimes we needed things, like sheets. When you live like that you have to have lots of things and I just couldn't make it with the money he gave me.

So I said, "This is the last time, Georgie, but I am going to work tonight."

"Go ahead," he told me. But when I came back he didn't want to sleep with me. He got out of bed and sat on the couch. When I went over to the couch and lay down with him, he went back to the bed and turned his back on me, saying that I had to change the sheets tomorrow because I had gone out. I told him that I didn't go with anyone. He was angry for about five minutes and then he got over it.

"I don't want you to go to work any more, Fela. I've been telling you that right along."

"But, Georgie, I didn't think you meant it. After all, you are not my husband. You have your wife and children at home. I don't think that you are going to keep supporting me and the children here like this."

"Look," he answered, "when a serious person decides to do something, he does it. I don't want you to think that I am like the others who have fooled you. I am an old man and I know what I am about."

"Well, then, all right. If you don't want me to go to work, then I won't." And I didn't.

After that, he would take me to the movies every night, or out dancing and even to see *un show*. And in the afternoon when he came back from work, I had to be waiting for him in my bathing suit so that we could go right down to the beach. We would lie down in the sand and kiss and get hot and then we would go to the water. Later we would get into bed and fuck.

Once, on Saint John's Day, I put on a new dress and shoes and waited to see if he would take me out. But he said, "Take all that off and let's go to the beach."

"But, Georgie, my bathing suit is back in the house in San Juan."

"Are you going to take that off or not?"

"No."

Paula said to him, "I bet you wouldn't take her down there with her clothes on."

"Oh, wouldn't I?" And he chased me all over the beach until he caught me and threw me into the water with my shoes and clothes on, and my necklace and hair curlers and everything. I grabbed a shoe and threw it at him and he began chasing me again and we kept throwing water at each other all night long. I didn't let him sleep. I got out ice cubes and threw them at him there in the house and he filled a pail with water and threw it at me. We got the whole place wet.

When he got paid he would make out a check for his wife and give me my money. I'd go shopping and he would say to me, "Tell me, Fela, are you happy with me?"

And I would answer, "Yes, Georgie, I feel happy with you. What makes you think I'm not?"

I hardly speak any English and he didn't know much Spanish. It was a problem for both of us. He would say to me, "Fela, I love you very much. I love you, Fela." Or he would try to say it in Spanish, *"Te ambro mucho, mucho. Pero, yo no comprendo, tu no comprende mi."* Then I would start to cry and think, "Oh God, please help me. If my happiness is with this man, help me learn a little more English so I can let him know what I feel in my heart."

There were times when I wanted very much to tell him, you know? Because I felt like a millionairess while I was living in El Condado. It was so diffcrent from my other life. Everything was clean and the people were very friendly and really nice. When we moved in there, the place filled up with neighbors who came to see us. Only Americans lived there. And Georgie was so nice to me. We never, never fought. We were always happy. We would talk and converse all the time, I felt so good when he took my hand or held out his arm for me or when he pulled out my chair for me to sit at the table. He'd call me *"child"* or he'd say, *"Honey,* do you want to eat?" or "Don't cook today. Let's go eat in a restaurant." I was the proudest woman in the world when I walked down the street with him. He took me to the Hotel San Juan and even to the casino and to all those luxury places for tourists. It was the first time in my life I was ever there.

I prayed to Almighty God from the bottom of my heart, "God, you helped me get out of La Esmeralda, don't make me go back. I'd rather starve to death." I didn't want the people to say, "Ah, look at her. She climbed up from La Esmeralda to El Condado, but the American left her and now she has to come back."

Georgie would take me to La Esmeralda to see my *mamá.* I didn't have any friends in La Esmeralda any more except my *mamá,* because everybody stopped speaking to me. I would get out of the car and they would just look at me. Cruz said, *"Ay,* imagine, people around here are saying that you are just like a tourist now." That's because Georgie would buy me those nice big purses and I went around in slacks.

Georgie had rented an Impala Super that had cost him eighty dollars *down.* It was a brand-new car, deep red, and it had air conditioning. We invited Fernanda and Junior for drives through the island lots of times, even though it cost a lot of money because you have to pay for the mileage on the car and for the time you keep it.

Once we took Fernanda and her husband to Arecibo. George was delighted with my *mamá* and would embrace her when he saw her. And she said she was fond of him. Georgie didn't like Junior but I didn't tell Fernanda that. Georgie bought sandwiches and beer for us and Junior didn't contribute as much as a soda. So I said to Fernanda, "Look, Nanda, Georgie never said a word to me, but when we leave here I want you to tell Junior to buy some beer or to offer Georgie something, just so he'll feel appreciated." So Fernanda said, "All right, all right." And when we got to Mayagüez, Junior said to Georgie in English, *"You want beer?"*

"That's not the way to say it," I told him. "If you want to give him a beer, go buy it and bring it to him, because he'll say no." Fortunately Georgie didn't hear Junior.

On the way home we stopped at Caguas and paid fifty cents apiece to get into the cockfights. Georgie had never seen one. I told him I never had, either. Then he says to me, "You really feel happy with me, don't you, because I take you everywhere?" I told him yes. Then he says, "You know something? I feel happy with you, because when I say to my wife, 'Let's go to such and such a place,' she says no. If a man is going to love a woman, she should do what he says, go where he goes. I like the way you behave, because you are not demanding and you don't make me do things that aren't necessary. And you don't say no to me, either. You always say yes when you should say yes." We had the nicest time! He drank a beer or two and I had one, and on the way back my *mamá* and I joked around.

Georgie took me through the El Yunque forest and we went to the very top of the mountain. We even went to see Edmundo's family in Salinas and I introduced Georgie as my husband. Edmundo was still away, working in the U.S. God forgive me, but I really laid it on when I saw his family. I felt so proud. Georgie parks this red Impala in front of Edmundo's brother's house and I say to him, "Let's go in here."

"Do you know these people?"

I said yes. Georgie knew that Edmundo was my husband but not that those people were his family. I introduced him and said, "Look, *comadre* and *compadre* Poncio, this is my future husband, but we are living together now."

"What about the children?"

"Ah, the children. They are with the girl who takes care of them."

So Poncio says to me, "And where are you living, *comadre?*"

"In El Condado," I tell him.

"Really? Then you moved out of La Esmeralda?"

"That's right. God presses hard, but he doesn't choke. You have no idea how happy I am now. This man's an elderly American, but he has it all over Edmundo."

"Then you really don't love Edmundo?"

"I wouldn't want Edmundo even to wipe my shoes." That's what I told him. The American asked me what I was talking about. He had an idea I was talking about Edmundo but I lied and said, "No, child, I was saying that you are my husband and we are thinking of getting married."

Then my *compadre* said to me, "Well, I wish you happiness. Bring the kids over here any time."

Everybody kept looking at me and at Georgie. I was wearing a new dress and I had a special hairdo and new shoes, and Georgie held my hand. When we went up the stairs he held my arm and helped me. And in Poncio's house I sat in Georgie's lap and he kissed me, American style, you know; Americans kiss anywhere.

"He really seems to love her, doesn't he?" they said.

"He has been all alone for three years," I told them. "And when you write to *compadre* Edmundo, tell him I want a divorce." When we were leaving I got into the car, leaned back and said, *"Adiós!"* What a kick I got out of it all!

Georgie used to talk to me about his wife. She was thirty-seven and he was fifty-seven. He said that they'd been sleeping in separate rooms for over two years because she liked to go to night clubs every night and she didn't want him to go with her. "When I get into bed," he told me, "she turns over and is cold, as cold as she can be, and doesn't want to move or even kiss me or anything."

I said to him, "Lord, what do you tell me that for? Who knows if you won't talk about me when you are with her."

"No, I don't talk about women in front of her."

"Ah, because you Americans are afraid of women and let yourselves be ordered around by them."

"No, I am the man in my house."

Georgie said his wife never showed him affection. He told me she didn't write to him, but one day I got hold of a letter from her and I read it. She didn't write anything about love but just something about her leg hurting her and she ended up with *"Love, Joan."*

When I asked Georgie whom his letters were from, he said from a friend and from relatives. Finally he said, "Look, Fela, my wife writes to me, but I don't know . . . She must imagine I have somebody here because she never wrote to me before when I was away from home. I have to send her the money orders because I have two little girls." Then he told me that she sent him a shirt on Father's Day. I had given him a shaving kit that cost me twelve dollars. "Look at this shirt," he said, and he threw it on the floor. "Look at this shirt! She never gave me anything before, never. She sends things so you can see them." He tore up her post cards without reading them and threw her letters down the toilet.

He told me that he didn't love her and only lived with her because they had been together for sixteen years. He said he realized now that she is very ambitious. She likes to have a lot of money in her hands. She knows how to drive and she wants new cars all the time and keeps buying things. He tells her to economize so that someday when he is old, his children will have something. He said that what he liked about me was that I didn't make demands on him and was always economizing.

He would kneel down and say, "Felícita, I swear to you that I was never the same with my wife as I have been with you. Listen, when I'd have relations with her she wouldn't do anything, so it would die on me right away."

But, you know, Georgie and I would do it five, six and seven times a night, one right after the other. Georgie is a very hot man. I'd put him up against any young stud at the track. The more he did it, the more I enjoyed it and the more he enjoyed it. We would take a bath together and he would begin kissing me on the ears. He would kiss my throat and suck my breasts and my navel and he would turn me over and knead my behind.

He acted as if he was very much in love with me. I don't know if he really was but it seemed like it. Sometimes when I was in the kitchen cooking, he would take off my shoes and kiss the soles of my feet. That's something no Puerto Rican ever did to me, ever. He would take off my shoe, just like that, smell my foot and kiss it. Then he would take hold of me and pull down my skirt and begin kissing me. I had to make sure the doors were locked all the time. If I happened to be out when he came home from work, dead tired as he was, he would bathe and shave. Then he would light his pipe and sit back in his armchair and read, waiting for me. It was one of those armchairs you can tilt back. I always had to eat with him, and if I didn't because I felt bad, he wouldn't eat that day either.

It was about a month since I had left my job. During the day I used to iron his clothes, but he didn't like me to wash because he said American women don't wash by hand the way I do. I would take the sheets and wring them out. And I really ironed his clothes nicely. At home he had to send his things to the laundry. It seems that he lives with a white woman, and those white women, oh, they don't like to wash clothes.

He used to buy me powder and perfume and everything, and I would fix myself up before going to bed with him. He would say to me, "You don't have to put on perfume, you smell good as you are." Then he'd put a pillow under me and I'd say to myself, "Now, he's after what I've been wanting for some time." He'd pull me down on the pillow and say, "Fela, I love you very much. I'm crazy about you." He kept pulling me down lower and kissing, and I acted as if I was asleep. Then in a sudden heat I kissed him on the neck and the chest, and when I sucked his nipples he got very excited and jumped up and kissed my cunt. And me, I was as happy as could be!

He asked if I wanted to do the same to him and I said I didn't. I just kissed his parts but I didn't take it in my mouth. And he said to me, "That's good, Felícita. You're a decent girl."

"And you're a dirty man."

"It's because I love you, Felícita."

So I said to him, "Don't worry. I'll do it to you one of these days. When you are my husband under the same roof and I know that everything in the house is mine. Not like here, because nothing here belongs to me, it's all rented. Someday I'll do it to you."

After that, he did it to me every night before we began. He'd say to me, "You have little titties, Fela, and you are nice and tight. That's what gets me so excited." I would kiss him and caress him, and hold his balls in my hand and play with them and then sprinkle powder on them. Then I would spray lots of cologne on him and kiss him all over and he would go crazy. He went out of his mind in bed. Sometimes when we were at the beach and I rode on his back, it would get hard, and he would say, "Let's go take a shower." And we would do it in the bathroom under the shower.

He didn't like any man ever to look at me or speak to me in Spanish. Everything I said had to be in English so he could understand. He got into a state where he thought every man I talked to was a boy friend. *"You fucking con ese man? You fucking?"* he would say, very angry and ready to start a fight with me. But he never laid a hand on me. When he got angry I was afraid to move and would wait for him to get home before I left the house. He would question me and want to know what time I got up, what time I went out, what time I got back, and what I did all day. He didn't want me to go out or anything. He just wanted me to wait in the house. So I did.

Georgie was getting fed up with Paula's cooking. All she prepared were Puerto Rican dishes, codfish and vegetables and *carne vieja*. He ate it but didn't like it much. Then the girl began acting up and saying that I hardly did anything around the house. I took care of my own work, washed and ironed my husband's clothes, cleaned my bedroom and dusted the living room, but she wanted me to fix her part of the house, and cook and wash the dishes and everything. I told her I couldn't because I had to go to San Juan every day to see the children and take them out. Georgie didn't like her attitude, so he decided to move. He said to me, "Let's get a place of our own." We would go out every night looking for an apartment.

Georgie talked a lot about the children. He liked little black Tany very much and said she was his favorite. He was fond of the others too, but we couldn't have them there with us and he couldn't live in La Esmeralda either because he is a very proud man. He doesn't like to live in slums or anything like that. I would say to him, "Look, Georgie, let's rent a little house and furnish it ourselves," and he would answer, "No, we'll stay in hotels or in El Condado." We put up with Mike and Paula for another month, then we moved to a small hotel.

One night not long after that, Georgie said to me, "Fela, I have to leave. I'm going to Florida because my work is finished here."

"*Ay*, Georgie, you're leaving me! I know you're going back to your wife."

Then he began to cry and said, "Fela, you have been the only happiness I have had in my whole life since I left my parents. I love you. I'll write to you every day. I don't love Joan."

Three days before he had to go, I said to him, "Georgie, did you buy *el ticket* already?"

"Yes," he said and tears came to his eyes. Oh, he would cry at anything. He is a *baby*. I began to cry and he pressed me close to him. Then he sat down on the floor, put his head in my lap, and said, "No, I'm not going to leave you, Fela. I'm going to send for you."

"All right," I said to him. By then I was resigned to God's will. I didn't believe he would do it.

"I'll write to you," he said.

"*O.K.*, Georgie."

"Is there anything you need?"

"Nothing." I told him that everybody tells me the same thing. "*Everybody say to me I come back and I write and nobody come back. Maybe you do it, too,*" I said to him in English.

"No, Fela," he told me, "I love you. I come back," and he said in English, "*No bring men here, no sailors, no Marines, because I have somebody downstairs see you every time and gonna write to me in Miami.*"

"*I don't care,*" I told him. "*You no my husband.*"

And he said, "*Yes, am your husband. And I gonna write to you and I put my last name for you, Felícita Arnold.*" And that is how he wrote to me.

That morning he said, "I don't feel like going."

"But you have *los tickets,* and you can't turn them back." Then I said, "*Puñeta,* you just said that to see what I would say."

"That no *bueno*," he said. He understood *puñeta* because I taught him to say a lot of things. We bought a little book with words in it in English and Spanish. I would say to him "*la chocha,*" and he would write down *chocha* in Spanish and next to it he would put *pussy*.

The Friday he was leaving he said to me, "Don't cook today. Let's go to a restaurant." And that farewell Friday we did it eight times. We did it toward dawn, we did it in the morning, and we did it in the afternoon. He lost fifteen pounds in Puerto Rico!

He said to me, "When I come back, I'm going to give you a *baby*."

"But I am operated," I told him.

"That doesn't matter," he told me. "I'll find where to give it to you." How do you like that?

He was leaving at six-fifteen, and at three in the afternoon he still hadn't packed his bags. He said to me, "Fela, do you remember when we first got together, after I gave you that perfume, I told you I was going to give you still another present?" I said that I remembered. I thought of it every Saturday when he got his pay check. "Well, let's go buy it," he said. *"Is something you have not too much and you need it. Maybe you like it."*

So we went to the jewelry store and he bought me earrings. "I want you to have something to remember me by." And he put them on me right there in the street. He bought them three hours before he left and they cost him twenty dollars. "Don't take them off," he told me, "because I am the one who put them on you and I am going to be the one who takes them off."

We got back to the house at three-thirty and I said to him, "Georgie, pack your bags." And he said in English, *"Fela is happy because Georgie goes."*

"The one who is *happy* is you," I told him, "because you are going to be there with Joan. *Joan is fucking another man, you bub."* I told him she was putting the horns on him.

We took a bath and did it once again. We were there for about an hour, banging away until we were through. "This is the last one for a long time," he told me.

"That's right," I said.

And then he held me very tight and said, "Look, if I can't come back, I'll send you some money and you can join me." I began to cry and said, "Oh, Georgie, probably you won't send me the money."

"Fela, you don't understand. I'm going to leave you a hundred and thirty. Pay for the children's food out of that and put a hundred away."

That's what I did and what I went through! I went for four days without eating in order to economize and have enough money left for my fare. I said to myself, "If I touch even one dollar of that hundred, I'll lose it all and I won't be able to go." I needed to buy clothes for the children and shoes for myself, so there I was, going through torture to be able to get to New York.

Nobody in La Esmeralda knew I was going hungry, not even my *mamá.* The only one was Cruz, but even she didn't know I had money put away. Cruz had moved and she took my children with her. I stayed alone in Georgie's apartment. I'd bring Cruz small amounts of money to pay for the children and when she asked me where I got it, I'd say that I had gone with a man the night before. May God forgive me, but it was a lie.

I waited out the two weeks. After a week and a half I received a telegram from Georgie saying: "Arriving Wednesday 11:45." I was getting dressed to go and meet him when there was a knock on the door. It was another telegram. It said: "Not arriving. Canceled." Without stopping to think, I rushed to the airport like a madwoman. I wanted to find out whether he had canceled his trip or if it was the flight that was canceled. The man told me that no flight was canceled.

The next day I went to see *doña* Alma, the spiritist. "Don't worry," she told me. "I'll help you. Go home now, and tomorrow you'll receive a letter."

Sure enough, the next day the letter carrier knocked and handed me a letter from Georgie. It said that he was in Florida and that his wife was very pleased with him and wanted him to take a vacation. He had asked her if she wanted to go to Puerto Rico but she said she didn't. He told me to keep his clothes for him and that if I had given up the apartment, to go and stay with my sister. So I did and he wrote to me at Cruz's house after that. The letters would come without any return address, and he would say: "I am in Philadelphia, but don't write to me at this motel because I will be leaving on such and such a day." Then I would receive another letter from somewhere else saying: "Don't write me here because I am leaving tomorrow." I could never write to any of those places.

It's over a month now that we've been apart. I haven't had relations since then and I haven't missed it. I can say from my own experience, when a woman gets a good man and knows he loves her and loves her children, other men do not exist. Now that Georgie has left me, I can't really accept it. I have a feeling in my heart for him, a joy, and I am hoping. Those four months were heaven on earth for me. I never had anything like that and I felt like I was going to die from so much happiness. I would lie in bed and think, "Is this a dream or is it real? Oh Lord, please don't let it ever come to an end."

I've always been afraid Georgie would abandon me like all the others. He had doubts about me because I was in the life. He didn't trust me, but I swear that if he had stayed with me I would be faithful to him to the end.

Since he left I haven't been able to go back to work or anything. I have no feelings, my heart is empty. I haven't the courage to go to bed with a man for money. All I can think of is Georgie and how good he was to me. I can barely eat and I ask myself, "What will become of my children now?" When you get the kind of opportunity that I had, when you can relax, knowing your children are eating, you feel at peace. But if you have to go back to your other life . . . I cry through the nights at the thought of it.

PART IV

SIMPLICIO

———

Days with Simplicio
in New York

Simplicio and Flora lived on a quiet street in the Bronx where once-elegant private houses had been converted into multiple dwellings. Simplicio paid sixty-four dollars for a third-floor furnished apartment which consisted of one room, a tiny kitchen, and a hall toilet shared with two other families. Simplicio and Flora had been living here for about six months, from the time they moved to New York from Pennsylvania.

One mild Friday evening in May, at about nine o'clock, Rosa climbed the three flights of stairs that led to their apartment. Flora opened the door to Rosa's knock. Flora was wearing a blue-striped dress and bedroom slippers, and her light-brown hair was elaborately arranged in waves, bangs and a pony tail.

"Come in," she said. "Simplicio isn't home, as usual."

Just inside the door, Gabi, the seven-year-old son of Simplicio's sister Felícita, was lying on a cot against the right-hand wall. He was reading a comic book and did not look up. On the left side of the room a woman was sitting at the dinette table. She, too, had on bedroom slippers; she was wearing a black-and-white checked skirt, white blouse and brown jacket.

"You know my neighbor Gina," Flora said. She placed one of the chairs from the dinette set in the center of the room and Rosa sat down. Gina nodded to Rosa.

The room was about fifteen feet square but seemed smaller because it was crowded with furniture. At Rosa's right was the mahogany-colored metal double bed in which Simplicio and Flora slept. It belonged to the house, but the white bedspread was Flora's. An orange curtain, fastened to a sprinkler pipe on the ceiling, hung part way across the room and gave some privacy to the couple when a guest slept on the cot. Two white-curtained windows with a steam radiator between them looked out on a small back yard below. Along this wall stood a pair of mahogany tables which Simplicio had brought from Pennsylvania, a television set, a ninety-nine-cent metal record stand, and another small table on which lay a red toy duck.

Gina said. "Well, here we are, sitting like two damn fools because our husbands went out and left us."

"They're a couple of good-for-nothings!" Flora answered. "Won't Simplicio ever get tired of drinking? I tell you I can't stand living with a drunk. That's why I left my other husband. That one really couldn't stop. He drank every night."

"At least ours only drink on *weekends,*" Gina said.

"I don't know what that bastard drinks with. I take away all his money on payday. Otherwise he wastes it and then complains all week long, 'Oh, I don't have money for lunch. Oh, I don't have money for anything,' " Flora said, mimicking her husband. "How does he expect to have it after he's thrown it away?"

"I wish I could get hold of at least part of Millo's check," said Gina sadly. "But he keeps it all, so I might as well forget about it."

"I don't know who pays for their drinks, but somebody does," Flora said. "You don't need money to drink. Hell, no! But if you're hungry, nobody'll treat you to a cup of coffee or a plate of food."

The door opened and Gina's six-year-old daughter, Mercedes, came in. She was very thin and she seemed frightened. She had been crying.

"Oh, so you woke up?" Gina said coldly. "Didn't the beating I gave you help you sleep?"

"Why did God have to give me you for a mother? I'll tell my *papá* when he comes home. I'll tell him to take me with him when he goes to work," the child said and began to cry again.

"*Ay,* wouldn't that be heavenly!" Gina said. She turned to Rosa. "These kids are driving me crazy. I wouldn't have any more for anything in the world."

"Yes, you can say that because you had that operation," Flora said.

"Well, I told Millo, 'If you don't have me operated on, I won't live with you any more.' I said it to him just like that. I had that last baby because he tricked me. We'd had a fight and then he wanted to—you know. He got up to find those tablets I used, and I put one in, but Millo didn't wait long enough."

Flora got up and moved restlessly around the room, rearranging the cheap decorative objects she kept on crocheted doilies on every available surface. Four panthers of black glass stood on top of the television set, a Philco with a twenty-one-inch screen. Flora had bought the panthers for three dollars on Delancey Street and she was particularly fond of them. Also on the TV set were a vase of artificial flowers, snapshots of friends and relatives, and a five-dollar Brownie camera. On a little table near the bed were an ashtray and a large array of ceramic animal figurines which had been bought or won at Coney Island. Heads or tails were missing from a number of them, but Flora kept them anyway. She also had a pair of Chinese dolls, one of which she didn't like at all. Simplicio had insisted on buying them on one of their visits to Chinatown. Another mahogany table, near the kitchen, held a record player, a radio, a lamp, a bottle of rubbing alcohol, a bottle of Vicks Vaporub and a key ring. Flora kept her collection of dolls on a shelf above the table. Fernanda had given her several of the dolls to comfort her for being childless and also in the belief that the presence of dolls in her home would help her to become pregnant.

On the first floor a record player was going full blast playing popular Puerto Rican songs. Now the women heard the beginning of *"El regalito"*— "The Little Gift"—which, with its double meaning, was the rage of the moment.

> Look, my love, I bring you a little gift.
> Care for it, it's yours. Kiss it, it's yours,
> Press it hard, it's yours. Caress it, it's yours.
> Oh, my love, won't you give me a little cure?

"I wonder when those two down there will be through for the night?" Gina said.

"Forget it. You know that on a Friday night they're never through until morning," Flora answered. "What I want that man to do is to give his woman a beating, because she's a no-good bitch with balls. Do you know, she wouldn't open the front door for the Blessed Virgin herself? Once I forgot my key, and Soledad and I stood there knocking and knocking and she wouldn't open up. Finally I had to go down to the basement and borrow Olga's key, and I wasn't even on speaking terms with her then."

"What those people need is to come up against the priest of their parish," Gina said. "He'd tell them how to behave."

"Soledad went and told that woman off. When Soledad gets into a rage it's better to be dead than to get in her way. She's the best there is, but there are times when even her brother is afraid of her."

"Well, I'm going home to bed," Gina said. "That queer is never coming."
She took her daughter's hand.

"Me too. Fuck Simplicio. I don't give a damn if he never gets home."

Flora closed the door behind Gina and her daughter. Gabi had fallen
asleep over his comic book, and Flora covered him with a checked blanket
which she took from one of the two closets at the end of the room. Standing in
front of the bureau, near the foot of Gabi's cot, she undid her pony tail and
began to brush her hair.

The bureau, which came with the apartment, was covered with various
objects. Religious articles were grouped together on the left, a statuette of
Jesus and His Sacred Heart which Simplicio had won at Coney Island, a figure
of Christ set in a sea shell, and one of Saint Martha, Flora's patron saint. A
votive light was set before these figures; to one side of them was a glass containing artificial flowers and pennies. Flora saved pennies so that she could
buy a new candle every week. There was also an unopened bottle of holy
water there, the gift of a neighbor. Flora kept it on hand in case of need. It had
the power to "calm a person," to chase out the "Devil inside" and keep away
unwelcome visitors. Near the bottle of water lay Flora's new brown purse, for
which she had paid two dollars at the factory where she worked. Beside the
purse were stacked two boxes which held a miscellany of hair rollers, bobby
pins, buttons and papers such as Simplicio's and Flora's social security cards,
and Gabi's birth certificate. Strewn over the rest of the bureau top was Flora's
considerable supply of cosmetics. Four novels in Spanish and Simplicio's shaving cream also lay there, along with pieces of inexpensive jewelry and several
pairs of Simplicio's cuff links.

Looking in the mirror above the dresser, Flora said, *"Bendito,* I wonder
how my poor *mamá* is? I must remember to buy a new candle for Saint Martha
tomorrow. Hell," she burst out, turning to Rosa, "if only God would let me
have a baby! I know Simplicio runs around the way he does because I can't
give him a child. I wonder why, because I like children so much. If only Simplicio would begin to love Gabi. I could love that child as if he were my
own."

Rosa and Flora put on their nightclothes and Flora turned down the bedspread, revealing clean white sheets. They got into bed and after a time fell
asleep, although the music downstairs was still playing full force.

At two o'clock Flora shook Rosa awake. "Listen to that noise!" she said.
"That man's breaking dishes. I'll bet there isn't a plate left whole down there.
Let's go find out what's up."

They went to the head of the stairs where Gina joined them. Other tenants
were on the landings or were poking their heads out of their doors. The quarrel
had awakened the whole house.

"Bitch! Whore! I shit on the bones of your mother!" a man screamed.
"I'll kill you! I swear I'll kill you!"

At this moment Simplicio and Gina's husband, Millo, came up the stairs. Simplicio was a handsome, light-brown, short, muscular young man. His black kinky hair was partly hidden by a narrow-brimmed felt hat. He had dark eyes, full lips, white teeth and an attractive smile. His companion, Millo, was older, short, fat and partially bald. Both men looked relaxed and cheerful.

"And where were the two of you?" Gina demanded.

"Oh, around," Millo said nonchalantly. "I saw only one of my sweethearts because I didn't have time to visit them all."

"Well, tell her to drop around Monday morning so she can make your breakfast and take care of your children."

"Forget it," Millo said, slapping her bottom. "You're my cook."

They all sat down together on the steps to listen to the fight.

"Those children are mine and I'll take them away when I please," the man below shouted. "And I please right now."

There were sounds of a struggle. Then something hit a windowpane and they heard the crash of broken glass.

"You go to hell, you damn bitch," the man yelled.

"Well, what a show!" Millo said.

"You hit me because I'm a woman," the wife screamed. "But never mind, God will punish you. I'm going to the police."

"Fuck it! Call them if you dare. Go ahead. I'm going to slit your throat."

Now they heard the voice of another woman. It was Olga, a fat middle-aged relative of the man involved in the fight; she must have come up from the basement. "Hit her again, you damn fool!" she shouted. "That woman left seven kids in Puerto Rico so she could come up here to fuck. Hit her! Those two kids aren't yours. She put the horns on you."

The man yelled back at her, "Shut up, you dirty old hag! You're the one who screws with every man in sight. Those three kids of yours aren't Xavier's and I can prove it."

"You dirty bastard! Look, that man told me he screws his wife in the ass." Olga was yelling now for the benefit of the whole house. "Yes, and she sucks his prick. That's how she holds him. How else could a woman of forty hold a man of twenty-one?"

"See here, you dirty old woman, she's my wife. And she gives me what I want the way I want it. And it's none of your business, see?"

A door slammed and suddenly there was silence. The tenants went back into their apartments. Simplicio lay down on the bed in his clothes. Flora went to the kitchen and brought him a plate of rice, beans and a pork chop.

"I don't want anything now," he said.

"Why not?" Flora asked belligerently, one hand on her hip. "Because you ate with that woman you were with?"

Simplicio grimaced, got off the bed, started to leave. As he opened the door Flora threw the plate of food at him; the pork chop sailed out onto the landing. Then she caught him and began to shake him by the shoulders. "Please do me a favor!" she cried. "If you were with that woman, go away and leave me in peace."

"But, Flora, what woman? How could I be with a woman? You know I'm broke."

"Don't pretend to be a saint," Flora answered. "I know you use your cousin as a go-between. Yes, and I know Chango told you to leave me because he says I henpeck you. Well, go ahead. He says I order you around, so go to Chango. He'll give you everything I give you."

Simplicio shrugged his shoulders and picked up the plate. There was still some food on it and he ate that, sitting on the bed and humming. When he had eaten he said good-naturedly, "Flora, get me a cigarette."

But Flora was still furious. "Get it yourself, you're not a cripple. I won't give you anything."

Simplicio found a pack and began to smoke one cigarette after another. Finally he said, "It's enough, Flora. I'm getting tired of this. One day I'll go and I won't come back."

"You can go right this minute. What do you expect me to do, cry?" Flora shouted. "If you leave me today, I'll get another man tomorrow."

"You'll see. Next week I'm going to borrow ten dollars from the *boss* and make a down payment on my fare for Puerto Rico. And when I go you'll never see me again, because I'm not going back to La Esmeralda. I'll go to New Jersey or Ponce and sign up as a sailor and forget you. I'll forget you, because every day it's the same old story. You kiss me good-bye in the morning and we're both happy. But by the time I get back in the afternoon you're ready to raise hell again. I don't even feel like eating when I'm here. Outside, I can at least eat my lunch in peace. I buy myself some food and go to some hallway where I can eat without anyone bothering me."

"Look at that! Fancy you chewing bones in hallways!"

"What do you mean 'bones'?" Simplicio was beginning to get angry. "If I go to a restaurant I have to pay double the money. A man can't eat in peace in this house."

"If I quarrel with you, it's only because you deceive me with that woman," Flora said, lowering her voice. "I don't cheat on you, do I? Well, you should respect me too."

"But, Flora, there's nothing between me and that woman. When somebody makes up a story, you believe it. But if a person tells you the truth, then you think it's a lie. I wasn't with that woman."

"If you could cheat me once, right under my very nose, you can cheat me a thousand times. Yes, and a thousand and three times too."

Simplicio grinned. "Well, I told that woman that the only one I really love is my wife. That's why she left me."

"Don't you worry, I'm going to write Nanda about this," Flora said.

"So what? What can Nanda do? Eat me up?"

"Maybe she can put some shame into you."

"Maybe I'm the one who should put some shame into her," Simplicio retorted. "Let's go to bed."

Simplicio carried Gabi, who was still asleep, and laid him across the foot of the big bed. Rosa took his cot, and Simplicio and Flora turned out the lights and got into bed.

All was quiet in the building when two policemen arrived and began knocking on every door. They could be heard asking, "What happened?" The invariable answer was "Nothing." When Simplicio opened his door to them he said, "I don't know what happened. I was sleeping."

"I wonder who called the cops," Simplicio said after the policemen had gone.

"That Jewish woman next door. Who else could it be?" Flora answered. "She's always making trouble. As if it was any of her business."

"Yes, she must have been the one because none of us in this building would do a thing like that."

"Of course not. Let them kill each other if they want to. They've got a right. That's what they're man and wife for, isn't it?"

Flora checked her watch. It was three-thirty. Everyone went to bed again and slept until ten-thirty. Simplicio was the first one to get up. He went to the kitchen and brought Flora a glass of water and half a cup of black coffee. Flora rinsed her mouth, spitting the water into a pink pail beside the bed. She drank the coffee and then got out of bed. On the way to the kitchen she stopped at the dinette table to push aside a set of small glasses that Simplicio had bought for her. Gabi woke up. Flora told him to put the chairs at the table, and she brought out coffee and crackers for everyone.

"Well, let's go shop for food," Simplicio said as soon as they had eaten. Saturday was the day Flora did the family shopping, not only for food but for whatever was needed. Simplicio usually accompanied her to help carry the packages and to wheedle her into buying the things he wanted. He enjoyed these weekly expeditions, as did Flora and Gabi.

"All right, I'll get dressed," Flora said. She was undecided what to wear. At first she considered putting on a new green dress that Simplicio had bought for her on Delancey Street, but she finally put on the same striped dress she had worn the day before. She slipped her feet into a pair of cream-colored shoes and combed her hair. Meanwhile Simplicio was dressing underneath the sheet. He emerged wearing black trousers and a brown-and-white shirt. He put on black shoes and slicked down his hair with oil from a bottle on the dresser. Flora gave Gabi a clean pair of jeans, a red-striped shirt and sneakers.

As they went downstairs Flora said, "Let's go to the A and P. Things are cheaper there."

"All right, I don't care, but those people don't sell on credit. When we're broke we'll be screwed up if we don't buy at a store that gives credit."

"So what!" Flora answered crossly. "We have to economize."

They passed a record shop. "Flora, give me a dollar," Simplicio said. "I want to buy 'La mano de Dios.' "

"Are you crazy?" Flora burst out. "We aren't going to have any money left over and you want to buy a record. Besides, you broke the arm of the record player, and that's expensive. So don't think we can get it fixed right away. I hope it's never fixed because when it works, all you do is play records so loud the whole neighborhood can hear."

"Ah, Flora, give it to me."

Flora opened her purse and threw a dollar bill at her husband. "Here, take it, but that's all."

"Oh, Flora, you never let me buy anything."

"Well, what do you want? More?" Flora said in a loud voice. "Here, take all the money and attend to everything yourself."

"No, don't be like that, Flora, please," Simplicio answered as though he were a child pleading with an adult.

At the big supermarket on Third Avenue, Simplicio and Flora bought two pounds of pork chops, two chickens, three frankfurters, two large cans of pineapple juice, three cans of Vienna sausages, two small cans of shrimp, three pounds of potatoes, five pounds of rice, half a pound of bread, three pounds of small kidney beans, and half a pound of salt picnic shoulder ham.

As they pushed their shopping cart toward the front of the store, they passed a shelf that held cans of dog food. "Mother of God!" exclaimed Flora. "To think of buying special food for a dog. Who'd dream of doing that in Puerto Rico? Down there you can't afford to buy enough food for people, let alone a dog. That's the good thing about this country, *chico*. If you work, at least you can eat. *Ay,* but how I'd like to have a salad of Puerto Rican lettuce and tomatoes! Well, we're through here. We'll buy the rest at the other store."

"But, Flora, aren't you going to buy me any beer?"

"*Ave María,* boy, if you had been a deaf-mute, you would have burst because you couldn't talk!" Flora said, "Go get them then."

Simplicio came back to the check-out counter with a dozen small bottles of Schaefer's beer, and two large ones. The total bill came to eleven dollars and five cents.

Flora told Rosa that she usually spent about twenty dollars a week on groceries, not including the cost of the quart of milk and quart of orange juice which were delivered daily. She said also that she was able to buy the same food here as in Puerto Rico. "But here you have to buy a lot of everything. In Puerto Rico I could buy a nickel's worth of coffee, two cents' worth of bread, three cents' worth of butter, and so on. But here if you can't buy a lot, you don't eat. If I don't have enough money for a pound of sugar, they won't sell me a half pound. In Puerto Rico you can eat a meal on a dollar, but here you can't do anything with that."

Back at the apartment, Flora, Gabi, and Rosa put away the groceries in the kitchen, which was small and crowded. Besides the stove and the sink, it was furnished with two standing cabinets, a refrigerator and Flora's wringer-type washing machine, which Simplicio had bought for her as a surprise when they lived in Pennsylvania. Simplicio's toy train, which had cost six dollars, was kept on the window sill.

Flora put the perishable food into the refrigerator. It already was half full of food, milk, juices, some meat, vegetables, cheese and eggs. The family used three dozen eggs a week, including those Flora took to the woman who cared for Gabi while she was working. "That's so she'll take good care of him," Flora said.

The staples were stored in a food-storage cabinet which stood beside the refrigerator. The cabinet contained a jar of salad dressing, dried peas, spaghetti, farina, a large can of Ajax cleansing powder, toilet paper, disinfectant, shoe polish, milk of magnesia, potatoes, cans of Campbell's soups, cans of tuna fish, cinnamon, and popcorn for Gabi. On the top shelves Flora kept an electric coffee pot which Gina had given her, a can that held kitchen knives, about six silver-plated place settings, all that was left of a larger set that Simplicio had bought for her in Pennsylvania, the remains of two sets of wine glasses, an old electric iron, and Simplicio's "junk," mostly old receipts and pay-check stubs. On top of the cabinet Flora kept her "everyday" plates, cups and glasses.

A cockroach ran across the floor and disappeared behind the refrigerator. "*Ay, Dios mío!*" Flora said. "These tiny cockroaches are worse than the ones we have in Puerto Rico. I throw down powder and the men come every month to clean them out, but they come back stronger than ever. You have to keep every pot covered. Everywhere you look you find more." She went for a can of roach powder and sprinkled it under the sink and behind the refrigerator. "The mice aren't so bad. At least they don't eat your clothes here the way they do at home."

In the second cabinet, which stood near the curtained doorway, Flora stored her "good" dishes which had been bought on the installment plan for forty-nine dollars. The cabinet was made of wood, and painted white. On the bottom shelves were cooking utensils, most of them battered and old. There were saucepans, three frying pans and a smaller skillet, a thirty-nine-cent coffee pot, and a *caldero,* a large, shallow pot with a heavy bottom used chiefly for boiling rice. The *caldero* had cost three dollars.

On one of the shelves lay a piece of hard, dry bread. It had been left by the previous tenants and Flora had not thrown it out "because as long as there is a piece like that in the kitchen, we'll never be without bread."

On top of this cabinet stood a small spice cabinet and several canisters decorated with decals of apples and pears. The latter held rice, sugar, coffee, beans and powdered milk. Flora told Rosa that she preferred to use Cremora, an instant cream that cost twenty-nine cents a jar, but that she planned to try the powdered milk sometime. It had been given to her by her sister. Two jars of vitamin pills were on top of the cabinet also. Simplicio had brought home a two-dollar bottle of vitamin pills a month before, when Flora was feeling weak, but she preferred the liquid, which, she said, tasted better.

While they were still storing the food, Simplicio came into the kitchen and said, "Flora, shall I make a pudding?"

Flora answered him angrily, "What the hell are you going to use for money to buy the mix with? If you were going to make something really good, you wouldn't be half as interested."

Simplicio turned to his nephew. "But don't I make good pudding, Gabi?"

"Yes, yes, make some," the boy said.

"You see, Flora? Gabi and I like my pudding."

"Later then," Flora said crossly.

"Look, Flora, we forgot to exchange the comics!" Simplicio said. "We have twelve here that we've read already."

"Yes, *hombre,* we did forget because you're always quarreling. We'll exchange them later."

"*Ay,* but give me some beer," Simplicio said.

"Get it yourself if you want it. I'm not serving anybody."

Simplicio took out some ice from the refrigerator and put it into a large glass jar. He also took one of the big bottles of beer. "Now I'm going downstairs for a while," he said. "Start roasting one of those chickens, Flora."

Flora brushed the chicken with oil, salted it and put it in the oven.

A short time later Simplicio came in with Soledad and her three little girls. It was about twelve-thirty.

"*Hola!*" Soledad called to Flora. "How's everything here?"

"*Ave María,* look at Soledad!" Simplicio said. "Go put on a brassière, you fresh thing. Flora, give my sister a brassière. I won't have any women around here looking like that."

"But *bras* bother me," Soledad said, laughing. "I'm not showing anybody anything." However, she took the brassière that Flora offered her and went into the bathroom to put it on. When she came back into the room she snapped her fingers. "Come on, let's dance, Simplicio!"

"You go ahead. I'll dance later."

"Well, put on some records then."

"How can we, when Simplicio broke the record player?" Flora said.

When the chicken was ready Flora began cutting it up into serving pieces on the dinette table just as Gina walked in, followed by Millo with a glass of beer in his hand.

"Hm, I must be a mind reader," Millo said. "I got here just in time."

"Say, mister, where's that chicken you were going to buy *me?*" Gina asked.

"It ran off and nobody could catch it. That's because New York's such a big place. It's not like the valleys back home where you can run after a rooster until you catch it."

"Well, too bad. You won't be able to eat either, see?"

"Never you mind," Millo said. "Say, would you people like some beer?" He went out and came back with a dozen bottles. "Now I'm going to bring something else over here, but don't laugh at it." He went out again, returning in a few minutes with a portable record player, the old-fashioned type that is wound by hand with a crank. "If you want to hear music, you'll have to grind coffee," he said, laughing.

Everyone helped himself to a piece of chicken except Soledad. She wound the record player, put on a record and began to dance again. "Come on, Gabi, I'll teach you to dance ballet," she said, lifting up her skirt. Her daughters began to dance too.

Gina and Flora were standing near the kitchen door watching Gabi. "Does the boy give you much trouble?" Gina asked.

"No, but he's so restless. He was running wild in La Esmeralda and now he feels caged-in here. You can imagine."

"He'll get used to it soon," Gina said. "He does seem to be hungry from way back, though."

"*Ave María!* That boy eats as if he had a tapeworm! He's making up for all the times he went hungry in Puerto Rico."

"My *mamá* didn't take care of me," Gabi said. He was chewing on a chicken leg. "She didn't fix up my clothes like you do, either. That's why I don't want to go back to Puerto Rico until I'm big. I don't want to be hungry all the time."

"Child, don't say those things," Flora said.

"But it's true!"

Simplicio and Millo meanwhile were talking together. "Damn it all!" Millo said. "They don't let me stay on here in my apartment because I have two children. You aren't allowed to have children in this fucking country, eh?"

"It's just that these apartments are too small," Simplicio answered. "You can't live comfortably here with two children."

"*Chico,* one lives as one can. Well, do you all like cider? Gina, go to our place and get the bottle of cider." When Gina returned with the cider, Millo poured a half glass for everyone. Simplicio drained his glass and then took the little that remained in the bottle. For a while everyone fell silent; no one seemed to have anything to say.

Millo finally said in an attempt to be gay, "There's one more beer left for each. Come on, who shall we drink to?"

"To the old lady," Simplicio said.

Soledad said, "Tomorrow's Mother's Day."

"Damn it, I never have any money," Simplicio said. "I can't even buy a present for my old lady."

"Well, I've already sent her ten nice little dollars," his sister said with satisfaction. She added maliciously, "And I sent her a letter really telling her off about Junior. I made it so bad she won't ever write to me again."

"Leave my mother alone," Simplicio yelled. "Don't talk like that about her."

"Oh, sure, sure, you're her little pet, aren't you?"

"No, I'm not, but I don't like to hear you talking about her that way."

"Oh, go roll in shit," his sister said.

"Stop quarreling and let's drink to your *mamá*," said Flora.

After they had made a toast to Fernanda, Simplicio suggested that they go to the park. "If we keep on sitting around here, we'll hatch chicks."

"You all go," Millo said. "I'm going to sleep. Those people kept me awake all night."

Gina also decided to stay home, and that meant her children stayed home as well. The rest strolled through the Bronx streets in the afternoon sunshine. As they passed a bar Soledad said, "Simplicio, do you remember when we used to come here?"

"Yes, and remember the time I had to carry you out because you were drunk?"

"How about the time I fought with a queer in there because he said you were a minor and he couldn't sell you a beer? Lucky I didn't have a knife that day or I'd still be in jail."

"And this isn't like Puerto Rico," Simplicio said. "Just ask Chango what it's like to be in jail here."

"Oh, I know," his sister replied. "Everything's worse up here except the money. It must be terrible to be in jail here. Think of it, not being able to talk to anybody. You might as well be a deaf-mute. They could be cursing your mother and you'd be thinking they were paying you a compliment. But maybe Americans don't know how to pay compliments."

Simplicio said with a laugh, "Well, if one of us is sent to jail, the rest will have to get themselves arrested too. That way we'll all be together."

Simplicio called to Flora who was walking alone some distance ahead. "Hey, Leila, wait for us!"

Flora stopped short. In a fury she ran back to Simplicio. "Oh, so you were with that woman last night after all. You damn *maricón!* Go on, go to her then, and stop screwing around!"

"But, Flora, that was just a slip of the tongue. Anybody can make a mistake."

"You queer! Idiot! You must have been thinking of her for her name to come out of your mouth. I won't let you go on making a fool of me. Does she suck your cock? Well, I can find a man to suck my cunt, see? I'm going to put the horns on you!"

As she stood there shouting at him, Simplicio took a clasp knife out of his pocket and opened it. Terrified, Flora started to run.

"Give me that knife!" Soledad said. "You want to show off, do you? Don't you know this isn't your country? You feel like cutting, do you? Well, cut off your prick then."

"I'm going to slit that woman's throat," Simplicio said, furious. "Didn't you hear what she said to me?"

"You can't hit her in front of me or cut her either," his sister said firmly. "Her or any other woman."

"Is that so?" Simplicio shouted. "You side with her against your own brother?"

"Well, I can wear her *panties* but not your undershorts," Soledad said. "Besides, real men don't hit women. Only sissies do. Go on, give me that fucking knife. Don't you have any respect for your eldest sister?" She grabbed the knife. Simplicio gave it up without much show of resistance. "Thank your lucky stars I don't have a razor on me," Soledad said. "If I had one, I'd give it to Flora so she could cool you off."

They walked on in angry silence until they entered the tenement where Soledad lived. Catín was sent to buy a dozen beers, but she came back empty-handed. *"Mami,* they wouldn't sell it to me. They said I was a minor."

"What do they mean, a minor?" her mother said, laughing. "Why, in no time at all you'll be old enough to marry. I guess I'll have to go myself." She went out.

In hostile silence Flora began to make coffee. Simplicio put on a record; he turned the volume up so high that the words of the songs were indistinguishable. When his sister came back, he downed three beers in rapid succession. "Let's go to Chinatown," he said. "I'm hungry."

"If you want food, lift your leg and suck yourself good," Soledad answered. "I don't have money to go to Chinatown."

"Well then, send out for some whiskey."

"Hell is what I'm going to send out for. Didn't you hear me say I don't have any money? Do you think I'm hustling?"

"Make me something to eat then. That chicken wasn't anything."

"All right, but you'll have to wait until it's ready," Soledad said grudgingly.

All this time Flora had sat sipping black coffee without saying a word. She was still furious; her eyes seemed to be popping out of her face. She was chain smoking.

Simplicio went over to her. "Goddamn coffee and cigarettes!" he said as if he were trying to provoke her further.

"Goddamn beer!" Flora replied. "Leave me alone. I pay for my vices with my own work."

"Oh, is that so? Well, look, you aren't going to work any more. You've gotten real fresh since you started working. But now you're out of luck because I'm going to make you stay home."

"Oh, sure," Flora said sarcastically. "We can afford that because you're so rich."

"Stop quarreling, you two," Soledad said. She was frying steaks and cutting potatoes for french fries. After a time they all sat down to eat a silent meal. Then Soledad again tried to make peace between Simplicio and Flora. "All right, Flora, come here. You and Simplicio wink at each other. Come on, let's all go to the park now."

Simplicio unexpectedly climbed up on the sofa and began jumping up and down on it like a child.

"What the devil are you doing?" Soledad said. "You're going to smash my sofa. If you don't give, at least don't take away. Well, are we going to the park or not?"

Once in the park, Soledad and Simplicio went to the swings; the others sat on the grass. Soon Soledad and Simplicio asked Rosa, Flora and the children to play hide-and-seek. They played hard for a while, dodging behind trees and bushes, and everyone seemed more relaxed. Simplicio was the first to tire. The others went on playing until Flora and Soledad were approached by two strange men.

"Let's go. I'm scared," Soledad said. She ran up to Simplicio.

"Who's going to eat you up, eh?" Simplicio said. "I don't want to go."

"Well then, you stay. I'm going."

Everyone left. Back in the apartment, Simplicio began to drink beer and play records.

"Are you deaf? Can't you turn that down?" his sister shouted.

"He's a drunk," Flora said. "I put the horns on that other man I had because he was a drunk and a bastard. If you go on the way you are now, you're asking for the same!"

Again Soledad intervened. "What the hell, stop it! Do you two plan to fight all day?"

Flora stood up. "Let's go. It's getting late."

"All right," Soledad said. "You two go, but you'll have to take Catín with you. If you keep on fighting, she'll come and fetch me. You'll have me there as quick as a fireman to a fire and as hot as water for chocolate. So behave yourselves!"

Simplicio went ahead, holding Catín by the hand. Flora, walking with

Rosa, said bitterly, "He doesn't respect his own wife, that's the trouble. He fell in love right under my nose in my own house. That Leila! There aren't words bad enough to describe what Simplicio and she did to me."

Apparently Simplicio had heard some of his wife's conversation. He turned back toward her. "Damn it, Flora, do you think I'm a woman? A man is a man, and he can have all the women he wants and he doesn't lose a thing. Now you, you have to stay home. Or do you want to wear the pants? Who said you had to be a woman, anyway?"

Flora ignored her husband and kept silent until they arrived home. She nodded curtly to a neighbor who was sitting on the front steps. As she and Rosa went upstairs Flora said, "Did you see that man? He's another son of a bitch. He was such a dirty dog that his wife had to leave him. I stopped taking care of Soledad's children so I could take care of his two, because he paid me more, see? But that's plain shit. I shouldn't have done it. I'm very fond of Soledad because she never keeps anything for herself. She gave me those red pajamas I wore last night, in spite of the fact that I've never been able to give her anything. I wish I worked all week. Working just three days a week is a waste of time. All I get is twenty-two dollars, and most of that goes for subway and lunch and paying the woman to take care of Gabi. Last week I only had three dollars left over. Imagine!"

Inside the apartment Flora said, "I'm going to rest for a while," and she flung herself down on the bed with her face to the wall.

Simplicio offered to walk Rosa home. They went down the stairs and walked for a few minutes in silence. Simplicio finally said, "*Chica,* a terrible thing happened to me last night, the worst that can happen to a man."

"Oh? What was it?"

"It's been on my mind all day. Last night I went to Leila's house and she wouldn't let me in. 'I don't love you any more,' she says. 'Oh, really?' I say. Think of it! I gave that woman everything. I even paid twelve dollars for her rent. Well, I left, but after I'd gone a little way she sent for me to come back. I thought maybe she was sorry and that now she'd be good to me, so I decided to go back and take my fill. When I got there I threw myself on her bed. I was wild, hot as fire, ready for anything. Well, I happen to look over at the bureau and I see a man hiding behind it. Quick as a flash I take out my blade and put it on my thigh. I start whistling. I pretended I wasn't scared, see, but inside I was trembling. The man comes over to me and asks, 'Listen, what are you doing here?'

" 'I was just about to ask *you* that,' I say. He tells me, 'Beat it!' I tell him, 'Beat it yourself!' The man just stands there, looking at me and pointing to the door. Then Leila says to me, 'Go away. I don't want to have anything to do with you any more. I love this other one.' That really made my blood boil. I fastened my pants and went away. When I got downstairs I yelled up at her,

'Never mind, I'll get even with you. You'll see.' And I will get even one of these days. I'll invite her to go out with me and I'll take her far, far away. Then I'll leave her there alone. That'll really screw her up."

They came to the block where Rosa lived and they went into an ice cream parlor on the corner.

Simplicio finished a chocolate soda before he spoke again. "I've had a lot of disappointments with women in this country but I don't let that worry me. The trouble is, I'm young. And you know how it is, a man's never satisfied with one woman. I'd have twenty if I could. Every woman is different and variety is the spice of life, right? But after all, I have my wife and she's for keeps. The others come and go. If I get sick or down on my luck, Flora is the one who's going to stand by me. Besides, Nanda's very fond of Flora. If she ever found out I don't treat Flora right, I don't know what would happen."

As they got up to leave, Rosa said, "Wouldn't you like to take home some ice cream, Simplicio? Chocolate?"

"Yes, Flora would like that. Thanks," Simplicio answered. "You know, Rosa, I run around a lot but I'd never leave Flora. I'm like a bird, I peck here and there but I always go back to my nest."

Simplicio shook Rosa's hand as they said good night. He accepted the paper bag containing the box of ice cream and walked off toward home swinging it in his hand.

Two Months Later

On a hot Friday in July, Rosa arrived at Simplicio and Flora's apartment at about ten o'clock at night and knocked on the door.

"*Who is it?*" Flora called in English.

When Rosa identified herself, Gabi opened the door. The boy was dressed only in a pair of white undershorts and rubber sandals.

"*Muchacha,* you come so late at night," Flora said. "Don't you know that the colored people are all stirred up around here? The streets aren't safe."

Flora was sitting in the big bed propped up with pillows. She was wearing an orange nightgown and her hair was neatly gathered in a pony tail. Her face was powdered but she wore no other make-up. She looked relaxed and cheerful.

"I've been listening to Don Ameche on television," she said. "I don't know what I'd do without television. I thought I'd go crazy when our other set burned up." Flora's favorite programs were *The Ed Sullivan Show, Candid Camera, Combat!* and a monthly movie in Spanish.

At the dinette table Gabi was drawing with crayons on a brown paper bag. Flora told Rosa to sit down beside her on the bed. Rosa noticed something new on the wall opposite the door, a pair of ceramic African heads. "I see you have some new decorations," she said.

"Oh yes, my Indian heads," Flora replied enthusiastically. "Simplicio bought them for two dollars at Smith's. I think they're too black, but *Rey* claims that black things in a house bring good luck. Well, here I am, waiting for him as usual. He's gone to the boxing matches."

The household must be a peaceful one right now, Rosa thought, for Flora never called her husband *Rey* (King) when she was angry with him.

"He'd better not come home drunk this time. If he does I won't let him in," Flora said. "I'm keeping this broomstick handy. Last Friday he came home from work, got himself dressed up the way he does every Friday, and went off. He left me here all by myself because Gabi was over at Soledad's house. You know what time he finally got home? Six in the morning. I had all my things packed, ready to leave. When he saw all the bundles, he burst out crying like a child. 'This time I'm really going,' I screamed at him. I was furious. I wasn't going to back out either, not for all the angels of Bethlehem, but the truth is, I didn't know where to go.

"Simplicio tried to talk to me and hug me but I just yelled, 'Go back to your other woman,' and I spoke to him *de usted*. That upset him more than anything. So do you know what he did? He said, 'All right, if you don't love me, look what I'm going to do.' And zing! he gave himself a cut on the arm with a *Gem*. I paid no attention and zing! he cut himself again. It made me even angrier to see his arms bleeding. I tell you, I could have killed that man!"

"But you didn't leave," Rosa said.

"Well, no, I didn't. Really, I got so angry that we just had to make up. That's when he promised not to take a drink for three months. But this business of cutting himself really upsets me. He's gotten so he'll do it for any little thing. That's why he has all those cuts on his arms. Just the same, he's a good man. He's not like Soledad's Benedicto, who's off sailing most of the time and drunk whenever he's ashore. I'm telling you, that one's just asking for the horns."

Flora offered a cigarette to Rosa and lit one for herself.

Gabi looked up from his drawing and said to Rosa, "Look at the new couch they bought me. It's really a good one."

"It really is," Flora said. "Last Tuesday night, about ten o'clock, somebody knocked on the door. And can you believe it? It was Elfredo with that couch. It's in very good condition and he sold it to us for five dollars on credit. We pay next week. The other one was falling apart. It was one my brother gave me because he was tired of it. Well, we've talked a lot and eaten nothing. Let's go make some coffee."

She sat down at the table with Rosa and Gabi while the coffee was percolating. "Say, I know how to wash dishes," Gabi said proudly. "Don't I wash the dishes now, Aunt Flora?"

"Of course you do. And you should learn to do everything."

"Sure, because I'll have to work," Gabi said matter-of-factly. He bent over his drawing again.

Flora and Rosa drank the coffee and then they lay down on the big bed for a while. Flora went on talking.

"I didn't go to work today because I was all worn out. I told Simplicio and he said 'Bendito, don't go then. You know I don't like to have my wife working. You do it because you want to.' But, Rosa, what I earn is for my family. I send money to my father, then there's my brother, and now one of my sisters wants to come up here. They all think I'm a millionaire. Listen, I sent my sister her fare and ten dollars and now she's asking for more. She has to buy a suitcase, she says, and she spent the ten dollars on a pair of shoes. I don't buy ten-dollar shoes for myself. The trouble with them is that they've never had to split their hides working, like I did. Young people have it soft nowadays.

"Well, speaking of working, did you know I joined the union?" Flora asked. "They practically forced me to. They started bothering me and making trouble until I had to join. But it's a good thing. They say that if you lose your job they'll find you another. They take out three dollars from my pay check, so they must do something worthwhile. They sent me a little book but it can lie there until the world ends because it's in English. I'll ask Rey to try and see if he can understand any of it. Well, let's go to bed. If we go on talking we'll be up all night, and I don't want Rey to think I'm waiting up for him."

She went to the bureau and took out a pink nightgown for Rosa. She got into the bed and Rosa lay down with Gabi on the couch. At three o'clock in the morning Rosa was awakened by the sound of the door opening. Simplicio came in and turned on the lamp. He was dressed in black pants, a checked jacket and black shoes. With a casual "Hello" he handed Flora a paper bag.

"Thank God you didn't get drunk," Flora said, smiling, "because, look, I had a stick ready for you. Oh, how nice, you brought me fried tripe. I love cuchifritos."

She got up for some plates and divided the food between Rosa, Simplicio and herself. Gabi had not awakened.

"Remember how good the fried tripe was that doña Minerva used to make?" Simplicio said. "I used to steal lots of it from her. She'd be furious but then she'd give me some more, to kill my hunger, she said."

"She's such a good woman, may God give her health!" Flora said. "She cured me of hunger often enough too."

"I bought this at the Spanish store. The man there told me he's going to have it every *weekend*."

"*Ay,* what I'd like to eat is some of Nanda's papaya in syrup," Flora said.

"*Ave María,* the fight was swell. José González lost by a knockout. People were betting like crazy, the dollars were flying. One man lost more than fifty dollars. If I'd had any money I'd have bet too."

"That's you all over, having to get into everything. Lucky I have a little money of my own."

"Didn't you see the fight on TV? I was right there in the middle."

"No, I don't like boxing," Flora answered. "What I like is wrestling."

"I don't like wrestling because it's all a fake," Simplicio said.

"I know it is, but I like it anyway. Boxing is worse because those men end up all bloody. Remember the time you took me to a match? We spent a lot of good dollars that day. Do you know, Rosa, this damn fool bought two lower seats and they cost three-fifty apiece."

"And you really can see better from the top seats," Simplicio said.

"Of course. You just wanted to act like a big-shot white. *Rey,* you should hear Gabi tell about the time Felícita left him in Lucelia's house. He says Lucelia beat him all the time."

"That old woman is all right," Simplicio said. "Her only fault is that she falls for *teenagers.* When I left she cried and cried. Once she got very sick, and Nanda wrote me that she kept calling my name and asking me for a doll. I bought one and sent it to her. It cost three dollars. And would you believe it, that woman got well as soon as she received it. Nanda says she still keeps it on her bed. Poor old lady, she only has one son and he's on dope. He doesn't even write to her."

"And what about your mother's letter?" Flora asked. "How much attention have you paid to it? Damn it, you know you hardly even read it."

"I know what she wrote," Simplicio answered. "She isn't coming to New York because she made up with her little husband. But I'm not mad at her. Let's see if we can have a bigger apartment by the time she does come. Listen, Gina's husband told me that some people are selling a seventy-five-dollar-a-month apartment. And they want to sell all the furniture cheap because the man lost his job and is going home to Puerto Rico."

"If only we had the money! But there's the deposit to pay and then light and gas. Forget it. And if we ever go back to Puerto Rico we'd practically have to give everything away. I want to go back someday unless you want us to stay here until we die of cold. We didn't come up here to stay. That's why I don't buy new saucepans or anything."

"What else did Nanda say?" Simplicio asked.

"Nothing much. Just that your sister Felícita is having herself a time with an American engineer and that she's left her children with *doña* Lucelia. What a mother! *Ave María!* I don't know why God gives children to women like that."

"She always did care more for Americans than for any of us. That's because she didn't grow up with us," Simplicio said thoughtfully. "And you know how our stepmother Hortensia is, so snooty she'd like to shit from higher up than her ass-hole. That's all Felícita learned from her, to be stuck up. She thinks she's better than the rest of us, maybe because her skin's lighter."

"But you don't know the latest," Flora said. "Marcelo is having an affair with a queer."

"What? I don't believe it! That's just malicious gossip. I know that boy. He's too much of a man to do anything like that, unless he's changed. And I was thinking of sending for him and getting him settled here. But if that's the way things are, he'd better not come. New York would be his ruin, with all the damn queers here. Flora, hand me my *coat.*"

Simplicio's coat was hanging on the back of the chair he was sitting in. Flora got up from the bed, walked two steps to the chair and gave him the coat. He fumbled in the pockets and pulled out a lipstick which he handed to her.

"Oh, peach color!" Flora said with pleasure. "Just the shade I like. I tell you, Rosa, this *negro* of mine is worth his weight in gold. But now let's go to bed. It's late."

"Tomorrow we're going to Coney Island," Simplicio said. "We haven't been to the beach or anywhere else this summer. And before we know it, that man-killer winter will be here. Say, speaking of the man-killer, we have to get a *coat* for Gabi. And I need a new one too."

"*Muchacho,* all your *coat* needs is to be dry-cleaned. It will come out like new."

"I'll put Gabi in with us," Simplicio said and carried the sleeping child over to the big bed.

Flora went to the kitchen and came back with a pail which she placed beside the bed. "This is to pee in."

Simplicio undressed in the kitchen; he kept his shorts on. Flora put out the light. For a few minutes there was silence, then Flora said, "Cross yourself. Put yourself in God's keeping. Don't be such an atheist."

It was ten o'clock before anyone awoke again. First Simplicio brought Flora her usual glass of water and cup of black coffee. A half-hour later she got up and went to the bathroom in the hall. She came back dressed in a peach-colored skirt, a flowered overblouse and low-heeled black shoes.

Simplicio, who had gone back to bed, asked Gabi to bring him some comic books. While he was reading Flora made breakfast; she set out orange juice, fried eggs, bread, and coffee for Rosa and Gabi. "Eat everything," she said, pouring the coffee. "You must learn the American way. They fill up on breakfast and don't eat lunch." She sat down at the table but ate little herself. "When could we ever have had a breakfast like this in Puerto Rico? *Bendito,* down there sometimes we couldn't even afford to buy the coffee."

When they had finished eating, Flora said to Simplicio, *"Rey,* shall I make your breakfast now? What would you like to eat, eh, *negro?"*

"Soft-boiled eggs, bread and juice, but not just yet. Listen to the dream I had last night. I had run away from home and I was lying on top of the house looking down at Nanda through a hole in the roof. She was searching for me but I didn't worry about it or anything. Then suddenly, instead of Nanda, I saw Erasmo, my stepfather, with an electric light cord doubled up twice in his hand. I screamed, 'No, no! I'd rather throw myself into the sea.' But when I tried to jump I woke up."

"I heard you scream," Flora said. "But don't think of that. I'm going to get your breakfast now."

Simplicio asked Gabi to bring his black pants. He put them on under the sheet. He pulled on a pair of black socks and went out to the bathroom.

"Aren't you cute, walking around in your stocking feet," Flora said when he returned. "It's easy to see you don't have to wash the socks around here."

Simplicio finished breakfast. While Flora was washing the dishes, he chose some records from his large collection; he had nearly a hundred records. He put one on and turned up the sound. Flora looked annoyed. She preferred the records she had bought—slow, quiet ones, such as *"Ave María," "Muñequita linda," "Última lágrima,"* and songs in English by Ray Charles and Ricky Nelson.

Simplicio went out to the bathroom carrying a single-edge Gem blade and a cake of Palmolive soap in his hand. He often shaved with only the blade, holding it between his fingers. Gabi began to draw pictures while Flora mopped the floor. When Simplicio came back from the bathroom, he put on a gray shirt and a pair of sandals. "Now let's go shopping," he said.

"See, you can wear those sandals with those clothes," Flora said. "They go well with sports clothes. He was angry with me yesterday, Rosa, because I wouldn't let him go out in them when he was all dressed up."

Flora gave Gabi a red striped shirt and from the closet she took two narrow-brimmed black felt hats. "Here, put these on," she said to Gabi and to Simplicio.

Just as they were about to leave, a middle-aged woman came to the door. Her olive-colored face was heavily made up with rouge, lipstick and eyebrow pencil, the low neckline of her dress revealed the curve and division of her breasts. She wore red high-heeled shoes and her hair was gathered into an incongruously youthful pony tail.

"What number came out?" Flora asked.

"Three sixty-six."

"Listen, I'm going to have to stop buying numbers from you, because I never win anything," Flora said. "You just come and ask for money."

"Do you expect to win so soon? Have patience, child. There are people who have been playing for years and never hit it. And here you, who began the day before yesterday, so to speak, are impatient already? Play a few cents on Múcura. Since she's being run at night, it might bring you luck."

Flora took a dollar and fifty cents from her purse and handed it to the woman.

"Well, I'm going," the numbers seller said. "I have to collect at a lot of places yet. Say, do you know that detectives are watching my boss, El Gordo? Things have really gotten hot. But one must take risks, right?"

They went downstairs together. The woman went on her way and Simplicio's family strolled toward the market. About a block from the house they met a slender, fair-skinned man, dressed in a checked shirt and gray trousers, and wearing glasses.

"Hello, friends, happy are the eyes that see you!" he said in greeting.

"Hello. How's your wife?" Simplicio asked courteously.

"She's well. Always quarreling with me because I drink a few beers now and then. As if she thought beer was made for washing horses! I'd better be going because she must be furious already."

"His wife is a Pentecostal," Simplicio explained to Rosa when the man was out of earshot. "That woman has more children! Every time I see her she's pregnant. Jehovah must help her take care of those kids."

"Simplicio, don't say such things," Flora said.

"Yes, because it's against her religion to use anything, you know. Anyway, not as long as *Welfare* supports the kids. It's *el Welfare* that helps, not Jehovah."

"The other day she came over and she almost made me dizzy talking about Jehovah. She talked and talked all the time I was cooking."

"Her husband is tired of it already. He just kids her about it now. He tells her that once when he went to church and the power descended on the people, they all started to jump up and down, and the minister just stood there looking at the women's *panties* when their skirts flew up."

Simplicio stopped in front of a shoe store. "Look, they sell sneakers here. You're going to buy Gabi some, aren't you? But the trouble is, I don't know how to ask for them in English."

They went into the store. Simplicio pointed first to the child and then to the sneakers. A woman clerk fitted Gabi with a pair. "Ask her how much they cost," Flora said.

"How much is it?" Simplicio asked in English.

"Two dollars and five cents."

"You see, Gabi, how good Flora is to you?" Simplicio said to the boy as they left the store. "I'll bet your *mamá* never treated you like this. Oh, Flora, buy me two little comic books, eh? I forgot to bring along some I had to exchange."

"All right, but don't keep on asking for things. You must think we're rich."

They came to a drugstore. This time Flora wanted something. *"Rey,* go and buy a roll of six-twenty film so I can take Gabi's picture. Nanda asked me to send her one." Simplicio went up to the counter while Flora looked at a display of hair sprays.

"I didn't know how to ask for it in English so I just said *'Photos,'"* Simplicio said, joining her. "They're going to bring me the film, I think." He saw a counter loaded with toys, and going over to it, he touched a small boat. He didn't need to say he wanted it badly; that was evident. *"Rey,* don't set your heart on that," Flora said sharply. "Remember we're short of money and we haven't paid the rent yet."

"Oh, I wasn't going to buy anything," Simplicio said hastily. "Here's the film. Pay for it, Flora. It's sixty-seven cents."

The next stop was a fruit store where Spanish was spoken. Flora asked for fifteen cents' worth of *ajis* and *recao largo,* herbs used in Puerto Rico for seasoning. An undernourished-looking boy of about sixteen doled out a little of each in a paper bag.

"Ave María! You people sure make a big profit up here," Flora said. "In Puerto Rico this stuff grows wild."

"The boss is the one who makes the profit," the boy answered. "I'm just a half-starved flea in this place."

"I know. But look at that! Fifty-nine cents for an avocado. Oh, well, what can one do. Give me one. After a while nobody will be able to eat in New York. Food is gold in this country. Give me two plantains. I won't even ask how much they cost because they never go for less than a quarter."

"Look, *Rey,* let's do all our shopping at the A and P. It's cheaper," Flora said as they went out.

"No. We'll shop at the Spanish store. The A and P is too far and I don't want to carry the stuff all the way home."

They passed a little park where some boys were playing softball. *"Ay,* how I wish I could play!" Simplicio said. "But I don't know those boys. They look like they're rich. In La Esmeralda we never saw a Spaulding ball, but the paper balls are just as good. Our bats were sticks that the sea washed up. We really played a lot of tricks there. If anyone tried anything crooked, we ducked him head first into the sea."

They came to the Spanish grocery store. The clerk was a short, fat white man who received them with a great display of courtesy.

"Can one buy on credit here?" Simplicio asked.

"The store is yours," the proprietor answered.

"Thank you, it was just a joke. We'll pay."

"If you need anything, food, money, it's no problem, believe me," the man said.

Simplicio and Flora picked out the things they needed. "Put six small beers in the bag," Simplicio said.

"No!" Flora spoke forcefully. "Don't sell beer to my husband. And don't go selling it to him on credit later on, you hear?"

"*Ay,* Flora, just two. Please, please say yes."

"All right, two beers."

"Here you have them, two beers to go and one on the house," the proprietor said with an ingratiating smile. "And how about you ladies? Won't you have a beer?"

"No, we don't drink beer and especially not away from home," Flora said.

"Well, how about a soft drink then?"

"Thanks, that would be all right, I think."

The man opened two bottles of Pepsi-Cola for Rosa and Flora. He said to Gabi, "You may take an ice cream out of the box."

When they had finished their drinks, the man bade them an effusive good-bye. Outside, Flora said, "He's not Puerto Rican. I think he's a Cuban, but at least he's a Latin and he speaks like we do. It's true he cheats us because look what our seventeen-twenty went for, but anyway, he pays you some attention. He's not like that *cabrón* of a Jew we bought from for almost a year. We spent seventeen to twenty dollars in his store every week, and then one day Simplicio needed ten dollars and asked him for a loan. Would you believe it? He refused. He said he'd sell us food on credit but he couldn't let us have any money. That was more than enough for us. We haven't gone back there since. Think of it! One gives those people a living and they won't lift a finger to help you out when you need it. Of course it had to be a Jew. Those people would shit on the very mother that bore them if there was any money in it. They won't even give their piss to the ground. Listen, my brother's *boss* was a Jew. Well, the day the *boss*'s mother died, everybody expected he'd give them the day off. But he opened the factory just like every other day. He couldn't afford to lose time, he said.

"Oh, *Rey,*" Flora added, "I forgot to tell you that the sister of your adored cousin Chango took off with another man. She left that husband she had."

"That's nothing, she's already had seven," Simplicio said. "Well, now she has eight. She can go screw herself for all I care. Her mother beat Nanda plenty. Nanda can talk for hours about the punishments she got from her Aunt Sofía and still not tell the half of it. Well, look, are we going to Coney Island or not? If we are, we better hurry and get ready."

At home, Simplicio made some sandwiches and Flora packed them together with the Pepsi-Colas into an insulated metal container. Gabi and Simplicio put on their swimming trunks under their pants and announced they were ready to go.

At the subway station on the way to Coney Island, Simplicio asked his wife for a quarter and bought a Dagwood and Blondie comic book and the New York *Post*. He turned the newspaper to the sports section. "Look, here's last night's fight. See what they did to Pagán!" Inside the station Flora took tokens out of her purse and gave them to Simplicio. He dropped one for each of them into the turnstile; he was the last to go through.

"Flora, give me a dime. I have to go to the toilet," he said.

"*Ave María!* In this country you even have to pay for that!" Flora exclaimed, taking a dime out of her purse.

When the train pulled into the station they entered an almost empty car. Simplicio and Gabi took a seat near the front, and Simplicio at once began reading his comic. Flora and Rosa sat down near the door.

"Simplicio's a good man, you know," Flora said to Rosa. "The best thing about him is that he gets along so well with my family. He never interferes. Sometimes I divide my whole pay check between my *papá* and my *mamá* and he doesn't even ask me what I did with the money. Any other man would insist I give part of my money for expenses. But I'm good to his family too. Come on, let's go sit beside *Rey*. I want to tell him something."

She interrupted Simplicio's reading. "Listen, *Rey*, we haven't been back to Delancey Street to make any more payments on the radio we have there. If we keep on this way, we'll lose it."

"Then we lose it. There's nothing we can do about it," Simplicio said. "You should have seen the record player they wanted to sell me yesterday for fifty dollars. It was worth at least three hundred dollars."

"It must be stolen goods."

"No, *hombre,* that's not it. This was a friend of mine who's set his heart on going back to Puerto Rico. He's selling everything so cheap, it's a giveaway. He's afraid of the cold weather coming."

"I don't know where the money goes to in this country," Flora said. "The best thing would be to go back to Puerto Rico. But I'm afraid of those friends Simplicio had in La Esmeralda. Do you know they almost got him sent to reform school? And then it's hard to find work there for a man! I wouldn't have much trouble getting a job, though, because I've been working there since I was born. I stick it out up here for Simplicio's sake."

"*Ay,* Flora, don't keep talking like that. I did those things when I was young but now I'm different."

When they arrived at Coney Island it was after two o'clock, and they found that the beach was very crowded. As they walked along, Simplicio said to Rosa, "You'll see a show and a half here! In Puerto Rico when a couple wants to put the fire in the can, they go to a special place on the beach and do whatever they please. Here they do it in front of everybody." As they spoke they passed a couple lying on the sand and pressing hard against each other. A little farther on another couple was lying under a sheet.

"Look at that shamelessness, damn them!" Flora said. "There's a time and a place for everything. Why can't they go somewhere else?"

Picking their way past other embracing couples, they found an empty space on the sand near the water. Flora spread a blanket and they sat down. Flora and Rosa took off their shoes, Simplicio and Gabi stripped down to their swim suits. Flora handed out the sandwiches and Pepsi-Colas.

After they had eaten, Simplicio and Gabi went into the water. Flora pointed to a very fat, short Negro woman with two children. *"Ave María!* What ugly little monkeys the Negroes are here. And how coarse! Puerto Rican Negroes are more refined, don't you think? These people are dirtier than the dirtiest person in Puerto Rico. I don't like to put on airs, but I wouldn't live where they live. They live like animals and don't give a damn. The truth is, they don't like us either. But if a saint doesn't like you, don't pray to him, that's all."

Simplicio and Gabi came up out of the water, both of them shivering. *"Ay,* that freezing cold water cuts into your flesh," Simplicio said. "And it's dirty besides. It's cleaner farther out, but who wants to go out there in this cold? *Ay,* I really could enjoy myself on Luquillo Beach with the warm water and the palms all around! *Let's go.* Let's walk around a little and see this damn Coney Island that I know by heart already." He began to dry himself. Flora handed a towel to Gabi.

"Where else can we go?" she asked. "Everything else is too expensive. Should we just shut ourselves in the house?"

"Damn it, some day my number will win and I'll have money, you'll see!" Simplicio said.

They strolled toward the amusement park. "Give me just a half dollar so I can go on the parachute," Simplicio begged.

"I knew it," Flora said grimly.

"All right, all right. But let's put Gabi in that Alice in Wonderland thing. It only costs a quarter. I'll go with him."

Flora relented and gave him the money. When Simplicio and Gabi came out of the building they were laughing. "I saw the fairy!" Gabi said. He was flushed and excited. "She had on a long dress and she was beautiful. When I get home I'm going to draw her. And there was a giant too. *Ave María,* he was so big you could have made three men out of him."

"It really wasn't worth it," Simplicio said.

"I told you so," Flora answered coldly. "If you want to waste your money, just come here and take in all these fool things."

"Let's go to the dock and take pictures," Simplicio said. The pier was crowded with people, many of them were fishing. A white sea gull flew very low and Simplicio snapped a picture. "If it turns out pretty, we'll put it in the living room," he said. He hunted among the fishermen until he found a small fish that had been discarded. Then he found a piece of string and put it through the gills. "Here, hold this," he said to Gabi. "I'm going to take your picture to send to Nanda." Gabi posed for two pictures.

"Now you, beautiful," Simplicio said to Flora. He took a photograph of Flora, and then Rosa took one of Simplicio and Flora together, their arms around each other.

"Now you take one of me by myself," Simplicio said to Flora.

"All right, but put your pants on. Or do you mean to go around in your swim trunks all afternoon?"

Simplicio put his pants on over his trunks. Flora took two pictures of him, one standing and one sitting. "All right, the last two are for Gabi," she said. "Put your pants on too, Gabi." The boy pulled his pants out of the shopping bag and put them on. "*Ay,* I forgot his hat," Flora said after she had taken the first picture. She placed it on his head and finished the roll of film.

They strolled along the pier, looking down at the bathers. Flora pointed out a dark-complexioned, full-bodied woman who was wearing a bikini. "Look at that *hispana,*" she said. "She's practically naked. I don't show my skin and bones to everybody, only to my husband. If she had a pretty figure it wouldn't be so bad, but look how ugly she is. Well, she would have to be a *hispana* to do such a thing."

"Oh, don't be such an old woman," Simplicio said. "I keep telling you to wear *shorts* but you never will."

They came to a roulette wheel and Simplicio looked at it longingly, but apparently he didn't dare ask Flora for money to play. Farther on there was a booth where for five cents a player bought five throws at a dummy; if he could hit the dummy's eye he won a prize. Simplicio asked Flora for a nickel and won on his second ball. His prize was a five-cent pocket comb. Still farther on, people were shooting arrows at a bull's eye about twenty feet away. Without even a glance at Flora, Simplicio went to the stand where the bows and arrows were being rented. "Flora, give me a quarter," he said. With no objection this time, Flora put a quarter in his hand, and Simplicio looked triumphant. After this game they all turned toward the subway. An ice cream wagon came up beside them. "I want some ice cream," Gabi said. Flora bought ice cream cones for everyone.

Simplicio paused before a photographer's booth to look at the display. "Ah, I take better pictures than those," he said. He put his arm around Flora. "We're going to the movies tonight, aren't we, Flora?"

"But what will we do for money?" Flora burst out. "We have to pay the insurance man today."

"Oh, let's drop that life insurance."

"And if something happens to us in this country, what will we do then? How will they get us back to Puerto Rico?"

"Forget it, *muchacha*. Nobody's going to die yet."

"I hope not, but who can tell? Better be safe than sorry."

"All right then," Simplicio said, laughing. "Better be safe than sorry, but if you don't buy me some of those little stuffed crabs there, I'll die of starvation." Flora laughed too, but she pulled him away from the delicatessen window.

Finally they reached the subway station. Again Flora gave Simplicio tokens for the ride. Since they were in the first car, Gabi went to the front window to look ahead as they passed through the tunnel. Simplicio sat by himself to read but he soon fell asleep.

"Poor boy, he likes to amuse himself," Flora said to Rosa, "because he's tied to that machine all week. You know, he isn't in *delivery* any more."

Flora was quiet during most of the long ride home. When they were nearing their destination she went over to Simplicio, shaking him gently, "Wake up, Simplicio. The next stop is ours." He woke with a start and ran a comb through his hair. Flora called Gabi and they left the train.

"Let's go to Soledad's house," Flora said.

"No, I'm going home to cook something," Simplicio answered. "You all go. But tell Soledad I want some comic books. Don't forget."

Just then someone threw an egg from an upper window and it struck Simplicio on the leg. He became furious immediately. "Who's the *maricón* that threw that egg?" he shouted. "I'll shit on his mother's balls! Come down here right away. You're not a man if you don't."

"*Rey*, stop it," Flora said. "Come on home and take off your pants. I'll sponge them off and press them and you can put them on right away, all nice and clean."

Simplicio stood waiting, but when no one appeared he walked off toward home. Flora, Gabi and Rosa went to Soledad's house. Sarita, one of Soledad's little girls, opened the door. Another child was taking a bath. Soledad came out of the bathroom. She was wearing a red blouse, a skirt with big checks, and sandals. Her hair was combed and parted on one side.

"We were just going over to call on you people," she said. "We'd lost track of you, it's been so long since you were here. Where have you been?"

"Well, *muchacha*, we went to Coney Island," Flora said.

"Why didn't you come by to get me?"

"Oh, we thought you were off enjoying yourself somewhere else."

"Oh, you're always thinking! I've spent the whole day cleaning this place. It was so filthy, I was ashamed. You see, I took a job all of a sudden, without having arranged things first. These kids' dirty clothes were piled up shoulder-high."

"What kind of a job?"

"It's a purse factory and it's wonderful. It's not the kind of junk we used to make. They're really good suède purses. They sell for twenty-five dollars apiece. It's a small factory and the girls made friends with me right away. They told me to ask the *boss* the very first day how much he was going to pay me. 'Don't work for less than sixty a week,' they said. So in the afternoon I said to the *boss,* 'I can't work for less than sixty.' And would you believe it? He said '*O.K.*' " Soledad laughed and hugged Flora.

"But you haven't eaten," Soledad said. "Here, have some of this soup. I made it from some fish my friend Elfredo brought me, good fish, the red kind, only he didn't bring me enough. Fish has lots of vitamin A, you know. It strengthens your brain and it makes you feel like screwing."

Flora said, "Oh, isn't screwing wonderful? Not at first, but after a while you'd like to keep it up all day long. Oh my, if Simplicio caught me talking like this!"

"Do you know what they used to call Simplico when he was little? 'Three for two' because his prick was so big. He had the biggest one in La Esmeralda. But Beni's is still bigger. *Ay,* this kind of talk makes me hot."

After they had eaten Soledad went into her bedroom and flung herself face down on the bed. She put a pillow between her legs and began to push against it, rhythmically.

"Hey, stop that!" said Flora, who had followed her. "What kind of thing is that to show to the children."

Soledad sat up. "Oh, it felt so good," she said. She sat there for a moment, looking around her smiling vacantly. Then she said abruptly, "Let's go into the parlor. I want to show you the underwear I'm selling."

They went into the living room. There, lying on a pillow on the sofa, five-year-old Sarita was making the same movements her mother had made in the bedroom. Soledad ran over to her and slapped her. "Look, if you want a man, I'll get one for you right now," she said harshly. "Just tell me if you want one with a long thing or a short one." The child began to cry and ran out of the room. Her mother let her go without saying anything more.

Rosalía looked in through the front window. Soledad smiled at her and said, "My love, where have you been hiding yourself? I haven't seen you all day."

"I've been in my house. Today I haven't lent my radiance to this blind old world. No, that's not true. I went to the cemetery to put some flowers on my husband's grave."

"*Muchacha,* why don't you use that money to buy meat for yourself? The dead don't need flowers. Look, I adore my husband Tavio who died. But he's there and I'm here."

"I'm willing to cut my throat if you weren't talking dirty here a moment ago," Rosalía said.

"And you were dying to be here so you could join in. Well, come on in so you can learn."

"As if those things could be taught? One learns that without teaching."

"Look, I'm selling these *panties*. Come in and see them."

"What *size* are they?"

"Your size. That's the only size I carry."

"Mine have to be *large*. Oh no, these are *medium*. Do you think I can't tell? Child, when you were just arriving, I was already coming back. I've been here in the Americas for forty-three years."

"And you're still as much of a Puerto Rican sweet-potato-eater as I am," Soledad said, laughing. "You can go to hell! Always talking about the Americas, the Americas. But come in and sit down, *chica*. We're talking like two kids who fell in love too young."

"No, I'm going to the park to cool off. I'll come back later."

When Rosalía had gone, Soledad noticed Gabi, who had come into the living room and was listening to the conversation. She said, "And how is my little lover Gabi behaving?"

"Don't say those things," Gabi said. "I'm not your lover. That's why I don't like to come to this house."

"Oh, is that so? Well, if you don't like it, don't come here. Go to hell then."

"You can go to hell yourself," Gabriel retorted.

"Gabi, have some respect for your aunt," Flora said. "I'm going to tell Simplicio on you. Soledad, darling, I have to go. Simplicio is all by himself at home, unless he's gone out to drink. Gabi, we're leaving now."

"Why don't you leave Gabi here with me? Maybe tomorrow I'll go to the beach too."

"Do you want to stay, Gabi?" Flora asked.

"Sure, as long as it's to go to the beach."

"You can stay then," Flora said, taking a nickel out of her purse and handing it to him.

Simplicio was standing in the doorway of their building, drinking beer. "Where's Gabi?" he demanded as soon as he saw them. "You left him there, didn't you? Who said you could?"

"Well, son, Soledad is going to the beach tomorrow and Gabi wanted to stay there so he could go with her. She'll bring him back tomorrow."

"Where are the comics? I'll bet you forgot all about them."

"Oh, *Rey*, I did forget." Flora was contrite. "If you hadn't mentioned it now, I wouldn't have remembered at all. Well, I've also forgotten what my first baby shirt looked like."

"You're always forgetting things I ask for," Simplicio said crossly. "And I'm starving."

"That's your fault for not coming with us to Soledad's house. Rosa and I are full. I thought you would cook something for yourself. But never mind, I'll fry you a beefsteak right now."

Flora and Rosa hurried upstairs. Flora dropped her purse on the bed and went quickly to the kitchen. "Let me fry this meat quick before Simplicio decides to go somewhere else," she said.

Rosa said she had to leave and Flora went with her to the door. "Do you see how nice Simplicio is?" Flora said, smiling. "He waited for me to come home. Simplicio's a good man and he loves me very much. It's the women who are bad and who tempt him. And I love him too. May the Virgin watch over him wherever he goes!"

Simplicio

I'm Proud to Be Poor

WELL, HERE I AM in New York and I'm doing fine. I earn sixty-five dollars a week in a *finishing* factory where they do all sorts of work—buttons, belts, everything except *coats*. I do many kinds of jobs. I sew with machines, make ladies' *scarfs,* big silk buttons, well, everything. I work very hard there, it's true, but I do it because they are considerate of me.

At first my job was *el delivery,* walking all over everywhere with a big suitcase, eight hours a day, for forty-five dollars a week. Soledad showed me how to take *el subway* to Manhattan where the factory is, and after that they just turned me loose. It's lucky that the streets in New York are numbered and easy to find. So I learned as I walked around, making my deliveries. I often got lost. But when I did, I just wandered around until I found my way back. It took me about a month to learn to go places on *el subway.* I got lost there, too, but that was plain stupidity. In my hurry I often caught the wrong train. But early rising has never hastened the dawn.

That's all I did when I started working there, *el delivery.* But I didn't mind because I know that if you don't have schooling you go down instead of up when you first come here. That's what many Puerto Ricans won't do and that's why they give themselves up to a life of vice. Because you feel lower than other people when you have to take a job as a delivery boy. And that might make you turn to stealing or to taking drugs, it might lead you to quit your job and become a tramp. And then you'd be a failure for sure. Because here in New York if you don't work, you don't eat. This isn't Puerto Rico, where if the neighbor sits down to a meal he'll send a plate of food over to you. Here people, even the Puerto Ricans, throw out food rather than give it away. That's because people change when they come here, on account of always having to think about working. That makes you use your mind, think of tomorrow, you know. If I have twenty dollars to last me all week, I can't go out and spend ten now. Because I wouldn't be spending only today's money but also tomorrow's and the next day's. And when the money's gone, there's nobody you can turn to for more. So we become used to that and lose our own customs little by little.

My *bosso* is a Jew, like most factory owners in New York. Those people expect you to work hard. But if you do a good job they're swell, because after a time they'll do any favor you ask them for. They never say no to you. Whenever I tell my *boss,* "I need this," he gives it to me. Right now, they often give me buttons for my wife and sister to cover. The pay is a nickel per button. Last week they covered fourteen hundred buttons. That's about eighty dollars, I think. My *boss* has even told me, of his own free will, that if I get myself a bigger apartment he'll help me. I want to do it but Flora doesn't. And after all, why should I pay more than the seventeen dollars a week I'm paying now for a place for Flora, Gabi and me? But that just shows you how good the *boss* is to me. He trusts me, too. He leaves me the keys and I am the one who closes the factory and opens it in the morning.

I've never been absent once in the year I've worked there. And I've never been late, either, in spite of the cold and the distance. This isn't Puerto Rico, where every place is near; it takes me at least half an hour to get from my home to the factory. I always get there an hour ahead of time. That way I can read *El Imparcial* and chat with my friends awhile before starting work. At seven forty-five I start working, and I'm happy to do so. Sweeping the place isn't part of my job but I like to have everything clean before I start. After that, I change my shirt and settle down to sew *scarfs* on the sewing machine. I stick to that until *el bosso* sends me out to deliver packages.

The only thing I don't like about my job is the way *el bosso*'s father comes around to hurry us. But I know him well enough to speak frankly. So I say to him, in English, *"I'm not coming to work to kill myself."* El bosso doesn't say a word. He's the old man's son but they're Jews and have their own customs. It doesn't seem strange to them that a son should order his own father around. And fathers treat their children like strangers.

They also have the custom of saving money. They won't eat a lollipop so as not to waste the stick! And they spit on coins for good luck so they'll get more money. For them, work is the thing. They kill themselves working, week in and week out. When they go out, they go alone. They never make love to women or anything like that.

For that reason, most of them are rich and able to send their children to school to get a good education. When the kids graduate and grow up, their father says to them, "We have such and such an amount of money. This is my share and this is yours, to work with or enjoy now, as you wish. Only remember, if you go broke you'll have to take a job with me like any other employee." It's as if they weren't very close to each other as a family. As if they don't feel they have a duty to help a relative who's badly off. That's the way they are; I don't know why. Maybe it's because they suffered so much because Hitler didn't like them. Hitler killed twenty million Jews, including newborn babies, for having killed God. Hitler was bad. He took no pity on anybody.

Look here, they say a lot of things about the Jews. That they killed God and spat on him and nailed him on the cross. But that's not their fault. Because the ones who killed God all died ages ago. There's not a single one of them left. All that's over and done with and it isn't important now.

They say that God died for us. Everywhere you go they tell you that. But how could he have died for us when we're Puerto Ricans and Christ never went to Puerto Rico? God didn't die in Puerto Rico, so it couldn't have been for us.

It isn't true that the Jews are bad. The trouble is that they have been labeled by history. But they are really good. Of course it's true they don't believe in God but they do have a religion. They believe in Moses, who saved them from a land where they were held as slaves. And they have churches of their own where they pray and sing. They don't have saints but they have everything else. And those people have been good to me. They have given me the chance to earn a lot of money. The only reason I don't earn even more is because I don't want to. I don't like to work *overtime*. Sometimes *el bosso* asks me to go to work Saturday and Sunday but I don't want to do that. I don't like to drive myself too hard.

Sometimes I get to thinking and I say, "Hell, it's a good thing I wasn't born rich." I wouldn't have enjoyed it. Because those people have everything, they have nothing to do with their time. Hey, I'm proud to be poor! We poor people may gossip about each other, but we're good-hearted. And after all, the rich depend on the poor and the poor on the rich. We're all flesh and blood, and when we die we're all stuck into a hole.

I would rather my wife didn't work outside the house, but Flora is ambitious that way. She leaves for work at seven in the morning and gets home at five-thirty every evening. I don't like that, because if I have a woman, it's so she can take care of my needs. Now my pants are all unpressed. Before, when she stayed at home, Flora kept my things nice, and the house was always clean and neat. Her working is no advantage to me in any way; I never see a cent of her wages. In fact, I never have asked how much she earns. When I get paid I give her the money to pay the bills, fifty dollars a week for rent, electricity and food. So Flora's money doesn't do anybody any good. We're going to have a big fight about that someday. I don't spy on her or anything, but I like to keep my woman at home.

With what I earn, I'm sure of a home, food, clothes and everything. I mean, I feel more settled here because I have a home where I rule. That's something I never managed to have in Puerto Rico. There I was like a waif. Nothing in the house was my own. Here, everything I have is my own, so I think of the future. I have responsibilities, see? I live with Flora, who is a good woman and satisfies me. So I have to make sure I have a decent life and that my woman doesn't ever have to go hungry.

It's true we have our arguments and all that, because when I buy a gift for her she never likes it. I always like the things she gives me, at least I never let her know any different. We quarrel, too, because she doesn't like me to go out with my own relatives. But I do as I please, no matter what she says.

What really drives her wild is my going out with other women. When she finds out she slaps my face. I control myself so as not to hit back too hard. She's suffered a lot, you see, because her first husband was a drunk. Fontánez gave her money, but he left the house on Thursday afternoon and never showed up until the following Tuesday. I mean, he never gave her love or anything of the kind. I have given her a little love and she has been good to me. With her advice and by controlling me, she has made a man of me. When I met her I was a street urchin. I didn't even wear underclothes. She made me wear them, instructed me, taught me how to dress. And then I'd go out with my girl friends and come back two days later, with lipstick on my clothes and kiss marks all over!

In spite of all that Flora has done for me, I won't marry her. If you marry a woman legally you have to stay with her even if it doesn't work out. You can't remarry. If you fall in love with another woman, you can't have her because you're married to the one before and she's the one who gives the orders. Of course, it's true that if you marry under the law the woman belongs more to you. But there's something forced about it. A man and a woman who marry legally have to put up with each other, no matter what. Suppose I wanted to divorce a woman and she didn't love me either, but refused, out of spite, to let me go. I couldn't do a thing about it. And one couldn't kill her or anything like that. I'd have to stay with her simply because she was my *missus*. And she couldn't leave me because I'd be her husband.

Flora and I stay together for love, because we do love each other. We can both be sure of that because we are under no obligation to stay together. If we weren't in love, each would go his own way. When I get to be thirty-five and, God willing, I have children, then I'll marry. By then I can be perfectly sure of what I want. But not now. I'm only twenty-one and I don't know what life may have in store for me.

Flora's family likes me and is good to me. There's not a two-faced one in the bunch except for that brother of hers. I tell him my secrets and he runs to repeat them to my wife. I spoke to him about it once. "You know how Flora is. Don't play that game of making my wife jealous. I don't go stirring up trouble at your house. I always show you the same face, I'm not changeable or a hypocrite. As I treat you today, I will always treat you." I haven't spoken to him since. I know myself and I don't want to risk getting mad at him. I'm not what you would call a violent man. I think before I act. But if I'm pushed beyond a certain point, I lose control of myself and don't know what I do.

I don't like to fight. Not me. I like to treat other people with respect and have them respect me too. But sometimes people like to make fools of others and lots of people have tried to make a fool of me. I won't stand for that. There's only one way anybody can make a fool of me—by being nice and getting around me that way. I'll do anything for someone who's good to me but you can't get anything out of me by force. And if anyone tries it, I'll get even. That's why I try not to get into a spot where I'll lose my temper, and I'm trying to break away from my old life. That's another thing I owe to Flora. She has helped me make a decent life for myself. Just think, all my old friends are in jail now, Pipo, Benito, Geño, Johnny, El Indio, the whole bunch except me. I'm the only one who's come up to New York.

Up here in New York the family doesn't mean the same as it does in Puerto Rico. No. Here you go to stay at the house of a relative and they're fond as can be of you, for the first few days. After that they kick you out. You can't do like you do in Puerto Rico, go into a relative's house and say, "Let me have a clean shirt, this one's dirty," and put on the shirt and go your way. Not here. I have gone to my sister and said, "Soledad, lend me one of your husband's coats." And she has answered, "No, I won't. Why should I go around lending things?"

Like when I first came to New York, I went to stay with Felícita. I was only sixteen then and I had left my woman behind in San Juan. Felícita threw her arms around me when I came; she was happy to see me. After a few days I got work and I always gave Fela fifteen dollars on payday. But she got real nasty about it; she thought I ought to turn over my whole pay check to her. She'd curse me and she never gave me anything to eat. If I happened to open the refrigerator she got mad. She's always been that way. When I got home, tired, at five o'clock, she never said, "Here's your dinner." So I went out again and came back about seven after eating a good meal at a restaurant. Sometimes I spent as much as ten dollars a week on food. And I had to pay to send all my clothes to el laundry too.

One week I sent Flora some money and Felícita got angry. She refused to take the money I gave her and she told me to get the hell out of her house. Then Edmundo, my brother-in-law, said I had to leave, and Felícita, my own sister, didn't speak up for me.

To show you how Felícita is: one night when I was in her house in La Esmeralda she was saying nasty things about all the Negroes around, especially her own brother-in-law, Crucita's husband, who was there. She went on and on, spoiling for a fight. Finally he couldn't stand it any more and knocked her down. Then I hit him and we started to fight. I really got into *trouble* that time. He picked up a handful of stones and I dared him to throw them. He did. I threw them back and hit his neck. He flung a bottle at me, but I stooped and it didn't hit me. I picked up a piece of the broken glass and drove it into his arm. They had to take him to the hospital.

After that I always went to see Crucita when he was out of the house. Crucita cooked my meals, washed and ironed my clothes, and gave me money. She was so good to me. If I wanted to do anything, she told me to go ahead and do it. She let me eat all I wanted and she never asked for anything in return.

But I have fought with that husband of hers. One time he asked me what was wrong, were we two going to fight? I said, "Fight with you? I should say so! Wait for me here." I went to my house to get a big knife and a baseball bat, but when I came back he was gone. I went looking for him but couldn't find him. Since then I've always been stand-offish with him, polite but distant.

One day he hit Crucita on the mouth. She came to me, bleeding. "Simplicio, my husband hit me."

"He did? But tell me, *chica,* how did that happen?" I asked her about it but I didn't go saying anything disagreeable to him on that account. I know how women are. Never have I interfered in his quarrels but when I was in New York I did send word to Crucita that if I were to go back to Puerto Rico and meet him, and if he were to say something to me, I'd shoot him. The next time we get into a fight, it's him or me. One of us is going to wind up in the graveyard.

Right now Soledad has Benedicto. You can see he's a real man, because he took her out of a bar and set her up in a place of her own. And he loves her children and everything. I say this even though I know he went around saying I was boastful and a queer. But he's good to my sister. Well, one day I was visiting them and they got into a fight. You see, she'd been to Puerto Rico on a visit and Benedicto found out she'd slept with an American there. And her a married woman. But that time Benedicto did something I don't like. He waited until I went home and then he beat her. I don't like that. I never mentioned it to him, though. One shouldn't butt into the affairs of a married couple.

I did talk to Soledad about it later. I told her she'd done wrong and if she didn't change her ways I'd stop going to see her. I said it was wrong to quarrel in front of me. When married people want to quarrel, they should wait until they're alone.

The truth is, I don't think much of my family, except for Crucita and my *mamá.* Because *mamá* is a woman and she has been a good mother, too.

She used to beat me. Well do I remember how hard, but she was right. This two-inch scar on my arm is from a blow she gave me. I even have a scar on my back, too, from that time. But that wasn't her fault, she can't help it if she's hot-tempered. That happened once when I got drunk and met Flora's brother. We both went to Fernanda's house and smashed everything we could lay our hands on. That made her mad and she struck at my face with a stick. I warded off the blow with my arm and the stick broke. But she herself took me to the hospital and everything.

Another time Catín went and told Fernanda that I was with a woman in a bar. Flora rushed over and I socked her. Cruz butted in and I fell on her too. Then Fernanda grabbed a bottle of Pepsi-Cola and hit me with that. I had a black eye for about a month. You can still see the scar where she split open my upper lid. And God help anyone who butted in! It made no difference to her that I was already a grown man with a woman of my own.

I don't give a damn about the rest of my family. I don't care for my sisters. None of them has ever been satisfied with only one man. They like to lead the gay life. I think that's wrong and I tell them so. I don't bother to explain that I say it for their own good or anything like that. No word recommending any special man ever passes my lips. I never say, "Look, this boy is my friend." I simply don't introduce my friends to them. And I don't say, "This or that would be good for you." They never pay any attention to me anyway.

But in spite of everything, I do love my sisters. And I won't let anyone speak badly of them in my hearing. Sometimes they even appear in my dreams. Now and then I dream that I'm in a wonderful, beautiful place full of dancing, singing people. I sit by the shore fishing when suddenly fish, or sometimes it's snakes, come and bite off my arm. And there I stand, with one arm missing, when Soledad appears and gets in beside the snakes, into a sort of puddle. And suddenly there are about a thousand snakes all over her. Seeing her in that fix, I fight and struggle with the snakes until finally I get her out of the puddle, out of the water, see?

Of course, I treat all my sisters as a brother should. I help them out with food and everything. I won't deny them my help simply because I disapprove of the life they lead. Because the truth is that whatever is going to happen when you grow up is predestined from the day you're born. Many are born to steal, others to be whores and some to loaf their lives away. Just like some are born to go to jail, and they do. But destiny isn't all. You yourself have a part in deciding what you are, and what you do. Before you can do that, you have to know yourself. And it's up to each one of us to know himself.

We Puerto Ricans here in New York turn to each other for friendship. We go out on Fridays because that's the beginning of the *weekend*. A whole bunch of us Puerto Ricans go out together. Because as far as having friends of other races goes, the only one I have now is an American Negro who owns *un bar*.

Lots of people here have relatives in New Jersey, Pennsylvania, well, all over. So they often spend the *weekends* out of town. Others go to dances or to the beach. That's what we mostly do for entertainment in summer, have picnics at Coney Island. A big group of us Latins go together. Coney Island is full of people—all sorts mixed together. There you find white and black Americans. But many other beaches are different; they don't want Negroes or Puerto Ricans.

We have our own clubs here too. There's one that holds a meeting every Sunday over the radio. They talk about the governors, what they're like and what they have done. That club is now trying to get rid of that law of Rockefeller's, the one that says a cop can go into your house at five o'clock in the morning or any hour he pleases and open your door for no reason at all. Rockefeller is a Republican, see? And he's in power in New York, but that law is bad.

The club wants to end racial discrimination like for example in that *World's Fair* where they didn't hire Negroes or Latins. The people at the club said Negroes should work there. But the whites wouldn't allow that and neither would the governor, that Republican, Rockefeller. The land where the *Fair* was belonged to the government but the *buildings* were private property. They belonged to companies, see? And if a private company doesn't want to hire black people, it's within its rights, isn't it? Like supposing a Latin wanted someone to work in his house. He'd look for another Latin, one of his own people. He has a right to. Well, the companies have that same right. Although it's bad because we all need to work and we're all equal.

I would like to work for the equality of Negroes and whites although I can't say that racial prejudice has really screwed me up much. But I don't agree with this business of the Negroes fighting. Many of them do it as a blind. They steal and shield themselves behind the race problem. I wouldn't get mixed up in those fights; they are Americans and understand each other. I'd let myself be drawn into something like that only if it was the Puerto Ricans who were in it. We have nothing to do with this business, so there's no need to get involved in fights.

If it were in my power to help the Puerto Ricans any way I chose, I would choose a good education for them, for the little ones who are growing up now. I would like them to have good schools where they would be taught English, yes, but Spanish too. That's what's wrong with the system up here—they don't teach Spanish to our children. That's bad, because if a child of yours is born and brought up here and then goes back to Puerto Rico, he can't get a job. How can he, when he knows no Spanish? It's good to know English.

But Spanish is for speaking to your own people. That's the problem the children of Puerto Ricans have up here. They understand Spanish but they can't speak or write it.

A good education would help them to get jobs. Because sometimes Puerto Ricans come here to get a job and they can't find one. They want to work and earn money but don't have any schooling at all. They find themselves in a tight spot and maybe they have school children to support, so they'll accept any job that comes their way, usually the worst ones. That's one cause for the delinquency there is among us.

Another thing I would like to work for is better housing. Puerto Ricans can't get good apartments here because the landlords begin raising the rent. They don't want us because they say we're dirty and messy. All pay for what a few of us do. What happens is that when a Puerto Rican rents a place he cracks the plaster on the walls by driving in nails to hang pictures. And then he paints the different rooms different colors. Americans don't like that. So if a Puerto Rican goes to look for an apartment in a pretty part of the city, he finds they charge a hundred and fifty or two hundred dollars' rent. How can we pay that? A Puerto Rican here barely earns enough to pay for rent and food.

It's easy enough for married couples without children to get apartments, but a family with three or four children has trouble. Nobody wants to rent to them. And we Puerto Ricans usually do have children. So we have to look for months and then settle for the worst, for apartments full of rats and crawling with cockroaches. The more you clean, the more they come. There are more rats than people in New York, where we Latins live, I mean.

Not me, I live well. But there are many Puerto Ricans who are much worse off than I am. Just take a look around El Barrio, the section where so many Puerto Ricans live. I went there once with my brother-in-law and Soledad, and I haven't been back since. There's too much vice in that place; children fifteen or sixteen years old smoking marijuana right out in public, streets full of people at all hours of the day and night, garbage cans all over the place! People throw bottles, tin cans, all sorts of rubbish onto the street. That place is a calamity.

When they see the way we live here, many Americans get the idea that we came over like the Italians and the Jews did. They have to come with a passport, see? They think we are the same. That and their racial prejudice are the things that make me dislike Americans. Whites here are full of prejudice against Latins and Negroes. In Puerto Rico it isn't like that. You can go any place a white man can, as long as you can pay your way. And a white man can sit down to eat at the same table as a Negro. But not here. That's why the United States is having so many troubles. That's why I say I don't like Americans. What I like is their country. The life here, the way, the manner of living.

Here one lives without gossip, see? You do your work and nobody interferes with anybody else. I also like the atmosphere here. You earn enough money so that you can go and see pretty things. You don't get bored, because you can afford to go to the movies or to the prize fights. When you're broke you can always go to Forty-second Street and look at all the pretty lights. Or you can go to Rockaway. It looks like La Esmeralda, like the Point at Stop 10, except that the people in Rockaway are rich.

Maybe if Puerto Rico became a state it would be like this country, but I don't think so. It's too small to have the things they have here. Why, Puerto Rico would fit into New York City, it's so small! Yet, I'd like to have Puerto Rico become State Fifty-One, just to see what would happen. Although when I left Puerto Rico, the governor was building roads, new hotels, new houses. Well, the people of Puerto Rico are progressing and I know that Muñoz Marín and the Popular Party have done good work. It's a pity that he doesn't want to be governor again next year.

But did you know that his party wants to do away with the slums? That's bad. It means they want to get rid of everything in La Esmeralda and in the slums at Stop 21. Now, if Ferré, the Statehood candidate, wins, he has promised to build new houses in La Esmeralda and let the people stay there. Ferré says that he's going to make a better Puerto Rico, with more work, a better life, more rights. That's what he promises but I don't know if he'll keep his word. His Republican Party was in power once and it fell because it didn't keep its promises.

Not that it makes any difference in the way I feel. I belong to that party because I believe in its ideals. And Nanda does too. Nanda worked in the registration of new voters for the Party. Afterward we would go to the meetings. She'd put on a dress made from a Republican flag and pin a sign on it saying she wanted Ferré to win. We used to go to different places on the island like that, talking the whole night through.

What Republicans want is to have the United States take Puerto Rico over completely, once and for all. Because right now Puerto Rico is half Puerto Rican and half United States. It flies both the Puerto Rican and the American flags. All they have to do to make us into a state is to add one more star to the American flag.

There's another party too, the *Pipiolos*.* They want Puerto Rico to be free like Mexico, Santo Domingo, Jamaica, Venezuela, and such places. That's bad. If that happened, we would need a passport to get out of Puerto Rico. What they want is a republic, which means that if you're a bad governor they'll get you out without an election or anything, with bullets.

The trouble with republics is that they have to defend themselves because they don't have another country to help them. Cuba used to be a republic, right? And what did it have to do? Call on the Russians for help. Now it's Communist. But Castro isn't bad. When he was in the Sierra Maestra with his guerrillas, he asked the Americans for help and the Americans refused because

* Partido Independentista Puertorriqueño (PIP).

they were on Batista's side. That's why he had to go to the Russians. If we became a republic now, Fidel Castro could take us over whenever he wanted to. All he'd have to do is send over a couple of Communist war planes.

If only Communism now were as it used to be! I don't know whether this is true or not, but I have read that Communism used to mean that if you had a plate of rice you shared it with everybody. If a man had a thousand dollars in the bank he had to share them with everybody else, and all were equal. That's what Communism used to be but it isn't like that any more. Now under Communism, what's mine is mine and what's yours belongs to you. The man who owns the most is the most respected one. If you have nothing, you're worth nothing. I don't like that kind of Communism. Why, besides all the things I've just told you, I also heard over the radio that in Russia they make children study from the time they are four months old! Besides, Russia is a military country. Do you know what that means? It means that at the age of fifteen a boy is already serving in the *Army* or the *Navy*. That's what's happening in Cuba today, people are forced to do things. You can't say no, because the government gives all the orders. And you can't change the government because there's only one party, the Communists. You can't say, "I don't like this country." You *have* to like it. It's not like here, where you're free. If you don't like one thing, you can go around the corner and get another.

If Puerto Rico were a republic we would starve to death. We have to buy everything from outside. Even our ships we have to buy outside. So if we were free, we would have to call on other republics for help. Naturally, the United States would help us if we were a republic, but it would be only the kind of help they give Mexico, Venezuela, and all those places. We'd have to submit to a lot of regulations.

Lately I have heard that the priests in Puerto Rico have formed a party of their own. It is called the Christian PAC.* It belongs to Rome, to Catholic people. If they win, who is going to govern Puerto Rico? The Catholics? I'm Catholic myself so I would be allowed to live, but what about all the people who are not? Religion has nothing to do with politics. President Kennedy was a member of the Catholic Church but that did not keep him from also being a member of the Democratic Party. Tell me now, suppose PAC wins the elections, what will become of Puerto Rico? Who's going to feed us? We would have to wait until ships came from Rome bringing us food. And when Rome falls, who will support us? We'll have to live on bread and wine, I guess.

Well, I live in New York and I don't meddle with what goes on here. I do see that Kennedy, the President who was killed, was pure gold. He was a Democrat and that's the same as being a *Popular* in Puerto Rico. But even so, he was good. Do you know what he fought for? For equality between Negroes and whites. For civil rights, which are the rights that belong to us, like not allowing a cop to come into your house and search it without your leave. The

* Partido Acción Cristiana.

privacy of the home is a right that every one of us has. And he was also for your right not to be stopped and searched by a cop for no reason at all as you walk quietly down a street, minding your own business. And for Negroes' rights to get a job as well as white men. All those are civil rights. President Kennedy was in favor of all that.

Imagine, he knew Cuba was Communist but he was willing to help them in spite of that. They were the ones who said no. And then, some of Kennedy's people were jailed over in Cuba and he exchanged them for a shipful of medicines. And that's when they killed him.

Now Johnson has succeeded Kennedy. Johnson is from Texas, where they killed Washington—I mean, Abraham Lincoln. There's a lot of racial prejudice in that state. Although it's so rich in oil wells and such, people have gotten scared of that place. Presidents won't dare to travel through Texas any more. Those people down there are too brutal. The way things are, Texas is having the same trouble as the Jews, one Texan killed Kennedy and now they're all paying for it.

Johnson doesn't seem to be like Kennedy, who was always talking about the Latins and looking out for them. But this one isn't like that. He's not talkative. And when he does talk it's only about politics for himself and his people. What's more, I don't think he writes his own speeches. Somebody else writes them and they give them to Johnson to read. He doesn't put ideas out of his own mind into them.

I have never voted, because I wasn't old enough. I was twenty-one this year and I'd like to vote, now that I'm of age. But I won't have the chance because I didn't register. I didn't know where to go or anything. I asked around but everybody said it was somewhere in Brooklyn, they didn't know exactly where. It isn't like Puerto Rico, where someone comes to your house and asks you which party you plan to vote for and then they send you a little card.

If I could, I'd like to vote for the Republicans because my *mamá* is a Republican. But not for Rockefeller. I'd vote for some other candidate, like Kennedy's brother, for instance. Rockefeller doesn't stand up for the Latins or the Negroes. And yet, if you stop to think, you'll realize that in New York there are more Latins and Negroes than whites. But when two men apply for the same job, a white man and a Negro, they hire the white man and push us aside. They treat us like they treat the Negroes, you see. And that in spite of the fact that the Puerto Rican works hard. If he sees a box that's meant to be carried by two men, he heaves it up and carries it by himself, even if it weighs a hundred pounds. We like the toughest kind of work.

CHAPTER

THIRTY-FIVE

Simplicio

———

That's When I Began to Be Bad

———

WHAT I DO MISS is not having had a father and mother to bring me up right. I wish I had grown up in a real home where they set me a good example and sent me to school and all that. When I was little, my sisters and I lived with my stepmother and my *papá* at Stop 26 in Santurce. Life there was bad because we lacked a mother's love, and a father's too, because my *papá* was a soldier and he would go and stay three or four months in Trinidad and other countries. It was then that my stepmother mistreated us. Not me so much as my sister Soledad. My stepmother whipped me with a strap or sometimes with her hand, but she never bruised me the way she did my sister.

I was two or three years old when I got sick with a weakness of the brain. I don't remember how it all started, but my *papá* tells me that one day I went to the beach and lay down in bed as soon as I got back. Then, when I tried to sit up, the base of my head, where the brain is, was bent. Once I was dead for over an hour. They had already lit the candles and were about to take me to the graveyard. Then I came to. I had an attack of some sort, it must have been an epileptic attack, I think. They took me everywhere, searching for a cure, but it was no use. They took me to the School of Tropical Medicine to take the liquid out of my tail—my spine, you know. *Papá* spent more than two hundred dollars, but nothing did any good.

Then, as a last resort, they took me to my aunt María's house. She's the aunt I love most, my father's sister. She wouldn't give up. You know, how those country people are. She kept on giving me different remedies until she cured me. I never saw her again after that. If I saw her today I wouldn't recognize her. They say she lives in Brooklyn now but I don't have her address. Soledad has her phone number, but she's never given it to me because my aunt insulted her once.

I was a good boy at home, see? I respected my stepmother because she was like a mother to me. But one day Domingo, her brother, wanted me to go with him to the market place at Stop 19. My stepmother said I couldn't go. He took me anyway and then he left me asleep in the entrance hall of a building. When I woke up and found myself alone, I sat on the curb and cried. Then I thought, "Maybe if I walk straight on I'll get home." So I walked and walked. This was about ten in the morning. I walked on until two o'clock. By that time I was so tired I sat down on the sidewalk again. Then a policeman came and asked me what I was doing there and I told him I was lost. After a while a lot of cops came and took me to the police station. I felt safe there in the station, and they gave me food and a bed. But then they told me that if they couldn't find my mother they would put me in an orphan asylum. That scared me and made me cry. I thought I'd never see my *papá* again. And my *papá* loved me. We would go riding in his battered old car, he and I. Why, even when he went drinking he took me with him. My uncles went too.

They kept me at the station about two days. Then they took me out in a police car and went around from house to house, asking if anyone knew me. At Stop 31 they found a lady who said she had seen me around Stop 26. They drove the car straight there and started asking around that neighborhood. Finally they found my house.

When I got home my *papá* was there. But he didn't beat me. My uncle Simón came at me with a strap. *Papá* grabbed his arm and stopped him. "I don't hit him, even though I'm his father," he said. "What right have you to beat him? If you want to whip somebody, whip your own children."

So you see, my *papá* defended me. He told me, too, that he had driven around to all the police stations in Santurce, looking for me. I don't know if he was telling the truth, but that's what he said. I calmed down then, and explained that it was Domingo's fault I got lost, not mine.

But after that, there was no stopping me. That's when I began to be bad. The very next day I ran away from home. I got on a bus and went to San Juan. There I saw a car parked in front of a house. It was night, and as the car was open, I got inside and curled up and went to sleep. I lived like that for a whole week. My *papá* had no idea where I had gone. But my *papá* was a soldier, and Fort Brooke is right in San Juan. One morning I was getting out of the car at the very moment when my father went by on his way to the fort. He picked me up in his arms and carried me back home. I was happy to be back. But the minute my *papá* left, my stepmother made me get up and gave me a beating that—oh, my God!

The only member of my stepmother's family whom I have nothing against was her mother. I called her "Grandmother." She was like a mother to me. When I ran away from home she went to look for me and took me home with her. She gave me food and money, and always fondled and caressed me. At night I shared her bed. When I left my stepmother's house I went naked. Although she had dressed me, I tore the clothes off. Then I'd go to Grandmother's house and put on the clothes she gave me. She always kept my clothes clean and pressed. And she would tell my stepmother not to beat me. The only reason I ever went back to my stepmother's house was because of my little sisters. I loved them very much. I got along best of all with Crucita because she's the one most like me and my *mamá* in color.

I remember the first time I ever saw Nanda. I didn't know her, and Soledad told me she was *mamá*. Then I put my arms around her and wouldn't let her go. I tagged after her everywhere. I snitched two cartons of cigarettes from my stepmother and took them to her. She was living then at the house of Soledad's godmother, at Stop 31. I slept with her there for about three days. But then she moved. After that she came to visit us once a month. Sometimes she went by the house and we were able to see her. When I saw her pass, I said to myself, "Where does my *mamá* live? Where? In what house? If she doesn't take me to live with her, it must mean she has no house or anything." Afterward she explained to us that she lived in La Esmeralda.

I remember as if it were yesterday how once, when I was about six years old, just before Mother's Day, I went to Sixto Escobar Stadium one morning to beg for money to buy my *mamá* a present. I went there two days and nights, begging. The people there gave me lots of money. That last night I stayed until eleven o'clock. I got fifteen dollars altogether.

I was going home at that late hour when a man called me, "Come here, little boy."

"What for?"

"Take this," and he gave me a breaded beef cutlet. "Here," he said. "This is for your *mamá*," and he gave me a dollar. So now I had sixteen dollars. When I got to my stepmother's house I gave her the meat and she gave me a beating. I had hidden the money in my pants and I didn't tell her about that. I took five dollars and hid them under *el caucho* where we slept. Out of the other eleven dollars I bought some cigarettes for my *mamá* and I bought my stepmother a present for three dollars. But Crucita had seen me put the five dollars under *el caucho*. She was little then and didn't know any better, so she told my stepmother. That one took the five dollars away from me and took me to the police station. So I ran away again. I went over to my *mamá* and gave her all the money I had left. I begged her to let me stay with her, but she said she couldn't because my *papá* didn't want me to. I insisted. Then she played a trick on me. She said, "Go home now and come back day after tomorrow. I'll be waiting for you and I'll take you in with me." When the day came, I bought a bunch of bananas as a gift for her, with money that I'd begged. When I got to the house it was empty. My *mamá* had moved and nobody could tell me where, although I asked and asked all over the neighborhood. So I just put the idea of living with her out of my mind.

I went back to the streets. I sold *El Diario,* a newspaper they had in Puerto Rico then, both morning and evening editions. I bought food in the street with the money I earned. When my shirt got too dirty I threw it away and bought a new one. I went everywhere, around the slums, into restaurants. In the evening I went begging for food. At night I spread newspapers in some doorway and that's where I slept.

One day they announced that a hurricane was coming. My *mamá* came to ask my stepmother whether I could stay with her for a few days. My stepmother said I could and my *mamá* took me to San Juan. I remember I was wearing shorts, shoes and a *sweater.* I took the pants and shoes and threw them away. I don't remember why, maybe I thought they were too much to wear, or perhaps I didn't want to return to my stepmother. I told my *mamá* that I wanted to stay with her. She said to me, "No, you can't. You are living with your stepmother."

"No, no," I insisted, "I'm staying here." The next day I ran away so she wouldn't take me back to my stepmother. I came back a day later and this time she let me stay. My stepmother kept asking my *mamá* to bring me back to her, but I wouldn't go because they wanted to take us to Panama with them. They hadn't said anything about it to us. But I knew, because before I left to go to my *mamá* they had vaccinated us and given us some shots they gave people who are going to Panama.

A few days later Nanda went to get my sisters. The only one of us who wanted to stay with my stepmother was Fela. So the three of us, Soledad, Cruz and I, went to live with *mamá.*

At that time Nanda was living in La Esmeralda with a man called Erasmo. Erasmo, my stepfather, was a bad man. He used to make me kneel on the food grater. He tied me like a dog to the bedpost to keep me from going out. He whipped me with strips of rubber from an inner tube and with electric light cords. That man was bad. He only had to see me to get after me and beat me. My *mamá* objected to that and quarreled with him. One day they even came to blows because he had struck me for no reason at all. While they were at it, I jumped out of the window and went to fetch the cops. So that time we had him arrested. But a week later he was out, worse than ever. I used to tell him, "If I were as big as you are, I'd fight you. You're nothing but a brute. You wait until my *mamá* goes out, to bully me." Yes, he waited until she left the house, then he practically killed me. Sometimes he didn't give me any food until my *mamá* got home. She had a job, so she was out of the house from six in the morning until five in the evening. He often punished me the whole time. He never did those things to Soledad, nor to Crucita, only to me.

I used to have to take his dinner to the Silver Cup Club, where he worked. But sometimes, instead of bringing it, I ate it myself. Because he was greedy, too. When he bought something good to eat, like a chicken, he didn't share it with anybody but gobbled it all up himself. If you asked for some, all you got was a tiny scrap.

Every time I had a chance to lay my hands on a shirt or a pair of pants, I left the house. And when I did, I would stay away for two weeks or a month. I used to beg, and sometimes I shined shoes or cleaned people's yards for them. I used to bury the money and sometimes I lost in that way, or bigger boys would steal it from me. I always ended up by going back home, after all. I'd give my *mamá* every cent I had and she would let me have fifty cents or a dollar for the movies. Whatever I did then, I did for my *mamá*'s sake. It was for her that I begged, although she didn't like it. When I got home, she would slap me and say we had plenty to eat and there was no need for me to go begging. And Erasmo was even worse.

Luckily my *mamá* had a boy friend, a young black boy called Alvaro—a sailor. One day Alvaro beat up Erasmo because Erasmo had struck me. And another time Alvaro came to call at our house and found me chained to the bed. He took off the chains and struck Erasmo across the face with them, saying, "That boy is not a dog." But that night Erasmo got even with me. He stripped me after Alvaro left and beat me terribly.

I kept going out to beg. What my *mamá* said to me went in one ear and out the other. She always told me that she had a job to support us and that I didn't have to beg. And besides, Erasmo earned twenty-one dollars a week at the Silver Cup bar. It's true that there was always food at our house, but it wasn't good food. I didn't like it and went out on the street instead. But at least Erasmo did have a home for us. That's why, if he ever came up here, in spite of everything I would receive him like a father.

You know, it must be nice to have a son of your own. I tell myself that if I ever have one, I will bring him up strictly but I will never beat him the way they did me. No. I will treat him with affection. I will reprove him if necessary, but never harshly. Beating one's child, that's bad.

I don't know exactly what was going on at home after that, because I was hardly ever there. But one day I went back, and Nanda told me Erasmo wanted to go to New York and she was leaving him. I said to her then, "Well, Nanda, I think that's the best thing you can do. He treats us very badly."

By then, Nanda already had her eye on Pedro. He was a member of the Police Athletic League when my *mamá* met him. I remember they took me along on their dates now and then. They would buy me ice cream and soft drinks to keep me busy while they kissed and so forth. Well, about three weeks later Nanda went to live with Pedro. Pedro was really good. He worked in a restaurant and he brought us food. He had a home for Nanda, one fairly large room, and he gave her every comfort and luxury: TV, radio, furniture, everything, see?

Pedro was very fond of me and treated me well. He gave me everything I needed. I respected that man, and he never had to beat me to earn my respect, either. He just spoke to me. When he found us in a place where we shouldn't be, he only said, "Go away." He never once struck me. I learned a lot from that man. It was then that I went to school. Nanda, like the good mother she was, always had my clothes and everything ready.

I learned to read but I can't write very well. I only stayed in school through the fourth grade. I never did like school. I would go, stay half an hour or so, and then slip out to the street, to walk all over town with my friend Marcelo. The two of us were always together. We would throw our books away and go beg for money or hunt crabs on the beach. In the morning I went out with a clean white shirt; by the time I got home it was black. I pretended at home that I had been in school all day. My sister Cruz was in school with me, and I asked her to tell my *mamá* that I had been there too. By four o'clock, when school let out, I was waiting for Cruz at the stairs, so we got back to our house together. Fernanda would ask Cruz whether I had been at school and Cruz always answered that I had. But every two weeks, more or less, my *mamá* would get a letter from the school. Then she'd beat me, but it never did any good. The next day I'd be at it again. And I wouldn't go home then, still less to school. My *mamá* would start looking for me; she went to the police station and everywhere.

Meanwhile I would go to the movies or shoot craps or play cards with my friends. There were five of us. We changed our clothes in the morning to go out. At midday we went begging for money or diving for the coins that Americans threw into the harbor for us. Fernanda found out that Marcelo shared these adventures with me. After that she wouldn't allow him to come to get me at our house. That's the reason why he and I did not speak to each other for three years. But the truth is that what we mostly did was just walk around.

That's all I cared about, walking around, because I was lonely. I needed somebody to love me. What I really wanted was to be at my *papá*'s side. I wished my *papá* and my *mamá* would make up. I used to dream about their living together again. I would see them together, but not for long. It was a very short dream.

After a time Pedro and Fernanda moved to a much smaller room, I don't know why. Then I, looking for affection as always, moved in with my cousin Chango. We were very fond of each other and always went around together. At that time he had a room in La Esmeralda. I stayed there with him until he moved to his sister's house in Salinas, about two months later.

I was about twelve then, and already a grown man. I shaved and had learned to drink. Wanda gave me my first drink, *ron coquito,* rum mixed with coconut milk. I drank and drank until I was dead to the world. The only thing I remember is that they took me to Fernanda's house and she started cuffing me. Next day she asked me, "Who gave you that rum?" "I don't know. Nobody." I didn't dare tell her. She's so hot-tempered, I was afraid she might go there. I kept on after that, but Wanda didn't give it away any more. I had to buy it. So I could only afford to drink now and then. Then people started giving me a little beer from time to time, even Nanda.

I was bad. And when I was drunk I'd do anything. Once a friend of mine stole some masks and gave me half of them. I took them to sell and get some money. I was arrested and taken to the police station. My *mamá* came and beat me right there in front of the cops, and after that they let me go.

Another time when I was drunk I broke a street light. I was caught and taken to the police station again, and I got another beating. Then they took me to the juvenile court. The judge let me go free because he could see I had been drinking.

About that time my *papá* came back. He loved me then, but I felt I should show him respect and I addressed him formally with *"usted."* I went with him because he offered to send me to my aunts in Philadelphia. He said, "If you want to go, get sixty dollars and I'll give you a hundred for the trip." Afterward I didn't dare speak to my *mamá.* I went to the house to take money to her but I never ate there or anything. I did that out of fear, of respect, see? Because I had left her to go with my *papá.*

As long as I was with him I had to stay in the house all day long and I didn't like that. And my *papá* gave me lots of advice. Finally I got used to his way of life. But I always went to visit *mamá.*

One day Fernanda told me that she had quarreled with Pedro but that they had already made up. When I was about to leave, feeling quite happy and carefree, Fernanda suddenly pushed Pedro. Then, so quickly that I couldn't do anything, she cut him twice in the back. I went to get the police myself. I thought they'd make peace and stop acting that way. But Fernanda hid at Papo's and it was three days before they finally arrested her. Then I went to Pedro and asked him not to press charges against her. He and I went to the police station together and he paid the twenty-five-dollar fine for her. Fernanda only stayed in jail half a day that time.

I went back to my *papá*'s house. But I found out they didn't have any intention of sending me to my aunts in Philadelphia. What my *papá* really wanted was to get me into the *Army* when I was old enough. I didn't like that. Some of my friends who had been in the *Army* told me that they treat you badly there. You suffer a lot at first because everybody orders you around. You have to get up and bathe at six in the morning and they only allow you two minutes to get dressed.

My *papá* said *army* life was the best in the world. I knew there were some advantages to being in the *Army*. Your meals are free and the clothes are cheap. But I thought it over. "No. Afterward my *papá* will go and leave me alone. Then I'll be all screwed up, not knowing anything and getting insults from everybody. No. That's not for me." So one day I told him I was going to visit Fernanda. And I never again went back to his house.

Nanda found me a little room where I could stay with Cruz. It was so tiny that there was only room in it for one little bed. Oh, well, what can you expect for a dollar a week? Usually Fernanda would get us food at the restaurant. When she didn't, I got money for food and Cruz would cook for both of us. That was her job, because I was the man.

At that time I managed to get myself about six dogs. I was good to them. I fed them and they slept in the little room with me. When I went to La Marina I took them with me. They followed me around and I taught them to bite anyone who hit me. I could leave the door to the room open because they watched it and didn't let any stranger in. At the beach I left three dogs watching my clothes while I went in for a dip.

I used to take them with me to get plantains, the kind they bring over to San Juan from Santo Domingo. On one of those outings, Papi, one of my dogs, lay under a *truck,* right in front of one of the back wheels. When the *truck* started, it ran over him. I went to pick him up and he was in such pain that he bit me, that's how badly hurt he was. I got furiously angry at the driver because when I told him about it he laughed. Listen, I went and got four long nails and stuck one in each of the *truck's* wheels. Then I went to work on the windows until there wasn't a whole one left. When the driver saw the windows he yelled at me, "You skunk, I'll get you for this." But when he started the *truck,* the four tires burst at once. I ran as fast as I could, with the dogs streaking along behind me. Then I stopped and called to him, "Get out of that *truck.*" If he had, the dogs would have eaten him alive. I took my little dead dog to La Esmeralda and buried him. For two whole weeks I cried for him.

After Fernanda got together with Héctor, she found herself a bigger room and took Cruz and me to live with her again. That man treated me well, like a father. He gave me clothes and money and everything. He also gave me much good advice, but I didn't pay any attention to that.

One day they were showing a picture in La Esmeralda about how an atom bomb is made. And you know what happened? The civil defense captain there was pushing all the kids. I was sitting there, quietly minding my own business, when all of a sudden he pushed me. He pushed me so hard that I fell to the floor. I grabbed hold of a bottle and smashed it on his head. All the kids jumped on me then, but I struck out and fought them off.

A friend of mine took me home. All this happened in front of a cop, but he was a great friend of mine and wouldn't have done anything to me. Only my sister put her foot in it. She began telling everybody I was her brother and that I lived in three different places. Then the sergeant asked the cop what it was all about. And he sent him with some papers that said I had to go to the juvenile court.

My *mamá* went with me. She was the only person who did right by me that time. We went to the court which was behind Padín's department store. The civil defense guy showed up with patches of tape all over his face. The judge asked me why I'd done what I did. I explained, but the captain said I was lying. He asked me, "Do you have a witness?"

"I have plenty of witnesses," I answered, "but they are all children."

After that they made me go and sign in at the juvenile court every Monday for five months.

One night when I was on my way home after having been away for ten days, I saw a man just as I was going up the stairs. He had a lighted cigarette in his hand and he tossed it right at my feet. That scared me and I took off as fast as I could go. I found myself at a four-way crossing in an alley and there I saw another man, a very hairy one, making signs at me. I lifted my eyes and there was yet another, with a face like a skull. I turned my eyes in another direction and there was another one. Finally I looked at the street that led to my house and saw it was empty. I streaked off and never stopped until I got home. Once there, I had to go to bed. For five days I couldn't get up. I told Fernanda everything that had happened. She told me those were the beings that were looking out for me, to keep me from acting the way I was.

After that I changed some. I wasn't quite as bad as I had been. I always told Nanda where I was going. I even went back to school. But I was already twelve, so I soon decided to go to work and try to help my *mamá*. At six in the morning I would go to the docks to shine shoes. Sometimes I didn't make a cent, but I kept on going to the ships because I loved them. Ever since I had been a very little boy I had wanted to be a sailor. I played at the beach, night and day, making wooden or paper toy boats and throwing them in the sea so they could sail away.

Alvaro was working in a sloop. I went and told him I wanted to work with him. He said he didn't dare hire me because I was too young. I was really out of luck that day. To top everything off, a red car killed Star, one of my pups. I made signs to the driver to stop but he paid no attention and ran over Star anyhow. I was with two of my friends, and we got our revenge. We threw stones at every red car we saw. Afterward I took my little dog to La Esmeralda and buried him beside the first one. But then I had only my little bitch, Fleas, left. The other had disappeared. Fleas got sick and Fernanda had her taken to the dog pound. She ran away from the pound and found her way back to La Esmeralda. She loved me, you see. She followed me everywhere. Then Fernanda paid a dollar to a man to take her in a sack to Cataño and turn her loose there. Would you believe it, the next day Fleas was back home. Then they killed her. I asked everyone I knew, one by one, but I never found out who killed her.

One day I was shining shoes aboard a sloop. There was cargo to be unloaded and all the crew members were drunk. I said to Gelo, the captain, "May I help you?" and he said I could. After that I always helped. One day I told him, "Look here, Gelo, I want a job sailing with you."

"But are you old enough?" he asked. I told him I was only thirteen and he said, "Well, get your father's and mother's permission in writing."

My *papá* refused. So I went to my stepfather, Héctor, and he signed. That man was like a father to me. I love him more than my own *papá,* even though he doesn't live with my *mamá* any longer. Then I took the papers to Fernanda. I told her that she had to sign so that I could go to see a movie, that if she didn't sign they wouldn't let me in. So she signed, too, and I took the papers to Gelo. A man there took me to Stop 22 to get my social security card. Gelo asked me who was in charge of me and I said my *mamá* was. He told me to pack my clothes and get ready to sail to St. Croix the following Wednesday. Then I told Fernanda, and she begged me to take good care of myself because that was a bad, dangerous thing I was doing.

St. Croix is a pretty place. I was able to see it all because we only worked until four o'clock. Then we bathed and changed and went on land. After that we loaded the ship again and sailed back to Puerto Rico. I spent the next two years sailing, to St. Croix, Santo Domingo, St. Lucia, Malvada, Tortola.

I have a son in St. Croix. That's where I came across the first woman I ever had. I arrived at St. Croix on a Friday. We worked all day long unloading gasoline drums. All I had to wear was the pair of *overalls* and the *sweater* I had been working in all day. So that afternoon, after I bathed, I put on the same sweaty clothes and I went out like that, all dirty. It was about five-thirty and they were celebrating a patron saint's *fiesta.* I had three dollars, so I bought myself a ride on the Ferris wheel. After that I went to the swings. All of a sudden I look to one side and see a girl standing there, laughing at me. She's saying, "Look at that dirty little *negro.* He must be Puerto Rican. I know he is, because he's so dirty."

That made me feel bad, so I went back to the boat. The next day we sailed for Puerto Rico. We arrived at two in the afternoon. I got my pay for the trip, sixteen dollars, and went shopping. I bought two shirts, two pairs of pants, new shoes. After three days in San Juan we returned to St. Croix with a cargo of rice and beans. We got there on Saturday. A boy who was sailing as a substitute on that trip told me, "Simplicio, I'm going to introduce you to my sweetheart." I said *"O.K."* That afternoon I bathed and fixed myself up real *nice.* When his sweetheart came, I looked at her and asked, "Do you remember me?"

"No, I don't."

"Remember that time you called me 'dirty little *negro*' when I was down there by the swings?"

Then she said, "Oh, are you that boy?"

"I am."

Luckily she knew a little Spanish. We talked awhile longer but then my friend took her off to a movie. I stayed on board and then went ashore and walked around awhile. I passed by a small movie theater and decided to go in.

About ten o'clock that night when I got out of the movie, I ran across her, all alone in the street. She called me. It seems she and my friend had quarreled or something. Anyway, we started to talk. She asked my name, my age, and things like that. I told her one lie. I said the captain of the sloop was my *papá*.

We sat on a bench in the park and went on talking. She threw her arms around me and kissed me. We made friends there.

"Tomorrow I'm coming to get you and take you to meet my *mamá*."

I asked her, "What about my friend?"

"I don't love him," she said.

"*O.K.* Come tomorrow."

She did come the next day, around ten in the morning, and I went to her mother's house. After that my friend got angry with me and changed over to another sloop.

I asked the captain to lend me five dollars and I took the girl riding in a car. That night we went to the movies. After we came out she asked me to come to her house. When we got there, her parents went outside and left us alone. She said, "Come to my room. You may sleep here if you like." That really scared me. "But where?" I asked. "Not here?"

"Stay and sleep here with me," she said.

I didn't want to. Or rather, I was afraid. I was scared because it was the first time I was going to be with a woman. And because she was beautiful, white and had long hair.

Luckily she told me what to do, step by step. "Take off your shirt, now your pants—" Well, in spite of my fear, I spent the night with her. It seems to me I did it well, like a man, although I was only thirteen at the time. She was eighteen, but already a woman, that is, she wasn't a virgin.

Next morning I got up early because the ship was sailing back to Puerto Rico. She begged me to stay and let her support me. I said, no, I wanted to work, just as she did. She earned a lot of money in a pineapple cannery. I told her that we would be back the following Friday just in time to spend *el weekend* together. All that week I was terribly restless. Now that I'd done it, the more I had, the more I wanted.

On one of my trips to Puerto Rico I told Fernanda I had a woman. Fernanda said, "Look, better forget about those things until you grow up." But I paid no attention to her. When we got back to St. Croix, my girl was waiting for me and we slept on board. You see, the captain liked her sister, so he slept with her sister and I slept with her.

I spent three very nice months that way. Then all of a sudden she told me I had made her pregnant. I didn't believe it. I said it wasn't so and she said yes, it was. I insisted, "No, no, it's a lie." But I spent all my money on her. I bought her dresses, petticoats, brassières, everything. During that time I never gave Fernanda a cent. You see, I had begun to love that girl a little bit.

But then one day I arrived with a beautiful dress I had bought her in Puerto Rico. When I took it to her I found a young man in her house. I greeted her but she didn't answer. Then her father called me aside and said, "I'm very sorry, but my daughter is living with that man now." I was practically a baby, and besides, there are lots of pretty girls in Puerto Rico. So I gave her father the dress and said, "Here, give it to your daughter." When I got to the ship I told the captain all about it. And on my return to Puerto Rico I quit that job and got one on another boat.

I was already earning quite a bit of money, enough to support myself. Sometimes we made one trip a week, depending on the sea and the weather. There were times when I earned as much as twenty dollars in one week, or forty dollars in a week and a half. And there were times when two or three weeks went by without our getting paid at all, because some trips lasted up to twenty-six days. When we went to St. Lucia it was different. That's so far away that we got paid by the hour, not by the trip. And they advanced us fifteen or twenty dollars.

St. Lucia is a French possession, see? It flies the French flag because France took it over, I think. Well, we got there. We went to buy rock salt, which is very common there and cheaper than in Puerto Rico. We needed about five hundred sacks of salt to toss into the hold to preserve the fish after we caught them. We worked a whole day loading the ship.

After we returned to Puerto Rico, a friend told me that my woman in St. Croix had had a son by me. I boarded a small lobster ship right away and went there. The moment the ship docked I got off. And there she was, waiting for me in a corner of the dock. "Every time a boat is due from Puerto Rico I come to wait for you," she told me. "Look, here's your son. Look at him."

"He's no son of mine," I said. And then I looked at him. He had ugly eyes and an ugly nose, just like mine. That kid is as homely as I am. Poor mite, I wonder if he got my hair, too. He didn't look a bit like his mother, because she was pretty. I thought, "Suppose I made him. Did I make him?" But then she said, "Listen, my husband accepted this child. I want to talk with you."

"I have nothing to say," I told her. I got on the ship and continued on my travels, seeing the world, Tortola, St. Lucia, every place. There I found all kinds of women who helped me forget.

And so for two years I worked as a sailor and helped my *mamá*. But one day we were on our way back from St.Thomas with a cargo of bronze bars for making bullets when we got caught in a storm and lost our mast. It was Hurricane Betsy. The captain came down into the hold and saw me fast asleep. "Get up, get up! You'll drown in there," he yelled and emptied a bucket of water over me to wake me up. "Take off your pants, the ship's about to sink." On deck everybody was going crazy. The ship stayed afloat but we couldn't steer a course. She just drifted with the current. The sky was cloudy and dark, the sea rough and wild. We drifted on. I was scared to death.

About six in the morning the next day we were just off the coast of Fajardo, but we couldn't land because at that moment we were in the worst of the storm. If we had tried to turn the ship she would have sunk. We drifted east and came abreast of San Juan, but we couldn't land there either. The sloop was shipping water, so we had to get out the lifeboat. But then the foremast snapped and the galley fell into the sea. The hold was full of water, the ship was done for. All hands started working the pumps, doing what we could to keep the water down. By dark we had drifted out of sight of land again. We couldn't see anything except the empty sea and the night. Much later the wind began to go down and we turned back. Long live God! But then a breaker hit so hard against the side that a pole fell on the captain's head and knocked him out. So then we were without a captain.

A friend of mine, praise the saints, took the wheel. He knew something about piloting, see? But much good it did! The water was already up to our armpits. "If I jump into that sea, I'll drown," thought I. "I'd better get into the lifeboat." But I was so tired that the minute I settled myself in that boat I fell asleep. I didn't know they couldn't lower the lifeboat.

When I opened my eyes again, the sea was calm. Far off I could make out El Morro. The ship had almost sunk when we saw the *coast guard* cutter drawing up alongside. The crew came on deck and emptied out the water with a sort of machine pump. Then they towed us into the harbor at San Juan. They brought doctors to examine us, but the only one they took to the hospital was the captain. The rest of us were doing fine.

I belong on the water. I don't believe I'll ever die on land. I'll probably drown. But I told the captain I wasn't ever going to sail on that ship again. I packed up and went home.

It was then that I became a really good friend of Marcelo's. Even before that, I was very fond of him because he always went about barefoot and ragged, and because he got such terrible spells of asthma. You'd have to see it to believe it. I had shoes and good clothes but I never wore them so Marcelo wouldn't feel bad. I didn't dare offer him a pair of my shoes because Fernanda might not have liked that. Sometimes I would give him a pair of shoes or a shirt on the sly but it did no good. He'd put on the shirt and wear it until it fell off his back in tatters. "Marcelo," I would tell him, "when your clothes get dirty, give them to me. Nanda will wash them for you. That way you can always be clean."

His stepmother treated him heartlessly and so did his father. That's why I helped him as much as I could. And so he was always with me. Except that sometimes I'd go out to look for a job and I would ask him to come with me. "Oh no," he always said, "I'm too tired. I'd better stay in La Esmeralda and run errands around here." So I went off alone. When I came back I always shared my money with him.

I took him to live at my house. We both slept on a *caucho* in the parlor. Nanda didn't mind. She was sorry for him too. And she always said, "Marcelo is one of the really good friends you have."

Sometimes we went together to shine shoes at the ships. One day we saw a ship with a strange-looking flag. I said to Marcelo, "I wonder what country's flag that is? Let's go there." We went and *el chief* came in and saw us. He took us to his cabin and started talking in a language we didn't understand. I was trembling, "They're going to kick us out, Marcelo," I said.

El chief talked on and we listened, hanging our heads. Then he made a sort of sign and I said, "That means we have to go now, Marcelo." But he took us down into the lowest part of the ship. There he found each of us white pants and a white shirt. When we had changed, the man pointed up. "Come on, Marcelo, let's go up and see what this is all about." *El chief* took us to the kitchen and set Marcelo to washing dishes and me to scouring the pots and pans. We stayed there all day, until six.

We changed back into our own clothes and were taken up to the captain's cabin. It was beautiful. Everything was so pretty, with lots of crystal, big rugs and all that. We sat down and the captain sent for a boy who knew some Spanish. The boy told us the captain was asking if we were good and I said yes. Then he said we were to come to work with them the following day.

The ship had a big dining room with long tables. First you lay a white cloth on the table. Then you set it with the plates, forks, spoons, cups, milk and everything. That's what we two did. Then the sailors sat down to eat. Among the men who were loading the ship were Reinaldo and Fontánez, two friends from La Esmeralda. We gathered all the leftover food and gave it to them. If we hadn't, it would have been thrown out.

We worked there for a week without getting any pay except for the food we ate. We got bored with the food there. That's why I say that I'm not very concerned about food because I have seen so much of it. On that ship we could eat whatever food we chose, even lobster. In moderation, of course, without greediness. On Friday we were still working on the ship, which was due to leave at four. Around two o'clock the captain sent for us. He gave us cartons of cigarettes, Ivory soap, undershirts and many other things. *El chief* gave us twenty dollars. And the sailors were generous too. In all, we made about eighty dollars, not counting the boxes full of cigarettes and all the other gifts. They gave us a little of everything the ship carried. They also gave us their addresses and asked us to write them, but who can write in Monrovian?

Well, we paid a taxi two dollars to take us to La Esmeralda with all that loot. When we got home we started unloading. They had given us all brands of cigarettes. "Five cartons are for Nanda," I said. We made a hole in the ground underneath a house and buried everything to keep it all together, see? Then I told Marcelo, "There are eighty-five dollars here. That's much too much. Let's share it between us." We each got forty-two dollars and fifty cents. I took out ten dollars from my share and said, "This is for my *mamá*." Marcelo pulled out a five-dollar bill and handed it to me, saying, "Give her this too." I finally gave Nanda twenty-five dollars and kept the rest for myself. I also kept some cartons of cigarettes. I smoked, but only behind Nanda's back.

Three days later I called Marcelo over. I was the one who always had ideas, so I asked him, "Do you have any money left?"

"A little—seven dollars."

"Well, look, I still have ten dollars. Let's buy a rowboat so we can go fishing." We went to a boy who had a boat and gave him the money. He said, *"O.K., the boat is yours."*

"O.K.," I answered. "It's mine and nobody can give me orders."

When we got into her, the damn boat started to roll as soon as we began rowing. She wasn't flat-bottomed, so she couldn't float properly. The slightest movement made her tip over. We headed into Cataño to get some stones for ballast. Once the boat was filled with stones, we rowed back slowly toward San Juan. But as we were rowing by Dock No. 1, the Cataño ferry crossed our path and the wave it made capsized the boat. There we were, clinging to the sides, when a thought came into my head. "What if a shark gets us now, eh, Marcelo?" Man, we really got to work in a hurry then! We turned the boat right side up and started to bail her out with a tin can that was tied inside. We dipped and dipped that can. Finally we got rid of all the water and rowed back. We anchored her at La Princesa and went home, dead tired.

Early next morning we were back at La Princesa. I was already taking out the boat when a man came up to me. "Listen, that's my boat," he says.

"Your boat? How come? We bought it yesterday."

"Tell me, who sold it to you?"

"A boy in Cataño." Then we pulled the boat ashore and I stood there and looked straight at the man. He pushed me.

I said, "Sir, this is my boat."

"No," he answered, "she's mine."

"How can she be yours? I bought her with my own money."

Then Marcelo butted in, "Never mind. Let him have her."

"No, Marcelo, no. This boat is ours." Then I tell the man, "Where are your ownership papers? Now, go away."

"Oh, Simplicio, what a mess!" Marcelo said.

"Shut up, *chico,*" I answered.

We went to work painting the boat. Then we left her there, ready for another day, and went home to sleep. The next day we went to get the boat, and she was gone. The man had taken her.

"Marcelo," I say, "let's go to Cataño and get our money back." We found the boy at home.

I told him, "Listen, the boat's owner took her back. I didn't ask you to sell stolen goods. So go get the money right away."

He said, "*O.K.,* come with me." He went into the house and got the money.

"Just give me back thirteen dollars," I said, "because we had the boat for more than one day." I gave Marcelo five dollars and kept eight for myself. And after that I put boats out of my mind.

Back in La Esmeralda, I loafed around for a time. Then I saw some men who were collecting old iron. One day I said to myself, "Hell, I'm going to find out what those men do with the iron." So I followed one and found out. "Oh, so they sell it. Now, wait!" I made a cart with big ball-bearing wheels. Then Marcelo, a friend called Teo and I began to pick up old iron to sell. We could get about six hundred pounds of iron in that cart. It was always breaking down because of the weight. Sometimes we left La Esmeralda at six in the morning and got to the old airport, where they bought the iron, twelve hours later. Because when the wheels didn't come off, the darn axle broke. We had to stop and look for wood to fix it. We had to run all the way from the airport to La Esmeralda to find a piece of wood for the cart.

Once I sent Marcelo to San Juan to borrow a hammer and nails, if he could. Five or six hours later he came back, exhausted. "Nobody would lend them to me." And there was I, starved to death. And to top it off, by the time we got to the airport everything was closed for the night. We left the cart in charge of *el wachiman** then, and came back to La Esmeralda on foot because we didn't have bus fare. We got to San Juan about ten o'clock, hungry and broke. I was sad for a little while but then I said to Marcelo, "Never mind. We've got the cart there and tomorrow's another day." We went to eat at my house because Nanda always saved dinner for me. I shared my rice and beans with Marcelo. Then we washed at the public faucet and went to bed.

The next day Marcelo didn't want to go with me. I went by myself and got six dollars for the iron. Then I shared it among the three of us, two dollars each. There wasn't much profit in that!

I was always full of ideas. One time Marcelo and I were walking along

* The watchman.

when the owner of a bathhouse called us over. He asked us to clean out the palm trees, you know, to climb up and knock the coconuts off. He offered to pay thirty-five cents for each tree, plus all the coconuts. I said, "O.K. Listen, Marcelo, get me a long stout rope." Then I went up each palm, tied the bunches of coconuts with the rope and lowered them for Marcelo to catch.

We really did well on that job, because the people around there were tourists and we sold the coconuts to them. We did that behind the owner's back. But he soon found out and stopped us. A man who worked there told on us, and he was from La Esmeralda too! The owner fired us and forbade us to come near the place again. But before leaving, I threw two stones at the man who had told on us, and I ran away.

After that we bought some fishing line and decided to go fishing. My ambition was to have a job where nobody could order me around. We fished from the shore, but we didn't get much of a catch because the tide was low.

There was a woman called Blanca who lived near by and saw us fishing. She sold cigarettes, the kind that come without a revenue stamp, four for a nickel. One day I gave Marcelo five cents and said, "Here. Go get me some cigarettes."

"Oh no, I don't dare. Go get them yourself," says he. So I did. I went up to her and said, "Blanca, give me a nickel's worth of cigarettes." She pressed my hand as she gave them. That made me nervous.

"I have to speak with you," she said.

"But you have a husband."

"That's nothing."

At that I ran off. When I told Marcelo he called me a liar. Next day I said to him, "Come with me, so you'll be convinced." It was morning and her husband, Alterino, was out playing billiards. The children weren't home either. "Come in with me, Marcelo."

"No. I'd better stand by the door. If Alterino comes, I'll whistle and you can jump out the window."

I went in, and right there she started kissing me. She told me she loved me very much and promised to give me anything I wanted. I said no, not then. She said, "I'll see you tonight." And I answered, "All right, I'll come."

We got there about eight o'clock. Marcelo crawled under the house to keep watch in case anybody came. Then I knocked on her door, sort of casually, as if I was going to buy cigarettes or something. "Is Alterino there?" I asked when she opened.

"No. Come in. The children are asleep." I went in and we got into bed and started kissing. Afterward she took off her clothes and all that—

We used to meet at night by the high wall near her house. From there we'd go to San Juan. She wanted to go to a hotel and offered to pay, but I didn't have the nerve. Once we went back to La Esmeralda and stayed there until about two in the morning. She sat on my lap. She showed me her thighs and I felt something like a sweetheart's love.

I was nervous about that business of her being married. She said she was willing to leave her children for me. I was fourteen at the time and she was twenty-six. We carried on an affair for about a year until a friend of mine told her husband and I got scared.

Alterino went to Fernanda and told her everything. When I got home from San Juan, Fernanda called me to her, "Come here, Simplicio, I have to talk to you. Look, you're going to break up a home. That woman has four children. You're doing wrong. You're young. Find yourself a girl who is a virgin."

I said to her, "But, Nanda, she's the woman I love."

"Oh, Simplicio, get yourself a virgin. I'll support her for you."

But I insisted, "Nanda, when one loves, one loves." That woman had been good to me. She kept me in clothes, shoes and everything. She could afford to, because her husband had a business of his own. She didn't love her husband, though. She loved me. She still does.

Finally her husband sent her back to her mother. She used to send messages to me, by Marcelo, asking me to come and see her. I ran to her whenever she asked me but somehow it wasn't the same any more.

In the meantime Marcelo and I kept on with our fishing. One day we were lucky and made eight dollars on our catch. We didn't spend a cent of that on ourselves. Instead we bought a harpoon, the kind that you shoot and it goes right through the fish. The spear is attached to a steel wire. We got it especially for night fishing. We sneaked into the docks at night when *el wachiman* wasn't looking.

One night we speared six fish in one throw. They were enormous. We had left La Esmeralda at eight in the evening to go fishing and by ten we were back, selling our catch. That day we made twenty-six dollars. We always sold in La Esmeralda. It's true people pay less there, but there are more customers.

Well, while I was still with Blanca I used to go to Fontánez's house to shine shoes and run errands. From one of the windows you could look right down on Blanca's house. I used to spend the whole day staring out of that window. Flora, Fontánez's woman, would come by and stroke my head and all that. Someone told Fontánez that I was in love with his wife. I went to the docks where he worked. "Look, Fontánez," I said, "I know they have told you this and that."

"I don't have anything to say to you. Beat it," he answered. So I went away.

Then one day Fontánez told Fernanda I was in love with Flora. That night Fernanda and I went over to his house to talk to him. I told him it was a lie. Fontánez began to talk and Flora started to curse and throw things. Then she left the house and went to stay with her aunt. After she left, Fontánez went around to my house to get me with a gun. He put the gun to my temple and said, "You dirty Negro! If you touch that woman I'm going to kill you like a dog. How could you support her? You'd just push her into the life."

I hung my head and walked away. I went to my *mamá*'s house and said, "O.K., Nanda, now I really am going to love that woman. I'm going to take off with her, to show her husband that I'm a man." I did it in revenge. Before that I hadn't especially liked the woman. I had never spoken to her of love. And she had never provoked me either. But that night I couldn't sleep.

Marcelo had the address of the place where Flora had gone. By six o'clock in the morning I was on my way to her. When I got there, Flora was in the house with her brother. "Flora," I said, "Nanda wants to see you, alone." She thought my *mamá* had sent for her to give her food, so she dressed and went downstairs with me. Then I asked her, "Flora, do you love me?" "I don't know," she said. "I love you," I told her.

We walked to Stop 26, talking all the way. Then I asked her, "Would you like to take off with me?" "How can you afford to keep me?" she asked. Right there we did take off. I got into a taxi with her. "You're going to my aunt's house," I explained. "And you're going to live with me." She said no and I said yes. So we went to Mameyes and I told my aunt Migdalia that Flora was my woman.

We were well received by my aunt, although I hadn't seen her in years. When she thought things over, she remembered Flora was Fontánez's wife. But even so she said, "All right, you two can sleep in this bed." The house was big and divided with curtains so we could be intimate without being seen by anybody. We had a week's honeymoon there. I only had ten dollars that I'd earned, so I borrowed from Flora. When the week was over, I told her, "O.K., let's go back to San Juan. I can't make a living in this place."

"No, not to San Juan," she begged. "I won't go there."

But I insisted, "Yes. We're going back to La Esmeralda!"

When we arrived in San Juan, I left Flora sitting on a bench in the plaza while I went to speak to my family. Fernanda refused to take us in. She said I had done a bad thing and besides, Fontánez was my stepfather Héctor's supervisor. So I said "O.K." and went to see Soledad. I explained things to her and she said we could stay there so I went to get Flora and we moved in with Soledad.

When Fontánez saw me, he went to *el bar* and got drunk. Afterward I went out to get some mangoes and soft drinks. We ran into each other. He stared at me but kept on walking. I stopped in front of my *mamá*'s house and was speaking to her when he came back. He stood there and said to me, "Why are you staring at me?" and pushed me. Then my *mamá* slapped his face. I went up into the house to get a pair of scissors to stab him. Just as I was about to strike, his new woman grabbed my wrist and threw herself on me, weeping.

Fontánez went up to my *mamá* and told her that she was the first woman who had ever slapped him in the face. "I slapped you once and I'll slap you fifty thousand times," she said. "You leave my son alone."

Then Fontánez offered his hand and said, "You're a man and a friend. Come to *el bar* and let me buy you a drink." I told him I didn't drink. "Well," he told me, "when you need anything, count on me."

I got along fine in Soledad's house except that she only had one small room for all of us, she, her children, Flora and me. We were very uncomfortable. She had a kitchen too, but she had lots of furniture and stuff. There wasn't room for anything more.

The children slept in the bed with Soledad. Flora and I slept on a *caucho*. Soledad treated us well. She got me a job at the Silver Cup *bar,* where she worked. We got along well together there. I knew just a bit more English than she did, so I helped her out with the Americans. I'd say to her, "Look, the American says he likes you."

"Tell him if he wants to be with me he'll have to pay such and such an amount of money," she'd answer. If the American agreed to the price, I would tell her. "Go with him." But she made me ashamed because she told people that I was her brother. I kept telling her, "Don't say that, I don't like it." But I might as well have kept my mouth shut, she never listens to me.

At *el bar* they paid me three and a half dollars a night, fifty cents an hour for seven hours. I didn't mind the low wages. Where I really made money was on the tips, twenty, sixteen dollars a night. They made allowances for me because Soledad was the sweetheart of the owner, old man Camacho. But even so they fired me four times in three months, and the last time they meant it. I was mischievous, you see. They kept finding me with the whores in the rooms. When you're young, if a woman says "Come!" how can you refuse? I didn't chase them, they chased me. Soledad knew all about it but she never told Flora, and I hope she never will.

We stayed on at Soledad's house, as uncomfortable as ever. Then I asked Fernanda again to let us stay with her. This time she agreed. I explained to Soledad that her house was too crowded, so we were moving in with Nanda. Soledad said it was all right.

It was crowded in Fernanda's house too. There were six of us: Héctor, Nanda, Flora, Felícita's twins and me. Nanda treated Flora well. They got along like mother and daughter, better, in fact, than Fernanda got along with her own daughters.

At that time, the most I could find was one day's work a week. I'd get up early and go out looking for a job but I couldn't find any. Héctor was like a father to me. He was the one who supported us. He let me wear his clothes and shoes. And when he could, he'd buy me shirts and pants. He even gave me pocket money, grown man though I was. Héctor's the best father I ever had. That's why I always gave him part of whatever I earned.

I was in New York when Fernanda and Héctor broke up and I don't know how it came about. But before that, while I was still in Puerto Rico, I saw my *mamá* cut Héctor. She did it right in front of me. That was wrong, see? The trouble with my *mamá* is that once she gets an idea in her head it stays there. A long time may go by but if she says she's going to do a thing she has to do it. It's a kind of mania.

I remember the night Fernanda cut Héctor. She and I were going to the movies in Santurce and our taxi almost bumped into another car. Then I said, "Let's go home. Forget the movies." Fernanda still wanted to go but I said no. Suppose we had gone on and had an accident, eh? My *mamá* also has that power; if she thinks something's going to happen, it does. So we decided not to go to the movies after all. When we passed by a *bar,* there was Héctor, sitting on a woman's lap. It was the woman's fault, not Héctor's, see? Fernanda went in and saw them. *"Pendejo!"* she spat on him. "I'm going to cut you."

"Nanda," I said, "it's not his fault." But she clung to that obsession. She threatened to cut the woman too. Because my *mamá* is like that—bad, terribly bad.

After that she went to La Esmeralda and began drinking beer. I kept after her all that night, "Nanda, forget it."

"No, no, no, never." She took a knife and hung it from her bracelet. I took it away from her. And all the while Héctor was sitting quietly at home. Then he came out and went over to Papo's. He and I were talking when Fernanda came and cut him with a *Gem.* He put his hand in his pocket. That made me nervous. I thought he had a gun. I got pale and began to tremble.

I said to them, *"O.K.* Now, Nanda and Héctor, let's go to the hospital," and I gave the knife to Héctor. Then the cops came and asked, "What's this?"

"A fight. Some men cut me," Héctor said. He whispered to me, "You shut up now. Don't tell them she did it."

As soon as we got home I gave Fernanda a good talking-to, because what she had done was bad. I grabbed her and scolded her. "Why did you do that to Héctor? Well, now you'll have to manage this mess as best you can." But I didn't hit her or even threaten her. After all, she's my mother.

Fernanda was born with that temper of hers. She inherited it, because I'm like that sometimes too. Whoever harms me pays for it. It's as if you have something that eggs you on, a sort of mania. It gets to be a kind of obsession and that's what makes us act like that.

For instance, I was told that Cruz's husband had slapped Nanda's face. That was two years ago but it's still in my thoughts. And I'll get even with him. When I see him I'll ask him, "With which hand did you hit my *mamá*?" And then I'll cut off that hand. Yes, he may be my sister's husband but I don't care. We'll fight it out.

I wish my *mamá* were a more peaceful kind of person. Calmer, you know. Deep inside me, I wish she were a better person. The way she is, there's no point my forbidding her to do something or even taking away her *Gem*. She'll always find something to cut a person with, once she's made up her mind. So I felt nervous inside. I felt bad. I tried to figure out why she did those things. And there was no reason. Héctor was good to her. But she's like that, the fool!

That made me suffer, yes. She's my *mamá*. I went to her and gave her good advice but she didn't like it, because I'm her son. Sometimes she'd stare at me and say that she could give me advice but not I her, because she's the mother and I the son. Nobody else ever tried to advise her. None of her daughters have. I'm the one who always goes to her. She's my *mamá* and I love her. I wouldn't dream of cutting her hands or anything like that for acting like she does. What's done is done. Wherever she may be, I'll always go to her. I mean, I'll help her out whenever she needs it. As her son, it's up to me to look out for her. Then, too, she's always been good to me and given me good advice.

It was about then that I got a job in a refrigerated warehouse in San Juan. I earned seven dollars a day. But it wasn't a *steady* job. And it isn't good for you to stay in such a cold place for eight hours a day, opening boxes and storing fish in the refrigerator. And the salt that the fish were packed in made my hands and feet raw and tender. Besides, I saw that some of the men who did the same work I did, earned more, as much as fifteen and twenty dollars a day. They claimed this was because they had worked there longer, but I got disgusted and hardly ever went to work. Why should I? After all, my family was supporting me.

What I really wanted to do at that time was to get my papers and be a sailor on one of the big ships. But things went from bad to worse. I was in a fix. My chain and watch, all I had that was worth anything, I had to pawn so I could give money to Flora and my *mamá*. So where was I going to get the hundred dollars I needed to get my sailing papers? Besides, I had to have the signature of the captain of a big ship. They send all that to Washington and then you have to wait about six months. I was still a minor, so I thought I'd better forget about it.

The best I managed to do was to get hired by a fishing boat, a bigger one than I had ever sailed on before. It was called the *Holy Ghost*. The captain had to make himself responsible for me before I was allowed to sail. He filled out the papers, saying I was his own son. I agreed to use the name Pablo and the captain's surname. The boat sailed and after four days we docked at Panama. The captain asked me to remain aboard because if I got into any trouble his own papers might be taken away from him. I said "O.K." and got to work. All I had to do was put meat into *el freezer*. From Panama we sailed to Peru. But I didn't see anything of those countries.

When I got back to San Juan they paid me a hundred and fifty dollars, the largest check I had received in my life. In spite of that, I said to myself,

"I'll never take that sort of a job again." I like to be my own boss, you see. When I tried to cash the check, nobody would accept it. I had to go with Héctor before they'd believe it was mine. When I finally cashed it, I gave Fernanda twenty-five dollars and Héctor fifteen. Then I bought lots of clothes.

I still had a craze for the big ships, but all I got was a job on a Bull Lines steamer, washing and drying dishes. I signed up to work on the ship as long as she was docked in Puerto Rico for repairs. I was paid from ten to thirteen dollars a day. I took some of the money home to my family and I also put away quite a lot of it in a coin bank I had.

After three weeks they told me to quit because they were going to break up the ship. All the sailors gave me money. They also opened the refrigerator for me and said, "Take anything you want there." I took two boxes of shrimp and filled two other boxes with different kinds of food. I showed all the stuff to the captain. "Look," I said, "all of you gave me this. But you'd better sign a form or something so they'll let me take it ashore." He gave me a card with the ship's seal to prove that all those things belonged to me and he gave me fifteen dollars too. And besides that, he gave me two very pretty cakes. Practically everyone in La Esmeralda got a taste of that food.

Afterward, with money in my pocket, you can imagine what a wonderful time I had! Marcelo and I would go dancing and looking for girls, or I'd go to the movies. When all the money was spent, I decided to fall back on my savings. I opened up my little bank and it was empty. I asked Fernanda about it. She said, "That money was to buy food for us here." I didn't say anything but I lost all interest in saving money.

I was broke again. So I thought, "*O.K.,* I'll make a trip or two in the sloops." But I only made one trip because the captain tricked me. He told me the ship would make a single trip from San Juan to St. Thomas. When we were halfway over, he said that we would spend three months sailing back and forth between St. Thomas and Ponce without ever touching San Juan. Listen, when I heard that, I broke down and cried. That's when I realized that I loved my wife. Day and night I cried out for her. When we got to Ponce after the first trip to St. Thomas, I couldn't wait. I jumped overboard and got to Ponce before the boat did. I waited for it, to get the twenty-four dollars they owed me for the trip.

At that hour I got a *público* to take me from the dock to the plaza. The fare was only a quarter but I paid the driver a dollar so that he'd take me right away, without waiting for other fares. Several cars were lined up by the plaza, with the drivers yelling that they were bound for San Juan. I said, "I'll hire a car all for myself. I'm in a hurry to see my wife. How much does it cost?"

"Fifteen dollars."

"*O.K.,* let's go. I'll pay."

I was home before two o'clock in the morning. When Flora saw me she ran into my arms. She kissed me over and over again, weeping, "Don't go away. Don't ever leave me alone again."

"No. I never will," I promised.

My *papá* was building a new house at that time and I went to work with him, making the window shutters. I didn't tell my *papá* about Flora and me. Cruz did. He came to me and said, "I know you're married." I denied it. He paid no attention to that but advised me to leave "that woman." I was young, he said, and I had no future with her. I should find myself a virgin.

Then I went off to San Juan. That's when Flora got pregnant and I didn't go back to my father. He sent me three dollars with Cruz for a whole month's work. I told Cruz to take the money right back to him, that I didn't want it. Then he sent me thirty dollars. I took that money because I really needed it.

Flora had to have a Caesarean section. They took twins out of her that time. She had to have blood transfusions. I was supposed to get donors but I couldn't find any. So I went to the hospital and asked them to take some of my blood. They said, "O.K. We'll take out a quart, and another day we'll take a second quart. Come tomorrow early, without breakfast."

The next day I went without having eaten a bite. They stuck the needle in my arm. The blood was already flowing into the bottle when they asked my age. "Fifteen, going on sixteen." That really made them jump; they rushed to the office. When they came back they took a good look at me and said, "Listen, you should be home and in bed. You're still a baby. Many men, real, grown-up men, have died this way. Go on back home." After that they operated on Flora and she came out all right. They told me, though, that the only way Flora could ever carry a child full term was by having her womb straightened out in the States. She was very sick and had to stay in the hospital several weeks before they finally sent her home.

I didn't have any kind of a job. I went to the docks regularly but there was no work to be had. At that time I got in with the wrong sort of crowd, dope addicts and the like. Everyone in my crowd except me used drugs. I never tried it. Never. Not once. I don't know where they got the money to buy it because they didn't steal. Not that I know of, at least. They did have lots of friends they sold the stuff to, though. When they sold it, they used the money to buy some more for themselves.

I was never mixed up in a gang. Not like other boys who got together to go fight the ones in Puerta de Tierra. The only time I ever did anything with a gang was when they beat up my aunt Migdalia's son. He was spending a few days at our house. Once he went out to bathe at La Esmeralda. While he was there, a gang came and fell on him. They made him eat dirt and everything. When I saw him come home crying, I rounded up about eight boys. We found that gang and beat them up good. But as long as people left me and my relatives alone, I didn't go out looking for a fight.

The trouble is that people began to talk. They said my friends were going to ruin me. They advised me to avoid their company because it was going to do me harm. One day my *mamá* talked to me about that. She said that boys who get in with that kind of a crowd get corrupted. I said to myself then, "Suppose they do corrupt me? What will become of Flora? No, I can't take those risks." That's why I decided to come to New York, to break away from that group. So I went and paid three dollars down on my fare. From time to time, whenever I was able to, I deposited two or three dollars with the agent. Fernanda paid in to the travel agency the money I gave her and added some of her own.

I wanted Marcelo to come over here with me, too. Then one day a sloop I knew stopped over at San Juan. I ran to Marcelo. "Look, Marcelo, ship out on that sloop! It's going to be four months in dry dock getting fixed. You'll earn twenty-nine dollars a month, plus free room and board, not counting *overtime*. So when you come back you can pay your fare to New York and help me pay mine. Then we can go to New York together. Get on that ship."

"Oh no, Simplicio. The captain doesn't want me."

I took him over to the captain, and he got the job. Then he said, *"O.K., Simplicio.* When I make a lot of money we'll both go to New York."

I was happy as could be and full of hope. And then, you know what happened? Marcelo was away for a whole month and only wrote me once. When he returned he came by plane. We met and he passed by without speaking to me. I asked him, "Marcelo, what's wrong?" No answer. He went to his father's house and gave the people there some money. On his way back he passed me again with never a word. I said, "Oh, *O.K.* What the hell!" But it hurt me all the same. After he spent all his money he looked me up. "Listen, I came by plane, it's true, but that doesn't mean I have money. I hardly earned anything at all."

"So now you've finally decided to speak to me," I said. "Aren't you ashamed of yourself? I guess you think that's nothing, what you did."

"No."

"Oh, well, never mind."

He went on speaking to me and I forgot my anger. We went to get his clothes at the boat but they had already been stolen. Then he came to me again but I told him, "No, Marcelo. I'm not as I used to be. Now I'm going to New York, by myself." But in spite of everything we kept on being close friends.

One day a ship burned at Dock No. 5. It was loaded with small cans of a special kind of sardine. They put a *wachiman* there but it did no good. The cans were worth fifty cents apiece and many people managed to sneak in and get some. I got sixteen dollars' worth the first day and sold them all. I set aside five dollars for my fare and gave Marcelo some money too. The next day was Sunday. We made a little cart and went back to the dock. We got twenty-five cans that time. We were almost out when a detective walked up to us. "What have you got there?" Marcelo was almost dead from fright.

I spoke up. "Sardines," I said.

"Let me see them."

Ave María! They made us get into the patrol car. They told Marcelo, "You wait here while we investigate." Can you believe it? Marcelo dashed off. He left the car far behind. They took me to the station and went and got the FBI. I said to myself, "That really screws me up." Because the FBI is Federal. At that point Flora came in, crying. I said, "Don't cry. Nothing's going to happen."

The insurance people came and asked me, "Why did you want that stuff? To sell it?"

I said, "Why else? To make money on it. I have a wife, see? Besides, who do those cans belong to, anyway? They're just there."

They said, *"O.K., you can go."*

I just looked at them. "What about the sardines?"

"Oh, take them. Leave five boxes here for us, and take the rest."

I did just that. I washed off my cans well, thinking, "These are mine." Like that, with no fear now. Then I went around selling them. I was never ashamed of selling anything. I left four boxes of sardines at home and made forty-eight dollars on what was left. Later on Marcelo came around to get his share. I said, "Here, take eight dollars and one box of sardines." I was so fond of Marcelo, you see. I'm telling you, I love him like a brother. He was a good friend to me. But he always leaves me in the lurch. Whenever anything happens, Marcelo leaves me to face it alone.

One day a cargo boat loaded with sacks of fertilizer touched San Juan. Héctor sent word to me about it. I went down but without much hope. There were so many men always hanging around the docks looking for a job that I was hardly ever chosen. That day, so great was my luck, most of the job hunters had left. Nobody wanted to work unloading such stinking stuff. It smelled worse than shit. And it was crawling with worms. So that day they took me on, see? I got right down to work, to earn money for my fare to New York. The first day I began at nine in the morning and worked until midnight. They paid me twenty dollars. I went right straight home and gave ten dollars to my *mamá*. The other ten I gave to my wife and said, "Here, save this money for me." Next day I got to work at six in the morning and worked till eleven at night. I kept that up for a week. The last day, Friday, I worked until two in the morning. When I got through with that job, I stank of fertilizer and my hands were raw from handling so many sacks.

The next day, Saturday, I paid my fare and got my ticket. How well I remember that day! It was in May. Then I went and bought myself pants and five pairs of shoes. When I got home that afternoon I said, "Flora, I'm going to New York. In a month or so, when I have a job, I'll send for you."

The day I was due to leave for New York it rained a lot. I remember there were fourteen or fifteen people to see me off at the airport. There were Flora, Nanda, Crucita, Marcelo, Alvaro, Papo, my *papá,* my stepmother, my half brothers on my father's side and many more friends.

Marcelo

I Never Had
a Mother's Love

I GOT TO KNOW Simplicio when he was about seven. He and I grew up together. Whenever I had money, I would share it with him and he did the same with me. Everything was half and half with us, *fifty-fifty*. We were the same size, so we wore each other's clothes. We went every place together. If I was going to the movies and he couldn't go with me, I wouldn't go either. It was as if we were tied together and couldn't separate to find other friends. Both of us worked, hunting iron or coconuts, or all kinds of stuff to sell, and we would share the money. We would give part to Nanda and we would drink up the rest or divide it. That's how the two of us grew up, somehow or other.

Simplicio lived with his *mamá,* and I used to go to his house all the time to sleep. He was the only son and the one she liked the best of her children, because if he had a dollar, half was for her and the other half for him. She never made demands on him, though. If he wanted to, he gave, but she never asked him. They shared like mother and son. They loved each other, that was it. Simplicio was happy because he had whatever he needed.

I didn't do so well because I was beaten in my house. My father and stepmother kicked me around a lot. And Junior, my stepmother's son, who was my age, practically never said anything to make them stop. He was the king in the house and *papi* treated him like that. *Papi* loved Junior more than he did me, and nobody touched him. Even Nanda tried to take my part. "Listen, don't abuse that child," she would say to my stepmother.

My stepmother, Celestina, was my hangman. She would pull my ears, spank me on the behind, beat me with a stick. And she used me like a slave. She got me up at five in the morning to fetch water. Every day I had to fill up a big drum, and if I didn't get it up to the top she would empty it out and I had to begin all over again. She never wished me anything but bad.

She took my *mai*'s husband away from her, that is, she took my father away from my mother. I never had a mother's love from my *mai*. It wasn't that she abandoned me but that *papi* took me away from her when I was two months old and brought me here to San Juan. My father told me so. But later he brought me back again. Then, when I was two, *papi* came for me again and took me to San Juan. He was already having relations with my stepmother.

Celestina cut my face one day. I was eating lunch and she says to me, "Virgin! What's the matter? Don't you like the food?"

"No, I don't want it," I told her, "because it tastes bad." It stank of soap.

"Well, you are going to eat, and right now."

There was a piece of soap in the food and I said, "I am going to tell *papi* when he comes home." So she hit me with a belt buckle and cut my face. When *papi* got back, he asked me what that was on my face and I answered, "Nothing, I fell down."

"That was not from any fall," he said. "Somebody scratched your face."

"When I fell, I scratched myself on a nail." Celestina was giving me a dirty look but then when I said that she got happy. "Watch out," I told her, "or I'll tell him the truth and then you won't laugh."

Well, she did laugh and so I said, *"Papi,* it was Celestina. She cut my face with a belt buckle." When he heard that he grabbed her and began beating her and I, little as I was, tried to stop him. "Don't hit her, *papi,* don't hit her!" I begged. "She didn't do it. I only said so to see what you would do."

"What happened then? I want to know the truth."

"It was nobody. I fell on a nail."

A week later I sat down at the table and was just about to put a spoonful of food in my mouth when this powder went up my nose and choked me.

"What is this, Celestina?" I wanted to know.

"Eat it," she answered.

I smelled it again and it was cockroach powder. "What is this, Celestina? Are you trying to poison me?" I asked. I was a pretty big kid and I realized what was going on, so I told her, "If that's the way it is, I'm leaving this house."

Then one day, when I was seven and a half or eight, my *papá* gave me a whack in the behind just for the hell of it. I was sitting down and when I stood up, I felt the crack. It hurt and I lay down. I stayed like that for a week because I couldn't sit and my stepmother didn't even make me a cup of tea.

When I felt a little better I got up. I said to my father, "*Papi,* I am still only a kid but this is the last time you are going to hit me."

"Why do you say that?"

"Because I'm leaving this house and I'm going to go at night. So it's better that I tell you now."

I set the clock for three in the morning and I went to bed. When it rang I quickly turned it off, got together the few clothes I had and jumped out of the window. Then I went to San Juan to beg.

I wandered around everywhere, all alone, with nothing. I begged for food and ate in people's doorways. And wherever the night found me, I slept, in doorways, in cars, on the boats, anywhere. There were times when I made five or six dollars begging for pennies in the streets. I bought myself shoes and clothes and I went to the movies every day.

My *pai* offered a reward to anybody who found me. He passed by me in the street without seeing me. But I saw him and heard him crying, "*Coño,* I must have been a bad father. I shouldn't have beaten him. If only I hadn't done it."

But I didn't go home. He didn't treat me right, so I took to the streets. I felt that I had no father or mother or brother or anybody and that I was on my own, come what may. And it was me alone who pulled myself up.

One day Simplicio said to me, "Come on, stay over at my house and sleep with me." So I went to live with them. Nanda was more to me than my own *mai.* She washed and cooked for me and did everything as if I were her own son and she didn't charge me a cent. When I had money I gave it to her, and I used to buy her cigarettes. Simplicio and I would go over to San Juan or to Santurce and get ourselves a couple of dollars. One would be for Nanda and the other for us, half and half. We shared with her just as if she were the mother of both of us.

Fernanda cared more for Simplicio and Cruz than for Soledad and Felícita. Simplicio and Cruz were the youngest and behaved the best to her. They got on together and Fernanda saw things in them she didn't see in the elder two. But she left them on their own and paid practically no attention to them. They managed the best way they could.

Fernanda hit hard, with whatever came to her hand, a stick, a bottle, anything. She never beat the children with a belt but with her fist or her hand, wherever she could land on them. Simplicio was the one who was always getting it. But since they loved each other, Simplicio never said a word to her. He would just laugh and go off some place with me.

Soledad was never a girl to behave herself. She never gave a damn about anything. And she never liked to be alone. She would go with one man today and a different one tomorrow. Fernanda used to say that Soledad was an indecent girl and she left her to shift for herself. Fernanda didn't show her much love.

Soledad, Simplicio and all the kids in La Esmeralda used to play house. Soledad was already in love with Arturo when she, Cecilia's cousin Teo and I were at the beach. I liked to dive down to the bottom and swim around to see what's there. And the next thing I knew I found Soledad and Teo under the water, kissing. When we came up for air, they just laughed.

I wanted to have an understanding with Soledad, and one time when we were alone together I told her so. "Soledad, I am not someone just painted on the wall," I said.

"No, you are too homely," she answered.

"O.K., but Arturo is homelier."

"Well, he's going to be the father of my children."

I never had relations with Soledad. I tried but never could get anywhere. Then, you know something? After that I felt affection for her like a brother for a sister, which we practically were.

Arturo lived like a king, with Soledad giving him everything he needed. She paid his rent, bought him clothes and shoes and a bed, and gave him money. He didn't do a thing, because he stopped working. It went on like that for six or seven months. She saw that the man had no intention of working and that he was old and ugly, and as she liked to put on airs and was always trying to go up in the world, they separated. She went to the devil, hustling at the Silver Cup. As they say, "a chip off the old block." Naturally, she had her *mamá*'s example. She knew that her *mamá* had been a woman of the world, a hustler, and so she went into the gay life, too, because she liked it.

Soledad was very good to her children when she was with them. If a child needed something, she would take any work at all to get it for him. Those kids had shoes and clothes and everything of the best. It was the same with Arturo. He would go out and buy whatever had to be gotten. If Quique started to cry and asked for a nickel, Arturo would reach into his pocket and give it to him right off. If it was Catín, though, he wasn't in such a hurry. Quique and Sarita were the ones he liked the best. Catín was adopted and her mother was a whore, so Arturo didn't care much for her. There were always fights going on over the children. If Soledad spanked Quique, Arturo would come and insult her, and if he beat Catín, she would insult him. But really, Arturo was very fond of all those children. He gave them a lot of father's love.

When Soledad fell in love with Tavio, I lived with them for a little while. Tavio was tall and dark, with straight black hair, green eyes and a lot of gold teeth. He was always coming around with a different watch and suit. He always like to be well dressed. He wore 7½, the same shoe size that I wear. He gave me lots of clothes. He liked me a lot.

While Soledad was living with Tavio she never hustled or went to the Silver Cup, because they loved each other. He kept her in the best style. She had good jewelry, rings, watches, chains, all kinds of things. That woman was like a millionairess. She had more chains than she knew what to do with, piles of them, and necklaces.

Tavio was a man who liked to do wrong things, to steal, that is. Until finally his number was up. Soledad tried to throw herself in his grave. Her feeling was strong, you know, because she loved him.

Well, when I was still just a kid, I lived with Fernanda and Erasmo in a house that belonged to *don* Mario, an old man who had lots of dogs. Then, for some reason, Nanda forbade Simplicio to go around with me, and as Simplicio liked me very much, he said he was going to, anyway. So Nanda said, "If you keep on with him, I'll give you the beating of your life and put you in reform school."

"Hit me if you want, but I'm going to stick with him."

I begged until I was thirteen, but then we went to work to try to earn money. Simplicio got a shoeshine box and I went with him to the Silver Cup to work at shining shoes.

One day while Simplicio was sitting there with me next to him, the door-man of the Silver Cup comes out and says, "Hey, kid, beat it, you can't stay here."

"I'm staying here," Simplicio told him. "I work here."

The two of us stayed there, but I was kind of scared. The doorman came out and gave Simplicio a kick. Simplicio grabbed a bottle of black polish and threw it at him, and that stuff ran down on his white uniform. I tried to get away but the police came and grabbed me by the shirt. They took all of us to the station. I told the judge what had happened and I said the doorman had no right to chase us away because we had been working in that same spot every day. Then the judge called the doorman and asked him why he had given Simplicio a kick.

"I did it because I felt like it," he said.

"Oh, so that's your answer!" the judge said. He sent us home and gave the doorman three months in jail.

By the time that man got out, I was a little taller and felt a little stronger. When he came back to work Simplicio said, "Come on, let's let him have it with the glasses." He picked up one of the big glasses they have in bars. I was a little braver then, so I got a glass, too. The doorman was in the middle of the bar. Simplicio went at him from one side and I from the other.

"You're a dumb shit," Simplicio said, "and you're not going to work here any more. I'm the doorman now."

"You're nothing but a shitty kid," the doorman said.

When I heard that, I hit him with the glass and ran behind the juke box.

He followed me and dragged me out by the hair. I got away from him and picked up a chair and hit him on the head with it. He was so tall that I had to jump to do it. Then Simplicio grabbed a baloney that was on the bar and hit him with that. Between the two of us, we pulled him outside, and the same cop came up.

"Fighting again?" he said.

"Yes, it's his fault. He tried to kick us out again."

So he went back to jail and we went on working. I was the doorman and Simplicio shined shoes.

One day when Simplicio and I were hunting palm seeds, we saw a real pretty electric sign that said "Cha-cri-la." As Simplicio is half crazy, he said to me, "Marcelo, let's bust that sign."

"No, Simplicio, don't do it. They'll put both of us in jail."

"All right then, if you won't, I will." And he began throwing the palm stones at the sign until he broke all the letters. Then we ran away. We went over to the Caribe Hilton Hotel, broke a window in a car and ran. We broke another car window near Sixto Escobar Stadium and kept running.

So we were arrested, and all on account of Simplicio. He had to show he was braver than anybody, so he had to get money for a lawyer. Nanda never knew about this. It was just between me and Simplicio.

One day I said to him, "Look, if you go on like this, we're going to have to break up, you and me. Because your *mamá* doesn't know anything about what happened, and if she ever finds out, she'll go crazy. And if *papi* finds out, he'll feel very bad. I don't want to do that to your *mai* or to my stepmother and *papá*. So maybe we'd better separate and stop being friends."

Simplicio answered, "Marcelo, I don't want to keep on the way I am. Let's change right now. Let's get a *steady* job and be respectable."

After that he became a good boy and we were even closer friends. We went to work on the docks. One day I was sitting on the wharf and a friend of mine passed by. *"Hola,* Marcelo," he said, "what are you doing here?"

"Just going around looking for work."

"Come with me to that schooner."

I went on board and the captain looked me over and said, "How old are you, young man?"

"Thirteen."

"Thirteen? You look a lot older. Have you ever sailed?"

"No, but I would love to learn."

"Oh, would you? All right. We're leaving on Wednesday, so you stay on and sail with us."

Man, I could have jumped, I was so happy. It was my first trip to sea. I signed my own name and shipped out as cook. Even though I didn't know a thing about it, I began cooking.

We were out for seven days and then put into San Juan, where I collected my first pay, twenty-two dollars.

I went down to La Esmeralda, really happy. We unloaded the boat the same night and after that we went to work caulking it. It was too hard for me and I said to the captain, "I haven't enough strength for this, I'm still too young. Give me another job."

"Get back to work or you're through," he ordered.

I didn't want to lose my chance, so I went back to work, even though I couldn't do it and something snapped in my back. I was all twisted. I couldn't straighten up for a week, but I unloaded the boat like that.

When Simplicio met Flora, he had not known anyone before. He used to go to Fontánez's house a lot, every day. He'd eat and drink there and everything. I didn't know anything about them being in love, so when it came out, it was like an explosion.

Flora's husband, Fontánez, called to me one day, "Hey, come over here. You're an accomplice in this, so I want you to tell me what's going on."

"If you think I know anything about it, hit me."

By then I had a little courage so I stepped forward to see if he would make a move, and if he did I would go after him. But Simplicio was behind me holding a bat three feet long. "Let's see if he swings," he said to me, "and then I'll crack him over the head with this bat."

When Fontánez saw Simplicio with the bat he pulled a knife.

"That's playing dirty," I said.

"You're the ones who are playing dirty, trying to take away my wife," said Fontánez.

"What do I want with your wife? Sure, I speak to her, but I haven't anything else to do with her," Simplicio said.

So Fontánez said, "All right, if that's how it is, let's forget about it."

By this time Fernanda was living with Héctor. One night I was lying around in shorts and Fernanda was reading a movie magazine. I was in my room and she was in the other room and we couldn't even see each other. Héctor got up drunk and said to Nanda, "What's going on, here? Are you waiting for me to go to sleep so you two can fuck?"

I burst out crying when I heard this and started out of the house. But he came after me, saying, "Come here, Marcelo. What I said was just drunk talk. Forgive me. Come back and lie down." So we went to sleep.

Soon after that we moved to another house. I was with them there for about two months when Héctor walked in drunk one day while Nanda was pressing a pair of pants for me.

"Who are you pressing that for?" he wanted to know.

"For Marcelo. He's going out."

"Oh, for your lover."

"Don't come around here with that kind of talk or we're going to have another fight."

"Then let's fight."

So Nanda picked up a milk bottle and hit him with it. I was in my room in my underwear and shirt, waiting for my pants.

"Nanda, give me my pants the way they are," I told her. "I'm leaving."

Simplicio knew that Héctor was jealous of me over Fernanda. "Don't be jealous of Marcelo, Héctor," he said to him, "because he has been very good to *mami* and she is like his mother."

"That's the truth, Héctor," I said.

I was there when Nanda cut Héctor. Héctor himself didn't know why she did it. The next morning she got up but didn't cook or anything. Instead she broke every plate she could lay her hands on. Then, to top it off, she threw a milk bottle at me and hit me in the shoulder.

I finally left Fernanda's house so that Héctor wouldn't have to be jealous of me any more, and I never went back to live with them again. We always remained friends, though. I would come around every once in a while and have something to eat or a cup of coffee if there was any. But then we drifted apart.

Simplicio and I didn't talk to each other for two years. Then one Christmas Eve I was roasting a suckling pig for a man and Simplicio was roasting another one, but we weren't talking. Well, as we thought a lot of each another, I sent to the house for a little coffee, and I stretched out my hand to him. Neither of us said a word. He took the coffee I handed him and drank it. Then he sent to his house for rice and beans and without saying a word to me stretched out his hand, that is, he gave me a little rice, and I ate it. We finished the work and they paid us. We wanted to talk together but couldn't find the way after two years of silence. So I went and had a shot of whiskey and so did he and then we embraced.

I went sailing again and my family never saw anything of me. I was all through the Virgin Islands, in Haiti, Cuba, Miami. Finally we went to Africa to look for certain fish and were gone for about six months. When I was about eighteen years old, I got tired of the sea.

I went back to La Esmeralda, near my *pai*'s house. It was Mother's Day. I was in the chips and wearing a suit that cost me one hundred and two dollars. I stood in the alley, leaning against a wall.

Papi called out to Celestina, "Celestina, who does that fellow over there remind you of?"

"Don't you know me?" I asked. My voice had changed a little, so they didn't recognize me.

Then Junior came and looked at me. "That's Marcelo, *papi*," he said. "Take a good look at his nose."

"Hey, young fellow," my father said. "Come over here."

"Not me. I'm nothing to you."

"Come here," he said.

Finally, because of the way he looked, I went over to where he was sitting and said, "Do you know why I don't come around here? Because you treated me bad."

"Where are you going?" he asked me.

"To Bayamón, to Ramona's house, to my *mai*."

"What for?"

"To bring her a Mother's Day present."

I had four hundred and ninety dollars in my pocket. Pulling out the roll from my pocket, I said, "Here's ten dollars for you, and give my stepmother Celestina these other five dollars."

I went to my *mai*'s house. I said, "Blessings, *mami*," but she didn't know me either. I lay down. I had a very bad cold and every time I coughed it was something awful. Around midnight a terrible rain and lightning storm broke and she said to me, "Get off the bed, because my husband will be here right away."

I got thrown onto the floor for that husband of hers! So I got out of bed, very hurt, and said, "*Mami*, pardon me, because this is Mother's Day, but I'm going." And I left. *Mami* had been amazed when she saw the pile of money I had, but I didn't give her any of it. Later she wrote me letters telling me this, that and the other, but I didn't answer. "You never throw out a son for some man," I said to myself. I felt very bad about this and for a while I didn't talk to her.

The parents are the ones who are to blame for the children. I had a sister and I fell in love with her. She was my full sister and I didn't know it! I liked the kid and she liked me. We were in love for five months and we never kissed and that was the only thing that saved me. It's a funny thing, but it was as if something was holding me back from kissing her. It never came into my head to ask her what her name was. Finally, one day I said to her, "Say, what's your full name?"

"Ana Celia Vilellas Castro."

"How can that be?" I said. "I want to meet your mother so I can talk to her about us being engaged."

When I saw that she was going along the same route I took to my *mamá*'s, I said to myself, "Now, where could that girl be going?" When we got to the house, there was my *mami*. I controlled myself and swallowed my tears.

"*Mami*, I want you to meet my sweetheart," said Ana Celia. I was waiting outside. I put on a pair of dark glasses.

"Tell him to come in."

When I walked in and took off my glasses, she said, "Marcelo, have you gone and fallen in love with your own sister?"

I told her that it was her fault and *papi*'s, because I never knew Ana Celia was my sister. Then I went to see *papi*. I said, *"Papi,* I nearly had an affair with Ana Celia on account of you and *mami*. You should always tell your children who their sisters and brothers are. I didn't know her and I fell in love with her, and when I asked to meet her mother she took me to my own mother, Ramona!"

So he said to me, "That's your problem over there. She doesn't live with me."

After that, whenever I saw Ana Celia I would lower my head, I felt so embarrassed. Finally, in time we got over it and we'd kiss each other like brother and sister.

Three months after my last visit, I went back to my *mai*'s house. She embraced me when I arrived and I said to her husband, "Say, you, come over here. Once my *mami* threw me out on account of you, now it's time that I threw you out. So get out of here."

"I'm the one who gives orders around here," he said.

"Oh no, you're not! I'm her son and I'm the boss here, and you'd better get out right now if you don't want to get thrown out."

He left. I sat down, and as I had a few dollars in my pocket, I said, "Take this money for yourself, *mami*. I didn't give you anything for Mother's Day, so take this." She was angry with me, so at six o'clock I said to her, *"Mai,* I'm going home, to *papi*'s house." After that I went to live with him.

I began drinking and drinking and drinking. I had made over two thousand dollars on one trip and I just drank it up or threw it away. Simplicio came around and stole money from me. He took about eighty dollars out of my pocket one night when I was drunk.

A couple of days later he said to me, "Say, you ought to take a little better care of your money." I gave him two dollars and then we started drinking until I was broke. Then I went back to St. Thomas again.

Felícita was in New York and she sent for Simplicio. He wrote me a letter saying, "Marcelo, I am leaving for New York and I want you to come to San Juan so you can go to the airport with me."

I took the plane from St. Thomas only a few hours before the time he was supposed to leave. When I got there, Simplicio was crying because I, his only friend, hadn't come to see him off. "I won't leave until Marcelo gets here," he was saying.

When he saw me he hugged and kissed me. He even kissed my feet. *"Coño,* it's been such a long time since I've seen you," he said. "I want you to ;ome to the airport. I'm leaving tonight."

"Of course I'll go with you," I told him.

Papo was there, and Ramón took us in his car. Two cars went. The other one was Fernanda's cousin's. We got to the airport and Simplicio just couldn't get used to the idea of his going and leaving me behind. "Don't you want to come with me, Marcelo?" he asked.

"No, Simplicio, I'm staying here. You make your way there and I'll keep on here."

Then he said, "Let me get my photo taken so I can leave you a picture of myself, at least." He had his picture taken and gave me one. You know, tears came to my eyes.

When they announced his flight he hugged me and began to cry, and I cried too. Then he got on the plane and in a little while it took off. When I saw it leave, I felt like I was going crazy. Nanda and I, both, felt like we were going to faint or something.

Simplicio and I wrote to each other for a while but then he stopped. He must have forgotten about me because he didn't write any more. I sent him letters but he didn't answer. I even insulted him about not writing, calling him all kinds of names, but that didn't matter. He always sent regards, though, and even wanted to send me a ticket to come there but I said no.

As men, Simplicio and I are different. Simplicio has stayed with one wife, I have had many. I have taken care of four wives from the time I was on my own in the world—Genia, Juanita, Santa and Tati. After them, I met that skinny one I have now, Cecilia, and she's the one who has lasted the longest of any under the same roof with me.

I had been alone for about four months when I met her. I went to a wake and a friend came looking for me there. "Come on," he said. "Fresh goods. A woman over in *don* Eduardo's house."

I went there all dressed up and I met her. She told me her name was Cecilia. She was Fernanda's *comadre*. We sat down to talk and she told me the story of her life and I told mine. She said I could come to visit her again some other day. About a week after that she sent me a message with Juan: "Tell Marcelo that if he doesn't show up now, not to bother coming around."

"Well, that gives me some hope," I said to myself and I dropped in on her. After that I came around every day and sometimes stayed until eleven or twelve at night. One day Cecilia said, "Marcelo, I'm going to wash the floors tomorrow. Will you help me?"

I stayed over that night and slept on the floor. The next morning we got up and went to work. We washed the floors and put the whole house in order. And so I stayed on, living there.

I didn't dare kiss Cecilia because, well, those things happen between lovers. Until finally, one day I came home half loaded. After I was in the house for a while, Cecilia came in and kissed me on the mouth, or rather, first she bit me. "*Coño*," I said to myself, "there's something doing here." So I grabbed her and kissed her and that was all.

About three months after that, I was drinking and thinking about it. Here I was living at Cecilia's without getting anything. You know how it is, there I was, living with a woman and yet not having her. And I always had to have a woman. So that night I sat in the room with her and we said things to each other, personal things, and after that I went to her room and lay down in bed with her. But we didn't do anything. And it went on and on and on like that until finally we had intimate relations. And now it will be three years that we have been together.

Fernanda was never mad at me, and always behaved the same, until she began living with my brother Junior. It was all because I mixed in.

I saw Junior and Nanda kissing under a house one night, so I spoke to him. "Look here, Junior," I said. "I'm your older brother and you should listen to my advice. You shouldn't be going with that woman. She's a woman who has been around a lot, a woman of the world, and the only one of her husbands she hasn't cut up is Erasmo, because he was too smart. She didn't cut Cristóbal because he left her in time. So you better be careful she doesn't cut you. You better break up with her."

Well, he went to live with her anyway. He was in third-year high school then and was going to graduate, but on account of her he left school.

Junior was jealous of me over Fernanda. Three different times he wanted to fight with me. Once I was on my way to the movies when I bumped into Fernanda and she asked me to take her with me. So I did, and on the way back from the movies, Junior came over to me and wanted to fight, saying that I had no business going any place with his wife. So I said to him, "Junior, I won't fight with you, because you're my brother. I went to the movies with her, just like you can go to the movies with Cecilia, which wouldn't make me mad." And that was the end of that.

Nanda has been very good to Junior, but they are always fighting. She wants to dominate him, to keep him shut up in a trunk. Junior isn't that kind, because it is the man who has to be the boss in the house and not the woman. If she asks for a new dress, he has to go out and get one for her, quick. The same with furniture. Well, they are over their heads in debt, paying for a refrigerator, a television, a stove, all kinds of things. Cecilia even had to give her signature so they could get a loan. And that money hasn't been paid back to this day.

In my opinion Nanda has Junior tied down with witchcraft. I have an idea she is having a spell put on him. He used to have a small photograph of himself as a kid and he took it out of his wallet once to show it to Fernanda, and after that it was gone. I don't know whether she has it and is using it to have a job done on him, or not. The kid is inexperienced and she must have done that to him to get him to go with her. You know, the boy can't find a way to shake loose. He wants to, but he can't. Something keeps him from being able to. He has told me so a lot of times.

CHAPTER

THIRTY-SEVEN

Simplicio

I'd Rather Be in Puerto Rico

I FLEW TO New York on *la Eastern*. That was my first airplane trip. When I got on I was drunk. I'd shared a bottle of rum and several beers with Marcelo and some of the boys at the airport. I had the seat to myself, so I lay down to rest. I fell asleep. I woke up when the plane was about to land. After it landed I got out, and there I was, lost. I didn't know where to go. I searched everywhere for one familiar face but I couldn't find anyone I knew.

About an hour later a man came up to me and asked, "Who are you?"

"I'm Simplicio."

"Felícita's brother?"

"Yes."

"I was looking for you," he said, putting his arm around my shoulders. He turned out to be my brother-in-law Edmundo, Felícita's husband. I had written so that they'd meet me at the airport. I'd sent a snapshot so they'd recognize me. "Come on, let's get your suitcase," Edmundo said. We got it and put it in the car. My brother-in-law had come with three other boys. As we drove down the streets, lined with tall buildings, I thought, "So many big buildings in this place, and this is where I'm going to live!"

We drove a hundred and fifty miles, to a place in the country in New Jersey. We stopped to eat at a restaurant because their house was too far away and we were hungry. I said, "I'll pay the bill," and paid out of fifteen dollars I had. They charged more than eight dollars, and then I had only seven left.

When we got to the house Felícita threw her arms around me. Then I said to her, "Here, take these five dollars and give them to Edmundo." That left me only two dollars.

My uncle Simón, *papá*'s brother, lived there too. They took me over to his house to meet him. He has always been good to me. I never met him until I came to the States, yet I address him familiarly as *tu,* never as *usted.* I feel closer to him than to my own father. I don't dare smoke in his presence, true, but we joke a lot. "If this one doesn't change, he won't live long," he said about me.

It was such a pretty, strange, different sort of place! After three days at my sister's house I got a job on a farm. I, who had never, never worked in the country before, got a job weeding around the *peach* trees with a tiny hoe. After the second day on that job I got so sunburned that the skin was peeling off my back. *Ave María!* I started to lose weight. I was paid nineteen dollars for the two days' work. I gave nine to Edmundo, sent five to Flora and kept the rest. My brother-in-law didn't like that. He expected me to turn my whole pay check over to him.

I started looking for another job. I didn't know much English but I did know a little. So I found a job packing tomatoes. I worked at both jobs at the same time, half a day in *el field* weeding *peaches* and half a day in *la packing.**
In all, I earned forty-nine dollars a week.

One day I decided to rest awhile. I was sunburned, sweaty and dead tired. To top everything off, *el boss,* who was Italian, came over and objected to my taking a break. He began to scold me, "I pay you a dollar an hour to work, see? Don't think things here are the way they are back in your country. You people come here because you're starving. You can't earn money back home—that's why you come here."

I stood up to him. "Listen, mister," I said, "I came here but it wasn't because I was starving back home, get it? I came from a country that's equal to this one, and American too."

"Where?" he asked.

"I'm a Puerto Rican," I answered, "and I have more right here than you do, because you're not American; you're not a citizen yet. But I'm an American and that's that. I can come and go as I please."

"Well, why did you come here?"

"I came to see the world, and because I thought there were good people here. There are good people too, good workers. And I know very well that he who doesn't work, doesn't eat."

* Packing house.

Then he said, "Why don't you go back where you came from?"

"I go where I damn well please, do you hear?" I answered. I told him off because they didn't like Negroes there. Then I walked away.

Luckily the head of *la packing* had asked me if I wanted a *steady* job. I worked in a room upstairs dropping cans into the machine. It was an automatic machine, so I had to be responsible and not lose even a minute. It was hard work and my fingers were full of cuts, but I earned a lot of money.

Then I had that argument with Felícita over sending money to Flora, and she and Edmundo kicked me out. So I went to my uncle Simón's house. He had a three-story house all to himself. I slept downstairs on a little *caucho* they had. My aunt washed and ironed my clothes and fed me.

One day I went with Uncle Simón's wife to the house of a spiritist in New Jersey. But I waited outside for her. I never do go into those places. I've always felt like that. When I was about twelve they used to hold séances at my cousin Virginia's house. If I was there, I'd disappear the minute I knew they were going to have one of those.

The thing is, I don't believe in spiritism. Well, I do believe, only I never go to those places. I also believe that if you think of something it can come true. That has happened to me many times. Like one Christmas Eve my brother-in-law invited me to a bar. I told him I wouldn't go, because if I did I'd get into a fight with some friends who worked where I did. I said to him, "I'm not going, there are some Puerto Ricans there." Finally I did go but I knew something was bound to happen to me there. Sure enough, a guy came and hit me on the back. I hit him, too, and we fought. I have a feeling about that. I'm superstitious.

I was very comfortable in my uncle's house. The only trouble is that he had two young daughters. They were my cousins, of course, but I didn't know them well enough to excuse their acting so familiarly with me. They would sit on my bed in their underclothes to talk to me. And at night they would come and lie down beside me and all that. I didn't like such carryings-on.

I never told Uncle Simón that this had anything to do with my leaving his house. What happened is that Edmundo sent for me. He was sick in the hospital, and he wanted me to move back into his house and take care of Felícita. After kicking me out like he did! But after all, Fela is my sister, so I went back. My uncle got huffy with me about that. But I explained to him that I wasn't the one who had gone to make up with Edmundo; Edmundo had come to me.

A week after I'd moved back with Felícita, Flora wrote. She announced that she, Soledad and Soledad's four children were coming up to the States. *Don* Camacho, who was Soledad's husband at that time, had paid all their fares.

That took me by surprise. *Don* Camacho did that because Soledad was dying to come to the States to see what it was like. She thought everything was *easy* up here. When they arrived—Flora, Soledad and the kids—I asked my sister right away, "*Muchacha,* how ever did you manage it?"

"Oh, it was easy," she said. "I wrote a letter saying things are good here and I signed it with your name. As soon as he read it, he gave me money for the fare."

I told her, "You shouldn't have done that. You should have known that if I didn't write such a letter it was because things are not good up here."

There were so many of us now, and Felícita's house was so small. There were fourteen people staying in the house at that time. Somehow we managed. When Felícita's husband came back from the hospital he didn't like it at all. And then, Felícita couldn't stand anything Soledad did. Finally Soledad found herself a husband. The trouble was that Fela was in love with the husband Soledad caught. Felícita was mad. Then Soledad said, "I have to make this arrangement because I can't stay here. I can't stand the way Felícita treats me any more." The boy she went with took her far away, about ninety miles from Felícita's house, way off at the end of nowhere. We didn't hear from her until sometime later.

I blame Edmundo, not Fela, for what happened. Someday I'll run into him somewhere and then we'll settle accounts. Want to know why I blame him? Because it's the man who gives the orders in his house and his wife has to obey him, right? And he didn't like Soledad. He said she was a tramp. So he made her life miserable until she had no choice but to take off with that man.

I stayed on with Flora. But the day Flora didn't prepare food for me, Felícita didn't either. So Felícita and I were on bad terms again. I didn't eat well or anything. When I got in from work and sat down in the front room, Edmundo was there, dog-faced and grim.

They moved into another house and we with them. It belonged to an American Jew who owned lots of houses. My uncle got me a job with the Jew but I never even got started on it because I got myself a job at *la packing* instead, at a dollar an hour. That was during the summer. At the beginning of the winter my sister kicked us out of her house. I had given her ten dollars and she objected; she wanted more. Well, that wasn't it, really. I'll tell you. You see, what happened is that Flora fell in love with a boy who worked at a hotel. I found a letter from him and I was going to kill her. I took a knife and cut all her clothes to pieces. She got scared and locked herself up in the bathroom. I tried to break in and get her. I didn't mean to kill her with the knife. I wanted to kill her with my bare hands, to strangle her. But then Felícita turned against me and that made me mad. I quarreled with her and said things. But then I went out, to forget.

When Edmundo got home Felícita told him what had happened. He began to talk. He said first we moved in with them and then we acted as if we were the owners of the house. I said to him, "Look here, I know I'm not the owner of this house and I don't have the right to give orders. But neither am I a hanger-on, because I'm Felícita's brother. Besides, I pay my way. The trouble with you is that you're greedy for money. You're a miser."

So without taking anything into account, he put us out in the street in winter. In the Christmas season. That's what he did. And Felícita didn't say a word.

Then I remembered that American Jew who owned a lot of houses. I went and knocked on his door. Another man would have told me that I wasn't any kin of his and had no call to go knocking on his door when I had *trouble*. But that man was like a father to me. I'm very fond of him, you know. People up here have been only too good to me. I can't complain.

When I called on him he opened the door. "What do you want, Simplicio? Come in."

"My sister kicked me out of her house."

"In this snow?"

"Yes."

"Why? Was there *trouble?*"

"No. It was all about money."

Then he told me, "All right. Stay here."

"I'm going back to get my wife tonight," I told him. I went to Flora and showed her the letter from her sweetheart. I told her, *"O.K. Come with me now. As soon as I can, I'll take you back to your family."*

That was on a Friday. Then the Jew gave me a job in his house, painting furniture and so on. He gave me a five-room place to live in, all furnished. There was a set of living-room furniture, bedroom furniture, rugs on the floors, washing machine, radio, TV, everything. On top of that he gave us all our food, and light, gas and water. He gave me all that for working for him. Besides, he paid me five dollars.

Then, through letters, we found out that Flora's sister was living in Breton, Pennsylvania. I said to Flora, "Let's go to your sister's house." This was on a Saturday. I had ten dollars with me. I didn't know the way to the railway station but we got there all right. I asked my two brothers-in-law to get me a job. Next day, Sunday, I went back to my job with the old man and left Flora with her relatives. I told them to keep her.

I went on working with the old man and everything was going fine. I had to work hard, so I was always tired when I got home. The American gave me my dinner. Afterward I lay down to listen to the radio. I also amused myself doing exercises with some dumbbells the Jew had in his house. I missed Flora some, not very much. I lived about a month like that, with no problems and nothing to worry about.

Then a letter came from my brothers-in-law telling me that I had a job at a hospital in Pennsylvania. They said I could earn good money there. I told the Jew I had to visit my relatives and he took me to Pennsylvania himself. When we said good-bye there he told me, "Come back soon."

I said, "Yes. I'll be there the day after tomorrow." I said it because I didn't know how to take leave of him.

There was an empty apartment in Flora's brother's house. It belonged to a woman but she couldn't rent it because it was too old and run-down. So I slept up there and Flora slept down in her brother's place. We were separated like that for a while. But then Flora begged me to forgive her and we got together again. After all, she had never gone to bed with her sweetheart or anything like that. I warned her, though, "You did that to me, now I'm going to do worse." That's why I behave badly to her up here. She did what she did and now she has to pay for it, with interest.

I started on my job at the hospital waxing and polishing the floor with a machine. The work was easy, much easier than my job with the Jew, and I earned good money, fifty dollars a week. The only Puerto Ricans working there were Flora's brother and me. *El boss* was an American Negro and he was good to me. In him I had a real friend.

Then we shared an apartment with Flora's sister and her husband, and I paid half the rent and half the food bill. Occasionally I also gave them cash. Then—I don't know what happened, it was something to do with Flora, not with me—they kicked us out.

I waited until I got paid on Friday, and with the fifty dollars I had earned that week I went around town looking for a place to live. I found a five-room apartment, unfurnished, and had to leave the whole of my fifty dollars there. I moved in that very night, with our bed and our clothes.

I didn't have a cent left, so I went back to the hospital and asked the *boss* to lend me twenty dollars. He was very good to me, he gave it to me right away. I set ten dollars aside for the week's expenses, then used the rest to have the gas and electricity connected so we could cook. There we were, living in that enormous apartment without a stick of furniture to speak of! And paying twenty-five dollars a month rent, plus eight dollars for water and electricity.

Then my friend, the Negro, gave me a sofa, and a little old man who worked with me sold me a refrigerator for twenty dollars. I had to pay ten dollars down and ten more later on. But the refrigerator was worth every cent of it; it was a big one, and new. Everybody said I had been more than lucky. I could put forty dollars' worth of food in it and it would still look empty. Then a little old American woman offered to sell me her furniture, a sofa and two chairs, for twenty-five dollars. So I threw mine away and bought hers.

No Puerto Rican helped me at that time the way the Americans and the Italians did. They gave me a carpet and a set of furniture for the bedroom. A woman who lived downstairs gave me some things too. Yes, they helped me a lot. My friend, the Negro, came to visit me. For *las Christmas* he gave me money, meat, pork and lots of other things.

We could even fish there in Pennsylvania. But it wasn't like La Esmeralda. Up here you need a license. You go to a place and pay three-fifty. They ask you where you live, how much you weigh, what your color is and things like that. Then they give you a piece of paper and that's it. Except that you have to get a fishing rod. You can't just dangle the string from your hand. Luckily, the Jew for whom I used to work had a lot of fishing rods and I'd taken one with me.

On my free days we'd go fishing in the river. I did it to amuse myself. I didn't make any money from it. There, if you don't want the fish for yourself, you have to throw them back in. Nobody else will take them. I loved it. In summer we got up at five in the morning and spent the whole day at the river.

In winter we took our rifles and hunted wild ducks and geese. It's easy to get a rifle there, not like in Puerto Rico. All they ask is your name and address. Then you give them a snapshot of yourself, pay two-fifty, and you have your license. My rifle cost thirty-nine dollars.

I had a good life there. I couldn't keep dogs but I had some white mice. I trained them, and you should have seen how clever they were! When I got home from work I called them. They'd run and jump on me and begin to tickle me. If I told them, "Come on and take a bath," they got into the tub. I filled it and bathed with them. They took food from my hands too. They ate their fill and crawled into their cage to sleep. When I woke up in the morning they were already standing beside my bed, waiting for me to feed them. They grew up, big and beautiful. I wouldn't have gotten rid of them if it hadn't been for Flora. She doesn't like animals. She kept nagging me about them, saying they shit too much and dirtied up the place. And it's true their urine stank a lot. So one day I took them out to the woods and left them there.

I had been working there for eight months, earning a hundred and eighty dollars every fifteen days, plus *overtime*, when I got a letter from Puerto Rico from Edmundo, Felícita's husband. He asked me to send money for his fare back to the States. After having treated me the way he did! I told Flora, "O.K. Write and tell him I'll buy his ticket." After all, I had money to spare. I was going to send for him, but by all that's holy, I was going to drown him when he came. I would say to him one day, "Come on, let's go to the river." And then I'd do it. But it all came to nothing. Flora refused to write to him.

Then I sent for my *mamá*. I wanted her with me because I lacked for nothing here. It was like a holiday when she arrived. We went to get her at the airport in the American Negro's car. Fernanda already knew him through my letters. I had written that I had a friend who was very, very good to me. And that day we ate and all that, and he paid for everything.

Flora had a job taking care of two children, and she turned it over to my *mamá* to keep her busy and amused and so that she could earn some money. Fernanda used that money to buy *Christmas* presents for her grandchildren in Puerto Rico.

I had a spare bedroom and space for two beds in the parlor. So I told

Soledad to come with her children and spend *Christmas* with us. So we all spent *Christmas* together.

I protected my *mamá* and took good care of her. I'd tell Flora to close the window against the cold in winter. Well, Fernanda would get up, still warm from the house heat, and would want to open the window and lean out. Then I'd tell her, "Nanda, that's bad. That's dangerous."

Fernanda fell in love with an old man whom I sometimes took to my house. I spoke to her about it. "Don't do that, Nanda. Look, people here aren't the same as in Puerto Rico. That man's Italian. Besides, he's married and has children."

"That's my business," she'd say, "not yours."

"Sure, it's your business, Nanda. I only advise you as a son. Don't fall for that man. You're up here with me, away from your husband. Don't let Héctor think that he was right when he said you came up here to chase an American Negro who was a friend of mine."

"Oh, don't bother me," she always said. "I only do this to amuse myself. There's nothing between that man and me."

But after about three months she got fed up with the States. For one thing, I went to drink at a *bar* once a week and she objected to that. And she hated the cold. But, *bendito,* what really made her go and decide never to come back was a fight I had with a boy. He fell and cut his face. After the fight each of us went to his own house. Up here the cops let you go home because they know who you are and where to find you. I didn't say a word about my trouble to the family.

The next day I went to work at the hospital as usual. In the afternoon the cops came and asked, "Are you Simplicio Ríos?"

"Yes."

"We're looking for you." And they snapped the handcuffs on me and took me to the police station. The first people I saw when I got there were Fernanda and Flora. The cops had been around to my house first. They handcuffed the boy and me. When Fernanda saw that, she had a fit of hysterics. They took us to the prison and shut both of us up in a cage. This was on a Friday. We spent the night there, and thank God, they took us to court on Saturday afternoon. The judge said we had to pay a total of one hundred and sixty-two dollars' fine. This boy and I got together and between us we managed to pay in full. So by two in the afternoon we were free.

When I got home Fernanda was crying. "You see what comes from keeping bad company? Now I'm really going back to Puerto Rico," she said. And she went. There was no holding her. She kept after me, "I want to go. Get me a ticket," until I gave in. I bought her a ticket and went to see her off at the airport.

Sometime after she got back to Puerto Rico she wrote that she had left Héctor. I asked her at once whether she wanted to come and live with **me** again but she said no. I knew she wanted to stay there because of the new husband she'd gotten. If she ever wants to come up, I'll send for her again.

After Fernanda left, Soledad had a nervous breakdown. She went crazy. She came to my house and asked me to take care of her little girls because she was sick and had to stay in the hospital. I said, "O.K., leave them here."

I had the children three months, until she got well. I gave those children everything they needed, as if they had been in their own home. That's why I tell her that she should leave those girls with me. Because I took good care of them and saw to it that they behaved, and all that in spite of Flora who didn't want to take charge of them. She said they kicked up a rumpus in the house and got on her nerves. I said, "Never mind. I'll see to it that they behave properly. That's what relatives are for."

I couldn't go and see Soledad while she was sick. The hospital was too far away. When she got well she came to get the children.

I was doing all right until I got into trouble on the job. Some fellows gave me a shot of rum. They forced it on me, see? I didn't even want it. Then a man broke a bottle of oxygen and accused me of doing it. I insisted that it hadn't been me. They were a bunch of American Negroes but I tangled with them. I fought three of them at once. The *boss* walked in while we were at it and he suspended me from the job for four months.

I said to myself, "In four months I'll starve to death. And I can't stand to have to ask for money." I was fed up with the place, anyway. I still went fishing but I was bored all the same. It was a dull life. By five in the evening I had to be home in bed, because if I went out I never met anyone. There were no people around at night, nobody at all. There was nothing in the whole city but hospitals, graveyards and bars. And it was a problem to get into the bars because they don't like Negroes there either. Near my home, a few miles away, there was a place called Morristown. They wouldn't allow a Negro to set foot there. I've passed through in a car but I never got out. It's better not to stop if you want to avoid trouble. Imagine, they won't even sell gasoline to a Negro there. I never once saw a Negro in that town. They have them in a place apart, you see, living in a separate section with *buildings* for Negroes only.

There were churches too. But I don't go to church. I'm a Catholic, but Fernanda sent us to church because they served a snack for children at four-thirty every afternoon. That's why she sent me. There I learned some prayers on my own, Our Father, Hail Mary—but I never got to take my First Communion because they made no preparations at home for it. They didn't get me clothes for it or anything. So I skipped the class for four days at a time and went to the movies instead. When Fernanda found out, she scolded me. I did go to confession, but that was thirteen or fourteen years ago. I haven't been to church since.

In spite of the fact that I don't go to church, I always light candles for the saints. And I believe in God. I pray to him every day as I go down the street.

But I'll tell you one thing, it's not good to go to church every day. I worship God in my heart. I go to church when I want to, because I feel like it. But this business of going every day or whenever the priest says you must, I'm against it. I'm a Catholic, of course, because that is the one religion I have known. And I know it was the first religion that ever existed. Most Protestants were baptized in the Catholic Church and changed later. Not that I blame them, every one has his creed and searches for God in his own way. But I can't agree with this business of forbidding people to smoke, drink or go to dances. And I don't like dancing and singing aloud in church and going into fits. I don't deny that if you have that religion you are unable to restrain yourself. But who knows? I might wind up in that church myself someday. Each of us has his own heart and his own way of thinking. But what I believe now, at this moment, is that it is a sort of fake religion. Who ever heard of not believing in the saints?

Although I'm not sure, sometimes I think God made Adam and Eve normal, like us. All human beings come from them, don't they? Then, where did those people with monkey faces and ostrich bodies come from? Another thing, Adam and Eve were white. So where did the Negroes come from, and the yellow people? Where did we Puerto Ricans come from? That idea is out of date. Because if each and every one of us is descended from Adam and Eve, how come there are so many different languages in the world? May God forgive me, but that somehow doesn't make much sense. A scientist once wrote a book that makes a lot more sense. He says that the world changed little by little. That we started out like the bugs and have changed step by step until the present. Now we are a little bit civilized but still not enough. So it may be that we, too, will go on changing—you know, evolving.

I like the saints and believe in them. I want them near me. But as for asking them for things, I only ask Saint Raymond and he helps me. I always ask him to give me health so that I can keep on working. I've never asked him to get me a job. That's something you have to get for yourself. Health is the most important thing of all.

And so, when they suspended me from the hospital, I commended myself to the saints and said to my wife, "Flora, we're going to New York." I had one regret on leaving. I knew I would miss my friend, the American Negro. He was like a father to me and he was my color, see? I was very, very fond of him.

I got Soledad's address, and without really knowing how to get there, I got on a train to New York. From there I took the subway at Thirty-fourth Street. That brought me to the Bronx, where Soledad used to live, but she had moved. Luckily, she had left her new address with some neighbors. After searching all over the place I found her house, but she wasn't there. I had to wait and wait until she came home. When she came, I told her what had happened to me. She said, "Stay here. I'll let you two have a room." So we did.

I went to a bar with Soledad's husband, Benedicto, and I liked it. After that I went every night. I was practically going broke. Then Benedicto sailed off on a ship. I got to thinking, and I said to Soledad, "What shall I do, Soledad? I guess I'd better go get my things in Pennsylvania and find myself a place to live." I looked until I found a place. I paid twenty-two dollars down, plus one dollar for the key. That was two weeks' rent. I paid it in advance, because my money was running out and I was afraid I wouldn't find a job. And if you at least have a place of your own, you're not too badly off.

After finding a place, I went to Pennsylvania to get my things. And you know, it's true that what's done in a year can be undone in an hour. The only things I brought here were the washing machine, the TV set, two lamps, the table and our clothes. I sold all the rest, for twenty-five dollars. And I left the apartment, after painting it and making it so pretty and fixing the bathroom. I left the refrigerator, bed, most of the furniture, new carpets for all the five rooms. I even had something to keep stuff in, a sort of desk, all made of glass. All of that I sold for twenty-five dollars so that I could come here to suffer.

When I finally got my bearings in New York I liked it better than Pennsylvania. It seemed different, see? There's more going on here, many big houses, lots of Puerto Ricans, all sorts of amusements. So I told Flora I was staying here, even though the job I have now is harder than the one in Pennsylvania. But that's not the important thing. Over there, that job was my only chance to work. If they had fired me, what could I have done? Here in New York, if they fire me I'll get another job right around the corner. The factory even gives me life insurance. That way, if something happens to me, my wife will be taken care of. She'll get ten thousand, maybe it's three thousand dollars. That will be some help.

I'm glad I'm a man. That way I don't have to bother with the monthly illness or getting pregnant or anything like that. Not that women are so bad off. They can make themselves pretty, and flirt and all that. And then, a woman doesn't have to go after a man. The man is the one who has to chase after the woman and give up his seat to her and so on. But even so, I'm grateful to have been born a man. Because that way I can work hard to get whatever I want and I can have fun, too, because a man, on account of being a man, can do anything he pleases.

If I fall for a woman, I let her see it. Right now I have one that I courted in our very house, right here in the Bronx. The woman I'm telling you about had moved into the same *building* where we lived. This was during the *Christmas* season and it was snowing. Flora's brother Sotero and I were downstairs. Then this girl came out and began to play in the snow. Her sister came out too. Sotero and I got into the game, Sotero with the other girl and I with mine—Leila she's called. Nothing came of it that day.

After that, both sisters came to call at my house. Then I looked at mine and fell in love with her. I asked Leila where she planned to spend Christmas Eve and said I was going to spend it with my relatives. She asked me if she could go, too. So we dressed up and went over to my cousin's through a heavy snowfall. On the way there I didn't say one word to her. After midnight we returned to my place and there we finally got to talking. Next day, every time I looked at her, we both had to laugh. On New Year's Eve I kissed the girl on the stroke of midnight, the first kiss I ever gave her. After that we drank and drank until dawn.

Flora realized what was going on and didn't want me to go to Leila's house. But our *toilet* faced the door of her apartment, so I would sneak out through there. When I went to see her we would dance. Flora would call out to me, "Come home now, it's time to sleep."

"Not yet," I'd say. "In a minute." One day Flora came over and punched me. I merely said, "Come on, Flora, be quiet." Then I took her home, put her to bed and went back to Leila.

Sometime later Leila moved to Third Avenue. One night I was there with her when Flora and Soledad appeared. Leila was pregnant and Flora saw she was wearing a maternity dress. The two of them tangled then and there. I simply walked out on both of them, went home to change my shirt, and then out to a bar to drink. But even after that I kept on seeing Leila. Hell, I have a lot of shirts and pants at her house and she washes them for me. I change my clothes over there sometimes. She respects me and does everything I ask her to.

That's why I say that I'm the one who wears the pants at my house. I don't deny that Flora slaps my face and curses me out and all that. I say "yes, yes, yes" to everything. Let her waste her saliva and beat her brain, I do as I please. I go out, have a good time. Then I go home and go to bed without even saying hello to her.

I do my duty as a man of course. I support my family and make people respect my home. I mean, if someone comes around to my place and starts speaking dirty or cursing I say, "Listen, I'm the only one who has a right to speak like that in this house. I'm the one that pays for it." That I do. And to do that, one has to work.

My ambition is to get enough money to go back to Puerto Rico. Then I'd buy a bit of land and make a home of my own to give security to my children, although I have no children yet. And all because Flora won't go to see a doctor and find out if she can be cured and give me a child. Maybe they can't do anything about it now. I have an idea they did something to her at the hospital the last time she miscarried, to keep her from getting pregnant again. She got so sick, you see. I think that's why she's never gotten pregnant again since then, although we don't do anything to prevent it. I guess I'll have to go make myself some children with some other woman.

I've asked Flora to go to the hospital, because I'm young and would like to have children some day. She says she won't go because she's scared. Well, if she doesn't want to, I won't force her. But she has no right to complain if I try to have children with other women. If I should have a child, ah, I'd take it home with me. If Flora won't accept the child, I'll go to the other woman, the mother of my child.

Seriously, I really have thought that. When Leila got pregnant I felt so good because the child was mine. Leila was seven months gone when she lost the baby. They went to get me at my house about five times that night. But I thought it was a put-up job, see? I didn't believe a word they said. But then I thought it over. By six in the morning I was at her mother's house. And it was the truth. Leila had been taken to that hospital where women go to have babies.

I rushed over but they wouldn't let me in. They said come back that evening at seven. I was so desperately eager to get in that I went ahead of time, at four o'clock, with a big bag of grapes, apples and all sorts of fruit. They wouldn't let me in. I waited there until seven and then they let me in, but they wouldn't let me take the fruit.

Leila stayed in the hospital three days. The baby died. He was a boy. They took him to another hospital to preserve him in alcohol. I felt the baby's death deeply, deeply. And think of it, she miscarried because of me, because I'd scared her half to death. I hardly ever get mad at anybody. But when I do, I go wild. I throw whatever I can get hold of. It's all over in a minute. But in that minute I'm not in this world; I don't know what I'm doing.

This happened on a Thursday when I was over at Leila's. She says to me, "Let's go upstairs. They're having a small dance."

"No," I say, "let's not."

"Oh, come on."

"Well, O.K." When we get there a little old man says to me, "I'm going to put on a record now, especially for your woman. I want to dance with her."

I said no. The old man punched me in the chest. I let it pass. We went back down to Leila's apartment and I locked the door.

About ten minutes later the old man knocks on the door, furious. He yells, "Come on out, you! I'm going to stick you like a codfish." * I opened at once. The old man was standing there with a steel knife in one hand and a small parrot-beaked blade in the other. "I came to get you," he says.

"Oh, forget it," I answered. He pushed on into the apartment. I went crazy. I grabbed a chair and smashed it over his head. I clobbered him. He's been covered with scars ever since. Well, that calmed him down, all right. Then his friends came and took him to the hospital. That was the night Leila lost the baby. She's never gotten pregnant again.

* Codfish are flattened out and piled up with a stake driven through them when they are put out to dry.

So, if I can't have children of my own, I'd like to keep Gabi, Felícita's son. If they give him to me for good, I'll take good care of him. But they'll have to give me a free hand to bring him up my way, according to my own ideas. I'll give him my name and teach and direct him as I think fit. I'll give him a good education. With me, he can feel he has a father. I'll give him everything he needs and take him places. I wouldn't want him to grow up as I did, with too much freedom. I'll give him freedom, but not absolute freedom. Let him be free, yes, but let him learn to respect me too.

I've had problems with some people here in the Bronx but not gang fights, or anything like that. One time, for instance, I got in between two of my friends who were fighting and one of them socked me over the lip. Another day a boy in a *bar* called me a queer. As far as I'm concerned that's the worst insult! Listen, if they call me *"cabrón"* I don't mind. Because *cabrón* means a man who likes to have a good time, who knows his way around and likes to dance and be gay and have women and more women. So it doesn't bother me in the least to be called *cabrón*. But I won't stand to have anybody call me a queer. Because a queer is a man who likes other men. You can imagine how I felt when that guy called me that. I told him not to call me that and he repeated it. "Oh, so you want to fight?" I said, and he answered, "Sure."

So we went outside. But he brought a friend of his along and they held me and hit me when I was helpless like that. They gave me a black eye and a swollen lip. Then the man who hit me ran away. I turned on the other one, the one who was holding me. "The other one escaped," I said, "but I'll be damned if you do." I socked him hard and broke his head. I'm even with that one now. And the other one is going to get his, too. I haven't seen him since, but I'm watching for him. If I'm sober when we meet, I'll get him. If you let someone make a fool of you, you're sunk. One has to be tough with a character like that.

Those things happen to me when I'm drinking. Truth to tell, I don't even know why I drink. I live my own life, see? I don't have any hard-drinking friends because I don't like that. What I like is going out alone and drinking by myself. I have many friends and I have my cousins, Chango and Tito, who are good guys and side with me. I could go with them if I wanted to. But I don't. I figure that my duty is not to go anywhere from Monday to Friday except to work and back to my home. Friday to Saturday, my entertainment is to drink and go places by myself or, at most, with one friend. Saturdays I'm out all night, calling on my sweethearts. There's a little American girl, Sandra, who's mad about me. She works with me. She's eighteen and a virgin. Know what she says to me? "Simplicio," she says, "we can't do anything now because I'm a virgin. But I'm going to marry another man so you can be with me afterward without getting blamed for anything." I say, "Gosh! Go ahead and do it," and I walk off.

I've had lots of things happen to me during these jaunts. Some places don't want you because you're a Negro. Once I went to a *bar* near *el Brooklyn Bridge* with a friend from New York. I'd been told that it was a place for whites. So I told my friend, "Wait outside for me. I want to see if they'll serve me." When I asked for a shot of whiskey *el bartender* said they didn't have it. So I say again, "Come on. Give me a shot of whiskey."

"We don't serve Negroes here."

"What did you say?" I asked and punched him in the face. When I struck out, all the glasses and stuff on the *bar* went crashing to the floor. The *bartender* cut me over the cheekbone. I had to beat it fast. If I'd stayed they would have killed me.

A lot of people here look down on a guy because of his color, see? But I don't know, sometimes it works the other way around. Because once I went with a white friend to a *bar* around here where they don't allow white men. That's not racial prejudice because I went in and they served me, but they refused to serve him because he's white. I don't understand it.

And there's something else. The only thing that has any value up here is money. You can't go out without money because nobody gives anybody anything. But nothing! In Puerto Rico, if you go to a cheap restaurant you can get a meal for thirty-five cents. And if you don't have that much, they'll give you the scrapings from the bottom of the pot or a dish of leftovers for fifteen cents. You can always get something, even if it's from the day before. But it's different here. If you're broke you starve. People are sour and talk rough, *"Hell, get out of here,"* without turning a hair. And if you accidentally bump into somebody, it gets you nowhere to say, *"I'm sorry."* If you bump into someone in Puerto Rico, you stop and say, "Excuse me. I didn't mean to do that." And you hold them so they won't trip saying, "I'm sorry, sir."

Nobody here bothers about things like that. Life is too hurried. You don't have time to do anything but work and eat. You walk along minding your business. And if you bump into the governor himself you just keep walking. Hell, in *el subway* they push you around and toss you about like a match stick.

The thing that shocks me most is, how can you act like a man up here—a gentleman, I mean—when women won't let you give up your seat for them? Not even the little ladies. No, not even the pregnant women. If you get up in a crowded *subway* and offer a woman your seat she'll just say, *"I'm sorry."*

If you give your seat to a woman in Puerto Rico, she sits down, and what's more, she's grateful to you and thanks you. In New York, if you do that, all you get is a rude answer. I say this because once I saw a little old lady and I said to her, *"Mrs., do you want to sit down?"* She snapped at me, *"I don't want to sit down."* I was so embarrassed. It seems that people here don't give up their seat even to a little old woman who hardly has strength to stand straight. But now I do the same thing. If I see a woman standing, it's just like seeing a man. I look the other way and keep my seat.

Yes, women here think they're men. You see them wearing pants and smoking in the street. They have no respect for their husbands; he goes his way and she hers. A man has no way of knowing what his wife's up to. He's away at work all day and his friends won't tell him what his wife is up to, the way they do in Puerto Rico.

And on top of everything else, women have more rights than men. If you hit your wife she can have you arrested. The law's on her side. So here, women are the ones who rule. It's not like in Puerto Rico, where the man gives the orders. And that's the way it should be. The man should rule his home and his wife has to respect him. If she doesn't, how can he make himself respected among men?

I have noticed that Americans are different from Puerto Ricans in everything, even in love. White Americans, I mean. Because here there are two races, and two kinds of love. A white American sees a girl passing by. He stops his car and calls out to her, *"Do you want a ride?"* And the girl climbs into the car. Then they introduce themselves to each other, kiss and drive on as if this were the most natural thing in the world. They drive around for a while, then they get off at the Park, to do whatever they're going to do. Afterward each goes his own way, as if nothing had happened.

Even with their own wives the Americans are different. Look, my *boss* has a beautiful wife. She's eighteen. Well, she goes to the factory and he acts as if nobody had come. When she leaves he says, *"See you at home."* Sometimes she calls him and asks how he's doing. He answers, *"All right. See you later, honey,"* and hangs up. Those things shocked me and made me mad at first. But then I realized everybody acted the same way and I got used to it.

Life is good here but I'd rather live in Puerto Rico. I like it better. It's so beautiful! But as long as I'm here in New York, my ambition is to make money. I'm going to enroll in night school and learn to speak English well. Then maybe someday I'll get my wish, to be in the *merchant marine.* That way I could work on a ship and get the money to go back to Puerto Rico and buy a house of my own, because you never do get to own one here. You pay and keep on paying, year in and year out, and you never do get to own it. No, what I want is a little cottage in Puerto Rico where I can keep hogs, chickens and all sorts of animals. A home. A place where I can look at the mountains.

If I'm able to build myself a house there, I'll take my *mamá* to live with me. I'll divide the house in two and keep her there. That would be a good life, living in the country in Puerto Rico with my wife and with everything that I own here, my TV set, the record player and all. And with the rest of my family near me. Every day I wake up with that hope. Although I have doubts, too, now and then. Sometimes I have a dream. I see myself leaving New York

and going back to Puerto Rico. But when I get there I find myself friend-
less and alone. Nobody looks at me. No one seems to know me. I'm all dirty.
And in my dream I think, "What am I doing here in Puerto Rico where
nobody knows me anymore." Then I begin to cry. I feel, oh, I feel I sort
of shouldn't be in Puerto Rico at all. That's when I always wake up and say,
"It was only a dream. I'm still in New York."

Flora

I'll Carry That Cross Until I Die

I WAS LIVING in La Esmeralda with Fontánez when I first met Simplicio and his family. Felícita and Soledad were married and Cruz later ran off with Emilio. I remember one evening I was standing on the steps of the house and Cruz was talking to some girls near Bonilla's store. She was wearing pants. Her husband came and knocked her down and pulled off her pants right there in the street. I tell you, I never did like that man.

Then Felícita came to live in La Esmeralda. Her house was a mess, with filthy rags everywhere. Her children ran around without clothes and shit all over the place. The twins would get up at five in the morning and go out naked in the street looking for someone to give them coffee. Sometimes they came to my house and I'd feed them, and sometimes they'd spend the whole day with me.

Felícita is everybody's friend to their face but she skins them alive behind their back, gossiping and throwing barbs. I was angry with her once for that. I had had a fight with my husband, Fontánez, and I wasn't speaking to him. But she was speaking to him, and like a fool she says to me, "Look, go and make some coffee for Fontánez." So I told her, "Don't say anything more because I don't want to hear about that man." And I got mad at her. Then she began making comments and needling me and she didn't want the twins to go to my house any more. She told them, "If I catch you there I'll give you a whipping." So they were afraid and stopped coming.

Simplicio was just a kid then and he used to come to my house, too. He shined shoes and I would ask him to run errands for me. But I disliked him so much I could hardly bear to look at him. I used to call him "dog" because he was so dirty and because his pack of dogs followed him wherever he went. But as time went on, I began to feel sorry for him. No one paid any attention to him and everybody talked about him, so I began to be fond of him out of pity. I remember the first time I really noticed him. He was dressed in old blue jeans, a torn white T-shirt, black sneakers and a cap. After that he began to dress better. He would stop by my house and we got into the habit of talking and kidding around with each other. We got fonder and fonder of each other, until we suddenly realized we were in love. He was sixteen and I was twenty-four. Oh, Holy Mother, I don't understand it. The world is full of surprises.

Reinaldo, a cousin of Fontánez, told him that I had Simplicio in the house when he was away at work. That was a lie. Fontánez's work shift ended at eleven, but one night he came home at ten, hoping to catch me at it. He began to drink and woke me and asked if it was true that I was in love with Simplicio. I denied it but he insisted, "Yes, it's true. It's true." He had a dagger in his hand and I lay there in bed, trembling. "I'll kill you." he said and I answered, "Kill me then."

Fontánez kept after me every day, "Why don't you tell him to stop coming to this house?" Or he would say, "If you run off with that man, how is he going to keep you? You'll suffer with him. He's not one to support a woman." Yet at that very time Simplicio was working on the schooner and giving me money, although he was hardly more than a child. He was very good to me.

One night when Fontánez returned from work, he called Reinaldo into the room. I thought they must be talking about me, so I went to the kitchen and got a long knife. Then I said to Reinaldo, "Look here, why do you have to go talking about me?" And I stabbed him so hard that I cut his hand open. They went to get the cops, and while they were gone I slipped out and went to my aunt's house.

When Simplicio heard I had gone, he burst out crying. He was such an innocent, he thought I'd left because I didn't love him. The next day I was sweeping my aunt's porch when I heard a whistle. I looked up and saw Simplicio. I began to tremble. "Fernanda says you are to go to her," he said. Right out like that, in front of my aunt. My aunt is a terrible coward. She said, "Oh, don't. If you go there, they'll kill you."

"Let them kill me then," I answered.

Simplicio didn't take me to Fernanda's house after all. We went to an aunt of his in Mameyes. I was crying on the way. I asked him, "Simplicio, where are you taking me? What will my aunt say?" But I went with him anyway. Simplicio's aunt was very nice to us, but she drank and fought all the time. She invited us to stay with her and said she would help us get jobs. But we didn't stay long because I didn't like her behavior. Besides, it's very hard to find work in Mameyes.

When we got back to San Juan I heard Fontánez was with another woman, so I wasn't worried. Soledad told Simplicio he could bring me to her house. She had a tiny room next door to *doña* Minerva. Most people wouldn't have taken anybody else to live with them in such a small room, but Soledad, being what she was, took us in. She is generous that way. I had known her ever since she began to live with Tavio. I used to buy a lot of things from him. He was awfully good. His only fault was that he stole. He was already dead when we went to live with Soledad.

Simplicio and I were getting along very well with each other. He's real hot and satisfies me. And he was always with me. He was out of a job and Soledad kept telling him that he didn't even try to look for work. Simplicio was only a boy then, but he did go out looking for a job. He got up real early every morning and was off to the docks. Then, not being able to get work there, he'd go over and help *don* Colón, who would pay him a couple of dollars. Simplicio always turned that money over to Soledad.

Soledad was down-and-out too, just like Simplicio. She with that tremendous belly, and no one to give her anything. She was pregnant with Toya and in mourning. There were times when she had no food to give her children. Arturo gave them nothing. He didn't have a job. All he did was gamble. Yet he objected to Soledad's falling in love with anyone else and they quarreled constantly. They lived in a state of war.

One day Soledad said, "Flora, I'm going out to try to get some money. Take care of the kids for me." She dressed in half-mourning and went to La Marina. She didn't put on any make-up and she was near the end of her pregnancy; yet, in spite of all that, she came back with money. Fifty or sixty dollars she brought. She's just plain lucky. I wasn't ashamed to use some of that money. Simplicio was out of work, and so was I.

Then Soledad got friendly with *don* Camacho, the owner of the Silver Cup, and she used to go to sleep with the old man right there. He gave her lots and lots of money, one hundred, two hundred dollars at a time. And he was planning to buy her a fourteen-room house so that she could take in boarders and live well, but Soledad didn't want to accept that. Maybe because he had a wife and children.

I had a hard time taking care of Soledad's kids. Sarita cried all the time. I had to get up several times a night to give her milk, but she still cried and I didn't know what to do. That went on for about a month. Then one day Fernanda spoke to me. She said she had refused to let Simplicio and me live with her because to get to her house, we would have had to pass through the alley where Fontánez lived. Then she asked me about the food she sent for Simplicio and me, and I answered, "I don't know. No one ever told me about it." Fernanda explained that she had been sending the two of us food all along. Soledad never told us. She gave it to her children. Then Fernanda invited us to move in with her. I hated to tell Soledad when she was so hard up, but finally I made up my mind and told her. Soledad cried, not because she was so fond of me, but because she needed someone to take care of the children.

At Fernanda and Héctor's house I felt completely at home. There was a parlor and two bedrooms. In one of them was Fernanda's bed and the twins' *caucho*. In the other she had a small bed for me and Simplicio. And she put a clothes rack up for me, and hung up curtains, and sewed me a bedspread. She was very nice.

I kept her house spic-and-span. She had bunches of artificial flowers all over and I was always washing the flowers. I really took possession of that house. When the twins were living there I used to get mad at them because they ate in the parlor and made it all messy after I had gone to such pains to have everything clean and neat. Fernanda would say, "Look at that, the kids have spilled rice all over the parlor." And she'd shoo them off to the kitchen. They were such pigs! Then she would barricade the door so they couldn't get into the parlor, because she always liked to have everything nice and clean. You know how Puerto Rican children go around barefoot and track up everything. Fernanda was always after the kids. "Get off that bed! You'll dirty up Flora's sheet."

Fernanda took me everywhere with her. She would take me to the movies. She would take me shopping and buy me whatever I needed. I still have a pair of shoes she bought me. She bought underclothes for me and all sorts of things, just as if she had been my mother. Nanda was always good to me.

I got pregnant at that time but I kept on menstruating. I just thought that my blood was weak. When I went to a doctor he told me I had to stay in bed. After that Nanda wouldn't let me do anything, not even take up a broom. She used to say, "The only child I'll ever take to raise is yours and Simplicio's— my son's child." She was wildly happy. She said she would buy the crib; she was already sewing little baby shirts. She would say, "That baby is the only one I love. After you bear him, if you and Simplicio should ever break up, the baby will be mine." And Simplicio. *Bendito!* He would stroke my belly and say softly, "My baby." He wouldn't let me do a thing for fear I would harm myself.

But in the fifth month I got pains. It was pains, pains, pains all the time. Fernanda called an ambulance and I was taken to the hospital. The baby was already dead and I had to have an operation to take him out.

They took me down to the operating room and I lost all my self-control. I screamed and screamed. Such a bad pain I had, oh God! I could see them operate on me. They had me there naked, with only a green sort of shirt on me. And I could see the doctor taking stuff out of me and all the blood. When I woke up and realized I was in the hospital, I tried to get out of bed but I couldn't. I looked down and saw my belly wrapped in bloody bandages and I tore them off. I screamed at the doctor, "You killed me! You killed me!" A nurse hurried in and held me down. There was a needle stuck in my arm and I tore it out, which made my arm swell up.

Simplicio came to see me but they don't let anybody into the surgical ward. He kept coming back every night. Finally he told a nurse to ask me to come out to him. I hadn't even tried to get up yet, but I put on my slippers and slowly, slowly crept out to Simplicio. When I got to him I couldn't say a word. So he said, "You don't love me any more."

"*Ay*, Simplicio," I wailed, "what do you want me to do?" He was on one side of the closed gate and I on the other. I stayed there for about five minutes. Then I said, "*Ay*, Simplicio, I can't stand any longer, I'm dizzy. Good-bye." So Simplicio left and I tried to find my way back.

The doctor scolded me and said I wasn't supposed to get up. But the next night when I rang for the nurse to give me the bedpan, nobody came. I had glucose dripping into a vein in each arm. I got up and took out one needle but left the other in. Then, holding a bottle of glucose in my hand, I got up and went barefoot to the bathroom. I really got chilled in that short hospital nightshirt with my whole ass out. *Ay*, dear God, that shirt really embarrassed me!

I stayed in the hospital for about two weeks but I couldn't get used to it. And then they didn't want to let me out until I had paid for the blood transfusions. But Simplicio was out of work and didn't have the money, so the doctor said I couldn't leave. "Then I'll stay here," I answered and they decided to let me go. Before I left, the doctor told me that I couldn't have any children and that he was going to take out my womb.

Fernanda was wonderful to me. She didn't let me do anything that might hurt me. About a month later I was pregnant again. It was the same thing all over again. They called the ambulance and sent me back to the hospital. I was in bed for a week without a bite of food. I was kept alive with glucose solution and whole blood. But the blood they gave me went bad inside my body. I watched it drip into my arm and it was very thick. It made me itch and break out in a rash all over my body. When they saw that, they took it away from me, but ever since then, the rash has kept coming back. It must have been bad blood.

Simplicio always worries about me and takes good care of me, but sometimes we fight. We had one terrible fight in Puerto Rico, and all over nothing. It was Catín's fault. That child made up stories. One Thanksgiving Day she went and told Simplicio that Fernanda and I were in San Juan drinking. I never drink. Then the child came back and told me that Simplicio was in

Papo's *bar* with a woman. Well, Simplicio came home and pushed me so hard that I fell over backward on the kitchen floor. I called him names, *maricón* and a lot of other things. Then everybody got into the fight. Nanda hit Simplicio with a bottle and Soledad went after him with a baseball bat. Then Simplicio threw a knife at Soledad and almost hit Héctor. Soledad struck out at Simplicio with her bat and hit Héctor instead. You should have seen the lump on his head! Nanda bit Simplicio. Then Soledad got hold of a knife and tried to stab Simplicio but she only scratched Héctor instead. Héctor was drunk, he wasn't fighting. He just said, "Well, I'd better get out of here before they kill me," and he left. Then *don* Camacho walked in, but seeing the fight, he turned around and went out.

I was so scared! All I could think was, "Simplicio's surely going to kill me." Then Fernanda hit him with a Pepsi-Cola bottle. "Now I'll go get the cops and have you arrested," she yelled. But she only said that to make him calm down. When Simplicio saw her go, he put on his shirt and went to the police station himself. "I'm the one who was fighting," he told them. About two hours later Fernanda and I went to get him and he came back with us as if nothing had happened.

One good thing about Simplicio was that he turned over to me every last penny that came to his hands. He didn't have a *steady* job but he gave me all he earned. Sometimes, if he gave me five dollars, I would keep three and give Fernanda the other two. Every night he drank a quart of milk with cookies. When I was mad at him I wouldn't buy anything and he would beg me, "Flora, give me some money to buy milk."

"I will not," I always answered. Then I fished out the money and handed it to him, because he really looked as if he would die! Yes, die. For fifteen cents! Because he couldn't bear to miss that milk for even one day! I've always been too soft with him because I pity him. Sometimes when he treats me badly I decide to walk out on him. But then I think, "If I leave him he will surely go to jail." I think I keep on living with him for his mother's sake, so that he won't land in jail. Because if I wasn't here beside him, that's what would happen.

When we were living with them, I saw for myself how good Héctor was to Nanda. *Ave María Purísima,* he was wonderful to me too! When I was in the hospital and Simplicio was out of work, Héctor gave Nanda money to buy me a nightgown and slippers. Anyone could see he loved Fernanda. When he came home from work he always brought some little thing for her. And Fernanda loved him too. I don't know what happened between them to make them break up. Héctor was no skirt-chaser, although it's true that he was sort of a drunk. But when he drank, all he did was go home, lie down and start talking nonsense, lying there in bed. That burned her up. She'd get real mad at him. Fernanda drank too, but not as much as Héctor, and she didn't get annoying. When she was drunk she slept it off and then went a long time without drinking. It never got be a vice with her, the way it is with some women.

After we had lived with Fernanda awhile, Simplicio decided he wanted to go to the United States because it was harder and harder to get work in Puerto Rico. Fernanda didn't want him to go but he was determined, and he reserved a plane ticket with a down payment of two dollars. Whenever he could, he would put down money on account. So then Fernanda helped him and he got ready to go.

The only time I met Simplicio's father was that day when he came to the airport to tell Simplicio good-bye. He's white, just like Soledad. His wife, Hortensia, came along, but I didn't bother to even look at her. They came in their car and we went in another one. They didn't speak to me because they consider themselves a little rich, so they're stuck up.

While Simplicio was in New York I lived with Nanda because my parents were country people and very poor.

My *papá* worked on the coffee plantation of *don* Leopoldo Rojas, who had given us a house to live in. Our little house was as poor as it could be, with a tar-paper roof and wooden walls. There was no furniture except the beds. My *papá* and *mamá* and some of my brothers and sisters all picked coffee, but even so we never had enough money and my *papá* also worked on sugar cane elsewhere.

My father is a very serious-minded man. He and my *mamá* were not married, yet I never saw him with another woman. My *mamá* was thirteen years old when she went with my *papá* and she bore about fifteen children, all but one of whom are still alive. When I was still a child I took care of my younger brothers and sisters when my *mamá* went out to pick coffee. I cooked, washed dishes, did the laundry and everything. And I really loved to do it. My *mamá* never beat me and she did not allow me to go coffee-picking because I was sickly.

My parents are people of good character. My *papá* was the one who taught me my prayers and he taught us to make the sign of the cross before going to bed. Both my parents prayed every night and they taught me Our Father, the Credo, and many things I don't remember any more. They also sent us to a tiny country church every Sunday. A *sister* came all the way from the town to teach us the catechism. She was very nice and I learned a lot with her, but I never got a chance to make my First Communion. My *papá* and my *mamá* sometimes went to the town church for the Holy Week, to see the procession. It was lovely, so many saints and Jesus looking so pretty, and lots of people!

I was seven when my *papá* took me to school, but I didn't like it. Often I left home as if to go to school but I went to play with other children. I didn't know anything, and the teacher punished me because when she asked me to read I couldn't. When I was in the second grade I myself decided to leave school.

My *papá* did not allow me to go out alone, and when I did he would scold me and hit me. I was also beaten for smoking. My *papá* and my *mamá* used to ask me to light cigarettes for them and that's how I learned to smoke. I used to take bits of paper and wrap them around tobacco and smoke them. When *papá* caught me he slapped my mouth until my lips were all puffed up. Sometimes I hid under the bed to smoke. I would watch to see where *papá* threw his cigarette butt so I could pick it up. That just shows what a hold the vice has. Sometimes he squashed his cigarette butts with his shoe and I cried tears of disappointment.

I never knew any of my *papá*'s relatives and nobody ever told me anything about them. I remember my mother's parents, though. They were rich. They had a farm with cows, horses and pigs. They lived on top of a little hill in a house much bigger than ours. It had four bedrooms, a sitting room and a kitchen. My grandmother had twenty children. Five died, I think. That lady didn't like her grandchildren. When we went to her house she'd say, "You kids come here to pester us." But children are shameless, and I kept on going there in the afternoon so that they'd give me dinner. They ate early. At my house we ate later and I got hungry long before dinnertime. When the old woman saw me, or any of us, she'd cover up the pot and say, "Listen, your *papá* is calling you. Run along now or you'll get a beating."

She did that because she didn't care for us. I would go and insult her. "You are a mean one. You cover the pot so you won't have to offer us food."

My uncles were fresh. You see, they were older men, twenty or twenty-five years old, and yet they had never married. I remember how my eldest uncle used to make love to me. I was a little girl, only about eleven. I didn't have breasts yet. He would set me down, then he'd sit in front of me where he could peek underneath my skirt. He said, "When you grow up I'm going to marry you." Then he'd hug me and try to kiss me. I used to go home crying. My grandmother said he was only joking. Being an ignorant child, I would think, "Maybe my grandmother is right."

I treated my uncles like brothers and I would be ashamed to tell an improper joke or to wear shorts in their presence. I wouldn't do it for anything in the world, not if Christ Himself came down to earth and asked me to. And yet, look at what that old woman did! If she encouraged her sons to act like that with their nieces, heaven only knows what she let them do to their sisters. And they have so many sisters! Every one of my uncles acted like that. I have never, never told any of that to my *mamá*. How could I tell her such a thing about her own brothers?

. . .

I was twelve years old when I went to work. I was still a little girl, but I wanted to work so I could buy the things I needed. My *papá* couldn't afford to buy clothes and shoes for so many children although it is true we never went hungry. We didn't eat much meat but we had plenty of rice and vegetables.

Doña Rita was the name of the lady I worked for. She was a schoolteacher. I had to clean, cook, do the laundry—everything. And I slept in.

I didn't like working there because *doña* Rita's brother bothered me all the time. He was an old man, about forty years old. I don't know whether he had ever been married or not. I didn't dare ask him. Sometimes he would follow me out on the porch, and the things he said frightened me. When we were alone in the house he would grab me and kiss me like a madman. I'd wriggle out of his grasp and run to the porch.

He knew that I liked to smoke and he brought me packs of cigarettes but Christ Himself couldn't have made me accept them. "No, no," I would say, weeping, "I don't want them," and I would run away, fearing he had put something in those cigarettes to harm me.

That old man used to say that he wanted to marry me, and that he was going to buy a car and we two would go riding in it all by ourselves. Oh, he offered me so many things! If I had known as much as I do now I would have married him, and I would be a millionaire today, with my own house. I think he really was a good man but I hadn't yet learned how to love. So finally I told my *mamá* that I wanted to leave that place because of the gentleman.

A friend got me another job, with *doña* Sole. She and her husband had two children; the smallest was only a month old when I went to work there. That child was fonder of me than of her own mother, so I had to take that blessed baby and rock and rock and rock. I really spoiled her, I loved her so. Many's the meal I cooked while carrying that child on one arm. At night I was the one who got up to give her her bottle. She got to be so attached to me that she didn't care for her *mamá*.

Doña Sole treated me very well and never once was unpleasant to me. But the work was hard anyway and I got pretty tired of working as a servant. I couldn't even buy clothes for myself because, *bendito,* my poor father was having trouble with his eye sight and he took most of my money.

My *papá* had turned me over to *doña* Sole on condition that she would never let me go out alone. So she used to take me everywhere she went. She often told me, "Whenever you feel like going to the movies, let me know. I'll take you." But I would have been embarrassed to ask her to do that. The only outing that ever occurred to me was to visit my parents at home.

Across the street from *doña* Sole's there was a garage, and a boy named Dionicio worked there. I got into the habit of sitting on the front porch to rock the baby. And as I rocked I watched Dionicio, and so I fell in love with him.

He had very fair skin and bright blue eyes. He was very handsome, a real *pollo,* a young cock. I fell in love with that damn boy because of his looks, and God punished me for it.

I hated working as a maid, always being ordered around by somebody. That's why I went off with that man, that *bum!* Dionicio had gotten a room for me a long time before. But every time he asked me to move in with him I put him off, "No, not yet." I was waiting for something better to turn up. But one day *doña* Sole and her family went on a trip and I found myself alone. I left the house key with a neighbor and went to meet Dionicio. I never went back to that house, not even to get my things. All I carried away from there were the clothes on my back.

Dionicio took me to live in a *barrio* near the beach. What a brute that man was the first night! He hurt me terribly. I said, "No, no," and tried to get up and run out. Then, seeing I didn't want to do it, he beat me with his fists. I cried out, "I do love you but I don't want to do these things."

He mistreated me from the very first. He was bad! He gave me food to eat but never any money, and I wanted clothes and shoes. And every night he wanted to get on top of me again and again. I didn't like that. It hurt so! All I wanted was for him to get off, to go away, to leave me alone. And every time, seeing I didn't want it, he beat me to make me do it.

My aunt Maritza lived in the same *barrio,* and so did a girl friend of mine who was also a housemaid. But I couldn't get to them to ask their help because Dionicio kept me locked up. I was lost, utterly lost. Then I got a chance to talk with the girl and I said to her, "Find me a job, will you? I'm leaving." She got a job for me and I walked out on him. I didn't take anything, only the clothes on my back. I had lived with him for a little over a month.

Dionicio tried to get me to come back to him. Once when the lady sent me on an errand, he came up to me with a *Gem* in his hand. "Come along with me," he said. "If you don't, I'll slash your face and your ass."

"Go ahead, cut me," I answered. "Only remember, if you do, you'll land in jail. And I'll walk in front of your cell window on another man's arm. I don't love you."

I don't know why it is, but I'm not afraid of anything. But if he had cut my face, I would never again have dared go out in the street. Because anybody who sees a woman with a scarred face is sure to think she's a whore. Thank God that has never happened to me and I pray it never will!

My family knew nothing of what I had been doing. I went and told my *mamá* all about it, but only after we had broken up. It was my duty to tell her. I had gone off with a man and it wasn't right to let her believe I was still a *señorita.* Well, she practically had a fit when she learned I had lost my virginity. She cried, "You! My eldest daughter!"

Papá never knew it. If he had, he would have killed me. Why, he practically killed my sister Arlín when she took off with her boy friend. As for my eldest brother, he would have slit my throat if he had known. So I went back to working and helping my family as before. I went home for visits and I didn't fall in love again for a long, long time. Not for years, in fact. I was fifteen or sixteen then and I thought, "I'm no longer a virgin, so I probably can't get married."

Then I went to live with my aunt Sonia, who had moved to San Juan. My aunt lived at Stop 27, where she rented a beautiful cement house with four rooms. There was a lovely garden, all full of flowers. My aunt's husband held two jobs. At night he worked for the electric light company and in the daytime he drove a milk *truck*. He earned good money that way.

I had never been in San Juan before and at first I was very homesick and wanted to go back to Arecibo. I didn't like San Juan because I had no friends there and nowhere to go.

My aunt got me a job in the house of some Spaniards, whose name I don't remember. They were bad as they could be. Oh, my! There were times when I didn't eat. They had an enormous house and I had to mop the floor of every room every single day. I don't want to talk about that, or even remember it. I earned twenty dollars a month, ten for me and ten for my aunt. I also wrote my family and sent them money, out of my ten. I thought about them all the time. I wanted to die! Nothing but work, work, work!

Then I met Fontánez. He passed by that house every single day. We saw each other, talked to each other, and fell in love. One day he asked me to go off with him and I did. I was so tired of working as a servant. He took me to his aunt Cristina's house at Stop 31.

My aunt Sonia said she never wanted to see me again because I had gone off with that man. She said, "You've ruined our breed, taking off with a black man. Aren't you scared of him?"

"Scared? Why should I be? He's a man like any other. And I like Negroes."

I sent word to my parents that I had gone off with a man and later on I took him home to meet them. My *papá* was crazy about Fontánez; they hit it off from the first. *Papá* would say to us, "Who cares if his lips hang down to his chin, as long as he's a good man?" And Fontánez was very nice to my parents. He gave them money.

They didn't know what was cooking in that pot, but I did. Fontánez never gave me one single penny. He stayed in his aunt's house and in the afternoon he'd bring me some food or else take me out to eat somewhere. I never ate a bite of that woman's food. I never spoke a word in that house either. And oh, that bunch of kids she had! I was up at the crack of dawn to take care of them. What a life! I lasted there one month.

Then I moved to La Esmeralda with Fontánez. I never had seen that filthy place before. It was a dung heap! The kids left their shit all over the place because the houses had no *toilets*. And the neighbors tossed their gar-

bage on the beach, without regard for anybody else's feelings. We lived on the
second floor and had no water, so we had to go down to *doña* Minerva's and
pay her a nickel for the use of her shower.

I never set foot out of the house because I was scared of the people in La
Esmeralda. There were so many drunks and whores! I cried, thinking, "People
will believe I'm one of them." I didn't dare go out for fear someone would
harm me. Fights were always starting there. I didn't know any dirty words
when I first went to La Esmeralda, words like *coño, carajo, puñeta*. It made
me so ashamed, I wanted to hide my face. I was timid, you see, a country girl
whose father had whipped her if she so much as said, "May evil lightning split
you."

As time went on I got used to life in La Esmeralda. In fact, I got to like it
so well I didn't want to leave. At first Fontánez and I lived in a tiny room, with
a bed, a rusty little stove and nothing to sit on. Fontánez used to bring a lot of
friends home and they had to sit on the bed. That made me so ashamed, him
acting like that with all the money he made. He was a foreman and earned
twenty-two dollars a day. I begged and begged him to take me out of that
little room, and finally we moved to another place where we lived for almost
a year. Then we moved again because the roof leaked and the house was full
of rats.

Fontánez had a wife but he denied it. The fact is, he had a wife and five
children. He used to go to sleep with her and then come back with the story
that he had been at a wake or had spent the night in jail. And I, like a damn
fool, believed him. I was still ignorant at that time. One day his first wife,
Teresa, showed up at our house, but nothing happened because he'd had another woman between the time he left her and the time he took me. He was a
real woman chaser.

Teresa was very nice to me. And as she was the mother of his children, I
always welcomed her. When she came to our home I always served her whatever food I'd cooked. If she saw that Fontánez was going to hit me, she always
stepped between us and said, "If you beat her, you'll have to beat me too."

"Ah, you women are all the same," he would answer.

Teresa always said to me, "If you want to leave and have no place to go,
remember you're always welcome at my house." I took care of her children
and she paid me ten dollars for that.

I didn't want to leave Fontánez, although I didn't love him. He and I
hardly ever did anything together because he was always out with other
women. He had me, yet he felt he had to have two other women at the same
time. He went into *bars* and squandered his money on other women. He used
to hide his money from me, but I got it anyway. He paraded his women in
front of me and that hurt terribly. He was a drunk too. Sometimes he drank
until daybreak.

That man even infected me. My womb was inflamed and my ovaries hurt, but Fontánez never bothered to take me to a doctor. It was his wife, Teresa, who gave me the money to go, although she earned only thirty dollars working in a factory. The doctor prescribed a long series of douches and some medicine to drink which took my pain away. And he advised me not to have intercourse with Fontánez nor live with him any longer. Later he infected me all over again. That's the reason why I can't have children.

Sometimes I hated Fontánez so much that I felt like walking out on him. It got so I didn't know where I could turn for help. Then Teresa took me to see a spiritist who told me everything there was to tell about Fontánez. That woman knows a lot, really a lot. I could hardly believe my ears. She asked me if I knew anyone called Zulma and I told her I did. Then she said, "Well, that woman wants to see you become a whore and if you don't want to, she'll cut your face." Then she added, "But she hasn't been able to work any evil on you because the spirit of your grandfather walks with you and because your little brother who died and who is now an angel lights your way." And that was true. But the thought rather scared me.

I stayed with Fontánez for five years. I get furious at myself every time I remember that. I hope our paths never cross again. I was grateful to Simplicio for taking me away from him.

When Simplicio was in New York he started working right away, because Edmundo found a job for him. As soon as he got paid Simplicio sent a letter with money for me and for Nanda. He didn't tell me anything about what it was like there. He only wrote that he was saving money for my fare so I could join him. Simplicio was very unhappy at first because he didn't know anyone there, and Felícita wasn't nice to him. She had a washing machine but she wouldn't put Simplicio's clothes in it. In fact, she'd throw some of his things away rather than take the trouble to wash them.

Then Soledad got it into her head that she wanted to go to New York and she made me come too. She said she would come only if I did. "I won't go," I'd tell her. "Why should I suffer? I'm a sick woman." I was almost dead after my miscarriage and I weighed only eighty pounds.

Finally I decided to come. Old man Camacho paid my fare as well as Soledad's and gave us each twenty-five dollars to buy a suitcase and clothes for the trip.

Then, after everything was ready, I changed my mind. Even when I got on the plane I wanted to get off. But the plane started just then and I fell sprawling on the floor. I hadn't fastened my seat belt, see? Afterward I fell asleep and knew nothing more until we landed. When I got out of the plane I burst into tears. Everything looked so sad and dull and I said to myself, "So this is New York." Simplicio and another man met us at the airport and drove us to Felícita's house. It took seven hours, and by the time we got there we were exhausted.

I can't even bear to remember that time we spent at Felícita's. We didn't get enough to eat. Felícita had boarders besides her family, so the rest of us got only leftovers and scraps. Simplicio bought food for breakfast, eggs, bread, and milk, yet I never dared open the refrigerator, so he usually left without breakfast. When he came back from work at about seven o'clock, I couldn't feed him, either. I didn't dare. All I could do was worry and suffer. Finally Felícita would ask Simplicio if he wanted any dinner and he's say no and go out into the street. My heart was torn with pity for him. I could never be so mean to a brother of mine. And over food!

Soledad had to leave. Eddy, one of Felícita's boarders, said he would take Soledad away from there and he wanted me to come with them. But I didn't know him well and I am very shy. I said to myself, "If I go with them, it will only be to suffer in a different place." Simplicio didn't want me to go and neither did Felícita. So I stayed.

Felícita wanted me there because I helped her out so much. I did the washing and ironing, and when Felícita went to look for a job, she'd find I had cooked the dinner while she was away. That's why she was so bent on my staying.

I never went out anywhere as long as I lived in Felícita's house. I just stayed in, washing and ironing clothes for all those kids, and cooking while she lounged in bed. Felícita looks clean but she's the dirtiest woman in the world. And always out of sorts and with a pout on her face.

Then I fell in love with a boy I met there. I never had an affair with him or anything like that. It was all platonic. He wrote me letters and I answered them. He asked me to go off with him, saying he had already rented a room for us. I thought it over very carefully and finally answered no, because I knew I still loved and always would love Simplicio. But then I changed my mind. I wrote him to come and get me, that I was willing. Not that I had stopped loving Simplicio, but he didn't earn enough to get a room for us and I was getting desperate. But I couldn't bring myself to send that letter after all. I folded it and put it away.

Then one day Simplicio began going through my letters. I grabbed that one and cried out, "Oh no, not that!" He snatched it from me and gave it to Fela to read. It didn't say anything bad, really. I only told that boy I would go off with him and asked him to come and get me. But Simplicio, ay, he nearly killed me! He tore off my clothes to keep me from leaving the house. Then he went out for a while and came back with a grim look on his face and a knife in his hand. I locked myself up in the bathroom because his first words were, "I'm going to cut you to pieces!"

By the next morning we had made up and Simplicio took me away. He went to work for a man who owned seventy houses. Hombre! Mr. Cohen he was called. That man let us have a nice apartment and he gave us our food. He had a wife and three children and they lived in a big house. I used to go there to clean on Saturdays and Sundays when their regular maid was off. But they all embarrassed me by speaking English to me. I used to beg Simplicio, "Tell them I have a headache today so they won't make me go over to the house." We lived in that place for about six months.

Finally my brother in Pennsylvania wrote to me and I went there to visit. My family was very happy to see me and insisted that I stay. They got Simplicio a job in a hospital and so we moved there. We found ourselves an apartment. The only piece of furniture we had was a bed. The electricity wasn't connected, so we moved in in the dark. We moved after Simplicio got home from work at eleven o'clock, with no help from anybody. Simplicio carried everything over himself. At the end of the week Simplicio got paid and we bought some of the things we needed. We kept on getting things like that, little by little, and made the house look very pretty.

We were doing quite nicely there in Pennsylvania. Simplicio had an American Negro friend named Charles. He was really good, he took me to his house and everything. He was very nice to me and so was his wife. They used to come to our house and sing and make tape-recordings. When Simplicio has a friend, he treats him like a brother and shares with him whatever he has. He always gets along well with his friends.

Nanda wrote to me that she wanted a wrist watch for Mother's Day and I told Simplicio, "Get the watch for Nanda." But then Nanda wrote to forget about the watch because she had bought one herself and instead, if he could, Simplicio should send her money for a plane ticket so she could come and have a little vacation up here. Héctor had no objection to her coming, she said, because she was going back to him afterward. So Simplicio bought her a ticket. The night she arrived, I was very happy. I've always loved her because she has been so good to me.

Simplicio wanted Fernanda to stay for good but she was homesick. She asked Simplicio to buy her a ticket to go back. She said she hated the States and would never in her life come back.

Soon after Nanda went back, she wrote us that she had left Héctor and was living with Junior. Simplicio's comment on this news was, "I wonder what made Nanda do that? She's really put her foot in it this time." Simplicio didn't know then that Fernanda had cut Héctor. He learned that from Catín when she came. And even then he couldn't quite believe it. That kid is such a little liar.

For me, life in Pennsylvania was simply divine. But Simplicio had problems in his work and we decided to move to New York. Simplicio sold everything we had bought, for only thirty dollars. Crazy! It made me terribly angry and it made me cry too, to think of all the trouble I'd gone through to get my things, all the expense, and then, to have them go for thirty miserable dollars! So we came here, to New York, and went to Soledad's house. She wanted us to move in with her but I said, "No, I only want to rent a room of our own. A room and a bed, that's all." I didn't want to stay in her house because of all those kids. So we got a tiny little room and we moved into it.

For a while I took care of Soledad's children for her and she paid me twelve dollars, although she used to pay another woman fifteen. But those kids didn't respect me. Sarita is a terrible brat. When I slapped her hands, she'd try to hit me. And so did that Toya. I was going crazy and I told Soledad to get somebody else to look after her girls, but no matter how often I told her, Benedicto would bring them over to me.

I begged and begged Simplicio to let me take a job so we could get a real apartment. He was only earning forty-six dollars a week, barely enough to pay the food bill. But no, not him. He didn't want me to go out of the house to work because he was afraid I'd fall in love. But he gave in, finally. He himself went with me to the factory where Soledad worked and waited there until they hired me. He even stayed on awhile after I had started working, until the *boss* told him to go because I was busy. Simplicio still gets angry when I work *overtime*. He wants to find me home when he arrives, with the house all neat and his dinner ready.

I have problems with Simplicio. If he has money he spends it right away. That man doesn't care about money. When he shops for food he buys and buys and never thinks of the cost. Listen, he once saw a twenty-two-dollar bedspread and he asked me, "Shall I buy that little bedspread for you?" I said, "No, I have more bedspreads than I need already. Forget it, we can't afford it." So then he got mad. That's why he gives me his money to keep, because he knows he'll squander it, and I save. Aside from little things like that, he's good to me.

Simplicio did play a dirty trick on me once, but he never has since. I had a friend named Leila who used to come to our home with her family. They were starving and I fed them. I treated them like my own sisters. There were three of them, the mother, Leila and her younger sister. I don't like to see anybody suffer, so when they came here I gave them some of everything we had to eat. I even loaned Leila some of my clothes.

Leila hung around the house a lot and I noticed that she often looked at Simplicio. She's one of those women who take one man today and another tomorrow. Man-crazy! I had my suspicions but I said to myself, "Until I catch them at it I won't do anything." And I did catch them!

One day we were at Gina's house. She's a friend of ours. I went out to do some shopping with Gina. "Simplicio, you stay here until I come back," I told him. But when we got back, Catín says to me, "Sotero told Simplicio to go over to Leila's place." Think of that, my own brother serving as go-between! He says that I am his favorite among all his sisters. And yet, look at what he did!

Oh, I got furious! I went to get Soledad, who was at a dance, and together we went to Leila's house. I pushed the apartment door open and there they were, Leila's mother, Sotero and my own Simplicio, talking with Leila in the kitchen. She was wearing a nightgown and one of those flimsy negligees. I went up to Simplicio and said to him, "What the hell are you doing here?" I grabbed him by the shirt and tore it and made a mess of his face, I slapped it so hard so many times. Then I turned on Leila and knocked her down. And the things I said to her: "You dirty bitch, what are you doing, talking to my husband in your night clothes?"

Simplicio broke in, "Look, Flora, I don't give a damn about this woman."

"You dirty bastard! If you don't give a damn about her what are you doing here?" I screamed. "Look here," I said to him, "if you're interested in her, pack up your clothes and go get her an apartment. Forget all about me. She's younger than I am, anyway. Go ahead, get out and leave me." While I raged, Simplicio just stood there weeping. "She's the one that chases after me," he sobbed. "I was just telling her that I would never leave you for her."

Simplicio tells everybody that he loves me too much to leave me, ever. He says, "Flora is the only woman who has been able to make a decent man of me." That is why I give him good advice and tell him, "Simplicio, do this," or "Simplicio, don't do that." Sometimes he grumbles, "Ah, leave me alone. You're always after me." But he always does what I say.

I have lived with Simplicio since he was a mere boy. I almost broke up with him once because he was so young and I so much older. I was ashamed. I still don't believe he loves me. But I love him. I love him truly. He says he loves me but it seems to me he must be lying. Because sometimes he gets drunk and starts insulting me the minute he gets home, "I know you have put the horns on me, so I'm going to kill you." The other day he pushed me in the presence of my brother. I tell him, "But, Simplicio, I haven't done anything wrong." I even cry and I wish I were a little girl again so as not to have to suffer with men the way I do. Then he asks me, "Do you love me?" And I say, "Simplicio, if I didn't love you, would I be living with you? I'm not married to you. If I wanted to leave you I'd do it in a minute."

Now he's set his heart on having a baby. Every time he mentions a baby, it tears my guts out. I keep talking about how hard up we are and how much it costs to bring up children. And I tell him we already have Gabi. But I'm under treatment to see if I can conceive. I want to bear Simplicio a son, a son to love. And besides, sometimes men are more apt to stay quietly at home if they have a child. Simplicio says that if he had a son he would be completely happy and would spend all his time looking after the child and not go out, not even to work.

Simplicio and I have made a solemn promise to each other and we've even shaken hands on it. We said, "When you die, take me with you. If I die first, I will take you." I feel happy now. I do still get into rages sometimes but that is because I love him so much. It's like a madness. I'll carry that cross for Simplicio until I die.

PART V

CRUZ

—————

A Day with Cruz
in San Juan

ROSA WAS on her way to La Esmeralda to spend a Sunday with Cruz. It was about seven o'clock in the morning. She passed Bonilla's grocery store, went down the cement steps on the opposite side of the road, and turned west onto a narrow cement ledge that served as a path for a row of decrepit houses. This ledge, carelessly constructed of rough cement from which large stones protruded here and there, was difficult to walk on. It led upward along the embankment until at Cruz's house it was twelve feet higher than the street below.

The two-story wooden building in which Cruz lived was gray and blank-faced, with tiny windows and doors. Although it had a cement base and was buttressed by two twenty-foot planks, it leaned out precariously over the ledge. Cruz's small apartment was the middle one of three on the ground floor. The second story also contained three apartments; the tenants of the upper story entered their rooms from a rear alley which was fifteen or twenty feet higher than the entrance to Cruz's house. A small red-and-white Popular Party flag flew from a stick over Cruz's window. Cruz and her family belonged to the Republican Statehood Party which advocated statehood for Puerto Rico, but she displayed the flag of Muñoz Marín's Popular Party because she received relief money from the Muñoz Administration.

When Rosa reached the house, she turned and looked down at the street below. It was quiet now, with only a few people out and about. Down the hill a little girl sat silently in a cardboard box. A man relaxed in a chair in front of his house, fanning himself. On a balcony a woman was combing her hair. *Doña* Yolanda was sweeping the street in front of her bar, while several drunks waited for her to open the doors.

Across the road in the vacant lot cluttered with rubbish, garbage and the rusty chassis of junked cars, three-year-old Mundito, the son of Cruz's sister Felícita, was banging on the fenders of a car. Gabi,* his seven-year-old brother, and his four-year-old sister Tany were playing nearer the house, apparently waiting for Cruz to let them in. Gabi was wearing white shorts and Tany a white skirt and a pink-trimmed blouse; their clothes were grimy with dirt. The children recognized Rosa and called out to her as she climbed the three crude, high cement blocks which led from the ledge up to the entrance of Cruz's apartment.

The entryway was low and dark and about six feet long. Without a light and without an outside door, it seemed like the entrance to a cave. Cobwebs laced across the ceiling, which was a patchwork of overlapping boards, old and new, of different sizes, shapes and colors, nailed there by various tenants whenever a small section rotted away. Here and there accumulated dust curls hung from rusty nails. The wooden walls were unpainted, their horizontal boards defaced with illegible scribblings in crayon, ink and pencil. On a door to the right was a cardboard sign which said, in Cruz's ill-formed printing, "Please pour water in the toilet. Don't be such a pig. And don't throw papers on the floor either." This message was for the other tenants on the ground floor, who also used the toilet.

Across the front of the little vestibule, Cruz had fastened the side of an old crib to protect her children from falling to the cement ledge four feet below. Cruz often used the entryway as an extra room, where she washed clothes, nursed her children or just relaxed. From this vantage point, high against the hill, she could watch people going back and forth on the streets below. She could also see the beach and hear the pounding of the breakers against the rocks.

Rosa stepped over the gate and made her way past various objects strewn on the entryway floor—two small dolls, an old broom, a glass jar, and a large stone which Cruz used to prop open the door to her apartment during the day. When Cruz made her rare excursions from La Esmeralda, she locked the door with a small padlock, sometimes leaving a note for her mother: "Fernanda,

* This day was observed in November, 1963, before Gabriel and Catín went to New York.

the key is in the toilet. Anyone who wants to come into my house may do so, but I'll shit on the mother of anyone who steals."

At the end of the entryway was the door to Cruz's apartment. Usually by this time Cruz had her door open and was already busy with her housework. Today the door was still shut, and Rosa knocked. "Who is it?" a woman's voice called from inside. Rosa identified herself and Cruz opened the door.

Cruz was a short, crippled mulatto girl of seventeen and a half, with a small oval face and reddish-brown kinky hair. She usually wore her hair pulled back in a pony tail but now it was uncombed and wild. Her face was flushed, making the little white scar on the left side of her chin more prominent. Her blouse was open and the hem of her skirt hung down in places.

"Come in," she said. Rosa walked through the tiny kitchen alcove and into the main room. Cruz's cot was rumpled and there were piles of unironed clothing lying on the floor next to it.

Cruz followed Rosa inside. Rosa sat down on a stool and Cruz limped over to her cot and flung herself down on it. Chuito, her six-month-old baby son, was wailing in his crib and Anita, her three-year-old daughter, looked as though she had been crying. Cruz paid no attention to them, although usually she was quick to attend to their needs.

Rosa was surprised to see Emilio, Cruz's ex-husband, sitting in a corner of the room. He was wearing a white T-shirt and red plaid shorts. His fly was open.

"Say, don't be so fresh," Cruz snapped at him. "Pull up your zipper."

Emilio turned his back to zip up his shorts. For a moment he tried to play with Chuito, then stalked out of the room.

"Ay, Rosa, you just saved me!" Cruz said. "Emilio came in like a wild man with such an erection I swear it could have torn out any girl's insides. Listen, *chica,* right in front of Anita he grabbed me, ripped off my blouse, and at one stroke I landed on the bed. He began kissing me and kissing me, and telling me to lock the door at this hour of the day. I wrestled with him and tried to get up. I said, 'But, *muchacho,* you have your woman. Stop bothering me and get out of here!' He told Anita to go out and shut the door. 'I'll buy you some candy in a minute,' he said to her.

"Then he gave me a push and we were fighting on the bed again. I grabbed him by the balls and shouted, 'Anita, go get Minerva!' *Bendito,* Anita was so frightened! And it looked like Chuito guessed what was going on because he started to cry.

"I got mad but Emilio said, 'I like it better when you're angry.' So I told him, 'You son of a great whore! You queer! Go to your woman and leave me in peace. I'll have to find a man who will put some shame into you. Things can't go on this way.' "

Little Anita, who had been listening to what Cruz was telling Rosa, came

and stood by her mother. The child was brown-skinned and very pretty. Her
dark hair was tied with strips of paper in knots all over her head and she was
dressed only in a pair of green rayon panties.

"Crucita, want titty," she said.

"Then come, child," Cruz said and went to the crib to pick up the baby.
With her free hand she straightened out the pink cotton spread and lay down
on the cot. Anita climbed up beside her and Cruz gave a breast to each child.
Lying between them she relaxed, and gradually began to look pleased. She
enjoyed nursing her children, especially her son, Chuito. She was sometimes
reluctant to nurse the older child, although it seemed to relieve Anita's asthma
attacks. The little girl resisted her mother's attempts to wean her and often
demanded to be nursed, especially when her little brother was at the breast.

While Cruz was lying with the children Rosa looked around her at the
familiar apartment. The room where she was sitting, the main living and sleeping area, was about nine by twelve feet. With only one small shuttered window
facing the sea, it was always dark and damp. Three of the walls were wooden,
but the back wall, which extended for another six feet across the kitchen alcove, was made of rough gray cement. The uneven floor was cement also. A
dozen colorful pictures of saints and several bright calendars partially relieved
the drab gray color of the room. Finally photographs were tacked on the two-
by-fours in the east wall. Below the pictures on a low table were snapshots of
Cruz's two children in a handmade wooden frame in the form of two hearts.
Another heart-shaped frame made of bright, folded gum wrappers, held a picture of Arturo, Soledad's former husband.

Next to the window was a shelf which served as a crude altar. It
held some votive candles and a prayer book which a spiritist had recommended. This was the only book Cruz owned. Above the altar hung a picture
of Our Lady of Providence, the patron saint of Puerto Rico, and a picture of
the Virgin which Cruz had found. Next to these were three pictures which
Fernanda had given her: a nativity scene, the Virgin Mary and the Our Lady
of Sorrows. A calendar picture of Christ entering the temple, and another Our
Lady of Providence, given away by an aspirin salesman, hung near the entryway.

The partition which divided Cruz's apartment from that of *doña* Rebeca
was made of new boards, although some of them had cracks and knotholes
large enough to peep through. This wall did not reach to the ceiling, and if
they stood on chairs, Rebeca and Cruz could talk face to face or pass things
to each other through the six-inch gap. Usually, however, they merely raised
their voices to banter or send insults back and forth. Unless they were very
careful, each of them could hear every sound in the other apartment. Cruz's
privacy was intruded upon in the same way by the apartment overhead, from
which she was separated only by the thin boards of a low, unfinished ceiling,

its rafters exposed and rotting. Here and there a patch of cardboard had been nailed to the rafters to absorb water that dripped through from upstairs.

Cruz changed the position of her furniture each month to bring her luck, but Chuito's large blue-and-white crib usually stood against the west wall, where the ceiling was in better condition. Her social worker had received the crib from a local furniture dealer as a donation for Cruz and it was the newest and finest piece of furniture in the little apartment. Otherwise the room was sparsely furnished with two metal cots and several small chairs and cabinets. Clothing hung from two wooden bars in the corners on either side of the window. Sometimes Cruz's room was in great disorder, with clothing and furniture scattered everywhere, but today it was neater. The chairs, stools and boxes had been lined up against the walls, leaving the center space free.

The kitchen was a tiny, windowless alcove about four by seven feet. Cruz usually kept the front door, which led into it, open for light and air. On the floor in front of the doorway was a small green rubber mat with the English word "Welcome" on it. The mat had been given to Cruz by her mother. On the inside of the door was a religious picture of Saint Martha which Cruz had stolen from a drunken peddler. Above the picture was a yellowed copy of the Prayer of the Door which a previous tenant had given her. A tin crucifix about seven inches high was nailed beside it. The crucifix had originally belonged to Cruz's grandfather and was her only "heirloom." On the beam above the door hung a glass-covered picture of Saint Expedito, the guardian of the home. The saint wore a red cape and held a cross in his right hand. Under his right foot was a bird symbolizing the Enemy. Before taking a trip or setting out to sell lottery tickets, Cruz turned Saint Expedito upside down to bring her luck.

The floor of the alcove was covered by a worn piece of linoleum. Here, too, holes in the ceiling were partially covered with plywood or cardboard to hold back water seeping from above and to keep out rats. Cruz had no refrigerator or icebox and all the shelves and "cabinets" were crudely improvised out of crates or old wood. Cruz cooked on a three-burner kerosene stove which stood on a table. A water faucet jutted out from the wall over a blue dishpan which rested on an enamel-topped table. This served as Cruz's sink. An old curtain hung like a skirt around the edge of the table to conceal the pile of dirty laundry Cruz took in to wash. The four-foot wall at the end of the alcove supported more shelves. A small box, nailed high on the wall out of reach of the children, held the medicines which Cruz received free from the Municipal Hospital. The box also contained a pair of rubber gloves used for tinting hair; a cloth coffee strainer which an old man had dropped as he passed by one day; a policeman's night stick which Cruz used as a pestle to grind spices; and Chuito's bottle.

The kitchen was in complete disorder. Pots which had been used to cook rice and beans, dirty plates and the tin cans from which Cruz and the children drank coffee were strewn over the table and stove. On the table were empty beer and soda bottles, cans of tomato sauce, several jars and a large bag of rice given to Cruz by the welfare agency. She received powdered milk, too, but she didn't like it and sold it or gave it away.

Cruz finished nursing the children, pulled her blouse together, and put Chuito in his crib. Anita began to jump up and down on the metal cot under the window.

"Stop that, Anita, and put on your shoes," Cruz said. Looking out of the window, she called to a little girl on the road below. "Julita, buy me three gills of milk, five cents' worth each of bread, butter, sugar and American cheese, and ten cents' worth of coffee." Cruz threw some coins down to the child.

When she turned from the window Cruz saw a rat running across the floor. *"Ay, Virgen!"* she said. "There goes a rat bigger than the baby. It's the *mamá* of all the others running around here. I caught six on Friday."

She went over to the cot and drew a basin of urine out from under it. "Whose piss is this?" she said to herself. "Oh, it's Anita's and mine." She took the basin to the toilet to empty it, closing the door behind her. The door slowly swung open and Rosa could see her urinating. When Cruz came out of the bathroom, Anita went in, pulled off her drawers and urinated on the floor. She came out naked.

"Put your *panties* on, you hear me?" Cruz said.

Cruz went to the door and called out to Lucelia, an impoverished old Negro woman who lived in *doña* Minerva's house. "Lucelia, come get my deposit malt-beer bottles. There's a lot. You'll have to bring a sack. Hurry, before Catín gets home and sells them." Catín, Soledad's foster daughter, had been living with Cruz for some time.

Lucelia poked her head in through the doorway long enough to say, "Bless the Lord! I'll be right back for them."

At the same time Julita returned from the store and gave Cruz what she had bought. "They wouldn't sell me a nickel's worth of cheese, Crucita," she said.

"Then run to Bonilla's. They'll give it to you."

Chuito began to cry softly. Cruz called, "I'm coming. I'm coming." Anita tried to slip out of the house. "You stay put," Cruz told her. "You're not going down, hear? *Ave María!* We have the nerviest mice here." Cruz paused for a moment to watch a small rat scurry across the room.

Lucelia came for the bottles. She brought a tin washtub, borrowed from a neighbor, in which to haul them away. When she saw the little fence stretched in front of the entryway she said to Anita, "So they've got you caged in, child."

Julita was back again. "Say, Crucita, Bonilla said I should buy the cheese in the same place I bought the milk."

"Oh, so that's what he told you, did he? Well, let him go take a shit for himself. He doesn't have to sell me anything." Julita returned the nickel and went home.

Doña Lucelia was delighted that there were so many empty beer bottles. Cruz dropped to her knees in front of the makeshift cupboard to collect them. "Come help me, Anita," she called. "There are more than three boxes of them." The little girl squatted beside her mother. When they had put the bottles into the tub, *doña* Lucelia began to pull it toward the entryway.

Gabi and Tany appeared in the doorway. "Look at those kids!" Cruz said to Lucelia. "I found them still running around in the street last night at eleven o'clock. I took them home and I was up with them until four o'clock in the morning. They shit in the bed and broke a bottle of medicine. You should have seen it."

She turned to the children. "You slipped out when Emilio came, didn't you? Isn't your mother up yet? What a disgrace! Go tell her I said she should get up and make breakfast for you." The children turned and left. "I don't know what goes on with that Felícita. She works but I never see signs of her having any money. Yesterday I was busy washing and starching and she comes around and says, "*Ay,* Crucita, cook for me."

"You shouldn't be doing it, *muchacha,*" Lucelia said. "Let your sister take care of her own children."

"Yes, I'm going to tell her to get someone to look after them. I'm not going to do it any more. Not me!" She paused. "*Doña* Lucelia, has your son written to you yet?"

The old woman stopped dragging the tub and straightened up, leaning against the wall. "Ah, that one," she said. "God gave me only one child and I've been so unlucky with him that he doesn't even write to me. New York has spoiled him. But never mind, all the little ones of La Esmeralda are my children. And seeing that I've grown old here, their parents give me authority over them. That's why I scold or even slap them when they get into trouble. But I don't really hit them hard because they all remind me of my son. *Ave María!* Now I'm an old woman whose hair is white as well as kinky. The only white thing I used to have in this coal-black face of mine was my teeth. But I'm losing those. On top of everything else, now even the children are afraid of me because I'm getting ulcers on my legs. But that's nothing. You still respect and love me, don't you, Anita?"

Lucelia bent over the tub of bottles again and dragged it outside and down the steps. When she was gone Cruz said to Rosa, "So he still doesn't write. Her husband's dead and all she's got is a little social security and what *doña* Minerva does for her. But she gets on. She stretches her legs according to the length of the blanket."

Cruz went into the kitchen and lit the stove to heat a mixture of barley and milk for the baby. The stove had belonged to Caridad, Rebeca's daughter, who had once been Cruz's next-door neighbor. Caridad had thrown it out because it leaked. Although it used more kerosene than it should—half a gallon (eleven cents' worth) every three days—Cruz had salvaged it for her own use.

Anita asked for some of the barley and milk. "Taste it and see if you like it," Cruz said, holding out a spoon with a little of the mixture in it.

"I like it," Anita said.

"All right, I'll give you a little." Cruz filled Chuito's bottle, adding vitamin drops. She went over to the crib, shaking the bottle gently. "Come here, Anita, and I'll give you some."

Anita grabbed the bottle from her mother and hid it behind her back. "Leave it alone," Cruz said. "I'll break your head for you." But she made no attempt to take the bottle away from the child. Instead she picked up the baby, crooned to him and tossed him into the air.

Then she went into the kitchen to make coffee. After washing the strainer, she filled one of her coffee pots with water and set it on the stove. Cruz owned two coffee pots. She explained to Rosa, *"Doña* Rebeca said to me the other day, 'Crucita, give me a quarter and keep this coffee pot.' So I gave her a quarter and now I have two."

While the coffee was coming to a boil, Cruz straightened the things in the open cabinet. The shelves held some dishes, the other coffee pot, lard, mayonnaise, salt, a cake of laundry soap, a carving knife, Clorox, soap flakes, a can of flour, a fork and some spoons. "Look, here's a half dollar of Héctor's and a half dollar of mine for tomorrow's lottery. Lord, I hope we hit it this time!"

It was after eight o'clock when the coffee was ready. Anita didn't want any; Cruz and Rosa drank from tin cans since Cruz had only one cup and one glass, both of which were dirty. Cruz said to Anita, "Let me know when you want some coffee so I can warm it up." Then Cruz was silent for a while, brooding over her coffee.

"Damn my life, I have the luck of a dog!" she said at last. "I have no husband and I can't fall in love. But what can I do with that man? Today I told him something I've never dared tell him before. And I sang it out at the top of my lungs, 'Look, you're nothing but a *cabrón!* I've been putting the horns on you.' "

"Do you have another sweetheart?" Rosa asked.

"I did, but Emilio managed to spoil it. There's a boy next door who is from the country. He's humble and good and you can see that he's really in love with me. I don't care for him but I was trying to because it would be the best thing for me. He has been very obliging.

"Yesterday he came over and the two of us were very happy. He had some photographs of me and I had many of him. I was looking at the pictures in his wallet when Emilio came by and saw me in the entryway. I tried to get the boy to leave but Emilio came up like a flash of lightning. He said to me,

'*Señora,* I came to see my children, whom you have abandoned. I want to talk with you. You know you still have to answer to me.'

"And I said to him, 'Why the hell do I have to answer to you, you heel?' I really came out with it.

"But he already had his plan made. He sent Anita to the store, and when I went inside with him he locked the door in that boy's face. The shame I felt! He grabbed me, and because I was so embarrassed and angry, I didn't even resist him. I gave in.

"When he had finished, he snatched my wallet, took out the pictures of that boy and tore them to pieces. He said, 'That's so you'll know that you don't let any man come up here but me. *I'll* satisfy you when you need a man.'

"At that I shouted, 'Cock-sucker! Queer! Cunt-eater!' He just opened the door and left.

"After that I didn't dare go out for a long time. When that boy saw me later, he said, '*Señora,* I'm sorry but you still have your husband to answer to, and I don't want to get involved in those problems.' So now I've lost him, damn it."

When they had finished their coffee, Cruz rinsed the cans under the faucet and turned energetically to the day's tasks.

"*Doña* Rebeca, you don't have a couple of little nails around, do you?" she called out to her next-door neighbor. "I want to fix the children's gate because everybody who goes by sticks his nose in."

"Nails?" a voice answered through the wall. "Yes, I think so. Wait a minute, let me look."

Doña Rebeca soon came in. She was about sixty-five, although she looked younger. "Here," she said, "I'll leave you these two hinges also. You have to fix it right, child, so that it opens and closes good."

Cruz marked with a nail the spot where she was going to secure the little fence more firmly across the entryway. Anita went over to look. "See?" Cruz said. "If I took this fence away, you'd fall down. You know that?"

Cruz went back to the kitchen, cut off a small piece of bread and gave it to Chuito. "He eats bread too. There's no holding him back! *Ave María!* Those children of Fela's have worms. They were grinding their teeth all night. Fela should take them to the clinic, but she doesn't want to be bothered. I had to give Mundo medicine last night so he could sleep."

She bent over the crib. "*Ay, bendito!* The baby has wet himself!" She picked him up, singing, "Dirty, dirty, Chuito," and laid him on the cot to change his diaper and powder him. When she had finished she put him back in his crib and stood on her cot, leaning out of the window to call to Anita, who had slipped out. Anita came running back, climbed into the crib with the baby and began playing with him. Cruz stayed at the window, leaning on her elbows. Her daughter got down from the crib and picked up an alarm clock.

"Look, you put that down," Cruz said, and gave Anita a slap on the head. "Hurry and put on your shoes, child, because we've got broken glass here. I'm going to sweep up this bottle your cousins broke."

She began to sweep up the pieces of glass, but interrupted herself to remove the baby's rubber sheet from the cot and place a pink spread over it. Anita picked up the broom. "No, Anita," Cruz said. "Put that broom down. You don't know how to sweep and besides you'll cut yourself." Anita then began picking up pieces of glass with her fingers. She had not put on her shoes. Cruz ignored this but shooed her away and finished sweeping.

Cruz's next task was to clean the bathroom "because people come in sometimes." Although she shared it with her two neighbors, she felt responsible for keeping it clean, since it was in her entryway. She often complained about the way it was left by the five men who lived on the other side of her. "I'm not so clean, but neither am I as bad as those pigs," she would say.

The windowless bathroom was about four by six feet. The floor was cement, sloping from the sides to the middle, where a drain caught water from the shower pipe. The walls were built of wood except for a cement ledge three feet high and a foot wide. The cement was the same dirty gray as Crucita's room, but here it had been applied more roughly so that the two-by-fours showed through in places. Decayed wooden planks in two of the corners supported the ceiling. Pieces of rotten wood had fallen into the room, leaving a hole through which one could see into the apartment above. Three large rusty drainpipes, littered with bits of cement, crisscrossed the ceiling above the toilet and shower. Here the cobwebs were thick, covering the pipes and hanging down into the room.

In the right-hand corner stood the toilet, seatless and usually in need of flushing. A large tin can near it held soiled toilet paper. To one side of the toilet, a water pipe stuck out from the wall. It was meant to serve as a shower but it was placed so low that Cruz had to stoop to get under it. This pipe was the only source of water in the room. Even the toilet had to be flushed with water drawn from it and Cruz used a large tin pan for this purpose. She had bought it from *doña* Rebeca for fifty cents.

On the ledge formed by the cement part of the wall, Cruz stored a wooden crate, the tin pan and two washtubs, one of which her mother had given her; the other she had bought herself. A wooden scrub board and a cake of soap lay on top of one of the tubs.

"*Ave María,*" Cruz called to Rosa. "Every morning that toilet is in the same condition. I clean and clean and every morning I find it the same."

When she had finished cleaning the toilet she ran water into one of her washtubs and rinsed out some clothes. "They are left over from last night. It's outside wash, but I didn't have time to hang it up to dry." Cruz preferred to do her customers' wash in the public laundry where there were large sinks and a ready supply of water, but it was often difficult to leave her home and the children.

When Cruz came out of the toilet, Anita was sitting on top of Chuito, apparently about to hit him with a paper shopping bag. "*Ave María Purísima!* I'll kill you if you hurt that child," Cruz shouted, slapping the little girl on the head again. Anita quietly rubbed the place where her mother had hit her.

A masculine voice called out, "Crucita, Crucita!"

"Ah," she said, "it's my stepfather Héctor. He wants his coffee." She called back. "Black or with milk?"

"I want it black."

"All right. Wait until I heat it up."

Chuito lost his bottle and shrieked with rage. Cruz gave it back to him. While the coffee was heating, she went into the toilet, coming out with a mop and the basin which had been used as a chamber pot the night before. She began to wash the floor of the living area. Anita, standing by the little fence at the entryway, was calling over and over again, "Nanda, Nanda, Nanda."

"You know how to say 'Grandma' now, Anita," said a voice through the wall.

"That's Rafael, one of the men who lives next door," Cruz said to Rosa. "He's very fond of Anita."

Cruz mopped underneath her cot. "I would have washed the floor before," she said, "but I couldn't because of taking care of Fela's children." Anita came back into the room, still barefoot. "Anita, you're going to cut yourself. And when you do, don't come around asking me to pick out the pieces of glass!" Cruz let the mop fall for a moment. Anita picked it up; her mother took it away and slapped her. "Leave that alone, stubborn! Get on the bed. Well, Héctor didn't come back for his coffee. He must be drunk, eh?"

She moved a large cardboard carton which stood under the ironing board and began to mop there. The box held clothes, even though Cruz did not like to store things in it. "Sometimes I don't clean out the box for weeks and I find cockroaches and little baby rats, and the clothing all dirty and eaten."

Above the box was the wooden bar that held Cruz's dresses on wire hangers. They were covered by a light blanket which Nanda had left. Overhead, Cruz had nailed several large pieces of cardboard to the rafters to protect the clothes. Taking a man's suit from the clothes rack, Cruz held it up for Rosa to see. "Fifty-five dollars!" she said. "My stepfather's. And another one for fifty-five dollars. Héctor brings them here for me to keep for him because he says they'll be stolen in his house."

She went on mopping the floor.

"Look, Crucita, Crucita!" Anita had found a yellow balloon under the cot.

"Ah, your balloon. Pick it up, pick it up. No, don't step on the floor. Pick it up from where you are." Anita lay on the cot, playing with the balloon and kicking her feet in the air.

It was after nine o'clock now. Cruz's face had begun to sweat from the work she was doing in the heat. She took down some clothes from the rack and went into the toilet to wash her face and neck and change her torn clothing. When she came out she was wearing a red, white and blue-striped blouse and a maroon, blue and brown skirt, a hand-me-down from her mother. She had put on a brassière which she had bought in Franklin's department store in San Juan for fifty-nine cents. She had three brassières but to make nursing simpler, she seldom wore one.

Cruz's wardrobe was rather large, considering that in the past twelve months she had spent only about thirteen dollars of her own money for her clothes. Almost three fourths of the clothes she owned had been gifts; half of them were new when she received them. Cruz's wardrobe included three skirts and blouses, four dresses, a pair of brown shorts that Soledad had sent her, a pair of slacks with a matching top that she had stolen from a down-town store, a black plastic belt that she had bought there, a bathing suit given to her by the Catholic sisters, two pairs of rubber-thonged sandals and two purses.

Cruz went to the kitchen for a bottle from which she poured some liquid into the basin of water. "This King Pine is very good for cockroaches," she said, "and it cuts the grease too." The odor of pine filled the room. Cruz began to mop the floor. "You know, Arturo took Catín to the country yesterday at seven o'clock in the morning. They are bringing her back today because she has to go to school tomorrow."

As she washed the floor Cruz sang:

> "If they tell you they saw me very drunk,
> Proudly, you can say it's on account of you."

Anita came back into the room and went to the cot to play with the yellow balloon. She threw it up and it fell on the baby, asleep in his crib.

A woman thrust her head through the doorway. "Look!" she said. "Give me a quarter. I'll put you down for five twenty-two, with another quarter for Héctor. That makes half a dollar."

"Ah! Let Rolando put Héctor down. Tell him I have only one quarter."

"That was Herminia," Cruz said to Rosa. "She runs numbers, and if the police catch her she'll get a year. She was already in once, so she'd get a year this time. Rolando is her husband. He was in once for the same thing. If they catch me playing, I'd get six months. Sure, we get punished for buying and for selling."

Just then Anita screamed. With her teeth she had been opening clothes pins fastened to wire hangers and had hurt herself. "Shut up, stupid!" Cruz shouted. "Stop that, Anita, or I'll hit you." Cruz turned to Rosa and said, *"Ave María!* I don't like crying children. When little girls start crying, I'd like to set fire to them and go away!"

"Crucita," Anita yelled.

"What's the matter?"

"I want to get down."

"Stay where you are. You're not going anywhere, stupid."

"Crucita, bread!"

"Bread? Okay. I'll give you some, but stay there." Anita climbed down from the cot. *"Ave María Purísima!* Are you deaf or something?" Cruz whacked the child on the head again. "Here. Here's bread." Anita climbed back onto the cot.

Cruz emptied the dirty water she had used for mopping and washed the basin in the blue dishpan. Driving a nail into the wall, she hung the basin among the fifteen pots and pans already hanging there. All but three of these had been given to her by relatives or neighbors.

Next, Cruz washed the dishes and pots in the same water, adding a little detergent. One by one she took the spoons, cans and plates from the dishpan and dropped them into a pan of rinse water. She then wiped the stove and the table with a rag and threw the garbage into an open can next to the cabinet. "I used to have just a small can," she said, "but one day Angelito went to dump the garbage in the public can and found this big one there."

"Crucita!" Anita called.

"What? If you make *pipí* in the bed or on the floor, I'll hit you, hear?"

Anita slipped off the bed. "Crucita, Crucita, I want water," she said. She was holding an ashtray in her hand.

"What? You're not getting down." Cruz picked up the black plastic belt and threatened the child with it. "Put that down!" Anita obeyed immediately. "And here's water." Cruz filled a baby bottle with water from the faucet.

It was now almost ten o'clock. Cruz carried the dishwater into the bathroom and poured it down the toilet, then hung the dishpan on the kitchen wall.

"Give me titty, Cruz, give me titty," Anita said.

"Wait a minute until I finish." Cruz filled a basin with water from a tub in the toilet and sloshed it over the floor of the entryway. Anita had started down to the cement path, dragging the mop after her.

"No, Anita, not down there. And give me the mop. All you're doing is dirtying up the place." Cruz took the mop and began pouring water on the cement at the foot of the stairs. She had to climb the steep steps and go back to the toilet to get more water. Farther down the hill three little girls played in the soapy puddles that Cruz's washing had made.

Anita had gone downstairs to play. Cruz called, "Come on up. Right away!" She put the mop back in the toilet. When Anita came in, she said, "Be careful you don't wake the baby or I'll hit you, hear?" Anita picked something up from the bed, and Cruz gave her another whack on the head.

Anita said, *"Mami, caca. Caca, mami."* Cruz pulled down the child's panties and set her on the toilet. "When you get finished, you wash up, hear? And don't come out without your *panties* on." In a moment or two Anita came into the room naked. Cruz took a pair of panties from the box and put them on the child.

Anita had more clothes than her mother. She had twenty-four pairs of panties, four pairs of socks, a pair of shoes, four pairs of shorts and a bathing suit. These had cost over fourteen dollars. In addition, little Anita had fifteen dresses hanging on one of the clothes bars, all of them gifts. She had also received a pair of earrings from Nanda, a religious medal from Alejandro, Cruz's recent lover, and a stone from her father to guard against witchcraft.

Chuito was awake now. "There! You see? You woke him up," Cruz said, giving Anita another slap on the head. Anita only laughed. Cruz rocked Chuito to see if he would go back to sleep. Anita began jumping up and down. "If you're not quiet," Cruz said, "I'll pull out your lungs through your mouth! Do you hear me?" But Anita was dancing to the music of a radio that was playing in a neighbor's house. Cruz watched her for a moment and smiled. "That girl is comical, you know?"

The baby began to whimper and Cruz examined her son. "It was this bedbug that woke him," she said. Anita came up to the crib but her mother pushed her aside. "Don't come around here pestering, please, or I'll hit you." Cruz brought a bottle of water from the kitchen and gave it to her son. Then she went to the bathroom for the clothes she had rinsed, and carried them outside to hang up. Cruz and *doña* Rebeca shared a clothes line which stretched between two electric poles along the cement path in front of the house. Cruz came back for more clothes. *"Ave María!* I'm going to have to pour some more water outside. Somebody emptied piss there and it smells awful and besides it's not healthy." She went out with the clothes. A slight breeze was blowing in from the sea. The ocean was calm but they could hear the sound of the breakers. In a street below some boys were playing marbles. "Hey, *puñeta,* it's your turn to shoot," one of them said. Another gang of boys was playing among the junked cars in the vacant lot across the street. As Cruz started back to the house for a third batch of clothes, an old woman stopped to talk to her.

Finally the clothes line was filled. Cruz came into the house to sit down. Anita was crying because Cruz had slapped her for sitting in a puddle of water.

"What an ironing I'll have tomorrow, and there's still more clothes to hang. No woman should take in washing and ironing. I don't recommend such a life to anyone. You know, a man whose wife is putting the horns on him came around yesterday asking me to wash and iron his clothes. I'm going to do it. At least it will pay what I owe at the grocery store. But I can work with a lot more peace of mind when these children are asleep. Anita has me dizzy. She worries me because it's so dangerous around here."

Cruz needed the money she earned from washing and ironing. She now received sixteen dollars a month from the Public Welfare; of this she paid eight dollars for rent and one-fifty for electricity to *doña* Rosa María, who lived in a second-floor apartment above her. Cruz benefited from this fixed rate, since it allowed her to iron and play her radio without worrying about the cost. However, Cruz, who had bought the radio on credit from a friend, did not play it very often so that it would last longer. The electricity came into Cruz's room by way of an extension cord which had a socket for a light bulb and two outlets to plug in her electric iron and radio. She hung the cord from a nail in the kitchen or from a ceiling beam that crossed from one far corner of the main living area to the other. Cruz used her mother's ironing board which she borrowed for weeks at a time. When Fernanda wanted to iron, Cruz would carry back the board. For a while she had borrowed a new iron that Felícita had bought for twenty-two dollars; now she had her own iron, given to her by the social worker.

"Think of it!" Cruz said. "One month *doña* Rosa María didn't pay the electric company, even though I paid her as usual. That's what you get for having to depend on neighbors, eh? They cut off the electricity and for days I couldn't iron and people kept asking me for their clothes. *Ave María!* You can be sure I told *doña* Rosa María what I thought. Yesterday I ironed eleven short pants and three long ones and two sheets, then twelve undershorts, two undershirts and twelve shirts. It all came to eight dollars and thirty-five cents. I took the clothes to *don* Norberto's house and he said he had no money and would pay me on Tuesday. Well—" she shrugged. She was not worried, because this had been a profitable week; she rarely earned more than five dollars.

Suddenly Cruz noticed that Anita was not in the room. "*Ave María!* That child has taken off. I can't let her out of my sight for a minute." She went to the window to call, but at that moment a very large Negro woman, who weighed almost two hundred pounds, came through the doorway carrying Anita. She was *doña* Minerva, Emilio's aunt. Minerva had spanked Anita because she found her crying face down on the dirty floor of the entryway.

Cruz took Anita, then lifted Chuito out of his crib and handed him to Minerva, who carried him under her stout arm as though he were a small package. Minerva asked whether Catín had come home yet, then went to settle her huge bulk in the entryway of the next-door apartment, where she began dandling Chuito up and down on her knees. Cruz followed her and sat down in her own doorway. Anita trailed after her mother, whining, "Crucita, want titty."

"A smack is what I'll give you. Minerva, yesterday my *papá* was in La

Esmeralda. He went to Felícita's house but he didn't come in here. He pays more attention to her than to me. Even when I talk to him he hardly ever listens."

Cruz smiled at Chuito as he rested on Minerva's knees. Playfully, she began to speak in a high-pitched baby voice, "*Ay, Virgen,* I'm in love, *mamita.* How many women are there in La Esmeralda, *mami?* I want to know because I'm all man. How many men are there in La Esmeralda? There is only one who's all man, and he is Chuito."

"Crucita, titty," Anita said again.

Cruz relented and let Anita unbutton her blouse. Anita sat on the second step and Cruz stood on the cement walk below while the little girl nursed. "*Ave María!* What a beating I gave this girl today. At four in the morning she was singing with Fela's children. They were singing, 'Not too much love in the beginning—' " Finished with one breast, the little girl wanted the other.

"*Ave María!*" Cruz said. "Now this damn girl is going after the other one."

"*Ave María!* Now she's going after the other one," Minerva repeated. "Say, aren't you going to leave anything for the baby? Leave him at least a drop, eh?"

Minerva continued to taunt Anita. Suddenly Anita made a noise. *Doña* Minerva, in spite of her great weight, jumped to her feet, as agile as a cat. "Phew," she said. "What a fart that girl let." She spat on the walk. "It stinks like rotten eggs. *Bendito!* If you want to get rid of me, do it some other way. You don't have to fart me out of the place." Cruz pulled her nipple out of Anita's mouth and buttoned her blouse. Embarrassed, the child hid her face in her mother's lap.

"Minerva," Cruz said, "Emilio was here today. He keeps coming even when I shut the door on him. If he goes on like this, I'll make him pay another three hundred dollars to get out of jail. *Ave María!* And he's doing nothing for his children."

"Ah, that Emilio! It would have been better if I'd never taken him from my sister and brought him up. It was the meningitis that made him this way because people who get that are never right in the head afterward. I'm his aunt, practically his mother, and I have to admit he's a low-down scoundrel. But you, Crucita, why don't you take the advice I give you? To begin with, stop keeping his shirts and photographs, and undo the spells you've cast on him. You bound him, now let him loose if you no longer love him. And another thing. If you want to have a sweetheart and hope to be happy, leave La Esmeralda so that Emilio won't see you. When the eyes don't see, the heart doesn't feel."

"No, no," Cruz said. "La Esmeralda is a public place. Why should it be me who has to go?"

Minerva shook her head. "Well, you don't take my advice the way many others in La Esmeralda do. Look, you can't imagine the nights I spend awake there in the alley, listening, because I'm afraid a tragedy might happen."

At this point, perhaps to escape *doña* Minerva's words, Cruz decided to go to the store. While she was gone, Minerva went on talking to Rosa. "Crucita's a sly one! To look at her you'd never imagine what goes on inside her. But she's the best of that lot, aside from Soledad. Women are like cows. You should pick them according to the breed, and what a breed hers is! Her mother never treated any of them too well and she gave all her daughters a bad example. I don't like to gossip, but the truth is, that woman was always beating her daughters.

"Well, Emilio's no saint, but Cruz isn't a bit better than he is. Cruz was more in love with him than he with her. She flirted and made eyes at him and I don't know what all. Who would have thought it? I always figured that because she is lame she would turn out to be more decent. It's true that he beat her, but she gave him reason to. She wanted to wear the pants in the family. She'd tell him, 'All right, if you have other women. I'm going to take on other men too. If you put the horns on me, I'll put them on you. If you go to the movies alone, so will I!' The shrew! Imagine acting like a man. A real woman doesn't say such things.

"You know what that lame girl did to get her way? She went to Loíza Aldea, to the spiritists, until she had him completely in her power. Then she started provoking him. One day he came home from work dead tired. I served his dinner and he sat in the doorway to cool off. A man came by and asked him, 'I want to know if you'll give me permission to buy your wife a beer because she's asking for one.' Emilio flung down his dinner and rushed away like a madman. I understand that he gave her such a beating he nearly killed her. But even then, every time she had any money she'd go to sorcerers to bind him to her even more. I know it's true because her sister Soledad told me so.

"And then, do you know what that girl did one day? She left for New York at ten o'clock in the morning without saying a word to Emilio. You can't imagine the state he was in. I thought he would kill himself. And do you know, she went off with another man, according to what I was told later. But that cuckold followed her, horns and all. *Ay,* there's no doubt it's better to have a thousand living men as enemies than a single ghost.

"She came back, but within a month she was living with still another man. What do you think of that? Lame and all. But this time she was really screwed up because that kid got her pregnant. Emilio's a dog because there are times when he doesn't give her a thing for those children, and whatever happened it wasn't the fault of those poor innocents. But Crucita can't claim that she has suffered too much. Every time my daughter Mónica got paid she put five dollars aside for Crucita. That money was sacred. And every time I cook, the first food I dish out is for Crucita and her children. I don't care whether or not the children are Emilio's. That makes no difference. And still less now that they all have Emilio's surname because he and Cruz are legally married. The girl Emilio lives with now is a very good little girl but Emilio can't stop interfering with Crucita and coming to her house, she has bewitched him so.

"Well, as to the rest I won't say anything because she's a good mother to those children. In that, she's a woman like me. But look here, Emilio already has a home of his own. If she just doesn't give a damn about him as she says, why doesn't she let him go?"

Cruz returned from the store with a can of fruit juice and a bag of "Japanese" rice, which she preferred to the rice she received from the welfare agency. Cruz picked up the can and held it up for Chuito to see. "Look at that!" she said. "Look how he watches it. He knows the juice is for him. Oh, what a lovely boy!" Minerva said she had to leave, and Cruz took the baby from her.

It was after eleven o'clock, time for the baby's bath. Cruz went to the toilet and brought back a tub of cold water into which she plunged Chuito without further ado. Then she went to get a diaper from a low wooden cabinet by the far end of the cement wall. The cabinet, made from a crate, held neatly folded piles of children's clothing. In the meantime Anita had soaped the baby's head and poured water over him. The baby shivered every time the cold water hit him, but he did not cry. Cruz came back and gave Anita a rap on the head. "I told you not to soap him, didn't I? All you want to do is see how close you can come to hurting him. You let any of that soap get into his eyes and I'll hit you, but hard. Just one little speck of soap in his eyes, eh?"

Cruz lifted the baby out of the tub and placed him on the cot, where she dried and powdered him. She sang, "I want to tell you in time, son, that you are my life." She stood back, admiring him.

Most of the time Chuito wore only a diaper, but Cruz had other clothes he could wear when she took him outside of La Esmeralda. She herself had bought him two dozen diapers, a dozen undershirts, five pairs of underpants, two pairs of socks, a pair of shoes, a little suit and a charm to prevent witchcraft. Fernanda, Felícita, the Catholic sisters, the social worker and a girl friend had given her other clothing for him: an expensive smocked shirt to use for special occasions, a suit, jackets, three white T-shirts, and a stocking cap to keep his curly black hair neat. Emilio had bought nothing for Chuito because he refused to recognize the child as his.

Cruz climbed on a stool to look out of the window. She needed someone to run an errand for her. "Pepito, Pepito!" she shouted. " 'Corporal' Pepito!" There was no answer. She saw Angelito and at once shouted, "Angelito, come up here. Come on, climb up."

"I can't climb up those steps," Angelito said.

"Bless me, but you're not a hundred percent male! A real man could do it." The boy came up to the entryway. "Look," Cruz said to him, "I want you to run an errand for me." Angelito was unwilling. *"Ave María!* You have to take a stick to these boys to make them do things. Listen, Angelito, you know where Recoveco's house is, don't you? The man who sells fritters? Get me a chicken there. Get going."

"I won't," the boy said.

"Oh, you won't? I'll give you a good slap and we'll see. How do you like these stubborn brats? They won't even do a person a favor." Angelito went out.

Cruz picked up a large stuffed dog from the floor and handed it to Chuito. *Doña* Ofelia, Fernanda's former employer, had given this and other toys to Fernanda, who had passed them on to Cruz. Cruz usually kept them stored on a shelf out of Anita's reach, because when Anita played with them, the toys were often stolen by other children.

Cruz saw that Chuito was almost falling off the bed. "Oh, my Lord, who put the baby there? Think what happened yesterday! I looked for him everywhere like crazy and there he was under the bed. He had fallen off. It's happened several times already, but he never cries. He's all man, this one."

Cruz shouted through the wall. *"Doña* Rebeca, you took the cigarettes last night, didn't you?"

"Yes, I took them."

"Oh, I was looking for them. Anita, stop upsetting the fucking house. I'm tired now. Stay still for a minute in one place or I'll give you a kick in the face."

Water had begun to drip down through the ceiling into Cruz's entryway. "Oh, for Lord's sake, those fucking women up there. I just get through washing the floor and they have to start dumping water. And if a person calls it to their attention, they want to eat you alive. They're looking for trouble and they'll get it." Cruz banged on the ceiling with the broom. The wood was rotted, and she broke through one of the boards. *"Ave María!* It's all rotten," she said in surprise.

Cruz went outside. Almost immediately she came back, muttering angrily, "He hasn't any money to feed his children, but he's able to buy himself a car. I'm talking about Emilio, the father of my children. He's down below right now with his car. That man is a good-for-nothing! You'll see, this time I really will go to court."

Two months earlier Cruz and her social worker had threatened to take Emilio to court for nonsupport. He had responded with a shower of food. Cruz's kitchen shelves had been crowded with twenty jars of baby food, eight bottles of malt beer, a big box of Kellogg's Corn Flakes, a bag of coffee, a huge tin of soda crackers and a number of cans of tomato sauce. Cruz had felt secure for a few days but now Emilio was neglecting the children again. And his friends had told her that his red and black Mercury had cost him a thousand dollars.

Anita had climbed onto her mother's cot and was calling frantically to her father through the window, *"Papi! Papi! Papi!"*

"You keep calling and I'll break your head for you," her mother said.

Angelito came in with the chicken. Cruz cut it up into small pieces, set them aside and placed a pan of water on the stove for boiling rice. She washed and drained the rice, fried it slightly, added water and set it over the flame to cook. She browned the chicken in lard and added it, piece by piece, to the rice. Then she drew out a small cardboard suitcase from under Catín's cot and rummaged around in it until she found a photograph of a woman who resembled *doña* Minerva. She handed the photograph to Rosa. "This is Emilio's mother and if you think she's fat," she said, "that's nothing. The whole family is like that and some of them are even fatter."

The suitcase was full of baby clothes. Cruz held up a frilly white-lace baby dress for Rosa to see. It was too small for Anita and rather worn-looking, but Cruz said she would never throw it out or give it away because it had been worn by Soledad's two daughters, Sarita and Toya, by Fela's Tany and by her own Anita. In the suitcase Cruz also kept a gold chain, a purse, Anita's and Chuito's shoes, a pack of cards and two registration cards for the pediatrics clinic of the Municipal Hospital. Whenever her children were ill, Cruz received free care for them at the clinic.

Cruz shoved back the suitcase, went to her own cot, climbed up and lit a votive candle which stood on the crude altar-shelf next to the window. She still seemed to be disturbed at having seen Emilio in his car. She sat down on a low stool and was quiet for several minutes, until Lucelia's voice from outside called, "Crucita, Crucita, lend me a pan."

"Eh? All right, Lucelia, just a minute."

"And bring me a plate to send you some tripe."

"Oh? But I'm cooking dinner myself." Cruz got up from her stool and carried a pan and plate to Lucelia.

When she came back she noticed that Angelito was sitting on Catín's cot. "Get up, don't sit there," she said. "That's what the stools are for."

It had become cloudy outside and looked as though it were going to rain. "Angelito, do you know what you have to do before the rain starts? Go to Bonilla's and buy me a quarter of a pound of lard, because what I have isn't going to be enough. And get two Pepsi-Colas."

"Here's your pan, Crucita," Lucelia shouted from outside.

"Coming!" Cruz called. In a moment she was back with a pan of stewed tripe and white rice which she offered to Rosa. Cruz said that she didn't like tripe, although Lucelia was a good cook. Rosa was hungry because it was past noon, and she ate some of the food.

Mami, see. I want to see," Anita said.

"What is it, my daughter? What do you want to see, my pet?"

Cruz picked up Anita and kissed her. With the child on her hip, she went over to the stove, uncovered the pan of rice and sniffed it. "My, the rice is just lovely," she said, "but it still needs to cook a little to be ready." She replaced the cover and gave Anita another kiss.

Angelito came back and said that Bonilla had refused to sell him anything.

"The bastard! Just because I owe him some money. What he's got there is a cockroach trap, not a grocery store. Well, go to another place. If you don't move fast, I'll give you a crack in the face, hear? But a good one! That Bonilla! All he wants to do is mix in the lives of all the women here and know everything. That's why I don't talk to him."

Angelito was soon back. "Here, Crucita," he shouted.

"Wait a minute, I'm coming."

"Crucita, it's raining."

"*Ave María!* Now, Angelito, go and buy me twenty cents' worth of beans. Go on!" The boy made a face but went, taking a small aluminum pot for the beans which were sold already cooked.

Cruz picked up Chuito, dropped him on her cot, and threw herself down on top of him, resting on her elbows to avoid crushing him. The baby reached up and grabbed his mother's cheeks. "*Ay!* Now I don't love you any more. You are a bad boy, scratching *mami*'s face." She played with his genitals, saying, "This is what you call a pair of balls. He's going to be a fresh guy, this male here." She kissed him on the mouth.

"Crucita," Angelito called from outside.

"I'm coming." She went into the entryway, took the beans and asked Angelito to bring in the clothes drying on the line.

"What?" the boy shrieked. "Something more to do?"

Cruz picked up Chuito again and began throwing him into the air. The baby laughed nervously but didn't cry. Finally Cruz dropped him into his crib.

Anita had taken off her panties. Cruz slapped her. "Put them on! Put them on!" She grabbed the child and put them on for her. Angelito came in with the clothes, and Cruz hung them on the beam overhead to finish drying. Angelito went to the toilet, shutting the door behind him.

Cruz called out, "Say, Angelito, where did you buy these beans?"

"At Casa Latina."

"Casa Latina! You certainly are a fool and don't know how to buy. They're the same kind we get from the Public Welfare and they aren't big enough. You're going to eat with us, aren't you, Angelito?"

"Yes. Serve me last."

"All right, but get a move on. Are you still 'cooking' in there?"

"Yes, still."

"*María Purísima.* You surely 'cook' a lot!"

In a minute Angelito called, "Say, Crucita, is it all right if I use this piece of cloth?"

"No, don't touch it, you might catch an infection. Wait!" She found an empty paper bag and opened the door just wide enough to slip it through. "Take this, you pig. Anita, do you want meat?"

"Yes, I want meat," *doña* Rebeca shouted from her room.

"Is that so? Well, go buy some, old lady, and stop pestering me. Oh well, come on over and get a leg."

On her way to Cruz's house Rebeca could be heard scolding her grandchildren. Cruz picked up a steaming chicken leg in a big spoon and handed it to Rebeca. "Here, and now have yourself a party." *Doña* Rebeca left, muttering something inaudible. "Angelito," Cruz shouted in exasperation. "Are you still shitting, damn it? *Ave María!* Hurry up."

"Yes, right away."

Cruz served Rosa and herself, then sat down on the floor beside Chuito's crib. From time to time she offered the baby bits of food. Because Cruz had only one fork, they all ate with spoons or with their fingers.

Angelito came out of the toilet. Cruz gave him his food on the lid of a pan. He took a spoon and went to sit in the doorway to eat. When he was not using his spoon, he held it between his toes. Anita, who had finished eating, joined him.

"Crucita, look at Anita," Angelito yelled. "She's pushing my food and she'll spill it."

"Come here, Anita," Cruz said. "Hurry up so you can take your nap."

Anita came crawling into the room on all fours, followed by Angelito, who handed the pan lid to Cruz and went out. She climbed onto Cruz's cot and held up her foot. Cruz looked at it. "There's a piece of glass in it. Didn't I tell you?" She squeezed the foot while Anita yelled in pain. "Shut up. Now it's out. Now go to sleep right away."

Cruz took Chuito from his crib and lay down on the cot between the two children.

"Want titty," Anita said.

"Such a little, little girl, my baby. *Mamá*'s baby is going to sleep now." Cruz spoke softly, trying to make Anita drowsy. "Close your eyes, Anita, but first say your prayers."

"Scratch me here, Crucita," Anita said. Cruz scratched her back, then took out her right breast and gave it to Chuito. "While you children are sleeping, I'm going to take a bath." Anita got up and took off her panties. "Crucita, Crucita," she said.

"Now don't go and shit. If you do, I'll break your head and pull your liver out through your mouth, hear?" Cruz brandished the belt and Anita lay down again, crying for Crucita's free breast. Cruz struck her lightly with the belt. "Lie still, child, and I'll give it to you. Just let the baby have another little bit. Look now, Chuito, you have to eat faster because you've got me all tired out. I haven't slept since four this morning. Hurry up, now."

Anita was still whimpering. Cruz said to Rosa, "I was just thinking, now that the rainy season is coming I'm going to have to start piling all those stools on the bed again because water leaks in on them through the shutters and walls." Cruz uncovered her other breast, gave it to Anita and both children nursed for a while. Chuito was the first to stop. "See, you silly boy," Cruz said. "Now you have lost the fuller one for being so slow." The baby was wide awake and Cruz gave him four quick kisses on the mouth.

Someone was coming into the entryway. "Who's there?" Cruz called.

"Me."

"Who's me?"

"Myself." Fernanda, Cruz's mother, came in with Angelito and she immediately went to pick up the baby. Cruz told her mother that Felícita's children had soiled the beds and floor the night before. "And I cooked on a dollar and a half today, Nanda. I had meat, rice and beans. Nanda, look over there." Cruz pursed her lips in the direction of the men's suits hanging in the corner.

"My Lord, don't tell me you finally got married, girl!"

"Sure. Those are my husband's suits." Cruz laughed to see her mother's expression of surprise. "They're Héctor's. He owes the rent but he has money for suits. How do you like that? Angelito, go ask Héctor if he wants dinner. When I'm broke he helps me out, thank God. I cooked for Fela one day last week so she would give me food. And Arturo gave Catín ten cents for juice at school. I only had a nickel to give her for a sandwich."

Fernanda said nothing. Cruz had complained before that Fernanda wasn't bringing food to her any more.

"When are you going to wean the baby?" Fernanda asked.

"When he reaches seven."

"My Lord!"

Rebeca called through the wall. "Listen, Nanda, that singing sounds like a man crying." The women listened for a moment to a radio that was playing in a nearby house.

"*Ay,* no," Cruz said loudly. "I like the way he sings. I like Salaman because he's so nice and big. He's lovely! *Doña* Rebeca, you have to like the ugly ones because you're an ugly old woman. You're a back number and not pretty at all. You're only one step from the grave."

Doña Rebeca mumbled something that Cruz couldn't hear. Cruz lowered her voice. "Listen, Nanda, Emilio bought a car but he has no money for his children. All I'm waiting for is for him to smash it up so he'll have two things on his head, if you know what I mean. That's when I'll get him in front of the judge. He's going to pay me for everything, but everything!"

She saw that Angelito was listening to her intently and she shouted, "Angelito, are you crazy or something? Go down to the beach and eat shit." When he left she continued, "Look, that car won't last because he has already begun taking parts out of it. He used to have a station wagon, a big one that holds a lot of people. They called it 'The Little Hotel' because it had a couch in the back of it and men went there with, you know, with a tramp. But I caught him at it one day and I let him have it right in front of his friends."

After a while Fernanda put Chuito, now asleep, into his crib and went out. Anita was asleep too. Cruz said to Rosa, "Did you notice how Nanda behaved? She acts more like a *señorita* than a grandmother. I'd be embarrassed if people gossiped about me. But not her."

Cruz paused. Then she called, "Rebeca, Rebeca! Sing me a song that will make me cry. *Ave María!* How I want some guava with white cheese! Does that mean I'm going to die, because I have such a craving?" Angelito had come in again and Cruz said, "Angelito, go get me some of that guava jelly." Cruz began to figure with paper and pencil how much the guava and cheese would cost. She gave her nephew a few coins and said, "Hurry, Angelito."

From Rebeca's room a child wailed, "Don't hit me, Grandma. I'll take it off right away. Don't hit me, Grandma." Four distinct blows followed.

Cruz picked up a towel and a pair of black panties trimmed with green flowers. "I'm going to bathe before the children wake up. Please, Rosa, put the nail in the door so it won't open." To hold the door closed, a long nail had to be bent over it on the outside. Rosa did as she was asked and soon she heard Cruz singing under the shower.

"Crucita, come here!" Angelito yelled from outside.

"Wait a minute, I'm bathing. Come on up, Angelito."

Angelito spoke to Cruz through the toilet door. "They don't sell fifteen cents' worth of cheese, only ten or twenty."

"Go to Bonilla's then. They have guava and white cheese for sure. Open the door for me, Angelito."

Angelito turned the nail, then ran down the steps, almost bumping into his mother, who was on her way up. Felícita was wearing a turban and a tight brown lace dress which was badly torn in front. Cruz came out of the toilet dressed only in the black panties. *"María Purísima!"* she said when she saw her sister. "Here comes living death. She looks like a Negro with that head."

"Say, did you cook today, Crucita?" Felícita asked.

"Yes, there it is." Cruz pursed her lips toward the stove. Felícita uncovered the pan and fished out a piece of chicken. She sat down on a cot, spreading her legs far apart.

"Look, Fela, that daughter of yours shit all over everything here."

"Ave María! They stop shitting during the day just so they can shit at night."

"You have to give Evita a physic. Last night I could hear the noise in her belly from the worms."

"Yes, the other day she showed me one she had shit out." Felícita went to sit in Anita's little chair, a wicker rocking chair that Minerva had given her on the Day of the Three Kings.

"Don't make so much noise, will you? The children are asleep."

"I'm not making any noise at all. I'm going now, right this minute."

"I'm not telling you to leave, but you can go if you want to. I can't stand you any more. You're so sloppy." Cruz sat down on her cot to comb out her matted hair. "My Lord, but that son of yours, Mundito, has eyes all sunken in. One of these days he's going to die on you, you'll see. Why don't you take him to the dispensary when you're not working?" Felícita acted as though she had not heard her sister.

A man outside began shouting in rage. "You fucking mothers and son-of-a-bitch fathers who don't take care of your children!" Both Cruz and Felícita went to the door to see who was shouting. Cruz said, "People get killed here and you can't find a policeman because they spend their time drinking rum and fucking whores. Well, screw those people out there. My family isn't in the fight."

As they went back into the house Felícita said. "Say, Ada and Freddy are sleeping on my balcony so as not to pay for a hotel."

"Balls, Fela, the thing is you don't use your head," Cruz replied. "You have children and still you let those people in."

"Well, she comes from a good family even though she is kind of black. The only thing is, she's a little crazy."

Gabi came in talking loudly and Cruz said, "Listen, Gabriel, don't talk all the time. You'll wake up the children. Shut up and don't screw around."

His mother imitated his slight lisp. "Lithen to the way that fairy talkth. Look at how you talk, you jerk."

"You look like a monster yourself," the boy said angrily.

"You do yourthelf, you fairy," Felícita said. She sent Gabi home to get her hair curlers, then said, "Say, Cruz, where do you keep the nail file?"

"Over there," Cruz answered, pointing toward a cabinet made from old orange crates. The nail file was in a small wooden box which had the name Soledad carved on its top. Soledad had given Cruz the box when she went to New York. It held a meager supply of cosmetics, an eyebrow pencil and two lipsticks, and some keys. Cruz spent almost nothing on cosmetics; what she had, Felícita or girl friends had given to her when they were ready to discard them.

"Yes, Fela," Cruz said, "you want to close your eyes to everything, but you're not taking care of those children the way you should. Those poor kids are running around the streets at night."

When Cruz upbraided her for her treatment of her children, Felícita's usual response was silence. This time Gabi's entrance was a distraction. He came in carrying the curlers in a green-and-red scarf. His brother, Angelito, had come in at the same time, without the guava and cheese. Cruz said, "Angelito, go get me some candy. Go on, hurry up." She saw that Gabriel had climbed up on the cupboard in the kitchen to reach the faucet. "Gabriel, if you're going to drink water, don't step on the cupboard or you'll break the dishes," she shouted.

Felícita, carefully creaming her face before a little mirror, ignored her sons. She was getting ready to go to work.

"*Ave María!* That girl upstairs must have the devil in her," Cruz said in exasperation. "Fucking people, jumping, jumping, all the time! But one of these days I'm going to get the police after them, you'll see!"

Rebeca came in. She was wearing a pink dress much too big for her. "Bless me, but that whore up above has more devil in her than me." When Felícita heard the word "whore," she lowered her head and pretended to fix her toenails. Unaware of Felícita's presence, Rebeca continued, "She and that man go too far, you know? And still she says, 'My husband, my husband.' A husband is one who sticks around steady for a couple of years, not just any jerk hanging around for a fuck."

As she finished speaking, Rebeca saw Felícita sitting in the corner, behind the door. "Say, don't be offended," she said now, but Felícita did not raise her head. Rebeca turned to Cruz. "She doesn't have to get offended. After all, she's in your house."

"For God's sake, leave her alone," Cruz said. "The thing that gets you sore is that she fucks and you don't. You're too old."

"Nothing makes me sore. I can't be a whore any more, and I can't be decent either. I am what I am, just an old woman."

"Yes, and an ugly one at that," Cruz answered.

"*Ay,* lay off it, child, you and I are finished any way you look at it."

"No, not me. I'm not finished. The one who's finished is the one who's gotten it up the ass, and they haven't done that to me yet. So I'm not finished, not a bit."

"The thing is, I have no one to look after me, so people can say whatever they want to me and I have to take it. I've lived sixty-five years and I've seen a lot in this life."

"And made a lot of shit too," Felícita said.

"That's nothing. I still intend to shit plenty more."

"Say," Felícita said, "you're practically in the cemetery already."

"Never mind about me being old, child. I can still hold my own. I shit on them all." Rebeca turned to Rosa. "What does a person like you think about the dirty way the people talk here? You'd better leave your face up in San Juan when you come down here. That's the way La Esmeralda is."

She pointed to Gabriel. "Say, look at that. He went and put cold cream on top of his head."

"That's the right place," Felícita said quickly. "It'll go in easy." Felícita, Cruz and Rebeca all laughed.

"Say, Fela, why don't you bathe the children now that you have a chance?" Cruz asked. In Felícita's apartment the bathroom faucet often did not work.

"Gabi, Angelito, go bathe," Felícita said indifferently.

"Hey, Gabi, fairy boy, masturbator, are you going to bathe or not?" Rebeca said.

"Don't use such language," Felícita protested. "The boy will learn things."

"Ah! That's nothing," Cruz said. "He knows more than that already. Yesterday he was kissing a little girl."

Felícita pointed to Anita, who was sleeping face down in a kneeling position so that her buttocks were raised. "Look at that, the way she is lying there. She's dreaming about a weenie and waiting for it with her behind up." Again the three women laughed.

"Say, will you let me press this dress?" Felícita asked Cruz. "And let me have a half a dollar?"

Cruz put her hand on her genitals. "Here's your half a dollar. Come and get it," she said while they all laughed.

"All right. I'll give *you* half a dollar if you hand it over."

"I'm not handing anything over. It stays right where it is."

Cruz lay back on her cot looking at herself in the hand mirror and picking her teeth. Felícita put the last curlers in her hair. Rebeca went to the toilet to take a shower.

Felícita said, *"Ave María!* The things I see every day over at the bar. This woman who owns a house over there came in yesterday with some old guy who looked like money. And what happens? After they are there awhile, a *teenager* comes in and she prefers him to the old guy. So the old guy ended up paying for everything and the *teenager* went off to fuck her. *Ave María!* I'm behind the bar, see? That's where I was, and I say to the customers, 'I'm going to let a small fart.' Then one of them calls me over and says, 'Look, sister, if you're going to let a fart, let it here in my hand for my collection.' *Ave María!* What a boy! In his hand! 'So as not to waste it,' he said."

"What a filthy woman!" Rebeca called from the toilet.

Chuito was now awake, and Cruz went over to the crib. He had moved his bowels, and she cleaned him with the diaper he was wearing. She handed him to Felícita, who held him for only a minute or two before she said, "Take Chuito, Crucita. Hurry up, I have to go soon or I'll be late, *chica!*"

"Oh, come on, you've still got time."

"Honest to God, I have to hurry."

Felícita, still holding Chuito, stood up. Cruz shoved her backward and Felícita stumbled into Anita's little chair, which stuck to her. Laughing, Cruz said, "Move your ass, girl, move your ass."

Felícita sat down and stood up two or three times until the chair finally slipped off. Then she placed the baby in his crib and went into the toilet, where Rebeca was still in the shower. Cruz followed her, and in a moment the three women were howling with laughter. Cruz shouted, "No, don't grab me, don't grab me." She burst out of the door and came running into the room. Felícita followed, laughing uncontrollably. Felícita managed to gasp, "And I always thought an ass-hole couldn't talk."

"Just look at them," Rebeca said. "They almost killed me, trying to throw pails at each other with me in the middle."

Felícita pulled the ironing board out into the center of the room and connected the iron to the extension cord. She lifted up the skirt of her dress to examine the torn places.

"Hey, don't lift your dress up like that," Cruz said. "Rosa's here."

"Bah!" Rebeca said. "She farted in front of Rosa and that's worse."

"No, it was Cruz who farted. She almost did it in my face. That's why I said to her that I didn't know a little ass-hole could talk. And Rebeca was yelling, 'They're killing me. They're killing me!' " Again Felícita and Cruz doubled over with laughter.

"Say, Fela," Rebeca said, "you should watch out for those kids of yours and not teach them dirty things."

"My God! I just like to joke about farts!"

"*Ave María!* If I let a fart in front of people I get embarrassed," Rebeca said. "Some people do it in front of anybody, just like that!"

Cruz rubbed the small of her back. "Felícita, what's in here, anyway?"

"Those are the kidneys there, you dumb jerk."

"The kidneys? Then, you know, my kidneys hurt."

"Maybe your monthly is coming."

"Well, don't make me laugh any more. My back hurts already."

Rebeca said she was going to the store. As she went out, Catín, Soledad's foster daughter, limped in. The lame child was undersized for her age and looked thin and wan in her pink-and-white nylon dress.

"*Ave María!* Here's Catín back from the country," Cruz exclaimed. "Well, did your *papá* treat you right?"

"Oh yes, I had a good time."

"Say, what about your slacks?" Cruz asked.

"I left them there."

"You left them? Well, the next time you can go naked. I'm not going to buy things for you to leave, see? Your father doesn't buy you any clothes, nobody does, and I'm not going to any more either." Catín edged toward the door and made her escape while Cruz was still speaking.

Rebeca rushed in, dropped the coffee she had bought onto the kitchen table, and hurried into the toilet. "My petticoats are falling down," she said.

Felícita picked up the dress that she had ironed and hung over the edge of the baby's crib. "How do you like that!" she said in disgust. "Don't I have good luck though? It's full of shit! Now I'll have to buy perfume to pour over it. Can you imagine what I'd smell like to anyone who comes near me? *Ave María!* What a shitty little boy!"

Cruz and Rebeca laughed as Felícita left. Rebeca took Felícita's place at the ironing board and began to iron a pair of child's pants. Cruz sat down at the end of the entryway, gnawing on a chicken bone. "Hey, come here, you little piece of cunt," she called to a short hunchbacked girl walking along the cement path.

Norma came up the steps, with her waddling walk. She was wearing a pink dress, vivid pink nail polish and a religious medal which hung down in back on her hump. Sometime before, a boy of about seventeen who professed to love her, had seduced her on the beach and had become her lover. Recently he had begun to avoid her. Norma and Cruz went into the house, where Norma immediately picked up the baby and kissed him repeatedly on his cheeks.

"Say, Norma, I have black coffee here. Would you like some?"

"Yes, Crucita darling, I'll have a little." Cruz poured some coffee into a can and handed it to her.

Anita awoke, climbed up to straddle Cruz's lap, and began to nurse. *Doña* Rebeca was still in the toilet. There was a sudden crash and Cruz wailed, "Lord, now I'm screwed! Yes, I'm screwed without a toilet or anything."

"It's all rotten in here," Rebeca shouted.

"Your ass is what's rotten, not anything in there," Cruz shouted back.

"*Ave María!* What a loud-mouth you are! You know that the wall behind the tub is rotted. That's why the tub fell."

"Norma, I saw your boy friend yesterday," Cruz said. "He had the tightest clothes on."

"Yes, I saw him too," Norma answered. "And when he passed by, I said to him, 'Don't bother me. I don't like fairies.' "

Norma began kissing Chuito. "Stop that," Cruz said. "He's not your boy friend."

"But he likes it, child, because he's all man," Norma said. "Aren't you all man, beautiful baby? Say, how are babies made, anyway? I mean, how does the thing begin?"

"Now that you're no longer a *señorita,* you should go see one of those pictures on how babies are made. What you see, for example, is how at one month it is like a pimple and then little by little it grows until it has hair, little testicles and everything. Imagine, Emilio brought a woman here and they wanted to put a tube inside me to get rid of this lovely Negro baby. But I refused. *Ave María!* How could I not want such a beautiful boy?

"I wish you could have seen when Raquel got rid of a five-month baby," Cruz went on. "She was in her house and she called to me, 'Crucita, Crucita, a lot of blood is coming out of me.' So I went there and looked and said, 'My

Lord! What do we do now?' Raquel said, 'Ah, that's nothing!' So she pushed and the baby came out. It had hair already and everything and it was alive. All it did was move its mouth, gasping like a fish. You've seen how fish do. So it kept doing that for about a half an hour. Then Raquel's husband came home."

"And then what? What did he do?" Norma asked.

"Ah! Nothing. He carried it off and threw it away like it was a dog. He threw it in the sea. That's why when Emilio wanted me to get rid of the baby I refused. I wish you had seen that. A puddle of blood in a white basin and that poor baby gasping."

Norma picked up a pair of bedroom slippers and tried them on. "You can keep those slippers," Cruz said. "They're the ones I wore when I went to the hospital to give birth to Chuito." Norma kissed Cruz on the cheek, and Cruz slapped her lightly on the shoulder. "My Lord! Giving me a kiss. Isn't she the fresh one, though."

Anita had gone to the toilet. A few minutes later she said, "Crucita, I finished shitting."

"Then wipe your little ass." But Norma already had gone to help the child and to dress her in a little playsuit.

"Catín, come here and let me comb your hair," Cruz called. The child came in and kneeled beside Cruz. Anita jealously asked to have her hair combed first. "All right, Anita, but I thought you didn't like your hair to be combed. Catín, what did you do at your *papá*'s house?"

"Nothing. We only went out somewhere in the country."

"Oh, listen to this, Norma," Cruz said. "A friend of mine came to see me yesterday and we made up a dirty poem. It's just nonsense. Listen:

> "My cock went and died on me,
> He's in mourning, the stupid jerk,
> Open that cunt, woman,
> To put the corpse inside."

Anita began to sing and Cruz said, "You like it, eh, Anita? It even makes you sing." Cruz finished combing her daughter's hair and began to comb Catín's. Tany and Angelito came in. "What's the procession for?" Cruz asked. "Stand still, Catín, I'm not finished yet." Cruz fastened Catín's hair in a pony tail. "All right, Catín, now you can take off. Go and buy an orange. Tany, go with Catín for an orange. Hey, Norma, come here. Now I'll comb you." Cruz went to sit in the door of the entryway where it was cooler. Norma sat on the step below her, leaning back between Cruz's legs while Cruz combed her hair.

Felícita stopped by on her way to work. With her face made up, her hair combed out and wearing a clean, fresh dress, she was a pretty, stylish young woman. She wore a red bow in her mahogany-colored hair, and red high-heeled shoes. Before she left, she gave Cruz a dollar bill; fifty cents was for two malt beers for her children, the rest was for Cruz.

"Hey, look at Anita," Norma said. "She's going into that man's house across the street."

"Let her go," Cruz answered. "If that man does anything to her, I'll kill him. There are all kinds around here, and they do things to little girls, eh? I would gladly kill anyone who did anything to Anita." A moment later they saw Anita coming home crying, but Cruz only shouted at her. Cruz went on singing as she combed Norma's hair, pausing now and then to watch the people go by. It was after five o'clock and at this time of the day the street below swarmed with men, women and children. Some of the men were obviously drunk.

When Cruz finished combing her friend's hair, she said, "Now I'll go get you a clip for a pony tail back here." Norma moved aside, but Cruz remained where she was for a moment, with her legs spread apart. A man was standing directly below her, and she shouted, *"Ave María!* Now you saw my pussy, didn't you, *Extraño?"* The man and Cruz both laughed.

Cruz went inside and came out again with the clip, which she fastened on Norma's hair. "You're finished now." Norma moved from her position and Cruz quickly closed her legs, saying, "No chance this time, *Extraño!"*

Norma's face was on a level with Cruz's knees. She put her head between Cruz's legs and sniffed, wrinkling her nose and winking. "Aren't you fresh!" Cruz said. They both laughed.

The voice of a race-track announcer was heard shouting over a radio. Norma and Cruz listened intently.

"Did you play today, Crucita?"

"No, not today."

"Lord, maybe you would have hit today."

A woman was selling breadfruit below. Cruz called down, "Angelito, get me ten cents' worth of breadfruit." She tossed him a coin. When Angelito brought the breadfruit, Cruz offered some to Norma and Rosa, saying, "These are grounds for divorce. They give you gas. Eat some of these and you won't be able to stand your own self."

Cruz ate some and worked her tongue around in her mouth. *"Ave María!* It's awful to have a tooth missing. The food gets in there."

Rebeca came up to Cruz to say that she wanted Catín to stop playing on the walk near her apartment. Cruz flared up immediately. "Leave her alone, you old bitch!" she screamed. "You have no business starting up with her. That dirty piece of cement over there in front of your house belongs to you, but not this one in front of mine, understand?"

"I didn't say anything."

"Oh no! You never say a word. Catín has a right to play here, and I'm not keeping her locked up in the house all the time. Look, her *mamá* is crazy there in New York; her father doesn't want her; Felícita won't keep her because she doesn't get on with her own children. But I want her and I love her as if she were my own blood."

"What are you talking about?" Rebeca said, spitting through her teeth. She was smoking a cigar. "Your own blood. Crap!"

"I mean, she's mine, my own blood. And whoever starts up with her is going to have trouble on her hands, Rebeca. So don't look for it."

"That's the way the people here are," Rebeca said. She spit again. "Yes, the young ones today who don't turn out to be whores are thieves or criminals. Better not to go near them."

"That's right. You've had yours already. You ate your banana. Now it's our turn to eat the bananas, and we don't give a damn."

Rebeca turned and went into her apartment.

"We're in La Esmeralda here," Cruz screamed after her, "and whoever doesn't eat shit smells it, see?"

"Keep quiet, will you, Crucita, keep quiet!" Norma said.

"You shut up! Leave me be!" Cruz said furiously. "The thing is, *doña* Rebeca has it in for Catín." She was talking loudly enough for Rebeca to hear. "Her granddaughter can do whatever she wants, but not Catín. And that granddaughter of hers has the dirtiest mouth, but she never says a word to her. Always complaining about Catín! Catín's orphan and has nobody except me and I'll shit on anybody for her."

Cruz and Norma went inside. But Cruz was not through with Rebeca. She raised her voice to be sure that Rebeca could hear her. "The people here have the damnedest gall! But I piss on them all. Let whoever doesn't like me poison my water."

Cruz dropped her voice and whispered to Norma, "I like to get Rebeca pissed off." Then, shouting, she said, "Just for that, I'm going to drink soda. Angelito, go get me three Pepsis. When I get mad, it makes me hungry."

Rebeca came out of her apartment and stopped in front of Cruz's entry-way. Her lips were trembling with rage. "Say, give me those pants I left inside. The ones I was ironing."

"Yes, girl, I'll get them for you," Norma said.

"Don't call her 'girl,' " Cruz said. "Call her 'devil.' That's what this old woman is and she's going to hell."

"Go screw!" Rebeca said and went back home.

It was after six o'clock. Cruz hunted for matches to light the stove. "Say, that bitch Felícita comes and uses the ironing board and then doesn't put it back where it belongs." Cruz raised her voice because Rebeca also used the ironing board. "From now on I'm not going to let her iron if she doesn't put the board back. She or anybody else."

Norma washed the tin cans and the coffee pot. Cruz stood on her cot to lean out of the window. She heard Anita crying and called, "Hey, what's going on down there?" There was no answer. Several girls came along to ask Cruz if the laundry was ready for the woman who sold scraped ices. "Tell her it will be ready tomorrow." Cruz turned to Rosa, "My Lord! They come for the clothes by 'seepage.' "

"Seepage?" Rosa asked.

"Yes, they seep in here one at a time. One comes today, another tomorrow, and a third one the day after. But when it comes time to pay, that's different. They disappear."

It had grown dark, and the street lights went on. Catín came in from playing, and Cruz told her to hang up the slip which Catín had thrown into a corner. When the girl fussed about it, Cruz slapped her on the mouth, saying, "Don't you shout at me! You aren't going to shit in my mouth." She slapped her again. "That's all I say to her," she said to Rosa, "and she gets like a mean dog. That's why she has to feel the weight of my hand, so she'll learn respect. *Ave María!*"

The rest of the children came trooping in. Tany and Mundito were naked. "Lord," Cruz said, "you kids must be fainting from hunger. I'll feed you right away. But you're going to sleep at home tonight because last night you shit in the beds here."

"Crucita, I'm leaving," Norma said.

"My Lord, why? Don't go. Have a drink first."

Cruz opened the Pepsi-Colas she had sent for. She gave one to Norma and another to Rosa. She handed plates of rice to Gabriel, Angelito and Anita. She spread an old blanket on the floor and set Chuito on it. Then she gave a plate of rice to Mundito, who had been sitting on the floor waiting. "You want some, Tany?" she asked.

"Yes."

"Then eat it all up, eh?"

The little girl was hungry and she quickly ate every grain of rice on her plate and those that had fallen on the floor as well. Chuito was kicking and trying to turn over. Anita went to lie beside him and to stroke his face but Cruz said, "Anita, you get away from him. You don't pet boys." Anita then put her buttocks against Mundito's face and tried to pass wind. "No, no," yelled the boy. "Say, Crucita, I want milk."

"*Ave María!* I'll have to buy another pint." Cruz partly filled a tin can with milk and gave it to him. "Here. And now I've got to get Chuito's bottle ready." Tany went to sit by the baby, smoothing his hair and petting his cheeks.

"Say, your mother didn't cook today, did she?" Cruz asked Gabriel.

"No, she bought food at the restaurant."

"What a woman! That's why you're in such a condition. That restaurant food is going to kill you."

Cruz hurried as she prepared Chuito's mixture of barley and milk because he looked as if he was going to cry. Catín said she was hungry. "You're hungry, eh? All right, be quick and I'll give you your dish. Give me that plate of Tany's to wash because everything is dirty. Gabi, your mother left money for malts. Go buy them and you'll all share them."

Anita had slipped out and Cruz went after her. "If you go down again, Anita, I'm going to call the monster to take you away, hear? I'm going to tell Lucelia to beat you." Cruz served herself some rice and beans and sat down on the floor to eat.

Tany said her ear hurt. Cruz tried to examine it in the dim light of the electric bulb that hung from the kitchen ceiling. Then she smelled the ear. "Look at that! The poor baby! The poor little girl's ear hurts and the mother pays no attention. Felícita says I am a gossip but that's what *she* is." She found a jar of Vicks Vaporub and put some into the girl's ear. Gabriel returned with the malt beer and Cruz poured it into cans for Felícita's four children. Cruz herself drank an entire bottle. Two fat rats darted in and out of the kitchen area looking for food.

"Come here, Catín. I'm going to take Fela's children home. I want you to keep an eye on the baby. But really watch him and be careful that he doesn't fall or I'll pull your liver out through your mouth, hear?"

It was seven o'clock when Cruz, Rosa and the children walked the short distance to Felícita's rooms. Since Felícita did not have electricity, a votive candle gave the only light in the house. A neighbor had already brought Evita, Felícita's year-and-a-half-old daughter, to the apartment and had left her there alone. Cruz hunted until she found Evita's bottle, smelled it, and said in disgust, "And Fela gives it to her just like that. I'm going to take this bottle and wash it and give the baby some food. You know, Fela said that Tany and Evita and Mundo should sleep on the cot and the twins in her big double bed. But when she comes home, she puts the twins on the floor and sleeps in the bed alone."

Cruz and Rosa walked back to Cruz's house through groups of teen-agers and drunken men and women. They passed four men who were taking army gasoline cans full of rum out of a car. A man with his long hair arranged in a pony tail ran past them. Some boys were banging on the junked cars with sticks and stones; another gang was playing cops and robbers. Radios were blaring, dogs were barking. The noise was deafening.

Back inside her apartment, Cruz washed Evita's bottle and filled it with barley and milk. She sent Catín to Felícita's house with the bottle, telling her to go in quietly. If the children were still awake she was to tell them that she would be right over. Catín soon returned, however, to say that the children were asleep and that she had left the bottle beside the baby.

In the meantime Cruz took off Chuito's wet diaper, kissed his buttocks and his penis and danced him up and down, saying, "I haven't been carrying you much lately, have I? No, I haven't." She put him back on the cot. Anita was asleep in the crib and Catín was urinating in a pot beside her cot. She then lay down with only her panties on, and began to suck her index finger.

Rosa and Cruz sat on the steps to watch the people in the street. Cruz was tired and did not speak for a long time. Finally, she said she was sleepy and she went inside to do the final chores. She set a rat trap with cheese and placed it on the table in the kitchen. She then lit two candles on the little altar shelf and went back to the kitchen to prepare incense. "I do this on Tuesdays too," she told Rosa, "because that is the witches' day."

First she placed pieces of wood in a pan, set the pan on the stove and lit the fire. She waited until the wood was very hot, then added herbs, sunflower seed, mint, *cundeamor* and *anamú*. When the herbs were smoking well, she shut the door and window shutters and passed the pan under each of the cots and under the crib. Then she placed the smoking pan in front of the closed door "because that's where the most danger comes from." Finally, she recited the "Prayer of the Blessed Shirt and of Peace for the Home":

"May the Holy Company of God be with me and the cloak of Holy Mary, His Mother, protect and defend me from danger. Hail Mary, full of grace, free me of all evil spirits, baptized and unbaptized. Christ conquer, Christ rule, He who was born in Bethlehem, wherefore I cannot be killed or involved with the law.

"Soften, my Lord, the hearts of my opponents. May those who wish me evil be unable to see me. They have hands but cannot reach me, their steel cannot wound me, their knots cannot tie me. May my enemies be as gentle to me as Jesus Christ was on the cross. Jesus Christ, speak and take my part. Jesus Christ, relieve me forever of my cares. Bless my bed, my body, my house, and all around it. Free me of the spells of witches and of men and women of evil intentions.

"This is the prayer of the Holy Shirt, of the Son of the Living God. It is this that I place against my enemies. By the three crowns of Abraham, I offer up this prayer together with myself. Amen."

The street outside had suddenly become very quiet. It was almost ten o'clock. *"Ave María!"* Cruz said and yawned, "and now I'm very tired too. *Ay,* but I almost forgot the blessing!" She went over to the crib, kissed Anita and said, "Anita, the blessing! Ask a blessing from *mami*, Anita." She kissed the little girl and talked to her for a minute or two until Anita was awake enough to ask for a blessing. Then she awoke Chuito, but for him Cruz did the asking and responding.

Rosa said it was time for her to leave. Cruz took off her clothes except for her panties, and lay down on the cot with Chuito. As Rosa went out, pulling the door shut after her, she heard Anita's voice.

"Crucita, want titty. Want titty, Crucita."

Cruz

"That Cripple"

I WAS ALREADY living with my stepmother Hortensia when I first became conscious of the world. She was the one I knew as my mother then, but they tell me that she didn't care for me and would beat me. My godmother says that one day when I was a year and a half old, I was sitting at the top of a high staircase and my older sister, Soledad, was keeping an eye on me. My stepmother called her in to wash the dishes and I was left alone. I asked my sister for a drink of water, but Hortensia came out in a mean temper. "What a pest this child is," she said and gave me a push. I was on the edge of the stairs and I went rolling down to the street below. There I lay on my back, crying at the top of my lungs. She just left me there. Neither my *mamá* nor my *papá* was around at the time. He was in Trinidad and I don't know where my *mamá* was living.

I was already walking when that happened, but after the fall I didn't walk again until I was five. My father and stepmother took me once to the clinic at Fort Brooke and some specialists examined me. They said I had broken my spine and they told my stepmother to bring me back for treatment, but she never did.

In some ways my stepmother was good to me. According to my godmother, Hortensia went to a lot of trouble when I got meningitis. She took me to the hospital and spent a lot of time with me there. After that I was in the hospital for two months with double pneumonia and bronchitis and the doctor told Hortensia to take me home to die because I didn't have a chance. So she took me to a spiritist in Manatí. I was stretched out cold as though I were dead, but the woman said that I was not dead at all, just very weak. She began to massage me and treat me, and they say she saved my life. It's a miracle that I'm alive today.

My *mamá* and *papá* separated when I was little but I don't remember that far back. One day my *papá* packed his clothes and left. Just like that, without saying a word. Later he divorced my mother and married Hortensia.

My *mamá* started working as a maid and my grandma helped her by taking care of us. I was always sick and so was my eldest sister; almost all of us were sick. My mother finally said, "There's just nothing else I can do," and that afternoon she left us at my godmother Elsa's house at Stop 27 and she took up with a man. You see, she wasn't able to feed us and we were crying from hunger. My *papá* wouldn't contribute anything for us, and my grandma had died. My *mamá* would have relations with men who gave her money and that's how she supported us. Yes, she went into the life, she became a prostitute. That's why my *papá* took us children away from her.

I was never very friendly with my father. We didn't spend much time together because he was never home for more than two or three weeks at a time. And he wasn't one to spoil us. He never fondled us, but he didn't beat us much, either. His character was one that demanded respect. Whenever it was necessary, he would spank us with his soldier's belt. When he was at home my stepmother sent us out of the house so that he could be with her and her children.

My *papá* never took to me because my stepmother told him I was a lot like my mother. Usually he paid no attention to me so as not to provoke my stepmother, who was very jealous. The one he got along with best was Felícita.

As my *papá* was in the *Army,* they sent money to my stepmother and she would buy things for her children and luxuries for herself but nothing for us. Whenever my *papá* came home, he brought lots of good clothes with him and left money with her to buy things for me and my sisters and brother. She'd buy some cheap twenty-five-cent material and make up a little dress for me, and that was all. And she was always calling me names, saying I had a face like a goat and that I didn't even look like a human being. That hurt me.

Then, for dinner, instead of serving the rice to us like the rest, she'd give us the part that stuck to the pan. And she didn't let us eat inside the house but gave us our food outdoors. Whenever visitors came, she threw us out and let her children stay inside. We weren't allowed back in until the visitors had left. Sometimes she punished us by making us stand behind the door all day long. One morning after breakfast she tied me up under the bed and didn't give me anything to eat until evening.

Once there was a big hurricane and my *mamá* came for us. She said that if anything happened she wanted to die with us. Someone told me she was my mother and we became friends. After the storm she took Soledad to live with her, then she took my brother, and then me. The only one who stayed behind was Felícita.

Well, we came to live in La Esmeralda with Fernanda. La Esmeralda is a good place. Yes, you see unbelievable things here all right, prostitutes, dope peddlers, and women and men loving it up right on the beach, but still, I like it. During the big celebration for the patron saint they shoot off fireworks and skyrockets from El Morro Castle. You can see it all from La Esmeralda and it looks just lovely over the water.

At that time my *mamá* lived with Erasmo, a stepfather of mine, who was a pimp. The first time I realized *mamá* was a whore was when I saw an American in the house. I asked her who he was and she said he was a cousin of hers. But as I was a little girl and liked to peep, I caught them doing it. I was amazed at what I saw and began to laugh and called my little friends to come and look. I called my sister and my brother too. "What are they doing?" my brother asked me. I said, *"Ay,* look at that there! How ugly a naked man looks!"

My sister looked and just stood there, paralyzed. I liked to watch just so I could talk about it to my sister and then tease my *mamá.* "Say, *mamá,"* I said to her, "what's the idea of that? Do cousins climb on top of one another?"

"What makes you ask?"

"Oh, because I caught you," I said.

My mamá would get into discussions with the neighbors and I would listen in. When the conversation got to its peak, as we say, she'd yell at me, "You get out of here," and I would hide behind the door. By the time I was eight, I knew all about such things.

I used to go to the bar where she made her pickups. I was just a little thing and, like a foolish kid, I felt happy there. My *mamá* would pick up men and then come and give me the money. And I would say, "Hooray! Now we'll have food tomorrow." I don't know how much she gave me because all she said was, "Here, hold this for me." I didn't dare look and besides I didn't know how to count. They'd lift me up on the bar and I would sit there watching the women go upstairs with Americans and come down again. People would see me and give me nickels and quarters; when the police came, I hid behind the bar and the women would run away and hide. They never caught my *mamá.*

When Erasmo took up with another woman, my *mamá* began living with Pedro. He told her that he would work to support her if she left the life. And so she did. He went to work and she stayed at home. But my *mamá* drank and Pedro didn't like it. They fought all the time and he beat us. I don't know why, but I was the one who got it the most, maybe because I was the smallest. I went hungry a lot while my mother was living with this stepfather. He would go out without leaving money for food, and I would crawl under the bed and cry from hunger until I fell asleep.

One day I went with my *mamá* to San Juan and when we came home we found our room empty. The bed was gone and the icebox too. Nothing was left. Nothing! Pedro had sold everything and had gone.

Mamá went on drinking, and when she was drunk she would get into a kind of fury with me, and sometimes she'd beat me. First she'd stare at me with "cow's eyes," as I used to call them. I don't know if it was because she hated me or because I reminded her of somebody she didn't like. I'd say to my girl friends, "Look, now the cow wants to swallow me." Then all at once she'd start insulting me and I'd know it was time for me to make myself scarce.

She'd punish me when she saw me sitting immodestly or when I did anything mischievous, like take the coins out of the basin in which she kept lodestones. She said it was good luck to leave the money there, but I thought, "Why should the lodestone keep the money when I can get candy with it?" And she never let me go outside either. I would sneak out to play after she lay down to sleep. Sometimes she would punish me for not wanting to tidy the house. She would get mad and beat me.

My mother treated me better than my stepmother did. Even though my stepmother was a decent and honorable woman and my mother was a whore, I consider my mother to be a better person and I've always preferred her.

When I got sick my *mamá* was good to me and would take me to the hospital right away. If I wasn't looking well, she would make me lie down. She gave me my medicines and took care of me, giving me Vicks and rubbing me with Mentosan if I had a cough. She really spoiled me. When I was afraid to sleep alone, she would say, "Come, get in with me," and she'd hold me close until I fell asleep. When I woke up, I would be back in my own bed.

I used to have asthma. It starts out with a lot of coughing and then the smothering gets you in the stomach very hard, and you gasp for breath as if you're choking to death. Once when I had an attack, my mother brought me to the hospital and stayed the whole night with me. They gave me oxygen and serum. The doctors told her to leave me there with them and they would take care of me, but she said that if I was going to die she wanted me to die at her side because I was her last treasure. That's what she said, but I don't know whether to believe it because her real favorite has always been Soledad.

On the Day of the Kings my *mamá* said to me, "You must get some grass for the Kings' camels and put out water for them." And silly me, I would get a glass and a saucer, a piece of paper for them to wipe their hands on, a fork and a spoon, and lay everything out neatly in a shoe box and put it under the bed. I went to sleep at six in the evening. When I woke up at about five in the morning I looked under the bed and found that the camels had eaten the grass and drunk the water, and there were the presents in the box, a coffee set and a doll. *Ave María!* I played all day long.

My *mamá* would do that every year, but once when she was living with Pedro, she had nothing to give me and so she cried. When I asked her what was wrong she said that her head ached. I went and put a bandage around her head. She said to me, "I'm sorry, but the Three Kings won't come to you this year." I began to cry and got all hoarse. I threw myself on my bed and cried and cried until I fell asleep.

Even though I didn't put out grass and water, I got up on the morning of the Day of the Kings and looked under the bed. The box was empty. So I thought to myself, "Aha! That's it! You have no money so you must be the Kings!" We didn't leave the house that day because everybody else had toys and we didn't. People would come and ask us what we had gotten and then my *mamá* would burst out crying, and I would go outside so as not to have to see her.

I started going to school for the first time when I was eight. My *mamá* took me. I remember I wore a blue dress and white shoes. My *mamá* got up early, dressed me and my brother, and registered us in school. I wanted to know why she was going to leave me in the classroom, because I thought they were going to spank me and make fun of the way I walked. When my *mamá* left I burst out crying. The teacher gave me some chocolate. Then when school was over, my *mamá* came for me. She brought us to school and called for us every day for a whole year, until I finally learned to go by myself.

In school they made me wear special high shoes with braces for about a year and my legs got stronger, but I still had to hold on to something when I walked. After they took off the braces I had to learn to walk all over again. I went to the hospital in Bayamón and they attached sandbags to my legs. I had to move back and forth, exercising with them, and then they put me in some machines to walk. I have been walking ever since, but with a limp.

Sometimes I'd feel very bad because my *mamá* would call me "that cripple." I would answer, "Then why did you make one out of me?" It would make me very sad to see the girls running about happy and well, and me the way I was. I didn't dare go around with them because people would point at me and make fun of me, imitating the way I limped. But actually, it never worried me much because I would say that God was there and it is He who disposes and that no matter what happened to me I would submit to His will.

My first teacher was called *Miss* Abril. She loved me very much. She was my best teacher. When I had no shoes or clothes for school, she would get some for me from *las sisters,* and every day she gave me chocolate or cake or cookies. She used to take me home with her almost every Saturday because she felt sorry for me. She had had a daughter, also a cripple, who was killed by a car. My brother went along to tend the garden. I wanted to wash the dishes and help her in the house but she wouldn't let me. She'd put chairs out on the balcony for us and sit there looking at me, and she'd begin to cry. On the Day of the Kings she bought me clothes and candy and toys and a great big doll.

One day while *Miss* Abril was my teacher I was jumping rope outside and my *mamá* was up in the house drinking. She called to me to make her a cup of coffee but I said I wouldn't. So she said to me, "I hope you break a leg on your way up here." I said, "If I break it, so what? You can eat it tomorrow with chickpeas." She said I was fresh and had no respect for her. She had a belt in her hand and she hit me with the buckle. I had to make the coffee for her. My eyes were so full of tears that when I went to take hold of the pot handle I couldn't see, and spilled the hot coffee all over myself. I managed to cover my face, but the coffee splashed over my hair and scalded my whole back. I still have the scar. *Mamá* just looked at me and said, "Let's see whether you die from it or not."

When I didn't show up at school the teacher came around to the house. She got a salve to put on the burn and told my *mamá* that I shouldn't be climbing on a stool in the kitchen to cook because it wasn't safe, and that if a policeman saw me in my condition he'd send my *mamá* to jail. She said that if anything else happened to me, she would hold my *mamá* responsible. So my *mamá* didn't let me cook any more and she rubbed me with grated potatoes and oil, and the mark faded a little.

I was pretty old for my group in school. Some of the children were nice to me and helped me, but others made fun of me. Some would make vulgar sounds at me, and I would throw erasers or hit them with a ruler. Once I had a fight with a girl by the name of Narda. It was during a test and I had studied everything and knew it all by heart, but she hadn't studied and wanted me to tell her the answers. She kept insisting and I wouldn't. So finally she said, "You lousy cripple!" She told me I had lice, so I asked her why she didn't pick them out down below because I had more there than up above, and as I said it I hiked my dress way up and pointed to where I meant. She said that I was dirty and a fresh thing, and she stuck the point of a pencil into my head.

Another time I cut open a boy's head. This boy kept making fun of the way I walked. My high iron shoes made me drag my foot because I couldn't stretch it out very well. I let him imitate me, but a lot of people were watching and laughing. I was with a girl friend named Ada, and I sat down, unbuttoned both my shoes and gave them to her to hold. Then I ran after him and hit him on the head with a stone and he had to have three stitches. They brought me to court because his mother made a complaint, but the judge said he had nothing to do with such a case and they sent me home.

Then the principal sent for my *mamá* so they could talk about putting me in a reform school. My sister Soledad went instead. She was furious and said, "The next time they make fun of you, pick up another stone and split his head in two." When we got to the office the principal said to her, "Cruz is a bad one. Give her a punishment she'll remember." But Soledad didn't do anything to me.

When they took X-rays of the children in school it turned out that I had a bad lung. It was just a spot but I was on the verge of tuberculosis. My blood was yellow too and I was getting very pale. I'd fall asleep in my seat every single afternoon and wouldn't want to eat in the lunchroom. I became bad-tempered and when the teacher spoke to me I would answer back. So she said that maybe there was something wrong with me mentally and she sent me to be examined. When they found the spot, they told my mother and she burst out crying. They told her to take me to the hospital at Aibonito. That is what she did and it was a good thing.

I was in the hospital for three months and my *mamá* came to see me only once in all that time. On Sundays when the visitors came to see all the other children, I would cry and say that I wasn't ever going back home but would wander around the world because I had no family. Then *las Mrs.* would try to console me, telling me that my mother was probably ill and couldn't come. I would say, "But I have sisters too," and they would answer, "Why, that's nothing. There are children who have been here for a year and nobody has come to see them yet." But I was heartbroken, and the Sunday my *mamá* did come, I refused to see her because I had learned from the visitors who came from San Juan every Sunday that she was all right but that she was drinking.

When it was time for me to leave, they wrote my mother a letter and she came to get me. I had rosy cheeks by then and I was nice and fat. I looked like a real American when she took me home.

We went back to the same house in La Esmeralda. Right then I told my *mamá* that I was not ever getting married but that I was going to study medicine and be a doctor. She said that God would help me and show me the right road.

I didn't have too many illusions, though, because I had been such a clown in school that for a long time I couldn't even read or write. When there was a test I would cross my legs, put my pencil in my mouth and puff on it as if it were a cigarette. When the teacher looked at me I'd say, "Who needs to work? Not me. It's my day off." But I didn't want anybody to know I couldn't read. When my boy friend in school would send me a note, I felt very embarrassed about having to give it to a girl friend to read for me.

One day when I was in the third grade I was passing by the church on San Francisco Street, and just out of curiosity I went in. I prayed to Christ hanging there on His cross. I started crying so He would help me at least to read and write, because I wanted to be somebody. I had twenty-five cents with me and I spent it on candles which I lit. Then I went and prayed to Saint Martha. I like the saints and have believed in them since the time I was little, and I believed in that Virgin very much because she had once granted me something I asked for. So I said to her, "Saint Martha, do everything you possibly can so I'll learn to read and write and earn a living with my own two hands. If you do, I'll burn a dollar candle for you."

I began by taking the reading book to the teacher and telling her I wanted to learn to read and write. But she said there was no hope any more. I felt very bad because I was the eldest one in the class and I was going to be left behind. Well, then a friend of mine said to me, "I'll teach you." And every day we went to the beach, and she taught me until I finally learned. The teacher was amazed when she saw that I could read. Well, at the end of the term the principal gave the final exam and I got a B. So I burned the big candle to Saint Martha as I had promised.

My mother sent me to the Catholic church often and sometimes I went to the Protestant Hallelujah in La Esmeralda. I never had my First Communion. When my *mamá* sent me to church on Sundays, I would go instead to San Juan Gate to play on the swings. She wouldn't permit me to swing on Sundays but I went anyway, and if she asked me if I had gone to church I'd tell her I had.

I believe I am paying back what I owe. I was a devil when I was a kid. I used to play with the boys all the time, doing things I shouldn't, see? We would play prostitutes or doctor. I would put a pillow over my belly and they would examine me as though I were pregnant. The boys would be my husband and the dolls the babies. We would tie a rag around the doll's waist saying that was its navel. Then the doctor would come and cut the strip of cloth with a piece of glass and say, "All right, the baby is ready. What's missing now is the *mamá*." So then they would pull my *panties* all the way down and look at my belly but without touching me, and say that now I was all right.

Then the boys would get hold of me and begin fooling around and dancing dirty with me, rubbing it in, and then I would dance by myself and sing. One day I went under the house, and this boy came along and grabbed me. I asked what he was doing and he said, "You had a child with Guillo González. Now have one of mine. It's easy." We were making believe I was a prostitute, and I would say, "*Ay*, I can't because I'm not well, and when I'm not well I don't go with anybody." My mother was upstairs all the while, watching through a crack and laughing. She came down below, still laughing, and said to me, "So you want to be a whore, do you?" But then she gave me a spanking and I didn't play that any more.

That was when I was nine years old. Almost all of the boys are in New York now, except for one, Johnny, who lives with my neighbor Caridad. He is the only one here who remembers how we used to play together. Some of the others in New York are married, some are in jail. The one they call Guillo González is in prison now because he would take drugs and steal, until they caught him and a girl by the name of Zulma.

When I was about ten, I played that same game with Hortensia's brother, Domingo. He's dead now. I went under the house with him and my sister Soledad, to play doctor. I was lying there and he had relations with me, not all the way, but a little bit. He was pretty old, about eighteen. He liked Soledad, but because I was growing up and everything, he said I was the one he liked the best and he began fooling with me.

Doña Bertha, a neighbor of ours, sold *bolita* numbers in La Esmeralda. The *bolita* is a forbidden game, an illegal lottery that competes with the government lottery. You buy a number for a quarter and if it happens to be a winning number, you get a hundred dollars. The winning number in the *bolita* is the one with the first three digits of the winning number of the government lottery.

I don't know why it's bad to buy numbers. The law says that parents spend their money on the *bolita* instead of on their children. But *doña* Bertha told me that numbers were a good thing because a person could make money selling them. Not knowing any better, I began to sell and I enjoyed it. I made a dollar when I sold a whole book, which was worth two dollars and fifty cents, and with a dollar in my hand I thought I had a fortune. Since I hardly ever got any money at home, I would sell numbers behind my *mamá*'s back. I went on my own to the house of the man who made up the books. He told me not to tell the police. I knew it was against the law and I said, "Don't worry, if they catch me I'll have to go to reform school." I went around with the books hidden inside the front of my dress. I knew a policeman wouldn't put his hand there.

I made three or four dollars a day. Sometimes you come out the loser if you have to put in your own money to pay for the books. I would give my *mamá* half a dollar and keep a half for myself. She wanted to know how come people were giving me half a dollar every Saturday, and I told her I made it running errands. Then one day I sold a winning number and she caught me with one hundred dollars in my hand. I told her a lady had given it to me to hold. My *mamá* took me to see the lady and then gave me a beating.

During the entire time I lived with my *mamá,* my *papá* sent her only one twenty-dollar money order for me and my brother, and he sent that only because my *mamá* had gone to the Red Cross to notify them that we were very badly off. They got him by the neck there in Panama and deducted the money from his pay. My *mamá* bought us clothes and shoes when the money came.

My *papá* is not a good father because he doesn't look out for us. When he comes on a visit to San Juan he doesn't even send for us. The only way we find out that he is there is if we happen to drop in at his house, and that's maybe once a year. A good father watches over his daughters no matter what condition they are living in, and he helps them out when they are in need. At least he should send a post card at Christmas time telling us where he is, but my father doesn't even do that.

He took my sister Felícita with him to a lot of places. After a while she got tired of traveling and one afternoon she came to stay with my *mamá.* I was washing the dishes when she walked in. I heard somebody outside asking, "Does Nanda live here?" I've always been nasty to the people around here, so I called out in a mean way, "Who the hell is looking for Nanda?" Then I saw Felícita and I hugged her and we kissed each other and I took her to Nanda. My *papá* and stepmother were waiting up on the Boulevard. I went there to talk with them, and I decided to bring my stepmother to the house. She and my *mamá* spoke to each other but just with their tongues, not from the heart.

My stepmother is very stuck up and always wants to go places. She hardly likes to be with us at all. Of her children, Thomas is the closest to me. When I go there he puts his arms around me and kisses me, but I don't like Hortensia's other son, Mariano. They live at Stop 26, on the outskirts of a mud flat. The house is high up on poles, but there is all kinds of filth down below. When I lived there we had an outhouse, but later my *papá* put in a toilet. A ditch runs alongside, by the window, and there was a shack where my stepmother's *mamá* lived. The people dumped garbage into the road, and you could see piles of shit all over the place, and drunks urinating. My stepmother's sister lived with her and sold rum, and so there were drunks in and out of the house all the time. I would see all that, the drunks pushing each other around and using foul talk. Whenever we went to visit my stepmother we'd come back with our shoes covered with mud and filth.

One day I went to Fort Brooke to see my *papá,* who was in the hospital recovering from an accident. That's when I met Felícita's husband Ángel. He was in the hospital there in Fort Brooke, too, and Felícita used to go and visit him every day. Some people told my *mamá* that he was not a good boy, that he beat women and was sick in the chest with tuberculosis. My *mamá* didn't want him for a son-in-law and she fought with Felícita all the time.

When Fela ran off with Ángel my *mamá* began to cry, but she let her go. Fela didn't come back to La Esmeralda until she was pregnant. When she had the twins, my *mamá* said to me, "Go there with her for a week to help her take care of the babies." I was on vacation from school, so I went.

As long as he wasn't drinking, my sister's husband Ángel was a fine person and very responsible and very attentive, too, but when he was drunk all he did was pick fights. He acted crazy and fought with everybody. Felícita didn't know what to make of him and just went along. One day while I was visiting, he started drinking heavily in the morning and she said, "There are going to be fights today." They began arguing about the twins, then he started to say bad things about her and worse things about my family, calling them all a bunch of whores and saying that I was probably worse than the others. Finally he gave Felícita a beating and locked us outside. One of the twins fell on the floor and cried, and my sister banged on the door for him to open. When she got in he began to slap her around. I went in too, to stop the fight, but he picked up a knife and I jumped over a pile of boards and ran out. I went back to my *mamá*'s in La Esmeralda.

We lived in one little room, my *mamá,* my brother and me. Soledad was already on her own by then. We had one little *caucho*, which was so small that when my *mamá* got into bed there wasn't room for both of us, so I would sleep on the floor with my brother.

We lived right across the way from Papo's bar. One day after my *mamá* was separated from my stepfather Pedro, she was in the bar dancing with some man and I was talking with a girl friend outside. Then all at once Pedro came along and wanted her to dance with him. She wouldn't and he hit her, so she pulled a *Gem* out of her mouth and cut him up. My stepfather was in the hospital for a month in a serious condition and my *mamá* went to jail. She was in for a month.

When Fernanda came out of jail she took up with Héctor. This stepfather of mine was really good to us. He bought me my school uniform and was always very affectionate. Whenever we asked him for anything connected with our studies, he would give it to us. Héctor was a good person. The only thing about him was that when he got drunk he insulted everybody. When he was sober he didn't talk to anyone and came straight home from work.

When my *mamá* went to live with Héctor, she said to Simplicio and me, "I'll pay the rent for this room, and you stay here to sleep for two or three days until I find a good big house to take you to. I'm not going to leave you; you're all I have left." So my brother and I stayed there. My *mamá* went shopping for us and I cooked for my brother and myself. Sometimes *mamá* would bring us food already prepared or we would go to a restaurant. My brother Simplicio had about twenty dogs that he had brought to the house, and we would sleep there in one big bunch with all those animals. Simplicio had girl friends, but not for long. He used to shine shoes and was always filthy dirty and surrounded by dogs, so hardly anybody would give him a tumble.

Sometimes I was happy to be living alone in that room without Nanda because when I was invited to a dance I could go. I must have been ten or eleven years old at the time. At first when my girl friends came by for me to go to a dance I'd answer, "I have to ask my *mamá*'s permission." My *mamá* would say, "No, no, she's not going anywhere. She's going to sleep." So I told my friends, "See! If I go without asking permission she doesn't say anything, but if I ask her she won't let me." After that, when they asked, "What do you say, Crucita, are you going to the dance?" I would answer, "Let's go, but first let my *mamá* lock me in." I would tell them to take my *mamá*'s key and open the door for me. Then I would come out and lock it again. My *mamá* would come by and peep through the door and say, "She's asleep."

I'd stay at the dance until eleven or twelve when my brother would whistle for me and I would leave. My brother didn't go to dances because he spent his time with the dogs and shining shoes at the docks. When he came for me he'd say, "Look, I've got the money here for breakfast. Give me the key so I can go home and sleep." And he'd give me fifty cents or a dollar. We were like husband and wife, and people would say, "There goes Cruz's husband."

Then my *mamá* sent me to live with my elder sister Soledad. She had been living in the country with Arturo but he gave her a bad time out there. He liked to beat her hard, and would go around with other women right under her nose. He's just a skinny little man, so one day she picked him up in the air and threw him down and broke two of his ribs. After that they came back to La Esmeralda and lived very happily for about two years, without fighting or anything.

They didn't have any children all that time, so Soledad took in another woman's baby. Then she got pregnant herself. I went to live with her and helped her so she wouldn't have to work so hard. Soledad treated me well while she was pregnant, but after she gave birth to Quique, she fell in love and put the horns on her husband.

There were two apartments in the house. My sister lived in one and a man and his wife in the other. Well, the wife would often go to the country to see her mother, and Arturo worked at night. Soledad would wait until I was asleep and then climb up over the roof and down into the other apartment. One night I got up and turned on the light and there she was, coming back naked. "Aha!" I said. "I'm going to tell Nanda." I ran to Nanda's house and told her. Then Nanda spoke to Soledad and said it was a dirty thing she was doing because she knew very well that her husband Arturo was working for her and why should she pay him back like that? Soledad's answer was that "what she had in the middle was for her to fiddle." It belonged to her and nobody else, and whatever she had to lose she had already lost.

Well, after Soledad did what she did, Arturo went back to the country. Then she went back with him for a while and they were happy and she got pregnant again. But she put the horns on him in the country too. She would say she was going to the river to wash clothes, but it was really to have relations with another man. So she and Arturo had a fight and they separated. She gave birth to Sarita here in La Esmeralda.

When Arturo saw Sarita he admitted she looked like his *mamá*, who had blue eyes and pretty blond hair, but still he didn't want to recognize her as his child. When he finally did, Soledad didn't love him any more and wouldn't live with him. He kept trying to get her to support him because he didn't want to work any more. He used to give her money and she bought everything she felt like buying, but he changed because she put the horns on him. She didn't do it for money but for love of the art, as we say.

I was still going to school but they took me out because I was suffering from asthma. My *mamá* said, "Go to Soledad's so you'll stop all this foolishness of being sick." I went to live with my sister at the housing project, but I didn't like being there. The house was nice and clean and comfortable and I had my own room, but I didn't like living with my sister because she was never at home. She was always running around, going from house to house as if she were a social worker.

One day my *mamá* came and found me doing all the housework and nobody even knew where Soledad was. "Pack your things," my *mamá* said. "We're going back home." So I went back to live with my *mamá*.

Nanda and I still fought a lot. Once she gave me a beating and I told her I was going to Mameyes before I came down with tuberculosis. My aunt Migdalia, my *mamá*'s sister, lives there. My *mamá* told me to go ahead and spend my vacation there, and so I did. I stayed for only one month because I had to go back to school.

My aunt was wonderful to me. I danced a lot, and went to the movies and to the beach. My aunt is short and dark, a very good person. Sometimes she is quick-tempered, but she is more affectionate than my *mamá*. Fernanda whacked me just for the hell of it even if I didn't do a thing. When I saw how much my aunt cared for me, bringing me things and sending me to the movies and taking me everywhere and being with me all the time, then I began to love her even more than my *mamá*.

There was one thing I didn't like about Mameyes, but I guess people are mean to outsiders everywhere. When I went out, people stood there looking at me and making fun of me, see? I was always getting into fights with people because they made fun of the way I walk. They called me "Cripple" and I didn't like it.

When I returned to La Esmeralda, I lived with my *mamá* and my stepfather Héctor and my brother Simplicio. Simplicio spent all his time with other kids, never with me. He was always good to me, though. Whenever he saw me sad or crying, he would tell me to stop because it made him feel bad. And when my *mamá* threw me out of the house, he would leave too, saying to her, "If you throw Crucita out, then I'm going with her." But he was very mischievous. He liked to make fun of people and throw empty cans at them, and to steal money from my *mamá*. When my *mamá* tied him up, he would jump out of the window with the rope and all and walk around San Juan like that.

I became a *señorita* when I was ten years old. The first time I got my period I thought that I had cut myself or that something had happened to me. I began to cry. I was watching television in my *mamá*'s house when I stood up and looked down and saw the blood. "*Ay,* Nanda, I cut myself," I told my *mamá*. She laughed and fixed a cloth which she put on me. I had seen her put *un Kotex* there and when I had asked her what it was for, she told me it was so she wouldn't shit on herself. She put the cloth on me and then took me to the hospital because I began to bleed very badly, as if I had a hemorrhage. They gave me some medicine for the pain. I had my next period when I was eleven years old.

Sometimes my *mamá* talked dirty, but she didn't dare to in front of me until I was a *señorita*. Then she would say, pointing first at my sexual parts, and then at my mouth, "Keep that covered and this open." And she told me not to show my breasts because that would only make them stop growing. Then, when I was about eleven and a half, my *mamá* said, "Here, put on this brassière, your breasts are big now." After that, sex became part of the conversation. When people talked about men, I would ask my *mamá*, "What is it like?" Then she would explain to me about men and their intimate parts. She told me all the names there are for the male and female organs. And when a woman was having her period, she said, "We have the babies in the cradle," or "The red light is on." She told me that there were men who had big balls, and I said, "But what is it that makes it get hard?" she said, "It gets hard when it stands up."

"But how does it happen?" I asked.

"Well now, feel this stick," she said.

She told me that if I were kissing my boy friend and I saw that his thing had begun to stand up, then it was time for me to be on my way, to run off, because that meant he was in a sweat already.

Now that I was menstruating, my *mamá* told me I could begin to think about falling in love. I told her that I wasn't going to get married because the men here never give any money to the women. If I got married it would have to be to somebody from New York. And that's the way it turned out.

Hortensia

They Don't Have to Love Me

MY FAMILY moved from Maunabo to Stop 25, Santurce, when I was seven years old. Nanda was our neighbor there. I used to go to her house once in a while, but I didn't know Cristóbal then. He was a soldier and was somewhere out of the country. I didn't get to know him until much later when he would come to see my sister Blanca Iris.

I lived with my *mamá* and *papá*, but in our house my eldest sister, María del Carmen, was the boss. She is nice to me now but she used to be very cruel. I was her slave. She worked in a *laundry* and whenever she felt like it she would send me in her place and stay home taking it easy. Then she would go and collect the pay and I never even saw the envelope.

After a while my sister got tired of *el laundry* and got a job doing house-work. But it was the same story. I'd work in her place and never see a cent of it. Those people had a daughter whose name was Hortensia, just like mine. They liked me very much and even asked my mother to give me to them. But she said no because I was very sickly and she didn't want to be separated from me.

Sickly and all, and with my *mamá* and me pulling against each other all the time, I got through school as far as the ninth grade. She didn't want me to go but I did. I loved school. It's a shame I couldn't finish!

When I left school I spent more time at Nanda's house. I helped her in the kitchen and I took care of her children, because she didn't. Nanda got a check for them from the *Army,* but those kids didn't get any of the benefit because Nanda would be going around with men. She was involved with a brother of mine and somebody else besides, whose name was Sereno. Nanda had a little girl whom she gave away. Sereno is the *papá,* I think, unless my brother is.

What Nanda did was throw away the money playing lottery with a bunch of girl friends and meanwhile the children were neglected. My sister would get so upset sometimes that she would take Felícita and bring her to the house. Hours would go by and the child would be starving but that didn't bother Nanda. She wouldn't get home until ten or eleven o'clock. Then my sister would take Felícita back to her.

That's what life was like until I was fifteen, when Cristóbal came back from abroad. I saw him a few times but paid no attention to him because I wasn't ready for those things yet. After he left Nanda he would stop in at my house every day. I really didn't have any idea that it was on account of me he came hanging around.

One day he invited me to the movies and I went. When we got back, you should have seen the row they raised! We were in the thick of the hullabaloo when in walked my sister María del Carmen, the one who was so mean to me. She laid down the ultimatum, right then and there. "All right, you're getting married, and fast," she told Cristóbal. Well, it was arranged and we were married. And to this day that man has been the cross I bear.

He had already taken those four children away from their mother and brought them to his brother Pablo's house. Pablo's wife, Elsa, didn't want them, but he did and I'll tell you why. Cristóbal had a little house and he told Pablo that if he would live in it and take care of the children, he would pay him eighty dollars a month. And as Pablo was working only at odd jobs for the *Navy,* he immediately said yes.

Well, it turned out that we went to live with them and right away they were using me as a servant. I soon realized that the reason Cristóbal had married me was to have someone to take care of his children. Inside of two days I was wiping up the shit of kids who weren't mine. Soledad was seven years old then, Felícita was four, Simplicio wasn't three yet and Cruz was less than a year old. And the trouble was that those children had very bad habits.

I had been married less than a week when I began to see what I was in for. One day I wanted to go to visit my *mamá,* so I got up early, washed the floor, put the house in order and stuffed those children with food. Then I went outside to take a bath, but first I asked them if they wanted to go to the bathroom because I had to lock them in the house while I was gone. When I came back, all in a rush to get to my *mamá*'s house, I found that Simplicio had left me about four piles of shit on the floor. I went blind with rage and beat that boy until the strap I was using, one of those *army* ones, fell apart. My sister-in-law came running right over. "You shouldn't be beating the kid like that," she said.

"If you don't want me to beat them," I told her, "take care of them yourself. Or let their mother come and get them. She's got it easy now. I'm young and still haven't had children. I'm the one who has to clean up the shit here." Well, after that I got dressed and went to my *mamá*'s house.

Cristóbal was going to come for me in the afternoon. I waited and waited, until finally he arrived very late at night with a look on his face like a dog. As we walked to the bus he came out with it and said, "Look, you shouldn't beat my children the way you did today, because they have a father, and besides, they will begin to hate you."

I stood right up to him and said, "So you went to check up on me, did you? Well, now I have something to tell you. Those are not my children and so they don't have to love me. If you don't want me to beat them, get them away from me. I won't mind a bit." He saw how furious I was and left me alone.

After that, problems started with Pablo and his wife. She was stepping out on Pablo, and not only with one man—she had a sweetheart from right around there, besides another boy friend. It seems that my being there interfered with her business, so she began giving Pablo an earful about me and he began to bother me.

One day I was in my *mamá*'s house talking to a boy who was courting my sister, when Pablo came in. If I tell you he insulted me, that would be mild. The nicest thing he said to me was that Cristóbal had always had bad luck with the women he picked and that I was going to follow in the footsteps of Fernanda or sink even lower. Cristóbal showed up at that moment and the two of them were on the verge of fighting, but Pablo's wife was able to separate them.

I was so full of fury that day that I went into the room, knelt down and prayed, "Oh, Lord and Holiest Mary, make them have to bow down before me." It poured directly from my heart because they had said so many humiliating things to me. Just imagine, Pablo said that the house I was living in then was like a cabaret. If it was true, it was because his own wife made it one.

What was behind the whole thing was that Elsa was planning to go off with a man, leaving a smear against my name. I knelt in my room and said, "I pray to God and the Virgin that they will have to come to me and beg to be taken in." And as God never keeps back punishment from someone who deserves it, that is just what happened. It wasn't two months before she had to come back to my house to live. Pablo lived in a flea bag across the street and she would bring his dinner there. That lasted until they were able to set up a house of their own. They took Cristóbal's children with them.

I was still unhappy. One day I said to Cristóbal, "Look, I'm pregnant.

But that doesn't matter. I'll manage. The thing is, I don't love you, and pregnant or not, I want a divorce. You stay with your children and your family and just leave me alone." He absolutely refused. So I stayed on with him. When I gave birth to my first son, Thomas, I was only fifteen.

And there I was, continuing the battle with Cristóbal. He didn't care about anything. He would take the money and gamble it away or drink it up. And listen to this! On account of my efforts he managed to build another house and one day while he was on a drunk he goes and sells it for eighty dollars so he could keep on drinking. He would come home whenever he felt like it and quarrel with me, but fortunately I never let him lay a hand on me. As my husband he could do whatever he wanted to me, but when he tried to be my father, too, that was too much.

I would see the poor children without anything over at Pablo's house. Cristóbal used to give Elsa the eighty dollars before he gave me my money, but she would give nice things to her family, and to those poor kids nothing but white rice soaked in a little soup that came out of an envelope. And that Simplicio had such an appetite he could eat three platefuls of food and still be hungry. He had nearly died of rickets when Nanda had him, so he was hungry from way back.

When I saw what was going on, my heart softened a little. So one day I said to Cristóbal, "Listen, those children of yours are going to end up in the cemetery or the hospital, because they are starving to death. Their *mamá* is just bumming around and doesn't even stop by to see them or anything."

"What do you think can be done about it?" he asked me.

"Bring me food and send them over here to me. I'll take care of them for you."

Instead of being grateful, he began to act worse than ever. Now Fernanda began coming to see the children and Cristóbal treated her better than me. He considered her very important. Whenever he saw her, Cristóbal would quarrel with me. When he came back from a drunk, he would take the children into a room with him, close the door and ask them whether I had done something to them or anything like that. That hurt me, as it would have hurt any woman.

The times Fernanda came around when Cristóbal wasn't home, she would talk to me about how she never had cared for him at all and that it was her *mamá* who had wanted them to get together. I have been told that if Luisa hadn't died they wouldn't have separated, because she had cast a spell on Cristóbal to make him stay with Fernanda.

Fernanda was working with evil or something, because I tell you that every time she came to the house the children all fell sick. Cruz and Fela both got asthma. Once she left Simplicio with such a fever that I had to run to the hospital with him. Even though she could see that the children got sick, she didn't want to leave the house. So what happened was that her friends turned into enemies of mine and went around saying that I had taken her husband away from her. God knows that is not true! I never liked to separate any woman from her husband, because I am a woman myself.

They began blackening my name, too, by saying that I had hit Cruz and made her lame. Now, when that child started to walk she was all right, but inside a year she was lame. She got paralyzed, you know. For more than three months I was trying to help that child. I gave her sun baths and cod-liver oil. Finally she began to walk again but she was lame.

One night I said to Cristóbal, "Look, they are going around saying that I crippled that child. I want us to take her to the hospital tomorrow just so there won't be any doubt in your mind about it being my fault."

So we took her and the doctors examined her from her toes to the tips of the hairs on her head and they said that it was a birth defect and that she never would get any better. They told me to get her special shoes, with one higher than the other so she would walk better. Later, when she was with Fernanda, they took her to another hospital. That hospital ordered some iron braces for her, like polio patients wear, and the same special shoes.

One day when Cruz looked more pinched than ever I called her over and felt her. She was like a piece of wax. I bundled her up right away and took her to the hospital, but they didn't want to accept her. So I said, "You have to keep her here because if she dies on me people will say I neglected her because I'm her stepmother." I put up such a fight that they finally took her in. That time she had whooping cough, and pneumonia too. For a person like me who never liked children, you should have seen how I went to visit that child every day.

Fernanda never went to visit her. She told people she did, but it wasn't true. When the hospital was going to discharge the child, I said to myself, "Now is the time to see what Fernanda has to contribute." So I went to her and said, "Listen, tomorrow they are going to discharge the child. I won't be able to pick her up because I have a lot of things to do. So you go and get her and bring her to me."

It was a waste of time. The next day I went there earlier than usual, and would you believe it, Fernanda didn't even show up! After the child was discharged I took her home.

The next day when Fernanda came around, I said to her, "I'm very sorry, but since you didn't bother to pick up your child, you needn't come around here any more. I don't want you in my house." So she disappeared for a long time. When she did return, Soledad wanted to go with her. The child had finished the first grade already. I don't know why she wanted to go. I think people had put it into her head that she ought to leave me and go with her mother. It made me so mad. But I let her go.

I had more peace of mind for a while but then Simplicio began to take Cruz and wander off with her. This was on the sly, and they would be gone for two or three days and sometimes even for weeks. The police sometimes made a complaint and I would have to go to the police station. And there was nothing that could be done about it. The more I beat Simplicio, the worse he was. Finally, during a storm, Fernanda came and took them because she wanted to be with them until it passed. As I was dying to get rid of them, I didn't object.

When the children were with me, they behaved themselves. They did whatever I said. I have no complaints. Whatever wrong they did was done behind my back. I used to leave Soledad in charge of all the children when I went out to the market. She was very hard on her brother and sisters and she used to hit them. But she never hit my boys. She loved them and they loved her a lot. She was a strong girl, not sick like Felícita and Cruz.

The one who was always closest to us was Felícita. She was a humble child and I was very fond of her because once when I was sick she stuck to the side of my bed until I was well. She was the only one who even gave me a drink of water.

The worst trouble I had on account of those children was that Cristóbal always seemed to prefer them to my two boys. I'll never forget how he beat Thomas on account of Soledad. She was a big girl then. What happened was that she was bathing the children and Thomas splashed water on her. Just because of that, Cristóbal gave the boy a slap that almost knocked him out. I was so furious I tried to do the same to Cristóbal. My poor kids! You wouldn't believe it, but I had to go behind their *papá*'s back to buy the things they needed. Fortunately, they were always humble and satisfied with what I gave them. Nobody knows it, but Cristóbal used to give my Thomas some terrible whacks. It didn't make any difference to him that the boy got frightful asthma attacks. He also whacked my Mariano. He favored the other children, the children of a mother who had been in jail and who could never get enough rum to drink.

I'll tell you the truth. I would advise any girl to stay single rather than marry a man with children and have to face such problems. It seems that a man always prefers his first children. As far as Cristóbal is concerned, Soledad is his eldest child. She may be, but she is not legitimate and so the one whose name has to appear on all the papers is Thomas. The proof of this is that before Thomas was born the *Army* used to pay that girl thirty dollars a month. Afterward they took it away from her and gave it to him.

What lives those four kids have led! The things they went through were either their own fault or maybe it was a matter of inheritance. Chips off the old block! They say that Soledad's first husband was a good man, yet she pulled a pistol and tried to kill him. That's how she is. Soledad would get into fights with Felícita right out in the street because Felícita would defend me. But I never let any of that stuff bother me. I lived my life as though they didn't exist.

When we went to Panama, I hardly ever saw even a hair of Cristóbal's. He had a bunch of women there and didn't bother about a thing. I received my little allotment and had to cover everything for the house out of it, dress Felícita and my children and everything. We went hungry lots of times because Cristóbal drank up his check. But I was proud and never let my spirit break. Even my own family never knew anything about it. Fernanda wrote to Cristóbal to send money for the kids or she would ship them all down to Panama. As he was so crazy, I was the one who had to take it out of my little check and buy the money order so he could send it to Nanda.

When we got back from Panama, I left Felícita at my *mamá*'s house. I intended to send for her from Baltimore, which is where Cristóbal was stationed next. But it seems that they were mean to Felícita, because when I came for her, she had already gone off with the father of her twins. I can assure you that if that girl had stayed with me she would have turned out as I wanted. She always behaved like a proper *señorita* when she was with me. But it was all for the best, because Cristóbal went from bad to worse in Baltimore. *Compadres* of mine had to keep after him to get five or ten dollars out of him for me. I endured it and didn't divorce him on account of my children.

A few years after that we went to Virginia and there I really suffered. I had no idea what I was in for. What happened was that Felícita sent word that she was coming and finally she arrived with her little girl, Tany. It was a martyrdom from the minute they set foot in the house. Felícita brought some kind of charm with her to break up my marriage. Right after she arrived she put a bottle of that *after shaving* on Cristóbal's dresser. "What is that for, Fela?" I asked her.

"Funny that you should always ask me that on Tuesdays or Fridays," she answered. Those are the days the sorcerers work their spells, so I told her, "Listen, you brought something here to do me harm. I'm going to write to my *mamá* and tell her to find out what it is." Well, then Felícita told me that Fernanda was the one who had sent it, after she had tried it out herself and all. And it did the job. It made trouble, the old story.

We would all go out to the *Bargain Center* and Cristóbal would carry that shitty little girl Tany, damn her, and he'd take Felícita on his other arm. They were like a married couple while I dragged along behind with my two children like I was nobody. And the way that one carried on, saying *papito* here and *papito* there! She was driving me crazy. Until finally she decided to go to New Jersey to see what she could do. So to get rid of her, and because Cristóbal insisted, I agreed to keep the baby. I'll tell you something, even though she was only about a year old, that baby wasn't bad. I would sit her on the couch and say to her, "Look, don't you move from there, hear? I'm going shopping." And when I got back she would be there right in the same spot. I took care of Tany for a year.

Cristóbal was the one who was unbearable with that child. If a person looked at her he would say they were putting the evil eye on her. If anybody touched her he thought they were killing her. One day my Mariano was taking care of her. Well, that damn kid had to go and fall down. So Cristóbal came in and gave my boy such a kick he nearly killed him. I was washing dishes at the time but I didn't lose my head. I dried my hands calmly and said to him, "You miserable wretch!"

Cristóbal said, "I let him have it and I'll do the same with anybody else who interferes, because that little girl has my blood and you don't."

I knelt at his feet right then and there and with my arms crossed I said to him, "You are my husband and so I have to submit to you, but I'm going to kill you like a dog." And I jumped at him and would have killed him. Fortunately, when he saw what kind of a mood I was in, he went and locked himself in a room. Since I wasn't able to get even, I knelt down again and put a curse on him. "I trust in the great power of God and Holiest Mary and I pray that they will kill you like a dog," I said. Inside the room, Cristóbal began to cry and said, "Nobody loves my granddaughter because she's black!"

I jumped up and said to him, "Naturally, if your daughter lay with a Negro, your grandchild couldn't come out white."

You won't believe me, but when Cristóbal left the house, he went to a garage across the street and a car that was backing out nearly killed him. Anyway, the gas pump broke. After that Cristóbal said to me, "Listen, if anything happens to me it will be your fault because you are always cursing me."

"I can't wait," I told him.

While I was living this martyrdom, Soledad would write to him, "Papito, see if you can't send for me, as I am having it lousy here. Maybe I could work there and do better for myself."

"Oh, sure," I thought to myself, "so you're going to work, are you? And who are you going to leave that gang of kids with? I'm supposed to take on that little job, right? Well, I'm not going to." And I went and tore up her letters and Cristóbal didn't even know that Soledad had written to him. I thought to myself, "If he's that gone on Felícita's little black kid, when Soledad comes over here with her pretty little blond girl there will be no talking to him any more." But I don't know, maybe I was wrong, because he isn't the same to Soledad as to Felícita. I don't know if Soledad realized that Cristóbal never had any idea that she had written to him. But I do know that she told her sister that I read her letters, and that I had no business mixing into her life. I don't know how she found out.

That Felícita broke all records. When we were in Virginia she would get dressed up in the afternoon and say, "Ave María, you get all fixed up around here and it's just as if you didn't, for all the difference it makes to anybody. Nobody says a word to a person." So Cristóbal would say, "Ay, daughter, you look lovely," giving me a dirty look at the same time.

"Maybe you look lovely to your father but not to me, because I am a woman." I told her.

I went back to Puerto Rico that Christmas and had a wonderful time with my family, especially with my kid brother Domingo, who was the light of my life. He took me to the airport, and when I was about to leave I said to him, "Listen, Dominguito, don't get into trouble. The holidays are here now and you have no idea how much we need to have you around." You see, they had told me he was involved with a married woman.

"No," he said, "don't worry about it. Christmas Eve is past."

"But not New Year's Eve. So be careful," I told him.

I thought of him all during the plane trip and wondered how I might have brought him back with me. I had a premonition. Something told me, "You're never going to see him again."

On New Year's Day we were going to Pennsylvania. Before leaving, I did something I had never done before. I told Cristóbal to leave a note that in case any message came for us they should leave it under the door. Even though I was desperate with worry, I went, because there was nothing else I could do. On the return trip I was driving and I made it to the house in forty-five minutes. When I opened the door there was the news waiting for me. It was too late for me to see him. They had already buried him. Since I never saw him dead, it is all like a dream, and I feel that he is still alive. Even now whenever I think of him, I cry. *Mamá* has been failing more and more every day since that boy died. They killed him in a friend's house, fifteen minutes after the last midnight of the year, in a house he used to visit every day. It was because of a woman. *Mamá* had said to him, "Son, don't go out tonight. Stay home. You know how things are tonight." And he answered, "Don't worry, *mamá*, I'll come right back."

They stabbed him. Once was enough, because he didn't last more than five minutes. Somebody ran to tell my sister María del Carmen. She has always been strong. She went to the drugstore, bought some medicines and went to *mamá*. When *mamá* saw her she said, *"Ave María,* what miracle finds you awake at this hour? You're always in bed before the New Year arrives. Domingo hasn't gotten back and I'm all alone."

"I know," said María, "Here, take this."

"You know where he is?" asked *mamá*.

"Yes. In the hospital, but we are going to get him out tomorrow afternoon."

"Don't lie to me. They killed him. Something tells me they did."

What bad luck I have had with my brothers who might have helped *mami*. Those who grew up were all killed. The only one who isn't dead is an *atómico*. Nobody worries about it at home, though. I would have liked to take him to that business of Alcoholics Anonymous but I am always the one who has to do everything and it shouldn't be like that because I can't divide myself up.

To get back to my life, we returned to Puerto Rico, but Cristóbal didn't change at all. At first we were getting along real fine, though something told me, "You are happy together now, but if it turns out that he has to go to Europe, the marriage is going to break up." A few days later he came home with the news that he was leaving for Europe. "So we'll go," I said to him. "That's the way it has to be when you are married to a soldier. You have to be ready for anything."

But he didn't want to take me along. The travel papers came for me to sign but he sent them back. "Don't try to come to Europe with me," he said. "It will be worse that way." What could I do? And so I stayed, but with a terrible pain in my heart. He was away for two years.

While he was away I got sick. It wasn't anything very serious and they took me to see one of those *Army* doctors. What a bunch of dogs those men are. Any cat-skinner is a specialist compared to them! Anyway, they had me with a drain inside for nine days. I don't know whether it was not clean or what, but I do know that I got phlebitis and nearly died. And my kidneys have never been right since. All on account of those doctors. That is why I have no faith in them and I believe in my own will power to cure myself.

There I was in death's clutches and all alone. My children came to visit me at the hospital every night but they were the only ones who did. My sister sent word to Cristóbal in Europe to try to come because she had never in her life seen me in such bad shape. And do you know what his answer was? That he wasn't coming because a kidney infection was something anybody could get and it didn't amount to anything, and that one of those Red Cross women had checked up and told him that my sister was looking after the children and that I wasn't so bad off. It was all a lie because nobody ever came around. I didn't care about dying because what's the good of a person living like this? When you've suffered a lot in life, more suffering doesn't affect you. It's all the same whether you live or die.

Finally Cristóbal came back from Europe. And just imagine, he left a woman in Paris! He said so himself. And she had the gall to write him here to my house! I got hold of him and I told him, "Listen, you tell that woman to drop that little game of hers of writing to you here at my house."

"Sure, I'll tell her not to write any more because my wife is jealous."

"No, not jealous, because you know I never did love you very much and now I don't love you a quarter of that. The thing is that it shows a lack of respect and I'm not going to allow that."

I have to keep pushing him all the time. He's a man who is lazy about everything except chasing women, drinking rum and gambling. Finally I convinced him that we should fix up the house. You should have seen me! There I was, mixing cement for the mortar with my two boys while he bummed around. As a result of all that heavy work my kidneys got sick again. And do you know what he said to me? "The house comes before you." How could anybody love a man like that?

Well, anyway, that's how it went until we moved to Texas. I didn't want to go and neither did Mariano, but Thomas did. He always liked to see new places. Until the last day I kept saying I wasn't going. I didn't give Cristóbal the travel papers, either, but left them in a place where he could see them and I went off in a car I borrowed from a friend. I got back at about four, and that man was going crazy because he thought I was going to leave him in the lurch.

He didn't improve any in Texas. We quarreled back and forth all the time. Just imagine, one day Mariano sat down on the bed and said to me, "Listen, *mami*, I know that you and *papi* are going to separate, but I realize it's not your fault. It's *papi's* fault."

Cristóbal had a pile of women in Texas and would go out and not come back until he wanted to. He acted miserable and cheap with the children and we even went hungry. But I didn't give in or let on to anybody. He would come to the house flat broke and want me to give him some of my money, but not me! So he said to me, "Yes, you're living off the fat of the land now, because you're receiving the allotment checks, but when I retire you'll be screwed because I won't give you the envelope that my checks come in."

I told him, "That's all right with me. Neither I nor my children will starve to death. I can work and will take any kind of a job." And that's how it was.

When we got back to Puerto Rico, Cristóbal retired from the *Army* and went to work in a garage. But then work got *slow* and they had to get rid of all the new employees, Cristóbal included. That was when his ulcers got worse and they were going to operate on him and all that.

You know, that big scoundrel kept writing to the French woman all that time. I found out because when he left his job and was sick in the hospital, they sent the letter there and I got hold of it and read it. As she never dreamed it would fall into my hands, she didn't hold back on what she said to him. I took it and put it away, just as cool as I could be. Then one day when he was out on leave he came home, but I didn't give him a tumble or even anything to eat. He had his dinner out somewhere and I wondered whether I should tell him or not. The next day, when he was leaving to go back to the hospital, I said to myself, *"Caramba,* if I don't tell him now, it'll be a long time before I get another chance." So I handed him the letter and he said very quickly, "How did this letter get into your hands?"

"It got into my hands because you are writing to each other. If not, it wouldn't have," I answered.

"Keep it then."

"Listen, you rat," I said to him, "I ought to kill you both like a pair of dogs, but I won't do it because you are not even worth a person's bother."

"Get away from me," he shouted. "It's on account of you that I'm sick. And what's more, don't even come to see me at the hospital."

"Stop breaking my heart," I told him. "If you knew how much I wanted to come to see you! Don't worry about that." But nothing happened. When

I didn't show up, he would send the children for me. One day when I didn't park right, the police took away my license. I didn't get to the hospital for a few days, so he wanted to know why I hadn't come.

Now we are living in the house together, but it's as if we were strangers. Yet he'll say to me, "Why don't you love me any more?"

"You've done so much to me," I told him, "that I don't even care about my own self, let alone anybody else."

While he was in the hospital I was the one who took care of all the expenses of the house and I brought him money right along. There were days when I took in fifty-seven and eighty dollars in the little business we have, selling groceries. It was killing me, though. Yet when I came to the hospital, Cristóbal would ask if I'd found a job yet. When was I going to be able to find time to go to work? I told him not to worry, that I was about to get a job. I knew inside that the reason he was so anxious for me to work was because he didn't want to give a cent of his money to me or to the children.

All right, if he wanted it that way! I spoke to an acquaintance of mine, a man I had worked for when he was just beginning a little business. He's rich now and he gave me a job as a clerk right away. I made forty dollars in six days. But in spite of how bad Cristóbal had been, I didn't begin working until a week after he was out of the hospital so I could take care of him. Now I'm working and I earn enough to cover my expenses and most of those of the children. As for him, he has to take care of the grocery. I'm working on the outside, so it's not fair that I should have to do that, too. But he complains about it and wants me to leave my job. Not me! It's too late now.

As I know how to drive, I don't worry about a thing, not even if I get out of work at eleven or twelve o'clock at night. I just get into the car and there's nothing to it. I tell you the truth, I don't need Cristóbal at all. I'm thirty-four now and people who know me say I can get along without him but he can't without me. We are just living a false show, as they say, because our marriage really broke up when he went to Europe. But I don't feel like getting a divorce. Fernanda and those kids have just been biding their time, waiting for me to divorce Cristóbal, but I won't give them the satisfaction.

I know that they don't love him. How could they? What they are after is the money, but I am smarter than they are. They think that if he dies, half of the property will go to them. That's not the way it will be, though, because it isn't fair. I was the one who pulled that man up out of the mud. He doesn't even know on what day he was born. They will have one-quarter coming to them and I am giving that to them so they will leave me alone and never cross my path again. It wouldn't be fair for them to get any more, because whatever Cristóbal made, he made with me. I even had to give him money of my own to buy that little store he has.

If they are not satisfied with that, let them go get a lawyer. He'll gobble up the little they get because that's all there is to it. I am the legal wife and half the property comes to me. Out of the other half, three-quarters go to my children because they are legitimate and the others can divide up the quarter that's left.

In the division I include the house and the store. The car is in Cristóbal's name, but I'll have him put it in mine so there won't be any problems. He'll do it, too, because he does what I tell him. I'll say in a nice way, "Look, Cristóbal, let's put the car in my name so you don't have to pay so much for plates this year." And he'll do it real quiet.

We're going to end up in good shape because we're going to get a pension, and his insurance policy is a pretty big one, besides. Of those children of his, Felícita is the one who is going to do all right. She is Cristóbal's favorite and he put her down as beneficiary for the thousand-dollar policy. She'll get that outright, no matter what.

Cruz

Life with Emilio

ONE DAY I was sitting with my *mamá* in the ditch alongside the Cantu Building, grating a coconut. I was going to make candy with it, as I like sweets. Well, this boy gets out of a taxi with his *papá*. The boy was tall and very dark and wore a white jacket and a big hat and looked very cute, so I said to my *mamá*, "Look, they are exhibiting a chimpanzee." We laughed and my *mamá* said, "No, that boy is from New York but he was brought up right here. He is Pabón's son." I didn't say any more but went on making my candy. Emilio knew my *mamá*, and he began talking to her. He had lived in La Esmeralda until he was twelve and now he was nineteen. And there I was, eating coconut.

That night I got dressed up and went to sit by the building. I was in the habit of going there to talk with the girls. Well, Emilio came that night and hung around with us. He got to know a girl friend of mine and they became sweethearts. Nemesio, my boy friend from school, began fooling around with me and threw me on top of Emilio, who grabbed me. I told him to let me go and I went home mad because he pinched me.

Emilio had made a lot of friends already. He was even friends with my sister Felícita, who had come back from Culebra because her husband mistreated her. She took a room for herself and the twins, and one day at her house, Emilio began talking to me about New York, because I loved hearing about it. So we sat there and talked. The next thing I knew he put his hand on my thigh. I took it off. He said to me, "Why don't you leave it there?"

"Because I don't want to," I answered. He had a girl friend and her family knew they were sweethearts. He told me about the people in New York and how much he liked it there and about the girl friends he had.

"Well," I said, "why didn't you get married?"

"Because I'm going to get married here." Then he told me he was only going to be around for a week. "Come to the Cantu Building tonight so we can have some fun," he said.

A month later he was still around. One day I was wearing a very tight skirt, and as I was crossing the street I tripped. He caught me and kept me from falling. I thanked him very much and kept on walking.

That night he sent me a note saying he wanted to talk to me and I said all right. He began by asking me if I had a boy friend and I told him I didn't want *him* because he already had a girl friend. He explained that it wasn't anything serious with her. So I left my boy friend, Nemesio, and Emilio and I began to go together. It was as if my heart told me that Emilio was for me, and I felt more love for him from the minute I saw him than I ever did for Nemesio.

Emilio gave me my first kiss. One day I was in Felícita's house playing with the twins, and the two of them were on top of me when Emilio came along. He pushed me over backward and kissed me. I slapped him, but I went hot and cold and began to tremble and my legs wouldn't hold me up. I had to stay sitting right there where I was. I began to think, *"Ay, my God, if my mother knew, what a beating she would give me!"* I felt such fear that I got a sick headache. I even felt like vomiting.

After that we began to make love. Emilio told me he didn't really know how to kiss and I said I knew even less. So he said, "I'll teach you then." But when we started to kiss again, he said, "You'd better teach me because you know more than I do." I'd seen Felícita and her husband kissing, and she said that if I didn't want to use my tongue, to keep my mouth closed. "What do you mean about the tongue?" I asked, and so she went and crossed tongues with her husband and let me watch.

One day I went to the beach with Emilio and a girl friend and her boy friend. Neither one of us really knew we were in love. When we were in swimming Emilio pulled me down under the water and kissed me. When I came out I was blushing and I got dressed. Emilio chased me until he caught me, lifted me up and threw me in the water with my clothes on. Then I stopped feeling embarrassed and we began to kiss and so did the other couple.

About a month and a half after I met Emilio, he left me. I said to myself, "I guess he's gone with some other woman. Well, I'll have to get myself another sweetheart. I'm still young." Then one day my *mamá* sent me to the bakery to buy a cake. I asked the girls if anyone wanted to go with me, but nobody did. A boy by the name of Andrés said he would. "Well," I said, "that's even better." So we walked along, with him playing up to me, and me leading him on hoping he would buy me a bun.

All of a sudden I saw a gang of boys and Emilio grabbed me by the neck. He said I was a whore and put a knife against my face as if he was going to cut me. Did I get scared! I told him if he did anything to me he'd go straight to jail. Since he'd never been in jail, he was afraid and put the knife away. But Emilio and Andrés began arguing and bought *Gems* to cut each other with. I told Emilio he had his sweetheart and to leave me alone. "You're going to walk with me now," he said. He was all dirty and stank of fish and sweat, and I had to walk back to La Esmeralda with him like that. I sure was scared!

Emilio and I quarreled about any little thing. He'd do something I didn't like and I'd stop talking to him. Or he'd say to me, "Give me a kiss," and I'd answer, "Not on that pig's snout," and we would get into a fight.

One day I was walking to school with Emilio and Norma, a friend of mine. Emilio and I had our arms around each other and the principal saw us from her car. When I got to school the principal said to me, "Who was that fellow you were walking with arm in arm?"

"A first cousin of mine."

"Holding you so tight?"

"I had a cramp, that's why."

"Hmm! You go to the office."

She kept me in the office for about two hours asking me and Norma all kinds of questions, but we said no to everything. Then she sent for my mother and Fernanda slapped me right in front of the principal. I cursed the principal and shit on her mother. Then I said, "Aren't you married? Don't you have children?"

"For the love of God, girl," she said, "can't you see that if a man that big and heavy falls on you, he will squash you?"

By then I was really angry and I said, "If you can have a 137-pounder one on top of you, I can take one who weighs 190. It's easy."

"You see how you have brought up this girl!" the principal said to my *mamá*. "Get her out of La Esmeralda before she becomes even worse."

I said, "Whoever is going to be a whore is going to be a whore. Anyway, God knows what you are doing behind your husband's back."

The principal also told my *mamá* that when I wore a cancan skirt and went up the stairs, the boys would stand below and whistle at me. Then I'd make a noise with my lips, lift my skirt in the air and say, "Take a bite, you skinny dogs. Look how the meat shakes." She told all this and more to my *mamá,* and my *mamá* said, "I'm going to have to keep an eye on her." But after that I ran around the school and talked back to the principal until she suspended me for a week.

One day my *mamá* gave me a terrific beating. Emilio had already bought the wedding ring and we were going to the movies that night at seven. My *mamá* said I could go. But she started drinking, and when I was about to leave she said, "Where do you think you're going? You aren't going anywhere."

I burst out crying. When Emilio arrived, Fernanda began to insult him in her drunkenness, calling him a son of a great whore. "Don't talk to him like that. He isn't doing anything to you," I said.

She grabbed me and gave me a slap and bit me on the neck and on the leg. I started to run but she came after me and cut my head open with a stick and scratched my face with a bottle. Next she picked up a knife to cut me with, but I hid and called to my brother to stop her. She said I was going to be a whore, and if I wasn't knocked up already, I didn't have far to go, and that I might as well go with that "scabby Negro" because I was a filthy so-and-so myself.

When my *mamá* came at me with the knife, Emilio grabbed her hand and told her to let it go. She took a swing at him with it but missed. Then she sent out for a *Gem* and cut up all my clothes and threw them out. I was left with only my *panties*. Emilio took off his shirt and put it around me. I told him not to mix in because it was a family affair, and he had a bad temper too. Emilio told me he wouldn't hit her because she was my mother. If she were a sister or a brother he would, and she should thank God she was my mother.

Emilio and I left with my brother to stay in the Cantu Building overnight. The people there gave me clothes, all too big for me, of course, but I put them on. I went back home after that, and my brother began working on the boats. When he came back, he brought me a pair of slippers, shoes, *panties* and other clothes. He brought me a little present from every trip.

My *mamá* said that I couldn't be Emilio's sweetheart because I was too young, and she kept throwing me out of the house. I went hungry a lot then because whenever my *mamá* beat me, she would throw out the food, pot and all, down on the beach. I asked her to at least let me go out and have some fun, the way other girls did, but she wouldn't let me out of the house, and I drank sugar water and went to bed. She gave me some terrible beatings. I don't know why, because she didn't do it to my sisters. She never touches Felícita or Soledad. God knows whether my *mamá* hates me or not, but she certainly never loved me.

People say she was in love with Emilio. He would drink with her and then she would be calm and relaxed, but as soon as she saw him walking to me she would start a fight. She never got to the point of having relations with him, though. They would only drink together and that made her very happy. I was embarrassed when people said she was in love with Emilio because he had asked for my hand and had bought me a ring. It made me ashamed and filled my heart with pain and I didn't even want to pass by the place where they were drinking. I would go down to the beach to cry and say to myself, "Oh Lord! This can't be true!" In the state I was in, if I had caught them in anything like that, I would have killed them. A lot of evil plans came into my mind, but for the time being I just cried and cried, and this seemed to calm my nerves.

I never said a word to my *mamá* about what people were saying. I was afraid I might offend her and I didn't dare. But my sister Soledad told her. One day those two were calling Emilio a "dirty Negro" and I told them they called him that because he hadn't had relations with either of them and that if he did, he would stop being a dirty Negro to them. They said they would rather put out for a dog. "You've put out for more mangy dogs than I can count," I answered. "He's eating sirloin steak. He isn't interested in you."

One time my *mamá* sent me for some meat tarts, and I was late getting home. It took me about an hour because there were a lot of people in the store. So at one o'clock in the morning my *mamá* threw my clothes out in the street, and that time I jumped out after them. I went to the cemetery and stayed there that night and the next day, sitting near a grave at the entrance, without a thing to eat. At about six in the afternoon three men came along and saw me. They threw themselves on top of me and began kissing me and pulling down my *panties*. I screamed and yelled until some people came and the men took off. I ran all the way home but didn't say anything to my *mamá*. I was sick for a week after that and right away people began to say that I wasn't a virgin any more.

I have to admit that I'm partly to blame for what happened later on. My *mamá* sent me to take care of Soledad's children while my sister was hustling in San Juan. I went to school in the daytime and took care of the children at night. Being sweet on Emilio the way I was, I let him come to my sister's house. I would bar the door on the inside and he would take off his clothes and stand there all naked. Then he would say, "All right, let's go to bed," and we would lie down, he naked and me in my *panties*. Sometimes he would say, "Take all your clothes off," and I would answer, "No, no, this way is fine." So we would lie there until after twelve o'clock at night like husband and wife, although I was still a *señorita*. Then we would go into the bathroom, and he would wash me and I would wash him. But he never had any intention of doing anything wrong in my sister's house.

When we were kissing and I saw he was becoming wild, I would get off the bed and say, "How would you like some chocolate?" He would get worked up every time we kissed and I thought he was going to do the worst to me. It wouldn't do me any good to call for help because screams were a dime a dozen around there. Well, I didn't want to have to fight with him or anything, so I would tell him to make that thing go down. He would answer, "Let him alone. He's learning to march. He looks like a soldier." At last he would say, "Go put on a bathrobe so I won't see you like this," and I would put on *un cotón,* a cotton robe of my sister's.

I finally began to have relations with him. But he didn't come inside me, and he didn't do it full force but little by little. It hurt me, so he left it only halfway in, and when he felt he was going to come he said, "Now, now, now!" and I pulled away to one side of him. He said it wasn't nice for a girl like me who was still in school to get pregnant. I was only thirteen years old at the time.

Then one day we told my *mamá* that we were going to the movies but instead we went to the beach. I guess he had it all planned because there was a big cardboard box flattened out on the sand. I thought it was odd. Emilio began taking off his clothes, but when he got down to his shorts I stopped him because people would be passing by. He said, "No, nobody comes around here at this hour. You take a swim too." Actually, it was very dark. So there we were, talking all kinds of silly things about being married, when he said to me, "Lie down so we can talk more comfortably."

I lay back on the box looking up at the sky and Emilio threw himself on top of me and began kissing me. I turned over on my side, but he grabbed me, locked my feet and crossed his legs over mine, keeping them folded, and with his great big hand held my hands behind my back. I couldn't move. Then he said, "Shall I take off your *panties?*" I said "No!"

"What do you mean 'No'?" he said and began pulling them off. I didn't want him to take me, and much less by force, but it was by force that he ruined me. I screamed and screamed but nobody heard a thing. He covered my mouth with his mouth.

When he did his damage, I poured blood. He bled a lot, too. When I stood up, everything was covered with blood. I had a lot of pain too, but finally I went and washed myself with sea water. I took off my slip and threw it away. Emilio took me home at about ten o'clock. He told me not to tell anybody what had happened because he was going to marry me. I had known him eight months by then.

We didn't have relations again after that, but we kept on going together. I stayed at my *mamá*'s house as if nothing had happened. I felt ashamed in the beginning, but I still went to school and Emilio kept coming to the house. Finally, I don't know how it happened, but he heard I had another boy friend. It was a lie, of course, but anyway, he decided to go to New York. And there I was, preparing for my wedding. He had done his damage and now he was going to leave me. It was then that I told my elder sister. I asked her, "Soledad, when a man ruins a woman and then wants to leave, what does that mean?"

"Well," she said, "it means that the man doesn't love her. He despises her and is running away so that he won't have to have anything to do with her."

"Emilio ruined me," I said, "and now he wants to go to New York and leave me."

Soledad began to cry and tremble and then she had an attack. She said that God only knew what was going to become of me now. When she asked Emilio if he had ruined me, he denied it. I told my sister Felícita also and she began to cry. Then my brother Simplicio said that things weren't going to stay like that and that if I had been ruined he was going to do his duty as my brother. So he began looking for Emilio, who hid from him. When my *mamá* came back from work at two o'clock, they told her. She went out and bought a *Gem* and said, "If he tries to tell me he didn't do it, I'll cut his throat for him." Evidently he knew my *mamá*'s intentions because when she asked him, he admitted it. So she said to him, "All right then. Now you're going to marry her."

"Yes, *doña* Nanda," he said. "All right, I'll marry her." My *mamá* told him that if he left me, she would have him put in jail. That was what scared him and helped me.

I found out later from his *mamá* and his aunt *doña* Minerva that Emilio had planned to leave me flat and go off to New York. *Doña* Minerva said, "You can thank the Lord that he didn't have money for his ticket because he would have gone off that same day and you would have been left with your rifle sitting on your shoulder."

My *mamá* sent a special delivery letter to my *papá*. He was in the *Army* and stationed in Philadelphia, where he lived with my stepmother. He wrote back saying that now that I had put my foot into it, I should take on my obligations and rights as a woman and give up being a little girl and marry Emilio. He sent no money for the wedding and he never wrote again.

Then my *mamá* spoke again. "Look, you have to go find rooms to take her to." He said he would but that at the moment he didn't have any money. I knew he was still planning to go to New York, because I saw the suitcases and tickets and everything.

Well, I went to San Sebastian Street to see a woman my sister Felícita knew about. Some women who deal in magic work for evil and some for good. This woman worked for the Enemy, the Devil. The Enemy hates the cross and all the saints. If you are working with the Enemy you can't wear anything red, only black, because the Enemy fears anything red, especially blood. The minute there is blood, the spell is broken. You can't have pictures of saints or good prayers, only the Enemy's book of black magic, a deck of cards, a little glass of water, and that's all. The one who works with good has the *Colecto,* a spiritist prayer book, the saints and a glass of holy water.

I told the woman that I needed her help and she said, "All right, I'll see if I can help you." She was a Negro woman with very dark skin, kinky hair and a twisted mouth. She always dressed in black. She had saints all over the outer room to hide that she was working for evil. In the inner room three saints had their faces to the wall. On the table were a crystal ball, a deck of black cards, and the book of black magic.

She opened the book and began shuffling the cards. Then she read out of the book as if she were asking Satan whether he would consider what I wanted. She said my first and last names and Emilio's last name. Then she began to shiver and talk in a man's voice. And tears came to her eyes when she looked at me. She said, "I'm going to give what you ask for, but you must do what I tell you." I said I would.

This woman said that Emilio would not leave me and that he was going to marry me. She gave me a white powder to put in a glass of water for him to drink. I was supposed to go to the ocean at night exactly at twelve o'clock and throw three pennies to the Devil. She charged me three dollars. I did as she said, and Emilio behaved himself and took me to live with him.

His aunt Minerva had given him an old bed that he fixed up and painted. His grandmother was letting him have a room in her house. We took the bed to the room that same night and at about ten o'clock we began living together. We talked about things we were going to buy, a new bed and a set of furniture. Emilio said, "You know what? This is like a movie. All we have are two glasses, two toothbrushes and a broken bed. It's like a picture that's just beginning, and God knows how it's going to end."

"God knows," I answered. "If the Lord helps us we'll be able to have better things than now, but you have to take your time. Don't be rushing into things and getting drunk. I'm going to be understanding of you so that you'll understand me too."

"All right," he said, "it's a deal."

We fooled around on the bed until about midnight and had relations three times. After that we took a bath and went to bed.

Emilio worked on the docks and made sixteen-fifty a day, but he didn't give me all of it. The second day he gave me fifteen dollars to buy some things, but after that he would give me ten or only five. He always kept at least half for drinking with his friends. On the day we bought the new bed he told me, "When you leave, I'll have my bed all set and won't have to pay for a hotel." He meant that if he got himself another woman he would bring her into the house and not have to pay for a hotel room.

My answer was, "You have to pay three dollars for the woman and two dollars for the bed, but if I leave I won't have to pay for a bed. They'll pay me." When I said that he beat me. After that we would quarrel and fight practically every day. He mistreated me because he said that I had forced him to live with me and that he was going to give me a hard time in return. That's how it was. But since I was a married woman now, I said to myself, "I can do as I like. When I break off with this one, I'm not going to take up with any other man. Good riddance to bad rubbish."

After living with my husband for two months or so, I began to enjoy having relations with him. We would do it in the night, in the morning, in the afternoon when he came back from work, before he left at six, and when he came from work at twelve. He took the whole thing as lightly as a song. But at the same time he didn't stop beating me. One day there was going to be a party and I was taking a bath. I was sitting in the tub when all of a sudden I felt something and there was blood gushing out of me like water. I didn't know whether I was pregnant or if something was happening to me, but I knew that I hadn't had my period. I asked Emilio whether he was going to the party anyway. He said he was going because he didn't want to miss it and if I was sick I should lie down in bed because that's where sick people belonged.

"At least get me an aspirin," I said.

"Ah," he answered, "you always want things brought to you."

"All right then, forget it. Don't do anything for me."

I sent for my *mamá* and she took me to the hospital. Afterward she told me it was a miscarriage. When I got back that husband of mine said, "You and your *mamá* didn't go to any hospital. You went off to Santurce and had an abortion done." He kept looking at me and the pills they gave me. He said, "I'm going to get dressed and go to the party." I was in bad pain and when I saw him getting dressed it got worse. At the party he danced until he was tired and came home drunk. He saw me lying there, and just for the hell of it he gave me a beating. He said I was pretending so as to get out of heating up his dinner.

"But I'm getting up to it," I said. "I'll fix your food so you can eat."

"Oh," he answered, "so you are forcing me to eat now." He slapped me and threw my clothes down the stairs. That's when I began to hate him. I told him that he was not my *papá* and shouldn't hit me. He began to beat me again, and that's when I left and went to my *mamá*'s.

I told my *mamá* what had happened and she said, "That's what you deserve for not taking advice." But she took me in and made me lie down and put a hot-water bottle on me. Emilio came around the next day and told my *mamá* that I had no respect for him, that I went wherever I pleased and that she could keep me. My *mamá* said, "All right, I'll keep her because she's my daughter and she's sick. But you should have more consideration for her."

After some time passed and I had calmed down, Emilio and I began living together again. But I saw that he wasn't taking care of me and I said to myself, "If this man doesn't do anything for me now he never will, so the best thing for me to do is to leave him." I loved him, but not the way I did at first. Then I was jealous of the breeze that touched him, but afterward I would see him go by with girls and it didn't bother me at all. After all the torture I suffered from him, the beatings and throwing my clothes out of the house, I asked myself, "How is this all going to end?" I wanted only one thing from God and that was to let me forget little by little. That was just what happened, because Emilio himself said to me, "You aren't the same as you used to be."

Before, when he came home, I used to take off his socks and wash his feet or bathe him all over when he didn't want to take a bath, and I sprinkled him with talcum powder. When he was sick and his glands swelled up like boils, I would lie next to him all night and keep bathing the place with hot water. Later on when I saw him sick it didn't mean a thing to me. I paid more attention to a dog being stoned than I did to him. So he said, "You must be in love, or something is going on with you."

"I have my reasons," I said.

One day I was making rice pudding in my *mamá*'s house and I went over to Soledad's to borrow some sugar. When I came back Emilio was there. He had heard that I had been drinking and dancing with a certain boy. Without even bothering to find out if it was true, he grabbed me by the hair, threw me down on the floor and beat me. Then he picked me up in the air and dropped me. That's when I lost consciousness, but they tell me that he carried me upstairs and poured bay rum and water on me. His family says they were really afraid he had killed me. I called the police and they arrested him, but he put up the bail and got out. There was a trial and I testified against him. The judge fined Emilio twenty-five dollars for assault and battery. We didn't talk to each other for a month.

I went to stay at my sister Soledad's house. This was after they killed Tavio. I said to my sister, "You're a widow now and need somebody around. I'll get a job and help you out with the house." She received some money from *el Welfare,* but my husband didn't give me any money, so I had to work.

"All right," my sister said, "go to work."

One day a woman came over and said, "They're looking for a girl to take care of a child."

"Fine, I'll go there tomorrow. How much are they paying?"

"Forty dollars a month."

"That's all right."

So I went to work for this couple, José Castillo and his wife. They lived in New York but had come to Puerto Rico to visit their families. I took care of their little girl and did the cleaning around the house. I behaved very well with them. Wherever they sent me, I went. If they said, "Press this for me," I would do it. And I cooked everything just the way they wanted it. One day their little girl wanted to visit a relative in Cataño and so I took her. When we came back at night, her mother had been worried. I told her that as long as the child was with me, nothing would happen to her. And so she began to be fond of me.

Even though my husband and I were separated, I used to sneak off to go to bed with him. But he kept on beating me. I told him that he wasn't going to have the chance to abuse me much longer and he answered that he would find me no matter where I went. One day I came to work with a black eye and they asked about it. I explained that my husband beat me and they told me not to take it. They said I was very young and should try to get into better surroundings even if I had to leave him. The *señora* told me that in New York I could earn good money. I could work, and God knows, maybe even have my leg cured, or I could live on *welfare.* The important thing was for me to live in peace without anybody beating me. I told her that I didn't earn enough to get to

New York. They said they would pay my way, but I didn't want to go because I didn't know a soul in New York.

One afternoon my husband got drunk and cut my face. I had been invited to a party that day by some girl friends who lived across the street from Soledad. She said to me, "All right, go, but be careful. You know what Emilio is like. He'll come there and beat you up." Well, I went. I wore a shiny black dress and shiny low-heeled shoes and Soledad made me a pretty hairdo.

On my way home my husband came along and said, "What are you doing out here at this hour? It's ten o'clock."

"Well, I was at the dance," I told him.

"God knows who you were with!" he said, and he slapped me so hard that I fell to the ground. Nobody could help me, because he was drunk. I picked up a bottle to try to defend myself. But then he kicked me in the face three times with the iron tips of his pointed shoes. When he saw the blood he pulled me up, saying, "Oh, my God! Look what I did!" He held me tight against him and his shirt got stained. I pushed away from him and got up. I left, stopping at the water faucet to wash off the blood.

My sister Felícita asked me, "Aren't you going to make a complaint against him?"

"No, and I'm not going to get first aid either," I said. "Now that my face is cut, what's the use of doing anything?" That night I slept in Felícita's house. I took the chamber pot and slept with my face over it. When I woke up the next morning, the pot was half full of blood, and when I looked at myself in the mirror, my God, what a sight I was!

My sister took me to the hospital and they got me ready to put in stitches. The lady doctor said, "The police will have to be notified. This is a mutilation." I didn't want to make a complaint against Emilio, so I told her that I had fallen down.

"I don't believe you fell," she said.

"Don't believe it then," I told her.

When she wasn't looking, I left. I didn't wait for them to put in the stitches but went home with the open wound and I took care of it there. And in spite of my fears, it turned out all right because I have just a little scar here under my chin. People hardly notice it. After that Emilio and I made up.

Then Emilio told me he had a mistress. I said, "I want to go to New York because what you're up to is Communism. You beat me and sleep with me, but you don't give me anything."

"That's because you don't deserve it."

"Why should I wait until late at night for you to come home for supper?" And why should I?

Well, since he had a girl friend, I gave up. I told myself there was nothing I could do. What was the use of my fighting with her? I would just end up the loser because she was a woman of the profession. So I said to him, "I'm going to give you what you deserve when you least expect it." Then one day he got drunk and threatened to cut my face again. I said to myself, "After what he did to me that other time, the sooner I get away the better."

Even though he always kept an eye on me, I began to get everything ready, my suitcase and my ticket, and I left for New York while he was at work. The Castillo couple was already in New York and had helped me with the fare. I didn't say good-bye to anybody except to Soledad, my brother and my *mamá,* who came to the airport to see me off.

I had never been in an airplane before, and when the plane was off the ground I began to scream that it was going to fall. The stewardess gave me a pill that made me fall asleep. When I woke up I asked her where I was.

"You aren't in Puerto Rico, now you're in New York," she said. I looked out the window and I could see New York in the distance. It looked so lovely. I said to myself, "My Lord, is this really where I'm going to be living?"

The Castillo couple was waiting for me at the airport. We got into a car and rode and rode to the Bronx, where they lived. But by the time it was night, I was dying to be back in La Esmeralda.

According to what my *mamá* and other people told me later, Emilio was furious when he found out I was gone and he drank for five days straight. My *mamá* told him she didn't know where I was. Because nobody knew when or where I had gone, they all said I had taken off with *señor* Castillo. But there was nothing, absolutely nothing, between me and that man, and there never has been.

In the beginning everything went well. I worked for my room and board, and to pay off my fare to New York. The couple was very fond of me and treated me nicely until I realized I was pregnant.

Before going to New York, I had skipped a period and gone to the hospital. They took blood from me and the doctor said I was pregnant. But he wasn't sure, and told me to come back in two months. I talked to *doña* Juanita, who lives next door to Emilio's aunt. I told her I wasn't sure I was able to get pregnant because I had already lived with Emilio for over a year.

She said, "Maybe you're barren."

"I hope I am," I said. "It's better that way than to have children who make you suffer."

One night I told Emilio, "I think I'm pregnant."

"A horse couldn't make you pregnant," he answered.

"Well, maybe it's not true. Doctors like to exaggerate."

I was doubtful myself, and the next month I stained blood twice. So I thought, "Whew, what luck! I'm not pregnant a bit."

But then, in New York, I began to have heartburn and to vomit every morning. I didn't dare say anything to the couple because I was ashamed, after all the money they had spent on me. I told the *señor* that something was wrong with my stomach and that I wanted to see a doctor. So he took me, and the

doctor said I was going to be a mother. I was past the third month. *Ave María!*
I began to cry. I said to myself, "Now what? That child is going to be a
bastard. Maybe Emilio won't recognize it."

I wrote Emilio a letter:

Dear Sir:
Pardon me for writing, but I have to tell you I am pregnant by you.
If you don't believe it, so much the better. If I have a bastard, it
won't be the first one in Puerto Rico, or here either.

And from there on I wrote him some nasty things.

He answered immediately by *especial delivery,* sending me twenty dollars. And he wrote, "The Bronx is not so far from Brooklyn, where my *mamá*
lives." I paid no attention, as I had no idea about places in New York.

The couple began to treat me very badly. They didn't give me a thing to
eat and fought with me all the time. I couldn't get a job to pay them back, so
all I could give them was the twenty dollars Emilio sent me. Then the *señora*
applied for *welfare.* There couldn't be anybody in the house when they came
to investigate, so she would say to me, "Look, go hide, because the social
worker might come today."

The Castillos had a grown-up daughter who didn't get along with me. She
was much taller than I and she never believed I would dare face up to her. But
one day when she cursed my mother I punched her in the mouth. She grabbed
my hand and began bending it backward, so I scratched her with the long nails
of my other hand. When she saw blood she began to cry. The couple told me
not to be so stupid, that I had been dragged in like extra baggage and now I
wanted to be boss of the place. I said, "I have no family at all here, but I'm
not going to let that little snot piss all over me. I may be smaller than she is,
but I'm not afraid of her." They said, "All right, get your things together and
leave." But I didn't go. Where could I have gone?

I really can't complain about that couple, though, because after all, they
made it possible for me to come to a country I never thought I'd get to know.
But I hardly went anywhere except to the movies. I learned only a few words
of English, mostly about how much things cost and how to count the change.

One day when I was washing clothes a woman came in, "Do you know if
a girl by the name of Cruz lives around here?" she asked.

"I happen to be Cruz."

She was Emilio's aunt. Emilio had written to his mother, Sara, who
began to check up. This aunt found me and invited me to go back with her that
same night, so I went and stayed with Sara. Emilio's mother felt sorry for me
when she saw how hopeless I was. She said, "You shouldn't be suffering in that
house. Don't go back to Puerto Rico either, because I know what kind of a

temper my son has. After you sneaked away from him, he'll kill you if you go back. Better stay here with me."

Sara treated me fine at first and I felt good. She was a hell-raiser, though, who loved to get drunk and fight and go off with different men. There was a woman in the house who lived very nicely with her husband, but my mother-in-law took him away. She would get him drunk, and then one day she and the wife had a fight.

I was upstairs cleaning, but according to what the neighbors said, the woman's husband came downstairs and Sara put her arms around him. The wife was chopping sugar cane with a hatchet, but when she saw the two of them walk off like that she went at Sara in a fury, grabbed her by the hair and cut her in the back with the hatchet. Sara was bigger than the wife and she took the hatchet away from her and cut her in the face. Then the husband's daughter came running and cut Sara on the nose and elbow.

They called me and I went down. When I saw my mother-in-law I said, "What happened to you?"

"Nothing," she answered. "That fucking woman is jealous of me on account of her husband, for no reason at all."

Suddenly I felt sad. "Let's go in the house. You shouldn't get into these rows," I said.

"No," she answered, "I'm going to get even." But the police came and took them both off to jail. Sara shouted to me, "Send *un especial* to Puerto Rico."

I immediately wrote *un especial delivery* to Emilio telling him that I was in his *mamá*'s house and that she was in jail and I didn't know what to do with his four half brothers. I kept feeling sad because Sara cut the other woman's face and that's the worst thing one woman can do to another. The first thing a man sees in a woman is her face, not her legs. To the men in La Esmeralda a woman whose face has been cut is not worth a thing.

When Sara got out of jail, she said she was going to make the wife move away and asked me to help her. She told me that all I had to do was throw some powder in the wife's house and read a prayer. Sara prepared a mixture of three powders, the powders of Saint Raphael and Saint Michael and the powder of the Seven Restless Spirits. She did it at midnight, wearing a red dress turned inside out and a red handkerchief on her head. Then she went outside, where the wind was blowing so it would carry off the smoke. She put the mixture in a paper and I threw it in the wife's doorway, saying:

> "With three I eye you up,
> With three I tie you up,
> Your blood I drink,
> And your heart I part."

Three days later the woman was gone. She left before the date of the big trial they were going to have.

My mother-in-law works with evil. While I was living there, I never saw her doing anything but evil witchcraft. I consider that bad. Evil shouldn't be done to anybody, because if you don't pay for it here you do up above.

Emilio's family raised the fare and sent for him. One day Sara and I were cleaning up some bedbug nests spraying Flit under the beds, when suddenly she said to me, "*Ay*, Cruz, leave that bed alone and take a bath. Something tells me my son will be here tonight."

"But it's ten o'clock already and that buffalo hasn't shown up yet."

She pulled me up bodily and said, "Go on. Take a bath and dress." I was wearing slacks, so I put on a crazy dress I had, and about half an hour later she said, "Look, here comes Emilio." I dashed into the bathroom and locked the door. I was afraid he had come to get even with me for leaving him.

Emilio came to the bathroom door and said, "Come on, open up."

"I'm not opening the door to anybody."

"Open the door," he yelled. "Come on out."

Finally I did and he picked me up in his arms and kissed me. I figured it was just to warm me up so he could screw me later. He wasn't angry at all. He was in a good mood and we slept together that same night. He went to work on the docks and began giving me money. It wasn't intended for both my mother-in-law and me, but I shared it with her. Emilio and I lived there with her and her husband and their children.

Emilio's stepfather was *un bum* who liked to drink. He tried to make love to me, and when I told my husband he started arguing and fighting with his stepfather all the time and Sara began to hate me. The stepfather would watch until my husband was downstairs, and then he would come up to annoy me. When my husband came up, he would go down. He spent the whole day like that. He said he wasn't giving up hope that I would be his, that he knew I was a good housewife, and that he needed a woman.

One day he tried to kiss me. I was in the kitchen cooking and I pushed him off and burned his arm with hot grease. When my husband came home, I told him and I told Sara too. The stepfather denied everything but as Sara loved her husband and my husband loved me, there was a big fuss.

My husband was good to me, but Sara hated me because he was giving the money to me and not to her. I had to get the baby's things on credit and when I got through with the payments, there wasn't any money left over for her. So she was angry at me or jealous, I don't know which, and she'd complain about me to him every day. If she had nothing to accuse me of, she'd make up something so that he'd give me a beating. Sometimes Emilio would come home from work in a good mood, but she managed to change that. That's the way it went all through my pregnancy.

But when the pains came, I must say she acted right toward me. Emilio and Sara were at a *party* upstairs and I had gone also to dance with my husband. There I was, belly and all, dancing the merengue. I had vomited all through my pregnancy and for a long time I could eat only lemon, but that night I drank two glasses of wine and ate a pile of things, blood pudding, turkey and suckling pig. All at once I felt a sharp pain. I told my husband and he bought me *Alkacerzer* which I drank, thinking it was just a stomach ache.

In a little while I said to him, "I'm going downstairs." He got angry because he wanted to keep on dancing, so I had to go down alone. I sent for him later but he wouldn't come. Finally he came in at about five in the morning, drunk.

Later my mother-in-law got up to go to the bathroom and asked me, "How are you doing?"

"I don't know," I said. "Something is leaking out of me." Emilio and I slept on *un matre* on the floor because there weren't enough beds to go around. When winter started, the cold gave me sharp pains and made me wet myself. But that night Sara took a look at me and said, "Oh, my God! Get up, Emilio, or this woman is going to give birth right here," and she called the police. They looked at me and called an ambulance which took me to a private hospital. They were going to charge a hundred and eighty dollars but I said I didn't have any money, so they took me to a city hospital. There I had pains for a day and a night. The doctors were examining me all the time because they thought they had to kill the baby. Everybody was dressed in white and the doctors kept coming in and sticking their fingers up me until I was getting sick and tired of it. Then a priest came in and I thought he was another doctor and I said, "What the hell, are you coming around to stick your finger in too?"

"No, daughter," he said, "I came to confess you."

"Oh, excuse me, Father," I said.

"I want you to say an Our Father and a Hail Mary." He sprinkled holy water on my belly and passed the cross over me and said, "God bless you and may you come through safely, now that you cannot have your child."

"All I want, Father, is that they kill me and let the baby live."

I was so fed up that I wanted them to cut my belly open. I said to them, "Cut me open and take out everything that is hurting me," but they were all Americans and didn't understand me.

The doctors decided to operate to see if they could take out the baby and save me. My husband and my mother-in-law had already signed that the baby should be killed. Then when the sac burst and wet my legs all over, I said to myself, "*Ay,* my Lord, they're going to kill the baby girl." I took it for granted it was going to be a girl and had bought everything yellow. The bed was high, but I got down and kneeled on the floor. "*Ay,* little Virgin, Saint Anne," I said, "if my daughter is born alive, I'm going to make you a promise. I'll go barefoot for a month and I'll name her after you. I'm putting my hopes in you, so I want you to get me out of this the best way." Whenever two tears come to my eyes I have faith that everything will turn out all right, and this time two tears came to my eyes.

A doctor came in, and when he saw me he shouted, "Get her out!" More doctors came running and put me on the table to wheel me off to the operating room. But right after they picked me up something went *"praaaa"* and the girl came out. Then a lot of doctors came. There must have been about twenty of them. They said, "It's not possible. It can't be!" They picked up the little girl and showed everybody that she was alive. After that, different doctors and specialists came to look at me every day. I was torn badly and had to have fourteen stitches. I named my daughter Anita, after the saint who had saved her.

I still think that if it had been necessary, it would have been better to let me die and save the little girl because she was a creature who came into the world fresh. With me dead, I could help her; if anybody did evil to her, my spirit would punish them one way or another. I believe that the dead can help the living, because whenever I have a big problem I kneel down and say, *"Ay, little grandmother,* I've never asked you a favor before but I want you to grant me this." I would ask, filled with faith, and things would come out right.

I had been in the hospital for a week when they discovered that Emilio and I weren't married. They wanted to know where I had met him. They had the idea he had kidnaped me from Puerto Rico without my parents' consent. The police sent a telegram to my *mamá* and she wrote a letter saying I had lived with him in Puerto Rico but they didn't believe her and thought it was all a plot.

So after twenty days, when I came out of the hospital, they put Emilio in jail. They treated him as though he were my boy friend and not my husband and made me sleep apart from him. They put me down as having no visible means of support. While he was in prison, they took me to court and locked me in all day. They asked me questions, trying to get me to say Emilio had brought mc to New York. I told them the truth but they said I was lying. Then the judge said, "Well, they have to get married. She says they lived together, so we'll have to marry them. If it's a lie we'll divorce them, and he'll go to jail and the baby will go to an institution." So they married us and we started living together. Sara had to sign as my mother because I was fifteen, a minor, and had no family. This was a big favor because if she hadn't, God knows where the baby and I would be now, and Emilio too.

We got married in a church in New York. Having it in the church was not a good thing because I was a woman already. But the law says you can't be married by a judge in New York, so it had to be in church. I was ashamed to be dressed in the lavender dress and black veil, but if you dress in white and are already a woman, you are deceiving the Virgin.

It had always hurt me to see my girl friends leave their homes, dressed in white, wearing veils and crowns, because it had been my dream to have a real wedding and to be taken out of my house properly married and to have at least a photograph of myself in my bridal gown. I used to dream that I would marry a good man and that we would never separate. I thought I would like to marry an elderly man who would give me whatever I needed and who would respect me and my children and my family. My idea of a good man is one who would be pleased if I gave my *mamá* a plate of food or brought her to my house when she got sick, a man who'd give me permission to put my family up in the house when they came from out of town, or let me rent a room for them somewhere and not interfere in what I gave them or they gave me.

I intended to help my husband and to be open with him. If he were out of work, I'd economize and respect him and have everything in order whether he was at home or not. When the husband is out of the house it's the wife who is in charge, and if she brings in disorder the home is not worth anything. It has to be the same way all the time. In the morning the wife has to fix her husband's bath, or prepare his breakfast and serve it to him in bed, then lay his clean underwear in a safe place where he can see it and put it on. As soon as he's gone she has to empty out the urine, straighten up the house, and wash and iron. When he comes home at midday, his food must be *ready* and everything nice and clean, including the dinner table. And the wife should receive him cheerfully and give him a kiss and a hug. It's more up to the man to make advances, but both should share. If the wife is busy in the kitchen he should come and give her a kiss, but if he comes and gives her a punch, she should clout him with a pot.

If the husband wants to go out and have some fun she should let him go, because you can't keep men tied down. She should say, "Go ahead, but just tell me where you're going in case something happens so I can get in touch with you." She shouldn't fight with him if he comes home drunk. Supposing the man tries to pick a fight, you should try to calm him down, but if he really wants a battle you have to give him one. If he comes home drunk or walks in talking nasty, you should say, "Take it easy. Go lie down," and give him a little plain black coffee. If he begins to drink every day, you should say, "Now what? Are you fixing to be *un bum?*" or "What's wrong with you? Don't drink so much." But it's not so bad if he goes out on a Sunday for a little amusement.

In bed, the husband and wife should approach each other equally. Supposing, as it has happened to me, that I don't feel like having relations with the man, I say, "*Ay,* no," and he should be satisfied. It should be the same the other way around. But we women come out the losers when the man wants to have relations and we don't. That's when they say we don't love them or are putting it out for somebody else, or that something is wrong. But when *they* don't want to, we have to keep our mouths shut.

After Emilio and I were married, I went back to my mother-in-law's house with the baby. Emilio didn't like Anita, because he wanted a very dark-skinned baby and she was lighter than he. His mother wanted a colored baby, too, with kinky hair. Sara told Emilio to take a good look at the baby because she wasn't his. My conscience was clear and I insisted that she was. Sara said that I had another man when I was in Puerto Rico and my husband believed her.

"All right," I said to Emilio, "as long as you're a dirty son of a bitch, we'll separate."

That night Emilio slapped me, so I threw a frying pan at him. He gave me a punch and I went after him with a bottle. Just then Sara appeared and said that if I cut her son's head I would get myself into a lot of trouble. At that I burst out crying, because it was two against one. So I said, "Well, what are we going to do now?"

"I'm the boss here and so you leave," she said.

I picked up the baby and wrapped her up warm. Then I took her little suitcase and left. But Emilio followed me. "Don't go," he said. "I'll get you a room."

I told him no, I wasn't going to live with him and he should go back to his *mamá* and leave me in peace. But he brought me back to Sara's house and I went to bed. The next day before he went to work, Emilio said, "Wait here for me. I'll get you a room with what I make today." I said to myself, "Whatever God wills."

When he had gone Sara said, "You can get out now. I have to leave, and I'm giving the orders around here. I want the house to be closed tight after you are gone."

"So let it be!"

"And you came without a *coat,* so you can go without a *coat.*"

I put on a sleeveless jacket, picked up the baby and left. This was toward the end of 1960 and a big snow had fallen. The people must have thought I was crazy, walking around like that in the deep snow. I had walked a few blocks when a policeman saw me and asked me what was wrong. I didn't understand him and he got an interpreter. I told him nothing was wrong, that I was going to a cousin's house. When I went on walking I fell down. The policeman picked me up, took the baby and said, "I'll take you to your cousin's house. But I know something has happened to you. Tell me what it is, and if I can help you, I will."

I didn't want to tell what had happened because my mother-in-law had done me a lot of favors. When they were going to send me to a reformatory, she signed that she was responsible for me. I was grateful to her and couldn't bring myself to make a complaint against her.

The policeman took me to the house of my mother's cousin Virginia. I explained everything to her and she gave me money. She had a ticket to Puerto

Rico and she let me have it. She found out when there was a seat and the next day I left under her name. I arrived at my *mamá*'s house at about ten-thirty at night. Héctor and Simplicio were living with her. Everybody was in bed already.

I knocked on the door and called out, "Let me have a little water, please, *señora.*"

"Look, go drink from the public faucet," my mother said. "These drunks coming around asking for water when a person is all tired out!"

Then I told her who I was and she opened the door.

"*Ay,* my Lord!" she said. She kissed me, took the baby, and began hugging her. She fixed a bed for me right away and I went to sleep.

The baby was only twenty days old and she caught a cold. It had been windy at the airport when I got off the plane and her little cap fell off and her covers came loose. A week later she got asthma and it has lasted right to this day. She gets it every single month.

A lot of men wanted to make love to me when I came back from New York because I looked white and had very long hair. If a boy who has been brought up among us goes to New York with his parents when he is twelve, his skin changes and he gets fatter and pink. Then when he returns to Puerto Rico, the girls go crazy about him because he is so handsome. It's the same with the women. I was as pretty as could be, but I kept off the men because I had a husband and I didn't dare.

My husband came back a month after I did, on January 6, the Day of the Kings. He brought Anita four dresses, a big eight-dollar doll that talked, a chain and earrings. She still has the earrings. I was living in my mother's house, and Emilio lived at his aunt Minerva's near by, almost across the street from me. Sometimes he would come to my house to sleep with me and sometimes I would go to his aunt's house and stay overnight with him.

Well, after about two months he took another woman. At first I had no idea what was going on, because I lived in my *mamá*'s house and didn't dare go out to check up on him. But one night he showed up with bite marks on his neck. I took the marriage license and tore it up, took the wedding rings and his clothes and went with them to where she lived. I walked right into the room, gave her a couple of slaps and hit him with a lamp. He gave me a real beating and threw me down the stairs. Later he told my *mamá* to get me to stop being angry with him and to talk to him. I said I wouldn't. But he came to the house one day and we began to talk, and that was it. We got together again.

I went hungry, though, while I was with Emilio. My baby lived only on my milk. I let her suck until my breasts hurt. Sometimes she wasn't able to get anything out of either breast and we would both fall asleep from hunger. A neighbor would sometimes give me food. Then one day Emilio said, "I'm going to leave this place. I'll save up money and see if I can take an apartment so I can send for you and the baby later." He told me he had *esteri** work in New York. I said, "All right. You're the man and have to do whatever is necessary. I'll be here waiting for you." And off he went to New York. He was away for nearly seven months, but I waited for him all that time without having relations with anybody.

My *mamá* and stepfather took care of me. Nanda bought me clothes, and I took in washing and ironing. Whenever I got sick or had to go out, she minded the baby. My brother gave me money, too, when he had it, and even bought food for the baby. But one day he hit Anita. I told him he had no right to lay a hand on her and not to be such a dirty bastard as to hit a tiny baby. He hauled off and slapped me and I scratched his neck and his face and tore his shirt and called him a son of a bitch.

"Whore! That's what you are," he said.

"And you're a cheap pimp! Go screw yourself!" Then I shit on his mother's name and there was *mamá,* right next to me. So then the two of them let me have it.

Ever since we were little my brother and I had fought with each other, but we really drifted apart after we were both married. This time we were fighting because I told him that Flora, his wife, had said he was a son of a bitch of a fairy and he wouldn't believe me. She and I didn't get along well. She was tall and straight, with long blond hair down her back, but she was a dirty louse. Her ex-husband, Fontánez, didn't speak to me any more because when my brother took away his woman, people told Fontánez I was the go-between. But I had already stopped speaking to Fontánez before that, because he would wink at me and make signs to me even when I was living with Emilio. You can see from his face that he's a ladies' man. He'd tell me between his teeth that he liked me and that I was a good piece. So I said, "I may be a good piece but I'm not to be eaten." Then he said, "What do you want? To be eaten by the earth?" And I answered, "I'd rather be eaten by the earth than by you!"

Fontánez was Felícita's *compadre* because he had sprinkled water on her little girl Tany. But he didn't speak to my sister either, or to any of us. We didn't know it at the time, but my *mamá* was putting the horns on Héctor with Fontánez.

After seven months in New York, my husband came back fat and elegant. He talked about New York all the time and I told him he was a show-off. The night he arrived we had relations seven times. I was satisfied after the second and didn't like the others because he insisted on my moving my hips and that was tiring but he forced me. When I told him there was no enjoyment

* Steady.

in it by force, he said he didn't care about that, because the madder he was at me the bigger kick he got out of it.

In my *mamá*'s house we were still in mourning for my grandfather and we owed for the rent, the furniture and everything. Then suddenly one day I hit a number. I had told my *mamá* I was going to sell numbers and she said all right. I offered her number 951 but she didn't want it, even though I reminded her it was a favorite of hers. The next day the winning number came out and I hit. I told my mother that she had no more debts because I was going to pay up everything. "May the Lord bless you," she said, "because your heart is pure." When I went to collect the money, my husband was there. He slapped me because he was having a jealous fit over the numbers seller, a *compadre* of his by the name of Felipe. But as I told my *mamá,* "Let him slap me twenty more times. I don't care. I have the money in my hands now."

I won two hundred dollars. "Let's count it," I said to my *mamá.* "Maybe that man clipped some of it." My *mamá* counted it and it was exact. I gave seventy-five dollars to my *mamá,* ten dollars to Emilio, five to his aunt Minerva, and I kept the rest for myself. I gave Emilio the money so that he could play pool, because there was a strike on the docks at the time and he had practically nothing. I didn't give anything to my sisters or brother because they weren't around, but I did give a dollar to each of Felícita's children and to Catín.

I bought dollar candles for the Virgin of Carmen and the Virgin of Everlasting Mercy because these were the saints to whom my *mamá* prayed, and she had asked me to buy them if I won. We had prayed a lot and kept promising the candles, so as soon as I won, I went and bought them and lit them myself.

Just one month after Emilio came back to La Esmeralda he took up with another woman again. He came home one day with kiss marks and that's how I found out. We had a fight and I refused to have anything to do with him from then on. I told him they had my blessing and he should get out. She had a room and he stayed there with her. A girl friend of mine told me that she was hustling in a bar. She kept on his neck, although, according to him, he didn't pay her even for the first time.

When I found out about it I said to myself, "If the saints don't favor you, just don't pray to them. I'm not going to fight for something that isn't worth the trouble." But I couldn't eat when I saw my husband running around with women all the time and never taking me out. I weigh one hundred and five pounds now, but at that time I weighed only eighty pounds.

My *mamá* wrote to my sister Soledad in Florida and she sent me a ticket to go there. What was the sense of my staying around and suffering? So off I went to Florida with my baby Anita.

FORTY-THREE

Cruz

———

To Florida and Back

———

SOLEDAD had gone to Florida with a married man by the name of Eddy, whom she met in New Jersey. But while she was on a visit to Puerto Rico, Eddy's wife had come very quietly and grabbed him back. When my sister returned she said, "I'm going to have to wind this up," and she sold the bed and furniture and everything he had left her. Then she began seeing a boy by the name of Jorge Luis Castro, a first cousin of Eddy's. He didn't get along with me because he had tried me before he got my sister.

On my sister's birthday they had a party for her. She was twenty-three and I was seventeen. Jorge gave her a good beating that day, cutting her head open with a tomato can. Soledad thought and thought about it and then went crazy. They sewed up the cut with three stitches and took her away to the insane asylum.

I stayed in the house with the four children, her three and mine. They told me that Soledad had done all kinds of terrible things when she got to the hospital. She dirtied herself and then played with the filth and smeared it on her face. Then she tore the sheets and broke the window and the chairs. After that she picked up the sheet and draped it around her neck saying what a lovely collar she was wearing. So *las Mrs.* put her in a sanitarium. I went to see her, but they wouldn't let me in because they don't allow Negroes there and I am dark-skinned. As she was lighter than any of us, they had put her with the whites but they treated me like a Negro.

There is racism in Florida. The Negroes and the whites live apart from each other. I've always liked the colored people and I didn't like this racism business at all. It made me sad that the Negroes didn't get along with the whites.

I lived with the *moyos,* which is what we call the American Negroes, but I couldn't talk to them since I don't know English very well. They didn't want Soledad to live among them because she is white. I'm a *trigueña* but they consider me Negro. A *trigueño* is a colored person but there's a difference between him and a Negro. The Negro is blacker and the *trigueño* more mahogany-colored. The *trigueño* has straight, "Indian" hair and the Negro's hair is kinky.

I cried a lot because I couldn't see my sister. I kept trying, until finally a man said I could see her but that it would have to be in a room by ourselves. I wasn't allowed to enter the part where the whites were. I brought her candy and crackers and she said, "Well, *comadre,* what are you doing around here? How are the boys?" She thought I was a *comadre* of hers. When I told her I was her sister, she just looked at me for a long time. "Here," I said, "I brought you some crackers." She took the box, opened it, crumbled up the crackers and threw them into her own face. They had to tie her up and give her an injection.

She had been in the sanitarium for about a month when she suddenly appeared at the house one day wearing a hospital bathrobe. She had escaped and come home. That night at around midnight I got up to see how she was and I found her in bed with Jorge. Afterward, she went back to the hospital.

I went to work. Sometimes I didn't get home until eleven at night and then I had to make supper for the children. I had a very rough life. I worked in the fields picking *las stróberi,* potatoes, beans and tomatoes.

I saved up fifty dollars after working day and night for a month. I wanted to send Soledad's girls back to Puerto Rico and I wrote my *mamá* a letter. She answered that Soledad should come home. I spoke to *el Welfare* that same day and they gave me three tickets for fifty dollars. I wrote to my *papá* and he sent me seventeen dollars, and I also sold the furniture. So I took the children to the airport and brought clothes for my sister. They brought her there with her hands tied and gave her an injection because she didn't want to leave. My *mamá* met her at the airport in Puerto Rico. She began to have treatments and got well again. My *mamá* wrote saying that Soledad was better but she didn't write much more because my *mamá* is kind of lazy about writing. Six months later Soledad was back in New York.

I stayed on in Florida for nearly a year, all alone with my little girl. I would leave the baby with some *moyos* when I went to work. They spoke a little Spanish and I a little English, so we managed. The *moya* who took care of Anita had known Soledad before I came to Florida and I liked her right away. We talked together a lot and she told me how much she wanted to visit Puerto Rico, to get to know it and to learn Spanish. She used to come to my house and we became good friends.

She wouldn't take a cent for taking care of Anita, so I gave her a little box I had with me and a watch. And I would buy her powder, earrings, bracelets, and clothing and shoes. Seeing how nice I was to her, she began to like me as much as she did the baby. Her husband kept telling me I shouldn't be spending my money because they would feed the baby anyway. They said she was their daughter because she was dark like them. I loved that lady like my own *mamá;* I could tell her all my troubles and she would give me advice. She knew the ropes around there and explained to me what I should and shouldn't do.

One day the baby was playing outdoors and a snake curled around her feet. I screamed and screamed until the *moyos* came and killed it. After that I didn't want to stay in Florida any more and I started thinking about how I could get back to Puerto Rico.

I met a boy named Antonio Borelli at a dance at a Puerto Rican girl friend's house. He was part Italian and was the same mahogany color I am. We danced together and he wanted to know why I was in Florida. He couldn't understand how I could bear being all alone. I said I did the best I could, with God's help.

"Well, I can help you too if you want me to," he said.

I said, "With no strings attached, though."

"All right, with no strings attached. Like a friend."

I lived out in the country and he worked in the city as a *foreman* in a shirt factory. He made a lot of money because he ran a numbers "bank" too. He had a car and an apartment, but I didn't want to live with him because I was planning to go back to Puerto Rico. I asked him to help me get out of my room because I was paying thirteen-fifty a week for it, besides the gas and light. He found me a room with two beds and a kitchen and with light and water besides, for six dollars a week.

He would take me out and go shopping with me and bring me groceries. The baby called him *papá* because he played with her in the afternoon. He would tell me to dress her up and he would take her out all alone, riding with him in his car. They would come back with toy dishes or a doll. When it came time for him to leave, he had to hide because Anita didn't want him to go.

Although my room was furnished, I didn't like the bed they had there, so he bought another one. It cost fifty dollars. Besides that, he bought me a stove and things for the kitchen. He was really very good to me, but I didn't love him because my thoughts were in Puerto Rico with Emilio.

I would look at Antonio and my heart would hurt because I had a husband and wanted to be with him. But I felt very sad when I remembered the beatings Emilio gave me and the bad things he said, and I thought how in the six months Antonio and I had been together we hadn't had one single fight. He would say, "Don't put on that dress, it doesn't look good on you." In the same quiet way I would go and hang it up in the closet. "Put on that outfit and shoes and carry this handbag," he would say, and whatever he said I'd do.

He never had any complaints about me and would tell his friends that I was the only one for him. If he changed his socks in the morning, they were washed and dry by the afternoon. When he took off his trousers they went into the wash immediately. And his dinner was always *ready*. I'd go to his house and clean the furniture and everything almost every day. His refrigerator was always kept nicely, his and mine both. He told me that he hadn't given up hope that I would come and live with him at his house, but that he was leaving things as they were for the time being because he knew I had a mania for Emilio. He'd say that I could be happy with him for the rest of my life.

God knows whether I would have been happy if I had stayed with him or what made me leave him. But because I was on the lookout for my own satisfaction and didn't find it with him, I acted like a fool. But I have nothing to regret. What I felt for him was gratitude because when I was all alone he was the only one who held out a helping hand. I really didn't love the boy and he deserved better than me. I'd say to him, "You're a young man and can get ahead. I'm not the woman for you because I don't love you." I had respect for him and didn't want to hurt him, but I didn't love him.

On Father's Day, Antonio gave me money to go to Puerto Rico. He said, "Take this two hundred dollars and go to Puerto Rico to see your *mamá*. Send me a telegram when you're ready to come back so I can get your return ticket." But when he left I said to a girl friend, "He'll see me go but not come back." I left behind eighteen dollars' worth of groceries, a stove, a hen with twenty-four eggs, two pounds of corn and a basin. I left absolutely everything and came on back to La Esmeralda.

When I arrived I went to Felícita's house. She was living with Edmundo and was pregnant with Evita. My sister was as good as could be to me. I was nice and fat when I got there. I returned on a Thursday and the celebrations of the Virgin of Carmen in Cataño were on Saturday. I planned to go and dressed up nicely, with high heels. When the boys are going to see you, you have to look elegant. I left the baby at my sister's and went to take the boat to Cataño.

I was standing in line to get on the ferry when somebody grabbed me and threw me down. It was Emilio. He pulled me by the hair and told me I wasn't going any place. I knew he was living with his woman and I said, "*Ay, Dios,* if I'm not your wife, why are you doing this to me?"

He forced me to sit down with him and he began talking and talking. He told me he was going to leave that woman and live with me. I accepted. I loved him and so I accepted. The next day he told the woman that if she tried to come between us, he would beat her up. But I stayed with Felícita for a while before we began living together.

Felícita was quarreling a lot with her husband. She said, "Look, Crucita, I live with him and I love him but he keeps talking against my family all the time. He asks whether Soledad has been a whore and if you are a whore and if I was a whore. He throws these things up to me because he's never willing to forget the past." So I said, "What you had better do then is think about your children."

I helped Felícita when she gave birth to Evita and also when she went to be operated on. We were always quarreling, though, because of our children. She didn't like it when Anita hit Tany but it was all right the other way around. She didn't want me to spank her children, but when the kids got into trouble she would always spank Anita and was nasty to her. When Felícita was pregnant with Evita she used to beat Anita a lot. That's why Evita looks so much like my daughter.

Felícita didn't want me to talk to my husband. She called him "that Negro." I said, "I don't interfere in your life, so don't mix into mine." This would start a big argument but then we would make up. Felícita never got along with Emilio and we couldn't have relations in her house. First we got together in a hotel on Luna Street. We stayed there all night for seven dollars. That was the night I got pregnant again, but of course I didn't know it then.

When my period didn't come, I thought that probably my blood was weak. Then I skipped the next month too and began getting the vomiting symptoms. So I said to my sister, "Fela, I'm pregnant."

"*Ay*, my mother! That man living with another woman and you pregnant. What a fix you're in!"

"That's nothing."

Felícita's husband Edmundo didn't get on with Emilio because he considered him a very bad type. Emilio was foul-mouthed in front of Edmundo and every place else too, but Felícita's husband was a hypocrite. Behind my back he would ask the children to tell me to pack my clothes and leave. To me he would say I could stay in the house and give birth to my child.

One day I caught him talking about me. I had been getting money together for a deposit on a room, and Felícita was telling him about it just as I arrived at her house. I heard him say, "Fine, if she wants to go, let her go. I can't stand her around here any more." I stood there on the other side of the door and they kept on talking. He said I should leave because they liked to live in peace and anyway I had been there a long time already, and if I was going around with that husband of mine, I should live with him. I slept there that night but the next day I left.

"All right, Emilio, give me money for a room," I said to my husband. I hadn't told him I was pregnant yet because I wasn't sure. He gave me eight dollars and I rented a room from Papo's Genoveva and I began living there. I had a little bed like the one I have now, a table that Emilio made for me, and a stove and dishes that he bought. But that woman he'd had began pestering him and so he took up with her again. Then he had the two of us, me and her. Finally I asked him whether he was going to stay with me or with her. He said with me, but it was a lie. He set up a room for me, but he kept on with her.

I asked *doña* Minerva where Emilio was and she told me he was at home. I said, "If he doesn't come to see me, it's because he knows very well I'm pregnant. Tell him not to act like a fool, because it's his."

Then he came around. "Ah, so you're pregnant by me, are you?"

"Yes."

"If you want to live happy, get rid of it."

I told him I wouldn't. Instead, I was going to take up with another man because I couldn't stand living the way I was. He said that would make the situation worse because he loved me as a woman. I said that when I wanted a man, I wanted him only for myself. He said that if I got rid of the child he would live happily with me. The thing was, he had to support himself and me and Anita, and the money didn't stretch. I said that if he could keep a woman he must have money and that I was going to give birth to the baby with just as much pleasure as I had when we made him.

"You're going to get rid of it because it's not mine," he said.

"How can you think it's not yours when I haven't been with anybody else but you? Whose could it be? It's certainly not your *papá*'s."

"God knows whose it is. I'm leaving and you'll stay here alone, so you have to get rid of it."

"I'm not getting rid of anything."

But one day when I was two months pregnant, he brought Zulma, the dope pusher, to the house. She had some suppositories, a rubber tube and two quinines. Quinines are white pills they sell in the drugstore for chickens with the croup. She was going to stick the rubber tube inside me and abort me. I refused because I don't like to be pawed, especially by a woman.

So Emilio slapped me and said what about the money he had to pay her. She got fifty dollars from him. She risked her neck, because if they catch her she goes to jail.

Three days later another woman came. She's in jail now for peddling dope. She had the same things as the other one and I refused again. She got thirty-five dollars.

Emilio said he would kick the baby out of me. He had never hit me in the belly during my first pregnancy, only in the face or on the arms, but now he gave me kicks in the belly that left me gasping for air. I believe God wanted me to have that baby because I didn't lose it.

Emilio kept insisting the baby wasn't his and one day when I was looking at pictures that friends in Florida had given me as remembrances, he saw one that said on the back, "To my beloved sweetheart from Antonio." He grabbed it and said that was the fellow who was the father of the baby. But I told whoever asked that Emilio was the father and sometimes, just to annoy him, I said that it was Emilio's *papá*'s.

Then, because I wouldn't get rid of the baby, Emilio wouldn't pay my rent or give me any money at all. He said I should go hustle at the water front, so I threw his clothes out the door. He hit me and put them back in and I threw them out again. But when he didn't come back I began to cry and cry. The landlady told me that I could pay the rent dollar by dollar, any way I could. After that Emilio would come to have relations with me by force, and to beat me. He didn't stay, and he let Anita and me go hungry.

It worried me when Anita said she was hungry. A neighbor gave me food for myself and I wanted to eat that food, but I gave it all to Anita. I went hungry because if either of us had to pass out, it had better be me.

I said to myself, "I'll have to find another man to help because I can't work." Who would take care of Anita? My *mamá* had gone to Philadelphia and none of my family was around. I could have written to Antonio in Florida to help me, but all I did was send word that I was pregnant and that it was too late now. He answered, saying it was never too late and that he would be willing to recognize the child as his and send me whatever I needed. He said I should come to Florida, as he was still waiting for me. I didn't write to him again, even though Emilio was doing nothing but abuse me. He enjoys hitting women. I would rather sleep under a stairway than live with him. The trip to the States had been wonderful for me, just to be separated from him.

One day a boy who had just gotten out of jail came to the house and said, "Cruz, wash these clothes for me, will you?"

I washed his things and then I said to Genoveva, "I'm going to take in washing and ironing and see if I can't earn a little something." She said, "Go ahead," so I spoke to a friend of mine and told her to let me know of any work I might get.

"I have five customers. You can have two," she said.

"Whose clothes are these?"

"El Gordo's and Tico's."

"*Ay,* no, I'm not going to wash for Tico. He dirties in his pants."

"Then take El Gordo."

So I did. Then my neighbor *doña* Rebeca notified a woman in San Juan and she brought me clothes to be ironed. After that I kept getting calls to iron at nine o'clock at night. Sometimes I didn't get through until one or even four in the morning. I washed during the day and ironed at night.

I began selling numbers again. Sometimes I sold seven dollars' worth of tickets a week. If I didn't sell all the books, I'd have to make up the money out of my own pocket. I'd lose money that way sometimes but usually I made some. I had regular customers because I'm lucky at selling. A little old lady who lives down near the beach bought three dollars and seventy-five cents' worth of tickets every week. I sold her a hundred-dollar prize. A lady at **Stop** 26 who was the "bank," would give the prize money to the person who sold me the books, and that person gave it to me. Then I'd give it to the winners, who'd give me ten or fifteen dollars. The first month I won a prize myself and I also sold a winning ticket to a man who gave me twenty-five dollars.

I would go into people's houses so they'd buy from me, but I never had many friends. Sure, the men wanted me to sleep with them, but I never went with any of them. Some of them said I was stuck up because I wouldn't put out for anyone. Almost no one around there talked to me. The only thing I did was play up to an old drunk who wanted to make love to me. We would drink and dance and fool around, and when he was good and drunk I'd get money out of him. I never spent a night with him. Everybody said that I was hustling, but I was afraid to hustle in San Juan because the police were picking up the women. I said to myself, "What's the use of hustling? What if they give me a sickness and Anita catches it too?"

I can do housework, and as long as I'm able to earn money honestly, I'll do it. It doesn't work out well for a woman to let a man use her body because there's always another one after him and another and another, until finally, when she wants to live a happy life, she can't any more. What happens is that a man begins to ask questions about a woman and then the gossip starts. So you have to tell a man everything before others do. But if a man loves a woman, the past doesn't matter.

Things were very bad for me because Emilio was throwing his money away on other women. One day I went to see a woman who works with evil. I told her I wanted something that would make Emilio give me money because I was going hungry. She said that if I did what she told me he would come to me all ashamed and give me everything I wanted. But I didn't do it. I always think things over before doing them. Suppose that later on I hated Emilio and he kept coming after me? We'd fight and if he didn't kill me first, I'd kill him. I didn't want anything like that to happen.

So I went to *doña* Rita, who lives in Loíza Aldea. She works with good and never charges. She gives prescriptions, though, expensive ones that cost almost two dollars. Felícita and my *mamá* go to her too and have a lot of faith in her.

When I went to *doña* Rita I sat down and she tried to contact my guiding spirit. Then she pushed me and said, "Get out! You shouldn't be here."

"My Lord, why not?" I asked.

"Because there's no solution to your problem and because I want to see you humiliated and working as a whore. I don't want you to be happy with any man. You won't live in peace with any man. Maybe for three months or six but never for a year, because I'll stand in your way."

"And who are you?" I asked.

"I'm your husband."

"All right, but what are you doing here?"

"The same as you, looking for help."

The spirit showed that my husband had put this spell on me so that I wouldn't take up with another man or be able to live in peace with anyone. The woman took off all my clothes, poured an herb bath over me and gave me massages. I had had a headache and a feeling of heaviness when I went in, but when I came out I felt light all through my body and I was relieved. I was very happy and when I got home I did the washing and ironing until four in the morning.

Cruz

Life with Alejandro

THEN I TOOK UP with a boy by the name of Alejandro Crespo. His nickname is Alejo and sometimes they call him El Negro because he's so dark. He was a boatman, and all boatmen had nicknames. He had hardly looked at me before but we were friendly. He was the sweetheart of a friend of mine by the name of Claudia, but he left her because the police were after him and he had to hide. There were charges against him because he had burned his wife. She had played him dirty and he set fire to *el matre* while she was asleep. She lived but was left with one leg paralyzed. The burn drew up the skin and she couldn't stand on her foot. The police finally caught Alejandro in St. Thomas but the trial hasn't been held yet.

I was living near Papo's *bar* when Alejandro came back to La Esmeralda. He used to drink there and I was always coming by to ask people for money for food. Then they told me that he liked me. He bought numbers from me and one day I sold him a winner and he won a hundred dollars. When I delivered the money to him, he gave me a present of ten dollars. I paid six dollars for the rent and I had four left. After I put Anita to bed that night we sat outside and talked and talked. The next day he brought me twenty-five dollars. I bought clothes for Anita, food and a pair of shoes for myself. Well, he helped me out for a whole week and even paid the next week's rent. After that, Genoveva told me he was a nice boy and I should get something out of him because I couldn't get anything out of Emilio.

I can't complain about Genoveva. She has behaved better than a mother to me. We have never had the slightest little argument. She would mind Anita for hours when I was out selling numbers. When I was sick she would prepare food for me and run errands and wash Anita's *panties*. She is nice to everybody. When anybody asks her for something she'll give it to them. When they want a room to make love in, she lets them go upstairs. Down below the people drink and horse around as they please. They can throw bottles and she never says a word.

Emilio said that she got men for me, because he saw her with me so much and because when he talked nasty to me she would defend me. She didn't like Emilio. Emilio was a longshoreman and the longshoremen don't get on with the boatmen who hang out at Papo's *bar*. Genoveva would stand at one door and Papo at the other with that revolver of his, and when a fight started they wouldn't let the longshoremen in. Papo was not afraid to use his gun. The reason longshoremen don't like boatmen is that the boatmen take the longshoremen's wives away from them. Alejandro said he wanted to take a room for me and him. I agreed and went with him. He said, "We aren't going to be able to live together in a regular way because I can't stay very long in one spot. I'll be coming and going." So we lived together but not under the same roof.

At that time I was having relations with three men, Emilio, Alejandro and a very lovely boy by the name of Armando. Emilio would arrive at eight o'clock at night and leave at nine-thirty, Armandito was with me from ten-thirty to eleven. Alejandro got there at midnight and left at about five in the morning. I handled all of them. It is not tiring if you like the men and I liked all three, although Alejandro was my favorite. None of them knew about the others. Emilio told me not to go out and I told him I never did. I told Alejandro not to tell anyone about us because I was a married woman and if Emilio found out he would make trouble. I told Armandito, "Look, you'd better not say anything to Alejandro because you know what a talker he is. If Alejandro says anything I'll know you told him, and you and I will be finished."

When I owed the rent they would give it to me. Armando gave me money for food and Alejandro helped me too. But I got nothing from Emilio. One night Armando came with a bottle of gin and left a kiss mark on my face. When Alejandro came he did the same but didn't notice the one I already had because it was dark. I always put out the light and wouldn't let them turn it on.

The next day Alejandro and Armando happened to meet at my house. They said to each other, "Hey, what are you doing here?" I flew down the stairs and Alejandro said to me, "Is it true that this guy slept with you last night?"

"With me! How? Didn't you leave here at five in the morning?" What a blabber mouth that Armando is! Armando went looking for Emilio and I told

Alejandro to get me out of there if he wanted to live with me. So he took me over to the old airport and we stayed there for two days.

When Alejandro was angry he'd get very serious. He hardly ever lost his temper, though. One day a boy was in the house and I was horsing around with him and he winked at me. Alejandro said that I winked back, but it wasn't true. Anyway, Alejandro was going to slap me and I threw a cooking pot at him. He didn't hit me then and he never lifted a hand to me after that.

Alejandro is more responsible than Emilio. I never saw Alejandro fooling around or drunk or talking foul. Alejandro's nature is to treat women nicely. He'd say, "Lie in this position," or "Put your legs like this." And he'd tell you when he didn't like something. Emilio would hit you right away. He is an unpleasant man and cold besides. In the beginning he was more manly than Alejandro and satisfied me, but afterward he was good for nothing. He doesn't wait for a woman but just gets in and comes. Sometimes the man comes before the woman but then he says, "Now you come," and the woman does because she still feels the excitement. When they said to me, "Now you," I would tell them I couldn't unless they helped me and they would.

One day Alejandro and I began drinking gin with beer—lots and lots of it. I really went under and had no idea what was happening. The next day I woke up with kiss marks all over my face and neck and breast. A friend of Emilio's told him about it and he came to the house.

"I didn't come because of those marks," he said. "I came because you gave me a disease."

There were a lot of people around and that's why he said that I had given him gonorrhea. I said, "If I gave you a sickness, then what condition would Alejandro be in and what about the child?"

"As a matter of fact," he said, "I came for her," and he grabbed Anita. I fought with him but he kicked me in the stomach and I fell down. I began to cry and then I called the police. When they came, Emilio said they should examine my face and chest.

They took us to the police station. Emilio and a friend of his told the judge I brought men to the house. The judge looked me up and down and asked what kind of an example was this to give my daughter. The judge said to me, "The child is his." Then he said to Emilio, "Your wife has the right to see the child, but you're the one in charge. Take her home."

I couldn't believe it. I went to La Esmeralda and had a talk with my friend Genoveva. She said, "Calm down, Crucita, I hope to God you'll get your daughter back because you're not a bad mother." Another friend of mine told me not to worry because I would forget the child little by little, but I told her that was impossible. Catín, my little niece who was visiting me for a few days, went around with a lighted candle saying, *"Ay, Dios mío,* bring Anita home so Crucita won't cry!"

Time was going by, though, and I saw that my daughter wasn't coming back. I wasn't able to sleep and I began to drink. I drank for three days without eating, and without changing my clothes or cleaning the house. Finally I said to Genoveva, "I'm going to Emilio's house to kill the baby. She can't be his, she belongs to me." I put a *Gem* inside my dress and said, "I'm leaving." Genoveva tried to stop me but I went.

At Emilio's house I opened the door, saw the baby there asleep and picked her up in my arms. His woman said, "What are you doing here?"

"I came to see my daughter. I have the right." She just looked at me and at the *Gem* and didn't say a word. "I'm taking her with me," I said.

"For the love of God, Cruz, don't take her. When Emilio comes home and doesn't find her, he'll beat me."

"All right, I won't do it because you're asking me to have pity on you. But if you try to screw me up, I'll let you have it."

"I'm not responsible for all this. I know that man loves you and lives with me just to get even with you. I'm going to leave him now."

"No, don't go. If something happens to the baby, you'll be responsible. Better wait until he comes back."

Emilio came from work at four o'clock and asked the woman what I was doing there. I answered, "I have as much right as you to see your daughter." He pushed me and I took a plate from the table and threw it at him. I went downstairs and threw two big stones at the house. *Doña* Minerva came and said to me, "Better get out of here because bedbugs are going to fall on you. You'll really get into trouble."

"Leave me alone. You're nothing but an old procuress and have no business advising that son of a bitch to take away my daughter! I gave birth to her and he's not man enough to keep her! I have a man who's more of a man than he is!"

"That baby belongs to me," yelled Emilio from above.

"Keep her then, but I won't be responsible for what happens when you come to my house."

Two days later he was at my house. "I'm not here about the baby," he said. "I just wanted to tell you something."

"What's that?"

"I want you to leave me in peace."

"I'm not bothering you, so beat it!"

When he left I began to drink again. I had twenty dollars, and in three days I spent it all, drinking beer and playing the juke box. I even smoked marijuana. Some boatmen friends of mine were smoking it and I snatched a cigarette away and smoked almost the whole thing. I felt I was the greatest thing in the world, as though if I were pricked I wouldn't bleed. I felt I was better than anybody else. Twice I fell and scraped myself but it didn't hurt at all. I saw blood and just cleaned it off. Then I fell down on the beach and a nail went into me but I didn't feel that either.

I was out of my mind. I went to Emilio's house three times. I said to that woman of his, "I'll show you who that man belongs to! Take a look at his neck and ask him who made those kiss marks. I was the one who made them. Take the T-shirt and shorts he left in my house last night. And you can have him too. I'll make you a present of him."

One afternoon I got drunk and went to a *bar* up in San Juan. "Don't go there," Genoveva said. "They'll beat you up." Emilio was there with his woman and Minerva. I was so drunk I didn't care about anything and I said to them, "You, Emilio, are a dirty son of a bitch! You, woman, are a whore! And you, Minerva, are an old hot ass! If you don't give me my little girl, you'll see what will happen to you. You tell me I'm a cheat and a whore. Maybe I'm a whore, but I have my rights." Emilio knocked me down on the floor. I picked up some figurines and threw them in his face. Minerva said that I was a procuress and not worth two cents.

I answered, "I may not be worth two cents, but you are the one who has heart trouble and can't catch your breath. Your trouble is really farther down, in that old cunt of yours. Tomorrow I'll bring you ten cents' worth of bobby pins so you can straighten out its wrinkles."

When I left *el bar* I cried and cried, thinking about Anita. A policeman friend of mine saw me and asked what the trouble was. When I explained he said, "Take this note and go to Family Relations. They'll help you. But don't say that Alejandro gave you those kiss marks. Say that it was the father of your children."

The next day I took Catín with me to Family Relations. I said to her, "Don't forget, Catín. You tell the judge it was Emilio who made those kiss marks." So she told him that.

The judge said to her, "Child, did you see this man enter the house of this woman?"

"Yes, I saw Emilio come in and lie down in the bed."

"Where were you sleeping?"

"In the other bed, with Anita," she said.

The judge sent me to the University in Río Piedras to see three lawyers, and I got a letter from them. When I gave it to the judge, he said that now he knew I really wanted my daughter because he had sent other mothers and they never got there. They had all turned back because it was too far away.

The judge heard my side and then Emilio's side. Emilio said I was a bad example for the child because I did bad things in front of her, and he wanted to bring her up properly. I said he shouldn't have her because Anita had always been with me and he hardly ever gave me anything for her.

That court almost always favors the woman if the man doesn't have much proof against her. If the woman is suspected of having a lover, the husband has to bring in a photograph of them together if he wants to do anything to her because the man's word alone isn't worth anything.

They began investigating. They investigated my life and his, and that woman's, too. They found out that Emilio hardly contributed anything to the child's care, that I was washing and ironing for her all the time, and that Emilio's other woman had been in the gay life.

Before the trial I went to Cristo Street to a spiritist who works with evil, and she prepared a spell for me. She took a lizard and opened it up in the middle and handed it to me. She said, "Throw away this lizard in the courtroom, and when the trial begins, say the prayer of the Holy Just Judge. That will be ten dollars." I paid her five, and I still owe her five.

The trial was going to take place on a Tuesday, but Emilio came the day before and turned the baby over to me. His woman was afraid he was going to be awarded the baby, and she had fed Anita something that gave her diarrhea. Anita had dirtied her bed and the woman refused to clean the baby, so Emilio beat her. She told him he was taking advantage of her, sleeping at my house whenever he felt like and leaving her to take care of the baby. She said to him, "Make up your mind. Choose between Cruz and me. I can't go on like this any more."

So that Monday morning Emilio came to my house with the baby all dirty and smeared with shit. He handed her to me and said, "Take the baby. You can keep her." I dressed the baby, wrapped her dirty *panties* in a bag and went to Family Relations that same day. I asked to see the judge and showed the *panties* to him.

"You didn't steal her away from him, did you?" he asked and immediately sent for Emilio. When Emilio came he said he had turned the baby over to me of his own free will. The judge told me that he had intended to let me have the child anyway and that he shouldn't take her away from me any more. Then he closed the case.

After that Alejandro and I were happy together and everything went well for us. He found me a larger room than the one I have now. One day I got sick and Alejandro stayed home from work and gave me medicine and massages. He cooked for me and washed the dishes, emptied my chamber pot and cleaned the house. He gave Anita a purge because I told him she had worms. He bathed her and cleaned up the worms, threw them in the toilet and then cleaned the toilet. He did everything the child's own father wouldn't do.

Alejandro said to me, "If we both get divorced, I'll marry you and recognize your new baby."

"How can you recognize the child if it's not yours?" I asked.

"Just as a favor. Supposing it were mine, I would recognize it. I would look after it always, even if your conscience says it isn't mine."

"Of course it's not yours. It's Emilio's."

Well, the month of December passed. For Christmas, Alejandro bought me a china closet and a whole bunch of other things. We were getting along fine and spent Christmas Eve at home. Emilio kept going back and forth, drinking, in front of the house to see if he could catch me outside. But Alejandro and I spent the time inside eating suckling pig, cakes and blood sausage that he had brought.

On New Year's Day Alejandro and I were asleep when there was a knock on the door. "Don't open," he said. "This is the end of the year and they might throw an evil powder at you or try to cut your face and there are no police around, so God knows." Later, when I was making the baby's bed, Alejandro picked me up in his arms and kissed me. While I was up in the air I glanced out the window, and there was Emilio, looking in. He made a sign as if to say, "Don't worry, I'll get you yet." I turned cold but all I said to Alejandro was, "Put me down. I want to finish making the bed."

I made dinner in the afternoon and after that we sat on the stairs playing with the baby. Alejandro kissed me, and Anita began to cry. At that moment Emilio passed by and said, "Look at those two dirty things." Alejandro didn't hear him and I paid no attention. Then Alejandro went out with some friends of his. He said, "I'll be right back. Wait for me here."

I finished straightening up the house, bathed and sat down with the baby in the entryway. She had gone down the stairs and fallen and cut herself. I was kissing her when suddenly I saw Emilio coming up the stairs. I went back inside and tried to shut the door but he pushed his way in and said, "Do you know why I'm here?"

"Why?"

He pulled out a pistol, put it to my temple and said, "If you don't take good care of that baby for me, I'll kill you!"

"Why do you say that?"

"Because I'm telling you!"

"All right, what more do you want me to do for her? You don't give me anything for her. I'm the one who has to take care of her, and she can't live on air." He hit me and I fell. I cried because I was frightened. I knew the pistol was loaded. I picked up a bottle and threw it at him and he left.

Emilio had bought the gun for twenty-five dollars and kept it under his pillow. Once I was going to kill him with it. He was asleep and I lifted the pillow. But when I had the gun pointed at him, he opened his eyes and punched me, and the bullet went in another direction.

When Alejandro came home and saw that my eyes and face were red, he asked what had happened. I told him I had been peeling onions. We were planning to take the baby and go to the movies, and Alejandro said, "I'm going out for a beer, then I'll come and get you," and he went over to Bonilla's for a beer. Later I looked out of the window and saw that Emilio was following Alejandro home.

I called out, "Alejandro, watch out!" As I said that, Emilio knocked him on the head with the butt of the revolver and they started to fight. I ran and got a policeman. The cop already knew Emilio and the way he mistreated me, and he said, "Is that fellow still bothering you? Let's take a look."

But when Emilio saw the cop, he ran off with the pistol in his hand. I said to the officer, "Look, I know where he lives," and I took him there but Emilio wasn't home. He had disappeared.

The next day they arrested Emilio and locked him up. I had pressed charges against him. Emilio said to the policemen, "She knows better than that, she wouldn't dare press charges!" The officer said, "Yes, you're under arrest." Emilio's family got him out on two hundred dollars' bail. They said to me, "What are you thinking of doing with this boy?"

"I think the same as he thought when he attacked Alejandro," I said. "Nobody is an angel as far as I'm concerned."

The judge asked me, "What were the facts, señora?" I told him and he said, "Now, did he touch you?"

"Yes, he touched me."

"Very well. Assault with criminal intent, carrying weapons, possession of an unlicensed weapon."

They fined him two hundred dollars and the lawyer took another one hundred for getting him out. In all, it cost him seven hundred dollars.

I don't know why, but after that Alejandro began to get annoyed. He said Emilio was going to keep the fight going and he wanted to leave. I told him I had no magnet to hold him with, and if he wanted to go, he could. I wasn't going to kill myself for him. I loved him, but he began saying things like "That guy is bothering me, I'm leaving." Or "Look, there goes your *macho*." Finally I got sore and I said, "If you want to leave, go ahead. I'm fed up with you." Then he joined the *Army,* but he visited me every day and we slept together at night. The *base* was near by.

Alejandro bought me a new bed because I like to have two, one for me and whoever comes over, and a separate one for the little girl. Alejandro said, "God knows how you can give birth in that little bed. I'm going to get you a new one so that you can have that baby right."

I went to all the furniture stores but as soon as I mentioned Alejandro's name, they refused to give me credit. So I spoke to my *mamá,* who had just got back from Philadelphia, and she went with me to a furniture store where she had credit and they gave him the bed. My *mamá* signed that he was a good boy and always paid up.

When he brought the bed Alejandro said, "This is for you, but I want you to know one thing, if I catch you with another man in it, I'll burn you!"

Then Emilio began coming into the house without Alejandro's permission, banging on the door and saying foul things. Alejandro isn't a fighter, so he got scared. He was kind of a jerk, because when a man feels he's a man, he'll stick his neck out for a woman. Alejandro doesn't like rows, but that Negro Emilio doesn't give a damn for anything. He's like the dog in the manger—if he can't eat, nobody else will. He told me he wouldn't let me live in peace with any man.

So Alejandro went to live with Gladys, a girl friend of mine. And I trusted my friends! This girl friend Gladys used to come to my house all the time and when she was sick I would take care of her. I even washed her *panties* when they were full of blood from her period. I gave her food, cleaned her house and lent her money. She would wear my clothes and leave me without anything to put on. Alejandro lent her money too.

She used to be in the life and has had a lot of men. She took drugs, too. She would ask me to hold the cloth while she injected herself and I watched. The police were after her but they never caught her. She was living with a boy they called El Flaco, who was an addict too. They took the drug at the same time and they would get into tremendous battles. Nobody could sleep around there.

I was lying down one day looking up at the ceiling and thinking, because Alejandro hadn't been home to sleep for three nights. He came around during the day but not at night. Suddenly it came to my mind that Alejandro went for Gladys and I said to myself, "My God! It's not possible!"

A few days went by and Alejandro didn't come to the house at all. I went over to *el bar* to look for him and there he was, alone.

"I want you to know that if I catch you with another woman I'll cut you up," I told him.

He laughed and said, "Beat it. I'll come to the house." But he didn't show up until nine o'clock at night. "Here, take this," he said, "and go pay the store and the rent," and he handed me a twenty-dollar bill. I hurried off to pay the store, as I always do the minute I have money. While I was there, my *mamá* came in and said, "I saw Alejandro taking all of his clothes out of your house."

"Alejandro?" I said, and I went to Gladys' house. It was as if something made me go there. "Is my *mamá* here, Gladys?" I asked. She said she wasn't. She shut the door of *el chiforovi** and just stood there. I stared at her for a while and then left for home. Later a friend of mine came and told me Alejandro and Gladys were in *el bar* dancing. I put on a pair of slippers and ran. Sure enough, I found them there. I grabbed Gladys by the hair and slapped her. People were saying, "She sure is strong, that little thing, lame leg and all!" When Gladys tried to grab me by the hair Alejandro held her back. Then he took me by the arm, pushed me and said, "You take a walk out of here." When he pushed me I picked up a bottle from the counter, broke it and went

* The wardrobe.

after Gladys to cut her face. He tried to catch hold of my arm and got what
was intended for her. I sliced him from wrist to elbow. "Piece of filth, don't
ever talk to me again," I said.

"I'm not going to live with you any more," he said.

"You can say that again! You can have her. I'm going to live with
Emilio, and this very night I'm going to sleep with him. Just think! Another
man will be sleeping in your sweat in my bed!"

Emilio already knew what was up, and was hanging around. So just for
the hell of it I said to him, "Hey, *señor,* come over here. What do you say we
sleep together tonight?"

"*Ay,* I'll be blessed! That's for me!" Emilio said.

I pay no attention to Gladys. She wants to fight with me, but why? I
haven't done anything to her. She took that boy and I didn't even try to get a
knife into her. When I go by her house she slams the door in my face, and
when she walks by mine she says foul things.

One day I said to her, "Stop putting your knife into me, because I haven't
done anything to you. You took that man away and what has it got you? You
have to hustle for him because he won't work for you. When he was with me,
he worked. Now if you want to fight with me, wait until I give birth. I'll look
for you when my forty days are up."

I went to see *doña* Rita and she told me Gladys had worked a spell on
Alejandro to make him go with her. *Doña* Rita said the spell would keep me
from being happy with any man. This spell had been thrown into the sea, and
to get rid of it I'd have to stay on the beach all night. I haven't done it yet
because I haven't had time. I would have to begin at seven in the evening and
stay until seven the next morning.

Emilio wanted me to live with him again but I refused because he had
another woman. I slept with him once in a while, when he forced me, but I like
things legal. He said that even if he had a hundred women, he would still go on
with me. But I asked him, "If you don't give me money, why do you come
around?"

"Because you're my wife. Before anybody else can enjoy you, I have to
get finished with you."

One day he said to me, "I'm going to bring my clothes."

"Not here you won't," I told him, and we began arguing. Then he said, "I
can't understand this woman. She's nice to me one day and fights me the
next."

There I was, eight months pregnant and all alone with my little girl. I
decided to bring Catín to my house because Arturo wasn't taking care of her.
He brought women into the house, and at her age, eight years old, Catín used
to fight with them. Just imagine! She would take a stick and drive them out.
Arturo likes women and he made passes at me too. I consider that a nasty

thing, because brothers and sisters-in-law should treat each other like blood relatives. As my sister's former husband, Arturo should have respect for me. I never let him touch me.

I said to Catín, "You go around like a beggar, all scabby with lice and sores and with your feet rotted. You're always causing trouble, and your *mamá* doesn't send you anything, but I'm going to straighten you out." I took her to the hospital and they cured her of the sores and we got rid of the lice. Then I put her in school. Arturo didn't give me anything toward her support. Arturo is stingy, and sometimes even when he has money and you need it, he won't give you any. When I got used to Catín, I loved her even more than Anita because I was giving my life for her, fighting with people over her, and once in a while even hitting Anita on account of her.

Very soon my *mamá* came to live with me too, because she broke up with Héctor. She was going with that boy Junior and we didn't know anything about it. My *mamá* can't live happily with one man, maybe because she's just hot in her old age. She has always been on the crazy side. When I heard that Fernanda was putting the horns on Héctor I didn't believe it until I saw it with my own eyes. The boy was eighteen and my *mamá* was forty. My *mamá* had known him since he was a child and she used to wash his diapers. I saw him growing up, because he lived across the street from us.

I wouldn't let Junior come to my house, because I'm very fond of Héctor and I didn't want him to have anything against me. After Fernanda left him Héctor would go around picking fights, but that was just to make her come back to him. To me Héctor has behaved well. He never said a bad word and he never made a pass at me. He was always respectful. To this day, I can ask him for help for anybody and he'll give it. The only thing he doesn't like is for me to have a man in the house. Then he won't give me money or anything. That's why he doesn't help Felícita, because she likes to have lots of men.

My stepfather likes fags. He isn't a fag himself but he is a *bubarrón,* that is, he likes men better than women. That was the cause of many fights between him and my *mamá*. Sometimes I'd feel sorry for him. He would come home with his hands stinking of shit. It seems that when he goes with fags he doesn't wash his hands well. I would pour lemon juice on them or bay rum and say, "Go on, get out of here." When he's drunk he won't give money to a woman, but he will to another man. When he's sober he won't even speak to a fag.

A week after my *mamá* came to stay with me, Felícita showed up with her five children. I saw this car full of lovely children and I wondered whose they could be. When I saw it was Felícita, I asked her what was wrong.

"Nothing, I just came from Salinas for a visit to see you and Nanda." Then she told me that Edmundo was beating her and that she wanted to come and live with me.

"As my sister you are welcome, but think it over." Felícita didn't like it in Salinas because she had never lived in the country and she said she wasn't a farmer. She let Edmundo think she was just going to visit her *mamá,* but she told me that she wanted to leave him.

My *mamá* told her that if she didn't love him deep in her heart, nobody was forcing her and she should do what she liked. I said to Nanda, "You're our *mamá,* but instead of being a good example for us you're a bad one. Here you are telling Fela she should leave her husband when you know she has five children, three of whom aren't his, and still he is bringing them up. How many men would do that?" *Mamá* didn't say anything but made signs behind my back that I was crazy. I went out and they stayed there chattering. I was angry because hardly anybody respected me, not even my *mamá* or my sister. They come into my house, take the iron and start using it without even saying, "I'm going to iron."

That same night Felícita said to me, "Crucita, I'm going to town."

"Let it be as God wills, but I hope you can hold out with that hot pussy of yours."

At about ten o'clock that night she came back with a man by the name of Rosario, the two of them slobbering all over each other. I said, "Lord have mercy! Look who's here! Look at that dirty whore! With her husband in Salinas, and look what she's doing!"

"Ay, you're always criticizing me and you are a big whore yourself."

"All right, if I'm a whore it's because I've followed the example of all of you. But I don't do the things you do. I may be a demon, but if I do it, it's out of need. You do it just to see the juice run." She burst out laughing. She was good and drunk.

I went on, "I wouldn't dare bring a man into my sister's or my *mamá's* house or make love in front of my *mamá.* And I wouldn't leave my children alone while I went out or bring men into the house, because that would set my daughter a bad example."

Felícita finally said, "All right, all right, forget it. I'm going out but I'll be right back."

At three in the morning I got up and there was Felícita, sleeping with that man on the floor, she in *panties* and he in shorts. Three of her children were sleeping on the cot, one was in the big bed with me and my *mamá,* and the other was on the floor. I said, "Now, what kind of a shameless thing is this? The mistress of the house doesn't bring men in, but the visitor does. Why don't you go down to the beach where you don't have to pay?" Felícita just laughed. I told Rosario not to do such a thing again, because if people saw Felícita bring men in, they'd think the men were for me and that would look very bad. So the fellow left.

A week later I got up at about eleven-thirty at night and there were Nanda and Junior on the floor. "How do you like this!" I said. "My house is getting to be a regular little hotel. *Mamá,* why do you have to bring a man into my house?"

"*Ay,*" she said, "the thing is, he was tired."

"Very tired! You in *panties,* and him practically with his balls hanging out!"

"*Ay,* stop criticizing. It doesn't mean a thing."

"That's what you say. I guess you old women have the hottest pants in La Esmeralda."

Junior saw I was really angry and put his trousers on.

I said to him, "Piece of trash, you're taking advantage of my not having a man around, but I'll show you I can defend my house. Let me catch you here again and I'll land on you with a bat."

"All right, Cruz. I won't do it again."

"I feel sorry for you if you do. Now, I'm going to tell your *mamá* and your *papá* and everybody else."

"Look, Crucita, you don't want to give your mother a bad name."

"She's an old hot ass. That woman is forty and she ought to control that pussy of hers."

He said, "But I love her."

"I don't want any romances in my house. Go down to the beach."

After that he and my *mamá* went to the beach. Down there they would get under a house, and Junior's stepbrother Marcelo would say, "The pigs are in the pen!" It embarrassed me. I said to my *mamá,* "*Ave María!* The things people say about you!" Her answer was, "I've got to live some way."

Nanda was angry with me for a long time.

Junior's mother said a lot of things against my mother, and she was right because Nanda is too old for that boy. My sister and I used to swap comics with him. That's why we didn't want her to go with him. Besides, I never got along with that *teenager.*

Soon after that, Felícita's husband Edmundo went to New York, saying he was going to divorce her and marry another woman. Felícita was left alone with five children. She went into the life and has been hustling ever since. It's the same story with my eldest sister, Soledad. She has four children and nobody to give her a helping hand. She had to pay twelve dollars' rent and couldn't work during the day because she had no one to take care of the children. My *mamá* didn't want to take care of them. She has always been very distant from us, and my sister went into the life out of necessity.

I wish I had had more brothers, because with men around we might have been kept busy and not gone out with other boys. And God knows, there would have been more of a feeling of shame in the house. The male can control the woman and that way we wouldn't have felt so alone.

·　·　·　·

I gave birth to my son, Chuito, in May, though the doctors had set April 5 as the date. Emilio said to me, "You will give birth in May." Then when April was gone, he said, "You have five more days before you give birth." Five days later, on a Sunday I felt like going down to the beach to bathe and so I did. I came home, washed the floor, straightened up the house, washed my *panties* and ironed. I was up almost until dawn. My *mamá* said, "Watch out. I see you're not being very careful."

"You know I behave the way I feel, like dogs do," I answered.

The next day I said to Catín, "Go get me an *Alkacerzer*. I have a stomach ache." Then in the afternoon a kind of white slime began coming out of me. I said to Catín, "Would you like any of this meringue?"

"I'm going to tell Nanda that you're taking the cream from the baby," she said. Then she called out, "Nanda, there's cream coming from inside Cruz."

Fernanda came running to the house. "You aren't going into labor, are you?"

"No, not me. It's a lie," I said, because I was afraid she'd take me to the hospital.

So I spoke to Felícita aside. "Fela, I feel bad. Give me an enema." So she gave me one on the sly.

A neighbor by the name of Yolanda gave me a plate of rice and beans which I ate between pains. For a while I held on tight to Catín. I kept saying to her, "*Ay,* come over here, you little devil, come over here." I just wanted to lean on her, but then I said she could go out and play. When Felícita came around again, I tore her dress in my pain. "Squeeze me tight, tight," Felícita said. Then Fernanda went out drinking and Felícita left for my *papá*'s house, where she was visiting.

Later on my *mamá* came back half drunk and took me to the hospital. "If you don't take care of her I'll make plenty of trouble," she told the doctor. After he examined me he said, "She isn't ready yet. Take her home." But the pains kept getting stronger all Tuesday.

At about seven o'clock in the evening I went out to the entryway, where my *mamá* was arguing with Junior. I said, "Nanda, send for Minerva. I'm feeling very bad."

"Minerva isn't talking to you and she won't come," Fernanda said.

"All right," I said and went back into the house. I lay down on the bed and began to cry. Fernanda sent for *doña* Juli, who put the washboard under me and examined me thoroughly. "The baby is doing all right," she said. Then she called the midwife.

While the midwife was examining me Anita took off her *panties,* lay down in the bed and began saying the same things I was. "Oh, my God! How it hurts! *Ay, papá! Ay, mamá!*" Instead of taking care of me, the midwife stopped to watch Anita. When my pains came every three minutes the midwife took me to the hospital. I began vomiting there, so I prayed to the Sacred

Heart. "Jesus, get me out of this and don't let anything happen to me. If God wills, let me have a son and I'll name him after you."

I had the baby and the doctor stitched me up. The next day, Wednesday, I just signed out and at nine-thirty I was back home. When Alejandro heard I had given birth he sent me ten dollars by a neighbor, but I wouldn't accept it.

Cruz

Living Alone

AFTER THE BABY was born I lived alone with Catín. Felícita got a place of her own and my *mamá* and Junior finally moved to a room in Cataño. I was getting help from the Mothers' Aid and I asked for help also from *el Welfare*. They said they would give me groceries. Every month I got eight packages of rice, two two-pound cans of lard, a big five-pound cheese and three cans of spiced ham. My husband was supposed to send me ten dollars every week for the girl and five dollars for the boy. At first he sent only ten dollars every two weeks and later sometimes two months went by without him sending anything.

I had gotten on *welfare* because my brother had been their case when he was little. His case was still in the files and one day they came to investigate. My *mamá* told them he was a man already and was married. They asked her if there wasn't somebody else in the family who needed help and they picked me because I had no husband. They investigated me and gave me nine and a half dollars a month. This was before Chuito was born. I was just seventeen. After Chuito came they increased it to eleven dollars a month and gave me the groceries besides.

One day there was a big fire in La Esmeralda and I was afraid it was going to reach my house. I went a little crazy and handed Chuito over to Emilio's aunt Minerva, even though I didn't want her to see the baby because everybody was saying how ugly he was. Minerva undressed him and all of them there began to laugh. I said, "Why don't you laugh at your own whoring mothers who bore you instead of making fun of my little boy?"

"No," she said, "we're laughing because he has skinny balls just like his *papá*. If that dirty Negro says this child isn't his, I wouldn't hesitate to scald him with hot water. Just look at him, he has Emilio's face and everything."

But Emilio wouldn't recognize his son. I had stopped loving Emilio from the time I was pregnant with Chuito, when he said my big belly wasn't his and he called me a whore. When he wanted me to get rid of the baby, I began to hate him. I tell you, he nearly made me vomit. Then all the love I had had for him went to the children.

Emilio's the kind of man who, when you tell him no, says yes. I stopped seeing him but he kept on bothering me. He would come to the house and stretch out on the bed and say, "I came to see my children." I would pick myself up and sit down outside until he left. Sometimes he would fall asleep, just to plague me, and so I would pour water on him to make him get up and leave.

But later, even though he didn't give me money for the children, sometimes I'd feel sorry for him because he'd come and tell me his problems. If he has a fight with his new wife he comes and says, "I came to get over my anger. I've just beaten up that woman and kicked her out of the house. She's a good girl but she goes in and out as she pleases. I'm a *macho* and I demand respect. I'm not going to let any other woman make a fool of me the way you did."

Once he asked me for some coffee and after a while he said, "What do you think? Should I have my car fixed? The motor doesn't work."

"Well, it's your money, not mine. You're the one who earns it."

That made him thoughtful and he said, "I'm going to get it fixed so I can be a tourist guide. Then I'll send some money to *mami* and get myself a few things I need."

"And how about the children? Aren't you forgetting them?"

"No, no, they always come first."

Caridad, my neighbor, had told me that Emilio said to her, "Cruz is a mess, that game-legged little bitch." So once I said to him, "When did you realize that I'm lame? Did you just notice it now, after I had these two children of yours? I was lame when I was a *señorita* too."

"Ah, I never said anything like that."

"Yes, you did."

"And if I did, so what?"

"One thing I swear to you and I swear it by the saint that I love most, the day you come back here again, I'm going to throw the kerosene bottle at you and mark your face for the rest of your life. I never want to see you because you've made me out worse than a whore and you've ruined my good name."

He kept looking into my face until finally he said, "How can you hate me when you love me so much?"

"Look," I told him, "if I were a millionaire and you asked me for a quarter, I wouldn't give it to you. You know why? Because I want to see you dead."

He just laughed and said, "All right, it's all finished." Finally he was tired of so much gabbing, and after tearing off the buttons on my blouse, he left.

But he came around the other day and said he was going to sleep at my house. I spoke to him frankly. "You think that if you make me pregnant again you're going to change my feelings? You'd go around saying that one wasn't yours either. That's what you did with both Anita and the second one. And now you want to give me a third one. I'd have to eat it!"

"Ah, you are just trying to make trouble."

"You're a big fake, boasting about all your women. Take a look at that hide of yours and see what you really are. With your color you ought to have a little spark of shame."

The walls in my room are just bare boards and a lot of them are broken, so my neighbors could hear everything we said and did. More reason for Emilio not to come. You can't keep a secret in that place. When my next-door neighbor Caridad has relations with her husband you can hear her moans and the creaking of the bed. It's the same up above. Then in the morning I'll say to Caridad, "Seems like you were stretched out like God on the cross last night."

"*Ay,* Crucita," she says, "you weren't watching?"

"No, not watching, listening. You were howling like a cat in heat."

"Oh, my Lord, I'm dying to move out of that room. You can hear everything."

"That's not the half of it."

"Well, the one with the hot pants is you because you're not doing it. Go get yourself someone too."

I hear everything they do. When he says to her, "*Mamacita,* let's knock off a piece," I say to myself, "A piece from where, in front or back?" Or he'll say to her, "*Mamacita,* give me a little piece of cunt," and I'll think, "With salt or sugar?"

Once when they were doing it I went outside and called, "Let me know every time you come so I can keep a record."

She said, "Oh, my God, Crucita, you know everything that goes on in a person's life. You have the ears of a consumptive. I don't like that. It embarrasses me."

"You didn't care when you used to bounce around on the beach, but now that you sleep on a *box spring* and *matre* you've gotten very refined."

Once they were doing it on the roof at about nine-thirty. I went outside and said, "My, how quiet it is. I wonder if anybody could have died." A minute later I heard a loud moan and called out, "Caridad! Have you got a toothache?"

"Come on, Crucita, what do you want from me?"

"What's wrong, my girl? You can tell me."

"Nothing. I'm fucking with Johnny and you resent it. You're jealous because you haven't any for yourself."

I went up on the roof and said, "Let me see how you do it." The fresh thing lifted up the sheet and I peeped. Anita likes to peep too.

Then I said, "Johnny, get up so I can see how long it is."

"No, Crucita, no. I have respect for you."

"How do you like that?" Caridad said. "She even takes my husband's measurements."

The next day while I was in the toilet rinsing off my pussy with water, they both sneaked in and peered at me. Suddenly, while I was peeing, Johnny said, "For goodness' sake, just look! Isn't that the reddest ass you ever saw?"

I jumped a foot high and tried to hide but a cockroach fell on me and I ran out naked into my room. Johnny laughed and laughed. I said, "Say, Caridad, aren't you embarrassed for your husband to see me naked?"

"No," she answered, "I trust you like a sister."

Later on that day Anita had been peeping through a knothole and called to me, *"Mami!"*

"What do you want?"

"Over there. Cunt and *bicho.*"

"You don't say!" I figured she must mean Johnny was on top of Caridad. I went to peep too. But Johnny had Caridad in such a position that I couldn't tell whether he was really giving it to her in the behind or not.

Later, when Caridad came by, I said, "Holy Mary, Caridad, are you taking it up the ass?"

"Me?"

"Yes, you. Do you think I don't know? I have a little birdie that guesses everything."

"Me? Look, drop that stuff."

"Yes, you. Anita, what does Caridad do?"

"Ah, Cari. Ah, cunt. Ah, ass."

Caridad looked at her and burst out laughing. "Where there's smoke, there's fire," I said.

Guisín lives upstairs. I don't know her husband's name because I've never spoken to him. Well, one night at about twelve o'clock I heard the bed rocking and creaking, and I listened. It was so quiet I could hear absolutely every sound. I heard her saying, *"Ay,* daddy! *Ay,* daddy!"

So I stuck my head out of the window and called, "Mommy, what's the matter with you?"

"Oh, you!" she answers. "You've gotten real dirty. Now that you're living there alone you don't want to miss a thing, and you spy on everybody through the cracks and through the ceiling."

Toward morning they began again. A glass fell on the floor and I went out and called, "Hey, now what? Are you using glasses and spoons? I have an old shoehorn down here I can lend you if you want, so he can get in easier." Her husband burst out laughing and we kept on talking that way, real rough.

One day I was home all alone, dressed in just my *panties,* when Emilio knocked on the door. I refused to open it and he threatened to break it down.

"Go ahead," I said, "but I'm not opening to you."

He gave two great tugs, the doorknob came off and he broke in. "Take those off," he said, pointing to my *panties.*

I said no and he said yes and I said no. Then he grabbed me and threw me on the bed and kissed me while I scratched and hit him. He laid me, but I didn't move with him. God is my witness, I didn't move. I would have given my life to have gotten him off of me. I was crying with fury afterward. Imagine how it is not to be able to defend yourself!

It seems as if God punished me, because I got pregnant. When my period didn't come I said to myself, "If I'm pregnant I don't know what I'm going to do!" But I knew how my eldest sister had gotten rid of some babies, so I drank rue with bicarbonate of soda and took two quinine pills. This made me menstruate, but I was in bed for two days. I would get up, do whatever I had to for the children and go back to bed.

If I had a chance I would be operated on. My sister Felícita did it, and for the kind of life she leads it's fine because it certainly didn't affect her pleasure. On the contrary, now she likes to have men on top of her all day long. But that wouldn't happen to me because it all depends on the person, right? I was alone for nearly a year and I didn't miss it.

Of the whole family I consider Felícita the best because she's my crying towel when I have problems. Besides, she's the most intelligent one in the family. Sometimes I'll say to her, "Felícita, this is what's happening to me," and she'll say, "Well, do such and such," and things turn out right.

Sometimes when I go out I say, "Felícita, take care of Anita for me," and I give her a dollar. When I get back I find the little girl nicely bathed and dressed, and when I ask her if she has eaten she says, "Yes, Fela fed me." And I am grateful to my sister for treating my daughter well while I'm away.

I love Felícita but she is vain. At times she seems to think more of her friends than she does of me. When I go to her house and they are there, she puts on a sour face. Then another time she'll say, "Imagine! I met the best-looking boy who's making love to me, but if you think you'd like him I'll introduce you to him." But she never does. She just goes on about the promises he made her.

Felícita dresses beautifully, and because I don't have the kind of clothes she has, sometimes she walks ahead of me when I go out with her, even though she invited me in the first place. How can I spend money on a dress if I don't even have food? If I have a dollar I'd rather eat with it and go on wearing what I have. Not Felícita. She wants nice clothes, so it's dresses for ten dollars or five or eight, and nothing for food. She prefers throwing away her money on luxuries, and if I talk about my being so poor, she makes a face and gets angry with me.

Felícita can be bad-tempered but she can also be gay and good. She's never the same. She'll behave well for a while, and then she'll act indifferent. We are always getting into arguments because she asks me to take care of her children so she can go fooling around. I'll say I can't because I have an infant of my own and I have to wash and iron for my *mamá*. Then she gets sore and won't talk to me for three or four days. Almost every night after she feeds her children and puts them to bed, she leaves to go to work, and I go to check on them even if it's late at night. Sometimes she'll say, "Crucita, take care of the children, I'll be right back," and at three in the morning the woman still hasn't shown up. I don't like that kind of thing. When a person gives me his word, I like him to keep it.

Sometimes I'll send dinner over for her children and she'll eat too. I can do it when *el Welfare* gives me a lot of rice and I've prepared plenty of food. But other times I don't have a thing, and neither does she! Sometimes she doesn't earn more than ten dollars all week. She almost always owes rent and hardly ever has money to feed her children. But when she has plenty of money she's not always ready to let loose of it if I ask her for some.

The other day I said, "Fela, I haven't a cent for breakfast, give me a quarter."

She answered, "Oh, for goodness' sake, when you see that a person has a few cents you're ready to jump at them as if a person is obligated to support you."

"You don't remember all the things I do for you," I said.

She said, "Here's half a dollar. Keep a quarter for malt beer for my kids and have one yourself." I bought a pint of milk and a quarter of a pound of codfish with the quarter. I made a meal for Nanda out of the fish and sent it to her so that she wouldn't keel over while she was ironing.

Sometimes Fela makes me angry because she comes home too tired to bathe her children or feed them. Other times I feel sorry for her because she gets home exhausted at five in the morning and then has to get up at six to give them breakfast and get them ready for school. So you see, I really consider her a good person. I consider any mother a great woman if she's willing to give her body to men for her children.

Now Felícita tells me she's thinking of marrying an American and going to the States with him. I hope to God he's a good boy. I keep telling her that she's not going to be happy with any man as long as her children are as bad as they are. Mundito talks dirty already. The twins are unbearable and so is Tany. The little baby Evita is the only one who's halfway decent. Not really though, because she has terrific temper tantrums.

I tell Felícita she should put her children in the nursery school. It's a school that takes care of children from eight in the morning until three in the afternoon and they teach them to read and to count. I have talked to them about taking in Anita, and they told me I would have to get her health record and her birth certificate. Felícita said she was going to send her children, but she never does a thing about it. She likes everything handed to her on a silver platter.

It was never Felícita's ambition to end up in the kind of life she has. She always said she was going to be an actress or a singer and she always hung around La Tribuna del Arte. She said that when she had children she would get somebody to take care of them for her. But she was never able to. She seems to have a curse on her.

Not long ago she made fifty dollars in one week and spent it all on luxuries. For herself she bought a dress for twelve dollars and a pair of shoes for seven, but all she got for the children were some little pants and undershirts and a few trinkets. And she won't pay me anything for taking care of her children. She just tells me to get a job because it's not her duty to support me. I tell her to stick her money up her ass and I go back home.

Soledad and her children came to La Esmeralda from the States for Christmas. She arrived at four in the morning. I was sound asleep when *doña* Lucelia woke me, saying, "Get up, your sister is here."

I went to Lucelia's house and kissed my sister and we talked until dawn. Then I said, "Come on back to my place with me and you'll see Catín."

Soledad walked into my house with an expression on her face that said, "What an awful way to live!" So I told her, "At least you're finding Catín well, compared to the condition you left her in. She's not living in a government apartment but it's better than nothing. At least she's alive and you can thank God for that."

"There you go, starting a fuss," she said. "And who is Nanda living with?"

"Who would it be? Junior, of course."

"For goodness' sake!"

"Come on. Stop putting on an act. You knew all about it."

"I'm going over to her house to bring her a present. Keep the baby here for me."

"Wait, I'll make you a cup of coffee." I went to Bonilla's and bought coffee and fixed it for her. Then she and Nanda went to Felícita's. I don't know what they discussed. The only thing Soledad said to me when she came back was, *"Ave María!* When I went looking for Fela in the bed, I couldn't find her. I thought it was a broomstick lying there."

I made more coffee and some breakfast, and we all ate. Then we went over to Nanda's, where we stayed until about nine o'clock. Soledad said to me, "I have to meet Ben. He's coming by boat. He works on a freighter."

"Who's this 'Ben'?"

"Benedicto."

"Ah, I see. I thought you were forgetting your Spanish."

Sometimes people come back from New York talking English, or what they think is English. They say *"Hi!"* and sound like they ate an American. Some of them really put it on thick. Most girls let some English words slip out the first few days, but Soledad came back no different from when she left.

Well, that same night she brought Nanda her present but I don't know what it was because she didn't show it to me. Soledad brought Felícita clothes, *un suit,* and three dresses for Evita. She brought me a little bottle of perfume and a lipstick, and that's all. And the dresses she bought for my daughter she put on her own little girl, Catín, and then later on she took them away. Oh, well! What can you do?

Soledad's husband didn't come that night. "Don't worry," I said. "The boat probably sank."

He appeared on Christmas Day. I had no money, so I went to the store and said to the girl, "Will you trust me for a few things? I have visitors at home and I want to give them a treat." I bought a pint each of anise rum, Superior, and Llave rum. We all drank and Benedicto got drunk. He's from Puerto de Tierra and they say that the people from there are nice but I didn't like him at all.

Soledad told me Benedicto was very good to her and gave her everything, and that he went off on trips and left her alone for a month or two at a time. I was sitting there listening when her little daughter said, *"Papá* hits *mamá* and makes her bleed." I have an idea that things haven't gone very well with her. She looked lighter-skinned and very thin to me. Also, she seemed much more refined and didn't act as if she felt at home. She objected to this and found fault with that and was particular about where she slept. She said, "Oh no, find me a white sheet."

"God knows what kind of flea trap she sleeps in," I thought to myself.

I heard that Soledad started taking drugs while she was in New York. A girl friend of hers, Zulma, told me she injected it into the sole of her foot. That made me very angry because I consider it a bad thing to harm yourself.

I didn't get along well with Soledad during this visit. She kept acting superior, as though she was looking down on me. Catín told me that while Soledad was here, she and Fernanda tore me apart. Fernanda said that she wasn't going to come to my house any more because I was Héctor's woman and because I was a troublemaker. When Soledad said, "You know, Cruz never changes, she *is* a troublemaker," I said to myself, "I have seven skins, one is my own and six are given to me by others."

One day I was sitting in the house with Soledad and we saw four little rats walking along in a line. Every few minutes we could see them file up and down the room. My sister looked and said, "Raising them, are you?"

"Yes, for New Year's Eve supper."

"*Ave María,* what a horrible thing!" she said.

It was awful. But I couldn't bring myself to kill them with the broom, nor could Soledad, so they walked right by us. I still think of that day sometimes. The rats kept going back and forth and I said to my sister, "Let them be. They're my family. Whoever kills them is an enemy of mine."

She said, "You pig, I hope they eat you up one of these days. Those rats are going to bite Anita or eat Chuito's penis. I'm not going to sleep here!"

I said, "The rats don't do anything to me. They know me by now. They like new meat, I guess." So even though I had a bed, Soledad went and slept with that old man, Cayetano, almost every night, and her children slept with me. Cayetano gave her about seventy dollars the day she left.

Lice, bedbugs and rats have always been a problem in my room. When I moved in here a year ago, the first thing I found were little baby rats in a hole. "Kill them!" my friend Genoveva said. "No, I can't do it, the poor little things look like children," and I left them there. The next day they were gone. I didn't kill them, they just disappeared. I cleaned up the house, and about a month later they were going back and forth through the room from one hole to another, with me just looking at them.

When Alejandro was here, more rats came because there was a hen with eggs under the house. A rat had given birth and had eaten some of the chicks. The owner took the hen and twenty-nine chicks out of there because there were baby rats underneath the hen too. The man threw them out but a week later they came back and were all over the place, even getting into the pan with the baby's milk and eating up whatever I left around.

One Sunday my *mamá* said, "Let's buy a rat trap and see if we can't get rid of some of them." Well, we tried it and that day between us and the next-door neighbor we caught twenty-nine little rats. After a while more came. Anita used to chase them across the room to see if she could catch them, and the boys who came to the house would say, "Look, look, a rat!"

I would tell them, "Let it be, it's one of the family. They keep me company, now that I'm all by myself. I'm raising them for soup."

So I left them alone, but before I knew it, there were great big rats here. They went back and forth, but as they never bit one of the children, I didn't pay special attention. One Sunday I said to Catín, who had just eaten a breaded cutlet, "Catín, you'd better go bathe or the rats will eat you up." Then I forgot about it and she lay down. Later I took a bath and went to bed. About midnight Catín screamed, "*Ay, ay, ay,* it bit me!" The first thing that came to my mind was that it was a snake or a scorpion. "What bit you?" I asked and when I turned on the light she said, "Look, look!" and I could see a rat running away.

She had been bitten on the arm and I could see the little teeth marks. I squeezed out the blood and poured urine and bay rum on it. Then I said, "Catín, you'd better come into my bed with me. God knows whether you were bitten because the crib is dirty or you are dirty." I was wearing only *panties*, Chuito and Anita were naked, but Catín was wearing a jacket and pants. Well, that same night the rat came and bit her again on the other arm. It was about three in the morning when she yelled, *"Ay,* it bit me again, it bit me again." I sprinkled bay rum all over the bed and rubbed it on her and nothing else happened that night.

The next day I went to the church and told *la sister* that the girl had been bitten by a rat. She told me that if she didn't start running a fever, to leave her alone, and if she did, to take her to the hospital. Then I said to Catín, "You see? That's what happens when you don't bathe." She took a bath every day after that.

At the end of the year, a rat bit Anita on the lip. I squeezed it out for her and it dried up and she didn't get a fever or anything. A few days after that, I was sitting in a chair with my arm hanging down when a rat came and *pra!* it tried to take off my finger. It wanted human flesh. I yanked back my hand and the rat ran to a hole and disappeared.

Well, then I said to myself, "Those rats have to be finished off. I can't live like this. There are more rats than people." I bought a trap from the man next door and I fixed the bacon myself and put it in the trap. First I caught a real big one, then another, and another. Three in all that same night. But there were still more left.

The next morning I heard screams coming from Rosa María's room up above. I said, "Rosa, what's wrong?" Her little boy was crying and shaking his hand, with a rat hanging from it. "Kill it," I said, but he answered, "I can't. Its teeth are stuck in my finger." Finally he got it off by dragging it along the floor. Rosa María attended him but the next day the child had a fever which kept going up. The doctor said the boy was getting tetanus and had to go to the hospital.

The people upstairs leave piles of rotting clothes and cans of food and rice lying about, and the rats make nests there. If they don't get rid of that filth, the rats won't leave. I asked the landlord to cover the holes because the rats keep going in and out as if they were in a bus terminal. He said he didn't live here and I should do it myself. So I answered, "Supposing another rat bites my daughter and I bring you up before the OPA."

He answered, "All right, you take me to the OPA and out you go."

"I'm going to stay right here, and I'm going to take you before the OPA.

From now on I'm going to pay only six dollars for this room because it's not worth eight dollars without light and with the water going off half the time."

"Do whatever you want, but I'm not going there to kill mice."

There are lots of cockroaches in my room too. And now fleas have come in, I don't know from where, except probably from the rats themselves. There are also crickets and salamanders. These houses are hollow underneath, and below the floor there's a lot of old boards and filth and all kinds of garbage that has accumulated, and at night the animals come crawling up.

I've noticed that it's on Thursday nights that the rats give us the most trouble. Every other Thursday, before the social worker comes, I clean my house from top to bottom so there are no crumbs on the floor for the rats to eat and no dirty dishes for them to clean. I've learned that unless I leave something for them, the rats come closer and closer to us. When the house is clean we are in more danger of getting bitten.

Soledad criticized the way I lived from the moment she set foot in my house. She told everybody how badly off I was, so I said if she would give me the money I would move to a government-project apartment. Yet on New Year's Eve, when she and Felícita went out on a binge, they showed up at my house with two Americans. All of them were drunk and they began to raise hell and talk foul. I told them I didn't want that in my house, so they went to Felícita's. I went there too, but they began talking dirty and my *mamá* said nasty things to me, so I said I wasn't going to spend New Year's Eve with them. I went home without seeing the old year out with my *mamá* and the family. I guess I shouldn't have done it but I locked my door and cried.

The only one missing from the family gathering was my brother. It will soon be three years since he left for New York. I love him very much because he's the only male in the family. He sent me a Christmas card but I didn't have the money to send him one. I was sad that night because of Simplicio and also because I thought how cruel the father of my children was. He didn't even come to see them.

The next day Soledad left for New York. Ben had told her that he would be in New York on January 2 and he wanted her there on the same date. So she made a plane reservation for that day. Then she told me Ben had given her money for Catín's ticket and she was taking Catín with her. When she said that, a chill went through me. I knelt down and said, "My Lord, may I not suffer on account of the girl. May I not miss her." I prayed with such faith that it seems as if God heard me because I didn't even cry when Catín left.

I don't hold a grudge against Soledad for taking Catín, because after all, Soledad is her *mamá* and what could I do? I told Catín she had to go with her *mamá* because she was a very rude girl and liked to fight with people. She was so naughty that I was afraid I might have to kill her someday. So rather than give her a nasty beating, I preferred her *mamá* to take her. Another thing is that Catín is almost a *señorita,* and any day she'll fall in love and go off and be dishonored. They will take from her what they have to take and then Soledad will say it was my fault. That's too much of a responsibility. He who brings up another's child loses his bread and his dog and gets nothing but grief. But any time Catín wants to come back I'll take her, because she's like my own daughter.

I saw Soledad off on the plane. She said, "You've put up with a lot."

"You know something?" I said. "I weighed a hundred and five pounds when you came and now I weigh eighty-five. And it's your fault."

"But why? Is it a question of food?"

"No, it's the bad time you've been giving me. That's why I can't wait for you to leave." We said good-bye in the plane and I didn't cry, because her behavior had been too much. She'd go out and not come home until the next morning. I was afraid her husband might come and find out. She had told him she was going to stay at my house, and if he heard that she put the horns on him, he might blame me. And the longer she stayed, the worse it would be. So that's why saying good-bye to her was no problem. Anyway, that bitch hasn't written since she left and I don't want to know anything about her.

I don't ever want to live in New York again. I'm better off in my own country because I went to the States twice and suffered a lot. I have suffered in Puerto Rico, but not as much. To me La Esmeralda is wonderful, better than New York or any other place. For me it's home. When I arrived here from New York I felt happiness rise up in me again. I kept telling everybody that La Esmeralda was like a magnet that drew me back. It's the same for all the rest who live here. When I came back, La Esmeralda seemed prettier and gayer. And when my house is fixed up nicely, it's a proud place because I feel happy living in it. Sometimes I dream that I'm packing and going to New York. I'm in the plane and I say to the pilot, "Turn back, I left the children's dresses behind." I never get to New York.

The only trouble with La Esmeralda is that there aren't any good men here. *Don* Luis, a neighbor, is considered a good man, but he can be very disgusting. When he gets drinking he sells everything in the house, beats his wife and throws the children out of the house. And he is a good man! All the men in La Esmeralda are women chasers. There's old Cayetano, my neighbor. First he had Soledad, then Felícita, then *mamá,* and then he wanted me. My eldest sister would take whatever money she found in his pockets, and he let her keep it. My *mamá* got money from him too. He gets one pension from the *Army* and another from Social Security. He's about seventy, very old, and can't even walk. My sister says he can't get it up and he just licks cunts. That's all he likes to do.

He comes around all the time annoying me, but I don't really pay any attention to him. What for? I don't like to have anything to do with men that my sisters or my mother have had. It doesn't look right.

I've had rough times in my life and I don't trust any man any more. I've given up hope of finding a good man. I keep praying to God not to make me fall in love but to let me remain alone. Maybe my fate will change, but for the time being I don't want anybody. What would be the good of finding a man who would be happy with me? No man really is going to love another man's children. He just wouldn't treat them like his own. He'd beat them for no reason and I don't like to see my children abused. I figure that the best thing for me is to work and struggle alone for them.

I am able to get by, with the help of *el Welfare*. The first thing I do with the money is pay one-fifty to the girl who gives me electricity, and the eight dollars' rent. That leaves me one-fifty. Then I buy a pound of sugar for fifteen cents and a quarter of a pound of coffee for twenty-four cents. The rest doesn't last me even two days. I have to start scrounging around so I'll have something for the children when they ask for food.

There are bad days. Sometimes it gets to be midnight and I'm still up, just sitting there, hoping a quarter will turn up for the next day's breakfast. When I get it, I go to bed. If I don't get it, I have to buy food on credit. I owe quite a bit that way, some months more than ten dollars. But when Emilio sends me money, I pay the grocery store. For instance, the other day he sent ten dollars and I paid seven to the store and kept three. I still owe two dollars to *doña* Yolanda and two more to her mother. Then there's the two dollars I borrowed at forty cents' interest from Genoveva. I borrowed it when both children had an asthma attack and I had to take them to the hospital. So now I owe six-forty. That's all. I don't owe anybody else a cent.

I hardly earn anything now because I can't do as much laundry as I did. I work sometimes, but at other times I can't because I have this pain in my spine and I get dizzy and tired and I faint. When I come to, I'm lying on the floor. And I keep getting such bad headaches that sometimes I can't stand the pain. Ironing all the time as I do, the brain gets worn out. Sometimes I feel sick all over. It leaves me exhausted. The other day Felícita was in my house when I suddenly fell over. *"Ave María,* my legs can't hold me up any more," I said.

"What's the matter with you?"

"I don't know. I got dizzy."

"It's too much. You're on the go all the time and you don't sleep or eat enough." So she gave me some money and I sent out for a breaded cutlet which I shared with the baby. Sometimes I eat sugar or drink sugar water so as not to feel hungry. I suffer so much that I think if I was with Castro I would kill people just to see the blood run.

Sometimes I feel very depressed. The way my nature is, I don't have faith in my own self. I depend on the saints but I have so many holy pictures I don't know which one to turn to for help. I really believe in Saint Martha and Saint Raymond and in no others. Those are the two saints I have in my mind all the time, or nearly. I've always liked them because when I ask them for something with very deep faith, they grant it to me. It seems as though they hear me and then suddenly somebody turns up to pay me back some money he owes me!

Once I was hungry and owed the rent besides. In La Esmeralda, if you owe two months' rent a policeman comes and puts your things out on the street. So I decided to appeal to Saint Raymond. I knelt down and begged the saint to help me out, saying that I would be satisfied with any little charity just to get me out of the pinch. I said, "*Ay,* Saint Raymond, please help me get some clothes to wash or something so I don't have to be asking people for things." The very next day I was washing and ironing until two o'clock in the morning!

Last year turned out to be an expensive one for me. When it wasn't me who was sick, it was the children. Whenever I had the money saved up to buy a bed or something I needed, I'd have to spend it on them. I didn't buy anything for them for the Day of the Kings because I had no money. I spoke to the social worker and she brought me a doll, a very little one, and one of those plastic turtles, a set of four little bottles, and a little cake of soap. I didn't even want Anita to bring her box of grass to my *mamá*'s house because once when she was smaller and I took her there, Nanda wanted to know why the hell I did that. Now that the child is more grown up and calls Nanda, "Grandma," she sometimes sends for her. But people tell me that Nanda says she doesn't consider Anita to be family and that hurts me very much.

It would be nice if I could get a good job and have somebody look after my children while I work. That way I could buy a good house where I could keep them properly. I'd buy a bed and the things the children should have, and give them their meals on time so that they can get a good start and grow up to be worth something.

I want to raise my children differently from the way my mother raised me. I love Nanda because she's my mother, but sometimes I get to thinking of some of the things she's done to me and I hate her. She has been mean to me and has let me down when I needed her most. And my sisters too. I won't be like that to my children. I want them to be somebody in the future.

I want my children to have peace and happiness, and I wish that none of the things that happened to me should happen to them. They shouldn't get into fights, they should behave themselves and they shouldn't drink.

My son should be whatever he likes, a soldier or a doctor. The same with the little girl. I had no opportunity myself, so I would at least like it for my children. I'd like Anita to be a respectable young lady, with a respectful character, not to be a loud-mouth or a tramp, and to have good manners, which is what I lacked.

I'd like Anita to marry an older man so he can be a better example for her because from a young man she'll get only punches and kicks. An older man can keep her in line just by talking to her. I'd like to see her get married dressed all in white, with a long veil and a crown, and a very pretty dress. But

I'd like to have her near me so I would be there if anything went wrong. I'd get the best place for the wedding. It wouldn't matter if it were in La Esmeralda. And I'd fix up a nice house for her.

I'd like Chuito to get married too because I don't want him to do to any girl what I wouldn't like done to my daughter. I hope my son is not a woman chaser like his *papá* and doesn't beat women, because if he strikes a woman in front of me I'll smash him. He should know that he was born of a woman, not of a cow. Men who beat women are more like women than the women themselves!

My children have been the greatest pleasure of my life. I've always liked children, even from the time I was a *señorita*. Anita is a good daughter. She's very affectionate with me. When she goes out she gives me a kiss. When she goes to bed she'll say, "Your blessing, *mami*." And if someone gives her pennies she always gives me one, or if she buys chewing gum she shares it with me. Oh, she's very good. And sometimes she'll say, *"Mami,* if you give me your tit I'll give you mine."

But it makes me mad when Anita nurses, because she's kept it up for four years and I don't like that. I don't know when I'll wean her. She asked for the breast as soon as I got back from the hospital and she enjoyed it so much. If she had her way she'd suck all day long. I've been trying to wean her since her second birthday. First I put pepper on my nipples, but she wiped it off and went on nursing. Then my *mamá* told me to smear chicken shit on them. Anita cleaned it off with her sweater and went on sucking. After that I used the baby's shit. She cleaned some of it off with a piece of paper and went on sucking, shit and all. Even when I had labor pains and the midwife was examining me, Anita was nursing.

Anita and Chuito both have asthma. My son's asthma is a family condition, because I had it when I was little and I have two half brothers on my father's side and two nieces who have asthma. But Anita's asthma is not inherited, it comes from worms. Last month when she got an attack, a woman told me to buy a bottle of vermifuge and give it to her. I did this and the following day she was better.

I have to take Anita to the hospital every month for an injection, and the baby too. I get up at seven and we arrive there at about nine-thirty. The first time, I handed in my card and we waited. At eleven-thirty they still hadn't called me. I noticed that the secretary was putting the cards of her friends and *compadres* and relatives on top so they'd be called first. I let out a sharp whistle, the way I can do. "Hey, what's wrong with you?" I said. "Do you think I don't see you? You're changing the cards. I'm going to tell the supervisor."

"What's the name?"

"Chuito Pabón."

"All right. Go on in."

"Now that you've let me in, you can change all the cards you want. I just don't like having tricks played on me."

One day when the baby was about five months old, I noticed that he was coughing and seemed to have a fever. I figured it was probably nothing very serious, but early the next morning I took him to the dispensary. Anita came along too. At the dispensary the lady doctor said, "We'll take an X-ray." So they did and then she said, "We're going to send him to the Municipal Hospital."

"*Ay,* my mother!" I said. "With this little girl on my hands." But off I went to the Municipal with my boy.

The doctor there listened to his chest and said, "You'll have to leave him here." As I had never left a child of mine before, I got an attack of nerves and burst out crying. They gave me an injection to calm me down. They took him upstairs at five o'clock that afternoon.

"He has bronchitis, complicated with asthma," the doctor said, "but it's nothing serious. He'll be here for two or three days. Go home, and come back tonight if you want to."

"No, doctor, I won't leave here until my son is well." Then Chuito began screaming and I started to cry too.

A little while later I got a taxi and brought Anita back to La Esmeralda to *doña* Minerva. I said, "They kept the baby in the hospital. He wasn't asleep when I left so I'm going back and I won't leave until he stops crying. Put the little girl to bed for me and give her a malt beer." I gave Minerva a quarter and I went back to the hospital. It was one o'clock in the morning before Chuito went to sleep and I was able to leave.

The next day they wouldn't let me in until seven o'clock and they told me I could stay only until seven-thirty.

When the nurse's aide came, I helped her clean the baby's crib and bathe him. She said, "When the supervisor comes around, hide under the cabinet." So I did, and when the supervisor left I crawled out and stayed there as happy as could be until one or two in the morning, when Chuito went to sleep. Every time he cried I fed him the breast or else a bottle. I had brought a balloon and I got into the crib with him and we played with it. The doctors came in but just laughed to see the baby on one side of the crib and me on the other. One of the doctors said, "She's one of those mothers who really loves her children. That child over there has been here for a year and I still haven't seen its *papá* or *mamá.*"

The day after that, I stayed from twelve until four in the afternoon. Then I went home, bathed Anita, fed her, went back to the hospital at seven and stayed until twelve, taking care of Chuito and the baby that nobody visited. The next day I was late and when I got there Chuito was gone. "My God," I thought, "they've taken him to the operating room!" I began rushing around like crazy when my *mamá* came out of the bathroom with him. "Oh, my God, what a fright you just gave me," I said. After a little while the supervisor came in and said, "Look, you, little one, you can take that kid of yours home now. I'll be glad to get rid of the two of you." I was so happy that I left a borrowed umbrella behind and had to go back for it.

When I brought the baby home from the hospital, Minerva stopped talking to me because she said Chuito didn't look like Emilio any more and must be Alejandro's.

"No," I told her, "he's Emilio's and I didn't make him with my finger either."

Emilio tells everybody the boy isn't his and that hurts me. My conscience is clear because I am sure he's Emilio's. Supposing he weren't, then God should punish me because I'm putting Emilio under obligation to support him. If he weren't Emilio's, I would do anything and go anywhere and sacrifice myself to support him.

I've had many a falling-out with *doña* Minerva over her nephew. She sees only what I do to Emilio and not what he does to me. She's always mixed up in arguments and criticizes the whole world. The truth is she has a tongue as long as from Cataño to New York. I don't respect her, because she doesn't respect me. It's true she's older, yes, but she says she shits on my mother and she tells me a lot of other rude things right to my face. When I left Emilio she went around saying I was going to be a whore just like my mother.

Sometimes I think of all the things people have done to me, of the bad treatment and the meanness. People still make fun of my lameness, and when they do I go inside and lock the door.

The thing that has made me suffer most was having to leave my husband. But that's fate. I don't like being beaten. Not long ago he asked me whether I wouldn't come back to him, as he had left his woman. I refused, and told him I was better off alone. You see, I don't love him any more. I used to think he was handsome. I've always liked dark people. And I like people with a humble manner, the way he used to be. But now he's changed a lot. I have developed a real feeling of disgust for him. I would like to kill him to get him out of my life once and for all. Because of my suffering I have a heart that is as hard as concrete.

Recently Chuito had bronchitis again and I asked his *papá*'s family why he wasn't giving me any money. They didn't even answer me. I didn't have a single cent to buy any food either for breakfast or for dinner. Anita kept saying, "*Mamá,* I want rice with milk. I want soup." I just stood there looking at her. Then I went to Genoveva and she gave me a quarter. She told me, "There's a man at the bar who wants a woman."

I thought and I thought, and then I said to myself, "Well, let it be as God wills."

"After all these months?" Genoveva said.

"I need the money for food for tomorrow, Genoveva, but I don't want to leave the baby alone."

"It won't be more than three minutes. Don't worry, I'll keep an eye on the baby for you."

So I went with the man. First I got a sharp pain because it seemed I was closed up inside, and I started bleeding. "It's been a long time since I had relations," I said. "Go little by little."

"I'm being considerate of you because you do this for your children," he said. He didn't come but he gave me five dollars anyway and I went home. The next day the man saw me and said, "You left me with the urge."

"Better get rid of it," I answered. I was very embarrassed. I hadn't enjoyed being with him at all. I didn't feel anything because it's no good without love. I was more furious than ever with Emilio because if he had helped me I wouldn't have had to do it.

I haven't earned anything to speak of by hustling because I don't go often. I could use the money, but I'm afraid of having any more babies. The men are scared of me because they say I get pregnant right away. And men don't like women to be sticking things into themselves. I know, because a short time ago a man called Gerardo wanted me to go with him. My sister Felícita had some of those suppositories and I asked him if I could use one. He didn't want me to, so I said, "Nothing doing."

Everything makes me angry. I blame both my sister Felícita and my *papá* for not helping me. It's not my *mamá*'s fault because she always gives me a dollar or two when she's working. When I was pregnant, she went out hustling herself and gave me money. Instead of buying herself a pair of shoes, she gave me the five dollars. I would like to see somebody else do that. I have a lot to be thankful to her for.

If my *mamá* sacrificed herself for us, it was our duty not to follow her example. They say that those things are in the blood, but I don't believe that's so. She went into the life because she had to. If she had gone to work and hadn't been a prostitute, God knows whether or not we would have made the slip. I might have thought, "Well, *mamá* worked like a slave on our account and wouldn't look at any man. She refused to give in. We should follow her example and make our way up." In that case none of us would even have gotten married!

Sometimes I feel happy and sometimes I feel sad about the way I'm living now. I'm full of worry because I have to work so hard. I feel hard pressed because of the children and I'm almost always unhappy because I'm alone, with nobody who cares about me. I feel so sad at times that I turn on the radio and don't even hear it. I just stand there with my eyes wide open, thinking, and I seem to see bugs and scorpions in my mind. It is as if the scorpions were stinging me. Sometimes I dream of snakes and I can see them, too, in my mind.

I have so many hopes for the future that I know none of them will ever come true. If God would give me a winning number, the first thing I'd do would be to take sixty dollars for an operation to keep me from having any more babies. And another dream is to have a better house for my children so I can bring them up right and give them everything they need. And I wish I had a TV set. I've never in my life had one. When I do get one, I'll take such good care of it I won't allow it to touch the floor. And I'd like to have everything I need of my own so I wouldn't have to play up to anybody.

They say he who goes after a lot, gets little. But most of the time I'm satisfied because I have a shack for my kids and for myself, a place where I can live in peace, where there's nobody to beat me or to treat me badly, nobody to say, "Straighten up the house, wash the dishes, sweep." If I do those things, good. And if I don't, who cares? I don't have to take orders from anyone now. Even though the rats bite me and the bugs bother me, at least I usually feel calm, now that I'm alone. I don't think of tomorrow. I live anywhere I'm thrown and I always land on my feet. Usually when I'm in a tight spot, all I do is entrust myself to the Lord and the saints. When I really put my trust in them, things come out right.

Epilogue

—————

Cruz Moves to a Housing Project

—————

THE SOCIAL WORKER told me it would be a good idea to get the children out of La Esmeralda because there's so much delinquency there. Moving here to the housing project was practically her idea; she insisted and insisted. Finally one day she came to me and said, "Tomorrow you have to move to the *caserío* in Villa Hermosa." I didn't want to upset her because she's been good to me, so I said *O.K.*

You should have seen this place when I moved in. It was spilling over with garbage and smelling of shit, pure shit. Imagine, when the social worker opened the door that first day, a breeze happened to blow her way. She stepped back and said, "Wait, I can't go in. This is barbarous." I had to go outside with her. I tell you, the people who lived here before me were dirtier than the dirtiest pigs. When I moved out of my little room in La Esmeralda, I scrubbed it so clean you could have eaten off the floor. Whoever moved in could see that a decent person had lived there. And then I came here and found this pigsty, and the place looked so big I felt too little and weak to get it clean. So, fool that I am, instead of sending out for a mop and getting right down to work. I just stood in a corner and cried. I locked the door and stayed in all day, weeping. I cried floods.

And this place isn't like La Esmeralda, you know, where there's so much liveliness and noise and something is always going on. Here you never see any movement on the street, not one little domino or card game or anything. The place is dead. People act as if they're angry or in mourning. Either they don't know how to live or they're afraid to. And yet it's full of shameless good-for-nothings. It's true what the proverb says, "May God deliver me from quiet places; I can defend myself in the wild ones."

Everything was so strange to me when I first moved here that I was scared to death. I hated to go out because it's hard to find your way back to this place even if you know the address. The first couple of times I got lost and I didn't dare ask anybody the way for fear they would fall on me and beat me. If anyone knocked on my door I thought four times before deciding to open it. Then when I did, I took a knife along. But I'm not like that any more. I've made my decision: if someone wants to kill me, let him. I can't live shut in like that. And if anybody interferes with me it will be the worse for them. I have a couple of tricks up my sleeve and can really fuck things up for anybody when I want to.

After a few days I finally started cleaning up the place. I scrubbed the floors and put everything in order. I even painted the whole apartment, although I had to fight tooth and nail with the man in charge of the buildings in order to get the paint. That old man wanted to get something from me in return, but I wouldn't give it to him. I never have been attracted to old men.

The apartment is a good one. I have a living room, bedroom, kitchen, porch and my own private bathroom. That's something I never had in La Esmeralda. I clean it every morning and when the children use it I go and pull the chain right away.

I never had a kitchen sink in La Esmeralda either, and here I have a brand-new one. It's easy to wash the dishes in these double sinks because they're so wide and comfortable. The only trouble is the water, because sometimes it goes off, and the electricity too—three times since I've been here.

I still don't have an icebox or refrigerator, but the stove here is the first electric one I've ever had in my life. I didn't know how to light it the day I moved in. I tried everything I could think of, backward and forward. Luckily, the social worker came in and she turned it on for me, but even so I didn't learn and Nanda had to show me again that afternoon. She has worked for rich people so long that she knows all those things. I really miss my own little kerosene stove, but Nanda wanted it, so what could I do? She's my *mamá,* and if she hankered after a star I would climb up to Heaven to get it for her if I could.

The main advantage of the electric stove is that when I have a lot of work to do and it gets to be ten or eleven o'clock, I just turn on the stove and have lunch ready in no time. In La Esmeralda I had to wait for the kerosene to light up well before I could even start to cook. And this stove doesn't smoke and leave soot all over the place, either. Still, if the power fails again or is cut off because I don't pay my bill, the kids will just have to go hungry. I won't even be able to heat a cup of milk for them. In La Esmeralda, whenever I didn't have a quarter to buy a full gallon of kerosene, I got ten cents' worth. But who's going to sell you five or ten cents' worth of electricity?

I haven't seen any rats here, just one tiny little mouse. There's no lack of company anywhere, I guess; rats in La Esmeralda and lots of little cockroaches here.

This apartment is so big that I don't have to knock myself out keeping it in order. And there's plenty of room for my junk. I even have closets here, and lots of shelves. I have so many shelves and so few dishes that I have to put a dish here and a dish there just to keep each shelf from being completely empty. All the counters and things are no use at all to me, because I just cook a bit of oatmeal for the children and let them sit anywhere to eat it since I have no dishes with which to set a table. Half of my plates broke on the way from La Esmeralda. I guess they wanted to stay back there where they weren't so lonely.

Here even my saints cry! They look so sad. They think I am punishing them. This house is so big I had to separate the saints and hang them up in different places just to cover the empty walls. In La Esmeralda I kept them all together to form a little altar, and I lit candles for them. They helped me there but here I ask until I'm tired of asking and they don't help me at all. They are punishing me.

In La Esmeralda I never seemed to need as many things as here. I think it is because we all had about the same, so we didn't need any more. But here, when you go to other people's apartments and see all their things! It's not that I'm jealous. God forbid! I don't want anyone to have less than they have. It's only that I would like to have things of my own too.

What does bother me is the way people here come into my apartment and furnish the place with their mouths. They start saying, "Oh, here's where the set of furniture should go; you need a TV in that corner, and this one is just right for a record player." And so on. I bite my tongue to keep from swearing at them because, damn it, I have good taste too. I know a TV set would look fine in that corner, but if I don't have the money to buy one, how can I put it there? That's what I like about La Esmeralda—if people there could help someone, they did; if not, they kept their mouths shut.

I really would like a TV, though, because they don't have public sets here, the way they do in La Esmeralda. I filled in some blanks for that program, *Queen for a Day,* to see if I can get one as a gift. Even if you aren't chosen Queen, those people give you what you ask for. It was Fernanda's idea, and she's so lucky that maybe I will get it. If I do, then at least I could spend the holidays looking at TV. And the children might stay home instead of wandering around the neighborhood so much.

The traffic here really scares me. That's the main reason I don't like this place. Cars scud by like clouds in a high wind, and I'm telling you, I'm always afraid a car will hit the children. If something should happen to my little penguins I'd go mad, I swear I would. Here there is plenty of room to run around indoors, but my kids are little devils, and when I bring them in through the front door, they slip out again by climbing over the porch railing. Back in La Esmeralda, where our house was so small, they had to play out in the street whenever people came over, but there were no cars to worry about.

Maybe I was better off in La Esmeralda. You certainly have to pay for the comforts you have here! Listen, I'm jittery, really nervous, because if you fail to pay the rent even once here, the following month you're thrown out. I hardly ever got behind on my payments in La Esmeralda, but if I did, I knew that they wouldn't put me out on the street. It's true that my rent is only six-fifty a month here while I paid eight dollars in La Esmeralda, but there I didn't have a water bill and I paid only one-fifty a month for electricity. Here I have already had to pay three-fifty for electricity, and if I use more than the minimum they allow for water I'll have to pay for that too. And I do so much washing!

It's a fact that as long as I lived in La Esmeralda I could always scare up some money, but here I'm always broke. I've gone for as long as two days without eating here. I don't play the races any more. I can't afford to. And I can't sell *bolita* numbers here because several cops live in this *caserío* and the place is full of detectives. Only the other day I almost sold a number to one of them, but luckily I was warned in time. I don't want to be arrested for anything in the world, not because I'm scared of being in jail but because of the children.

Since I can't sell numbers here, I sell Avon cosmetics. I like the pretty sets of china they give away and I'm trying to sell a lot so that they'll give me one. But there's hardly any profit in it for me.

In La Esmeralda I could get an old man now and then to give me five dollars for sleeping with him. But here I haven't found anything like that at all. The truth is, if a man comes here and tries to strike up a conversation I usually slam the door in his face. So, well, I have this beautiful, clean apartment, but what good does it do me? Where am I to get money? I can't dig for it.

In La Esmeralda we used to buy things cheap from thieves. They stole from people who lived far away, in Santurce or Río Piedras, and then they came to La Esmeralda through one of the side entrances to sell. And who the hell is going to go looking for his things down there? Not a chance! You hardly ever saw a rich person in La Esmeralda. We didn't like them and we scared them off. But so far as I can tell, these dopes around here always steal from the *blanquitos,* the rich people, nearby. Suppose one of them took it into his head to take a look around here for his missing things? What then?

Since I've been living here I'm worse off than I have ever been before, because now I realize all the things I lack, and besides, there are so many rich people around, who always want everything for themselves. In La Esmeralda you can bum a nickel from anyone. But with these people, the more they have, the more they want. It's everything for themselves. If you ask them for work, they'll find something for you to do fast enough, but when it's time to pay, you'd think it hurt them to pull a dollar out of their pocket.

Listen, to get a few beans from some people who live in a house near here I had to help pick and shell them. People here are real hard and stingy. What's worse, they take advantage of you. The other day I ironed all day long for a woman and all I got for it was two dollars and my dinner. I felt like throwing the money in her face but I just calmly took it. At another lady's house near here I cooked, washed the dishes, even scrubbed the floor, and for all that she just gave me one of her old dresses, which I can't even wear because it's too big for me.

Right now, I don't have a cent. The lady next door lets me charge the food for breakfast at her husband's *kiosco,* the yellow one out there. She's become so fond of me, you can't imagine. Her husband won't sell on credit to anybody, but there's nothing impossible for the person who is really interested in helping you out. She trusts me, so she lets me write down what I take and I keep the account myself.

I buy most of my food at the Villa Hermosa Grocery. It's a long way from here and I have to walk it on foot every time I need something. It's a supermarket, so they don't give credit, but everything is cheaper there, much cheaper. A can of tomato sauce costs seven cents there and ten cents in La Esmeralda. Ten pounds of rice cost a dollar and a quarter in La Esmeralda and ninety-nine cents here. The small bottles of King Pine that cost fifteen cents each in La Esmeralda are two for a quarter here.

The minute Chuito landed in Villa Hermosa he started turning up his nose at everything he used to eat in La Esmeralda, even rice and beans. He must have smelled out the fact that this is a rich neighborhood. I don't know what to do with this little penguin of mine. It is harder to feed him than to buy the food. And he gets sick here more often because it's a cold place. What he needs is the sea air.

One day he was feeling fine and then during the night he was burning up with fever. I thought he was going to die. By two o'clock in the morning he couldn't talk any more and there I was, all alone, not knowing what to do. I looked at the saints and fell on my knees. "Oh, my God, oh, my saints, if you save my child I'll repay you with a Mass on my knees, holding my son in my arms. I'll have an evangelical service here in my house and I'll have a seance, too. But you must save my child. That's what you're there for."

I left Anita and Angelito asleep here and took my little boy to the hospital at that hour of the night. When the doctor saw him, he undressed him quickly and examined him and called the other doctors and they began to whisper. I said to myself, "My God, my son is dying."

They gave him an injection and put him in an oxygen tent and then they said to me, "*Señora,* we're sorry but the child must stay. You may go now."

"Fuck your mother. She's going, not I. I don't leave so long as my son remains." I was getting angry with the saints until I heard my boy say, "Crucita." Then I thought, "Ah, the saints are answering my prayers. Now he won't die. This is a miracle!"

At six o'clock in the morning I went home because if the children woke up and found themselves alone they would yell like a couple of street vendors. I called my *papá* at that hour to come and take care of Anita and Angelito until Chuito got better. I was afraid to call *papá* but he came right away and took them to his house.

I went back to the hospital and didn't leave any more. They told me that the baby needed blood and that I would have to pay for it. I thought, "Pay! Just try to get it out of me. I don't have even one cent." I was dying of hunger all the time I was there. I sent a message to Nanda and she had a peso and went and spent it on a toy for Chuito instead of giving it to me for food. I was furious with her.

Finally they let me take the baby home but my heart sank when they told me that he was sick in the chest. Oh, my God and saints! My poor little son is going to be an invalid when he grows up. Do you know what they told me to do? To keep separate the dishes he eats from, as though he were infected! But I'm not doing any separating for anyone! In this house no one is afraid of anything!

I'm supposed to feed him well on milk with chocolate, and eggs. They told me that if I wanted to keep him with me I had to feed him well. But what food did I have to give him? Even if I dropped dead I had nothing to give him. But for my son I'd go out hustling even if it means getting pregnant. At least it would solve things for the moment.

The baby is much better now, thank God, and I am fulfilling my promises. On Sunday the Pentecosts came and had a service here. But they told me that I had to get rid of the saints. I'd make *them* get out before I'd throw out my saints. These saints cost me a lot of money. They're the only things here that have any value, and when I'm hard up I can sell one without any trouble at all.

El Welfare still gives me food, but not always, and I don't like most of the things they give. That long-grain rice doesn't taste like anything. It's like eating hay. The meat they give has fat on top and it comes in a can and it's real dark. They say it's corned beef, but I don't know. The same goes for that powdered milk. Who could drink the stuff? In La Esmeralda I saved it until I was really hard up and then I sold it to anybody who was willing to shell out a quarter for it to feed it to their animals or something. But I don't dare do that here because it's Federal Government food and it's against the law to sell it. I could get into trouble that way in a place like this, where I don't know anybody. I might try to sell that stuff to a detective without realizing who he was and I'd land in jail.

I haven't been to La Esmeralda often since I moved here, because I can't afford it. Every trip costs forty cents, twenty cents each way. I want to pay off all my debts in La Esmeralda so that I can hold my head high and proud when I go there. I want people to think I've bettered myself because one can't be screwed all one's life. Even now when I visit, still owing money as I do, I put on my best clothes and always try to carry a little cash. I do this so that Emilio's aunt Minerva won't get the idea I'm starving or anything. She really suffers when she sees me in La Esmeralda and I do all that just to bother her. I dress up the kids real nice and take them to call on everybody but her.

When I first moved out of La Esmeralda, nobody knew that I was leaving, in the first place because it made me sad and in the second place because that old Minerva had gone around telling everybody she hoped I'd clear out. She even said it to my face. I'd yell back at her, "What right do you have to say that? Did you buy La Esmeralda or something?"

Another reason why I hardly ever go to La Esmeralda is because Emilio spies on me. He has come after me in the *caserío* just the way he did in La Esmeralda, though not as often. He likes to use the shower in my new apartment when he comes. When I start home after visiting La Esmeralda, he gets into his car and drives along behind me, offering to give me a lift. But listen, I wouldn't get into that car even if I had to walk all the way from San Juan to Villa Hermosa. I put a curse on that car, such a tremendous curse that I'm just waiting to see it strike. I did it one day when Anita had asthma and I had no money to take her to the hospital. I happened to glance out of the window and I saw Emilio stretched out in his car, relaxed as could be, as if he deserved nothing but the best. I let go and yelled at the top of my lungs, "I hope to God someday you'll wear that car as a hat. I hope it turns to dust, with you all fucked up inside it." Now I can't ride in the car because I'm afraid the curse will come true at a time when both of us are in it.

You can't imagine how lonely I feel here. I have friends but they're sort of artificial, pasted-on friends. I couldn't confide in them at all. For example, I got pregnant a little while ago and I had to have an abortion. I nearly went crazy thinking about it. Having a baby is nothing, it's the burden you have afterward, especially with a cowardly husband like mine who takes the easiest way out, denying that the child is his. So there I was, pregnant, and you know, I was ashamed. I was already out of La Esmeralda, see? Well, I know that my

womb is weak, so I took two doses of Epsom salts with quinine and out came
the kid. You can't imagine how unpleasant that is. In La Esmeralda you can
tell everybody about it and that sort of eases your heart. But here I didn't tell
anybody. These girls I know here are mere children, and something like that
—*ay, bendito!*

But to tell you the truth, I don't know what they call a *señorita* here in
Villa Hermosa. The way it is in La Esmeralda, a girl and boy fall in love. For
a few months they control themselves. Then they can't any more, and the boy
does what he has to do to the girl. The hole is bigger than the full moon, and
that's that. They tell everybody, and become husband and wife in the eyes of
all the world. There's no trying to hide it. But here you see girls, who by rights
should have a couple of kids at least, trying to keep from being found out.
They call themselves *señoritas* but they'll go to a hotel with their sweetheart
and let him stick his prick into every hole in their body except the right
one. And they'll suck his prick and he'll come right in her mouth or over her
thighs. The girls do all that and then they're so brazen as to come out of that
hotel claiming they're still *señoritas*. It's plain shameless.

There are some policemen here who make love like this to some girls I
know. Well, the policeman who did it to my friend Mimí told me that if I
loaned him my bed for a little while he would give me three pesos. As that
money wouldn't be bad at all and as he wasn't going to do it to me, I rented
him the bed and grabbed the three pesos. Let them go screw! They locked
themselves in the bedroom for a little while and then they went away. It was
none of my business. If they didn't do it here they would go and do it somewhere else. And she didn't lose her virginity or anything here. So my hands are
clean.

Sometimes I want to go back to La Esmeralda to live and other times I
don't. It's not that I miss my family so much. On the contrary, relatives can be
very bothersome. But you do need them in case you get sick because then you
can dump the children on them. Sometimes I cry for loneliness here. Sometimes I'm bored to death. There's more neighborliness in La Esmeralda. I was
used to having good friends stop by my house all the time. I haven't seen much
of this neighborhood because I never go out. There's a Catholic church near
by but I've never been there. And I haven't been to the movies once since I've
been living here. In La Esmeralda I used to go now and then. And in La
Esmeralda, when nothing else was going on, you could at least hear the sea.

In La Esmeralda nobody ever made fun of my lameness. On the contrary, it was an advantage because everyone went out of his way to help me:
"Let me help the lame girl. Let me buy *bolita* numbers from Lame Cruz,
because cripples bring luck." But it isn't like that here, where people just
laugh. That's why I'd like to live in La Esmeralda again or have Nanda move
in here with me.

The social worker told me that I could have an operation to fix my back.

Imagine, I'd have to go to the doctor and to the hospital. Who could I leave my little baby crows with? And suppose what they do is take my guts out in order to make me look right? But still, now that I live in a place like Villa Hermosa, I would like to have an operation to make me straight.

ABOUT THE AUTHOR

OSCAR LEWIS was born in New York City in 1914, and grew up on a small farm in upstate New York. He received his Ph.D. in anthropology from Columbia University, and taught at Brooklyn College and Washington University. He was until his death in 1970 Professor of Anthropology at the University of Illinois.

Oscar Lewis was Field Representative in Latin America for the United States National Indian Institute, consulting anthropologist for the Ford Foundation in India, and the recipient of two Guggenheim fellowships. His field work took him from the Blackfoot Indians of Canada to Texas farmers, from a Cuban sugar plantation to Spain, and from Mexico to a village in northern India. The research for his studies of the culture of poverty in Puerto Rico and New York was supported by grants from the Guggenheim Foundation, the Research Institute for the Study of Man, the Social Security Administration and Welfare Administration Research Grants program, and the Research Board of the University of Illinois.

He was the author of numerous articles and, in addition to *La Vida,* published seven books—among them *Five Families, The Children of Sánchez,* and *Pedro Martínez,* which have become landmarks in anthropological studies. (*The Children of Sánchez, Pedro Martínez,* and *Village Life in Northern India* are available in Vintage Books.)

La Vida received the National Book Award.

VINTAGE WORKS OF SCIENCE
AND PSYCHOLOGY

VINTAGE BIOGRAPHY AND AUTOBIOGRAPHY